MEMORIAL MANIA

Memorial Mania

PUBLIC FEELING IN AMERICA

Erika Doss

THE UNIVERSITY OF CHICAGO PRESS Chicago and London

The University of Chicago Press, Chicago 60637
The University of Chicago Press, Ltd., London

Paperback edition 2012
Printed in the United States of America

20 19 18 17 16 15 14 13 12 2 3 4 5 6

ISBN-13: 978-0-226-15938-6 (cloth)
ISBN-13: 978-0-226-15941-6 (paper)
ISBN-10: 0-226-15938-8 (cloth)
ISBN-10: 0-226-15941-8 (paper)

Library of Congress Cataloging-in-Publication Data

Doss, Erika Lee.
Memorial mania : public feeling in America / Erika Doss.
p. cm.
Includes bibliographical references and index.
ISBN-13: 978-0-226-15938-6 (cloth : alk. paper)
ISBN-10: 0-226-15938-8 (cloth : alk. paper)
1. Monuments—United States—Public opinion. 2. War memorials—United States—Public opinion. 3. Collective memory—United States. 4. World War, 1939–1945—Monuments—United States. 5. Victims of terrorism—Monuments—United States. 6. Clayton Jackson McGhie Memorial (Duluth, Minn.) 7. McGhie, Isaac, ca. 1900–1920—Monuments. I. Title.
E159.D67 2010
355.1'60973—dc22

2009046951

∞ This paper meets the requirements of ANSI/NISO Z39.48–1992 (Permanence of Paper).

In memory of Masumi Hayashi (1945–2006)

Contents

Figures

Acknowledgments

The debts incurred in writing this book are numerous and I have many people and institutions to thank. Research for this project was supported in part by the Council on Research and Creative Work, Dean's Fund for Excellence, and Graduate Committee on the Arts and Humanities at the University of Colorado, Boulder, and the Institute for Scholarship in the Liberal Arts, College of Arts and Letters, University of Notre Dame; I would also like to thank the Institute for Scholarship in the Liberal Arts and John McGreevy, dean of the University of Notre Dame's College of Arts and Letters, for generous publication subvention funds.

Memorial Mania took shape at the Ohio State University's Institute for Collaborative Research and Public Humanities, where I was a visiting scholar in spring 2000, and was further honed in 2005–2006, when I was Fulbright Distinguished Chair in American Studies at the University of Southern Denmark, and in spring 2007 at Depauw University, where I was Lee G. Hall Distinguished Visiting Professor of Art. Thanks to faculty and students at these schools who graciously allowed me to air my ideas, including Christian Zacher, Rick Livingston, Barry Shank, Barbara Groseclose, Vibeke Schou Tjalve, Sharon Millar, Jørn Brøndal, Torben Huus Larsen, Rikke Schubart, Catherine Fruhan, Cindy O'Dell, Melanie Finney, and David Worthington.

I have greatly benefited from presenting portions of my work at conferences held by the American Studies Association; College Art Association; American Association of Geographers; Americans for the Arts; International Association for Media and Communication Research; International Conference on Media, Religion, and Culture; European Association for American Studies; American Studies Association of Norway; Preserving the Historic Road; Colloque Mémoire Sculptée de l'Europe; and John F. Kennedy-Institut für Nordamerikanstudien, Berlin. Likewise, I am deeply grateful to audiences who listened to versions of this project at the Denver Art Museum, Wichita Art Museum, Boulder Museum of Contemporary Art, Snite Museum of Art, Scottsdale Museum of Contemporary Art, Boston Public Library, Columbus Museum of Art, Amon Carter Museum, and Milwaukee Art Museum, and at schools and institutes, including the University of Colorado, University of Notre Dame, Kent State University, DePauw University, Washington University, New Mexico State University, University of Iowa, University of Cincinnati, George Washington University, Kenyon College, Dartmouth College, University of Kansas, Carnegie Mellon University, Institute of Sacred Music at Yale University, University of Texas at Austin, Colgate University, Belmont University, Roger Williams University, Goucher College, Valparaiso University, University of Copenhagen, University of Aalborg, University of Aarthus, Netherlands Academy of Arts and Sciences, Danish Institute for Military Studies, University of Helsinki, and University of Warsaw.

Conversations with friends and colleagues have been indispensable to this book. Thanks to Bill Anthes, Elissa Auther, Maoz Azaryahu, Judy Baca, Michele Bogart, Julian Bonder, Gretchen Buggeln, Melissa Dabakis, Dennis Doordan, Greg Esser, Vivien Fryd, Julie Greene, Kristin Haas, Patricia Hills, Steven Hoelscher, Martha Hollander, Andrew Hoskins, Amelia Jones, Evelyn Kane, Jerzy Kutnik, Adam Lerner, Peter Jan Margry, Joan Markowitz, Cynthia Mills, David Morgan, Lisa Nicoletti, Mark Pittenger, Sally Promey, Harriet Senie, Sarah Schrank, Marita Sturken, Stephanie Taylor, Selma Thomas, Ellen Wiley Todd, Joe Traugott, Randall van Schepen, Laurel Wallace, and Beth Wilcox for good advice and constructive feedback. Thanks also to Sylvia Grider, David Kieran, Victoria Langland, Margaret Malamud, Bernard Mergen, Andrew Shanken, and Irene Stengs for sharing their work on memorials and public culture.

Colleagues in a writing workshop at the University of Notre Dame, including Gail Bederman, Annie Coleman, Jon Coleman, and Sandra Gustafson, provided enormously helpful criticism, and Bob Nauman and Garrison Roots were similarly helpful at the University of Colorado at Boulder. Sherri Brueggemann, director of Albuquerque's Public Art Program, kindly shared files on the city's Quarto Centenario memorial with me. Judy Baca, Lisa Blas, Bob Bednar, Heather Bowling, Heather Butler, Jonathan Doss, Sam Durant, Eric Fischl, David Frech, Leigh Ann Hallberg, Edgar Heap of Birds, Jim Hirschfield, Dean Keesey, Jennifer Geigel Mikulay, Paul Murdoch, Cindy O'Dell, Christopher Pardell, Bob Reece, Sharon Ringer, Carla Stetson, and Elyn Zimmerman generously shared photos and images used in this book. I am especially grateful to Michele Bogart and Edward Linenthal, whose valuable insights and critical prodding have helped make *Memorial Mania* a much stronger book.

Thanks to Susan Bielstein and Christopher Westcott at the University of Chicago Press for support and help throughout. And, as always, thanks to Geoffrey, Devon, Zoe, Deleuze, Lesley, and Vanessa for road trip companionship, good humor, and general willingness to explore the American Scene.

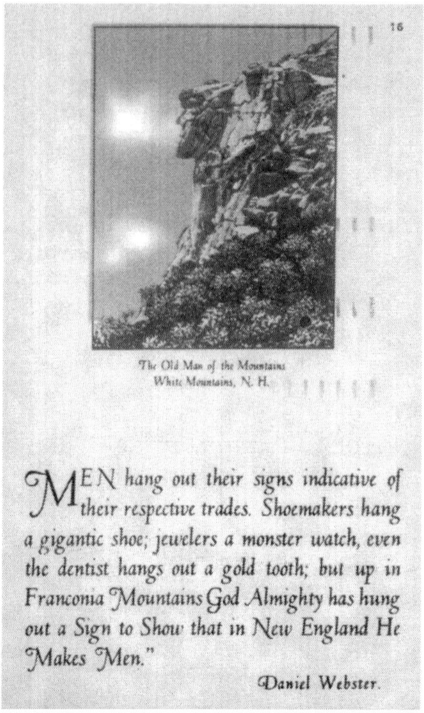

0.1. "The Old Man of the Mountains, White Mountains, N.H.," postcard, ca. 1950. (Originally printed by Tichnor Bros. Inc., Boston. Collection of the author.)

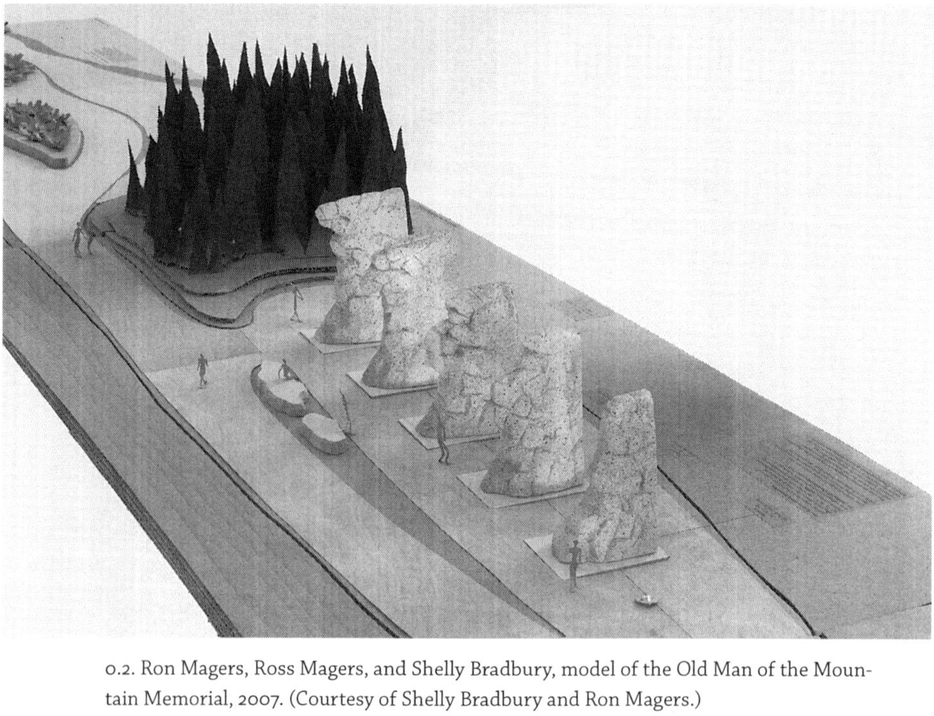

0.2. Ron Magers, Ross Magers, and Shelly Bradbury, model of the Old Man of the Mountain Memorial, 2007. (Courtesy of Shelly Bradbury and Ron Magers.)

INTRODUCTION

In May 2003, the Old Man of the Mountain fell down in New Hampshire. A multi-ton rock formation that looked like the craggy profile of an elderly Yankee, the Old Man was venerated by Nathaniel Hawthorne as the "Great Stone Face" and was later memorialized on the Granite State's license plates and highway signs. Finally, however, the Old Man slid from his perch in the White Mountains and collapsed, a victim of erosion (fig. 0.1). New Hampshire natives and visitors went into deep mourning, "deeply saddened" by the memorial's disappearance, which some likened to "losing a member of one's family." So many were so distraught that the New Hampshire Division of Parks and Recreation organized an online "scrapbook of condolences" for those who wished to "share their feelings" about the "loss of this familiar icon."[1] In 2007, the division, along with the Old Man of the Mountain Legacy Fund, organized a national competition for a $5 million memorial to the lost memorial (fig. 0.2). At a press conference announcing the winning entry, the commissioner for the state's Department of Cultural Resources declared: "This is truly a magnificent design which will create new memories for young people who've never experienced the Old Man while bringing back pleasant old memories for those who've made Franconia Notch a regular visit."[2] The new Old Man of the Mountain Memorial is scheduled for unveiling sometime in 2011.

Why do we make memorials in America today—and why do we make so many of them? Just in the past few decades, thousands of new memorials to executed witches, enslaved Africans, victims of terrorism, victims of lynching, dead astronauts, aborted fetuses, and murdered teenagers have materialized in the American landscape, along with those that pay tribute to civil rights activists, cancer survivors, organ donors, Rosie the Riveter, U.S. soldiers in any number of wars, U.S. presidents, the end of Communism, Martin Luther King, Jr., and the Indian victors of the Battle of Little Bighorn (figs. 0.3–0.10). Equally ubiquitous are temporary memorials: those seemingly spontaneous offerings of flowers, candles, balloons, and teddy bears that precipitate at sites of tragic and traumatic death, like Columbine High School in 1999 and the World Trade Center in 2001 (fig. 0.11).

Memorials of all kinds—including memorials to memorials, as in New Hampshire—are flourishing in America today. Their omnipresence can be explained by what I call *memorial mania*: an obsession with issues of memory and history and an urgent desire to express and claim those issues in visibly public contexts. Today's growing numbers of memorials represent heightened anxieties about who and what should be remembered in America. The passionate debates in which they are often embroiled represent efforts to harness those anxieties and control particular narratives about the nation and its publics. If wildly divergent in terms of subject and style, contemporary American memorials are typified by adamant assertions of citizen rights and persistent demands for representation and respect. Memorial mania is disposed to individual memories and personal grievances, to stories of tragedy and trauma, and to the social and political agendas of diverse numbers of Americans. Driven by heated struggles over self-definition, national purpose, and the politics of representation, memorial mania is especially shaped by the affective conditions of public life in America today: by the fevered pitch of public feelings such as grief, gratitude, fear, shame, and anger.

September 11, 2001, certainly heightened feelings of urgency and anxiety in America, feelings that were quickly revealed in all sorts of memorials. Within hours of the attacks on the World Trade Center, New York City was filled with handmade memorials in parks, on street corners, at firehouses. Within days, the entire country was dotted with temporary memorials, and many people began to talk about how September 11 would be *permanently* commemorated. As early as September 30, 2001, the *New York Times* published a number of memorial proposals from well-known artists and architects. Shirin Neshat, John Baldessari, and Barbara Kruger argued for a park on the site of the former towers, while Richard Meier and James Turrell wanted "new buildings" that would be "higher than the old ones." Louise Bourgeois suggested a seven-story stone column topped by a star, with the names of the dead chiseled in vertical rows. And Joel Shapiro, whose sculpture *Loss and Regeneration* (1993) is featured at the entrance to the United States Holocaust Memorial Museum in Washington, D.C., said leaving the World Trade Center site in ruins would be "the most effective" form of remembrance and commemoration. "It's like Berlin," Shapiro observed, recalling the blocks of rubble that permeated that German city for decades following World War II. "You see the devastation."[3]

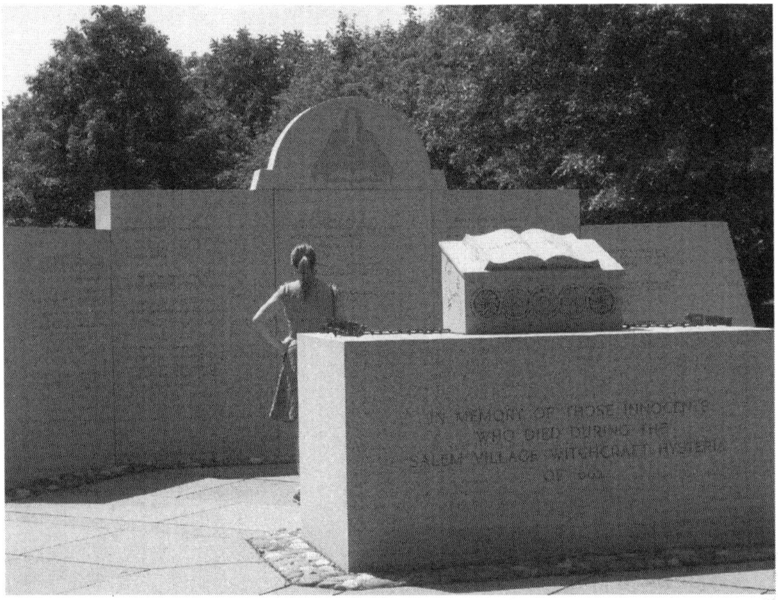

0.3. Salem Village Witchcraft Victims' Memorial, Danvers, Massachusetts, dedicated 1992. (Photo by the author.)

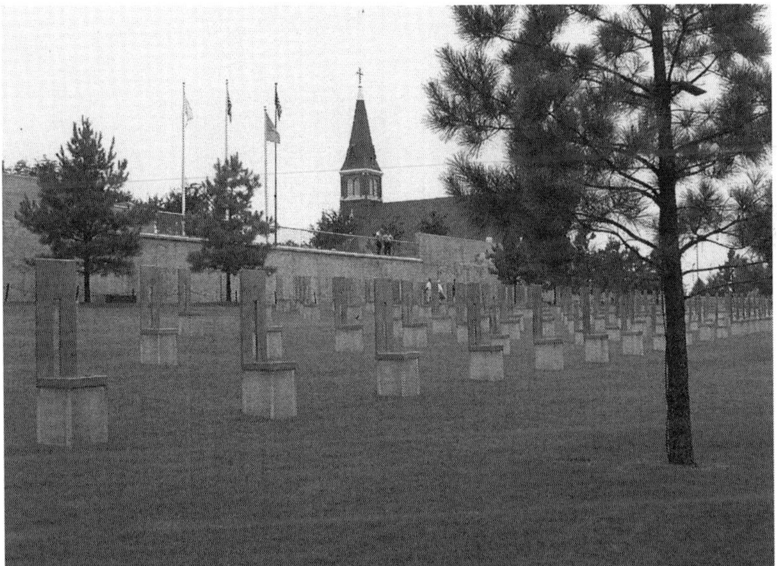

0.4. Hans Butzer and Torrey Butzer, Oklahoma City National Memorial, Oklahoma City, Oklahoma, dedicated 2000. (Photo by the author.)

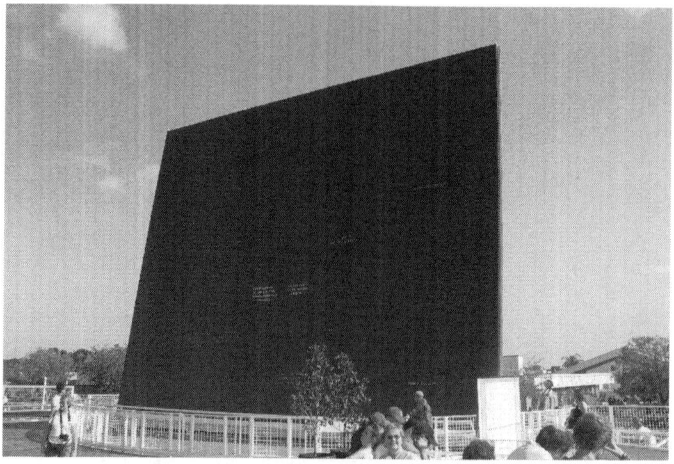

0.5. Space Mirror Memorial, Kennedy Space Center, Merritt Island, Florida, dedicated 1991. Mirror-finished granite. The memorial features the names of U.S. astronauts and pilots killed during space missions. (Courtesy of Seth Buckley, Creative Commons.)

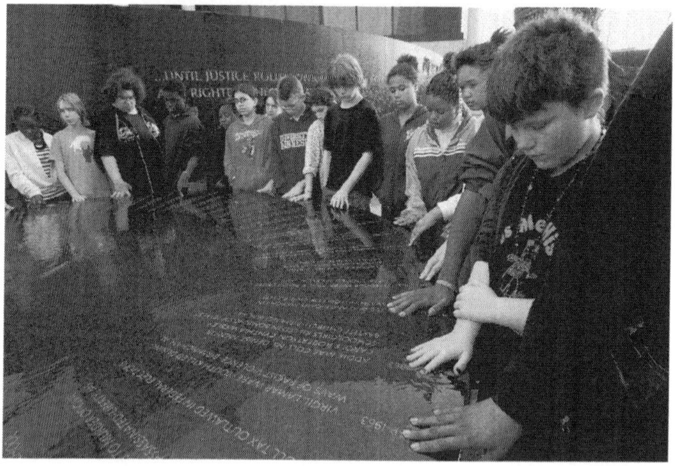

0.6. Students from Minneapolis Southside Family Charter School visiting the Civil Rights Memorial, Southern Poverty Law Center, Montgomery, Alabama, March 2008. The memorial was designed by Maya Lin, dedicated 1989. (Photo © Dudley Edmondson / raptorworks.com.)

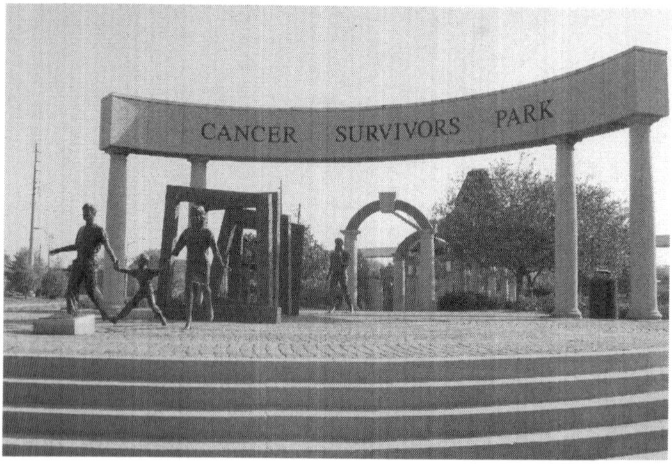

0.7. Victor Salmones, *Cancer . . . There's Hope*, Richard and Annette Bloch Cancer Survivors Park, Indianapolis, Indiana, dedicated 1997. (Courtesy of Lesley A. Sharp.)

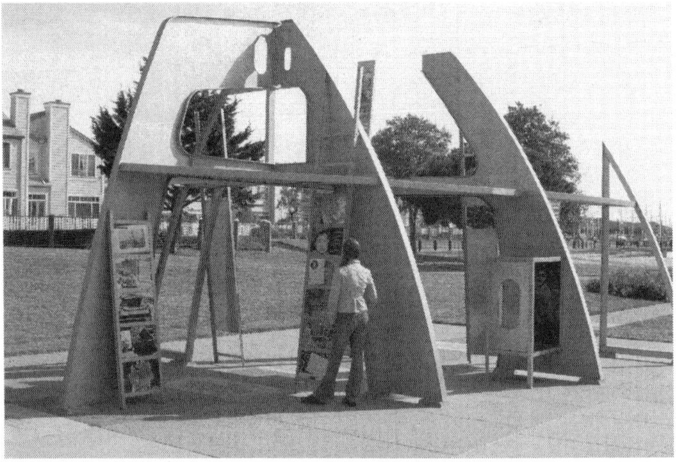

0.8. Susan Schwartzenberg and Cheryl Barton, Rosie the Riveter Memorial, Rosie the Riveter / World War II Home Front National Historical Park, Richmond, California, dedicated 2000. (Courtesy of Geoffrey Thrumston.)

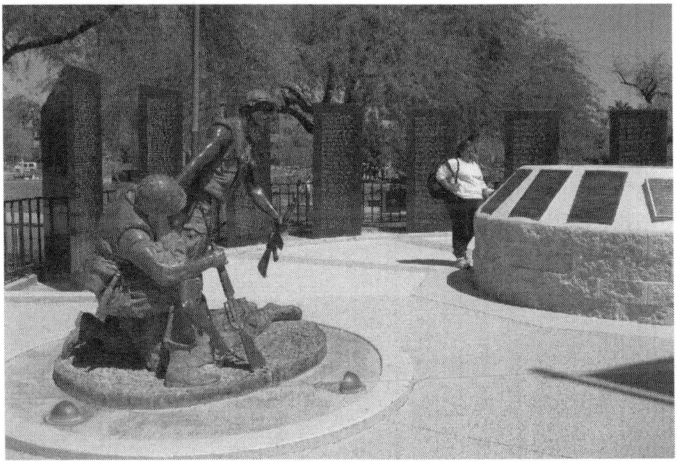

0.9. Vietnam War Memorial, Phoenix, Arizona, dedicated 1998. (Photo by the author.)

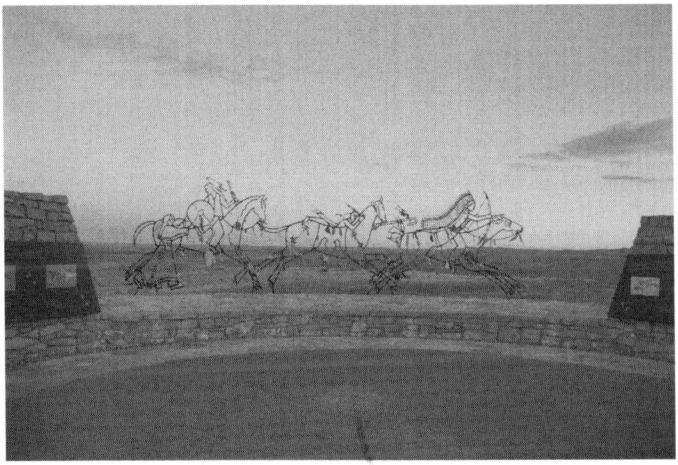

0.10. Colleen Cutschall, *Spirit Warriors*, Indian Memorial, Little Bighorn Battlefield National Monument, Crow Agency, Montana, dedicated 2003. Metal armature sculpted of bronzed steel rods. (© 2005 Bob Reece. All rights reserved.)

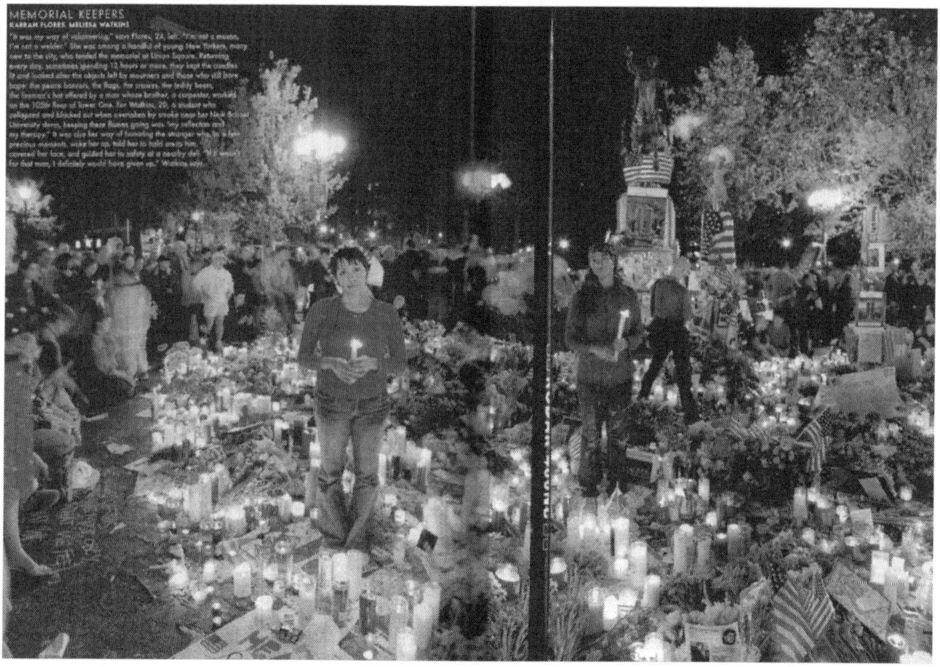

0.11. Jonas Karlsson, photo of a temporary memorial, Union Square, New York, September 2001. (Originally published in *Vanity Fair*, Special Edition, November 2001. Courtesy of Jonas Karlsson.)

There was never any doubt that there would be a permanent memorial at what was quickly dubbed "Hallowed Ground Zero," an assumption that tells us how prevalent, and sacrosanct, issues of memory and acts of commemoration have become in America today. It also indicates the particular privileging of New York's 9/11 memories: neither the Pentagon Memorial nor the Flight 93 National Memorial in Shanksville, Pennsylvania, nor countless 9/11 memorials have received the intense mass media and public attention as New York's 9/11 memorial, now called the National September 11 Memorial & Museum at the World Trade Center. If this relates to the sheer numbers of 9/11 dead in New York (2,752) as opposed to Washington (184) and Pennsylvania (40), it also represents a prevailing sentiment of "recovery through rebuilding" particular to the financial district of New York's Twin Towers.[4] Demands for newer and bigger buildings, erected as soon as possible, overwhelmed more introspective memorial designs that favored leafy parks and melancholy ruins.

In 2003, more than 5,200 entries were received in the World Trade Center Site Memorial Competition, managed by the Lower Manhattan Development Corporation and juried by a thirteen-person panel, including artists Maya Lin and Martin Puryear. (This was three times the number of entries submitted for the Vietnam Veterans Memorial competition in Washington in 1980—which Lin won.) The winning design, a multi-acred minimalist memorial that architects Michael Arad and Peter Walker call "Reflecting Absence," features a tree-lined plaza punctuated by two huge spatial voids located on the footprints of the former Twin Towers (fig. 0.12). Inside the voids are recessed pools of water whose outer walls are inscribed with the names of the dead; bordering the pools are narrow ramps descending into an underground museum filled with artifacts recovered from the rubble (fig. 0.13). The memorial's selection in January 2004 was front-page news all over the country.

So, too, was the selection of architect Daniel Libeskind for the redevelopment of the World Trade Center. Libeskind's master plan featured a "Wedge of Light" (a scheme to orient the new buildings so that each year, on the morning of September 11, "the sun will shine without shadow"), a "Park of Heroes" (a space commemorating the 343 firefighters who lost their lives at Ground Zero), and a "Freedom Tower" that was a symbolically patriotic 1,776 feet tall. The design (now mostly abandoned) was a calculated response to Lower Manhattan Development Corporation site plans featuring the word "memorial": Memorial Plaza, Memorial Square, Memorial Triangle, Memorial Garden, Memorial Park, and Memorial Promenade.[5] Repeatedly appearing on TV talk shows and in the popular press, Libeskind himself became something of a memorial guru. Reverently intoning that architecture was the "future of memory," Libeskind implied that anything and everyone was subject to memorialization. In 2003, for example, while discussing plans for the Denver Art Museum, for which he designed a swanky $110 million addition, the issue of what to do with an outdoor space came up. Libeskind immediately proposed a memorial garden. Museum staffers responded: "Memorial to what?"

Indeed, memorial to what? What is driving this contemporary American frenzy to memorialize, and who is being remembered? At the most basic level, memorials are designed to recognize and preserve memories. They are typically understood as acts and gifts that honor particular people and historical events. In 1957, for example, some nine thousand members of the American Bar Association paid for a memorial to the Magna Carta, which was erected near the site in England where the Great Charter of Freedoms was issued in 1215. Gift-giving, of course, is rarely altruistic; memorials, like most things in capitalist and commercial economies, are informed by systems of production and reception, by expectations of exchange and reciprocity. In 1965, the British National Trust gifted an acre of land near the Magna Carta Memorial to the United States, on which a new memorial to President John F. Kennedy

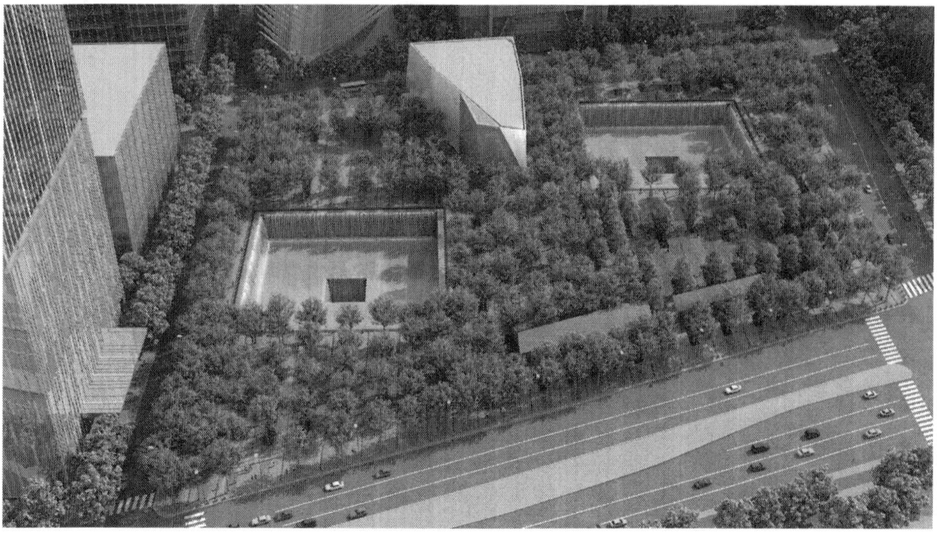

0.12. Aerial view of the selected design for National September 11 Memorial & Museum at the World Trade Center, including "Reflecting Absence," by Michael Arad and Peter Walker. (Renderings by Squared Design Lab. © 2004–2008 National September 11 Memorial & Museum at the World Trade Center Foundation, Inc. All Rights Reserved.)

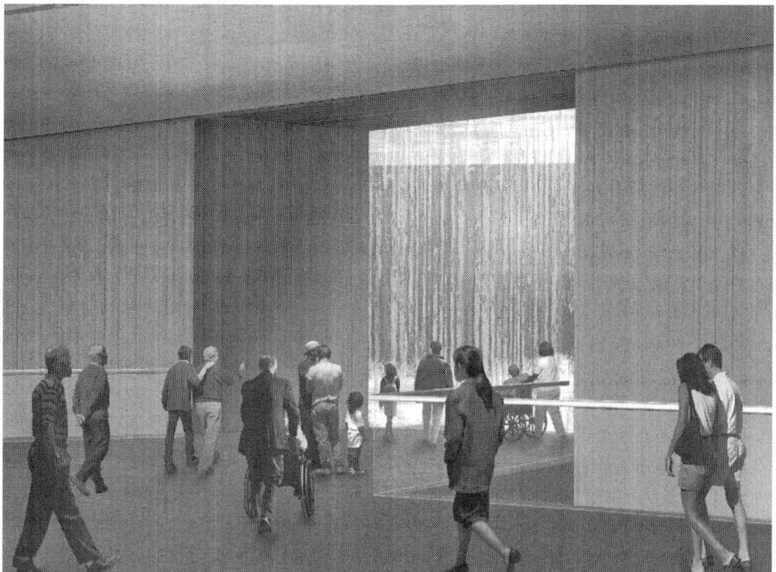

0.13. Memorial Hall, National September 11 Memorial & Museum at the World Trade Center, New York, New York. (Renderings by Davis Brody Bond. © 2004–2008 National September 11 Memorial & Museum at the World Trade Center Foundation, Inc. All Rights Reserved.)

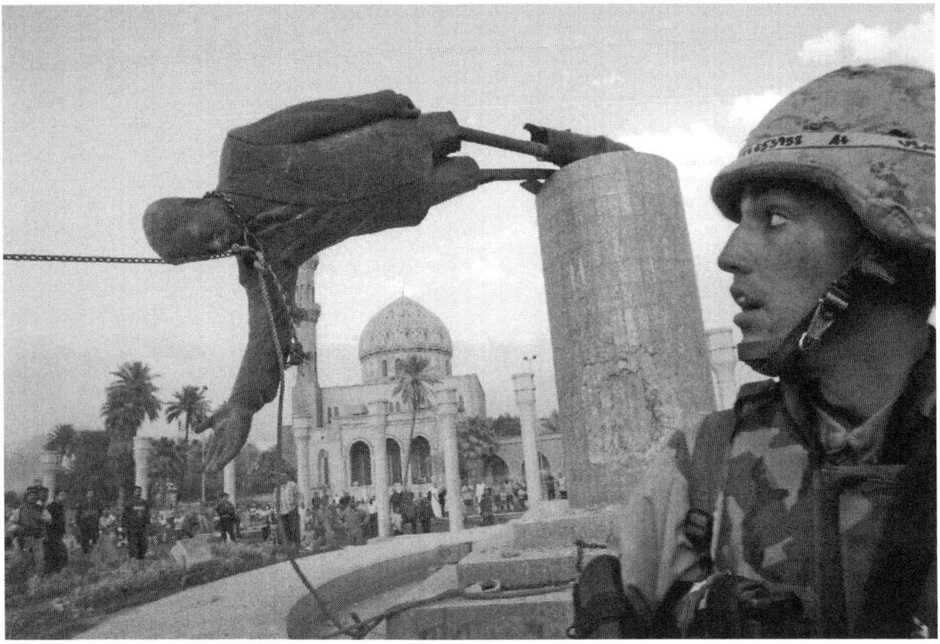

0.14. Goran Tomasevic, "U.S. Marine Corps Assaultman Kirk Dalrymple Watching Statue of Saddam Hussein Topple in Baghdad, April 9, 2003." (© Goran Tomasevic / Reuters.)

was erected. Put in the context of cold war political frictions between the United States and England, both memorials can be seen as symbols of American authority on British soil.

Marking social and political interests and claiming particular historical narratives, memorials can possess enormous power and influence. The American military certainly knows this: when the United States invades or occupies another country, it often destroys their memorials, thereby erasing their symbolic authority from the social and political landscape. In 1946, for example, Allied forces in Germany issued Directive No. 30, "The Liquidation of German Military and Nazi Memorials and Museums," and ordered that they be "completely destroyed and liquidated" within eighteen months.[6] In 2003, U.S. soldiers in Iraq pulled down multiple monuments to Saddam Hussein. One of the most widely reproduced images of the invasion was the toppling of a forty-foot statue of Saddam in central Baghdad (fig. 0.14). While initial media accounts credited joyous Iraqis with the memorial's destruction, later reports showed that U.S. Marines had destroyed the monument as a "target of opportunity," and "a quick-thinking Army psychological operations team" made it look like a "spontaneous Iraqi undertaking" rather than a

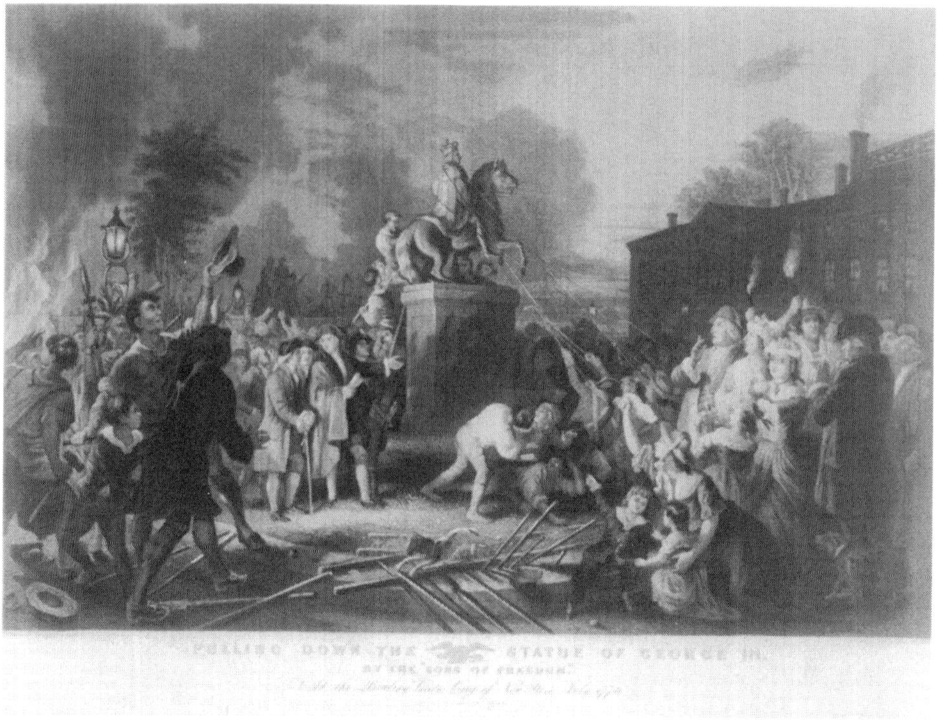

0.15. *Pulling Down Statue of George III by the "Sons of Freedom" at the Bowling Green, City of New York, July 1776*, painted by Johannes A. Oertel, engraved by John C. McRae. (Library of Congress, Prints and Photographs Division, reproduction no. LC-USZ62-2455 [B&W film copy negative].)

staged performance.[7] However they are initiated, such actions intuitively acknowledge the "symbolic capital" of memorials and the fundamental roles they play in shaping and directing perceptions of social order, national identity, and political transition.[8]

But consider this contradiction: on its own turf, the United States allows—or more accurately, ignores—memorials to the defeated states and underlying white supremacist politics of the secessionist Southern Confederacy. There was, by comparison, no such tolerance following colonial America's declaration of independence from Great Britain. On July 9, 1776, an equestrian statue of King George III was toppled in New York's Bowling Green at the southernmost tip of Manhattan (fig. 0.15). Originally designed by British artist Joseph Wilton and erected in 1770, the gilded lead memorial was pulled down from its fifteen-foot pedestal and disembodied, some pieces snatched up as souvenirs and others eventually melted into musket balls for the Continental army. Paintings and prints of the memorial's destruction—what one art historian calls an "iconography of regicide"—were especially popular in the 1840s and 1850s, when various democratizing revolutions swept through Europe.[9]

In the decades following the Civil War, countless Confederate memorials were built in the United States, from simple granite shafts commemorating common soliders to towering bronze statues of Southern heroes like Robert E. Lee and Jefferson Davis (fig. 0.16). In 1883, Washington and Lee University in Lexington, Virginia, dedicated its Shrine of the South, a mausoleum housing Lee's body and the bones of his favorite horse, Traveller, for whom visitors often leave gifts of apples and carrots (fig. 0.17). Sixteen miles east of Atlanta stands Stone Mountain Confederate Memorial, a giant bas-relief designed by Gutzon Borglum (who also designed Mount Rushmore). This memorial commemorates both the Southern Confederacy and the Ku Klux Klan, which funded the memorial and was politically revitalized in a ceremony held at the base of the mountain in the fall of 1915. Borglum, who joined the KKK during the course of the commission, originally planned to include an altar to the Klan in the memorial.[10]

Confederate memorials also dot the north and the nation's capital. Gettysburg National Military Park features an entire avenue of Southern memorials, including the Louisiana State Monument (1971), which depicts a ten-foot female figure ("The Spirit of the Confederacy") blowing a trumpet and grasping a flaming cannonball while the fallen soldier below her clutches a rebel battle flag to his chest. Arlington National Cemetery includes the similarly audacious Confederate Monument, a thirty-two-foot memorial decorated with a frieze of Greek gods and goddesses, handsome Confederate officers, and stoic slaves seeing their owners off to war (fig. 0.18). Best described as "a pro-southern textbook illustrated in bronze," the Confederate Monument was dedicated on June 14, 1914 (the anniversary of Confederate president Jefferson Davis's birthday) in a ceremony attended by President Woodrow Wilson.[11] In 2002 and 2003, the Bush White House paid its own homage to the Southern Confederacy by ordering a floral wreath laid at the base of this monument on Memorial Day. In 2009, the Obama White House did the same—although it also sent a second wreath to the African American Civil War Memorial (see fig. 4.28 on p. 231).[12]

Do these memorials to the secessionist South obscure the history and meaning of the Civil War? Does their abiding presence speak to a national faith in freedom of expression? Do they embody "heritage not hate," as defenders of various forms of Confederate commemoration (like the rebel battle flag) have vigorously asserted in recent years? Do they legitimate racism's ignoble presence throughout American history? Inconsistent and intensely passionate responses to these questions,

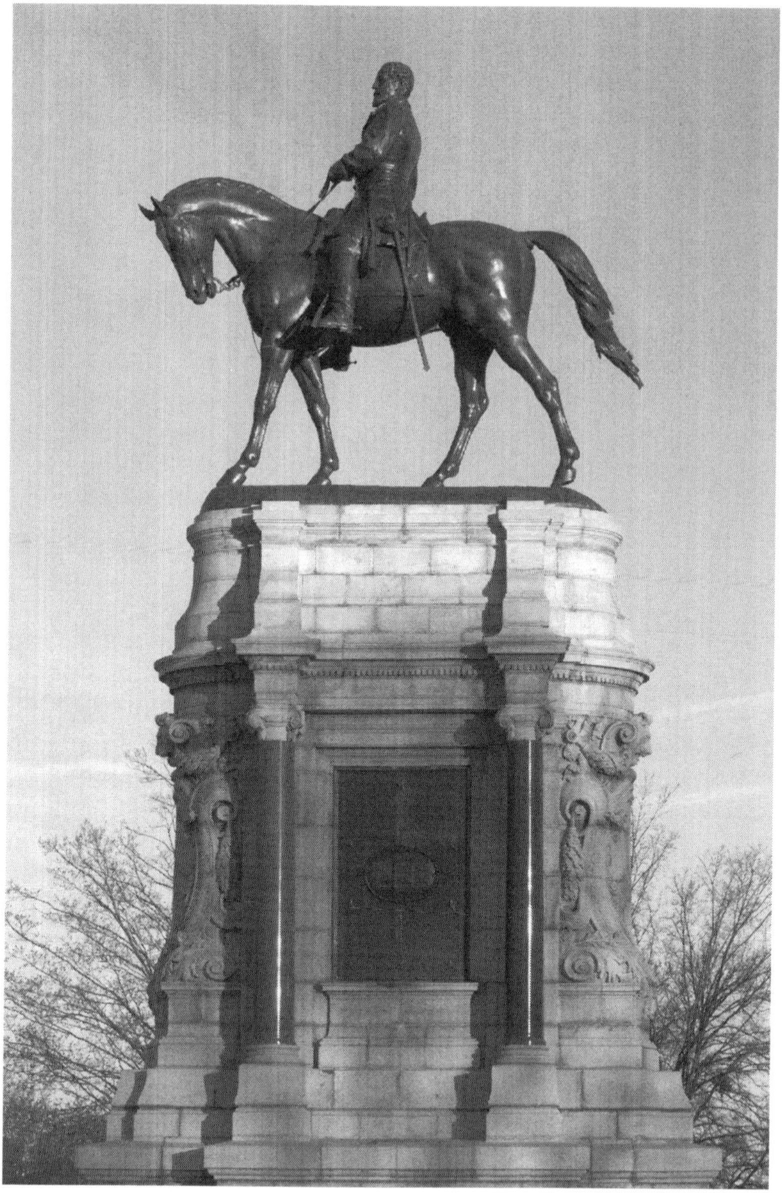

0.16. Antonin Mercié and Paul Pujol, Robert E. Lee Monument, Richmond, Virginia, dedicated 1890. (© Lee Sanstead.)

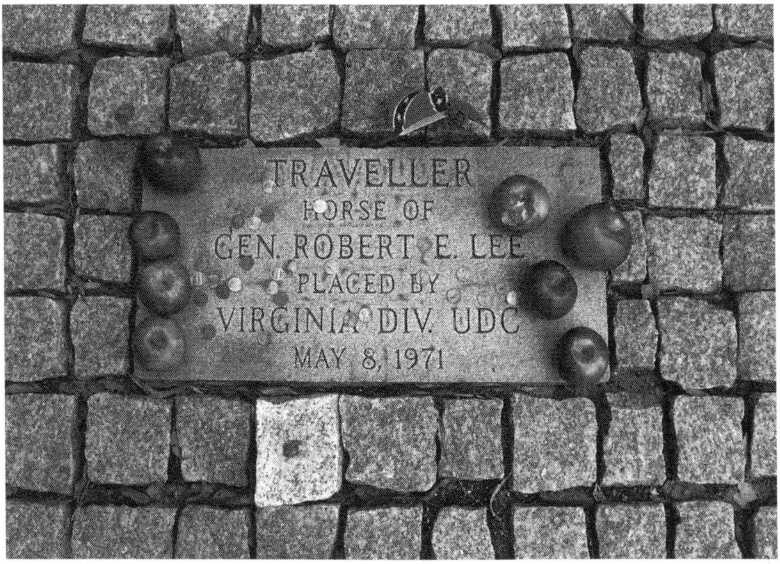

0.17. Lisa Blas, "Untitled," 2006. Photograph of the grave of Traveller, Robert E. Lee's favorite horse. (© 2009 Lisa Blas. All rights reserved.)

much like the neo-Dixie mania that Tony Horwitz documents in his survey of Southern memory, *Confederates in the Attic: Dispatches from the Unfinished Civil War* (1998), suggest the highly contested stakes of commemoration in America.[13]

Memorial Mania explores the cultural, social, and political conditions that inform today's urgent feelings about history and memory. Starting with the assumption that much of today's memorial making is excessive, frenzied, and extreme—hence manic—this book traces how modern America's obsession with commemoration developed and why it is so prevalent today. Memorials, I argue, are archives of public affect, "repositories of feelings and emotions" that are embodied in their material form and narrative content.[14] Pairing discussions of particular memorials with the affective conditions in which they are imagined, produced, and received (or experienced and understood), I contend that fresh insights about American history, memory, and self and national identity are especially realized through the lens of public feeling.

Increasing numbers of temporary memorials, for example, including shrines erected at the sites of car accidents and public school shootings and installations displayed during antiabortion rallies, suggest how new understandings of grief, mourning, and citizenship are being framed in America today. Memorials that commemorate the victims of terrorism, like the Lockerbie Cairn in Arlington National Cemetery (1995),

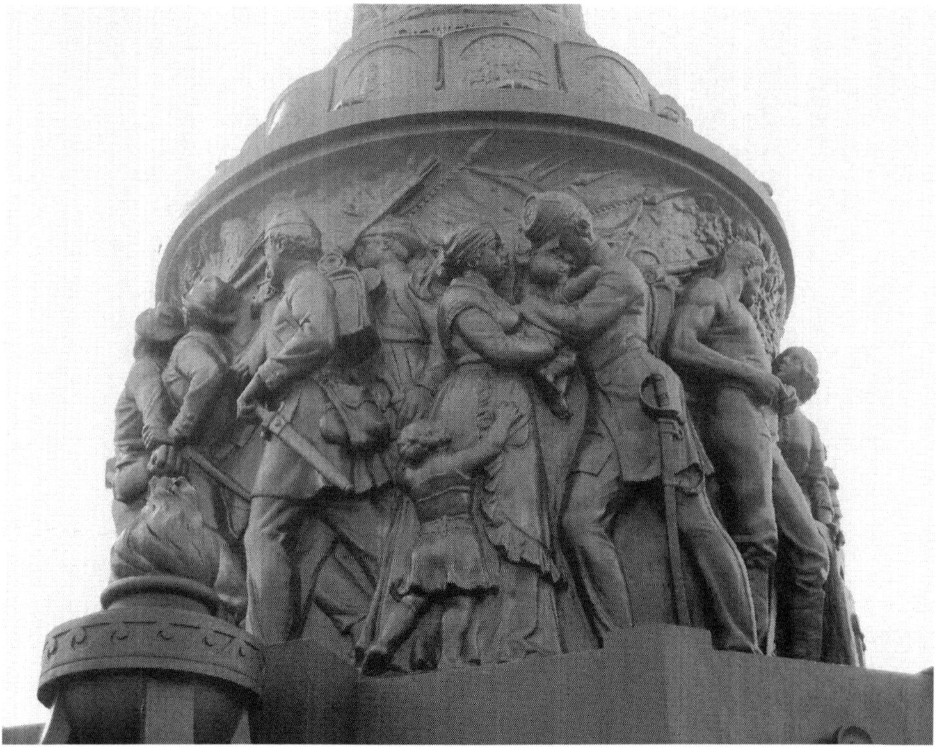

0.18. Moses Ezekiel, Confederate Monument, Arlington National Cemetery, Arlington, Virginia, dedicated 1914. (Courtesy of Heather Bowling.)

the Oklahoma City National Memorial (2000), and increasing numbers of 9/11 memorials, simultaneously embody widespread fears about the state of the nation and equally emotional narratives about social stability, civil unity, and national security. Scores of recently dedicated war memorials, including the National World War II Memorial (2004), negotiate the terms of gratitude and what it means to say "thank you" in today's America—and to whom. Likewise, a growing body of shame-based memorials, including those that address the subjects of slavery, lynching, and war relocation, challenge standard accounts of a progressive national narrative and raise questions about how to remember, represent, and perhaps redeem the nation's shameful histories of racial violence and intolerance. And a number of especially controversial memorials, including the newly reconfigured Little Bighorn Battlefield National Monument in Montana, a series of statues that pay tribute to Spanish conquistador Juan de Oñate in New Mexico and Texas, and the Martin Luther King, Jr. National Memorial in Washington, speak to the intersection of revisionist histories, origin myths, and feelings of anger in contemporary America.

These public displays of affection prompt various questions. How, for example, are feelings of grief, fear, gratitude, shame, and anger mediated in America's memorial cultures? How are sociopolitical concerns such as racism, violence, and terrorism negotiated? How do the metaphors of agency, subjectivity, rights, and citizenship work in visual and material cultures? How do memorials represent and also repress national consciousness? What does memorial mania tell us about how Americans feel about themselves as Americans today?

Recognizing the range of feelings that frame contemporary commemoration, each chapter of this book explores the making and meaning of affect in American public culture today. Derived from the Latin word *affectus*, meaning "passion" and "disposition of mind," and also "to afflict" or "to touch," "affect" is perhaps best understood as physically expressed emotion or feeling. If especially familiar in psychoanalytic circles, affect has become increasingly salient in disciplines ranging from neuroscience and philosophy to literary studies, art history, and political science, and has emerged as its own distinct field of study. Theories about the "transmission of affect," about how feelings and emotions flow between individuals and their social and physical environments, and about how certain affects mobilize social groups and activate cultural and political modes of production (and vice versa), are widespread.[15] Foregrounding affect as a fundamental element in contemporary commemoration, this book understands affect in terms of public feeling, and focuses on how emotional attitudes and practices inform—and are informed by—cultural conditions like memorial mania. The feelings of loss and sadness that followed the Old Man of the Mountain's passing in 2003, for example, certainly fueled the memorial's regeneration a few years later.

Affect—Frederick Jameson notwithstanding—is omnipresent in contemporary American culture and society. Contrary to a Habermasian vision of a public sphere in which rational citizens exchange ideas and come together in shared and progressive actions, contemporary American public life is especially marked by emotional appeals and affective investments.[16] Consider how public feelings have been manipulated in recent political elections; consider the amplified emotional tenor of ongoing debates over reproductive rights, health care, the war on terror, and immigration. Memorial mania is one feature of this affective culture, although its link to a "statue mania" craze of more than a century ago suggests that today's public display of affection may be more a national continuum than a uniquely contemporary condition.

1 STATUE MANIA TO MEMORIAL MANIA

Scope of the Subject

"The notion of the monument as memorial or commemorative public event has witnessed a triumphal return," cultural critic Andreas Huyssen observed in the mid-1990s. Reflecting on the "current obsession with memory" and what he called a "memory boom," Huyssen commented on the "surprising" contemporary resurgence of "the monument and the memorial as major modes of aesthetic, historical, and spatial expression."[1]

No American city better embodies these conditions of memorial mania than the nation's capital. Washington has seen a glut of built and proposed memorials in the past few decades, all approved by Congress and each managed by the National Capital Planning Commission, the U.S. Commission of Fine Arts, the National Park Service, and / or fifteen other federal agencies claiming some degree of control over the city's built environment.[2] Since 1995, the following memorials have been dedicated in Washington: the Pentagon Memorial (2008), Air Force Memorial (2006), National World War II Memorial (2004), George Mason Memorial (2002), Tomas G. Masaryk Memorial (2002), National Japanese American Memorial (2000), Mahatma Gandhi Memorial (1999), African American Civil War Memorial (1998), Women in Military Service for America Memorial (1997), Franklin Delano Roosevelt Memorial (1997), Korean War Veterans Memorial (1995), and Lockerbie Memorial Cairn (1995).[3] In 2007, President George W. Bush dedicated the Victims of Communism Memorial, located just a few blocks from the U.S. Capitol (fig 1.1). Orchestrated by Heritage Foundation fellow Lee Edwards, the $950,000 memorial consists of a small plaza centerpieced by a ten-foot bronze called the *Goddess of Democracy*, a replica of the Statue of Liberty erected by Chinese student dissidents in Tiananmen Square in 1989.[4]

More memorials destined for the nation's capitol—all similarly authorized by Congress—include the American Veterans Disabled for Life Memorial, Benjamin Banneker Memorial (commemorating an eighteenth-

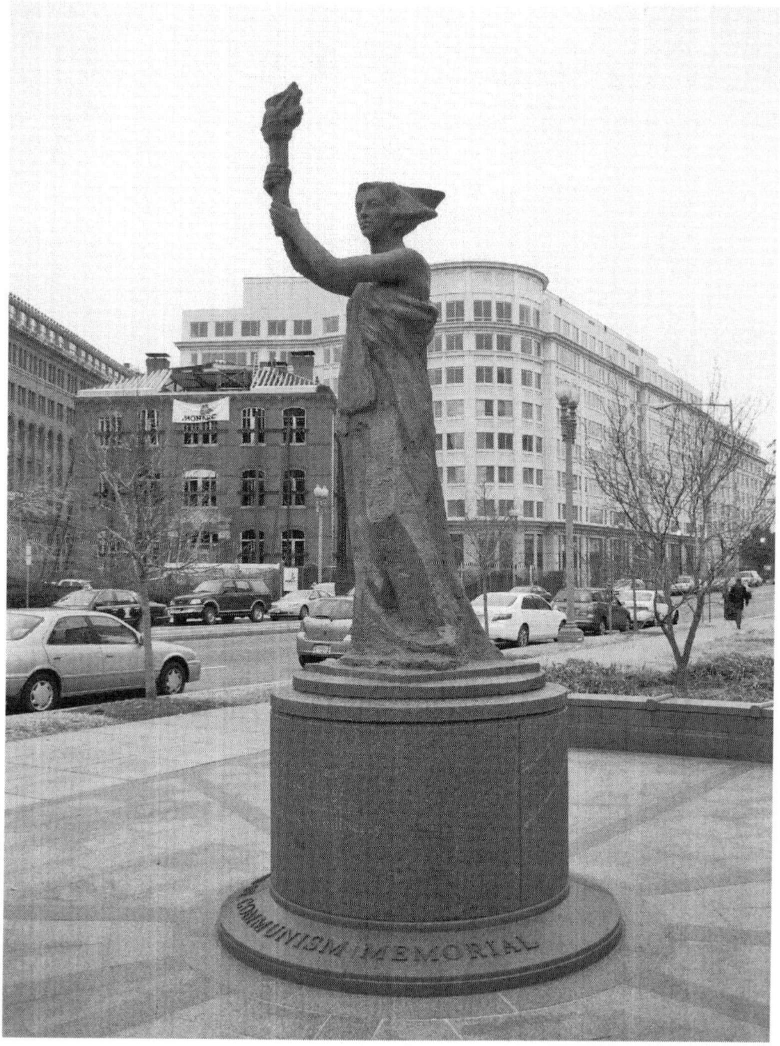

1.1. Thomas Marsh, Victims of Communism Memorial, Washington, D.C., dedicated 2007. (Courtesy of Heather Bowling.)

century African American scientist), and Adams Memorial (a memorial to the second and sixth presidents of the United States and their wives). The Dwight D. Eisenhower Memorial, Black Revolutionary War Patriots Memorial, Monument to the Victims of the Ukrainian Famine-Genocide of 1932–1933, and Martin Luther King, Jr. Memorial (see fig. 6.3, p. 320) are also on the lineup.

In 1986, worried that too many memorials might "get in one another's way, competing for attention among themselves and against the landscaped beauty of the Mall," Congress passed the National Commemorative Works Act, aimed at "severely restricting" the numbers of memorials intended for the nation's capitol. Yet legislative management of public commemoration is offset by countless constituent demands for national recognition. The act's rather sweeping mandate, after all, is to promote commemorative works that evoke "the memory of an individual, group, event, or other significant element of American history."[5] That covers a lot of territory.

Memorial mania is not just a federal issue, of course. In her study of monuments and memory in Lowell, Massachusetts, Martha Norkunas documented some 252 memorials erected in that northeastern textile town since the mid-nineteenth century. More than 65 were erected in the last two decades of the twentieth century.[6]

This dramatic increase in memorial numbers is explained in part by expanded understanding of commemoration itself. American memorials are as protean today as their American patrons and publics, and range from multi-acred properties like the National September 11 Memorial & Museum at the World Trade Center to single monuments like the David Berger National Memorial in Beachwood, Ohio, an abstract sculpture dedicated to an American athlete killed during terrorist attacks at the 1972 Munich Olympics. From permanent memorials intended as timeless national fixtures to temporary shrines erected at the sites of school shootings and car accidents, contemporary kinds of commemoration include plaques, parks, cairns, quilts (the NAMES Project Foundation AIDS Memorial Quilt), trees (the seven oaks planted at the Johnson Space Center in tribute to the crew of the *Columbia* space shuttle), and Web sites (there are thousands of online memorials to the victims of 9/11, Hurricane Katrina, and the Virginia Tech shootings, among others).

By extension, today's "obsession with memory" and memorials is grounded in a vastly expanded U.S. demographic and in heightened expectations of rights and representation among the nation's increasingly diverse publics. As the following overview details, memorial mania is contextualized by a highly successful public art industry, burgeoning interests in "memory studies" and "living" or experiencing history, and shifting understanding of American national identity. In particular, memorial mania embodies the affective dimensions—the structures of public feeling—that characterize contemporary life. And as Huyssen alludes in his comments on the "triumphal return" of commemoration, today's memory boom has precedence in an earlier historical moment when monuments and notions of the monumental similarly dominated public art and public culture.

STATUE MANIA

Today's memorial mania parallels the "statue mania" that gripped nineteenth- and early twentieth-century Americans and Europeans alike. In France, historian Maurice Agulhon explains, "statueomania" was especially realized in countless memorials to "Marianne," a feminized symbol of revolution and liberty. Determined to unite the French body politic around a consensual national mythology, Third Republic patriots unleashed an army of Marianne memorials in public squares throughout France in the latter decades of the nineteenth century. They also stirred a "patriotic fervor" for laudatory statues of local and national French figures from Louis Pasteur and Denis Diderot to Berlioz, Danton, and Voltaire. In 1870, there were fewer than a dozen statues of "great men" in Paris; by 1914, there were over 150. Statue mania, the monumental impulse of France's Third Republic, was "an inherent feature of modern urbanism and liberal and secular society," Agulhon remarks, and the parallel processes of forging the modern French nation-state and raising statues were seen as one and the same.[7]

Statue mania erupted in the United States from the 1870s to the 1920s for similar reasons. After the divisiveness of the Civil War, countless American cities and towns vied for statues (and other symbolic markers) that helped reimagine what Benedict Anderson terms the "affective bonds of nationalism."[8] Statues not only embellished the postbellum public landscape but encouraged passionate and consensual understandings of nationhood. Frederick MacMonnies's Pioneer Monument (1911) in Denver, Colorado, for example, a multi-tiered fountain featuring an equestrian statue of Kit Carson and other figures labeled "The Hunter," "The Prospector," and "Pioneer Mother and Child," promoted a national history defined by manifest destiny, American exceptionalism, Anglo-Saxon supremacy, and heteronormative family values (fig. 1.2). Commissioned by a Denver real estate outfit as a tribute to Colorado's first territorial governor, MacMonnies's original design featured a statue of a naked Indian on horseback, "his palm extended in a gesture of peace." But Denver newspapers angrily objected, contending that Colorado "has no love for the savage redskin" and that the sculptor's decision to depict a Native American was a "sad mistake."[9] MacMonnies revised his plans, substituting a fully-clothed figure of Kit Carson for the Indian, and the $72,000 monument was dedicated in Denver's Civic Center Park in a ceremony attended by some ten thousand people.

Likenesses of American explorers, inventors, statesmen, and soldiers were commonly commissioned in the era of statue mania, as were "great men" valorized by different Anglo-European ethnic groups. Baltimore,

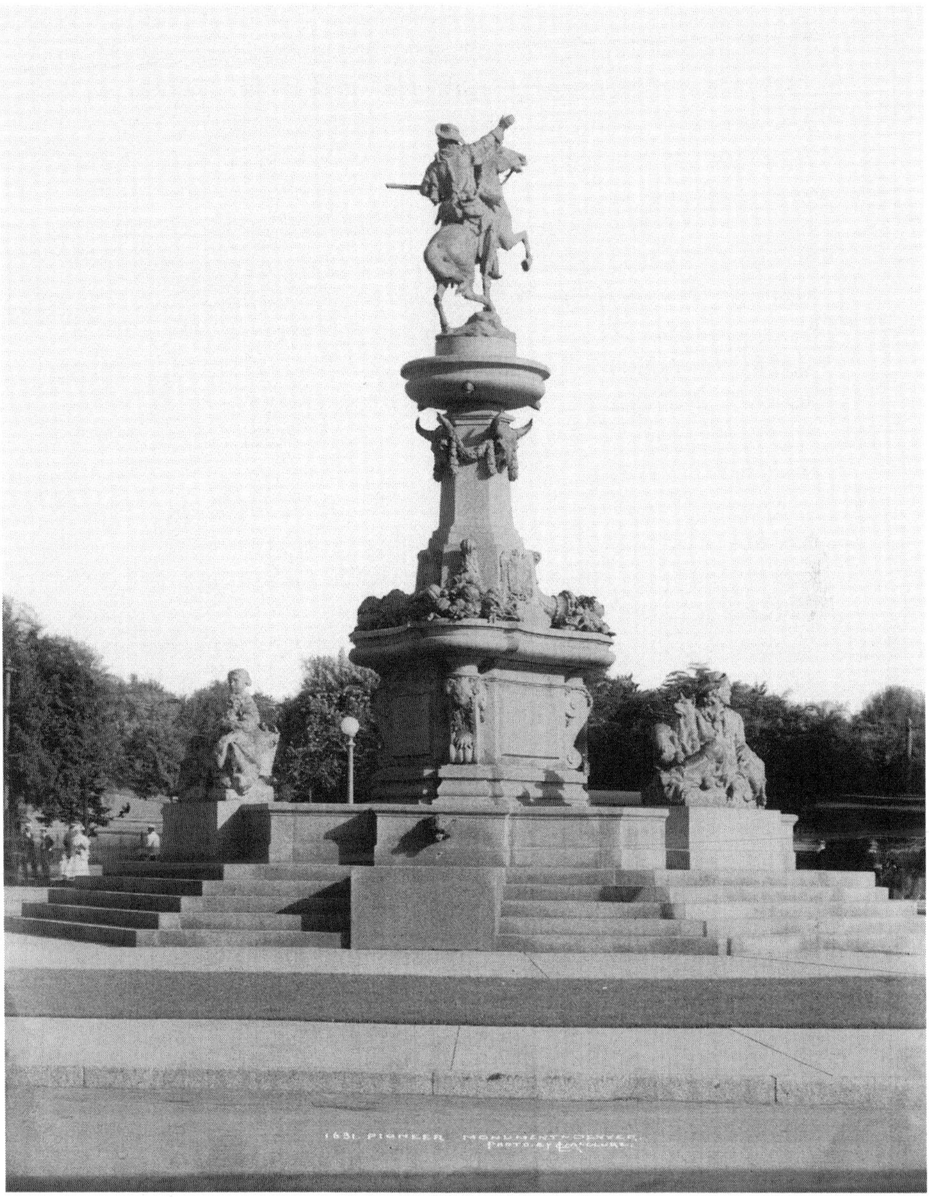

1.2. Frederick MacMonnies, Pioneer Monument, Denver, Colorado, dedicated 1911. (Courtesy of the Denver Public Library, Western History Collection [call no. MCC-1631].)

nicknamed "the Monumental City" in the early nineteenth century, was dotted with memorials to men ranging from George Washington and Edgar Allen Poe to Thomas Wildey (founder of the Independent Order of Odd Fellows in North America) and John Mifflin Hood (president of the Western Maryland Railway). Cleveland's Cultural Gardens, a narrow strip of urban parkland first developed in the 1910s, was outfitted with statues, busts, and plaques commemorating the city's Czech, German, Hungarian, Italian, Polish, and Russian literary and musical legends. Staking their own claims to America's historical memory, civic groups elsewhere erected memorials to founding fathers like Leif Erikkson (sculpted by Anne Whitney for the cities of Milwaukee, Wisconsin, and Needham, Massachusetts in 1887), Thaddeus Kosciusko (Boston, 1899; West Point, 1913), Giuseppe Garibaldi (New York, 1888), and Sam Houston (Houston, 1924).

Christopher Columbus was statue mania's most popular "great man." As early as 1849, Missouri senator Thomas Hart Benton proposed that the forthcoming transcontinental railroad be commemorated by a colossal statue of Columbus "hewn from a granite mass or a peak on the Rocky Mountains . . . pointing with outstretched arm to the western horizon, and saying to the flying passengers—'There is the East; there is India.'"[10] (Although never built, Benton's grandiose scheme surely sparked Gutzon Borglum's similarly ostentatious interest in carving memorials like Stone Mountain and Mount Rushmore.) Hundreds of other Columbus monuments, statues, busts, and fountains were built in other cities, including Baltimore, Boston, Brooklyn, Chicago, Columbus, New Haven, New York, Peoria, Providence, Sacramento, Scranton, St. Louis, and Willimantic, all of them honoring the four hundredth anniversary of the Italian explorer's "discovery" of America. In 1912, Lorado Taft's Columbus Memorial Fountain was erected in front of Washington's Union Station, and dedicated in an elaborate civic ceremonhy that the *New York Times* said was "second only to the inauguration of a President" (fig. 1.3). Over 150,000 spectators listened to an address by President William Howard Taft and watched a parade of 15,000 troops, 2,000 cars, 50,000 Knights of Columbus, and numerous floats depicting notable moments in Columbus's life.[11]

Statue mania was not unique to the nation's white ethnics: postbellum black communities were also deeply engaged in what the *Washington Bee*, an African American weekly, called "monument fever" in 1889. Local and national drives (not all of them successful) to erect memorials to African Americans such as William C. Nell, Crispus Attucks (honored with a statue in Boston Common in 1888), Nat Turner, Frederick Douglass (Rochester, New York, 1899), Harriet Tubman (Auburn, New York, 1914),

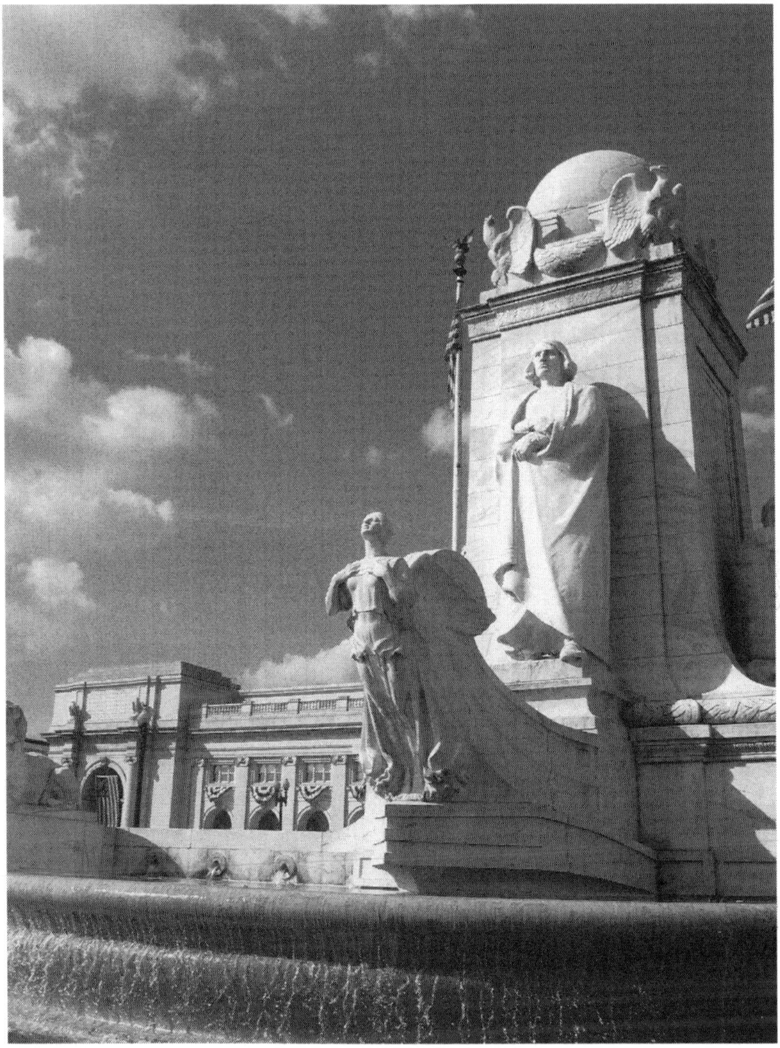

1.3. Lorado Taft, Columbus Memorial Fountain, Washington, D.C., dedicated 1912. (Photo by the author.)

and John Mercer Langston were frequently covered in the *Bee*. The newspaper's editor, W. Calvin Chase, was an avid memorial enthusiast who as early as 1883 had pushed for a monument that would honor black Civil War veterans and "be erected at government expense in the nation's capital."[12] While a bill to support it was introduced in Congress a few years later, such a monument would not be built until 1998, when the African American Civil War Memorial, featuring Ed Hamilton's *Spirit of Freedom* was dedicated in Washington (see fig. 4.28, on p. 231).

Thousands of war memorials erected in the late nineteenth and early twentieth centuries paid tribute to America's soldier dead and reified a national ideology of militarism and masculinity. Most were produced by a burgeoning commercial monument industry that provided mass-produced memorials to muncipalities all over the country. In the fifty years following the Civil War, for example, northern and southern cities purchased "standing soldier" statues of Union or Confederate warriors: common soldiers, generally lone infantrymen, standing on top of stone columns and grasping a rifle. Selecting stock examples from catalogues published by companies like the Armes Foundry in Chicopee, Massachusetts, or the Muldoon Monument Company in Louisville, Kentucky. Civic associations such as the Daughters of Union Veterans of the Civil War and the United Daughters of the Confederacy paid anywhere from $1,000 to $10,000 for the Civil War statue of their choice. In 1870, the Colored Women's Lincoln Aid Society of Philadelphia laid the cornerstone for a proposed $2,000 "monument to those [black soldiers and sailors] who fell fighting to perpetuate our glorious Union."[13]

In the early 1900s, many U.S. cities purchased stock statues of Spanish American War soldiers, called "hiker statues" after the animated march of American troops up Cuba's San Juan Hill. In the 1920s, they spent their civic dollars on "fighting doughboy" memorials depicting rifle-thrusting World War I infantrymen seemingly lifted from the European trenches of the western front.[14] Ernest Moore Viquesney, who made funerary monuments for commercial firms in Georgia and Indiana, was one of several American sculptors who designed World War I memorials and produced hundreds of fighting doughboy statues for cities ranging from North Canaan, Connecticut, to Beaver, Utah (fig. 1.4). Each of Viquesney's bronzes, which cost $2,000 to $5,000 and were called *Spirit of the American Doughboy*, featured a seven-foot soldier boldly striding through a no-man's-land of barbed wire and shelled tree stumps, hoisting a bayonet in one hand and a grenade in the other. Capitalizing on their popular appeal during the era of statue mania, Viquesney also marketed $6 fighting doughboy statuettes ("endorsed and recommended by the National Memorial Committee of The American Legion"), desk lamps, and candlesticks.[15]

Other cities boasted the individually commissioned and much more expensive memorials of sculptors such as MacMonnies, Taft, Daniel Chester French, and Augustus Saint-Gaudens—professional artists who saw themselves as the cultural custodians of American taste and viewed their statues as ways to educate the public about "official" and hence appropriate national histories and ideals. As John Bodnar argues, "Official culture relies on 'dogmatic formalism' and the restatement of reality in

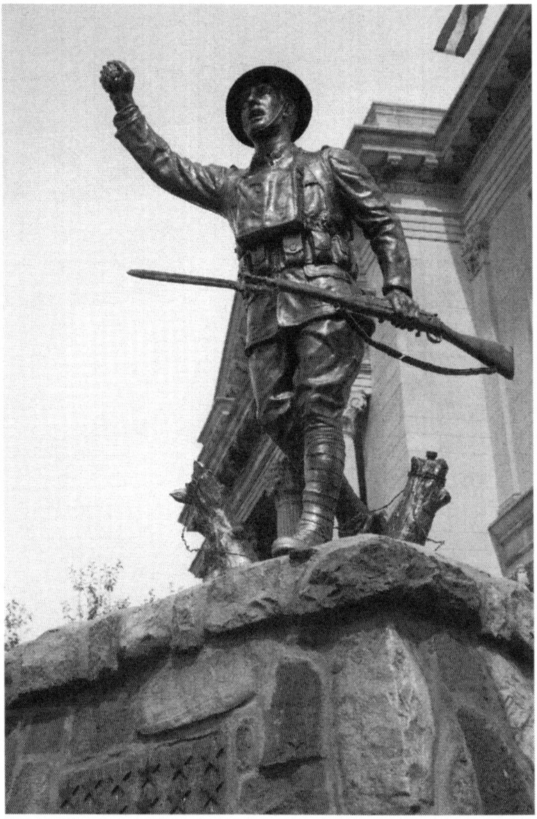

1.4. Ernest Moore Viquesney, *Spirit of the American Doughboy*, Greencastle, Indiana, dedicated 1920. (Courtesy of Cindy O'Dell.)

ideal rather than complex or ambiguous terms . . . Cultural leaders, usually grounded in institutional and professional structures, envisioned a nation of dutiful and united citizens . . . and never tired of using commemoration to restate what they thought the social order and citizen behavior should be."[16] Statues played a vital role in championing collective national ideals, as did a widespread public culture of national anthems, holidays, festivals, and fairs.

French's *The Concord Minuteman*, for example, a life-sized bronze of an alert Yankee farmer ready to do battle with the British at a moment's notice, was unveiled in 1875 in Concord, Massachusetts, at a Revolutionary War centennial celebration (fig. 1.5). A replica was displayed a year later at Philadelphia's Centennial Exhibition, a world's fair attended by some ten million people who saw, among other memorials, the gigantic arm of the Statue of Liberty, a gift from France that would be dedicated in New York in 1886. The Pledge of Allegiance, a ritualistic act of fealty to the U.S. flag ("and the Republic for which it stands") was written in 1893. It was popularized that year at the World's Columbian Exposition in Chicago,

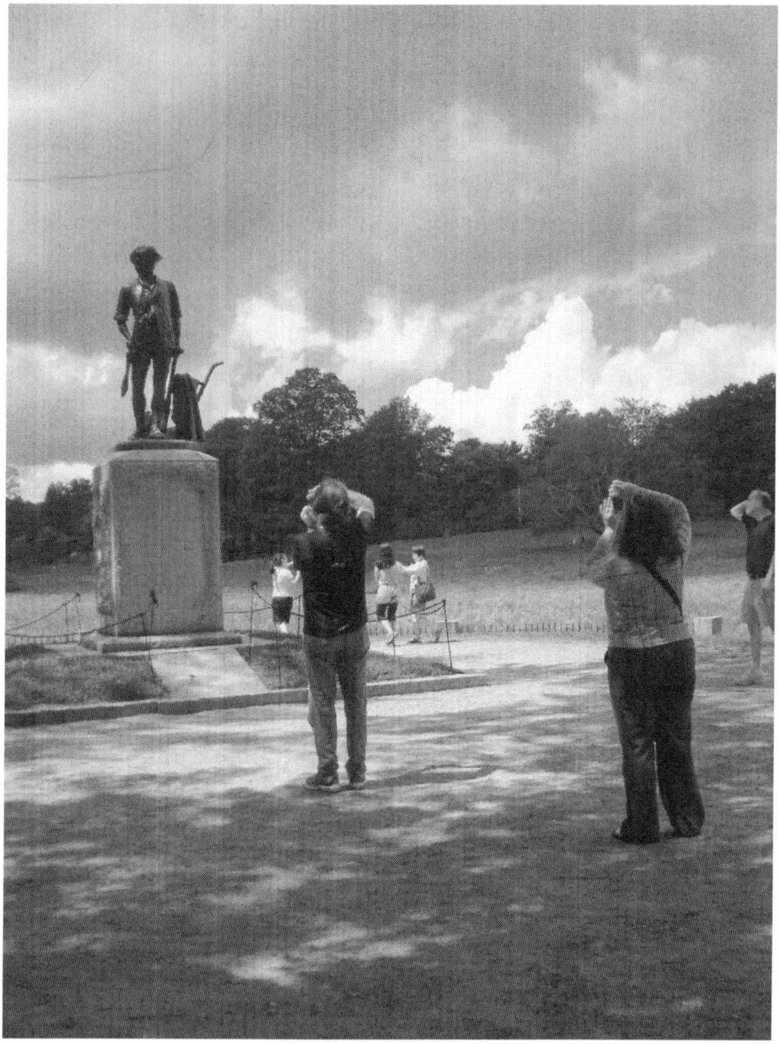

1.5. Daniel Chester French, *The Concord Minuteman*, Concord, Massachusetts, dedicated 1875. (Photo by the author.) More than one million people visit the Minute Man National Historical Park each year.

a world's fair that while ostensibly a tribute to Christopher Columbus was mostly a monumental spectacle of renewed national self-confidence and a proclamation of America's late nineteenth-century technological innovations, cultural ambitions, and global economic leadership.

These commemorative cultures aimed at evoking intimate, emotional, and authentic ties between different American publics and the United States, encouraging an affective allegiance to the nation that would be as strong and as sacred as that extended to family, region, religion, and / or ethnic and racial group. Naming practices—such as listing the names of the nine thousand Cuyahoga County residents who served in the Civil War on the walls of the Soldiers' and Sailors' Monument (Cleveland, Ohio, 1894)—were further employed to generate shared feelings of nationalism.[17]

Statue mania was symptomatic of turn-of-the-twentieth-century anxieties about national unity, anxieties unleashed by the rapid advance of modernism, immigration, and mass culture. Cultural efforts to assuage those anxieties included, among other things, reordering the nation's urban landscapes. From New York to Cleveland to San Diego, urban America was revamped in an idealized "City Beautiful" aesthetic that appropriated Greco-Roman and other styles in order to evoke Progressive Era political ideals. Grand boulevards, spacious squares, and manicured parks were centerpieced by oversized statues—like Denver's Pioneer Monument—that promoted "official" cultural perceptions of national values and virtues as they simultaneously belied the sociopolitical frictions that mandated their making in the first place. Many newly revised urban spaces became the staging grounds for highly ritualized civic festivals like "The Pageant and Masque of St. Louis" (1914), which was performed in St. Louis's Forest Park by a 7,500 person cast and viewed by an audience of some 350,000 people. Featuring costumed processions of American ethnics and newly naturalized citizens, these carefully choreographed "Dramas of Democracy" rarely critiqued the terms of civic inclusion or how and why "other" Americans were often excluded from national subjectivity (like much of St. Louis's African American population).[18] Similar sorts of social, political, and cultural anxieties undergird memorial mania today.

Likewise, a century ago the nation's proliferation of public monuments—and public commemoration in general—was seen on "manic" terms as a worrisome problem of irrational emotional zeal and material excess. "The country's gone pageant mad," one reporter observed in 1912.[19] This was not a uniquely American condition. In the mid-nineteenth century, the British press voiced concerns about "monument mania" following feverish plans to memorialize prime minister Sir Robert Peel, who died in 1850.[20] Prior to the 1800s, "mania" was mostly understood as a synonym of "furious madness," as a chronic collapse of reason and self-control and the appearance, instead, of generally deranged behavior. In the nineteenth century, however, "mania" became more broadly understood as a "primary disorder of affect" or as an emotionally driven (if also physically presented) illness.[21] Used as a psychological diagnosis for various forms of addiction, including alcoholism and sex (for example, dipsomania and nymphomania), "mania" was also typically understood as the manifestation of social and cultural excess—hence, statue mania.

In France, increasing anxiety—and outright hostility—about statue mania prompted one journalist to declare, "as concerns the many commemorative statues, I would like to state the same as Marat once did—I need 300,000 heads." In 1911, Paris's Municipal Council took the "remarkable step," noted the *New York Times*, of stopping its statue mania "epidemic" by banning any new statues, busts, and bas-reliefs for the next ten years, "no matter what may be the claims to immortality of the candidates for honors."[22]

As statue mania spread, *Leslie's Weekly*, one of the major illustrated weekly magazines at the time, complained that the United States was "being covered with monuments . . . which are, in many cases, absolute deformities, designed in utter defiance of every principle of good taste, and lacking every element of appropriateness." (The magazine later called Cleveland's Soldiers' and Sailors' Monument one of the nation's most "inartistic public monuments.") In 1919, the *American Magazine of Art* bemoaned "the plague of war memorials now sweeping over the land." The editors despondently concluded, "Must we suffer not only war but also the commemoration of war?"[23]

Problems of poor craftsmanship, indifferent placement, civic congestion, hyper-commercialism, and general public irrelevence prompted this criticism of statue mania. Writers at the *New York Herald*, for example, took issue with the "painful lack of originality" conveyed by the "entirely spectacular" statuary displayed at the Columbian Exposition. Protesting that there was "hardly an American idea" among the Chicago fair's many memorials, reporters gleefully maligned the Greco-Roman conceit of statues like French's sixty-five-foot sculpture *The Republic*: a gilded goddess clothed in a toga crowned with a laurel wreath and holding a staff topped by a liberty cap in one hand and a globe topped by an eagle in the other (fig. 1.6). Critics were especially impatient with MacMonnies's overblown Columbian Fountain, a cluttered sculptural display that was effusively—maniacally—decorated with prancing seahorses, plunging dolphins, playful putti, and other allegorical froufrou. Such sculptors were admonished to "unbend for awhile from the commercial and monumental attitude in which they have stood so long."[24]

Statue mania backlash was furthered by growing weariness with old-fashioned art styles (especially at a moment of nascent modernism) and heavy-handed proselytizing by art elites who overestimated the

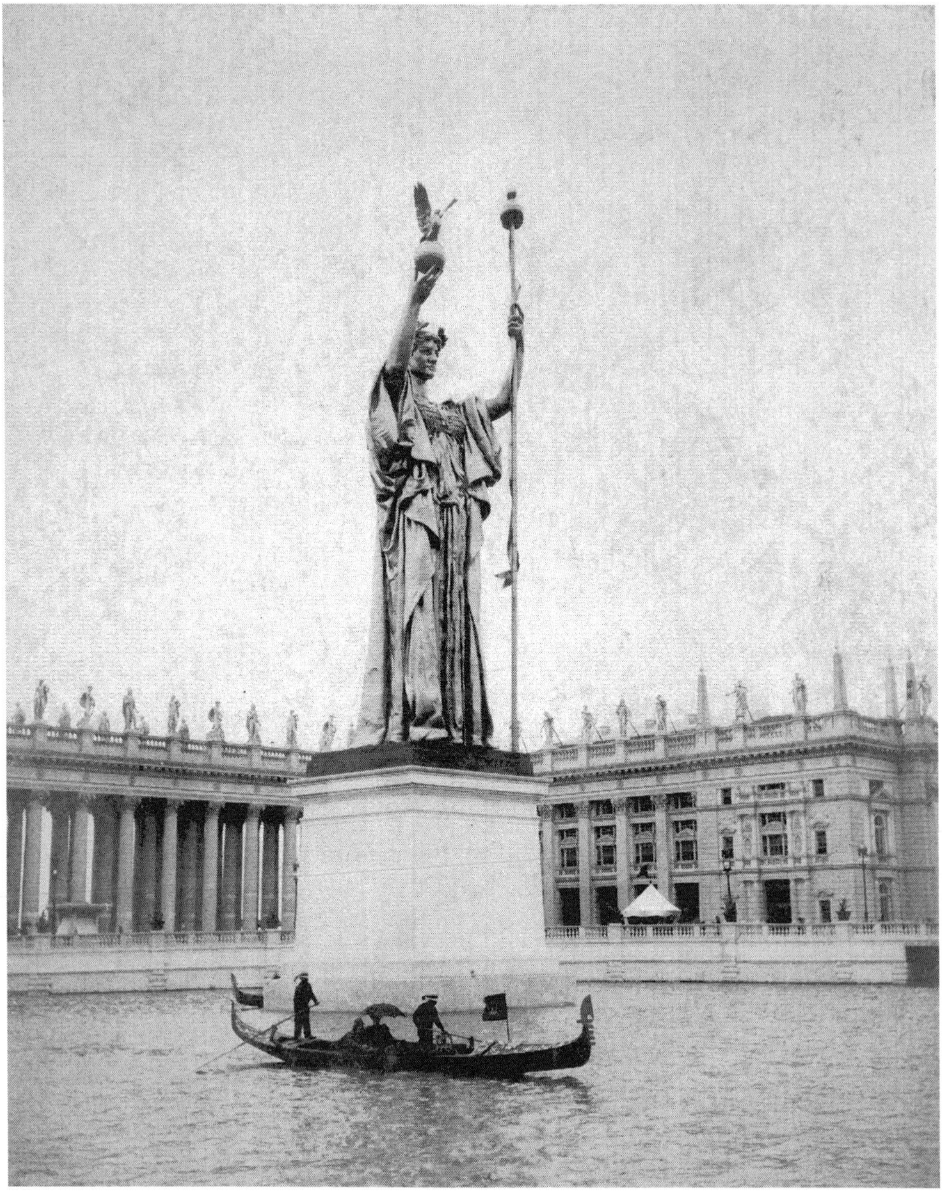

1.6. Daniel Chester French, *The Republic*, World's Columbian Exposition, Chicago, Illinois, 1893. Destroyed. (Photograph reproduced courtesy of the Chicago History Museum [ICHI-29874].)

unifying capacity of public monuments. As Michele Bogart argues in her discussion of the "protracted negotiations" that ensued over a memorial to Samuel J. Tilden (finally dedicated in New York's Riverside Park in 1926 after several decades of debate), "the fact that certain turn-of-the-century groups took commemorative statues seriously and succeeded in placing some of them on public property is proof of neither consensus nor success."[25] Assumptions about appropriate standards of cultural taste and monolithic accounts of American history typically failed to reckon with other, more diverse and dynamic visions of the nation and were increasingly challenged as the twentieth century unfolded. In 1925, for example, American sculptor Janet Scudder, who began her career making allegorical statues like *Nymph of the Wabash* for the Indiana Pavilion at the Columbian Exposition, pointedly condemned the "obsession with male egotism that is ruining every city in the United States." As Scudder protested, the nation was overrun "with rows of hideous statues of men-men-men—each one uglier than the other—standing, sitting, riding horseback—every one of them pompously convinced that he is decorating the landscape!"[26]

Statue mania was eventually defeated by the temporal politics of American memory. However much they were meant as timeless vessels of permanent national values and beliefs, turn-of-the-twentieth-century public statues embodied presentist ideals and interests that became irrelevant and even irreconcilable in later decades. Wandering through America in the 1960s and 1970s, photographer Lee Friedlander shot hundreds of statue mania's bronze and marble offspring: the sculptures, fountains, obelisks, shrines, and plaques that were installed—and often abandoned—in the nation's parks, squares, cemeteries, and public streets (fig. 1.7). Compiled in the oversized volume *The American Monument* (1976), Friedlander's sardonic photographs of statue mania's founding fathers, U.S. presidents, American soldiers, Sons of Liberty, and volunteer firemen reflect on the fleeting faith that Americans place in the stuff of historical memory, revealing the neglect of posterity and the litter of modernity.[27]

By the 1920s, statue mania was seen as a crisis of emotional excess, a troubling public spectacle of intemperate affect. Comparable criticism about memorial mania is voiced today, especially by those who are alarmed by the proliferation of statues, sculptures, monuments, memorials, and other kinds of commemoration that occupy (or are scheduled to occupy) the nation's capital. Anxieties about how America's burgeoning memorial culture can be managed and how its affective excess can be controlled are common. Worries that memorial mania signals the nation's emotional unraveling are rife.

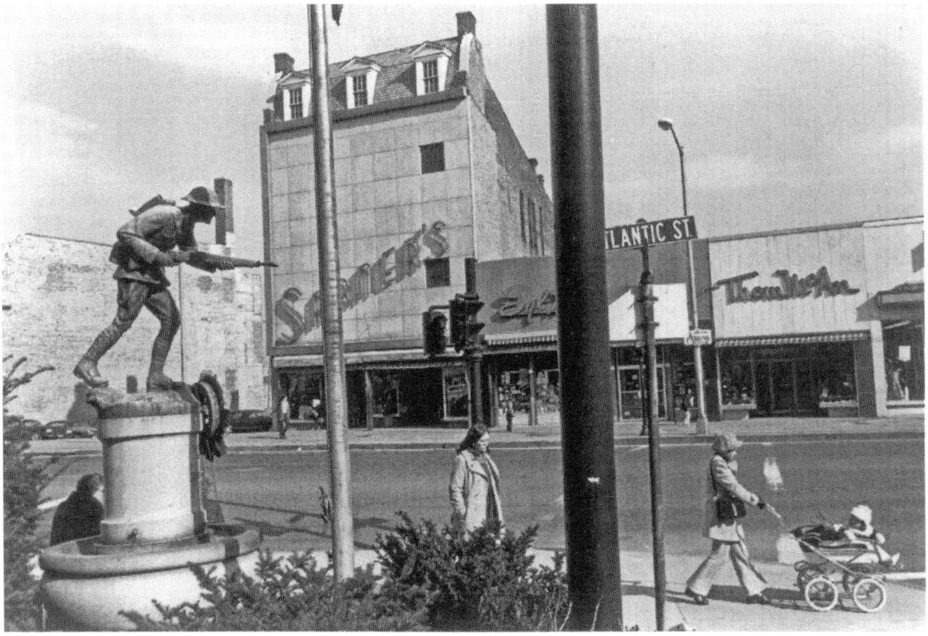

1.7. Lee Friedlander, "Doughboy, Stamford, Connecticut," 1973. Gelatin silver print. (© Lee Friedlander. Courtesy of the Fraenkel Gallery, San Francisco.)

PUBLIC ART/PUBLIC RIGHTS

Much of today's memorial mania relates to the recent mushrooming of the public art industry—"the fastest-growing industry in the United States," art critic Grace Glueck speculated in 1982. With the advent of Percent for Art ordinances in multiple American cities and states, whereby certain percentages of capital construction costs are dedicated to public art, millions of dollars have funded thousands of public art projects across the country.[28] Supported by local and state art agencies, national organizations, degree-granting programs (at the University of Southern California and the University of Washington, among other schools), and a growing body of artists, architects, and designers specifically attuned to the rules and regulations of the field, public art has become ever more visible and professionalized in America. Its visibility rests especially on its "functional utility": since the 1970s, as Miwon Kwon explains, public art has been charged with generating a sense of "place-bound identity" and lending an aura of distinction and authenticity to the nation's increasingly homogenous and indifferent public spaces.[29] Occasional arguments for the sheer existence of "art" in America are countered by presumptions of public art's civic and social responsibilities, and its efficacy

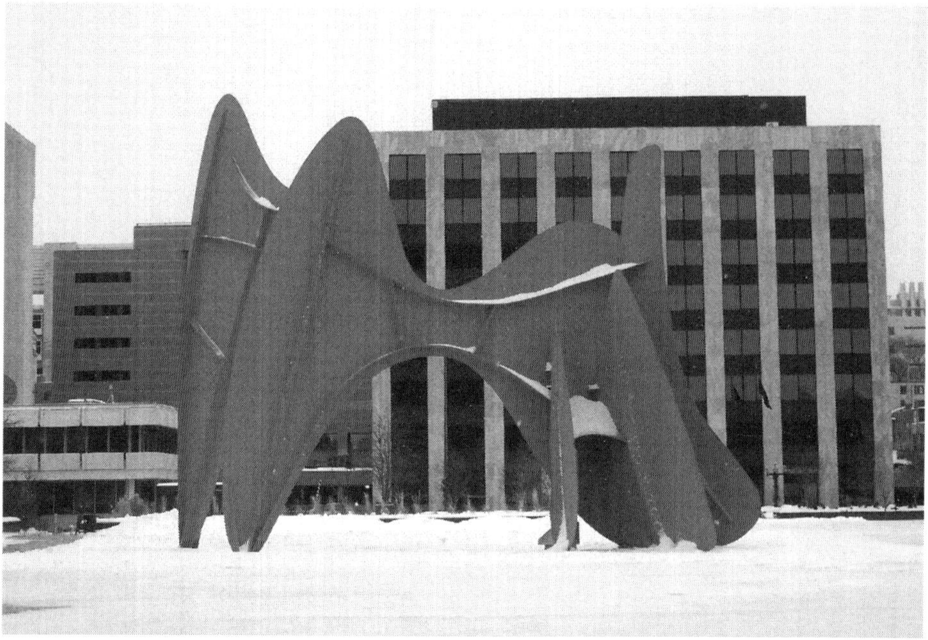

1.8. Alexander Calder, *La Grande Vitesse*, Grand Rapids, Michigan, dedicated 1969. (Courtesy of Jennifer Geigel Mikulay.)

as symbolic capital. Contemporary public sculptures that fail to generate some sense of spatial and/or social relevance are snidely dismissed as "plop art."

The expectation that today's public art "stand" for something stems from its origins in an earlier memorial culture. Long before Alexander Calder's *La Grande Vitesse* (1969; fig. 1.8) was installed in Grand Rapids, Michigan, to broker modernist sophistication and engender civic identity, American cities were liberally sprinkled with the pragmatic stuff of statue mania. In 1905, for example, lumber baron Benjamin Franklin Ferguson bequested $1 million for the "erection and maintenance of enduring statuary and monuments, in the whole or in part of stone, granite, or bronze, in the parks, along the boulevards, or in other public places within the City of Chicago, Illinois, commemorating worthy men or women of America or important events in American history."[30] For over a century, the Ferguson Fund has financed numerous statues and monuments in Chicago. The Art Institute features Lorado Taft's *Fountain of the Great Lakes* (1913), an allegorical concoction of five comely ladies dribbling water from giant seashells. The University of Chicago hosts Henry Moore's *Nuclear Energy* (1967), a twelve-foot bronze monolith erected on the site of the school's former Stagg Field Stadium (under which the first controlled nuclear chain reaction took place in 1942). More recent sculptures, such as Isamu Noguchi's *Fountains* (1976), Louise Bourgeois' *Helping Hands* (1996) in Jane Addams Memorial Park, and a commemorative statue of Haitian-born fur trader Jean Baptiste Pointe du Sable by Martin Puryear that is planned for DuSable Park, suggest the relative indistinction between memorials and public art. Indeed, in 1957, Ferguson's will was subject to legal wrangling over the suggested ambiguity of the words "statuary" and "monuments" when fund administrators at the Art Institute petitioned to bankroll not just public sculptures but a new wing for the art museum to be called the "Ferguson Memorial."[31]

In the early years of the public art industry, the 1960s to the 1980s, many of its champions struggled to distinguish public art from the memorials and monuments of statue mania. "Public art isn't a hero on a horse anymore," Arlene Raven asserted. "The bronze memorial, the most enduring public art form of the past century, gave way to large-scale abstract sculpture that flooded the public domain in the United States when the National Endowment for the Arts launched its art-in-public-places program in the 1960s." Likewise, promoting a "new vision for public art" in the 1983 exhibition Beyond the Monument, curator Gary Garrels wrote:

> Until very recently public art and the monument were closely linked terms, with one essentially implying the other. The notion of public art, almost without exception,would call forth an image exemplified by a traditional stone or bronze statue of a hero or by a geometric welded steel abstraction . . . a number of artists increasingly have challenged these ideas and forms . . . there has been a movement toward art which invites active participation, which becomes a functional part of the environment, and which claims purposes inclusive of, but not limited to, aesthetic or formal issues.[32]

Writer Douglas McGill similarly described the "new public art" as "art plus function, whether the function is to provide a place to sit for lunch, to provide water drainage, to mark an important historical date, or to enhance and direct a viewer's perceptions."[33]

Yet even as they made these distinctions, such writers implied the similarities and continuities between the "new" public art and seemingly old-fashioned memorials: McGill's description of the commemorative function of public art is, at base level, the definition of a civic monument. Whether figurative or abstract in style, public art and public memorials both take as their subject what Rosalind Krauss describes as "the public, conventional nature of what might be called cultural space."[34] Public needs, public participation, and public response are their shared tenets.

Similarly expected to perform on utilitarian terms and funded from the same sources, whether private monies or Percent for Art dollars, public art and public memorials are practically synonymous.

Both are also ubiquitous today because American demands for the symbolic expression of particular concerns have never been stronger. As demonstrated again and again, contemporary conflicts over public art are typically linked to localized struggles over cultural, social, and economic authority in the public sphere; as Rosalyn Deutsche argues, public space is "inseparable from the conflictual and uneven social relations that structure specific societies at specific historical moments." By extension, heated civic debates over public art styles, subjects, and costs correspond to the public's perceptions of representation, or the lack thereof.[35]

Of course, as Michael Warner argues, the notion of the "public" is itself highly unstable: "No one really inhabits the general public. This is true not only because it is by definition general but also because everyone brings to such a category the particularities from which she has to abstract herself in consuming this discourse."[36] Thus, while the concept of the "public" is and always has been a naturalizing (and normalizing) construction of American national identity, "being" a public depends on the shared assumptions of its participants, or would-be participants, that *they* comprise the public sphere and are therefore entitled to its rights and privileges.

Consequently, one explanation for today's memorial mania is the sense of entitlement, or "ownership," that pervades today's public sphere: increasingly, self-interest groups view the nation's memorials as the direct extension of their particular causes. The Franklin Delano Roosevelt Memorial, a $48 million project designed by Lawrence Halprin and dedicated in Washington, D.C., in 1997, is a prime example. Shortly after the 7.5-acre memorial opened, Congress, responding to the demands of the National Organization on Disability, passed a joint resolution requiring that the site visibly depict the thirty-second U.S. president's physical handicap. In 2001, a bronze sculpture of FDR in a wheelchair was placed at the memorial's entrance, where people gather before beginning their journey through its four "rooms" (symbolizing the four terms of Roosevelt's presidency). Placed at ground level and looking, as Sally Stein observes, "less definitive than diminutive," the sculpture is the source of innumerable photo ops, as visitors pretend to push the president's wheelchair (fig. 1.9).[37]

Stricken in 1921 with a paralytic illness believed to be polio, Roosevelt himself downplayed and disguised his impairment, believing that its social perception as a disability would negatively shape his public image and limit his political abilities. Only a few photographs show him

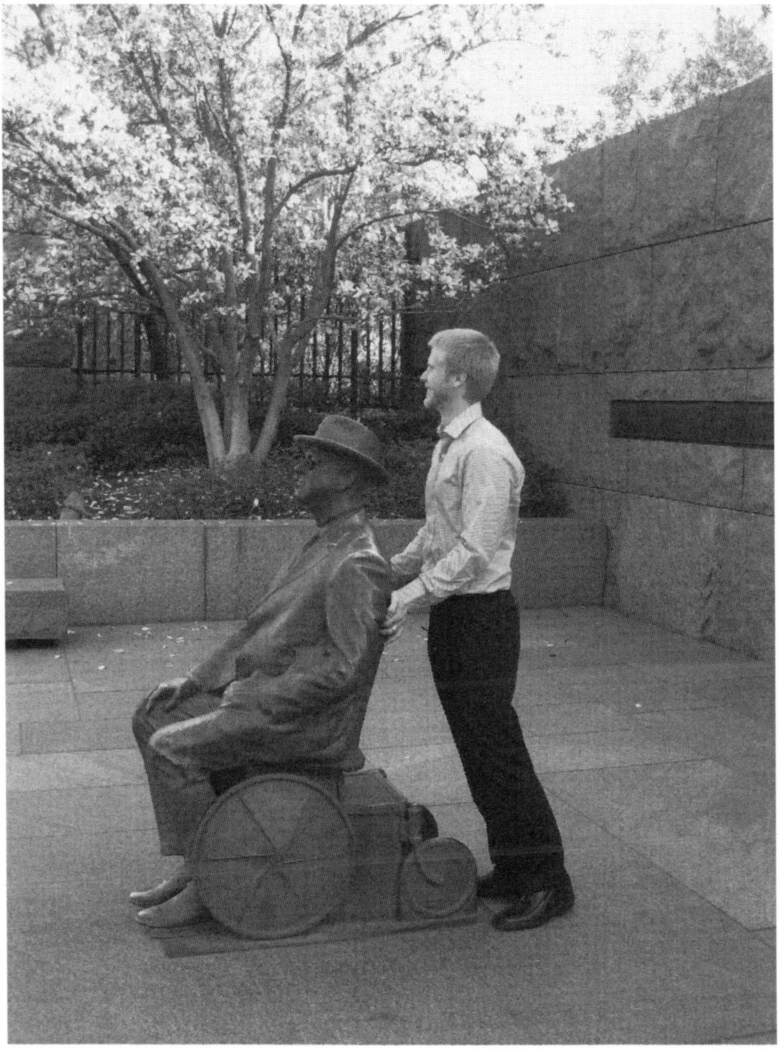

1.9. Robert Graham, statue of Franklin Delano Roosevelt, Franklin Delano Roosevelt Memorial, Washington, D.C., statue dedicated 2001. (Courtesy of Heather Bowling.)

in a wheelchair and FDR went to great lengths to refigure himself as a healthy, competent, and powerful presidential body.[38] Sculptor Neil Estern conveys this commanding figure in his oversized statue of FDR in the memorial's third room, which depicts the president wrapped in a long military cape, seated on a high-backed armchair equipped with small casters (one of which can be seen at the back of the sculpture), and attended by his faithful dog Fala (fig. 1.10).

Yet this statue was deemed inadequate by disability activists who

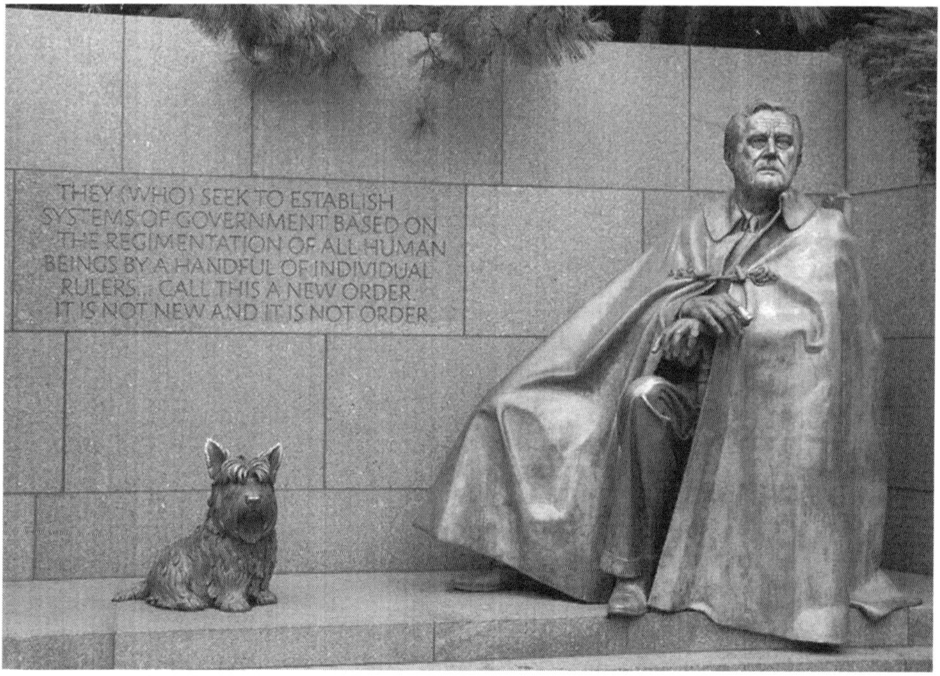

1.10. Neil Estern, *FDR and Fala*, Franklin Delano Roosevelt Memorial, dedicated 1997. This statue of FDR is almost nine feet tall. (Courtesy of Heather Bowling.)

insisted that Roosevelt's memorial more blatantly commemorate their own interests. Theirs were not the only claims to symbolic representation—and erasure—at the site: antismoking lobbyists succeeded in eliminating any references to FDR's cigarette habit, and animal-rights groups managed to suppress the inclusion of a fox stole in a statue of Eleanor Roosevelt, who stands alone and furless in an isolated niche of the memorial's fourth room. All of these claims and, in fact, the entire memorial ignore the president's own preferences regarding his public commemoration. As Supreme Court Justice Felix Frankfurter related in a 1961 issue of *Atlantic Monthly*, FDR never wanted an elaborate or conspicuous memorial and left plans for only a modest block of stone no bigger than his desk and "without any ornamentation," to be placed in front of the National Archives Building.[39]

Efforts to control the symbolic terms of national commemoration extend from a broader emphasis on citizen rights in America. Writing about current understandings of citizenship, Michael Schudson traces the growth of "rights consciousness" in the wake of the civil rights movement, as American courts and legislatures became increasingly attuned to the obligations of law and government regarding the claims of individuals. Today's model of citizenship is more rights-oriented—for example, the activism of the disability rights movement—and today's public sphere has become a "playing field of citizenship" where rights are asserted and claimed. Importantly, this "triumph of democratic sensibilities" has vastly expanded understandings of American citizenship and nationalism: of who counts as an American today, and of what causes are now deemed constitutionally fundamental to the nation—such as civil rights. Yet, Schudson cautions, rights consciousness also "legitimates individual and group egoism and emphasizes at every turn the individual, self-gratification over self-discipline, the economic over the moral, the short term over the long term, the personal over the social." As Halprin observed of the congressionally mandated inclusion of the additional sculpture of FDR in the memorial he designed: "Special interest groups were able to override thoughtful processes and established procedures. The results dilute the art and send equivocal messages to the future."[40]

Memorial mania is shaped by individual impulses and factional grievances, by special interest claims for esteem and recognition, and by efforts to symbolize and enshrine the particular issues and aspirations of diverse and often stratified publics. Today, the pace of commemoration has quickened, and the number of memorials has escalated, because growing numbers of Americans view *public art* as a particularly powerful vehicle of visibility and authority. Their preference for memorials, as opposed to monuments, further clarifies contemporary understandings of public commemoration.

MEMORIAL VERSUS MONUMENT

Art historian Horst Janson explained that the traditional Western monument falls into three categories: the funerary monument, the monument to historical events or ideas (for example, "Liberty"), and the monument to great men. In terms of style, the traditional monument was typically figurative and vertical, placed high on a pedestal that mediated between the physical site it dominated and the symbolic capital it embodied.[41] Intended as permanent fixtures in distinctive spatial and social landscapes, and thus usually made of enduring materials like marble, granite, or bronze, monuments were meant to perform specific didactic functions. As Alois Riegl put it in his classic 1903 essay "The Modern Cult of Monuments," "A monument in its oldest and most original sense is a human creation, erected for the specific purpose of keeping single human deeds or events (or a combination thereof) alive in the minds of future generations." The purpose of the monument, echoes Françoise Choay, was essentially affective: "It is not simply a question of informing, of calling to mind a neutral bit of information, but rather of stirring up, through the emotions, a living memory." Consequently, Eric Hobsbawm observes, monuments became central to the construction of shared national ideologies and identities by operating as "open-air museum[s] of natural history as seen through great men." Their "function as social magnets," Marvin Trachtenberg asserts in his discussion of the Statue of Liberty, was a crucial means of transmitting "communal emotions."[42]

Distinctions between monuments and memorials are tenuous: if monuments have traditionally functioned to commemorate great men and moments, memorials—in the public culture context discussed here—have similarly served to remember and honor the subjects they address. Both monuments and memorials are memory aids: materialist modes of privileging particular histories and values. Some scholars argue for their difference: Marita Sturken explains that "monuments are a means to honor the past, whereas memorials focus specifically on paying tribute to the dead." Wilbur Zelinsky finds that monuments "verge close to sacredness, not unlike the temples, shrines, and historic landmarks with which they are often associated," whereas memorials are more multivalent entities like "parks, gardens, forests, bridges, auditorea, stadia, highways, benches, government buildings, and institutions of every description."[43]

In the United States today, the terms "monument" and "memorial" are used interchangeably. Monuments can be massive stone obelisks like the one on the National Mall, or figurative sculptures like the Robert E. Lee Monument in Richmond (see fig. 0.16, p. 12). Monuments are also federally managed parks such as the Muir Woods National Monument north of San Francisco and the Devil's Tower National Monument in Wyoming (designated America's first national monument by President Teddy Roosevelt in 1906). Likewise, memorials include national parks like the Coronado National Memorial in Arizona, and figurative projects like the Cuarto Centenario Memorial in Albuquerque (2005), a multi-statue narrative of Spanish conquistador Juan de Oñate's trek through the Southwest in the late sixteenth century (see figs. 6.18–6.19, pp. 357, 358). Memorials also denote national days of remembrance (Memorial Day), sports arenas (the Spokane Veterans Memorial Arena), libraries (the Martin Luther King Jr. Memorial Library in Washington, D.C.), hospitals (Union Memorial Hospital in Baltimore), and highways (Jane Addams Memorial Tollway, Illinois).

Despite their interchangeability, the word "memorial" is used more often and has greater cachet today than "monument." Almost all of America's recent commemorative projects are called memorials, not monuments: consider the Pentagon Memorial, Victims of Communism Memorial, National World War II Memorial, Oklahoma City National Memorial, New England Holocaust Memorial, Franklin Delano Roosevelt Memorial, and Korean War Veterans Memorial. As Maya Lin, who designed the Vietnam Veterans Memorial in Washington, D.C. (1982; see fig. 3.6, p. 128) and the Civil Rights Memorial in Montgomery (1989; see fig. 0.6, p. 4), remarks: "I consider the work I do memorials, not monuments; in fact I've often thought of them as anti-monuments." Or as architect James Ingo Freed commented on his design for the United States Holocaust Memorial Museum, situated on the National Mall and near the Washington Monument: "I choose to call it a memorial and not a monument because monuments celebrate things. Here there is no celebration. Also, monuments tend to be too unified, too unitary, restricting different possibilities of readings and interpretations. So 'memorial' seems to be better."[44]

As Freed observes, disengagement from the word "monument" relates in part to perceptions of its "monolithic" character. Today, in an American scene especially disposed to individuals and special interests and focused on self-expression and personal feeling, the traditional monument's invocation of a "unitary" mass ethos may seem oppressive and exclusionary. These critiques are not particularly new: discussions of the inadequacy and even impossibility of the traditional monument were frequent throughout the twentieth century among historians, critics, and artists responding to the compromised polemics of statue mania and eager to advance seemingly more authentic forms of modern art. In the late 1930s, Lewis Mumford argued that monuments were completely out of sync with modern times: "The notion of a modern monument is veritably a contradiction in terms. If it is a monument, it is not modern, and if it is not modern, it cannot be a monument." Forty years later, Rosalind Krauss dismissed "the logic of the monument" amidst the apparent triumph of modern and contemporary sculpture's "functionally placeless and largely self-referential" conditions.[45] Photographers like Lee Friedlander found monuments similarly passé.

Some raised objections in terms of their perceived stylistic deficiencies. In 1958, when he chaired a jury to select a monument at the Auschwitz-Birkenau concentration camp (a public competition in which 685 sculptors and architects from 36 countries participated), British sculptor Henry Moore questioned the "almost insoluble" problem of making "a monument to crime and ugliness, to murder and to horror." After reviewing the 426 proposals, he wrote, "Is it in fact possible to create a work of art that can express the emotions engendered by Auschwitz? It is my conviction that a very great sculptor—a new Michelangelo or a new Rodin—might conceivably have achieved this. The odds against such a design turning up among the many *maquettes* submitted were always enormous. And none did." Moore could not imagine his own style of modernist representation memorializing the horrors of the Holocaust. Nor, apparently, could he and other members of the jury convince the memorial organizers (an international group of Auschwitz-Birkenau survivors) of the value of Polish architect Oskar Hansen's more radical proposal to pave the grounds of the former death camp with a long black road—a proposal that Moore termed "exceptionally brilliant." Cutting diagonally across the ignoble landscape, Hansen's horizontal design challenged the very notion of the traditionally vertical and figurative monument-on-a-pedestal with its "open form" aesthetic.[46] Earlier, in 1949, Theodor Adorno had similarly questioned the possibility of any art or poetry after Auschwitz, worried that whatever its stylistic tendencies, emotional entreaties to pleasure or to beauty risked redeeming and thereby affirming—or commemorating—the conditions and values that had manufactured the Holocaust to begin with.[47]

Shared perceptions of the symbolic collapse of multiple cultural conventions, including lyric poetry, narrative styles of painting, and figurative monuments, were prevalent in the years during and after World War II. Apprehensions about whether any kind of representational art could adequately express the horrors of the war and anxieties about the hubris of even attempting to do so were widely shared. As one *New York Times* journalist pleaded in 1943: "No! No victory arches! It's all too terrible a disaster to make into a public emblem. Half the world mad to kill and the rest of the world struggling to recover civilization . . . No memorial arches shall keep us reminded." The editor of *Pencil Points*, an architectural journal, asked his wartime readers how best to remind "future generations about the common men who died in the cause of human freedom. Can it be done by 'monuments'? We think not . . . Let there be memorial parks and playgrounds and schools and community buildings . . . Let whatever we do have a truly social purpose and a practical social result." Likewise, in a 1945 essay in *Atlantic Monthly*, architect Joseph Hudnut declared, "Build no monument, but a civilization fit for free men. Build something that is simple and considered, useful to the community."[48]

World War II *was* commemorated in America—despite claims to the contrary by the backers of the National World War II Memorial, dedicated in Washington in 2004. But as Andrew Shanken explains, from the mid-1940s through the 1950s, the war was mostly commemorated via "living memorials": "useful" public buildings and social spaces like libraries, auditoriums, hospitals, swimming pools, and parks that included the word "memorial" in their names and typically displayed bronze plaques listing the nation's soldier dead.[49] In 1948, for example, Omaha's Memorial Park, a 65-acre site with a golf course, was dedicated to the men and women of Nebraska who died in the war. In 1950, the University of Wyoming's War Memorial Stadium ("The War") opened, a living memorial to Wyoming's World War II soldier dead and veterans. In 1953, the University of Colorado's Memorial Center was dedicated to the state's wartime servicemen. However much it changed in design and purpose, memorial making continued in post–World War II America: neither modern artists nor architects, and certainly not the American public, abandoned commemoration. Even Adorno, who questioned the efficacy of traditional aesthetic styles and conventions, enjoined postwar artists to pioneer new modes and new concepts of creativity.

Many followed his lead. Isamu Noguchi proposed immense utopian earthworks like *Memorial to Man* (1947, also titled *Sculpture to be Seen From Mars)*, and collaborated with architect Edward Durell Stone in the Jefferson National Expansion Memorial Park competition in Saint Louis.[50] Over 172 entries were received in the competition, which Eero Saarinen handily won with his design for Gateway Arch, dedicated in 1968. Other postwar memorial competitions were more fraught. In 1953, British sculptor Reg Butler, winner of the International Competition for a Monument to "The Unknown Political Prisoner," was broadly condemned for "insulting both taste and intelligence" with an avant-garde design that blended abstract and figurative elements. Butler competed against some 2,000 other proposals by artists from 52 nations (including American sculptors Alexander Calder, Naum Gabo, and Richard Lippold), and received a $12,500 prize for his design. But his highly publicized memorial, disparaged as "an emblem of Defeat" by John Berger (then writing as an art columnist for the *Daily Worker*) and "an emblem purged of pity and terror" by British writer and critic Herbert Read, was never built.[51] More successful was pop artist Claes Oldenburg, who has toyed with the metaphors of memorialization since the 1960s. Commemorating mundane things like electric plugs and clothespins in absurdly gargantuan public sculptures, Oldenburg pokes fun at the grand scale and celebratory symbolic authority of many memorials (fig. 1.11). His earliest work especially satirized the heroizing sensibilities of traditional monuments: *Proposed Monument for Park Avenue, New York: Good Humor Bar* (1965), featured a colossal sculpture of a melting ice cream bar plunked in the middle of one of Manhattan's main boulevards. Another design, *Proposed Colossal Monument to Replace the Washington Obelisk, Washington, D.C.: Scissors in Motion* (1967), featured a gigantic pair of red scissors whose blades slowly

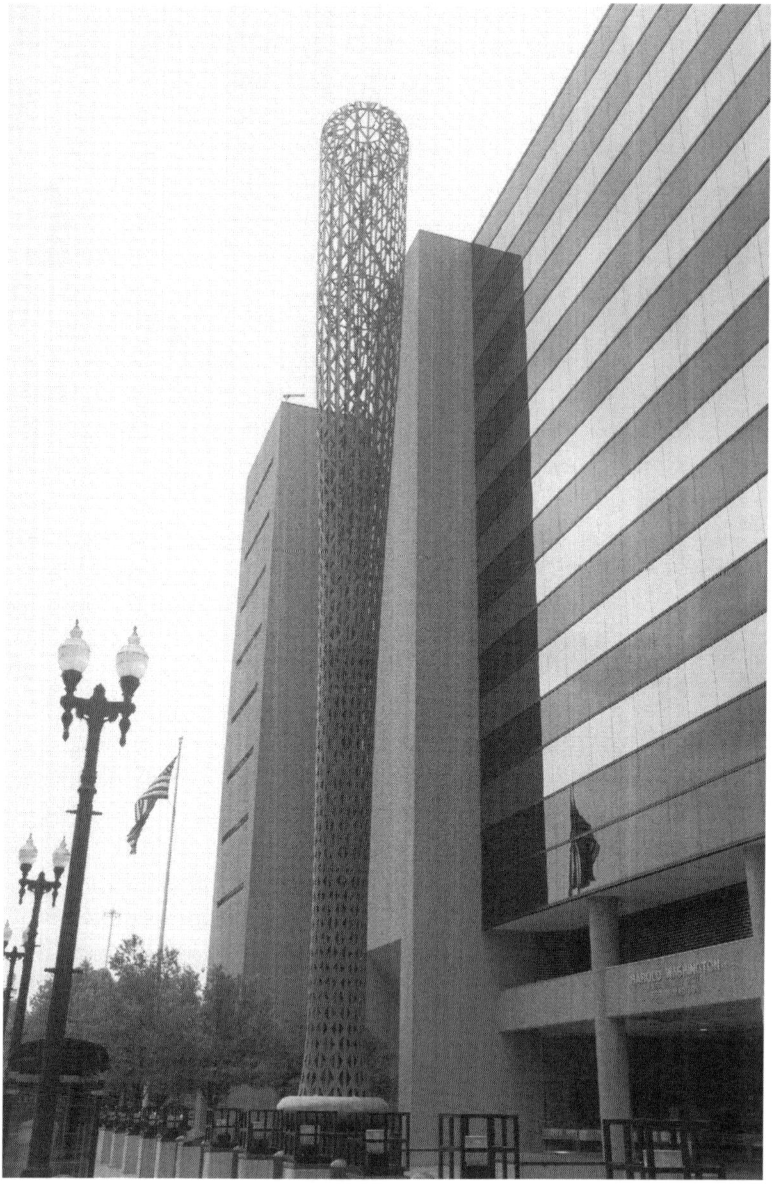

1.11. Claes Oldenburg, *Batcolumn*, Chicago, Illinois, dedicated 1977. Cor-Ten steel painted gray. (Courtesy of Geoffrey Thrumston.)

opened during the course of a day and then slowly closed all night until dawn, when, Oldenburg wisecracked, they "joined, forming a structure like the obelisk, catching the sun's light at the tips."[52]

In the 1970s, the traditional monument was declared moribund; as Janson remarked, "I am the first to admit that the public monument, as a species, is dead today." Likewise, in 1973, architect James Wines announced, "The age of monuments . . . is finished and most attempts to perpetuate the tradition are pretentious and extraneous no matter how well conceived. We presently lack the cultural estate and unifying ideology necessary to lend any significance to these heroic icons."[53] Such declarations were, of course, greatly exaggerated and failed to recognize a major shift in American commemorative practices from the monument to the memorial, from "official" national narratives to the subjective symbolic expressions of multiple American publics. Further, they failed to recognize how modernist concepts, such as irony, ambivalence, interruption, and self-criticality were often situated within these new modes of memorialization. Public and artistic interests in commemoration never died.They did, however, shift in shape, subject, and style.

While Oldenburg, for example, cynically spoofed the traditional monument, he remained keenly attentive to memorialization itself. He wasn't alone: soon after he first imagined his "proposed colossal monuments" as "playful personal fantasies" in the mid-1960s, Oldenburg "became aware that practicing architects had taken some interest in the monuments" and wanted to realize them as public projects. When students at Cornell University estimated that one of his proposed monuments "would weigh 5,000,000 lbs., if concrete were used; and that the memorial would sink through the surface the way a pat of butter melts in a baked potato," Oldenburg was pushed to decide, as he later recalled, "whether I really want to convert my fantasy to real projects." He opted for conversion and soon multiple American (and European) cities began sporting Oldenburg-designed memorials like *Clothespin* (1976, Philadelphia), *Flashlight* (1981, Las Vegas), and *Free Stamp* (1991, Cleveland), all made of lighter metal materials. Oldenburg remained focused on the memorial as a form of critically engaged public expression, observing, "Proposing monuments is like composing with a city. For example, in Chicago I feel the Hancock building needs something to balance it; perhaps a heavy fireplug monument at the end of Navy Pier . . . many of my monuments reintroduce the idea of the monument as obstacle or disruption in the city."[54] The giant bat he made for Chicago is a prime example of this "disruptive" sensibility.

Oldenburg's first fully realized memorial was *Placid Civic Monument* (1967), a temporary project built in New York's Central Park (behind the

Metropolitan Museum of Art) for the citywide exhibition Sculpture in Environment. Made at a moment of gaining public protest against the Vietnam War, Oldenburg's monument consisted of a six-foot-long, three-foot-wide, three-foot-deep trench dug by professional gravediggers—who then refilled it three hours later. The pit clearly conveyed the artist's political views; as he remarked in his notebooks at the time, "Grave is a perfect (anti) war monument, like saying no more." *Placid Civic Monument* was also built within sight of an Egyptian obelisk nicknamed Cleopatra's Needle, a seventy-one-foot-high memorial (ca. 1500 BCE) that Oldenburg had played under as a child and considered "a great monument" as an adult.[55] Looted from Alexandria, the colossal monolith was gifted to the United States by the Khedive of Egypt after the opening of the Suez Canal in hopes of cultivating trade relations; it was erected in Central Park in 1881. Typical of the affective sensibilities of Gilded Age statue mania, over ten thousand New Yorkers attended the dedication ceremonies for the ancient memorial's reinstallation, during which U.S. secretary of state William Maxwell Evarts waxed eloquent about the obelisk as a trophy of conquest, an emblem of imperial power, and a cautionary symbol of national mortality:

> Who indeed can tell what our nation will do if any perversity is possible of realization; and yet this obelisk may ask us, "Can you expect to flourish forever? Can you expect wealth to accumulate and man not decay? Can you think that the soft folds of luxury are to wrap themselves closer and closer around this nation and the pith and vigor of its manhood know no decay? Can it creep over you and yet the nation know no decrepitude?" These are questions that may be answered in the time of the obelisk but not in ours.[56]

Whether or not Oldenburg was aware of Evarts's moralizing on the imperialist perils threatening the postbellum nation, his *Placid Civic Monument* was similarly intended as a contemporary critique of unexamined political loyalties and national malfeasance. Oldenburg's ephemeral civic grave simultaneously heeded and questioned the conventions of commemoration, including memorial practices surrounding death and mourning and uncontested assumptions of triumphal nationalism. Importantly, the ironic, ambivalent, and disruptive tenor of Oldenburg's antimonumental aesthetic, which embodies both traces of the traditional monument and its critical undermining, set the pace for many subsequent examples of public art and commemoration in America. From Oldenburg's own *Lipstick (Ascending) on Caterpillar Tracks* (1969; fig. 1.12), an antiwar memorial featuring a giant lipstick-like obelisk perched on top of an army tank, to Lin's Vietnam Veterans Memorial, the modern

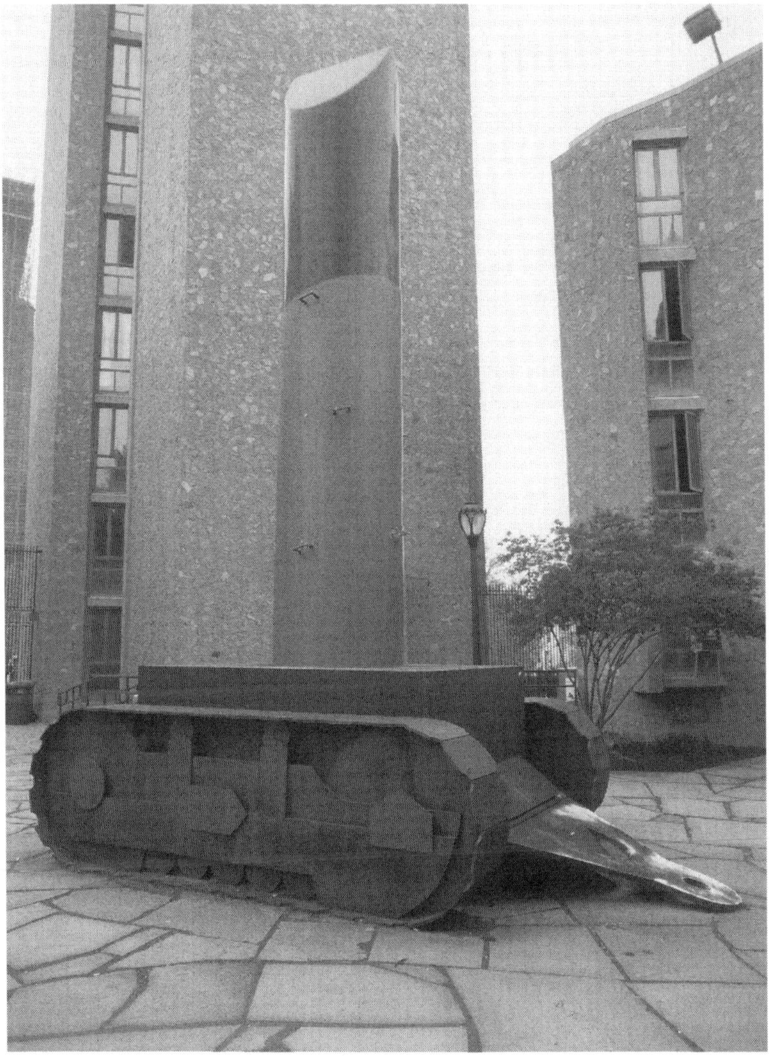

1.12. Claes Oldenburg, *Lipstick (Ascending) on Caterpillar Tracks*, Morse College, Yale University, New Haven, Connecticut, 1969–1974. (Photo by Aaron Carico.)

American memorial is often equivocal, unresolved, and ambivalent. Its meaning is neither inherent nor eternal but *processual*—dependent on a variety of social relations and subject to the volatile intangibles of the nation's multiple publics and their fluctuating interests and feelings.

Following on the relational nature of works of art and how they are produced, experienced, and made meaningful, contemporary American commemoration is understood as a locus of organized human activity that produces visual and material bodies (memorials) that represent particular interests and symbolize certain claims. Memorials are bodies of feeling, cultural entities whose social, cultural, and political meanings are determined by the emotional states and needs of their audiences. Memorials also determine those felt states; as Teresa Brennan argued, the "transmission of affect" is unbounded.[57] As cultural bodies, memorials have particular life spans and biographies: few memorials possess constant or consistent meaning or create the same sort of public response that they did when they were first dedicated. Likewise, because they depend on the fluctuating interests and feelings of their public patrons, memorials have no stable or timeless agenda. Today, for example, victims are commemorated as often, if not more so, than heroes. And themes of irony, contradiction, and conflict—among the key tropes of modern cultural consciousness—typically guide contemporary commemoration.

There is no single style of public commemoration in today's America. Figurative memorials include the world's largest equestrian bronze, a controversial monument dedicated in El Paso in 2007 that was originally intended to honor Juan de Oñate (see fig. 6.20, p. 359).[58] Many memorials are realized in abstract and minimalist styles, most notably the Vietnam Veterans Memorial, New England Holocaust Memorial (see fig. 3.10, p. 136), and Oklahoma City National Memorial. Despite their stylistic differences, their general reliance on modernist aesthetics, and their embrace of contingent and even contradictory meaning, contemporary American memorials are as much engaged in the ideological concerns of national identity as were the representational monuments of statue mania a century ago. The terms of that identity, however, have changed considerably.

Commemoration has been customarily viewed as the product of shared national beliefs. In the 1980s, architectural historian Spiro Kostof argued that public monuments "derive their authority from some unified vision—or its presumption," and earlier, James Wines stated that the age of monuments was "finished" because of the apparent lack of a "unifying ideology" during the divisive era of the Vietnam War.[59] To some degree, these premises stem from notions of collective memory advanced by French sociologist Maurice Halbwachs, who argued that memory was mostly a social phenomenon, a dynamic agent that linked atomized individuals to communities and nations. "It is in society that people normally acquire their memories," Halbwachs wrote in 1925. "It is also in society that they recall, recognize, and localize their memories." Halbwachs believed that certain collective memory "frameworks," like religion and nationalism, both reconstructed the past in terms of presentist social needs and helped maintain social continuity and equilibrium. He noted, "society tends to erase from its memory all that might separate individuals, or that might distance groups from each other."[60]

If helpful in terms of articulating memory's debt to the present and explaining how immediate sociopolitical concerns typically dictate the scope and shape of what is remembered, Halbwachs's emphasis on social unanimity does not completely account for the affective conditions of contemporary commemoration. Memorial mania does not rest on a coherent, collective, or even consensual ideological framework. Many contemporary memorials are marked by conflict, rupture, and loss and by a recognition among artists and audiences that memorials have the power to stir things up as much as smooth them out. Commemorative works like the Vietnam Veterans Memorial, Michael North observes, "achieve their aesthetic distinction and their emotional power from their political complexity" and "place their viewers in a public space that is articulated in terms of political controversy so that to view the piece is not simply to experience space but also to enter a debate."[61]

Memorial mania's discursive ambitions; its experientiality, irresolution and ambivalence; and its tendency to express social contradictions and historical traumas make it different from past modes of commemoration in America. Nineteenth- and early twentieth-century monuments to heroic men and historic moments "were not meant to revive old struggles and debates," writes Kirk Savage, "but to put them to rest—to show how great men and their deeds had made the nation better and stronger. Commemoration was a process of condensing the moral lessons of history and fixing them in place for all time." Public monuments like Washington's obelisk (dedicated in 1885) and Lincoln's memorial (1922) "sought to purify the past of any continuing conflict that might disturb" a "carefully crafted national narrative" of historical progress, heroism, and confidence. Even occasional memorials to tragic episodes in that historical narrative reaffirmed themes of "noble self-sacrifice" and courageous masculinity: a memorial to the *Titanic*, for example, sculpted by Gertrude Vanderbilt Whitney and dedicated in Washington, D.C., in 1931, features a thirteen-foot statue of a partially clad male figure who resembles the crucified Christ. It includes this inscription: "To the brave men who perished in the wreck of the *Titanic*, April 15, 1912. They gave their lives that women and children might be saved."[62]

Representing a shared national consciousness, or the striving for one, statue mania embodied a seemingly shared faith in a unified national history. American memorial making at the turn of the twentieth century, much like the simultaneous emphasis in American public schools on memorizing speeches and oaths (such as the Gettysburg Address and the Pledge of Allegiance) and the dates of significant foundational moments (like the landing at Plymouth Rock in 1620 and the defeat at the Alamo in 1836), was rooted in consensual "allegiance to the past."[63] Statue mania's emphasis on great men, great moments, and great ideas demonstrated an allegedly collective commitment to a celebratory, monolithic, and mostly masculine national history.

Memorial mania, by contrast, is less convinced of a seamless—or shared—American historical narrative and is less engaged in collective understandings of a progressive American history. This is not a hard and fast rule, of course; the National World War II Memorial, for example, evokes a unified, triumphant, and romanticized American past. Importantly, too, notions of American nationalism have not been abandoned in today's memorial cultures but have been redefined to reflect particular assertions of entitlement. Contemporary American commemoration is increasingly disposed to individual memories and personal grievances, to representations of tragedy and trauma, and to the social and political agendas of a diffuse body of rights-bearing citizens.

MEMORY STUDIES

"Welcome to the memory industry," Kerwin Klein bids in a discussion of the swell of "memory studies" in academic scholarship and the influence of theorists and historians such as Halbwachs and Pierre Nora. The study of memory—the word comes from the Latin *memor*, meaning mindful—is fairly recent, originating in late nineteenth-century cognitive psychology and understood by Freud, for example, as the private agent of unconscious mental processes, as a tool that individuals could use to retrieve personal information from the past. Today, the study of memory "extends considerably beyond psychology," observes Barbie Zelizer, and is a salient feature of academic discourse in disciplines ranging from anthropology and mass communication to art history, cultural geography, and literary criticism. Likewise, incipient concepts of memory's essentially privatizing agency have shifted to considerations of its public performativity and, especially, to how acts of remembering are key to the formation and reformation of social identity. As Jay Winter remarks, today's "memory boom" is directly related to today's identity politics: to diverse social and political groups claiming voice and vying for representation in the public sphere.[64]

The past few decades have seen a burgeoning of theoretical, social, and cultural projects centered on memory, ranging from the publication of Nora's multivolume anthology *Les Lieux de mémoire* (*Realms of Memory*, 1984–1992), to heated psychotherapeutic and legal debates surrounding repressed and recovered memory.[65] Memory work today includes flourishing popular interests in autobiography, memoirs, and genealogy, and growing public commemorations of the Holocaust in memorials, museums, and rituals of remembrance, such as ceremonies held in 2005 recalling the sixtieth anniversary of the liberation of Auschwitz-Birkenau by Soviet troops on January 27, 1945. Memory today is defined by all sorts of cultural practices, material artifacts, and national narratives: from family reunions, Facebook, and scrapbooking to civic celebrations including Cinco de Mayo, Memorial Day, Juneteenth, and the Fourth of July. For many Americans, memory is defined by generational recollections of traumatic historical moments: JFK's assassination in 1963, the explosion of the *Challenger* space shuttle in 1986, the attacks on the World Trade Center in 2001. For others, memory is all about the self: many blogs, for example, practically function as self-memorials, as narcissistic recitations of the most banal details of their makers' daily lives.

Memory's montage of meaning—collective social ritual, redemptive agent, subaltern expression, vanitas, and / or identity politics—dominates contemporary cultural sensibilities. Memory seems to evade timeless categories, which helps to account for its broad appeal in a cultural climate where category challenging, and shifting, is the norm. Among other clichés, memory is valorized for refusing to "stand still"—for being elusive and unstable, open-ended and unresolved. It is further embraced as an active agent that is performative, personal, and presentist. Memory's contemporary dominance certainly stems from its material and visual presence. "Modern memory, is, above all, archival," Nora remarks. "It relies on the materiality of the trace, the immediacy of the recording, the visibility of the image." Or as Juliet Mitchell explains, "Memory comes into being only after the trace which marks it: there is no thing, no event, experience, feeling, to remember, there is only that present which an empty past brings into being."[66] It is no accident that an online resource of the Library of Congress that includes animated films, audio recordings, baseball cards, New Deal photographs, and panoramic maps, among other things, is organized in a huge directory (over seven million digital items) called "American Memory."

Memory's popular and academic appeal has a lot to do with recent perceptions of history's repugnance. "Our sudden fascination with memory," Klein observes, "goes hand in hand with postmodern reckonings of history as the marching black boot and of historical consciousness as an oppressive fiction. Memory can come to the fore in an age of historiographic crisis precisely because it figures as a therapeutic alternative to historical discourse."[67] Following this binary, history is condemned as hard, cold facts and monolithic master narratives, while memory is welcomed as the feelings of "real people"—especially those formerly excluded from grand historical projects. History is demonized as the remote and dusty past; memory is extolled as its immediate and intimate alternative. Memory, Nora contends, is "affective and magical," while history, "because it is an intellectual and secular production," is dispassionate "analysis and criticism." History, he adds, "is perpetually suspicious of memory" and is bent on "deforming and transforming it, penetrating and petrifying it."[68]

Obviously, these sorts of reductive distinctions depend on which, or whose, history and memory are under consideration. Both can be careless and capricious; neither is necessarily more authentic than the other. Paul Ricoeur insisted that memory was the "bedrock" of history and argued for reconsiderations of their reciprocity.[69] Indeed, contemporary concepts of memory and history are largely inseparable because of changed understandings of how knowledge and identity are acquired and understood on experiential and affective terms. While some forms of history are deemed suspicious, others are viewed with pleasure.

After interviewing several thousand Americans for a study of popular history in the mid-1990s, historians Roy Rosenzweig and David Thelen found strong affective connections regarding the "presence of the past."[70] From high school reunions to heritage tourism, the history that is most meaningful to Americans today is personal and participatory and keyed to individual and family memories. For many Americans of color, history means shared experiences particular to race and ethnicity, including tribal and community traditions, the struggles of slavery and civil rights, and forced incarceration on federal reservations or in World War II internment camps.

Today's "memory boom" reflects less an abandonment of history than a cultural shift toward public feeling as a source of knowledge. As Alfred Gell argued, "To see (or to know) is to be sensuously filled with that which is perceived, yielding to it, mirroring it—and hence imitating it bodily."[71] Consider the popularity of Civil War battle reenactments, where players dress, eat, and talk like long-dead Union and Confederate soldiers. Consider the popularity of "living" museums and interactive exhibitions, where audiences emulate historical persons and actions. At the United States Holocaust Memorial Museum, for example, visitors carry identity cards of Holocaust victims and walk through a Nazi-era freight car. At the Sixth Floor Museum in Dallas, visitors can stand near the "sniper's nest" in the building's southeast corner, where Lee Harvey Oswald shot President John F. Kennedy. At the National Civil Rights Museum in Memphis, visitors walk into the rooming house bathroom where James Earl Ray fired at Martin Luther King, Jr. Across the street, they can peek inside the motel room where King died—and where his unmade bed and unwashed dishes from his last meal are on display. As the museum's Web site notes, "the emotional focus of the museum and the historical climax of the exhibit is the Lorraine Motel, where Dr. King was assassinated. Dr. King's room can be viewed as it was on April 4, 1968."[72]

Interests in "experiencing" history, especially histories of trauma and tragedy, are faciliated by contemporary artists, architects, and memorial makers. As Maya Lin observes of her memorial aesthetic, "I don't make objects; I make places. I think that is very important—the places set a stage for experience and for understanding experience." Likewise, in his design for the FDR memorial, Lawrence Halprin explained that he "hoped to evoke as many emotions and approaches" as possible in commemorating Roosevelt's twelve-year presidency:

> No single image could capture the multiplicity of events, challenges, difficulties, and successes. No simple statement could adequately express the achievements. Somehow I needed to evoke in each visitor, through his or her experience of the Memorial, a deep and emotional understanding of how these years changed the lives of the people who lived through them. I wanted this Memorial to be an experiential history lesson that people could grasp on their own as they walked through it.[73]

Similarly, just a few months after 9/11, several New York architects, including Liz Diller, Rick Scofidio, and David Rockwell, designed a public viewing platform at the edge of Ground Zero, a temporary wooden stage where up to three hundred people at a time could survey the ruins of the World Trade Center. As New York mayor Rudy Guiliani said during the dedication ceremony held for this memorial platform, "This is hallowed ground, sacred ground. We decided to put up these platforms because there's been so much of an interest in seeing this site . . . This gives you all kinds of feelings of sorrow and then tremendous feelings of patriotism."[74]

As Alison Landsberg explains in her work on "prosthetic memory," new forms of public cultural memory informed by mass-mediated technologies enable anyone to personally experience the past, no matter how remote or distant.[75] The desire to do so—the desire to "experience" the Great Depression and the New Deal by walking through the various rooms of the FDR memorial, or to "live" the history of Jewish persecution and genocide in the United States Holocaust Memorial Museum, or to "feel" sorrow and patriotism while standing above the rubble of Ground Zero—stems from the affectively enlarged dimensions of contemporary American culture.

Today, sight alone, or just "seeing," is not considered sufficient in terms of how Americans make sense of themselves and the world. Sight still reigns as the "sovereign" sense: some estimate that three-quarters of what we know comes from predominantly visual sources, and as Tom Mitchell observes, we live "in a culture dominated by pictures, visual simulations, stereotypes, illusions, copies, reproductions, imitations, and fantasies." But other sensual and affective domains constituting what Caroline Jones calls the "modernist sensorium" are also regarded, indeed demanded, as necessary pathways to knowledge, comprehension, and identity.[76] Their heightened relevance in memorial cultures relates in part to the complicated terms of visuality. After more than a century of modern mass media, multiple publics today are certainly aware of how visual images are the products of fluctuating sociopolitical conditions, and are wary of the crucial roles they play in representing and determining identity. Moreover, as "sensory historian" Mark M. Smith argues, "some phenomena—the aural dimensions of religious experience, the gustatory history of food, the role of smell in elaborating questions of race and class, the relevance of tactility in understanding the difference between freedom and slavery—cannot be understood through vision alone."[77] In contemporary America, felt experiences and public feelings, or an expanded economy of affect, are increasingly considered more genuine, and more substantial, in shaping contemporary understandings of self and nation.

Of course, as Joan Scott argues, discourses of experience are both illuminating and highly problematic: they give visibility to often marginalized historical subjects (women and people of color, for instance) but may also buffer these subjects from critique when "experience" is understood as "authenticity" and is thereby rendered beyond reproach in terms of critical analysis. By extension, experiencing history in a "living museum" may put audiences "in touch" with the past but it can never actually be the past, or their past. The solution, says Scott, is to "attend to the historical processes that, through discourse, position subjects and produce their experiences. It is not individuals who have experience, but subjects who are constituted through experience." Experience, she clarifies, "is at once always already an interpretation *and* is in need of interpretation."[78] Explaining, then, how and why contemporary Americans are drawn to experientially based memory practices, and how those practices help to define self and national forms of identity, is central to understanding memorial mania.

MEMORY NATION

Contemporary understandings of self and nation, like those of memory and history, are typically blurred and overlapping. As Rosenzweig and

Thelen observed, "Our respondents often made national stories personal, personal stories national, and formal settings for studying the past intimate."[79] This confounding of categories has had a striking effect on contemporary commemoration. If nineteenth-century statues were especially engaged in reimagining nationhood and promoting consensus, today's memorials represent a shift toward more subjective and personalized narratives. Yet contemporary memorials still serve as enabling agents of national identity. While there may be no single national paradigm or single style of national memorial, there are various efforts and positions—a kind of "critical re-membering"—that represent interests in defining, and redefining, the terms of national belonging.[80] Persistent anxieties about those terms help to account for the abundant forms and manic dimensions of contemporary commemoration.

Whether understood as "an imagined political community" (according to Benedict Anderson), as "a soul, a spiritual principle" (Ernest Renan), as "political movements seeking or exercising state power" (John Breuilly), or as "a large social group integrated not by one but by a combination of several kinds of objective relationships (economic, political, linguistic, cultural, religious, geographical, historical) and their subjective reflection in collective consciousness" (Miroslasv Hroch), notions of "the nation" are wide-ranging and, as Anderson notes, "notoriously difficult to define."[81] Generally shared, however, are understandings that the nation, as well as concepts of nationalism and national identity, are cultural constructions rather than timeless certainties, and that as such there is a profound difference between the idealized sociopolitical principle of "the nation" and its lived, felt, reality.

As an academic discipline especially engaged in critiquing the discrepancies between what the nation is and what it aspires to be (a "more perfect Union," for example), American studies aims to deconstruct the myths of American nationalism. Exposing the flaws within national paradigms of exceptionalism, egalitarianism, and autonomy, the field resists previously dominant models of "consensus"-based national identity and posits more expansive and often conflicted concepts attuned to multicultural and multivocal narratives.[82] Subsequently, some regard the very idea of national identity as retrograde, or as only the property of a political right disposed to discourses of moral superiority, religious fundamentalism, and unblinking patriotism. But we need to continue to take the nation seriously as a category of analysis. From the attacks of 9/11, which were perceived by the American government, the American media, and the American people as attacks on the nation, to President Barack Obama's postracial narrative of national unity, "the nation" remains a powerful and authoritative structure of belief. As Anthony Smith argues, nationalism may be the "most compelling identity myth in the modern world."[83]

Because it is a historical, political, social, cultural, religious, and psychological construction, nationalism is also a highly *unstable* identity myth. While the basic components of the modern nation-state include political independence, centralized authority, military might, geographic consolidation, and the formation of a collective ideology, words like "contingency" and "contested" are also central to contemporary understandings of nationalism. Notions of the nation as a totality representing a unified and cohesive social subject are largely untenable; as Prasenjit Duara remarks, "nationalism is best seen as a relational identity" and continually shifting historical configuration constituted within a "fluid network of representations." National identities, he explains, arise when individual groups "mobilize particular representations of nation or community against other representations and, while doing so, appropriate the dispersed meanings and pasts as their own." That mobilization, adds Thomas Scheff, is inherently emotional and often stems from feelings of pride, shame, and anger. Emotions are the lifeblood of contemporary American politics, George E. Marcus argues, and the emotional agency of the nation's "sentimental citizens" profoundly impacts the course of democratic practice.[84]

Likewise, notions of nationalism are no longer confined to those of geographic place and space. If older concepts of "being" Japanese, Mexican, or American were rooted in the physical territories owned and occupied by Japan, Mexico, and the United States of America, understandings of national identity today are far more fluid. National identity is shaped as much by language, religion, ethnicity, and race as it is by the geographic coherence of a homeland, real or imagined. New global technologies and new forms of social organization (for example, transnational advocacy networks and nongovernmental organizations similarly challenge fixed notions of nationalism. And while neoliberalism—the reorganization of capitalism into economic and social policies that favor the privatization of public resources and promote corporate profits—is often described in terms of transnational globalization, it depends on the dynamic mix of collective identity, competition, and market protection that the nation-state provides.[85] The intently nationalistic focus of today's global sports contests, like the Olympics and the World Cup, are prime examples.

Nationalism's inconstancy contextualizes contemporary American memorials, explaining why certain American histories are privileged by public commemoration and others are not. It further articulates how certain representations of American identity dominate at certain moments in time, and in certain American landscapes.

Consider the dueling memorials of Crazy Horse and Mount Rushmore, both hacked out of mountains in the Black Hills of South Dakota (see figs. 6.14 and 6.15, pp. 344, 347). Rushmore, the colossal carving of the heads of four American presidents (Washington, Jefferson, Lincoln, and Teddy Roosevelt), was dedicated in 1941. Crazy Horse, the representation of a nineteenth-century Lakota warrior, is a work in progress begun in 1948. Almost two million people visit Mount Rushmore each year, exploring its museums, walking its grounds, and attending its highly popular Evening Lighting Ceremony, which features a half-hour talk by National Park Service (NPS) rangers followed by a multicolored light-show projected on the side of the mountain. Simon Schama reminds us that Rushmore was designed by the racist, fascist, and sexist Gutzon Borglum, a sculptor who viewed his "National Shrine to Democracy" (his term) as a testimonial to white supremacy, manifest destiny, and American masculinity.[86] In addition to being a KKK member and a Mussolini fan, Borglum rebuffed a mid-1930s campaign to include Susan B. Anthony's visage on the mountain and similarly dismissed suggestions to showcase legendary American Western figures like Buffalo Bill Cody and Oglala Lakota Chief Red Cloud.

Today, the National Park Service—the major institutional body charged with shaping national identity through its management of America's national parks, memorials, monuments, and historic sites—downplays these details of Borglum's biography in favor of Mount Rushmore's sweeping national subjectivity. The opening paragraphs of the NPS's Mount Rushmore Web site intone:

> The sheer size of the mountain carving on Mount Rushmore evokes a sense of awe in those who view it. We are also amazed when we see ourselves in the faces of the presidents. The four presidents carved in stone represent all Americans. They represent our courage, dreams, freedom, and greatness.[87]

As such rhetoric suggests, the NPS sees Mount Rushmore as a symbol of collective American identity predicated on elite white male leadership (I am / we are George Washington). Meanwhile, about seventeen miles away, the equally bombastic Crazy Horse Memorial—a project begun by former Rushmore stone carver Korczak Ziolkowski and now visited by one million people a year—seemingly renegotiates that national narrative by heroizing a nineteenth-century Native American warrior. Yet both of these pretentious mountain memorials aggrandize the "awe"-inspiring artistic and technological feats of their respective sculptors. Neither reckons with the audacity of carving up rocky peaks held sacred by American Indians or embracing manifest destiny, militarism, and masculinity as appropriate tropes of national allegiance and identity.

Memorials have long played central roles in shaping and defining understandings of America: the Washington Monument, Statue of Liberty, Lincoln Memorial, USS *Arizona* Memorial, Gateway Arch, Vietnam Veterans Memorial, and National World War II Memorial are all symbolic markers of the nation. For Americans, the touristic experience of visiting them, whether as an obligatory civic exercise in middle school or while on family vacation, is a primary means of learning about and becoming an emotionally engaged member of the nation. American memorials help to create and celebrate an imaginary national citizen: the representative American, the "good" citizen that all American citizens aspire to become.

America's political leaders certainly see them this way, issuing passionate proclamations about their national importance and proudly accepting them "on behalf of the American people." During his terms as president, Bill Clinton dedicated eight national memorials and designated twenty-one national monuments, including the controversial 1.9-million-acre Grand Staircase-Escalante National Monument in southern Utah. During his presidency, George W. Bush dedicated the Pentagon Memorial, National World War II Memorial, Air Force Memorial, National D-Day Memorial, and Victims of Communism Memorial. He also authorized the World War II Valor in the Pacific National Monument: a noncontinugous three-state memorial administered by the National Park Service (and the U.S. Fish and Wildlife Service) that includes battlefields in Alaska's Aleutian Islands, military installations in Hawaii's Pearl Harbor and nearby Ford Island, and the Tule Lake Segregation Center National Historic Landmark in California, where thousands of Japanese Americans were relocated and incarcerated during the war.[88]

Yet memorials often occupy precarious positions in the national landscape—or so it seems in countless American movies in which memorials typically signal disaster. In *Planet of the Apes* (1968), the Statue of Liberty is buried in sand up to her midriff; in *Deep Impact* (1998), she is toppled by a tidal wave; in *Cloverfield* (2008), she winds up decapitated and dislocated on 42nd Street. In *Logan's Run* (1976), the Lincoln Memorial and the U.S. Capitol are found ruined and covered in vines by twenty-third-century futurists; in *Mars Attacks!* (1996), the Capitol is blown up by aliens. In *The Deadly Mantis* (1957), the Washington Monument is besieged by giant grasshoppers, and in *Earth vs. the Flying Saucers* (1953), the entire National Mall is mowed down by extraterrestrial invaders.[89] Mount Rushmore is another favorite target: destroyed by lasers in *Richie Rich* (1994), ruined by an earthquake in *10.5: Apocalypse* (2006), blown up by terrorist missiles in *The Peacekeeper* (1997), annihilated by Michael Moore (playing a suicide bomber) in *Team America: World Police* (2004), and defaced (or rather, refaced) in movies like *Superman II* (1980) and *Head of State* (2003).

Besides showcasing Hollywood's obsession with special effects, destroying national memorials on screen most obviously signifies national dystopia. Abandoned memorials are metaphors for an abandoned nation; vandalized memorials signify national instability and imminent collapse. Steeped in feelings of remorse and anger (best captured in Charlton Heston's tortured oration at the end of *Planet of the Apes*: "You maniacs! You blew it up. Damn you! Damn you all to hell!"), ruined national memorials symbolize anxieties about a ruined national body.

Memorial mania's affective conditions may call attention to those facets of American national identity gone awry, or bordering on ruin, or in need of revision. Nora argues that sites of memory "only exist because of their capacity for metamorphosis, an endless recycling of their meaning and an unpredictable proliferation of their ramifications."[90] Many American memorials are sites of reformation and transformation: spaces and places where history and identity are frequently reconsidered in order to cultivate, or revive, citizen identification with an inconstant nation. Many new memorials managed by the NPS, for example, focus on previously marginalized American subjects. The Manzanar National Historic Site (dedicated in 1992), located in an isolated desert valley in central California about 220 miles northeast of Los Angeles, commemorates the forced relocation and internment of Japanese Americans during World War II and calls attention to the tenuous nature of citizenship and civil liberties in America. The National AIDS Memorial Grove (1996), an affiliated area of the National Park Service in San Francisco's Golden Gate Park, is a "dedicated space in the national public landscape where anyone who has been touched by AIDS can grieve openly without being stigmatized, can find comfort among others whose lives have been affected by AIDS and HIV, and can experience the feelings of renewal and hope inherent in nature."[91] The Indian Memorial at the Little Bighorn Battlefield National Monument (2003, see fig. 0.10, p. 5) pays tribute to the Native American victors of this 1876 battle and revises legendary accounts of "Custer's Last Stand" in American historical consciousness. Vastly expanded beyond statue mania's commemoration of great American men and grand national moments, memorial mania is steeped in the continually evolving terms of American national identity, the experiential dynamics of today's "memory boom," and the affective conditions of contemporary American life.

MEMORIAL MANIA

Although new memorials are dedicated with surprising frequency, memorial mania itself has been curiously underexamined. Public art is the focus of many historical surveys, case studies, and theoretically engaged analyses on the social production of space, "new genre" paradigms, the rhetorics of display, cultural democracy, and issues of site-specificity.[92] The Vietnam Veterans Memorial, Franklin Delano Roosevelt Memorial, and Oklahoma City National Memorial are the subjects of recent monographs. Commemoration of the Holocaust, an extension of the voluminous discourse on the Holocaust itself, has generated numerous books, articles, and exhibition catalogues focused on issues of memory, history, representation, and redemption.[93] But missing from this historiography is a synthetic critique of contemporary American memorials that considers commemoration within the relational dynamics of physical space, social practice, cultural theory, national identity, and public feeling.

Modernist assumptions that once distinguished ideas from feelings—the basic binary of the Cartesian mind/body thesis—are increasingly challenged by new understandings of their synergism, of how cognition is embodied, sensate, interested, and invested; and emotions are, as Martha Nussbaum asserts, "upheavals of thought." Especially in the past few decades, many fields have developed methodologies and interpretive frameworks that assess public displays of emotion and explain how feelings like joy, grief, shame, and anger inform the making and meaning of particular cultures, societies, and nations.[94]

Historian Henry Rousso, for example, reflects on the felt conditions of collective memory in *The Vichy Syndrome* (1987), a study of Gaullist-inspired amnesia in France during and after World War II. Utilizing terms such as neurosis, obsession, repression, projection, and transmission to analyze a rich array of "memory vectors" including monuments, annual remembrance ceremonies, movies, public school textbooks, and personal testimonials from prisoners of war, members of the resistance, and concentration camp survivors, Rousso critiques the "tactical and emotional motives" that led the French to "falsify" their past.[95] Likewise, drawing on funerary inscriptions, poems, letters, and liturgical readings in her consideration of various medieval "emotional communities," Barbara Rosenwein posits a complex culture of affective bonds, systems of feeling, and emotional expressions that challenges understandings of the Middle Ages as emotionally childlike (a basic presumption of modernist historiography). In *Feeling Italian: The Art of Ethnicity in America* (2005), Thomas J. Ferraro explains how "patterns of intelligent emotion and articulate gesture played out in Italian America." And in his study of greeting cards and American business culture circa 1840–1960, Barry Shank considers how "feeings of longing and desire" and strategies of "emotional eloquence" were shared (not separated) by private and public social spheres.[96]

As these and other writers argue, feelings and emotions are expressions and representations that are created, learned, and used by particular cultures and societies. We are not born in grief, we are not born ashamed; we learn how to feel, we learn how to be emotional. Emotions are among the tools that we use to manage and mediate our lives: conditions, styles, and forces that help to determine and explain our attitudes and behaviors. Contextualized by the shifting values and concerns of certain communities at certain times, emotions are varied and dynamic. Grasping their complex sociocultural circulation, as well as the sociopolitical implications of this "sensual turn," requires our empirical consideration, as Lauren Berlant recommends, of "what feelings are made out to mean; and which forces, meanings, and practices are magnetized by concepts of affect and emotion."[97]

As this book argues, contemporary American memorials embody the feelings of particular publics at particular historical moments, and frame cultural narratives about self identity and national purpose. Such narratives are especially relevant in today's so-called Prozac nation, a portrait that captures both the prevalence of emotional tensions in contemporary America and multiple efforts to manage those tensions. The explosion of interest in the psychological character of the American nation and the emotional states of its citizens, manifest in the prescriptive popularity of antidepressants and sexual enhancement drugs on the one hand, and memorial mania on the other, begs serious analysis. Emotions are hyperrealized in contemporary America. Understanding them calls for a critical pedagogy of public feelings—an emotional epistemology—which shrewdly considers how and why (and which) public feelings shape historical moments, concepts of citizenship, and understandings of self and national identity.

Does this critical focus argue "against" memorials or imply that their typically fraught circumstances are untenable? Not at all. The affective conditions of contemporary commemoration—and public culture in general—do not foreclose the possibilities of social and political transformation. Rather, feelings are cultivated and as such can be mobilized: affect has agency. Recognizing how affect can generate creative structural change, each chapter of *Memorial Mania* closes with the "affective possibilities" of public feelings, and a consideration of how public commemoration can be emotionally productive.

Memorials embody the histories and feelings that respective Americans choose to remember at particular moments. The public grief expressed at recent sites of tragedy and trauma, such as the shootings at Columbine High School in 1999, is one example of an emotional history deemed memorable by Americans today, and where *Memorial Mania* next turns.

2 GRIEF

Temporary Memorials and Contemporary Modes of Mourning

On April 20, 1999, two teenage boys, Eric Harris and Dylan Klebold, opened fire on their classmates and teachers at Columbine High School in Littleton, Colorado, a suburb southwest of Denver. Brandishing 9-mm semiautomatic rifles, TEC-9 semiautomatic handguns, double-barrel shotguns, pump-action shotguns, and pipe bombs, the two boys killed twelve students and one teacher, and seriously wounded another twenty-three students.[1] At the end of their murderous rampage, Harris and Klebold killed themselves.

Within hours of the shootings, while police and firemen were still evacuating the building, a temporary memorial emerged in Clement Park, a 325-acre grassy knoll next to the high school's parking lots. It started when students—more than 1,900 attended Columbine—began piling personal mementos on the cars of their murdered classmates (fig. 2.1). Victim Rachel Scott's red Acura Legend was blanketed with flowers, stuffed animals, and balloons; John Robert Tomlin's brown Chevy truck was draped with similar items and a high school letter jacket, on which was inscribed: "To all the people of CHS [Columbine High School]. You are all creations of God. You are beautiful people."

Within a few days, much of Clement Park was carpeted in four-foot-deep mounds of various offerings (fig. 2.2). Cellophane-wrapped bouquets of flowers and condolence cards were placed next to class photos, stuffed animals, butterfly-shaped balloons, personal letters and poems sealed inside plastic bags, crosses, framed religious prints, laminated Bibles, posters of rock stars and sports legends, bed sheets inscribed with tearful comments and Biblical passages, origami cranes, a mile-long paper chain (made by school kids from Fort Wayne, Indiana), American flags, sneakers, soccer balls, votive candles, school jerseys, and lots of T-shirts featuring the high school's mascot, an American Revolutionary War soldier nicknamed "Rebel," holding a rifle (fig. 2.3).

During its two-week presence in Clement Park, tens of thousands of

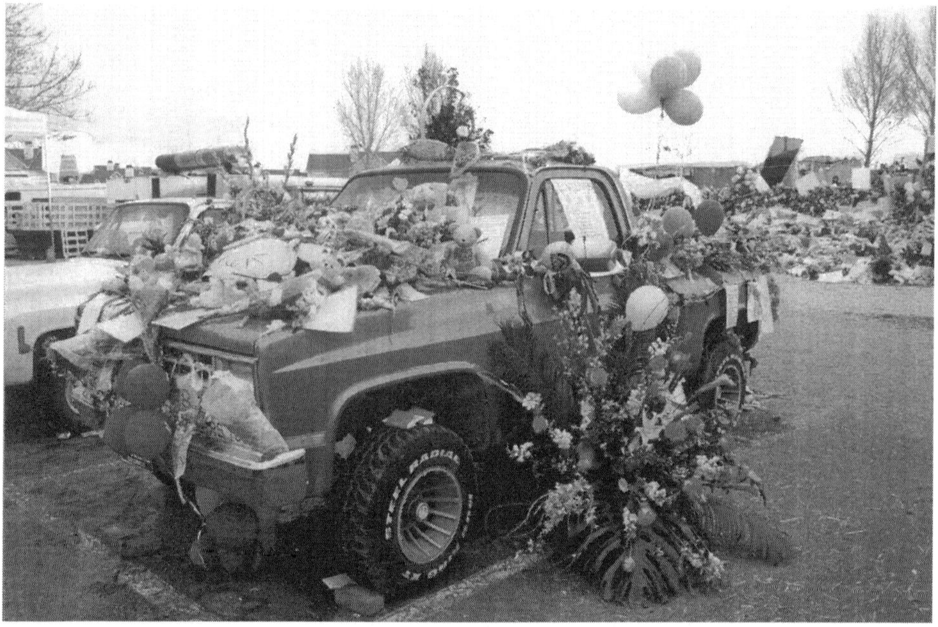

2.1. Flowers, balloons, teddy bears, and other offerings on a truck belonging to student John Robert Tomlin, who was murdered at Columbine High School, Littleton, Colorado, April 20, 1999. (Photographer unknown.)

people wandered through the makeshift memorial. Many brought something to add, recording their experiences with cameras and buying sodas and hotdogs from the fast-food vendors who quickly set up shop around the site. (The local parks and recreation department set up portable toilets, too.) Some people left messages on scraps of paper or cardboard, including warnings ("the millennium is approaching") and prayers ("Heavenly Father, hear our cries. Heal our children. Help our country"). The park was filled with dozens of TV vans, satellite dishes, mobile-phone towers, and roving reporters who broadcast the "terror in Littleton" to viewers across the nation and around the globe. Trees were dressed with wind chimes, blue and silver ribbons (the high school's colors), crepe paper, and rosaries. Fences were strewn with banners declaring "Love and prayers from the employees of US West" and "Our thoughts and prayers are with the students, faculty, and friends of Columbine High School. From your Littleton Wal-Mart."[2] An Illinois carpenter planted fifteen crosses on top of Clement Park's Rebel Hill, the highest point in the park. Staff from Schwinn Cycles & Fitness left a Sting-Ray bike painted in blue and silver with a card that read, "The darkness will lift. The ride will go on." The entire memorial, wrote one *Rocky Mountain*

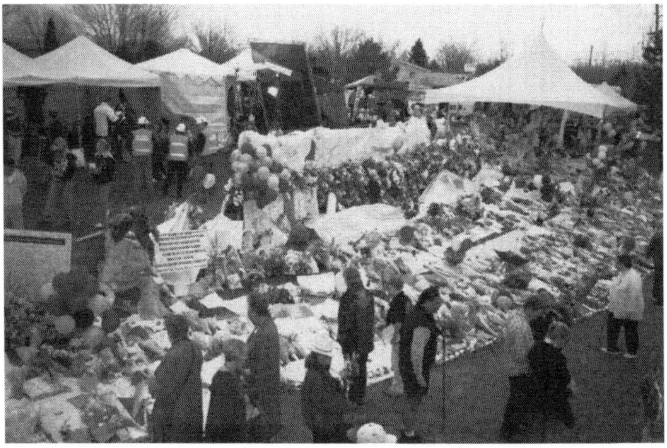

2.2. Large temporary memorial created in Robert F. Clement Park next to Columbine High School, April 1999. (Photo by the author.)

News reporter, was a "perfect suburban shrine, sprawling, growing without boundaries and taking on a life of its own."[3]

Despite its spectacular size and carnivalesque atmosphere, Columbine's temporary memorial was neither uniquely American nor particularly contemporary. Roadside memorials marking roadside fatalities have been a global phenomenon for thousands of years and are found today in Australia, Greece, Ireland, Japan, the Netherlands, Peru, and elsewhere. In the American Southwest, roadside memorials called *descansos* (Spanish for "resting place") date from the eighteenth century.[4] Similar sorts of temporary memorials have been made throughout the nation's history, typically at sites of tragic death. In San Francisco, for instance, just hours after several striking longshoremen were murdered on "Bloody Thursday," July 5, 1934, the stained sidewalk where they died was circled in chalk and marked with bunches of roses, American flags, a sign reading "Police, murder, two men shot in the back," and banners from the International Longshoremen's Union.[5]

Decades earlier, Abraham Lincoln's assassination on April 15, 1865, was met by a national deluge of grief manifest in elaborate eulogies, processions, and temporary memorials. The funeral train that transported Lincoln's body from Washington, D.C., to the Springfield, Illinois, cemetery where he was buried was met at the numerous stops along its two-week journey (it traveled at five to twenty miles per hour) by thousands of mourners, many of them wearing mourning badges and adding flowers to the specially constructed catafalque in which the dead president was placed on public view. The funeral train itself, bedecked with bunting, floral wreaths, and black-fringed presidential seals, featured a photo-

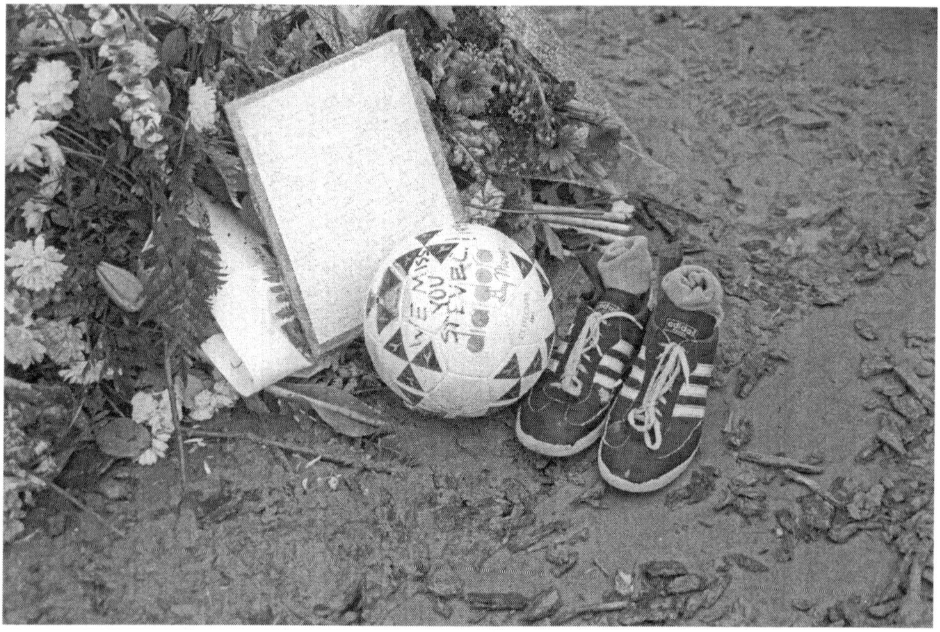

2.3. Temporary memorial in Clement Park, April 1999, detail. (Courtesy of Heather Butler.)

graph of Lincoln over its cowcatcher and traveled on tracks festooned with memorial arches draped in black crepe and American flags. Lincoln chronicler Lloyd Lewis likened the funeral cortege as "half circus, half heartbreak." Poet Carl Sandburg called it "garish, vulgar, massive, bewildering, [and] chaotic."[6] Both descriptions seem apt for today's similarly spectacular, and growing, public culture of temporary memorials.

Their rising numbers suggest that traditional forms of mourning no longer meet the needs of today's publics and prompt questions about what death, grief, and memory mean in the new millennium. More specifically, how are feelings of grief mediated in contemporary America? What do temporary memorials tell us about who and what is deemed memorable in American history, and in terms of an imagined national future? By extension, is grief a useful or productive public affect? Or are there psychic and political dangers for a nation seemingly "too attached" to public expressions of grief?

TEMPORARY MEMORIALS

Temporary memorials are flourishing in contemporary America, especially at sites of tragedy and trauma. In Detroit in 1992, for example, an

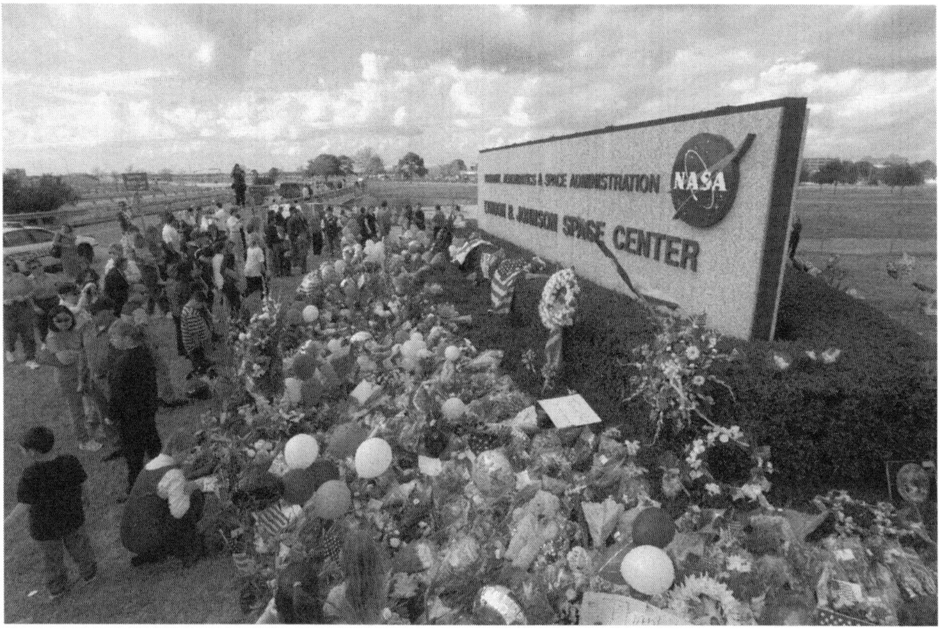

2.4. Temporary memorial to *Columbia* space shuttle, Johnson Space Center, Houston, Texas, February 2003. (Courtesy of NASA.)

impromptu memorial was erected in front of an abandoned storefront at Warren Avenue and 23rd Street, where motorist Malice Green was beaten to death by local police. In 1994, the South Carolina lake where Michael and Alexander Smith were drowned by their mother became the site of a shrine decorated with teddy bears, toys, and trinkets from McDonald's Happy Meals. In 1996, after TWA flight 800 crashed off Fire Island, New York, killing all 230 people on board, nearby beaches were dotted with makeshift memorials. In 1998, a wooden fence outside of Laramie, where University of Wyoming student Matthew Shepard was left to die, was marked by small baskets of flowers, teddy bears, and a horizontal cross made out of pebbles. In 2003, following the tragic loss of the *Columbia* space shuttle, a temporary memorial featuring flowers, stuffed animals, U.S. flags, and a banner reading "Pres. Bush, Please! Don't let them die in vain . . . Keep NASA alive!" was erected at the entrance to the Johnson Space Center in Houston (fig. 2.4). Smaller memorials sprouted up all over Texas following the trajectory of *Columbia*'s debris.

Similarly ephemeral memorials were made at the site of the Alfred P. Murrah Federal Building in Oklahoma City, which Timothy McVeigh bombed in 1995, leaving 168 dead; at the site of Texas A&M University's Aggie Bonfire Stack collapse in 1999, which killed 12 students; at the Station nightclub in West Warwick, Rhode Island, in 2003, where 100 people died in a fire; and at Virginia Tech University in Blacksburg, Virginia, in 2007, where 27 students and 5 teachers were shot to death before their killer, a student at the school, committed suicide. The most visible temporary memorials in recent memory were those that developed after the death of Princess Diana on August 31, 1997, and after the attacks on the World Trade Center on September 11, 2001. Memorials were made at both the sites of death or relatively near them: on a pedestrian bridge at the Place de l'Alma just above the Parisian traffic tunnel where Diana died in a car crash, and on the Manhattan streets and sidewalks closest to where the Twin Towers once stood. They were also made at other sites all over the world.

Temporary memorials erected at the homes of suddenly dead celebrities are common. In 1995, the fence surrounding the home of Tejano singer Selena in Corpus Christi, Texas, was covered with flowers and cards from fans after she was murdered. In 1999, the street in front of John F. Kennedy, Jr.'s Lower Manhattan apartment was clogged with piles of flowers and crowds of mourners following his death in a plane crash. In 2008, a makeshift memorial similarly marked the entrance to Heath Ledger's New York apartment after the actor was found dead. The backyard gravesite where Elvis Presley is buried at Graceland, the Memphis home where he died of a drug overdose in 1977, is always filled with floral bouquets and handmade gifts from fans.[7] Likewise, Strawberry Fields, the shrine in Central Park across the street from the New York apartment building where John Lennon was shot in 1980, is decorated daily with fresh flowers and other offerings.

Unexpected, violent, and televisualized death especially prompts this sort of commemoration, not just celebrity status: consider the temporary memorial that literally engulfed the Sarasota, Florida, home of Carlie Brucia, an eleven-year-old girl whose abduction at a carwash in February 2004 was captured on surveillance cameras and broadcast nationwide. Or the similarly huge memorial in Tracy, California, to eight-year-old Sandra Cantu, whose murder in April 2009 drew throngs of media and whose funeral service drew over three thousand people.[8] Indeed, the memorials made when Princess Di died and after 9/11 became the most visible and most discussed temporary memorials in recent memory in large part because of the extensive and repetitious mass media coverage that they received. Temporary memorials are often glimpsed in TV crime shows like *Law and Order* and *The Wire*, too, looping "real" and "virtual" demonstrations of the public grief that follows violent death in contemporary America.

While obviously omnipresent, there is little agreement about what temporary memorials actually mean or represent. The subject is confounded by the problem of definitions.[9] Some call them "vernacular memorials" to distinguish them as individual, handmade, localized, and grassroots projects rather than officially sanctioned or institutionalized kinds of commemoration. Some refer to them as "performative memorials" to emphasize their fundamentally active and social nature.[10] Some use the terms "spontaneous memorials" and "spontaneous shrines" to evoke their seemingly abrupt and unpremeditated appearance, and to reference their religious overtures.

But any nomenclature does well to remember the mercurial nature of temporary memorials: they may originate as ephemeral forms and sites of commemoration, but as they are visited, photographed, and collected they enter into new taxonomic registers. Likewise, the formulaic and increasingly universalized terms of their production call into question their vernacular sensibility. By extension, the use of the term "spontaneous" is a misnomer; however impromptu they may seem, temporary memorials are actually highly orchestrated and self-conscious acts of mourning aimed at expressing, codifying, and ultimately managing grief. Their spontaneity is only in their origination, in their swift response to the sudden and unexpected events of tragic and traumatic death. And if "spontaneous shrine" has a certain charming alliteration, it generally bears little relation to the scripted and often secular dimensions of these kinds of commemoration.[11] Given this, I opt for the term "temporary memorials," recognizing that what we are especially considering is the cultural production and consumption of ephemeral forms of commemoration, some of which are eventually transformed into permanent memorials.

The literature on temporary memorials is substantial, especially in the fields of anthropology, communication, and folk and performance studies.[12] The term "spontaneous memorials" was originally coined by folklorist Jack Santino in a 1992 essay on murder sites in Northern Ireland that had become shrine sites—places visited by the families and supporters of victims of political assassination; places physically transformed by their gifts of flowers, notes, and other objects; places accorded special, even sacred, status by the ritualized acts and offerings of everyday urban pilgrims.[13] Following linguist John L. Austin, Santino has since refined his initial thoughts on these temporary public displays, arguing for their conceptualization as "performative commemoratives" that mark instances of untimely and especially traumatic deaths, become places of communion between the living and dead, and invite broad public participation. As Santino observes, such memorials "display death in the heart of social life. These are not graves awaiting occasional visitors and sanctioned decorations. Instead of a family visiting a grave, the 'grave' comes to the family—that is, the public. All of us."[14]

Some recent scholarship on temporary memorials similarly argues that these public displays of death and disaster represent civic and communal practices that are distinct from official or mainstream commemorative practices. For some, temporary memorials constitute acts and places of social agency and even social challenge. As art historian Harriet Senie remarks, "Spontaneous memorials are populist phenomena, ways for people to mark their own history. They create a public place for individuals and communities united in grief and often anger."[15]

Examples abound, including the international array of temporary memorials to Princess Diana. Dubbed "the People's Princess" by British prime minister Tony Blair, Diana's unexpected death generated an equally unexpected outpouring of public grief, represented in the vast sea of flowers, pictures, notes, and other offerings that materialized at Kensington Palace (her official London residence) and Buckingham Palace (the Queen's London residence), as well as a multitude of smaller, if no less deeply felt, tributes to her all over the world. Some see the public mourning of Diana's death on oppositional terms, as populist expressions of grief that signaled strains of collective civic protest. Santino, for example, describes the temporary memorials erected in London to Diana as a kind of "cultural-political contestation" to the elite trappings of the British royal family. Others have likened them as a "floral revolution": a popular grassroots uprising against the policing of mourning in modern Great Britain and a populist demand for heightened levels of inclusion in a bounded and class-divided society.[16]

There is no doubt that temporary memorials represent changed cultural and social practices regarding public mourning, if claims that they represent *new* practices are countenanced by the ongoing scholarly recovery of their historical origins.[17] Their meaning lies especially in their affective dimensions, and the ways in which these fundamentally material memorials negotiate the crisis of grief.

THINGS MATTER

Temporary memorials are often scorned for their obsessive materiality and manic displays of mourning. Their excessive physical and emotional properties are deemed "too much" and even fetishistic; their overwrought sensibilities seemingly strain boundaries between good taste and vulgarity. In 2004, the conservative British think tank Civitas mocked temporary memorials and public displays of grief as "conspicuous compassion" and "mourning sickness."[18] Yet as material culture theorists from Jules

Prown to Daniel Miller argue, “things matter,” and the fact that many people have made temporary memorials a priority among their many diverse “object worlds” matters a great deal.[19] Rather than being viewed as cultural pathologies, temporary memorials can be seen as the creative products of profound personal and public feelings. More directly, temporary memorials help to mediate the psychic crisis of sudden and often inexplicable loss.

The palpable stuff of which they are made both describes and defines them; temporary memorials are exemplars of Nora’s observation that “modern memory is, above all, archival.”[20] An estimated fifteen thousand tons of flowers and other things made up the temporary memorials created at London’s royal palaces in memory of Princess Diana. Some two hundred thousand items were left at Columbine’s temporary memorial. Perhaps as many as one million items were left on Oklahoma City’s Memory Fence, an eight-foot-tall chain-link fence that circled the large area formerly occupied by the Murrah Federal Building (fig. 2.5). Built immediately after the bombing to restrict public access to the crime scene, the fence became covered in “tokens of remembrance,” including stuffed animals, plastic flowers, laminated poems, hand-drawn pictures, license plates, military medals, and religious mementos that were left by thousands of visitors from 1995 to 2000 (when a permanent memorial was dedicated on the site). Local residents who lost family and friends in the bombing claimed particular areas of the fence and added personal belongings, including toys, photographs, baby blankets, and prom flowers. Tourists visiting the site either prepared offerings in advance or added items closest at hand when they got there (fig. 2.6). These included T-shirts and hats on which people often inscribed their names, the dates of their visit, and sentiments such as “Brian and Jerry, We Remember, We Will Never Forget, July 14, 1997” and “Richard, Meg, Sherry, Senatobia, Mississippi TaeKwon-Doe, God Bless, June 22, 1999.”[21]

Links between material culture and mourning are timeless, of course, and the rituals of observance that are central to temporary memorials stem from long-standing materialist practices that memorialize the dead. Rituals of death abound in materialism, from the basic consideration of what to do with the dead body to the literal matter of coffins, cremation urns, gravestones, cemetery plots, *memento mori*, photographs of the deceased (especially common in the late nineteenth century), mourning clothes, mourning jewelry, and more.[22] Floral wreaths are typical offerings at Christian funerals; small rocks or pebbles are often left at Jewish gravesites; gifts of food and other items are expected during Day of the Dead observances in Latino Catholic cultures; gifts to honor ancestors are typically brought to Japanese Shinto shrines. “Dead man shirts,”

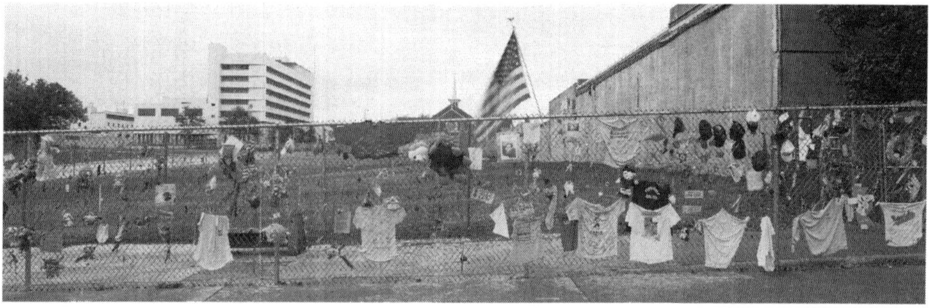

2.5. Memory Fence, Oklahoma City, Oklahoma, 1995. (© 2009 Visions of America / Stock Connection. Courtesy of World of Stock Media.)

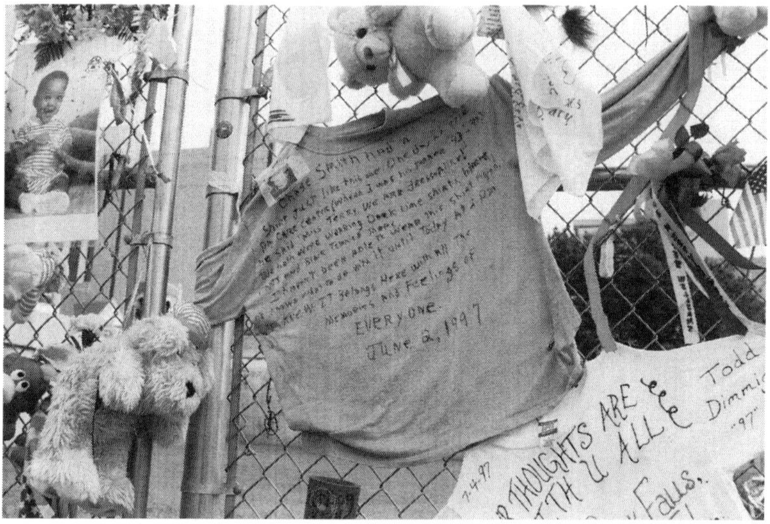

2.6. T-shirt and other things left at the Memory Fence, 1997. (Courtesy of Ken Kraeske.)

T-shirts that feature photos of the deceased, are gaining in popularity throughout America, handed out at funerals and often worn again later at remembrance services and family reunions. Cars and vans display custom-designed "In Loving Memory" decals that turn them into mobile memorials, or "rolling tombstones."[23] And more and more graves in American cemeteries are decorated with the personal effects of the dead, from toys, blankets, and baby bottles, to high school sports trophies, yearbooks, car keys, lipsticks, war medals, and guitar picks.

The materiality of temporary memorials is widespread, sharing cultural and social practices that transcend religious, regional, racial, and ethnic differences. In part, this stems from how easy and inexpensive it is to participate in this memorial culture. Corner grocery stores are conveniently stocked with the usual cheap stuff of temporary memorials: bouquets of flowers (real and artificial), stuffed animals, balloons, votive candles, condolence cards. Just as we don't go empty handed to dinner parties, we don't go empty handed to temporary memorials. A quick dash into the Kwik-Stop provides everything we need.

More significantly, the material culture of grief at sites like Columbine embodies the faith that Americans place in *things* to negotiate complex moments and events, such as traumatic death. Things satisfy the emotional needs of this negotiation. Flowers symbolize the beauty and brevity of life, as do balloons. Handwritten notes, cards, poems, and letters give voice to the grief-stricken and permit intimate conversations with (and confessions to) the dead. Stuffed animals, teddy bears in particular, intimate lost innocence. These things are central to contemporary public recollections of loss and performances of grief not only because they are inexpensive and easily available but because they resonate with beliefs in the symbolic and emotional power of material culture. Things, especially public things, map political cultures and shape political bodies; things, as Bruno Latour argues, constitute "atmospheres of democracy" and *dingpolitik* (literally, the politics of things) provides clearer and more credible possibilities than *realpolitik*.[24]

Things also, of course, constitute a modern mass culture that valorizes impermanence and disposability in order to fuel patterns of consumption; as Arjun Appadurai argues, one of the hallmarks of modernity has been the organization of consumer desire around "the aesthetics of ephemerality." Still, however ephemeral the stuff of temporary memorials (and such stuff is not, actually, that ephemeral), significance is found in how it mediates, permits, and encourages the social release of grief. However fleeting, spontaneous memorials shoulder "a great deal of social weight."[25]

The meaning of material culture rests in how things evoke memories, sustain thoughts, constitute political conditions, and conjure states of being. Like other forms of commemoration, temporary memorials are memory aids. They specifically function to remember the recently, suddenly dead, to make their loss visible and public, to render their deaths memorable within the realm of social responsibility. Cards and signs stating "we will never forget" and "we remember" suggest that the duty of memory is to acknowledge loss.

Temporary memorials flood the memories of their visitors; the mundane, familiar things of which they are made trigger personal associations. Their materialist dimensions mediate between the living and the dead as flowers, photographs, and other objects "have connotations of transience as well as permanence which feed into the metaphors used to describe and account for the capabilities of memory." These things are meant to bind the living and the dead and "preserve a material presence in the face of an embodied absence."[26] And because their ephemeral nature might sever this psychic bond, temporary memorials are increasingly being saved and preserved.

Temporary memorials rarely feature precious materials and, generally being outdoors, are subject to weeks of ruinous environmental conditions (it snowed during the first week that Columbine's temporary memorial was created). Yet today they are increasingly regarded as unique, valuable, and irreplaceable things. Most of the stuff affixed to Memory Fence and amassed in Clement Park was saved. In Oklahoma City, it was collected, catalogued, and stored in a local warehouse maintained by a museum-trained archivist; in Colorado, it was archived within collections maintained by the Littleton Museum and the Colorado Historical Society. Like the thousands of offerings left each month at the Vietnam Veterans Memorial, which are regularly culled by the National Park Service and preserved and catalogued in a suburban Maryland storage facility, the things left at temporary memorials are treated as things worth saving.[27] As staff at the Colorado Historical Society were advised during a "Columbine Memorial Recovery Strategy Meeting":

> We are working for the public and this event will be documented by the media . . . We will save everything. Everything will be collected and removed from the site. Later decisions will be made as to how the mementoes will be handled. There will be no dumpsters. We need to be sensitive. Members of the volunteer teams may have been directly affected by this event. Everything will be recovered.[28]

In early May 1999, over one hundred volunteers spent three days collecting the items left at Columbine's memorial. Rotted flowers became compost for Denver area parks; fresher flowers became potpourri for victims' families. Everything else was archived.

Materialist responses to tragedy are prevalent now: overwhelmed by 9/11's catastrophe of traumatic death, for example, grief-stricken Americans built temporary memorials, visited New York's Ground Zero (and also the Pentagon and Shanksville), took photos, bought souvenirs (see fig. 2.14, below), and collected scraps of the ruined remains of the World Trade Center.[29] Much of the stuff they made and saved was displayed in various post-9/11 exhibitions, including The Day Our World Changed: Children's Art of 9/11 at the Museum of the City of New York in 2002, and Elegy in the Dust: Sept. 11th and the Chelsea Jeans Memorial at the New-York Historical Society in 2006.

In today's "scramble to curate disaster," as Bill Brown puts it, increasing numbers of public institutions are being called upon to save, store, and otherwise mediate America's temporary memorials.[30] In December 2001, Missouri senator Kit Bond introduced a measure authorizing $5 million in federal funding for the Smithsonian National Museum of American History "to collect and preserve items of historical significance" specific to 9/11, including six million tons of debris from the World Trade Center. "It makes sense that since this was a national tragedy," Bond remarked, "our national historical repository get on top of it and organize it."[31]

One such repository is the September 11 Digital Archive, which uses electronic media to "collect, preserve, and present" a plethora of 9/11 materials. Organized by the American Social History Project at the City University of New York Graduate School and the Center for History and New Media at George Mason University, the archive has partnered with the Library of Congress, the American Red Cross, uReach (a leading communications provider), and Seagate Technologies (the world's largest manufacturer of disk drives and magnetic disks), among others, and includes more than 150,000 digital items relating to 9/11. Understanding public memory as an "evolving process" of democratic participation and materialist accumulation, the archive urges browsers to contribute their own stories ("Tell us what you did, saw, or heard on September 11th") and to upload their personal photos and other data on its Web site.[32]

These impulses are driven in part by the ever-expanding scope of information technology. With camera phones, digital image management software, and increasingly larger data preservation mechanisms, capturing and storing information has never been so easy, affordable, and expected. "Just as social networks and weblogs flip the question of publishing from 'Why publish this?' to 'Why not?'" observes Clay Shirky, "the availability of cheap storage flips the question of whether to save information from 'Why keep this?' to 'Why throw this away?'"[33] This segues with contemporary assumptions that everything—every bit of information—is valuable and must be saved. This, in turn, helps direct the contemporary historical archive and the stewardship of history toward the terms of personal experience and public feeling. Responding, for example, to the online query "How do I know if this item is factual?" the September 11 Digital Archive asserts: "Every submission to the September 11 Digital Archive—even those that are erroneous, misleading, or dubious—contributes in some way to the historical record. A misleading individual account, for example, could reveal certain personal and emotional aspects of the event that would otherwise be lost in a strict authentication and appraisal process."[34] Historical veracity, in other words, is not a huge concern, because whether real or imagined, the ways in which individuals experienced, or felt, 9/11 are automatically assumed to be important. While admirably inclusive, this curatorial approach is also critically vacuous: by refusing the risk of interpretation it fails to interrogate how and why (and which) experiences and feelings constitute self and national identity.

If especially ubiquitous because of the enormous media attention granted these objects, images, and exhibitions, 9/11's material archiving is not unique. Following the *Columbia* space shuttle disaster, for example, staff at the Smithsonian National Air and Space Museum organized a temporary memorial in the museum's main hall, near a fifteen-foot model of the spacecraft. Visitors brought bouquets of flowers, candles, cards, and a copy of the Torah, signed their names in the public comment books that the museum provided, and posed for photos in front of the display. Collecting and displaying this sort of space shrine material—called "grief's memorabilia" by Smithsonian staffers—has now become part of the National Air and Space Museum's curatorial agenda.[35]

Expectations that temporary memorials should be saved—and even made—by America's public museums raise enormous practical and ethical questions, which museum professionals themselves struggle to answer. Can we realistically expect already underfunded and overburdened public institutions to process and house the vast stuff of temporary memorials? Should museums be "managing" these memorials, which means removing them from their original public environments (when? after how long?) and then storing them in sanitized and often less accessible archives?[36] However these questions are considered, the fact remains that memorials made of ephemeral and base materials have assumed honorific status in contemporary America. Their prestige lies in perceptions that they embody important public emotions, and that these emotions are eminently worthy of attention and preservation. More directly, temporary memorials are valued as the literal manifestation of public grief.

Their privileged symbolic value today relates to how they are made to be felt—not simply seen. As Carole Blair observes, memorials "work on the body" by directing "the vector, speed, or possibilities of physical movement."[37] This is especially true of temporary memorials. Usually erected at unexpected sites of unanticipated tragedy, temporary memorials are often aggressively physical entities: spaces that must be walked around (literally, if they block a sidewalk or occupy vast acres in a park) and demand our physical interaction. Like most memorials, temporary memorials are destinations: places to be visited. Fixed commemorative sites like Mount Rushmore and the Statue of Liberty are mostly memorials to visit and look at, although they may also host annual ceremonies. Viewed with binoculars and cameras or visited in cyberspace at the National Park Service Web site, these memorials are typically experienced indirectly. Mount Rushmore has always been a site to see, not actually climb (the 1959 movie *North By Northwest* notwithstanding), and following 9/11, direct physical access to the Statue of Liberty (among other national memorials) was severely restricted. Temporary memorials, however, are performative public spaces. People bring things to these memorials, not only making them but orchestrating their affective conditions. They walk through and around them; they read the cards and poems that are left at them; they kneel down to caress the other things that have been brought; they photograph and videotape what they see; they cry; they are physically and emotionally moved—affected—on multiple levels.

Kinesthetic sensibilities have long informed commemorative cultures: consider the rituals of circumambulation at ancient Greek funerals, or in honorific ceremonies conducted around Trajan's Column in imperial Rome. Consider the Christian practices of touching the crucifix at the altar, stroking the hem of a clothed statue of the Virgin, or kissing the revered icon of a saint. Consider how visitors touch the names of the dead on the Vietnam Veterans Memorial, and make rubbings of those names on pieces of paper. Consider the compulsive obligation to frame and capture memorials and rituals of commemoration on camera—and how these acts of visual documentation have become the social norm. If photos of the dead were common a century ago, photos and videos of *mourners* of the dead are typical today.

These physical, intimate, and performative gestures shape the sustained meaning of temporary memorials. As C. Nadia Serematakis maintains, memory "is a culturally mediated material practice that is activated by embodied acts and semantically dense objects."[38] Today, as knowledge and understanding are equated with felt experience—with being there and touching something, with "feeling" the pain and suffering of others—temporary memorials are especially meaningful because of their particularly kinesthetic dimensions. This is not to argue that embodied memory is inherent or unmediated in temporary memorials, or any memorials, but to recognize that relationships exist between memory, the body, and material culture.

MEDIATING COLUMBINE

Fundamentally physical, intimate, and experiential, temporary memorials embody an ostentatious display of public grief that today's museums and mass media deem particularly valuable. Tens of thousands of people visited the makeshift memorials erected in Oklahoma City and at Columbine High School because within moments of the murderous events that

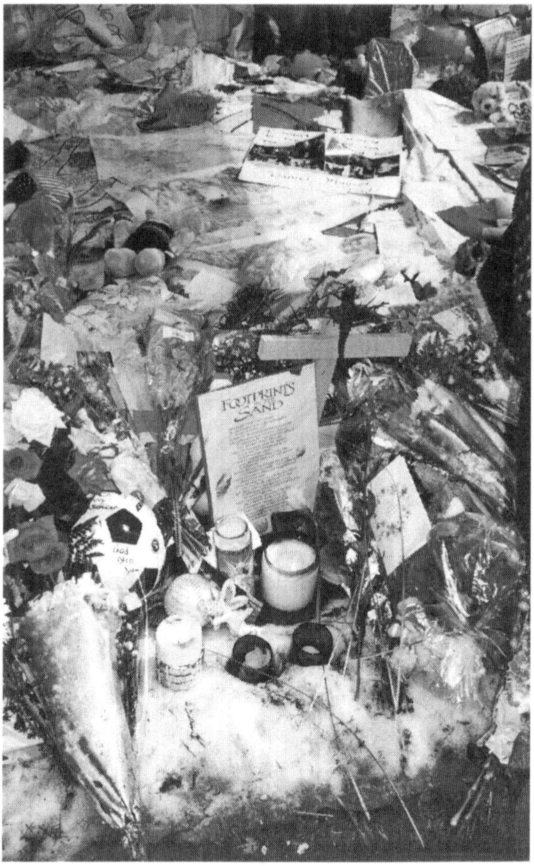

2.7. Votive candles, flowers, teddy bears at the temporary Columbine memorial in Clement Park, April 1999. (Photo by the author.)

redefined the meaning of these places, the media were "live" and on the spot, shaping and directing that meaning—and finding it primarily in the affective conditions of the memorials themselves (fig. 2.7).

In recent years, newspaper and television coverage of tragic and traumatic events has consistently and rather formulaically focused on the material offerings and public rituals of local residents and visitors. At Oklahoma City, Littleton, and death shrines that regularly sprout in the hallways, playgrounds, and front lawns of American public schools from Jonesboro, Arkansas (where in 1998, four girls and one teacher were shot to death by two middle-school boys, ages eleven and thirteen) to Red Lake, Minnesota (where in 2005, a sixteen-year-old high school student killed ten people, including his classmates, his kin, and himself), mass media interpretations of violent and unexpected death typically center on the emotional responses of survivors, bystanders, and tourists as conveyed in temporary memorials.

Television especially is the witness and conduit for ritualized expressions of public grief. At temporary memorials, victims and visitors eagerly chat with TV reporters and openly share their experiences; indeed, doing so is prescribed as curative. The shootings at Columbine, for example, began at 11:20 a.m. on Tuesday, April 20, 1999 and "Breaking News" coverage began within minutes. By 11:55 a.m., CNN and MSNBC were broadcasting live footage captured by Denver NBC affiliate KUSA-TV, including shots of students jumping out of windows and cell phone calls from terrified students still trapped inside the school. By noon, every TV channel in the Denver metro region was fixed on the story. For hours, they featured nonstop images of the SWAT team siege of the school and recovery efforts by firemen and paramedics.[39] In the mid-afternoon, one TV reporter spoke with an obviously distraught father, waiting with hundreds of other parents to determine whether his teenage daughter was safe. Later that evening, the same station featured a live broadcast of their tearful reunion, wherein father and daughter turned to the television cameras and talked about how they felt.

As a "special report" anxiously interrupting TV's regular programming, Columbine was what media analysts Daniel Dayan and Elihu Katz call a "festive viewing" experience, one that producers and audiences alike observe as the "high holidays of mass communication." It was quickly framed as a "media event": a captivating televisual spectacle like the *Columbia* space shuttle disaster and the hijacker attacks of 9/11.[40] In the hours and days following the shootings, an estimated 750 news organizations sent media representatives to Colorado to cover the story. CNN alone sent seventy staffers; NBC and ABC, fifty apiece.[41]

Littleton became "Network Row West" as TV anchors including Tom Brokaw, Katie Couric, Peter Jennings, and Dan Rather descended on the Denver suburb. (*Nightline*'s Ted Koppel was dispatched to Jonesboro, where he talked with families still grieving from their own school shooting a year earlier about their reactions to this latest "media event" in Colorado.) Within twenty-four hours of the shootings, Columbine students, parents, and teachers were making the rounds of national TV programs like *Today*, *Good Morning America*, *Entertainment Tonight*, and *Oprah*. Eyewitnesses and survivors were thoroughly comfortable with what Jessica Seigel calls the "axiomatic wisdom of our talk-show culture: Talking heals pain." *The Montel Williams Show*, for example, flew eight students and six parents to its New York studios for an hour-long special that aired three days after the murders; as Williams put it, "They wanted a good and safe place to express their grief." It wasn't apparently that safe: a comment by the show's "consulting psychologist" about students taking "responsibility" for their attitudes and actions erupted into a heated off-stage shouting match between parents and *Montel* staffers.[42]

Nonstop TV coverage of the Columbine shootings—variously titled "Killings in Colorado," "High School Massacre," and "Terror in the Rockies"—gave local stations their highest ever viewership; likewise, TV newsmagazines centered on the Columbine story earned peak ratings. A special two-hour *Dateline* anchored by Brokaw on April 21 scored NBC its highest seasonal rating in that time slot; coverage on the Fox News Channel drew the highest twenty-four-hour ratings in that network's then three-year history. "Every night we go home and watch it on the news," the mother of a Columbine High School senior told one reporter. "It's helping us heal."[43]

Television is time bound, a steady presence organized around predictably scheduled programs and planned events. Ostensibly an instantaneous medium of mass communication, television operates within a conventional structure of storytelling, thereby relating narratives from local news to soap operas within carefully framed formats featuring beginnings, endings, and plot development called "content." While an unpredictable crisis like Columbine validates television's self-promoted significance as a "live" and seemingly impartial source of information, it also disrupts TV's temporal flow, puncturing its regularly planned programming and forcing producers and anchors to scramble for new modes of storytelling. This explains TV's repetitious visualization of catastrophic events—footage of the explosion of the *Challenger* space shuttle in 1986, for example, or of planes crashing into the World Trade Center on 9/11—and its quick and often facile analysis of these events. Steadily replayed images and reports are strategies aimed at restoring television's narrative and time-bound sensibility.[44] Simultaneously, they create social consensus about media events themselves, reconciling (or collapsing) competing or differing accounts of crisis and tragedy within a shared historical and national memory.

Lacking a single iconic image that might neatly summarize the shootings at Columbine, as well as a conceptual understanding of why the shootings occurred, many journalists explained that the story of Columbine was the story of public grief. "You don't want to stick a camera in a crying person's face, but you have to get used to it," said one CNN intern. Whether repeatedly broadcasting footage of grief-stricken students piling flowers on the cars and trucks of their murdered classmates, soliciting graphic details of the murders from shell-shocked survivors, or airing images of people sobbing at Columbine's temporary memorial, TV networks generally avoided the subject of why the murders happened or how similar tragedies might be avoided in the future. Issues such as school bullying and gun control were downplayed, although

Harris and Klebold's murderous anger may have been exacerbated by their reputations as public school pariahs and social outcasts, and their murderous actions certainly stemmed from their effortless ability to buy firearms.[45]

Political causes and connections were also overlooked—such as the fact that Harris and Klebold targeted their high school near the date that Timothy McVeigh blew up the Murrah Federal Building (April 19, 1995), which was itself a calculated response to the murders of more than eighty Branch Davidians two years earlier in Waco, Texas (April 19, 1993). Although Katie Couric, who spent several days in Clement Park anchoring for *Today*, did ask Colorado governor Bill Owens if he "wondered" about the easy "accessibility of guns" in America, her unedited seventeen-minute interview with Michael Schoels (stepfather of Isaiah Schoels, the only black student who was murdered) and Craig Scott (teenage brother of Rachel Scott), was considered "the poignant highpoint" of Columbine's media event, made more so by "the memorable scene of Schoels reaching over to grab the hand of the shocked teen, who was having trouble expressing his pain to Couric." As Couric herself remarked a few years later, "That interview remains one of the most emotional experiences of my professional life."[46]

Mass media attention to mourning at Columbine generated peak ratings but skirted the social and historical dimensions of these visibly public deaths. Perhaps television is simply incapable of addressing these causal dimensions; as Patricia Mellencamp argues, TV's time-bound organization largely prevents it from recognizing, let alone reckoning with, the particular contexts of crisis and catastrophe.[47] Television's storytelling focus allows it to dwell on the intrinsically dramatic manifestations of public affect, on heightened emotional performances of suffering and sorrow. Yet the lack of analysis accorded the most often repeated lament expressed by Columbine's mourners—"I don't understand why this happened"—suggests the mostly superficial nature of mass media's "coverage" of grief.

Failure to understand the outburst of public grief at Columbine, grief in no small part shaped, of course, by the media itself, underscores a general inattentiveness to the critical meaning of mourning and the changed nature of its objectification and display in contemporary America. Further, while mass media and mourners may understand temporary memorials and emotional talk-show interviews on curative terms—as emotionally powerful ways to express and "heal" the grief caused by sudden and traumatic death—questions remain about what is actually being expressed and what needs to be cured.

GRIEF

Grief is the most obvious affect in the making and meaning of temporary memorials. Grief is generally understood as the expression of deep emotional anguish, usually about death and loss, while mourning is defined as the ritualized practices that help assuage that anguish. Modern Western assumptions that grief is a private, internal emotion and mourning is an external, social behavior are increasingly challenged today—as the widespread presence of temporary memorials suggests. In fact, temporary memorials problematize supposed distinctions between grief and mourning, as they embody both visibly public expressions of grief and rituals of mourning. They also embody contemporary understandings of continued, rather than severed, bonds between the living and the dead.

In "Mourning and Melancholia" (1917), Freud argued that mourning was crucial in terms of "working through" grief; indeed, mourning was necessary in order for the grief-stricken to free themselves ("decathect") from psychologically dangerous attachments to the dead. "When the work of mourning is completed," said Freud, "the ego becomes free and uninhibited again." Those who failed to do this, who could not take measure of their loss and separate themselves from the deceased, were considered dysfunctionally subsumed by self-serving melancholia, which Freud regarded as a pathological form of grief.[48] This was a modernist approach to grief and mourning, prompted by assumptions about rationality and early twentieth-century urges toward order and efficiency. Grief was viewed as a disruptive and debilitating emotional response, one that had to be dealt with—"worked through"—as quickly as possible, hence the emphasis on severing ties with the dead by "letting go" and "getting over it," and moving on with one's life.

Although Freud's thesis stemmed from his own interests in ego development and Oedipal crises (the detachment of the child from the parent), not from the physical and emotional contexts of death and loss per se, this "breaking bonds" presupposition became the cornerstone of modern Western psychoanalytic understanding of bereavement. It remains common in the rhetoric of grieving today: Columbine's temporary memorial was repeatedly described in curative and healing terms, as part of a process of "working through" and "finding closure" for grief. Yet Freud's own experiences with grief eventually led him to recognize the limitations of his original argument and to subsequently revise his understandings of mourning.[49] More recent theoretical and clinical analyses of grief are based on how and why people actually grieve, and emphasize the inseparability of life from death—or the "continuing" bonds between the living and the deceased.

Some contemporary theorists argue, for example, that melancholia and bereavement are constant, if not central, in the formation of African American and / or homosexual identity. As José Esteban Muñoz writes, "melancholia, for blacks and queers of any color, is not a pathology but an integral part of everyday lives . . . a mechanism that helps us (re)construct identity and take our dead to the various battles we must wage in their names—and in our names."[50] Mourning is particular to personal experience, and injunctions against it, such authors argue, constitute injunctions against the bereaved. Clinical researchers such as Dennis Klass and Phyllis Silverman similarly maintain that bereavement is a persistent cognitive and emotional process that "affects the mourner for the rest of his or her life. People are changed by the experience; they do not get over it, and part of the change is a transformed but continuing relationship with the deceased."[51] Grief, in other words, is often endless, although it need not be endlessly obsessive or pathological.

Recognition of grief's enduring presence has fostered a great deal of popular interest. A veritable "grief industry" has developed, replete with bestselling books like *How to Go On Living When Someone You Love Dies* (1988), *Tuesdays with Morrie* (1997), and *Talking with Children About Loss* (1999). Online chat rooms and "grief-share" Web sites (including griefnet.org, webhealing.com, and petloss.com) are also popular, providing support from volunteer traumatologists, extensive bibliographies on any number of "grief-related topics," and directions on how to create a virtual memorial.

While obviously attuned to today's cultural renegotiation of what grief means in America, the prescriptive tendencies of the grief industry are simplistic and highly opportunistic. Rather than recognizing causes, determining preventative measures, or considering the continuous and nonpathological dimensions of grief, many of the industry's professionals see grief as an abnormal period of psychic pain and emotional damage, as a problematic "stage" or phase of trauma that must be "worked through" in order to generate "closure" and return to normalcy. Their assumptions that grief is basically a disease that can be healed strike many as arrogant. As Edward Linenthal observes in his study of public feeling and commemoration following the bombing of the Murrah Federal Building, "closure" was "a word that many in Oklahoma City came to detest."[52]

The grief industry is also insidious. Armies of grief and trauma professionals are typically deployed to American public schools today to "address the emotional needs of students" and "help them cope" with death and loss following school shootings, car accidents, and murders. Following the murder of six-year-old Jon Benet Ramsey in 1996, the elementary school that she had attended in Boulder, Colorado, organized three days of grief counseling for its students. Following the shootings at Columbine, hundreds of grief therapists were dispatched to nearby churches and community centers; when Columbine students returned to school a few weeks after the murders, a mental health counselor was present in every classroom to guide "psychological debriefing."[53] Following the attacks on the World Trade Center, several thousand grief and crisis counselors descended on New York, many trained in critical-incident stress management (CISM, also called "emotional first aid") and taught to ask questions like, "What was the worst part of the incident for you personally?"[54] Whether a high-profile media event like Columbine or a more typical if no less heartbreaking daily tragedy such as the deaths of American teenagers in car accidents, grief industry professionals are on the scene.

The benefits of extensive grief counseling are speculative, and some conclude that "generic interventions, targeted toward the general population of the bereaved, are likely to be unnecessary and largely unproductive." Some question the self-promotional tendencies of trauma therapy; as one grief industry professional observed, "There were far too many helpers at Columbine. Perhaps we need to look at our own egos and motivations. Do we all need to be at the front lines of a public tragedy?" Others worry about the "threat" that grief therapy poses to self-reliance and national confidence, cautioning that contemporary Americans are "too attached" to a pathology of trauma and to a self-interested industry of mental health professionals who overestimate the nation's psychological fragility.[55] Nevertheless, public discussions and displays of grief are flourishing in America, as seen in the popularity of bereavement counseling and the ubiquity of temporary memorials. Both are increasingly considered critical components in the management of grief.

MANAGING MOURNING

In its *Crisis Communications Guide & Toolkit* (2000), the National Education Association advised school districts and parent-teacher associations on how to "manage" the temporary memorials now commonly made after school shootings:

> There is a need to develop and implement systems for depositing, warehousing, cataloguing . . . It is a very healing process for the community to participate in as givers and receivers. Outside Columbine High School, hundreds of thousands of spontaneous memorials sprung up, growing higher and more beautiful by the minute. The fences were papered with

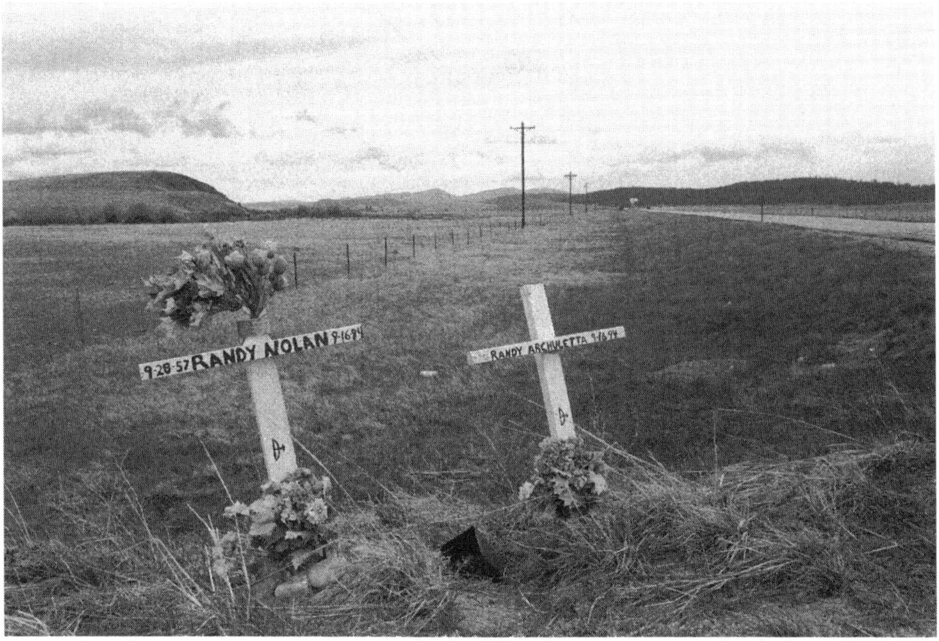

2.8. David B. Nance, "Randy and Randy, U.S. Hwy 285 south of Fairplay, CO, 2000," photograph of roadside memorial to two friends, both bow-hunting enthusiasts (note the bow and arrow motif on the crosses) killed in a car accident in 1994. (© David B. Nance.)

> posters, pictures, artwork, and symbolic expressions of the entire nation's profound loss. There was a significant need to preserve and display these items."

Following the National Education Association's lead, many American public schools have implemented "crisis management policies" that include guidelines on "appropriate" post-trauma memorials. In Springfield Township, Pennsylvania, temporary memorials at public schools may not exceed 8 feet by 4 feet in size and thirty calendar days in duration; in Jonesboro, memorial trees are preferred. In a 2007 newsletter, a U.S. Department of Education spokesman said public schools "need to monitor messages left at spontaneous memorials and be ready for unusual or unexpected circumstances."[56]

Roadside memorials are also increasingly subject to mourning "management" (fig. 2.8). In the American Southwest, temporary wood and stone *descansos* were originally erected to commemorate those who died suddenly on the road, did not receive last rites, and were buried in unconsecrated ground, in hopes that other travelers might stop and say prayers for the souls of the deceased. Eighteenth-century territorial governors and bishops tried to ban these handmade memorials, worried that they might scare off potential settlers or that the practice constituted a threat to prescribed political and / or religious authority.[57] Yet making roadside memorials continued and, especially in the twentieth century, burgeoned along with the growth of America's car culture.

In 1922, temporary memorials to children killed in traffic accidents—a leading factor in child mortality at the time—were erected in New York's Central Park; in 1926, a Monument to Traffic Accidents was placed at the intersection of Broadway and 72nd Street, bearing the inscription "In Memory of 256 Persons Killed by Reckless Drivers in New York City Since Jan. 1 1926."[58] In the 1930s, the Arizona Highway Department began erecting markers at the sites of fatal roadside accidents; in the early 1950s, the American Legion began installing small metal crosses at such sites in Montana. In 1941, a letter writer to *Life* magazine commented on how roadside fatalities along U.S. Route 17 near Savannah, Georgia were marked by clusters of small white crosses "in mute testimony that danger lurks not only around the corner, but along a straight stretch too." In his Louisiana-based novel *All the King's Men* (1946), Robert Penn Warren described how "the boys from the Highway Department" would "mark the spot" of car crashes "with a little metal square on a metal rod stuck in the black dirt off the shoulder, the metal square painted white and on it in black a skull and crossbones."[59]

Thousands of Americans die each year in car accidents: over forty-three thousand in 2005; over thirty-seven thousand in 2008. There is no national monument to these deaths—because, as Michael Warner observes, it is *mass* disaster that commands national subjectivity.[60] But there are thousands of local roadside memorials, usually erected by family members and friends. They typically mark the site of random automobile, motorcycle, truck, and bicycle fatalities and consist of crosses decorated with flowers, teddy bears, and photos and mementos of the dead (fig. 2.9). As visibly public modes of mourning, roadside memorials help to manage, order, and control the psychic disaster of death and loss.

Their heightened presence has generated a lot of popular and critical attention: recent films on roadside memorials include the suspense thriller *Descansos* (2006), starring Gary Busey, and the documentary *Resting Places* (2007), narrated by Liam Neeson. Recent songs include Don Morrell's folkie ballad "Roadside Cross" (1999). Roadside memorials have also been examined in detail at academic conferences, in scholarly articles, and on Web sites. Various Internet entrepreneurs sell ready-made "Roadside Memorial Crosses" with personalized nameplates and mounting stakes "for easy installation."[61]

Their abundance and agency—some see roadside memorials as "ex-

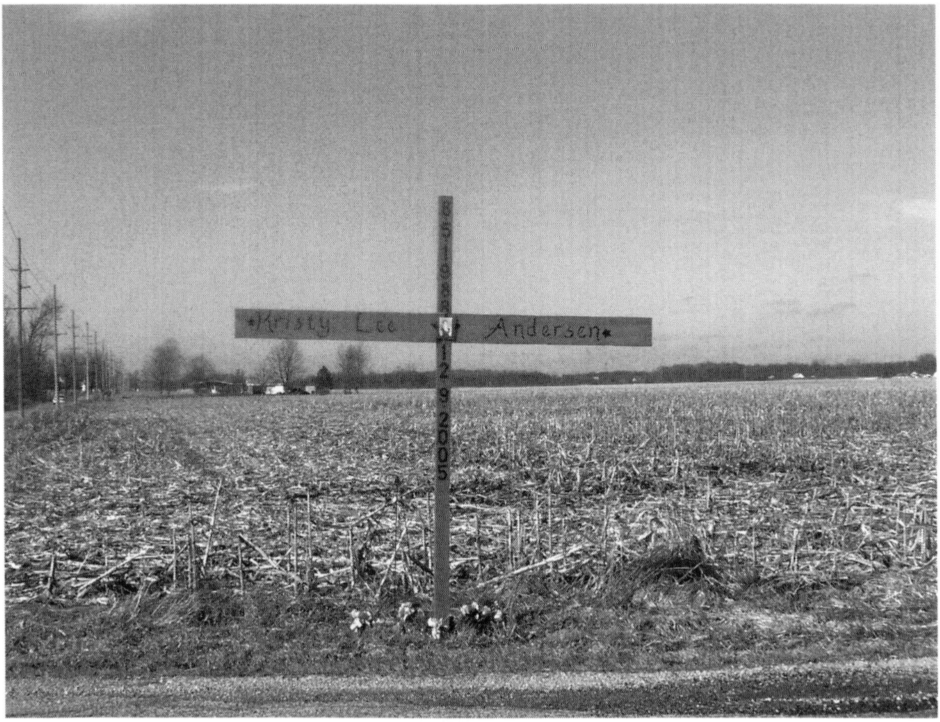

2.9. Roadside memorial, U.S. Highway 6 near Teegarden, Indiana, 2009. (Photo by the author.)

pressions of alternative authority drawn from the intensity of grief [and] from a belief in the spiritual presence of the deceased"—has also generated considerable state and legal scrutiny.[62] Many states have passed legislation banning or restricting roadside memorials, arguing that they are driving distractions. Massachusetts, Missouri, Oregon, North Carolina, and Wisconsin are among states that prohibit handmade roadside memorials, encouraging mourners to participate instead in Adopt-a-Highway roadside cleanup programs that recognize victims in approved signage. Other states, including Colorado, Florida, Texas, Virginia, and Wyoming, permit only "official" roadside memorials that are ordered by the families of victims and installed for limited periods (one to six years). These typically require a fee and feature metal or plastic signs (sans crosses) that include the name of the dead and cautionary inscriptions such as "Drive Safely" and "Please Don't Drink and Drive" (fig. 2.10). In 2007, Oregon legislators adopted "Eric's Law," approving roadside memorials that warn drivers to "share the road" with bike riders; the law was enacted in memory of Eric Kautzky, a teacher who was struck and killed by a car while riding his bike.[63]

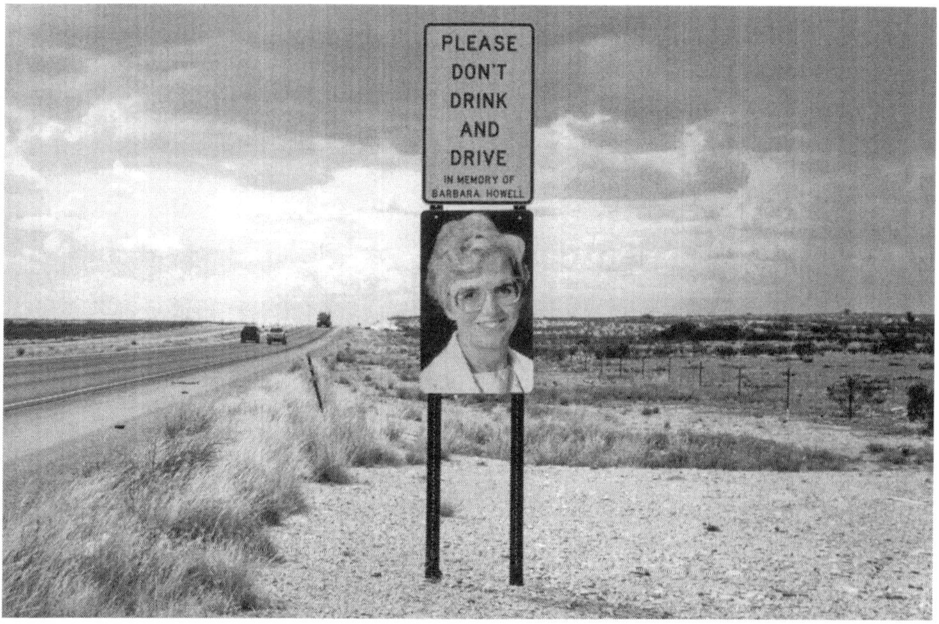

2.10. Bob Bednar, "Please Don't Drink and Drive." Photograph of U.S. Highway 285 / 84, north of Carlsbad, New Mexico, August 2003. (Courtesy of Bob Bednar.)

Florida's Department of Transportation estimates installing four hundred to five hundred highway safety memorial markers each year, and Wyoming's Department of Transportation erected ninety-eight such signs (designed by elementary school students and depicting a broken heart and a dove in flight) between 2003 and 2005. In October 2007, the Delaware Highway Memorial Garden, a $239,000 project, opened at the state's Smyrna Rest Area. Intended to replace all of the state's roadside memorials, the eleven-thousand-square-foot park features a reflecting pool and hundreds of memorial brick pavers provided free to the families and friends of those who have died in state highway accidents, each engraved with the names of victims and with inscriptions like "In Memory of All Souls Lost, Rest in Peace."[64]

Regulatory debates over roadside memorials represent classic struggles over public expression in America, over whether or not vernacular memorials featuring religious symbols are permissible on public property. Colorado resident Rodney Lyle Scott didn't think so, and in April 2000 decided to remove a roadside memorial made of crosses and artificial flowers that he had driven past every day for several years. "I had gone through a lot of personal turmoil myself," said Scott. "I didn't appreciate somebody else throwing their hurt and sorrow out for the public view, as if it was more important than someone else's hurt or losses." The state saw otherwise and charged Scott with "desecration of a venerated object" after the family who had made the roadside memorial complained that it was missing. Scott's attorney, a member of the Wisconsin-based Freedom from Religion Foundation, questioned the legality of "using public lands to endorse religion," and moved for dismissal, which was granted.[65] A few years later, the Colorado legislature voted to ban privately erected roadside memorials altogether, opting instead for the nondenominational blue and white markers of the state's Roadside Memorial Signing Program.

While increasing numbers of states have adopted them, official roadside memorials seem to have had little impact on curtailing highway deaths or managing public acts of memorialization. They have, however, intensified public resentment about statist intervention. "This is the bureaucratization of love. I don't like it one bit," complained conservative Virginia assemblyman Robert G. Marshall whose son was killed in a car accident in 2001. Challenging Virginia's official roadside memorial policy, Marshall declared: "I intend to put a cross up for my son. Period." In Wisconsin, the Department of Transportation modified its ban on handmade roadside memorials after grieving families persisted in remaking them each time officials took them down at the site of the state's deadliest highway accident—a fifty-car pileup near Sheboygan that killed twelve people in 2003. And in Alaska in 2003, grieving parents persuaded the state to legalize privately made roadside memorials, such as the six-foot cross decorated with flowers and photos that Barbara Dowdy erected at the spot outside Fairbanks where her daughter died in 2000. "My daughter was seventeen," Dowdy explained. "An official road sign wouldn't have been her. It was not a statement of her life."[66]

Other mourning management practices gaining popularity in contemporary America include those centered on pregnancy loss. These often feature the use of "memory boxes" to store "cherished mementos that connect with the tiny child," such as hospital I.D. bracelets, photos, locks of hair, and hand and foot prints. Corresponding rituals include gifts to the dead child on his or her birthday, adding charms to a "Miscarriage / Pregnancy Loss Charm Bracelet," wearing blue and pink pregnancy and infant loss awareness ribbons, participating in hospital memorial services, and organizing funeral ceremonies with tiny caskets called "burial cradles."[67] Web sites like angels.4ever.com, emptycradle .org, and honoredbabies.org offer virtual memorials "for those who have lost a baby due to miscarriage, SIDS, stillbirth and other infant deaths." Shifting social perceptions of "the fetal subject," shaped by advances in reproductive technologies and neonatal medicine, and by the recognition that pregnancy is a personal choice rather than moral or medi-

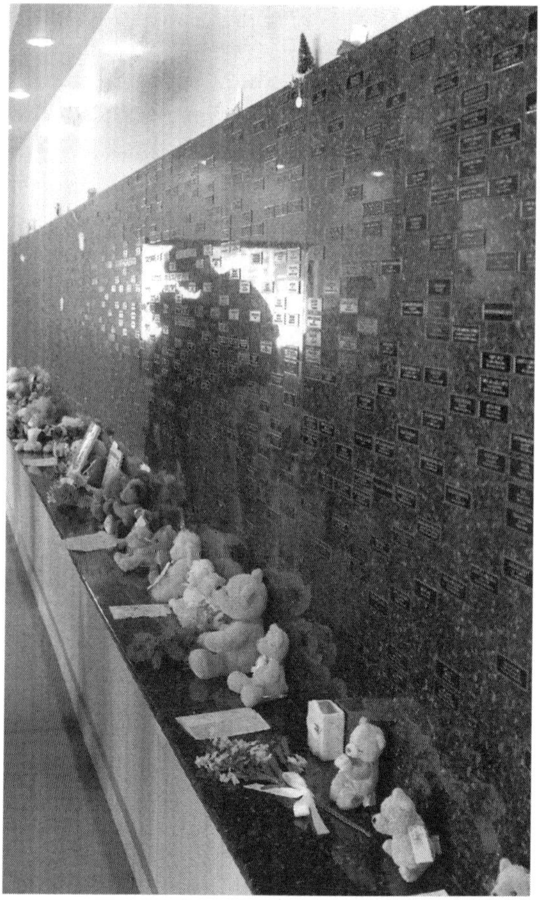

2.11. National Memorial for the Unborn, Wall of Names, Chattanooga, Tennessee, est. 1994. (Courtesy of the National Memorial for the Unborn.)

cal obligation, contribute to the growing movement to commemorate pregnancy loss. Since 2001, more than twenty-one states have enacted laws—called "Missing Angels" bills—allowing birth certificates for stillbirths. Mourning rituals and material culture products play similarly instrumental roles in constructing and commodifying neonatal identity and parental grief.[68]

Constructing fetal personhood, making the fetus a member of the American body politic, is the goal of the National Memorial for the Unborn in Chattanooga, Tennessee (fig. 2.11). Established in 1994 on the site of a former abortion clinic, the National Memorial for the Unborn is "dedicated to healing generations of pain associated with the loss of aborted children" and offers "abortion recovery services" featuring Bible studies, post-abortion stress support groups, and ceremonies focused on "ending the denial, admitting the sin, facing the pain, and experiencing God's forgiveness." The memorial itself features a Remembrance Garden, a Pool of Tears, and a fifty-foot Wall of Names dotted with small brass plates ($35 each) inscribed with "Words of Remembrance" from their donors.[69] Similarly, Rachel's Park Memorial in Waco, Texas, erected in January 2006 by Elijah Ministries, includes a Wall of Remembrance on which women are encouraged to "inscribe the names of their aborted children." Sponsored by Operation Save America, an aggressively right-wing antiabortion group that insists that "Jesus Christ is the only answer to the abortion holocaust" and has issued an "Emancipation Proclamation for the Pre-Born Child," the Waco memorial is intended as the first of many. As its backers proclaim, "Our goal is to see the vision and mission of Rachel's Park Memorial spread throughout America, one park in each state of the Union."[70]

Antiabortion memorials are thriving in contemporary America because, as Brian Massumi observes, "In North America, at least, the far right is far more attuned to the imagistic potential of the postmodern body than the established left, and has exploited that advantage for at least the last two decades."[71] Their strategies of affective visual exploitation include temporary memorials featuring hugely enlarged color photos of aborted fetuses and plots of small white crosses, often displayed on the lawns of college campuses during antiabortion rallies. In the spring of 2009, Operation Rescue and other antiabortion extremists protested Barack Obama's commencement address at the University of Notre Dame, calling Obama America's "most anti-life president." For several weeks, trucks displaying graphic antiabortion images circled the city of South Bend and a small plane flew over the campus towing a banner depicting a bloody fetus and the words "You'r [*sic*] Honoring This." Randall Terry, the founder of Operation Rescue, was arrested on the Notre Dame campus for trespassing while pushing a baby stroller containing dolls coated in fake blood.

In 1992, New York Cardinal John O'Connor advised the Knights of Columbus (a Roman Catholic men's group) to begin erecting more permanent antiabortion memorials; within a decade 1,700 had been built (fig. 2.12). Most are located on the grounds of Catholic churches, cemeteries, parish halls, and community centers and consist of small markers inscribed with phrases like "In Loving Memory of All Unborn Children" and "All Life is Sacred, Born and Unborn."

One proposed antiabortion memorial is The Arch of Triumph of the Immaculate Heart of Mary and International Shrine of the Holy Innocents, a gigantic golden arch in Buffalo, New York, that aims "to honor the Virgin Mary and unborn fetuses which were terminated through abortion." Unanimously endorsed by Buffalo's city council in 2002, the seven hundred-foot tall antiabortion arch—taller than the Gateway Arch—is

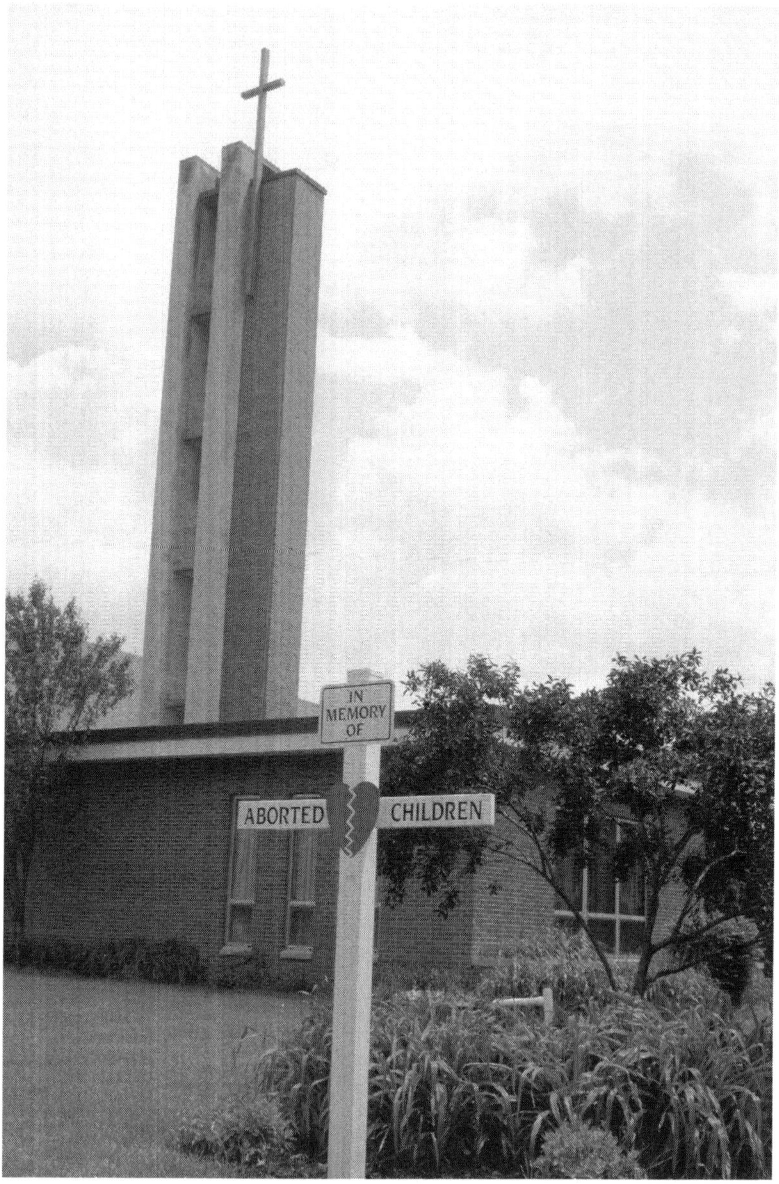

2.12. Antiabortion memorial, St. Anthony de Padua Parish, South Bend, Indiana, 2009. (Courtesy of Geoffrey Thrumston.)

to be erected on the eastern shores of Lake Erie and will include an observation deck, three chapels, and an enormous golden crucifix. Estimated at a cost of more than $100 million, the memorial is intended to "substantially enrich Buffalo's cultural and economic status" and is proposed as "an international signal call to conversion and a return to God, and to an ever-greater love of purity and detestation of abortion and immorality." Critics level words like "arrogant," "extravagant," and "folly," but the arch's antiabortion backers appeal to contemporary understandings of the fetus-as-citizen-body when they declare:

> [A] memorial to victims of abortion runs counter across pro-choice philosophy like nails across a chalkboard. Memorials by nature exist for people as opposed to formless blobs of fetal tissue. And people have feelings, souls, and rights. Consequently, this memorial in a way revives the status of abortion as a moral crime against humanity.

In *Boomsday* (2007), a satirical novel about generational entitlement and Beltway politics, Christopher Buckley references the similarly ostentatious pet project of a pro-life senator named Gideon Payne: The 43 Million Memorial, "a memorial on the Washington Mall to the 43 million unborn souls since the Supreme Court's Roe v. Wade ruling in 1973."[72]

As highly affective "geographies of faith," antiabortion memorials are obviously vehicles of Christian proselytizing. The Memorial Wall for the Unborn, for example, dedicated in 2000 in Boulder, Colorado, on the grounds of the Sacred Heart of Mary Catholic Church, features a seven-foot statue of the risen Christ and includes several gravestones adorned with tiny brass plaques reading "I'm Sorry," "Forgive Me," and "No Less Real, No Less Loved." Buried near the memorial wall are the ashes of several thousand fetuses aborted between 1996 and 2005 at the Boulder Abortion Clinic. The ashes were obtained from a local mortuary in violation of its contract with the clinic prohibiting the use of cremated remains in any religious or political ceremonies. "They have taken it upon themselves to make a macabre ritual out of this," clinic director and doctor Warren Hern angrily told reporters when news of the church's antiabortion memorial was publicly announced in January 2005—just days before the thirty-second anniversary of the 1973 *Roe v. Wade* Supreme Court decision establishing the legal right to abortion in America. "Antiabortion zealots, Catholic or otherwise, have shown that they will stop at nothing to inflict guilt and to compound the grief, sadness, and sense of loss that these women experience," Hern added. Others were incensed that this Boulder church presumed that its Christian / Catholic modes of mourning and memorialization were appropriate for all.[73]

New social understandings of what and how to mourn in America

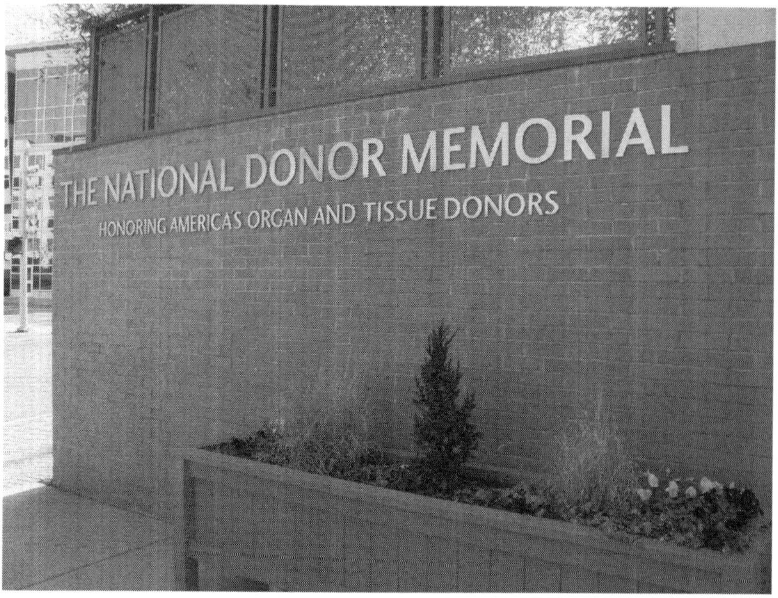

2.13. National Donor Memorial, United Network for Organ Sharing, Richmond, Virginia, dedicated 2003. (Photo by the author.)

and who counts as a citizen worth mourning extend to the organ transplant (or transfer) community. As Lesley A. Sharp explains, many organ donor recipients remember the dates of their transplants in elaborate ceremonies called "rebirth" days, sometimes with cakes in the shapes of their new kidneys or hearts. Yet donor kin, the families of the dead who donated those kidneys and hearts, also want to memorialize their "gifts of life" and to mourn the loss of those who gave them. Although medical professionals insisted for decades on the total separation of organ recipients and donors—adhering to modernist assumptions regarding the psychic, social, and legal distinctions of life and death—the past few years have seen a radical shift in their relationship. Today, donor kin publicly mourn their losses with memorial trees (a regenerative symbol that, Sharp points out, serves in the "greening of the body") and memorial quilts like Patches of Love, a 1,500-panel quilt produced under the auspices of the National Donor Family Council (the leading lobby for organ donor kin).[74] In 2003, the United Network for Organ Sharing dedicated its 10,000-square-foot National Donor Memorial (fig. 2.13), an outdoor site with "three metaphoric rooms" symbolizing "the emotional process of donation and transplantation: the Wall of Tears and Water Garden (hope), the Butterfly Lawn (renewal), and the Memorial Grove (transformation)."[75] Insisting on continuity between organ recipients and organ donors, and thus between the living and the dead, such memorials grant personhood to previously marginalized subjects of grief.

All of these modes of mourning—temporary memorials, roadside memorials, pregnancy loss memorials, antiabortion memorials, and organ donor memorials—are public. If modern Western social and cultural conventions insisted on private and individual forms of grieving throughout much of the twentieth century, viewing the bereaved as psychologically disabled social pariahs, today's mourning practices are public and participatory. Changing understandings of the enduring trajectory of grief and the performative terms of mourning, as well as repetitious media attention to the felt experiences of traumatic death and loss, have made grief a permissible public emotion in America. Likewise, revisionist understandings of trauma discourse and collective bereavement within particular communities, within communities of color or among those with AIDS, for example, have significantly altered how much of America negotiates grief.

Localized losses are often claimed today on national terms. "What happened in Littleton pierced the soul of America," President Bill Clinton proclaimed one year after the shootings at Columbine High School. Likewise, as Linenthal observed in 1998, the grassroots grieving following the bombing of the Murrah Federal Building intimated "that the deaths in Oklahoma have become, like the deaths in the Holocaust, public deaths that count not only for the families but the nation." Bereavement, he notes, "is one of the only ways Americans can imagine themselves as one; being 'together' with millions of others through expressions of mourning bypasses or transcends the many ways in which people are divided—by religion, by ideology, by class, by region, by race, by gender."[76] And bereavement tourism is a growing industry.

TRAGIC TOURISM

"What are we to make," asks Lucy Lippard, of the apparent popularity of "tragic tourism"? Why are Americans, among others, so drawn to sites of tragic and traumatic death, to "celebrity murder sites, concentration camps, massacre sites, places where thousands have been shot down, swept away in floods, inundated by lava, herded off to slavery, crushed by earthquakes, starved to death, tortured, murdered, hung, or otherwise suffered excesses the rest of us hope we will never experience?" Sarah Vowell considers similar sorts of questions and quests in *Assassination Vacation*, a bloodstained travelogue of the murders of three nineteenth-century American presidents (Lincoln, Garfield, and McKinley) and irreverent exposé of seemingly insatiable American appetites for journeying through a national landscape of violent death.[77]

Tragic tourism—the "catastrophe walkabout," one author calls it—is burgeoning today.[78] Often physically and emotionally insulated from death and disaster, people visit sites like Columbine High School and New York's Ground Zero to see and touch tragedy. Their grim fascination with the deaths of innocents and unfortunates is accompanied by feelings of grief, guilt, and gratitude: with sorrow over sudden, unexpected, and senseless loss; with worries about personal responsibility; with thanks that they were not inside that high school or office building. These feelings are ritualized, becoming shared and socially permissible through performances of public mourning.

These affective conditions become even more memorable through acts of consumerism. Tragic tourism, like most tourism, privileges the souvenir as a primary agent of remembrance, and even the sites of the most obscene deaths feature gift shops and street vendors. Just a few days after 9/11, salesmen took to the streets near Ground Zero, turning Lower Manhattan into a veritable open-air market where tragic tourists could purchase photographs, postcards, glass figurines, T-shirts, coffee mugs, and all sorts of other mementos featuring images of the smoldering ruins of the Twin Towers (fig. 2.14). Souvenirs are the trace of authentic experience, Susan Stewart argues, and Americans are certainly drawn to the sites and things of tragedy and trauma because of their authenticity.[79]

Visiting such sites is tantamount to slowly driving past car accidents and scanning crash scenes for signs of death, for evidence of the unknown. Visiting the bombed remains of the Murrah Federal Building, said the widow of a man who was killed there, "just makes it real."[80] A few months after it was first erected, officials in Oklahoma City actually moved Memory Fence a few feet closer to where the federal building had been, thus enabling public interests in interacting with the authentic milieu of death. Made out of chain-link steel, the fence prohibited visitors from literally touching the site of death but still provided a window onto what Bataille termed "the reality of the impossible."[81]

Palpable desires for visceral experience—for intensified modes of sensation that may permit empathetic response, encourage ideological attachment, and, especially, confirm our own reality—draw people to the spaces and places of tragic death. "The core power of this site, the reason it resonates with so many people, is that this is where the tragedy took place," explains the president and CEO of the September 11 National Memorial & Museum at the World Trade Center in New York. "The notion of authenticity and using actual artifacts that have a connection

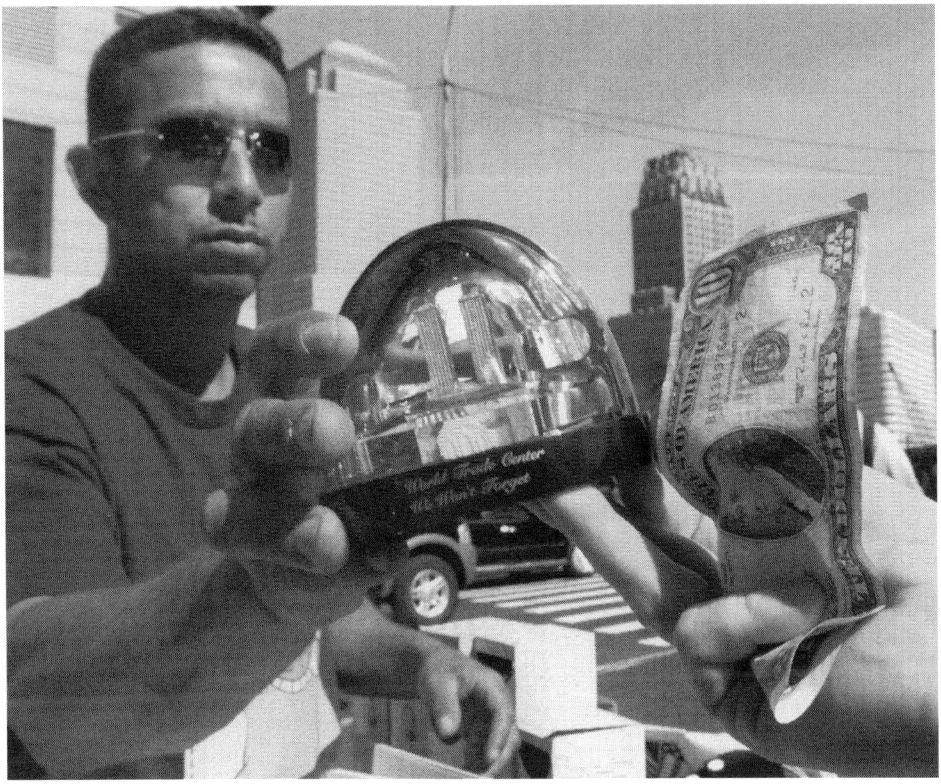

2.14. Selling World Trade Center souvenirs near Ground Zero, 2007. (Photo by Tina Fineberg/AP Images.)

right back to that event is something this museum will be exhibiting and showcasing as much as possible," he adds. If this seems disrespectful, a kind of tourism tainted by "insidious elements of voyeurism and sensationalism" says Lippard, it is also the experiential and "authentic" kind of tourism out of which modern Americans make meaning of tragic death, traumatic loss, and a national legacy of violence. As Joan Scott argues, these experiences are constitutive: visiting memorials, tragic or otherwise, is not simply something touristic Americans do: it is who contemporary Americans are.[82]

It is crucial, then, to determine who and what is deemed memorable—and who is forgotten. Focused on personal experience and contemporary narratives, American memory is awash in historical forgetfulness. Why was Columbine commemorated while similar sites of violent death in American schools have largely been forgotten? In 1908, for example, one hundred seventy-five children and teachers were killed when a fire swept through their elementary school in Collinwood, Ohio. In 1927, forty-five students, teachers, and townspeople were killed in Bath, Michigan, when a local farmer and school board member targeted the local public school with a lethal concoction of home-brewed bombs. In 1937, a natural gas leak led to an explosion at a school in New London, Texas, killing three hundred students and teachers. In 1958, arson at a Chicago school left ninety-five schoolchildren and teachers dead.[83]

The issue of who counts in the national imaginary is largely determined by presentist understandings of their national historical significance. In 1995, Timothy McVeigh's bombing of the Murrah Federal Building was defined as the "worst" act of terrorism on American soil. In 2000, the dedication of the Oklahoma City National Memorial sustained that claim. On September 11, 2001, that claim was usurped. In April 2007, the shootings at Virginia Tech were widely pronounced on CNN and elsewhere as the "worst killing spree in U.S. history" and the "deadliest mass shooting in U.S. history." Those claims ignore the nation's many, many instances of far deadlier shooting "sprees," including the 1857 Mountain Meadows Massacre in Utah, the 1864 Sand Creek Massacre in Colorado, and the 1890 Wounded Knee Massacre in South Dakota. Likewise, although American history is dotted with public school disasters, Columbine is the name and the place that the nation remembers today.

The appeal of touring America's tragic landscapes lies in their commemoration of deaths that fracture, and critique, the nation's seemingly calm front. Over a hundred Americans die each day in car accidents. While roadside memorials commemorate some of them, most are forgotten in the public landscape. However tragic, their deaths are simply not that unusual or unexpected; however large their numbers, they die separately rather than en masse; however much we mourn their loss, we neither obliterate the roads and highways where they died or stop driving on them ourselves. Collectively shared and toured, the nation's memorials to grief are those that bear witness to unfathomable, unexpected, and sensational deaths—or at least to deaths that are seen on those terms by particular American publics.

Circumstances of race, gender, and class further determine the public reception and touristic potential of tragic death. In 1994, the remote South Carolina lake where Susan Smith drowned her sons quickly became a makeshift memorial visited by some two hundred people a day. A year later, several permanent memorials were erected at the site, including one with a photo etching of Smith's children and another featuring a fourteen-inch solar-powered light in the shape of an angel. As the woman who commissioned the second memorial and raised money for playground equipment at the site remarked, "So many people are looking at that lake as a horrible place. I don't want families to feel they can't go there. That's what families are missing now, spending time together. I want to help parents realize how special a gift they have that they'll take time to be with them." In a truly macabre twist on tragic tourism, a family doing exactly that—visiting the memorials and spending time together—died at the lake in 1996, when their Chevy Suburban rolled down an embankment, ran over a tree planted in memory of the two Smith boys, and plunged into the water. Three adults and four children died, although their deaths are not commemorated at the site.[84]

However notorious, Susan Smith's story—made into, among other things, the award-winning musical *In the Lake of Fire* at Williams College in 2000—captured the imagination of the nation. In part, it generated tremendous response because Smith herself, a young, white single mother, held the nation hostage with her fantastical account of being kidnapped by a black male carjacker. Repeated TV and media coverage of Smith's sons, young murder victims like Carlie Brucia and Sandra Cantel, and the mostly white teenagers killed at Columbine High School (where students of color comprised only 3 percent of the high school's population in 1999 and only one of the murdered students was black), suggests the conflicted racialized dimensions of contemporary national grief, of whose death counts the most, and who is mostly commemorated, in America today.

Satire about memorial mania's many conflicted dimensions, including its excessive emotional currency and its televisualization, is also burgeoning. Consider "Bob Fuller's Roadside Memorials" (2006), a Web site and pseudo public service announcement offering an assortment of "handcrafted" memorials (including "The Jogger" and "The Retiree") for the "not-so-safe driver." The brainchild of a Chicago advertising agent determined to promote safe driving, the site's droll video ends with the words "Stop the spread of memorials. Drivewithcare.com "[85] In 2007, the *Onion* produced a clever story on the Folsom Disaster Remembrance Statue, a "pre-emptive memorial" built to honor the "future victims" of an "imminent dam disaster" in Folsom, California. Etched with the names of the victims, "once they are killed," the $20,000 memorial "is intended to provide comfort for those who are about to lose their family members, friends, or even their own lives in the disaster." Equally cynical is the Buildings of Disaster collection from Boym Design Studio, a series of bonded-nickel replicas, each just a few inches tall, of buildings like the Oklahoma City Federal Building and the World Trade Center. Canny about the affective dynamics of touching—and owning—sites and symbols of tragedy and disaster, designer Constantin Boym explains that these $110 "souvenir buildings" are "important cultural objects which can store and communicate memories, emotions and desires." He adds:

"These small monuments make a different, populist history of architecture, one based on emotional involvement rather than on scholarly appreciation."[86]

MOURNING CODES

However cynical some are about memorial mania's heightened emotional conditions, the period immediately following traumatic death—or death in general—is viewed in any number of cultures as psychologically uncertain and hence socially and politically dangerous. "The passion of grief is volatile," remarks Gail Holst-Warhaft, and mourning rituals are devised to wrest order out of disorder, provide structure and give meaning to the ineffable, and prevent psychic and social anarchy.[87] From the moment of eruptive trauma to the collection of their wilted flowers and soggy teddy bears, temporary memorials are manufactured according to particular cultural codes. These include making the memorial directly at or as close as possible to the site of death; making offerings of culturally and socially symbolic objects such as flowers, photos, condolence cards, and stuffed animals; demonstrating emotional behaviors such as sobbing and hugging; and making references to religious intervention. These codes are socially reinforced through mass media coverage and advanced by expanded understandings of permissible public emotions.

To some degree, mourning codes are instituted in order to objectify and depersonalize grief, thereby assuring "that the psychic crisis engendered by loss, especially in its initial stages, will not plunge the mourner into sheer delirium or catalepsy."[88] Socially shared and culturally familiar, these codes are central to contemporary understandings of America as a nation touched by tragedy. They shift local traumas—the bombing in Oklahoma, the shootings at Columbine—into nationally mediated events, and also curtail the threat that violent death and disaster might pose to the collective American psyche. Conducting interviews immediately after 9/11, for example, historian Mary Marshall Clark found that local understandings of the attacks in New York were "characterized by ambiguity, uncertainty, and contradiction." Temporary memorials, and the various commemorative cultures that appropriate their affective conventions, help to orchestrate consensual understandings of tragic death's meaning. Indeed, as an affect conditioned by what Alistair Thomson terms "popular memory," the public mourning embodied in temporary memorials "demonstrates the ways in which expressions of grief, far from being 'outside' politics, are always framed within dominant narrative forms and genres."[89]

Consider the narrative codes of mourning devised by the *New York*

Times in its nationally syndicated "Portraits of Grief" column, which first appeared three days after 9/11 and continued until late December 2001. Initially called "Among the Missing," the *Times*' series originated with the missing-person flyers that circulated immediately after the collapse of the Twin Towers. Featuring personal details and photographs, these Xeroxed flyers were posted on every public surface near Ground Zero, and then, as the missing became the dead, formed the basis for many temporary memorials. Impressionistic and ritualized, much like the memorials on which they were modeled, "Portraits of Grief" were snapshots of affect: two hundred–word profiles, usually accompanied by tiny headshots, which casually sketched the preferred pastimes (parties, dancing, golf, fly-fishing) and endearing qualities (loved to laugh, loved to cook) of 9/11's victims. Intimate and anecdotal, these sketches were the seeming antithesis to the cold eulogies of the typical newspaper obituary—much as temporary memorials are often cast as the emotional opposites of permanent stone and bronze monuments.

Yet "Portraits of Grief" were also informed by formulaic codes of bereavement, or what David Simpson likens as the "Taylorization of mourning." Few of the *Times* portraits included the details of death (not that these were actually known in more than a few cases), and most emphasized cheerful, upbeat moments in the lives of the dead. Assuming that the victims of the attacks of 9/11 were an essentially heteronormative group (few of the newspaper portraits alluded to sexual difference), the *Times* sketches "were almost all versions of the same story—happy people, fulfilled in their jobs, fountains of love and charity, pillars of their family and community . . . a flourishing civil society indifferent to race, gender, and economic category."[90] The potentially disordering grief of 9/11 was thereby managed as a tragic national ordeal that was experienced and endured by all Americans. More critically engaged questions of why and how 9/11 happened were sidestepped in deference to a consensual national discourse that ultimately permitted the war on terror.

DEAD MATTERS

Temporary memorials are almost always memorials to the dead, and as such are best understood in terms of highly conflicted American attitudes about death. For most of the twentieth century, the United States was characterized as a death-denying society in which public discussions of dying, death, and bereavement were largely taboo, and death itself was relegated to the institutional and private settings of the hospital. Sixty percent of Americans, for example, die in hospitals today, and an additional 16 percent die in nursing homes or hospices.[91] Contemporary debates about abortion, euthanasia, gun control, living wills, organ transplantation, and stem cell research, as well as popular interests in "good death," the afterlife, and bereavement therapies, suggest heightened attention to issues of death and dying. The growing national trend toward funeral preplanning and the global explosion of cyber memorials and online death tributes suggests this as well.[92] The absence of explicit references to death and dying in contemporary commemoration, however, suggests abiding public anxieties about the finality of fleshly existence and uncertainties about an afterlife, as well as the causal dimensions of tragic and traumatic death.

In 1994, George Soros's Open Society Institute launched its Project on Death in America, which, over the course of nine years, awarded $45 million in grants to health and humanities initiatives focused on improving palliative care for the dying. In the past two decades, the interdisciplinary field of thanatology—the study of death and dying—has yielded some four thousand publications, including essays and reviews in the journals *Death Studies*, *Mortality*, and *Omega: The Journal of Death and Dying*.[93] The Open University Press in the United Kingdom offers a special series on the subject, titled "Facing Death." The temporary memorials created in Littleton, Oklahoma City, New York, and innumerable other places similarly suggest intense American interests in "reclaiming" death: in making death more meaningful on personal and individual levels and challenging an "American way of death" largely dominated (since the mid-nineteenth century) by the purviews and professionals of medicine, science, and technology.[94]

Still, however much they validate new American attitudes about death and dying, temporary memorials are typically less oriented to critique—such as asking why Timothy McVeigh bombed the Murrah Federal Building in 1995, or why two teenage boys killed their high school classmates in Colorado in 1999—than to the immediacy of felt experience and emotional catharsis. This may relate to the often elusive and incomprehensible nature of trauma itself, which Cathy Caruth argues presents an epistemological challenge that cannot be immediately processed or represented: "the event is not assimilated or experienced fully at the time, only belatedly, in its repeated possession of the one who experiences it. To be traumatized is precisely to be possessed by an image or event."[95] It may further relate to how Americans perceive traumatic death on sacramental terms. As Georges Bataille wrote:

> The victim dies and the spectators share in what his death reveals. This is what religious historians call the element of sacredness. This sacredness is the revelation of continuity through the death of a discontinuous being

to those who watch it as a solemn rite. A violent death disrupts the creature's discontinuity; what remains, what the tense onlookers experience in the succeeding silence, is the continuity of all with which the victim is now one. Only a spectacular killing . . . has the power to reveal what normally escapes notice.[96]

Likewise, however much temporary memorials commemorate trauma and grapple with the spiritual and psychological terms of human finality, death itself is absent. Images of victims in pain, dying, or dead are generally banned; references to the circumstances of their deaths, or to the traumatic struggles of survivors and rescuers, are taboo. Rather, temporary memorials—like the *Times*' "Portraits of Grief"—focus on the dead as they were once alive. They are, as Roland Barthes observed about photographs, "certificate[s] of presence" that ratify what has been rather than what is no longer.[97] The flowers, letter jackets, concert posters, sneakers, and Bibles left at Columbine's temporary memorial summoned the taste and faith cultures of those who were killed at the school. The flowers, T-shirts, teddy bears, and religious ephemera that made up the memorial at Virginia Tech in April 2007 similarly evoked the personalities and spiritual beliefs of the thirty-two students and teachers who died in that school shooting.

While temporary memorials commemorate sudden death, and speak to loss and absence, the dead themselves remain present—visible in the photographs, clothes, and possessions left by mourners, "persistently social" in the cards and poems addressed to them.[98] This might suggest the denial of death, or the inability to acknowledge human finality and reckon with loss, at least in the period immediately following death. It also suggests a primary motivation in the making of temporary memorials, which is to commemorate grief. Obviously, all memorials commemorate the interests and ambitions of their makers; the dead, after all, are dead. But the materialist, kinesthetic, and emotional dimensions of temporary memorials *are* their raison d'être, and much of their meaning lies in the performance of bereavement.

It also lies in the symbolic authority of those being grieved—the dead. Over the past fifty years, the United States has "invested heavily" in managing and controlling death:

> We [the United States] have eradicated many previously fatal diseases and control others with medical technology. Infant mortality rates have plunged while adult life expectancy has surged. We have developed automobile air bags, emergency response systems, warning devices, and safety standards for nearly everything that could put our lives at risk. Even our risk of dying in war has been reduced by strategies such as air-

strikes rather than deployment of ground troops. We have gained such control over death that we now expect to die only of old age.[99]

In 2007, the Centers for Disease Control and Prevention announced that the average life expectancy for Americans had reached 77.9 years (75.3 years for men; 80.4 for women).

Thus, when sudden, violent, senseless, and traumatic death does occur, especially in "safe" settings such as public schools and office buildings, and especially among young people, Americans are shocked. Temporary memorials convey this shock and simultaneously organize social and cultural understandings of the dead. As Robert Pogue Harrison remarks, "obligation to the corpse" is a particularly revealing social index, and multiple cultures have long operated under the assumption that human remains demand appropriate ceremonies of burial and prayer to facilitate the psychic release and alleviation of grief. Recovery and ritual observance of the dead is crucial, argues Zoë Crossland, in order to properly situate them within the realms of individual and collective memory, and thereby "remake" the world of the living.[100] Bodies that are not properly mourned and buried become specters, haunting and restless reminders of life out of order.

This helps to explain the exhaustive recovery efforts undertaken after the attacks on the World Trade Center in 2001, where rescue personnel focused on finding the dead—after it was determined that there would be few survivors—at great detriment to their own health and welfare. Record numbers of firefighters deployed to the Twin Towers developed serious respiratory ailments and symptoms of posttraumatic stress disorder.[101] For ten months after 9/11, authorities in New York sifted through millions of tons of debris searching for human remains, eventually recovering some nineteen thousand fragments. Millions of dollars were spent trying to match them to the names of the missing, and while more than half of those who died in the World Trade Center were eventually identified, thousands of human fragments remain unidentified. In 2005, members of WTC Families for a Proper Burial filed a federal lawsuit against the City of New York, demanding that Staten Island's Fresh Kills landfill, where most of the debris from the World Trade Center was deposited, be reopened for further recovery and removal operations. City plans to convert the 2,200-acre site into a huge public park (three times the size of Central Park) and 9/11 memorial were contested by grieving families suing over the right to recover and bury their dead. "Our loved ones need to be put in a final resting place with dignity," one woman demanded. "Our family will not stop fighting this until we have a proper burial place."[102]

Desires to possess the dead explain the demands of the bereaved following other tragedies, such as when EgyptAir 990 crashed into the waters off Nantucket in October 1999 and grieving relatives insisted on the immediate retrieval of bodies although debris had sunk in nearly three hundred feet of water, a bad storm generated twenty-two-foot waves, and the entire area was described by the Navy's senior salvage expert as "pitch black."[103] And they explain how the USS *Arizona* became a national memorial in Pearl Harbor, Hawaii. Since the Civil War, the United States has made the recovery, identification, return, and proper burial of military fatalities a national priority. Despite military protocol and public expectations, however, most of the bodies (over a thousand) inside the USS *Arizona*, a ship struck by Japanese bombers on December 7, 1941, were simply unrecoverable. The shock of the sudden attack made the slogan "Remember Pearl Harbor" the rallying cry of World War II; the battleship burial of its crew legitimated the dedication of the USS *Arizona* as sacred ground, as a war grave and national memorial, in 1962.[104]

Dead bodies, Katherine Verdery explains, have enormous symbolic power: evoking "the awe, uncertainty, and fear associated with 'cosmic' concerns, such as the meaning of life and death." Dead bodies have sacred obligations but are also malleable and ambiguous. As such, they are particularly efficacious political symbols that help to determine national identities and narratives. Today's recovery of the victims of the Spanish Civil War, of the prisoners of the Soviet gulag, of those slaughtered in German death camps, Cambodian killing fields, and Rwandan forests is oriented to the remaking of national history and memory in those places; as Verdery remarks, "dead bodies animate the study of politics."[105] This is no less true in the United States, where Abraham Lincoln's assassination and the "half circus, half heartbreak" spectacle of his body traveling from town to town on a two-week tour helped revivify nationalist feeling after four years of civil war. Lincoln's body simultaneously served as the primary object over which Americans grieved their personal losses and celebrated the union's endurance. Likewise, as Franny Nudelman recounts, John Brown's body—both literally and figuratively "mouldering in the grave"—played a key role in the formation of Northern understandings of nationalism during the Civil War.[106]

In more recent times, mass mediated images of the dead have played similar roles. Jim Crow–era photographs of lynchings, for example, both sustained assumptions of white superiority and, under the guidance of political activists like Ida B. Wells and the editors of *Crisis* magazine, fueled a national crusade against racial violence. Photos of Emmett Till's horribly mutilated and disfigured body, which his mother insisted be publicly displayed in an open-casket funeral, were published in the

Chicago Defender and *Jet* in 1955 and are credited with radicalizing the post–World War II civil rights movement.[107] Photos of the 504 Vietnamese civilians killed by U.S. soldiers in the 1968 My Lai Massacre, like the Pulitzer prize–winning photo of a young woman kneeling in anguish over the body of a college student slain by National Guardsmen at Kent State University on May 4, 1970, are similarly credited with escalating national outrage against the Vietnam War. Widely distributed photos of the naked body of al-Qaeda leader Abu Musab al-Zarqawi, displayed during a U.S. military press conference in Baghdad in June 2006 (and circulated on the U.S. Department of Defense's Web site) were intended to rally declining public support for the war in Iraq; indeed, al-Zarqawi's death, stated President Bush, "give[s] us renewed confidence in the final outcome of this struggle: the defeat of terrorism threats, and a more peaceful world for our children and grandchildren." Suppressed photos of the bodies, coffins, and funerals of U.S. soldiers—in 1991, the Department of Defense banned the media from taking pictures of U.S. soldier dead—serve the same purpose.[108]

Dead bodies similarly perform political roles in contemporary American commemorative cultures. Even if the dead are not physically evident, they exert a powerful ideological presence. At Columbine, for example, the bodies of the dead served to validate tenets of contemporary Christian evangelicalism including the authority of the Bible, the necessity of being "born again" and finding personal salvation through Christ, and the importance of proselytizing on behalf of the faith. At Columbine, the bodies of the dead—or rather, the bodies of twelve murdered students and one murdered teacher—were viewed less as victims of a terrible crime than as modern-day martyrs with the post-corporeal power to spark a "potential religious revival" in America.[109] The bodies of their killers were damned as satanic monsters, as agents of evil.

DYING FOR JESUS

Often called the "Bible Belt," Denver's southwest suburbs host an active evangelical community and flourishing youth ministry, many of whom viewed the killings at Columbine "as a God-given marketing opportunity, a chance to save souls." While Littleton itself hosts a diverse religious population with churches ranging from Baha'i Faith Assembly to St. Timothy's Episcopal, Christian evangelical students had a high profile at Columbine High School. Four of the twelve who were murdered were members of the Columbine Bible Club, which met daily at the school.[110] The day after the shootings, hundreds of students met in Clement Park to sing contemporary Christian songs and shout, "We feel the presence of Satan, operating in our midst!" Eyes closed and arms raised to the sky, the students were featured the next day on the front page of the *Rocky Mountain News* in a color photograph captioned "United in Prayer."[111]

As Columbine's story unfolded, some students related that seventeen-year-old Cassie Bernall had been killed because she affirmed her faith in Christ at gunpoint. Although challenged by credible witnesses and investigators, this account of her death immortalized Bernall as Columbine's most visible martyr, made more so by her recent conversion to evangelical Christianity, by the bestselling book her mother wrote shortly after her death (*She Said Yes: The Unlikely Martyrdom of Cassie Bernall*), by the many references to her in Columbine's temporary memorial, and by the comments of her pastor at her funeral service, held at West Bowles Community Church and attended by more than two thousand people. As Reverend George Kirsten declared, "Cassie died a martyr's death. She went to the martyrs' hall of fame."[112]

Bernall's body was not the only one seized for symbolic purposes by Denver's Bible Belt; Rachel Scott was also claimed as a "Christian American martyr" at her funeral service. Over half of the funerals for those killed at Columbine High School were held at evangelical churches in the area. The service for John Robert Tomlin at Foothills Baptist Church included, at his parents request, an invitation to be born again, which Reverend Bill Oudemolen later described as "an incredible opportunity not only here, but through the live [television] feed that we had." Cassie Bernall's pastor similarly remarked "Millions have been touched by a martyr" and advised, "Pack that ark with as many people as possible." At the nationally televised memorial service for Columbine's dead, held in a shopping center parking lot near Clement Park, pastor Jerry Nelson of the Southern Gables Evangelical Free Church announced, "Whether you are a family member grieving the loss of a loved one, a neighbor hurting deeply for them, or a member of this community that is shocked by the evil that has been perpetrated in our midst, we your pastors urge you to seek Jesus."[113]

At the same memorial service, Reverend Franklin Graham (son of evangelist Billy Graham) invoked "the name of Jesus seven times in under 45 seconds" and demanded the "return of prayer" in America's public schools. As Graham preached, "It is time for this nation to recognize that when we empty the public schools of the moral teachings and the standards of a Holy God, they are indeed very dangerous places." Attended by some seventy thousand people, including Vice President Al Gore, retired General Colin Powell, and Congressman Richard Gephardt (D-MO), and watched by millions more, Columbine's public memorial service featured performances by Christian musicians Amy Grant, Michael W. Smith, and

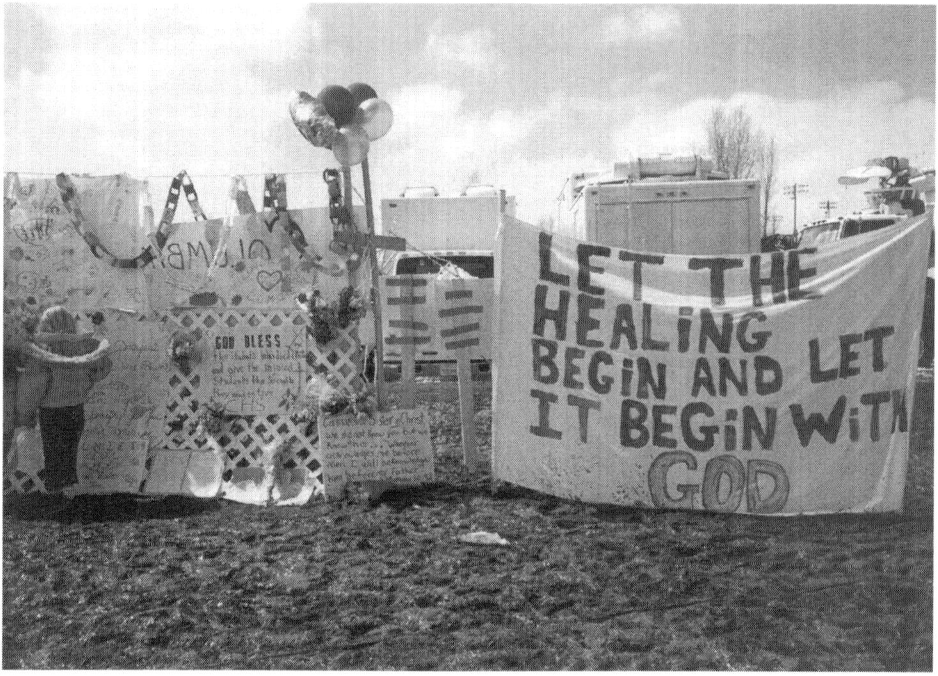

2.15. Banner and other items at temporary Columbine memorial in Clement Park, April 1999. (Photo by the author.)

Phil Driscol (singing his Christian music hit "Christ Remains"), a collective sing-along of "God Bless America," and the release of thirteen white doves by Colorado governor Bill Owens. At a taping of the Christian Broadcasting Network's TV show *The 700 Club* a week after the shootings, the pastor of Littleton's Celebration Christian Fellowship declared, "Prayer in schools was officially reestablished on April 20, 1999, because it was accompanied by bombs and shootings. It is always the blood of martyrs that acts as rocket fuel for the church."[114]

Evangelical Christianity similarly marked Columbine's temporary memorial. Repeatedly described by journalists in sacred terms as "tear-stained hallowed ground" frequented by tens of thousands of reverent "pilgrims," Clement Park took on all the appearances of an outdoor revival meeting, a little muted maybe by police barricades and yellow caution tape but still an "amazingly public and unselfconscious display of Christian piety."[115] Signs and banners reading "What Would Jesus Do?" "Servant of Christ," "Heaven is a Place," and "Let the Healing Begin and Let it Begin with GOD" were widely represented (fig. 2.15). So were crosses, pictures of Christ, and evangelical booklets titled "What Matters" and "Where's God Now?" published by the International Bible Society, a group based in Colorado Springs that calls its mission "evangelism through Scripture" and distributes thousands of such tracts at sites of tragic death each year. Candlelight vigils, prayer and worship services, and scripture readings (many of them televised) were constant. Visitors to the memorial were encouraged to pray; more than a few placards and posters urged them to accept Christ as their personal savior.

Mourning for the dead at Columbine's temporary memorial, in other words, translated into a celebration of their "new life" in Christ, as evangelicals maintain that Christ saves believers from eternal death and damnation by granting them providential dispensation. "Well, Rachel, you have graduated early. You have graduated to life eternal," eulogized Rachel Scott's pastor, adding, "And the diploma is signed by the shed blood of Jesus Christ."[116] Like most temporary memorials, direct references to death and dying were absent in Columbine's shrine, but at this particular memorial proclamations of the better life in Heaven promised by being born again were especially prevalent. Other religions were also represented in Clement Park: Scientologists handed out flyers, Hare Krishnas offered sanctified food, and Mormons offered counseling services. But evangelical Protestantism and visual and rhetorical references to Jesus Christ as personal savior dominated. Like the televised memorial service and the funerals of the slain, Columbine's makeshift memorial substantiated "the re-emerging evangelical hegemony over American public rituals of mourning" and served to legitimate evangelical Christianity in contemporary America.[117]

As evident in the combative tone of Columbine's mourning rituals, perceptions of menacing external threats and compulsions to convert nonbelievers are fundamental aspects of America's thriving evangelical Christian community. "Distinction, engagement, and conflict vis-à-vis outsiders," observes Christian Smith, "constitute a crucial element of what we might call the 'cultural DNA' of American evangelicalism."[118] Social problems are seen on atomistic levels, solvable only in terms of personal relationships with Christ. Victims of crime are viewed as martyrs to the cause; their killers as irredeemably evil. As Rachel Scott's father put it when he testified before Congress on May 27, 1999, arguing against gun control a month after his daughter was shot to death: "Columbine was not just a tragedy—it was a spiritual event. We need a change of heart and a humble acknowledgement that this nation was founded on the principle of simple trust in God."[119]

The oppositional tenor of contemporary American Christian evangelicalism was especially realized in the angry fight over the Columbine crosses (figs. 2.16 and 2.17). A week after the murders, Greg Zanis, a carpenter from Aurora, Illinois, erected fifteen wooden crosses on Rebel Hill

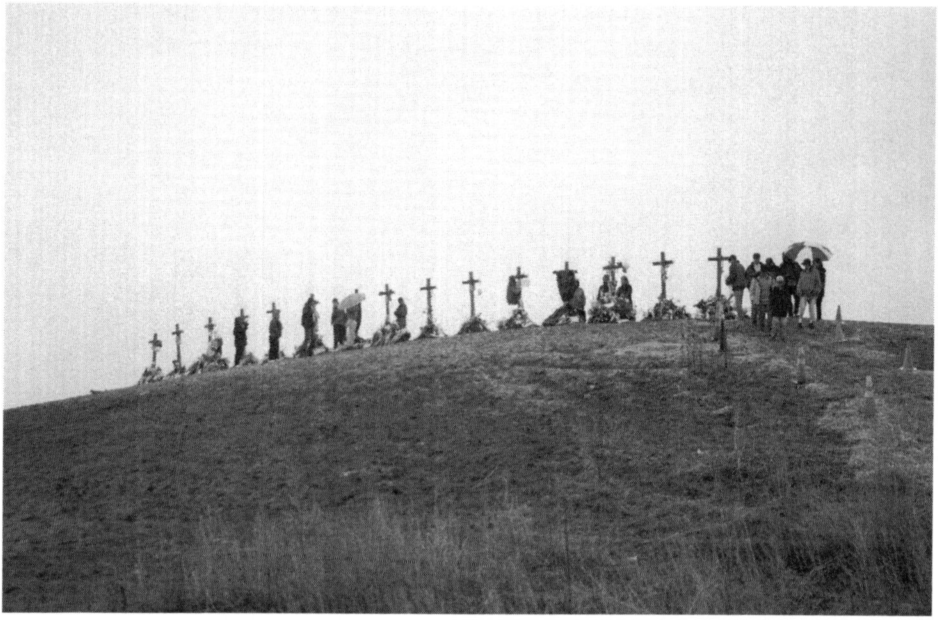

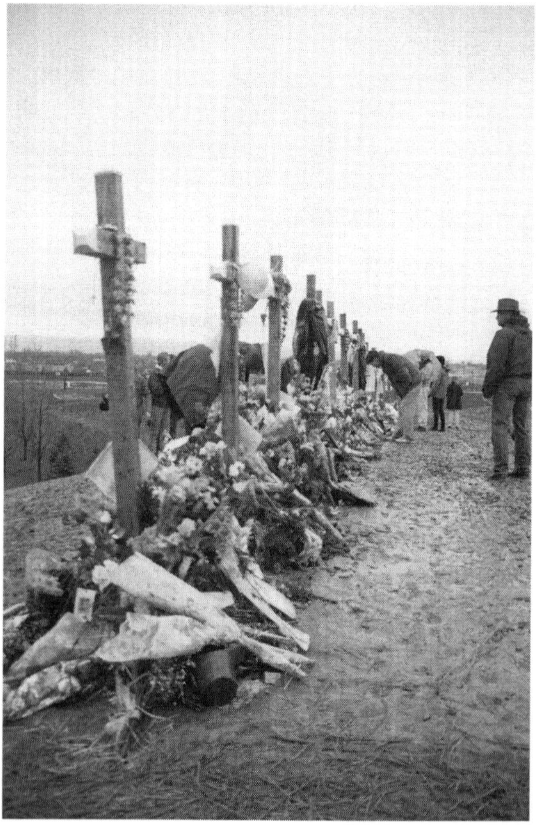

2.16. Crosses on Rebel Hill, Clement Park, Littleton, Colorado, April 1999. (Courtesy of Heather Butler.)

2.17. Crosses on Rebel Hill, Clement Park, April 1999. (Courtesy of Heather Butler.)

overlooking the high school, each one eight feet tall and etched with the names of the dead. Zanis began making crosses in 1996 following the brutal murder of his father-in-law. A born-again Christian who views his cross making as a ministry, Zanis remarks, "I make crosses to help people heal and to remind them that Jesus gives peace and grace." He has delivered thousands of them (an estimated seven thousand by 2005) to sites of tragic death all over the country, from crime scenes to car crashes.[120] Explaining that he viewed all of Columbine's dead as victims and that he saw the two killers in particular as "victims of society," Zanis made fifteen crosses for Clement Park. Yet he also etched Harris and Klebold's names in a different font to "disassociate them from Christ," because "they were nonbelievers of the Lord."[121] Zanis's crosses were the only visible markers to Harris and Klebold at Columbine's temporary memorial, and visitors left flowers, T-shirts, rosaries, and penned inscriptions such as "May God Forgive You," "He is Still God's Child and Is Loved," and "You Also Deserve Our Compassion."

Some visitors also wrote derogatory comments like "Evil Bastard" and "Unrepentant Murderer," and covered the crosses dedicated to Harris and Klebold with black garbage bags. Angry arguments broke out over who should be memorialized at Clement Park: all of the dead, including the two killers, or only the twelve students and one teacher who were murdered. Zanis maintained that his crosses were intended to bring everyone under God's judgment and into Christ's blessing: "Any cross I put up shows that Greg Zanis cares for them, and that the Lord loves them and he's there for them. These crosses are not put up for dead people. They're put up so your sister won't go to hell, so she'll wake up and say, 'Hey, I could die this very minute. Somebody could aim a gun in my face and I'd be dead.' Children know so little about Christ. We need to lead them back." Others disagreed and at one point a fight broke out (broadcast on local television stations) between mourners visiting the crosses of the thirteen slain and mourners visiting the crosses of the two killers. Two days after they were installed, Brian Rohrbough, the father of one of the students murdered at Columbine, posted signs on the two crosses dedicated to Harris and Klebold reading "Murderers Burn In Hell" and then tore them both down and tossed them in a dumpster. Rohrbough told the reporters who followed his performance "it was an outrage to use a Christian symbol to honor the murderers at a victims' site." He added: "We don't build a monument to Adolf Hitler and put it in a Holocaust museum—and it's not going to happen here."[122]

If Brian Rohrbough's actions stemmed from the temporary memorial taboo regarding direct reference to the circumstantial details of death, including the names of murderers, they also followed from his oppositional evangelical Christian beliefs. Zanis views his cross-making ministry on pastoral terms and saw Harris and Klebold as dead bodies and lost souls worth mourning. But Rohrbough saw them as killers and nonevangelical nonbelievers who were undeserving of any commemoration or consideration. Interviewed after the incident, Rohrbough stated that gun control was a "side issue" and the real story of the murders at Columbine was in "knowing the difference between right and wrong" and seeking answers in Christ. When Columbine's temporary memorial was dismantled a few weeks later, all of the crosses in Clement Park came down as well.[123]

Yet conflicts over Columbine's memory and meaning, over who to mourn and who to blame, continued. On May 2, eleven days after the shootings, eight thousand gun control advocates rallied at the Colorado State Capitol, carrying signs reading "Cradle Children, Not Uzis" and "Prom or Funeral? You Decide." Tom Mauser, whose son was killed at Columbine, addressed the crowd: "It is time we own up to the fact that we have a violence problem in this society. Something is wrong in this country when a child can grab a gun so easily and shoot a bullet in the middle of a child's face, as my son experienced."[124]

The rally took place in downtown Denver at the same time that the National Rifle Association held its annual convention, which Denver mayor Wellington Webb had asked the NRA to cancel. The NRA refused, using the meeting instead to defend the further deregulation and expansion of gun ownership in America. "NRA members are, above all, Americans," NRA president Charlton Heston declared. "That means that whatever our differences, we are respectful of one another and we stand united, especially in adversity. We have the same right as all other citizens to be here . . . to help shoulder the grief . . . to share our sorrow . . . and to offer our respectful, reasoned voice to the national discourse that has erupted around this tragedy."[125] Ignoring the gun as the instrument of Columbine's grief, and hence their own complicity in Columbine's "tragedy," the NRA argued that guns were not to blame in the nation's epidemic of gun-related deaths—despite the fact that in 1999 alone there were 28,874 gun-related deaths in the United States.[126]

At the end of May 1999, the father of a Columbine student who survived the shootings mounted a protest in favor of a permanent Christian monument at Clement Park (one with thirteen crosses), by hoisting an eight-foot cross (also made by Greg Zanis) for an entire day at the park. "As long as I keep my hands on it, nobody from the ACLU or Freedom of [*sic*] Religion Foundation can take it away from me," the man stated, adding, "It's Memorial Day and I have freedom of speech." In September 1999, Brian Rohrbough and the relatives of another student slain at Columbine chopped down two of the fifteen trees that the West Bowles

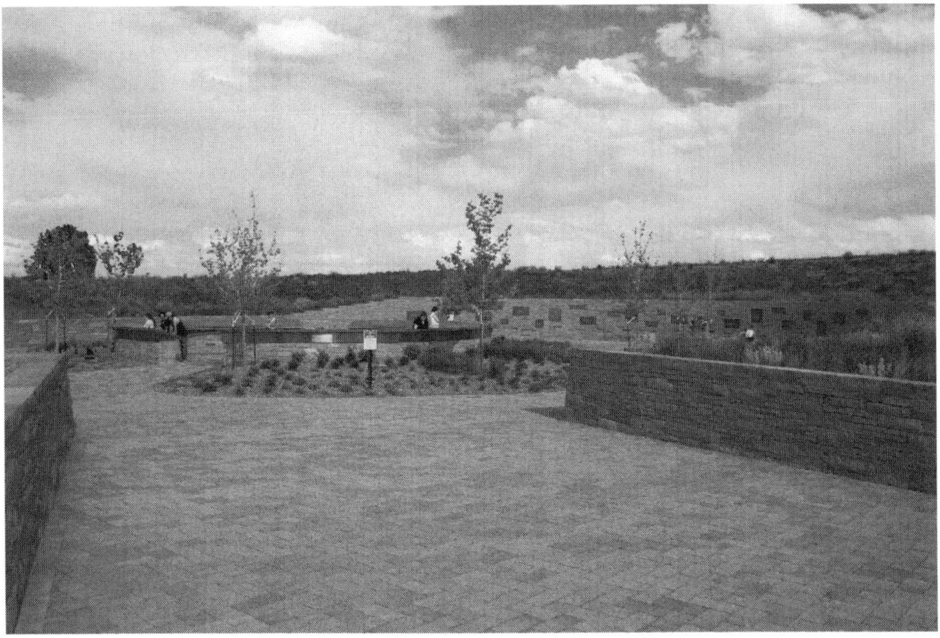

2.18. Columbine Memorial, Clement Park, Littleton, Colorado, dedicated 2007. (Photo by Jeffrey Beall, May 2008. Courtesy of Creative Commons.)

Community Church had planted (on its own property) as a memorial "Prayer Park" dedicated to Cassie Bernall and all of those who died at the high school. Before their act of vandalism, Rohrbough and a group of about forty people protested in front of the church with signs that read "Unrepentant Murderers Honored Here" and "No Peace for the Wicked." As Rohrbough told the *Denver Post*, "The Bible tells us that if someone sins against us, then rebuke them." He also vowed to monitor any "similar memorials" that might also address inclusion, tolerance, and forgiveness, adding: "This is not an issue that's going away. We can tell the rest of the world what's right."[127]

The "issue" of how Rohrbough's son died, the issue of gun violence in America, was ignored at Columbine's temporary memorial. It was dismissed by Littleton's evangelical community, who mourned their dead as Christian martyrs. It was manipulated by the NRA as the "respectful, reasoned voice" of Second Amendment rights. The permanent memorial for Columbine, a $2 million project dedicated in 2007, similarly excludes references to Eric Harris or Dylan Klebold and their murderous rampage (fig. 2.18). A sunken oval space configured out of thick red flagstone and nestled into a hillside at Clement Park, the permanent memorial consists of two circular stone walls: an outer Ring of Healing that features dark tablets etched with quotes from students and teachers, and an inner Ring of Remembrance arranged in thirteen stations, each marking narrative remembrances and personal messages written by the families of those who were murdered on April 20, 1999. "Steve, you are forever in our hearts. Soar high, and fly straight. We love you!" wrote the parents of Steven Curnow. "We miss her immensely, but know she's in that better place," wrote Cassie Bernall's parents. The inscriptions written by Brian Rohrbough relate that his son was murdered "in a Nation that legalized the killing of innocent children in the womb; in a Country where authorities would lie and cover up what they need and what they did; [and] in a Godless school system."

Managing the psychic crisis and social disorder of tragic death, temporary memorials like the one made at Columbine demonstrate how grief is negotiated in contemporary America. Such memorials do not yield the results some might prefer—such as a cultural economy of radicalized social protest, or ritualized performances of "cultural-political contestation" that affirm democratic solidarity. Cultural geographers Kate Hartig and Kevin Dunn explain, for example, that some roadside memorials in Australia to young men killed in car accidents are "conservative memorials of youth machismo [and] heroic aggression" that serve to glorify "dominant and problematic strains of masculinity."[128] Likewise, Columbine's temporary memorial helped proselytize on behalf of intolerant and oppositional strains of evangelical Christianity.

THE AFFECTIVE POSSIBILITIES OF GRIEF

Undertakings like the NAMES Project Foundation's AIDS Memorial Quilt reckon with the affective possibilities of grief on more inclusionary terms (fig. 2.19). Conceived in 1985 by a San Francisco activist determined to bear witness to friends who had died of AIDS, the quilt consists of tens of thousands of three-foot by six-foot colorful cloth panels, each naming—and helping to humanize—its subject. Most of the grave-sized panels incorporate objects and images particular to them: photographs, favorite items of clothing, poems, teddy bears. Some are solemn and sobering, others are funny, outrageous, sad, and angry; each is an individual memorial patched to a larger project of grief and remembrance. As the epidemic grew, the quilt became a huge national (now international) art project centered on politically mobilizing the fight against AIDS and against homophobia—a combination of "mourning *and* militancy," as Douglas Crimp called it. The last time it was entirely displayed—in October 1996 in Washington, where it covered the grounds of the National Mall and was visited by an estimated 1.2 million people, including

President Bill Clinton and Hillary Clinton—the AIDS Memorial Quilt featured over forty thousand panels (fig. 2.20).[129] Intimate, elegiac, and collaborative, the quilt is a collective portrait of contemporary America. As Simon Watney observed, "To have Liberace alongside Baby Doe, to have Michel Foucault alongside five gay New York cops. In many ways it's a more accurate map of America than any other I've ever seen."[130]

The NAMES Project Foundation's AIDS Memorial Quilt reworked American modes of mourning and revised American national subjectivity by including queers and people with AIDS. Christopher Capozzola relates that when "existing cultural forms of mourning" were unable or unwilling to address their bereavement, AIDS communities developed "new cultural products that could accommodate the urge to memorialize and mourn those who had died." Activist AIDS projects like the quilt, remarks Ann Cvetkovich, countered "the invisibility of an indifference to feelings of loss by making them extravagantly public as well as building collective cultural practices that can acknowledge and showcase them."[131] With its reiterative naming and jumbled patchwork aesthetic, its combination of public mourning, consciousness raising, and community building, the AIDS Memorial Quilt refused the silencing of its subjects. Mobilizing the material culture products and emotional practices of mourning, the quilt made grief ethically, socially, and politically beneficial.

In the wake of its extraordinary influence—seen by an estimated five million people by the mid-1990s, popularized even more by extensive media coverage—other marginalized Americans have turned to memorial quilts to fortify their claims to mourning, personhood, and national inclusion. The Agent Orange Quilt of Tears, a project founded by the widow of a Vietnam vet whose death was exacerbated by exposure to the toxic herbicides used in wartime bombing operations, is similarly engaged in social accountability.[132] And while the AIDS Memorial Quilt is now too large to be seen in its entirety—a depressing testimonial to the devastating scale of AIDS—it has by no means disappeared. Today, the NAMES Project Foundation is a worldwide foundation with multiple chapters and affiliate organizations focused on AIDS research and HIV infection-prevention education. Tens of thousands of Americans continue to "tour" the AIDS Memorial Quilt, which is continually on display (albeit in smaller blocks of panels, about eight panels to a block) at schools and community centers all over the country (fig. 2.21). And the quilt itself continues to grow, a panel at a time.

Temporary memorials are among the most visible manifestations of grief in contemporary America. Their emotional, materialist, and public dimensions are just the point of departure, however, for more affective possibilities that remain largely unrealized; the problem with tempo-

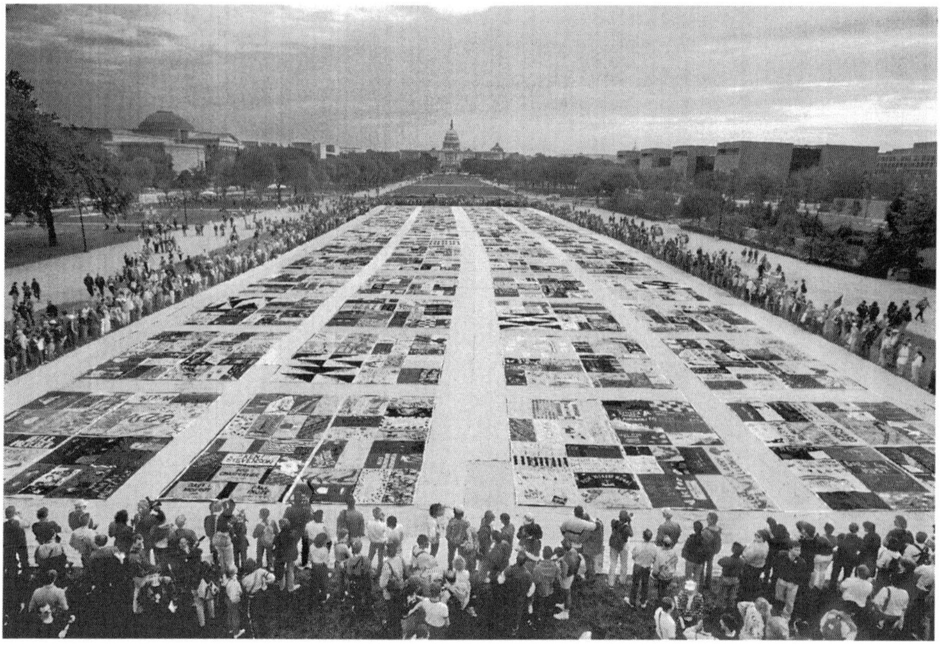

2.19. Thomas Michael Alleman, "The NAMES Project Foundation's AIDS Memorial Quilt displayed on the National Mall," Washington, D.C., October 11, 1987. (© Thomas Michael Alleman.)

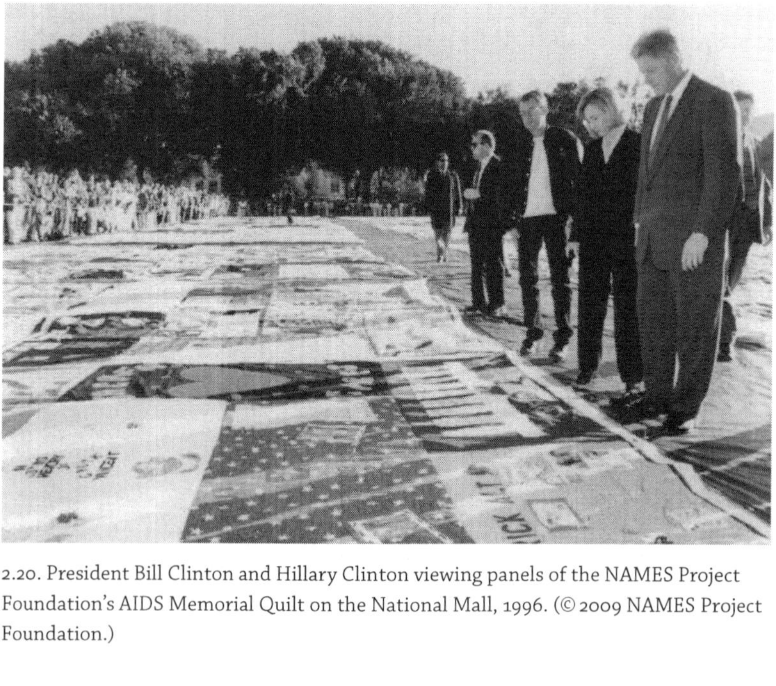

2.20. President Bill Clinton and Hillary Clinton viewing panels of the NAMES Project Foundation's AIDS Memorial Quilt on the National Mall, 1996. (© 2009 NAMES Project Foundation.)

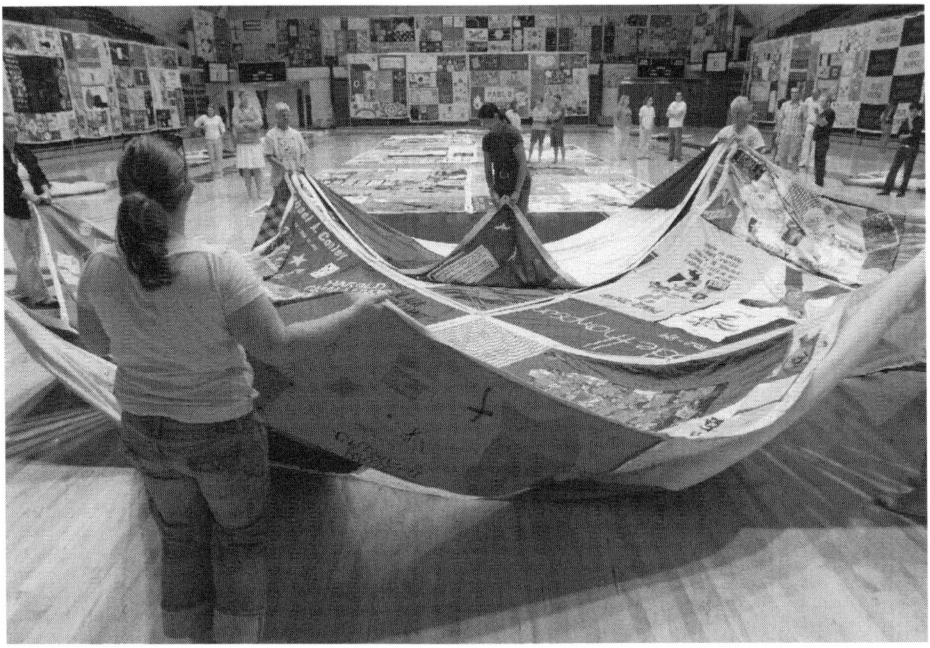

2.21. Tom Bauer, "Volunteers practice unfolding a quilt panel prior to the opening ceremony of the NAMES Project Foundation's AIDS Memorial Quilt exhibit at the University of Montana in Missoula, Mont., Sept. 18, 2008." (Courtesy of Tom Bauer.)

rary memorials is not that they are "too much" or that they intimate a nation "too attached" to grief but that they often fail to magnetize the social forces and political actions of democratic reform. Some temporary memorials engage social and political transformation—granting personhood to previously silenced subjects, demanding inclusion for those subjects within an expanded national imaginary. Grieving is thus a form of claiming, an insistence on belonging, too, in America and subsequently reshaping and reforming American national identity. Yet other temporary memorials are frozen in emotional catharsis, fixated on exclusionary religious and political tenets and / or beholden to grief industry experts who promote them as ways to "work through" trauma. They are the material and emotional testimonials of a nation grief stricken by violent death and yet seemingly disengaged from the social and political initiatives that might check such violence.

Grief's affective potential in America lies in its ability to mobilize social and political action, and to orchestrate productive change. It is hardly surprising that grief has an expanded presence in contemporary America; because its performative power can challenge and overturn established national norms, grief is both highly appealing and highly threatening.

Controlling and manipulating grief are ways of accessing its power, hence the gaining presence and authority of state-mandated roadside memorials and grief management policies in American schools. Hence, too, the oppositional religious dynamics of Columbine's temporary memorial, where the bodies of the dead were exploited as Christian martyrs. If Columbine's temporary manifestation of grief succeeded in legitimating evangelical Christianity to a larger national audience, it failed to question the nation's legacy of gun violence. Despite strong public support for gun control following the shootings at Columbine High School, state and federal legislators failed to challenge the NRA. Despite the outpouring of grief at Clement Park, it seems neither the American people nor their political representatives are aggrieved enough to demand the legal interventions that might prevent future school shootings. This failure to affectively marshal grief stems in part from public cultures of fear, the subject of *Memorial Mania*'s next chapter.

3 FEAR

Terrorism Memorials and Security Narratives

In December 1995, the Lockerbie Memorial Cairn was erected in Arlington National Cemetery (fig. 3.1). Made of roughhewn blocks of Scottish sandstone, the ten-foot cairn's marble base was engraved with the following words: "On 21 December 1988, a terrorist bomb destroyed Pan American Airlines flight 103 over Lockerbie, Scotland, killing all on board and 11 on the ground. The 270 Scottish stones which compose this memorial cairn commemorate those who lost their lives in this attack against America." At groundbreaking ceremonies for the memorial (December 21, 1993), President Bill Clinton vowed that the United States would "never stop pursuing justice against those" who had bombed Flight 103. At the cairn's dedication ceremony two years later, Clinton declared, "We know that each act of terrorism is a terrible assault on every person in the world who prizes freedom, on the values we share, on our nation." He added, "It is fitting that this memorial to the citizens of 21 nations has been erected here in the sacred place of our nation, surrounded by so many who fell fighting for our freedom."[1]

A similar memorial was also erected in 1995: a fountain at New York's World Trade Center dedicated to the six people who died and more than one thousand who were wounded in the first attack on the building in February 1993 (fig. 3.2). Designed by Elyn Zimmerman, the memorial was placed directly above the spot in an underground garage where a truck filled with 1,500 pounds of explosives detonated. Its outer walls were decorated with "symbolic cracks" representing the devastation of the explosion; its inner rim featured the names of the dead and this inscription: "On February 26, 1993, a bomb set by terrorists exploded below this site. This horrible act of violence killed innocent people, injured thousands, and made victims of us all." On 9/11, the memorial was destroyed during the second terrorist attack on the World Trade Center.

Terrorism memorials—memorials that commemorate the victims of terrorism—have escalated in contemporary America. Memorial mania is

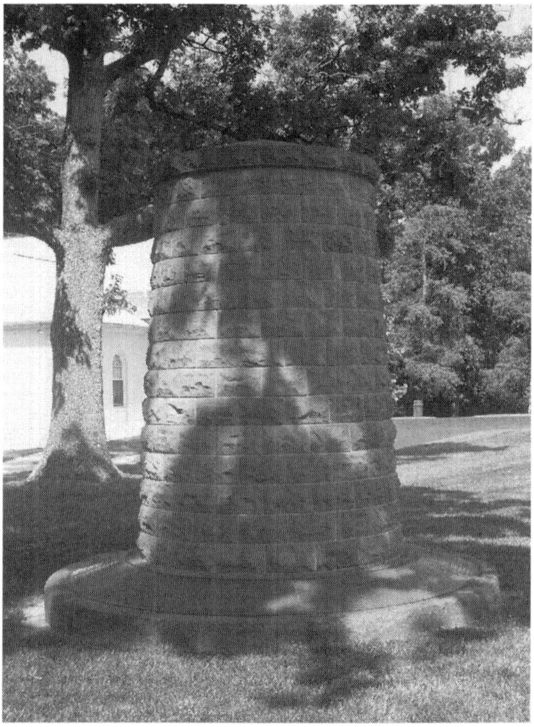

3.1. Lockerbie Memorial Cairn, Arlington National Cemetery, Arlington, Virginia, dedicated 1995. (Photo by the author.)

typified, in fact, by projects that commemorate two acts of terrorism on American soil: the bombing of the Murrah Federal Building in Oklahoma City on April 19, 1995, and the attacks of September 11, 2001. The competition to design the Oklahoma City National Memorial received 624 entries. Its dedication on April 19, 2000, was broadcast nationwide and included a speech in which President Clinton described the new memorial as a "public stand against terrorism."[2]

Interests in designing the three major national 9/11 memorials in Washington, D.C., Shanksville, Pennsylvania, and New York City were similarly strong: the Pentagon Memorial and Flight 93 National Memorial competitions each received over 1,000 proposals, and jurors for the World Trade Center's memorial design sorted through 5,201 entries. The winners were officially announced at televised press conferences with politicians, corporate spokesmen, jurors, families of the dead, and members of the winning design teams. Subsequently, each memorial was the subject of intense public scrutiny and media coverage, including blogs featuring furious comments from those who felt "hoodwinked and betrayed" by how the memorials were selected, what they looked like, and who was—or was not—commemorated.[3] Angrily protesting what she

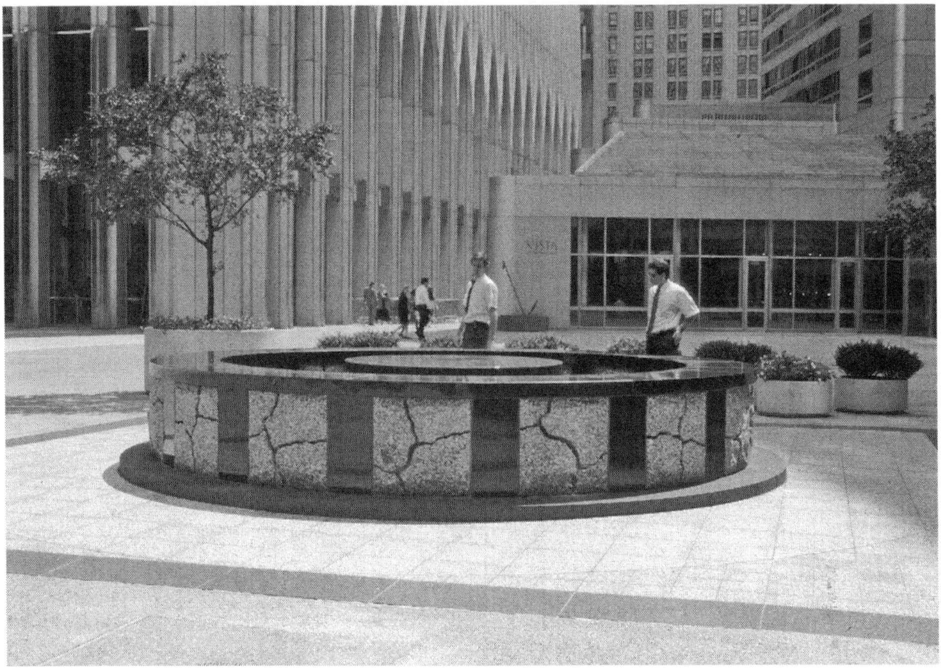

3.2. Elyn Zimmerman, World Trade Center Memorial, Austin J. Tobin Plaza, New York, New York, dedicated 1995. Destroyed. (Courtesy of Elyn Zimmerman.)

called "The Great Ground Zero Heist," Debra Burlingame, the sister of a pilot who died at the Pentagon, lambasted the Lower Manhattan Development Corporation for proposing the inclusion of museums like the International Freedom Center in the new World Trade Center complex. "They're trying to hijack the meaning of 9/11; we're trying to rescue it," Burlingame declared, insisting that the sixteen-acre site that once contained the Twin Towers be solely dedicated as a memorial to those who died there, and not to cultural and economic redevelopment schemes more consistent with the trade center itself.[4]

From hyperbolic presidential assertions of their unifying nationalism to populist obstructionist claims on their designs and purpose, terrorism memorials are among the most heated sites of public feeling in contemporary America. Not since the fury over the Vietnam Veterans Memorial in the early 1980s has the nation been so passionately engaged in memorial culture, and various Americans felt so strongly entitled to its control. This is not surprising: if reckoning with the Vietnam War preoccupied the nation in the 1980s, terrorism dominates understandings of national identity today. As this chapter details, America's terrorism memorials embody widespread public fears about the state of the nation and the vulnerability of its citizens. While they ostensibly counter those fears with particular security narratives geared toward national unity and social stability, they also reinscribe them.

TERRORISM

Terrorism has dominated American political, media, and public discourse in recent years. Shortly after 9/11, President George W. Bush declared that his "primary focus" was to "rout terror wherever it exists." Concurrently, the U.S. Department of Justice declared that protecting Americans "against the threat of terrorism" was "strategic goal one" for the FBI, INS, DEA, and other agencies under its jurisdiction.[5] Statistics compiled by the Tyndall Report show that coverage of the war on terror commands contemporary American media attention. Introduced in 2002, federally mandated color-coded terror alerts (red for "severe," orange for "high," yellow for "elevated") are announced every few minutes in America's airports. "The nation has danced ever since between yellow and orange," Brian Massumi observes, and public feelings of fear and insecurity have become the "new normal."[6]

Indeed, a 2005 survey by the National Center for Disaster Preparedness found that more than three-quarters (78 percent) of Americans were "concerned that there will be more terror attacks in the United States." Less than half (49 percent) had confidence in the government's ability to protect them. Another survey, conducted in 2006 by Scripps Howard/Ohio University, found that more than one in three Americans (36 percent) believe that the U.S. government itself had a hand in orchestrating the terrorist attacks of 9/11.[7]

National fears about terrorism are understandable, because terrorism is repeatedly framed on national terms, as "an attack on America." While the bombing of Pan Am flight 103 killed people from twenty-one countries, their commemoration at Arlington National Cemetery was remembered on American terms. While the 9/11 attacks on the Twin Towers killed people from ninety-two countries, their deaths were obscured within a largely uncontested appraisal of the *World* Trade Center as a symbol of only America, and the attacks in New York as attacks on the entire nation. Further characterized as a "national trauma," 9/11 was perceived as an assault on American innocence—a devastating blow that victimized all Americans and simultaneously mandated their shared therapeutic recourse in the war on terror. Images of a tearful but angry American eagle posed against the smoking ruins of the Twin Towers popularized these ideas on T-shirts, bumper stickers, and decals (fig. 3.3). As Lauren Berlant argues, these presumptive manifestations of a "na-

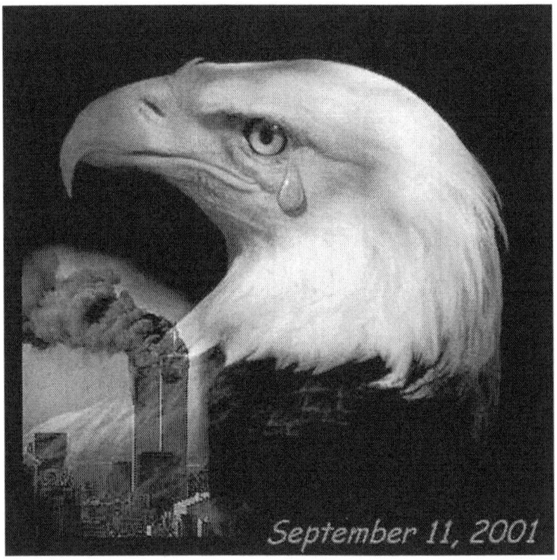

3.3. Dennis Waldron, *Crying Eagle*, 2001. (© Dennis Waldron.)

tional symbolic" help transform all Americans into the "subjects of a collectively held history."[8] Local deaths and regional tragedies become the register of an official national culture, and acknowledging them becomes the purview of national political claims on their meaning and memory. Clinton affirmed this in 1997, when he remarked after the design selection for Oklahoma City's terrorism memorial: "This tragedy was a national one, and the memorial should be recognized and embraced and supported by the nation."[9]

From a larger historical perspective, national fears about terrorism are understandable because of America's long-standing legacy of violent extremism. Political terrorism is not new—the term itself comes from the French Revolution's Reign of Terror (1793–94)—and its history in the United States just since the late nineteenth century includes the Chicago Haymarket bombing of 1886, the racial terrorism of white supremacists during the era of Jim Crow, the dynamiting of the offices of the *Los Angeles Times* in 1910, and the bombing of Wall Street in 1920, which left thirty-three dead and over four hundred wounded. Since the 1950s, an estimated three thousand acts of terrorism have taken place in the United States, including murders and bombings by the Ku Klux Klan, Aryan Nation, Posse Comitatus, antiabortion fanatics, the Armed Forces of Puerto Rican National Liberation, Jewish Defense League, Weather Underground, Symbionese Liberation Army, and Earth Liberation Front.[10] Terrorism in America is most often committed by Americans against other Americans. Between 1980 and 2000, some three-quarters of the extremist acts of violence classified by the FBI as "suspected or confirmed" acts of terrorism in the United States were carried out by American citizens.

Nor are America's terrorist histories unknown. Capitalizing on "star-spangled fear," the exhibition The Enemy Within: Terror in America, 1776 to Today opened at the International Spy Museum in Washington, D.C., in 2004, and at the Oklahoma City National Memorial Museum in 2006.[11] Yet these histories are generally marginalized by political, media, and popular assertions that 9/11 was "the worst" act of terrorism ever to occur on American soil. Jean Baudrillard described the 2001 attacks on the World Trade Center as "the absolute event, the 'mother' of all events."[12]

Contemporary coherence about terrorism is further undercut by assumptions that terrorism in America is either done by demonic foreigners and alien others or by maniacs and misfits like Timothy McVeigh, whose bombing of Oklahoma City's federal building was seen as the insane act of a social deviant, not the rehearsed performance of a decorated Gulf War veteran. By extension, attempts to contextualize 9/11 within narratives of either domestic or international terrorism, or within the nation's larger history of violence, are deemed disrespectful to the memory of those who died, and traitorous to the national duty of patriotic revenge. As George W. Bush proclaimed in a speech at the Pentagon on September 11, 2002: "The murder of innocents cannot be explained, only endured. And though they died in tragedy, they did not die in vain. Their loss has moved a nation to action, in a cause to defend other innocent lives across the world."[13]

The willful incoherence, or "enlightened false consciousness," as Peter Sloterdijk puts it, of dehistoricizing 9/11 as an exceptional event and casting it as a uniquely American trauma that "cannot" be understood further augments public fears about terrorism.[14] Cynical and fatalistic sentiment naturalizes terrorism's violence as unpredictable and indiscriminate, as inexplicable actions by unknown outsiders that can only be "endured" in America. It also posits a trope of innocence that absolves the victimized nation from reflecting on issues of historical responsibility and resorting, instead, to retribution.

Terrorism memorials are the primary public sites where the nation remembers the victims of violent acts of extremism. For family members and survivors, they are sacred sites of bereavement and, often, burial. For politicians, they are ideological rallying grounds. For millions of tourists, they are "authentic" destinations marked by tragic death and traumatic loss. Bearing witness to unfathomable death, these memorials serve to offset the threat and fear of terrorism and its rupturing of American invincibility by reproducing national narratives of social stability, unity, and endurance. The minimalist aesthetic adopted by many contemporary terrorism memorials helps to manage these security narratives by simultaneously expressing and containing affective conditions of fear.

MINIMALIST MEMORIALS

In 2002, Michael Kimmelman observed that minimalism, "of all improbable art movements of the last 50 years," had become the "unofficial language" of contemporary commemoration. In an essay headlined "Out of Minimalism, Monuments to Memory," Kimmelman asserted, "Minimalist abstraction, with its allegorical pliancy, turns out to function in a memorial context as the best available mirror for a modern world."[15] Recent decades have produced a plethora of minimalist styled memorials including the Vietnam Veterans Memorial, the Space Mirror Memorial (see fig. 0.5, p. 4), the Oklahoma City National Memorial, and "Reflecting Absence." This is not, of course, an exclusively American phenomenon: Berlin's Memorial to the Murdered Jews of Europe (2005) is an immense minimalist project of 2,711 disorienting gray concrete pillars that architect Peter Eisenman describes as a "field of memory" (see fig. 3.8, below).[16]

Many artists and critics feel that minimalism is, in fact, the only adequate art style for today's memorials, and in particular, for the commemoration of traumatic histories. Yet how and why did minimalism—an abstract style of modern art that originated in the 1960s—become aligned with the contemporary commemoration of terrorism, trauma, and tragic death? How did such a seemingly "cold" art become so thoroughly attached to these "hot" topics?

As noted, perceptions of the inadequacy of traditional forms of representational art were widely pronounced in critical and intellectual circles after World War II. Henry Moore's inability to imagine a figurative monument at Auschwitz-Birkenau in 1958, for example, and his (unrealized) preference for the Holocaust's commemoration as an expanse of tarmac, was concurrent with the American refusal to commemorate World War II with victory arches. While the U.S. Marine Corps honored its soldier dead with the monumental Iwo Jima sculpture in 1954 (see fig. 4.1, p. 188), World War II was mostly commemorated with "living memorials" like auditoriums, parks, highways, and museums. As Andrew Shanken observes, "Few memorials built in the years after World War II are figurative or iconic."[17]

The general rejection of representational styles in postwar American commemoration is contextualized by the cold war, when the nation loudly and repeatedly pronounced its political, social, and moral superiority—especially over Communism. In cultural terms, this amounted to championing art styles that touted American values like freedom and individuality and rejecting those that suggested otherwise. Because representational art was directly, if simplistically, linked to manipulative strands of political propaganda—both earlier, in Nazi Germany and in New Deal America, and after the war, in the Soviet Union where idealized statues of farm workers and party leaders helped promote Stalinist-style Communism—it was critically rejected in cold war America. By extension, representational art's particular role in commercial advertising, as the visual culture pimp of mass consumerism, deemed it both corrupted and lowbrow in a postwar era obsessed with rigorous distinctions of taste, class, and aesthetic hierarchy.[18] Because abstract art was naïvely lauded as a seemingly apolitical and noncommercial form of personal expression or as the binary opposite of ideologically tainted modes of representation, it became the style choice for any number of postwar American cultures, including commemoration.

Yet coupled with this cold war shift from representational to abstract and eventually minimalist modes of memorialization were critical and artistic assumptions of abstract art's utopian possibilities as a "witness to the unpresentable" and an agent of radical change. Jean-François Lyotard, for example, equated abstract art—and in particular, the abstract expressionist paintings of Barnett Newman—with the sublime, the affect of pleasurable anxiety that accompanies our confrontation with overwhelming and confounding experiences. Lyotard argued that the sublime was a powerfully subversive modernist sensibility that had the capacity to disrupt outmoded thoughts and behaviors and spark the search for new meaning; as such, the sublime held transgressive possibilities for bearing witness to unfathomable and "unpresentable" histories, repressed (or denied) traumas and marginalized subjects.[19] In contrast to cold warrior assumptions about abstract art's political efficacy as an exceptional weapon against Communist totalitarianism, critics like Lyotard privileged abstraction—or some style of avant-garde art engaged in something other than mimetic representation—as an agent of social difference and cultural resistance.

Minimalist art discourses in the 1960s were similarly engaged in oppositional practices and politics, and similarly viewed abstraction or nonrepresentational forms of art on utopian terms. There were, of course, as Anna Chave observes, "multiple Minimalisms" with many "different discursive configurations."[20] Still, a particular minimalist canon emerged in 1960s New York: a nonfigurative, geometric, and serial style that centered first on the "matter" of matter—on what art was made out of and how it was made—and second on art's phenomenological and performa-

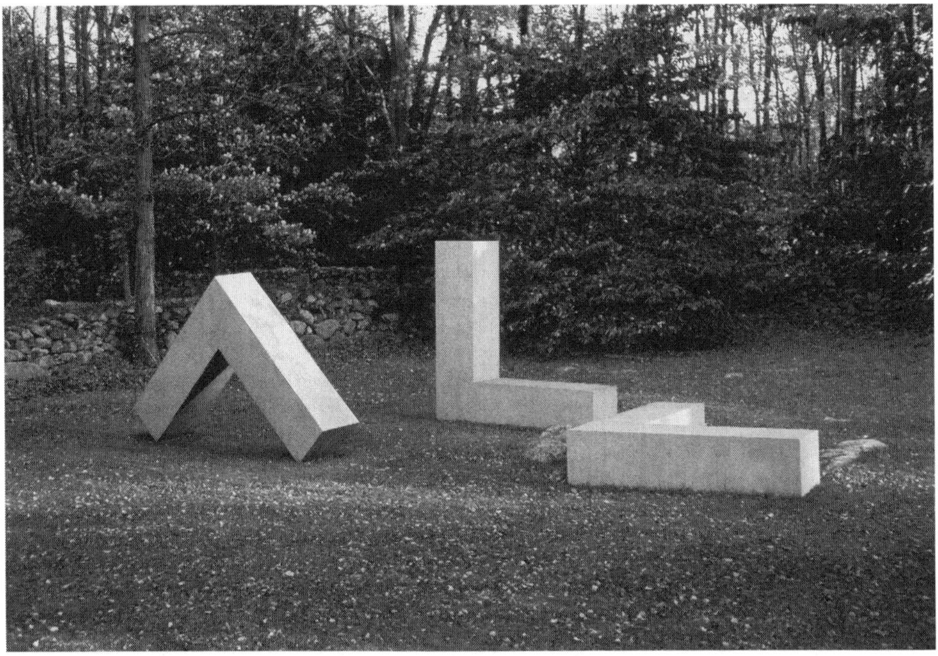

3.4. Robert Morris, *Untitled (L-Beams)*, 1965. Whitney Museum of American Art, New York. (© 2010 Robert Morris / Artists Rights Society [ARS], New York.)

tive dimensions. No illusions, no allusions: minimalist art was "direct, unadulterated experience . . . minus messages."[21] Shunning traditional art media like bronze and marble in favor of base industrial materials like concrete, steel, aluminum, and plywood, minimalist sculptors like Robert Morris (fig. 3.4) and Donald Judd (fig. 3.5) made untitled boxes and modular forms that "force the audience to an awareness of existence," remarked one critic. Minimalist sculpture "goes beyond the presence of any particular art object . . . [W]hat is most important is what the sculptural object *does*—in terms of [our] response—rather than what it *is*," he added. Or as Morris described minimalism in 1966: "the better new work" is "a function of space, light and the viewer's field of vision." The "situation" of sculpture, he observed, "is now more complex and expanded."[22]

Focused on felt conditions and refuting traditional distinctions between art object, artist, space, place, and viewer, minimalism launched a "fundamental reorientation" of modern art.[23] As such, it was a transgressive modern aesthetic aimed at a blunt critique and radical transformation of institutional and cultural authority. Its context was the Vietnam War; its critique included the deconstruction of industrial modes of production and the mass technologies of American militarism. Many mini-

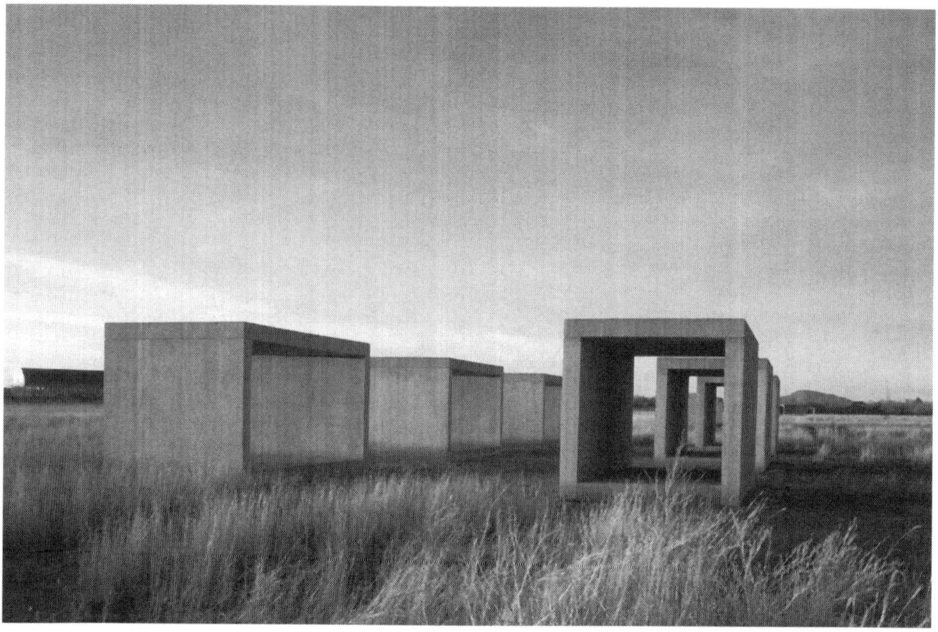

3.5. Donald Judd, *15 Untitled Works in Concrete*, 1980–1984, detail. Permanent collection, the Chinati Foundation, Marfa, Texas. (Photo by Florian Holzherr, 2002. Art © Judd Foundation. Licensed by VAGA, New York, NY. Photo courtesy of Chinati Foundation.)

malist artists participated in the antiwar movement and were deeply opposed to "establishment" values of consensus and consumerism. Some chose to make art outdoors, seeking a world outside of "cultural confinement." Artists like Robert Smithson created gigantic minimalist earthworks in remote locations of the American Southwest—like *Spiral Jetty* (1970) in Utah's Great Salt Lake.[24]

This is not to argue that minimalism's intended unseating of traditional artistic authority was actually realized; as both Chave and Alex Potts detail, minimalist art was as deeply ingrained in issues of biography and personal (or signature) stylistics as any other form of modern art.[25] Moreover, minimalism was undermined by its problematic reliance on mass industrial materials and means, its muddled understandings of institutional and political authority, and the ambiguity of its own critique. Despite dissident ambitions, minimalism's forceful aesthetic was deemed especially, if ironically, fitting for corporate offices, government buildings, and modern museums, many made out of the same steel and concrete materials and adhering to the same sharp and sober designs. As Francis Frascina relates, minimalism's countercultural politics were marginalized by critics and curators who sensed the threat they posed to mainstream accounts of modern art as cultural commodity.[26] Its emphasis on experientiality deeply troubled critics like Michael Fried, who condemned minimalism as theater, not art, and worried about the growing role that the viewer—the public—might play in the meaning of modern art.[27]

In fact, minimalism is the style of choice for many contemporary memorials precisely because of its theatricality, its emphasis on felt experience and audience engagement . Today, when public feelings matter, and public art is deemed especially successful when it generates strong feelings of social relevance and public "ownership," minimalist art is considered the "best" aesthetic because of its participatory and experiential dimensions. Of course, as political theorist Carole Pateman observes, "participation" is often championed as an expedient tool of consensus rather than a transformative vehicle of democratic action; participation does not, in other words, guarantee public agency.[28] In any case, "what used to be men on horses with thrusting swords has morphed more or less into plain walls and boxes," Kimmelman observes. "Once considered the most obstinate kind of modernism, minimalism has gradually, almost sub rosa, made its way into the public's heart."[29]

Distinctions must be made, however. As the neoclassical style of the National World War II Memorial makes clear, the United States continues to valorize great men (like "the greatest generation") and "thrusting swords." And while the nation turns to minimalism to perform the memory of modern trauma, the minimalism it turns to is profoundly different from the oppositional and transgressive modernism originally imagined by artists like Judd, Morris, and Smithson, and championed by critics like Lyotard.

The most visible national memorial in recent history, the one that Paul Goldberger calls "the best American memorial of modern times" and Kimmelman credits with making minimalism the "presumptive sculptural style for memorial design," is the Vietnam Veterans Memorial, dedicated in Washington, D.C., in 1982 (figs. 3.6 and 3.7).[30] Designed by Maya Lin as a project for an undergraduate seminar at Yale University on funereal architecture, the $4.2 million memorial consists of two intersecting walls of black granite set directly into the earth, each about 250 feet long and ranging in height from eight inches at their ends to ten feet at the center. To be fair, the memorial also features several elements mandated during acrimonious federal hearings on the project: a 60-foot flag pole erected at the entrance, and *Three Fighting Men,* a seven-foot bronze sculpture designed by Frederick Hart.

Originally notorious, "the Wall" is one of the national capital's most popular memorials (over 4 million visitors were counted in 2008), if less because of its abstract style than its mandated listing of names and focus

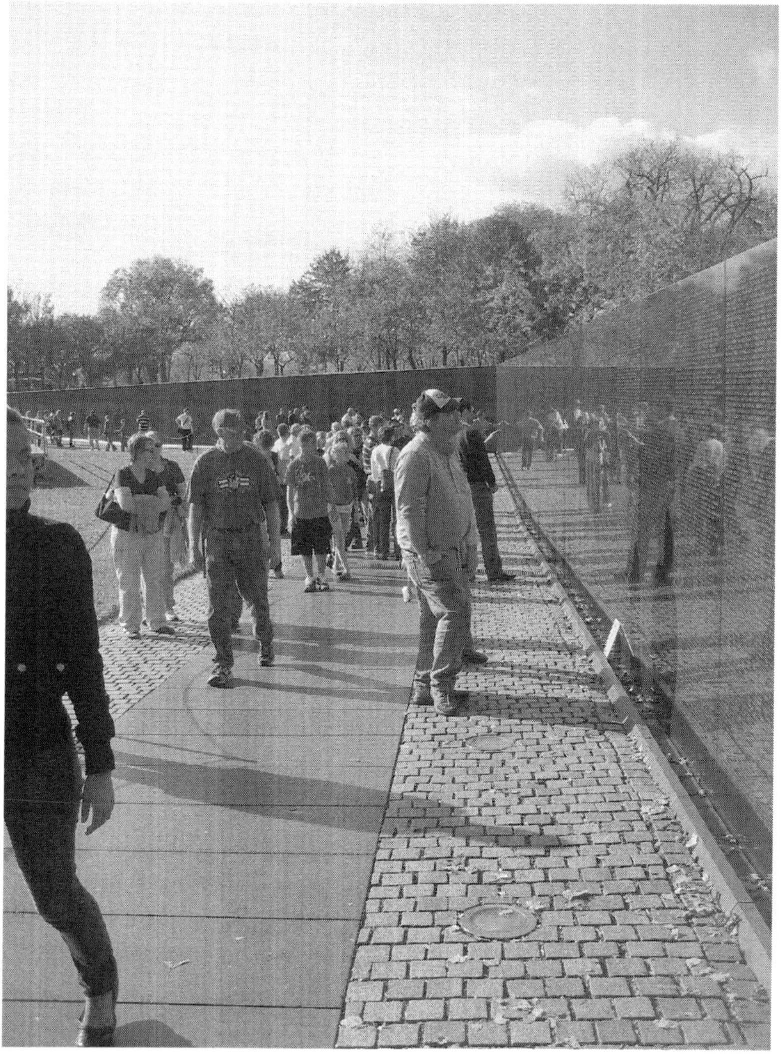

3.6. Maya Lin, Vietnam Veterans Memorial, Washington, D.C., dedicated 1982. (Photo by the author.)

on felt experience. As Lin relates, "I didn't want a static object that people would just look at, but something they could relate to as on a journey, or a passage . . . I had an impulse to cut open the earth . . . an initial violence that in time would heal." Visiting the Wall is akin to descending into a dark void and then walking out "into the light;" other experiential aspects include reading and touching the names of the 58,253 dead inscribed on its symmetrical slates, seeing one's own body reflected on its mirror-like surfaces, and leaving "tokens of remembrance," such as

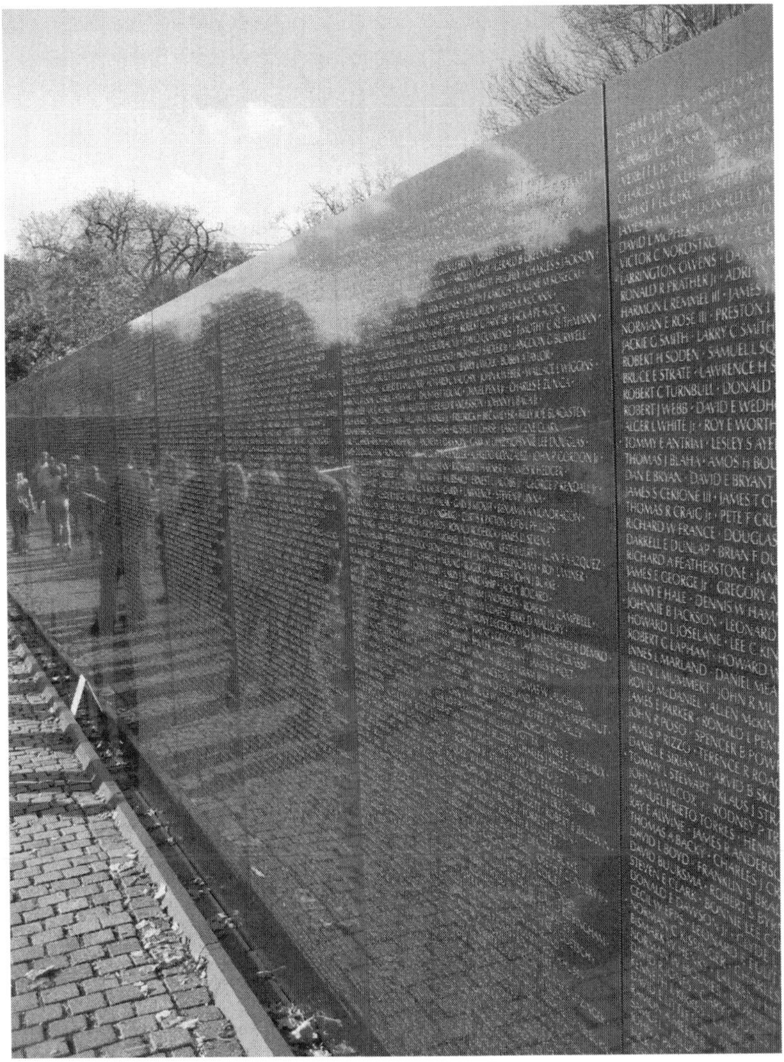

3.7. Vietnam Veterans Memorial. (Photo by the author.)

flowers, poems, photographs, and medals. "I really did mean for people to cry," Lin remarks.[31]

Its horizontal design and black stone challenge conventional styles of commemoration on the National Mall like the Lincoln Memorial and Washington Monument, both nearby. Yet if the Wall is minimalist by design, it does not posit an oppositional or "transformative social critique."[32] Rather, Lin's decorous memorial is oriented toward national reconciliation, a position clarified by the text inscribed at its vertex, where the two walls meet: "Our nation remembers the courage, sacrifice, and devotion to duty and country of its Vietnam veterans." The memorial acknowledges the trauma of a particularly divisive, much despised, and publicly protested war by listing the names of America's soldier dead in incantatory fashion. But it avoids any assessment of the war, and how it so profoundly disturbed and divided the nation. In an odd disconnect that separates it from its reason for being, the Vietnam Veterans Memorial is not even claimed as a "war" memorial; the word "war" isn't even part of its official name. This relates in part to the rules of the commissioning agency (the Vietnam Veterans Memorial Fund, Inc.), which insisted that the memorial "make no political statement about the war." Conceiving of the memorial as a place of "common ground" for "both supporters and opponents of the war," commissioners called for a design that would be "conciliatory" and "harmonious" within a "spacious garden" landscape. As jurors wrote following their selection of Lin's design: "This memorial with its wall of names becomes a place of quiet and reflection, and a tribute to those who served their nation in difficult times. All who come here can find it a place of healing."[33]

Lin, who also designed the Civil Rights Memorial in Montgomery, Alabama (see fig. 0.6, p. 4) and was a particularly persuasive member of the jury that selected "Reflecting Absence," employs a revised minimalist aesthetic to insert affect into the discourse of national memory. Despite the nation's multiple moments of crisis and dissent, the affective narrative that most informs her influential memorial aesthetic is the revelation of loss and the reaffirmation of stability, both self and national. The Vietnam Veterans Memorial is framed by a highly selective sense of what is remembered and what is forgotten; as one veteran observes, "Our healing here is therapeutic, but not historic." Or as Jan Scruggs, the veteran who initiated the memorial in 1979 and wrote a book about it titled *To Heal a Nation* (1985), asserts: "The memorial says exactly what we wanted to say about Vietnam—absolutely nothing."[34]

Kimmelman suggests that minimalism pervades contemporary forms of commemoration because of its "ambiguity:" that the "bare walls" of today's memorials "are blank slates onto which we project our deepest commonly held feelings." Marita Sturken similarly argues that the walls of the Vietnam Veterans Memorial "act as a screen for myriad cultural projections," and Tom Mitchell sees the memorial as a polysemous site that "provokes an indefinite series of narratives and counternarratives" and hence has subversive social potential.[35] Yet the minimalism of the 1960s was never fixed on "feelings" (and certainly not "commonly held" feelings) but on the transgressive possibilities of felt experience. Moreover, presumptions of a polysemous minimalist void beg the question of what we actually bring to the blank slate: abstract art, like all art, is informed by presentist beliefs and expectations.

Today's minimalist styled memorials are not at all ambiguous, but are carefully orchestrated narratives of select traumas aligned with notions of social reconciliation and national redemption. As President Ronald Reagan declared during Veterans Day ceremonies held at the Vietnam Veterans Memorial in 1988: "We remember the devotion and gallantry with which all of them ennobled their nation as they became champions of a noble cause . . . Their love for their country lives. This memorial has become a monument to that living love."[36] This was no ambiguous statement: Reagan saw the Vietnam Veterans Memorial as a symbol of American patriotism and military sacrifice. He was not alone; in recent years, the Wall has been the destination for an annual Memorial Day pilgrimage of thousands of Vietnam veterans intent on revising national memories of that traumatic war by shifting perceptions of "lost cause" to "just cause." Many contemporary terrorism and trauma memorials are similarly engaged.

TRAUMA

"If every age has its symptoms, ours appears to be the age of trauma," write Nancy Miller and Jason Tougaw.[37] Trauma is prioritized in today's cultural imagination as the project (some would say preoccupation) not just of commemoration but innumerable scholarly studies, national surveys, popular television shows, and a burgeoning industry of clinical and critical theory. Mark Seltzer describes the omnipresent circulation of traumatic imagery—nightly news roundups of disaster narratives, for example, or the popularity of TV shows such as *CSI* and *NCIS*—in terms of "wound culture," a "pathological public sphere" marked by a "collective gathering around shock, trauma, and the wound."[38]

Some of trauma's contemporary symbolic capital stems from its own broad trajectory as an event of extreme and devastating violence, an injury to a living organism (the word "trauma" comes from the Greek *traumat*, meaning "wound"), and the intense emotional suffering and psychological disordering of the wounded. Trauma, in other words, is both agent and affect, mechanism and result. Its discourse is especially modern, a new explanatory vocabulary for modernism's multiple wounds (total war, genocide, terrorism) and abundant anxieties (shell shock, survivor guilt, posttraumatic stress disorder). Modernist inquiries into trauma's manifestation and meaning were especially framed by Freud and Pierre Janet, among other early twentieth-century psychoanalysts, who theorized about the destabilizing power of "traumatic memory" and the manner in which such memory was repressed (Freud) or dissociated (Janet) as being too painful to bear, and yet remained present, if subconsciously, in the form of nightmares, flashbacks, hallucinations, and other repetitive and incapacitating symptoms.[39] Failure to resolve the disordering symptoms of traumatic memory was viewed as inimical to psychic and physical health. In today's therapeutic cultures, this has led to a particularly literalist focus on "recovering" trauma by "working through" its pain and suffering and thereby coming to "closure" in order to restore personal (and collective) stability.

As a concept and a culture, trauma's heightened presence in contemporary America dates to the wake of the Vietnam War, when the war itself was repeatedly described as a "national trauma" and its symptomatic impact on veterans led to the American Psychiatric Association's recognition in 1980 of posttraumatic stress disorder, defined as an anxiety disorder triggered by traumatic memories both experienced and witnessed. Hence, the dedication of the Vietnam Veterans Memorial in 1982 was understood by many as the nation's attempt to "work through" the trauma of the war. Trauma gained further social currency with the rise of recovered memory therapy (recovering repressed memories of childhood sexual abuse, in particular) in the 1980s and 1990s.[40] Similarly, personal testimonials and memoirs, "writing wrongs" and bearing witness, and especially Holocaust studies, have been central to contemporary trauma discourse, from theoretical considerations by literary critics and historians including Cathy Caruth, Shoshana Felman, and Dominick LaCapra, to sociopolitical analyses which claim trauma as an authenticating mark of identity among diverse publics.[41] "We are implicated in each other's traumas," Caruth asserts in her influential *Unclaimed Experience: Trauma, Narrative, and History* (1996), arguing that modern history is a shared and haunted history of trauma. Among 9/11's many narratives—including anger, crisis, disbelief, sorrow, and vengeance—trauma is especially employed.[42]

In public policy, clinical psychiatry, and law, trauma is typically perceived on pragmatic terms as a devastating psychic blow that can be accessed and must be cured; trauma is a problem, but it can be resolved. In literary criticism and social theory, trauma is also problematic but mainly because it is so overwhelming that it exceeds comprehension. In other disciplines, trauma is increasingly utilized to reframe historical conditions and political interests. Including the trauma of slavery in the American historical narrative, for example, profoundly disrupts national paradigms of freedom and liberty. Trauma's disruption "brings us to the limits of our understanding," Caruth contends, but it also portends transgressive possibilities: new modes of reading in literary studies; new concepts of evidence and interpretation in history; new narratives of identity and purpose in the national imaginary.[43]

TERRORISM MEMORIALS

Competing accounts of trauma are played out in contemporary commemoration and explain both minimalism's use in terrorism memorials and the heated public debates that surround them. While trauma is the organizing theme of terrorism memorials, its representation is often superficial and mostly oriented toward the restoration of social order and the revitalization of presumably shared national norms. Trauma's historical terms—and transgressive possibilities—are generally overlooked, if not entirely ignored.

Trauma is dissonant, confusing, and chaotic, a kind of dismantling that its victims describe in terms of physical and emotional modes of detachment: time and space "out of order." Trauma's inexpressible pain "unmakes" the body, Elaine Scarry agues, shattering the unity of the subject and plunging victims into silence and grief.[44] Minimalism is often selected to commemorate trauma because it simultaneously evokes this disorientation and resolves it; it conjures trauma's profound dissonance and also speaks to the recovery and reaffirmation—the remaking—of individual and collective harmony. The Vietnam Veterans Memorial's long cuts of black granite, for example, embody both the wounds of the war *and* its reconciliation in the national narrative: time and space are disrupted when we descend into the memorial's disorienting depths and then are returned to normalcy as we exit along an inclined path facing the Washington Monument. It is no surprise that the Wall has become *the* model for contemporary trauma memorials: since its unveiling in 1982, artists and audiences alike have learned to read its redefined minimalism in terms of an experiential procession or pilgrimage from grief to mourning to healing.

Eisenman's Memorial to the Murdered Jews of Europe similarly relies on minimalism to evoke trauma's disruption of time and space (fig. 3.8). Featuring a grid of several thousand concrete stelae of varying heights and inclines (each plinth is about three degrees off plumb), all densely packed within a five-acre field, the memorial's physical space is profoundly disconcerting. There is no marked entrance or exit into its sober stone landscape—nor is there a center—and meandering through the memorial's labyrinthine terrain is claustrophobic and confusing. Daniel Libeskind's Garden of Exile and Emigration (1998), a section of the Jewish Museum Berlin, is similarly discomfiting (fig. 3.9). Cramped and nar-

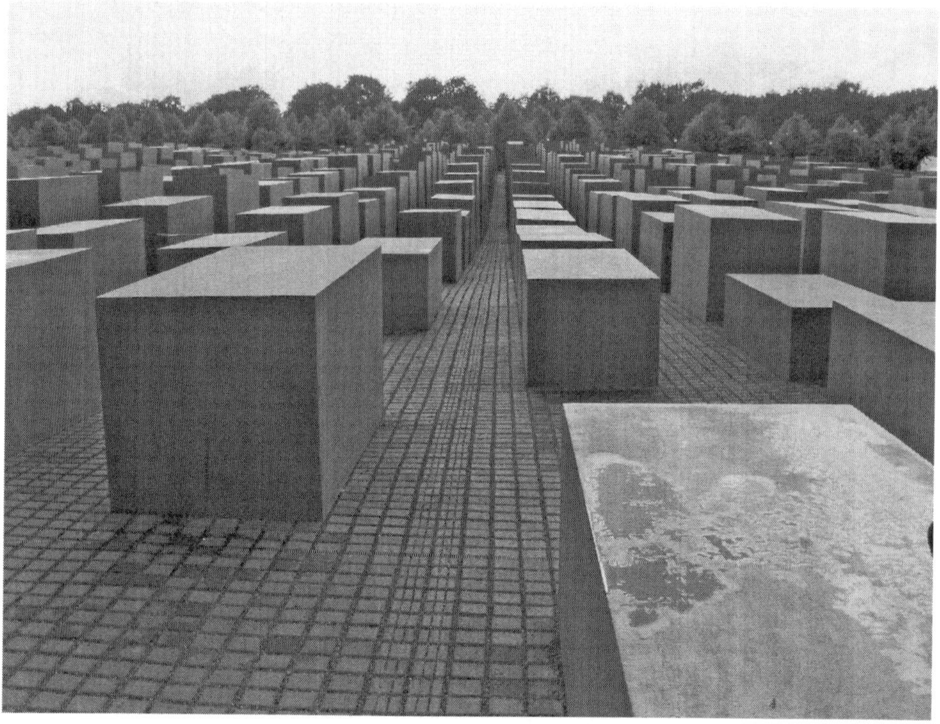

3.8. Peter Eisenman, Memorial to the Murdered Jews of Europe, Berlin, Germany, dedicated 2005. (Courtesy of Beth Wilcox.)

row, the memorial consists of tilting twenty-foot-tall concrete columns, each topped with trees and shrubs. Audiences inside the "garden" look up to see the trees—and realize they are trapped below the ground, buried inside the gloomy confines of a memorial void.

The New England Holocaust Memorial (1995, fig. 3.10), located along Boston's historic Freedom Trail and near Faneuil Hall, combines towering monolithic forms and unexpected physical juxtapositions to evoke the ineffable. Designed by Stanley Saitowitz, the memorial features a linear grid of six fifty-four-foot-tall glass towers perched on a black granite walkway and etched with a ghostly pattern of six million numbers (referencing the number of Jews murdered during the Holocaust). Beneath each tower is a steel grate covering a six-foot chamber, at the bottom of which small lights illuminate the name of a Nazi death camp, and from which warm air—turning into smoke and fog in colder months—comes out, as Saitowitz says, "like human breath as it passes through the glass chimneys to heaven."[45]

Sharing a revised minimalist aesthetic, America's terrorism memorials are similarly informed by disorienting design elements aimed at

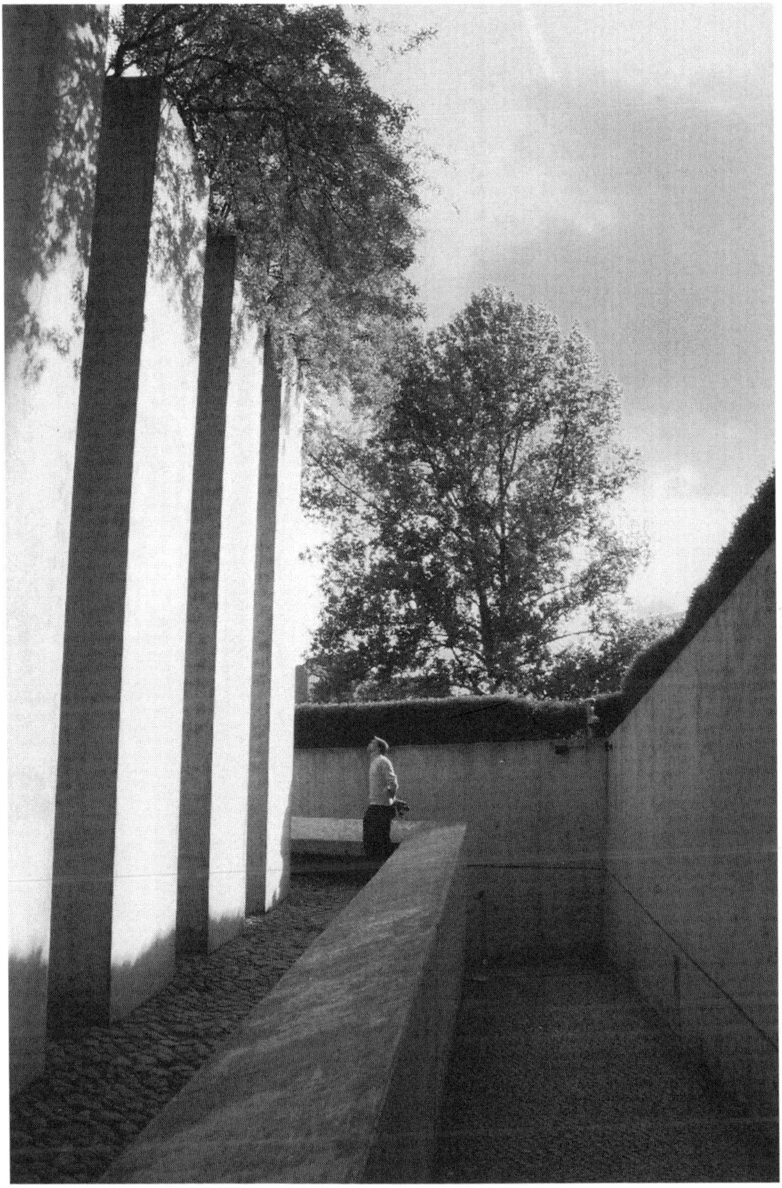

3.9. Daniel Libeskind, Garden of Exile and Emigration, Jewish Museum Berlin, Berlin, Germany, dedicated 1998. (Photo by Ruben Joye. Courtesy of SXC.)

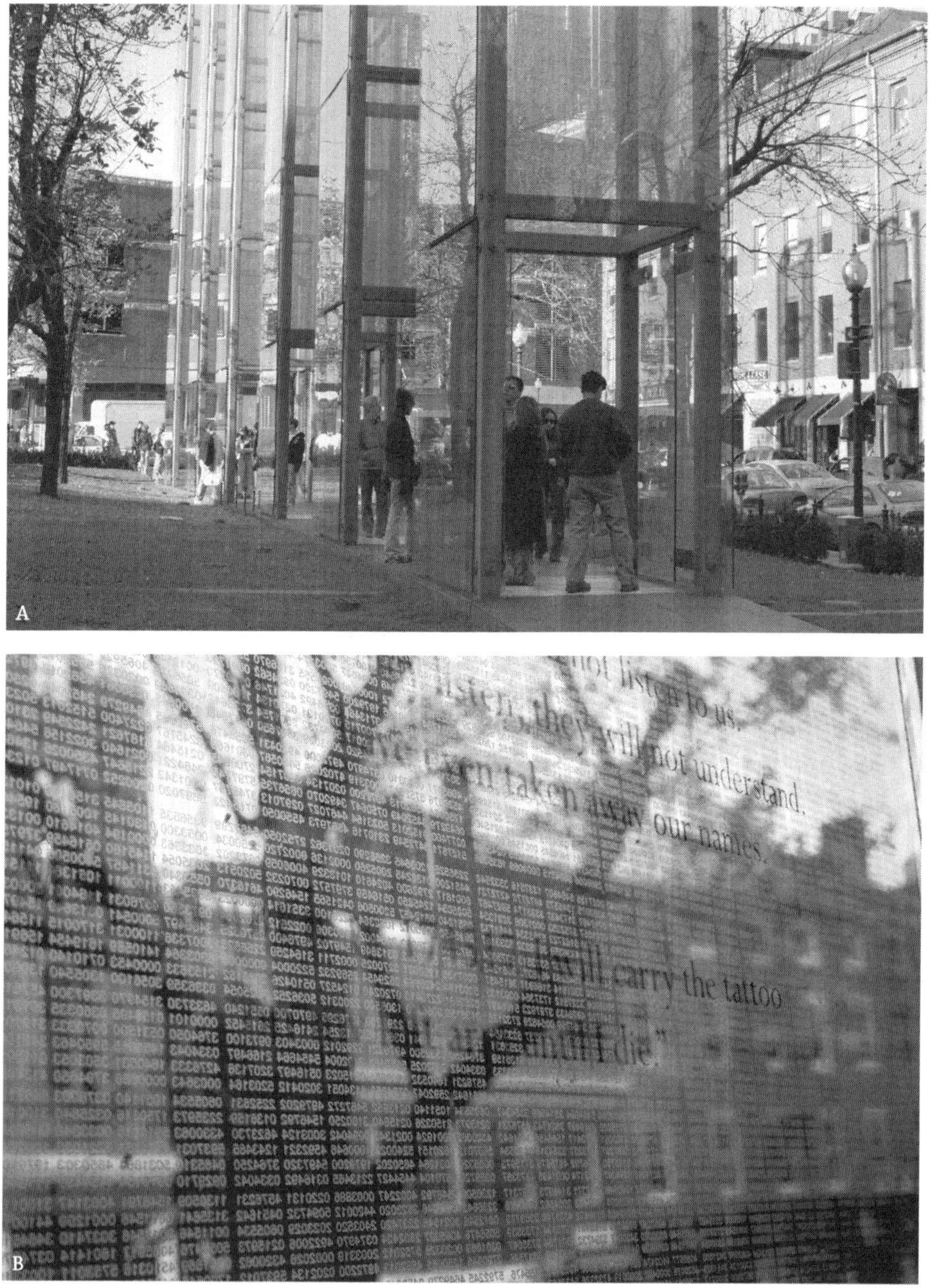

3.10. *A*, Stanley Saitowitz, New England Holocaust Memorial, Boston, Massachusetts, dedicated 1995. (Photo by Sharon Ringer.) *B*, New England Holocaust Memorial, detail. (Photo by Sharon Ringer.)

evoking trauma. But unlike the Holocaust memorials designed by Eisenman, Libeskind, and Saitowitz, America's terrorism memorials are also dominated by a curative or therapeutic sensibility centered on "working through" trauma. However much artists and critics hold faith in minimalism's transcendent possibilities, that faith and the style itself have been diluted to evoke social stability, not radical transformation. Audience participation at the Oklahoma City National Memorial, for example, is highly prescribed. Visitors enter and exit the 3.5-acre, $29 million memorial through monumental Gates of Time, each 42 feet tall and clad in bronze tile (fig. 3.11). These tomblike monoliths frame both the actual physical location where the 168 victims of the bombing died and the moment of the blast that killed them, 9:02 a.m. on April 19, 1995. The East Gate reads "9:01" and the West Gate reads "9:03," meaning that the memorial recreates, and its visitors re-experience, the temporal and spatial dislocations of Timothy McVeigh's terrorist act and the deaths he generated. Yet each gigantic gate is also etched with the memorial's mission statement, which reads: "We come here to remember those who were killed, those who survived, and those changed forever. May all who leave here know the impact of violence. May this memorial offer comfort, strength, peace, hope and serenity."[46]

Between the gates is a 318-foot long reflecting pool, tiled in black granite and likened by the memorial's designers, Hans and Torrey Butzer, as "gently flowing water [that] soothes the HEALING wound caused by the fiery blast" (fig. 3.12). The pool is faced on one side by the memorial's dominant design feature: 168 bronze and glass chairs, each etched with the name of a victim of the bombing (fig. 3.13). Standing on a grassy footprint of the former federal building, the chairs are arranged in nine rows representing the building's nine floors and are placed according to where each person was in the building at the moment of the blast. The nineteen children who died in the building's daycare facilities are represented by smaller chairs grouped together in a single row. With its tidy grid of headstone-like chairs fixed at the site of each death, this section of the memorial resembles a well-ordered necropolis (see fig. 0.4, p. 3). At night, the chairs are illuminated by small lights that the Butzers describe as "beacons of hope [that] will inspire Oklahoma City, the State, and Nation to rebuild and prepare for tomorrow."[47]

The Oklahoma City National Memorial's grand scale, select symbolism, and revised minimalism—Kimmelman describes it as "a grid of chairs lined up like Donald Judd's boxes"—is echoed in terrorism memorials in Washington, Pennsylvania, and New York. Designed by Julie Beckman and Keith Kaseman, the Pentagon Memorial cost $22 million and was dedicated on September 11, 2008. It occupies a 2-acre site about

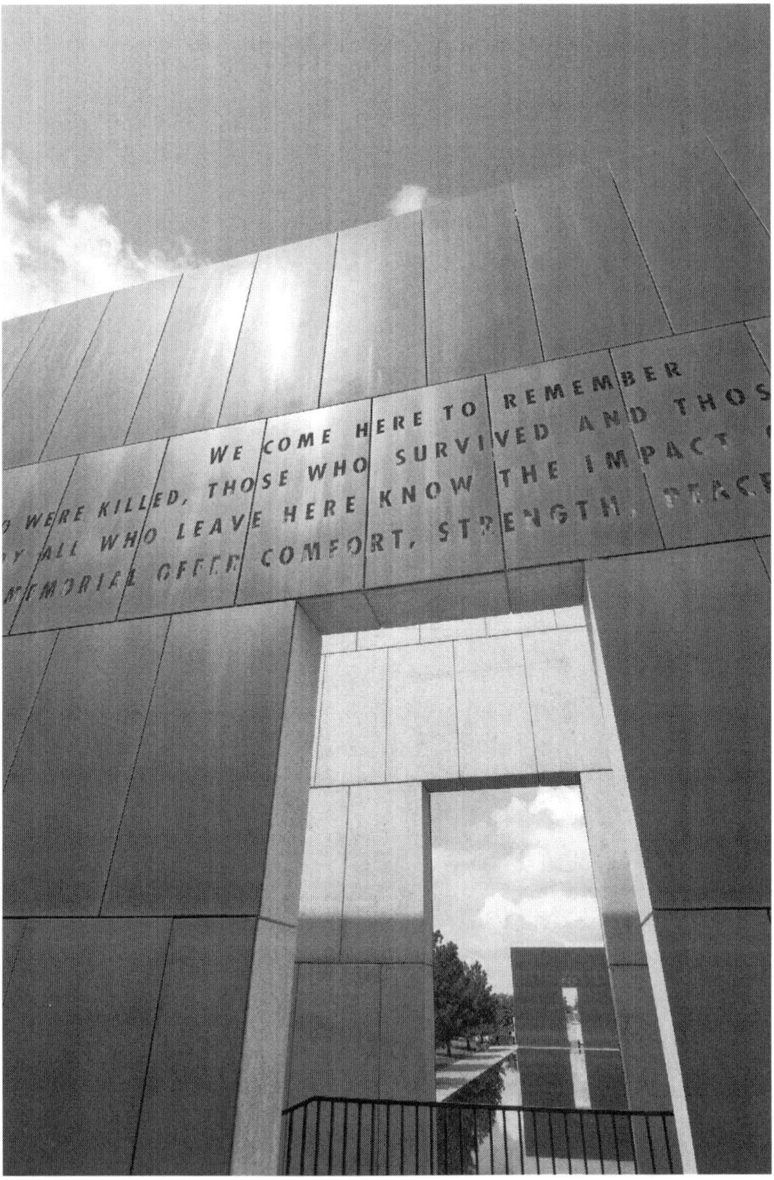

3.11. Gates of Time, Oklahoma City National Memorial, Oklahoma City, Oklahoma, dedicated 2000. (Courtesy of the Oklahoma City National Memorial Foundation.)

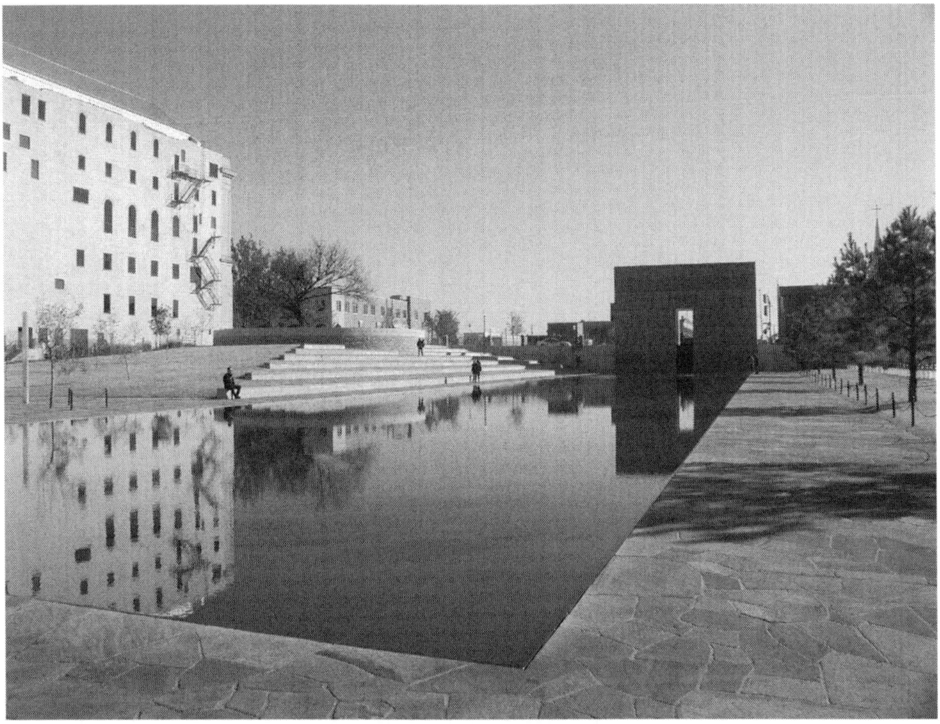

3.12. Reflecting pool, Oklahoma City National Memorial. (Photo by the author.)

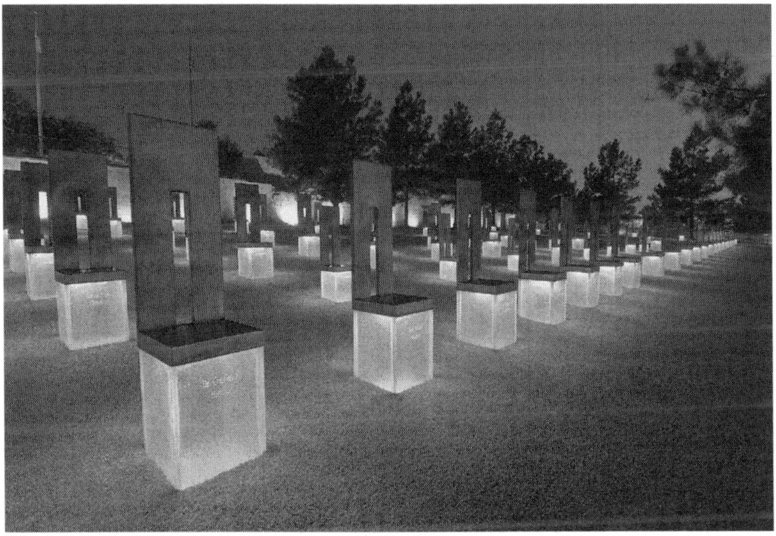

3.13. Chairs, Oklahoma City National Memorial. (Courtesy of the Oklahoma City National Memorial Foundation.)

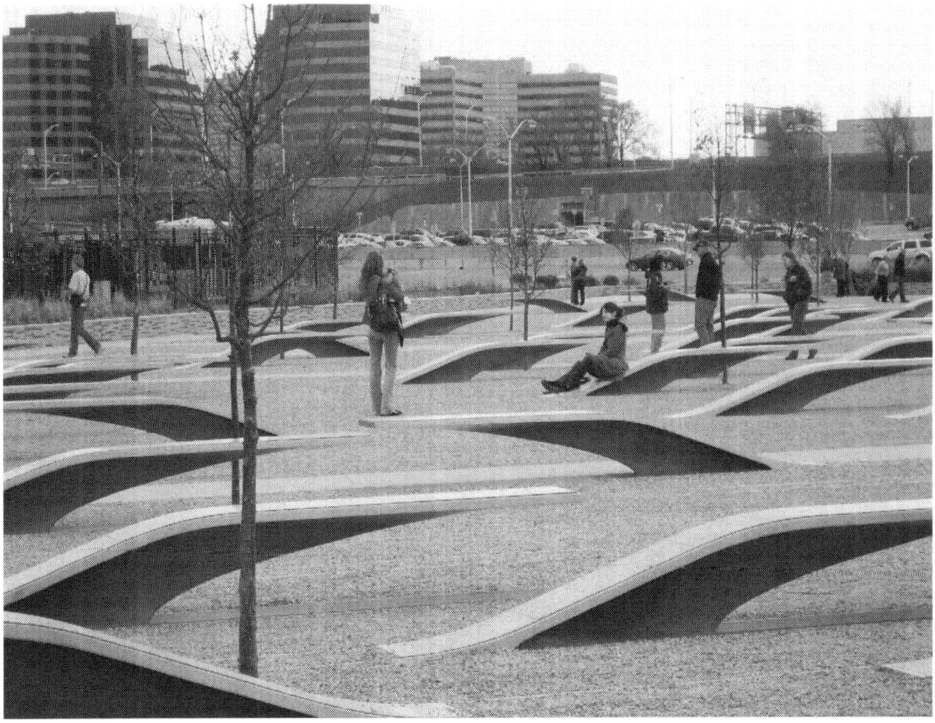

3.14. Julie Beckman and Keith Kaseman, Pentagon Memorial, Washington, D.C., dedicated 2008. (Courtesy of Heather Bowling.)

165 feet from where American Airlines flight 77 hit the building and features 184 cantilevered stainless steel benches, each engraved with the name of one of the victims of the crash (fig. 3.14). Each bench is part of a "memorial unit" and hovers over a rectangular pool of water that is illuminated at night; a longer, continuous bench frames the perimeter of the memorial's wedge-shaped space, and the memorial grounds are landscaped with clusters of maple trees. The named benches are organized according to the age of the victims and whether they were on the plane (59 people) or inside the Pentagon (125 people); the memorial also features an Age Wall that references the victims.

The Flight 93 National Memorial is an immense $58 million project located near Shanksville, Pennsylvania, about eighty miles southeast of Pittsburgh (figs. 3.15 and 3.16). Mandated by Congress in 2002, the memorial is managed by the National Park Service and guided by the slogan "A Common Field One Day . . . A Field of Honor Forever."[48] Spread over 2,200 acres, the memorial was designed by the Los Angeles architectural firm of Paul Murdoch and features a Field of Honor enclosing the entire site, a Tower of Voices housing 40 white wind chimes, and a ceremonial

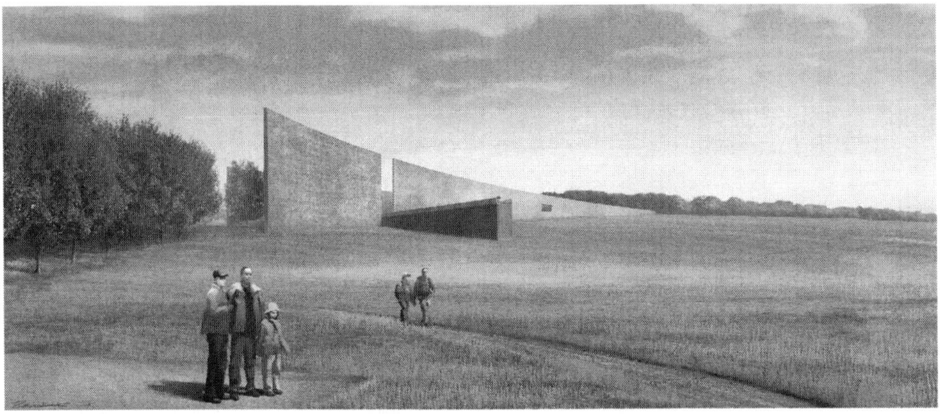

3.15. Overview, Flight 93 National Memorial, Shanksville, Pennsylvania (design selected 2004). (Drawing courtesy of Paul Murdoch Architects and Aleksander Novak-Zemplinski.)

gateway leading to Sacred Ground, a walled space marking "the final resting place of the passengers and crew" of United flight 93.

The 4 hijackers of flight 93 are unnamed; likewise, the Pentagon's 9/11 memorial does not reference the 5 terrorists who orchestrated the crash that killed 184 people and themselves, and New York's 9/11 memorial makes no mention of the 10 terrorists, 5 on each plane, who hijacked American Airlines flight 11 and United flight 175 and slammed them into the north and south towers of the World Trade Center. These omissions are hardly surprising; these are memorials, after all, to the *victims* of terrorism. Yet the absence of historical referents to the perpetrators of terrorism helps shroud these memorials; by effacing the agents of terror, terrorism memorials efface their intentions and encourage a blurring, or evasion, of causality.

All three memorials claim national status and therefore national significance. Following the "national symbolic" presumptive that the September 11, 2001, attacks on the World Trade Center were attacks on all America, New York's World Trade Center Memorial was renamed the National September 11 Memorial & Museum at the World Trade Center in 2007. Responding to charges that Shanksville's memorial had been officially designated by Congress as 9/11's "national memorial," New York mayor Michael Bloomberg remarked, "I think the country is big enough to use the word 'national' multiple times." As the memorial's foundation explains, the name change "reflect[s] more fully" the attacks of 9/11 "as a national tragedy that changed the course of history." Or as its chief executive put it, "We are building a national symbol that, like the Statue of Liberty, tells us something about who we are as Americans." In Septem-

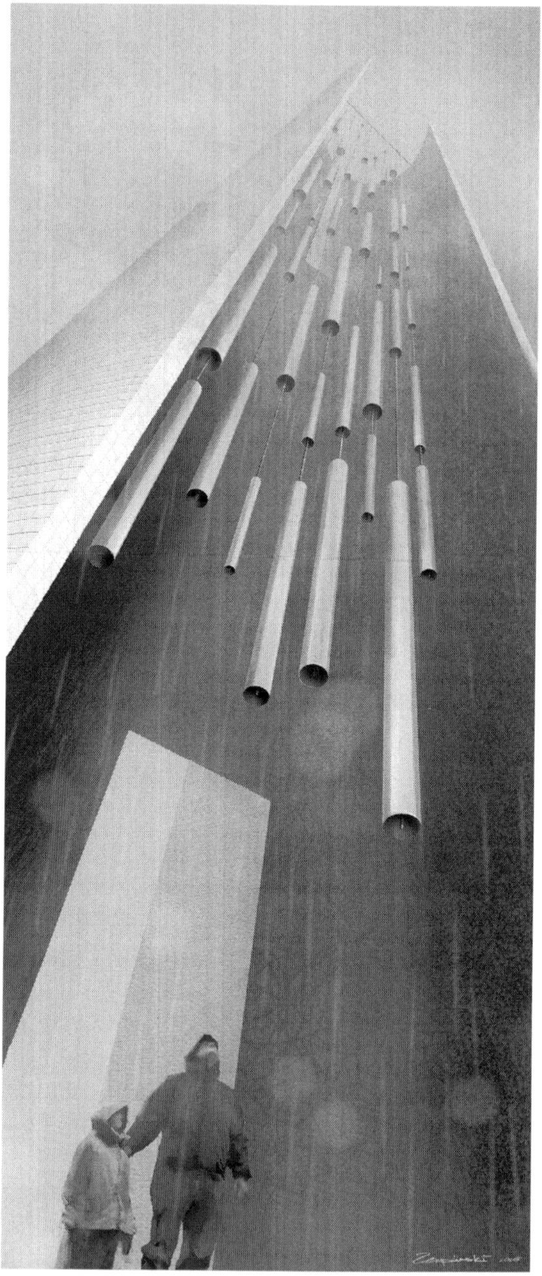

3.16. Tower of Voices, Flight 93 National Memorial. (Drawing courtesy of Paul Murdoch Architects and Aleksander Novak-Zemplinski.)

ber 2007, the foundation launched a "national awareness tour," exhibiting 9/11 photographs and artifacts across America and giving audiences "the opportunity to become a part of the project's history by signing their names to steel beams destined for the construction of the Memorial."[49] New York's memorial also features *all* of the names of 9/11's victims, as well as the six people who were murdered in the first attack on the Twin Towers in 1993.

New York's 9/11 memorial is the most expensive of the nation's three major terrorism memorials, and perhaps the most expensive memorial in modern American history. Construction costs for the memorial and adjoining museum, a massive 120,000 square-foot space that one critic likens as "a storehouse for relics of the dead," are expected to exceed $1 billion (which is what the entire World Trade Center originally cost to build in the 1970s). Annual operating costs for the memorial, museum, landscaped plaza, and visitor's center are estimated to be $57 million.[50]

Minimalist designs were typical among the proposals submitted for New York's 9/11 memorial, and as Harriet Senie relates, "I overheard many who viewed the models at the World Financial Center observe that they could barely tell them apart."[51] Maya Lin's influence was palpable, both as a member of the jury and designer of one of the nation's most popular memorials. Lin championed "Reflecting Absence," which will occupy an 8-acre site with two huge spatial voids—actually, sunken pools bounded by walls of water—on the footprints of the former Twin Towers (fig. 3.17; see also fig. 0.12, p. 8). (The site's remaining acres are occupied by World Trade Center skyscrapers and a subway terminal.) Each void is 176 feet square and bordered by 30-foot ramps descending into a series of underground walkways and exhibition chambers, some of them 70 feet below ground and some intended only for 9/11 families and survivors (fig. 3.18). As jury member James Young recounted, "Reflecting Absence" was picked "because we liked its simplicity, its Minimalist aesthetic . . . The voids themselves really seemed to be in keeping with a postwar vocabulary that attempted to articulate absence, which is a very difficult thing to do."[52]

The "presence" of absence is a dominant metaphor in memorial mania.[53] Just a few days after 9/11, New York was plunged into feverish debate about how the shockingly empty space formerly occupied by the World Trade Center would be remembered and redeveloped. The site was largely disliked during its lifetime: designed by Minoru Yamasaki and built between 1966 and 1977, the World Trade Center's complex of seven buildings, including the 110-story Twin Towers, was considered overbearing, bland, and dated, especially as more fluid and "networked"

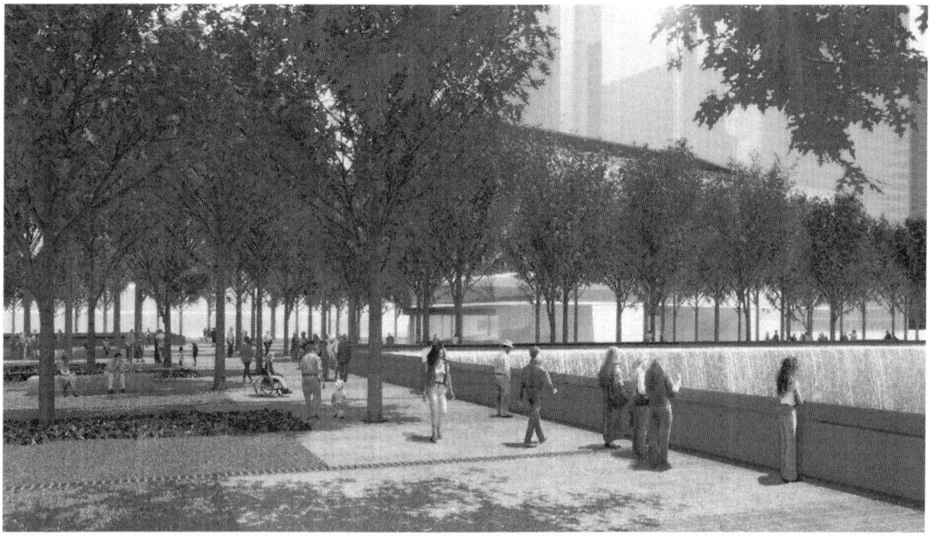

3.17. Memorial Plaza parapet, National September 11 Memorial & Museum at the World Trade Center, June 20, 2006. (Renderings by Squared Design Lab. © 2004–2008 National September 11 Memorial & Museum at the World Trade Center Foundation, Inc. All Rights Reserved.)

paradigms of urban space and postmodern architecture developed. And it was a predictable target—twice—for al-Qaeda, which saw its towering "pillars" as *the* prime symbol of American capitalist arrogance. As Osama bin Laden declared a few weeks after 9/11: "I swear by God, *who has elevated the skies without pillars*, neither America nor the people who live in it will dream of security before we live it in Palestine."[54]

Still, the World Trade Center's sudden absence was met by widespread calls for its immediate replacement. Arguments in favor of the area's new openness, such as reshaping the site into a memorial park and retaining the reopened view to the Hudson River, lost to those insisting on the World Trade Center's instrumental importance in Lower Manhattan's, and the entire nation's, economic recovery—especially in the recessionary climate of the early twenty-first century. Worries that rebuilding the towers might trigger more acts of terrorism were brushed off as the whimpers of cowards and traitors—of "giving in" to terrorists. Architects Elizabeth Diller and Ricardo Scofidio pleaded, "Let's not build something that would mend the skyline, it is more powerful to leave it void." But local politicians and real estate developers insisted on "recovery through rebuilding," on new and loftier buildings that would serve as economic catalysts and reaffirm American national authority, while

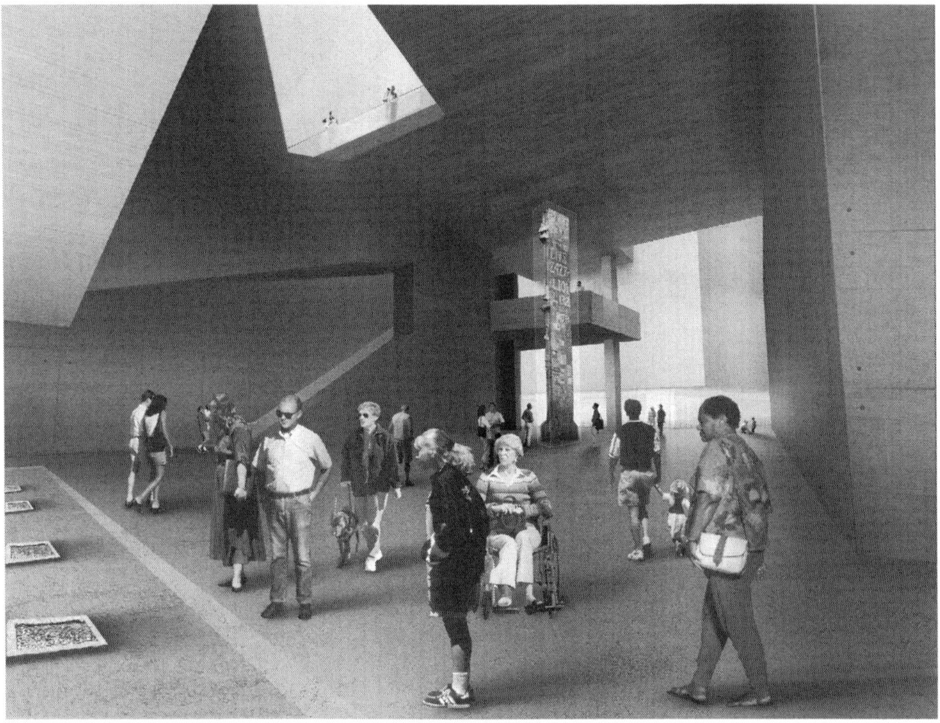

3.18. Memorial museum, National September 11 Memorial & Museum at the World Trade Center, June 20, 2006. (Renderings by Davis Brody Bond. © 2004–2008 National September 11 Memorial & Museum at the World Trade Center Foundation, Inc. All rights reserved.)

simultaneously representing the "absence" of the original buildings and several thousand people.[55]

Representing absence is the primary mandate of New York's 9/11 memorial, whose twin voids occupy the spatial footprints of the former Twin Towers and thus reconstruct them on metaphysical terms. Yet as Dominick LaCapra argues, "losses cannot be adequately addressed when they are enveloped in an overly generalized discourse of absence."[56] Loss connotes destruction and disappearance, whereas absence suggests vacancy and lack, or "nonpresence" and the anxious possibility of reappearance. Contemporary preference for "absence" over "loss" not only suggests a general confusion about their distinctions but an inability to address their specific forms, and meanings, on historical and sociopolitical levels. "Reflecting absence" comes close to "reflecting amnesia."

Like Oklahoma's terrorism memorial, New York's 9/11 memorial is framed by a mission statement that reads, in part: "May the lives remembered, the deeds recognized, and the spirit reawakened be eternal beacons, which reaffirm respect for life, strengthen our resolve to preserve freedom, and inspire an end to hatred, ignorance and intolerance."[57] Many memorial proposals, including "Reflecting Absence," literally referenced this reassuring directive by making light and water, traditional symbols of hopefulness and regeneration, their primary design motifs—"Mass murder dulled by architectural Musak," Maureen Dowd chided in a *New York Times* op-ed titled "The Unbearable Lightness of Memory." She added, "The designs are reflections of our psychobabble culture, exuding that horrible and impossible concept, closure . . . Even the names of the models sound like books by Deepak Chopra and Marianne Williamson: 'Garden of Lights,' 'Inversion of Light,' 'Votives in Suspension,' 'Suspending Memory,' 'Reflecting Absence,' 'Passages of Light: The Memorial Cloud.' All ambient light and transient emotion—nothing raw or harsh or rough on which the heart and mind can collide."[58]

Many terrorism memorials employ a redefined minimalism that manipulates normal understandings of space and time in order to evoke trauma's dissociative affects of fear and anxiety. Towering monoliths, angled walls, recessed forms, reflective surfaces, and gridded units strewn throughout enormously scaled sites lend these memorials their purposely disconcerting impressions. Pits, voids, and an aesthetic of "absence" further their destabilizing sensibility; tensions between their overwhelming spatiality and their simultaneous emphasis on intimate experience heighten their anxious affective conditions.

Yet they are also framed by sociotherapeutic assumptions that trauma can be represented and must be cured, hence the affirmation of hope, healing, renewal, and closure in design elements such as reflecting pools, waterfalls, manicured lawns, and clusters of trees. Likewise, such memorials rely on refined materials such as granite, marble, and bronze rather than the ignoble materials more typically employed in 1960s minimalist sculptures. However informed, in other words, by original minimalist tropes of disruption, experientiality, and radical transformation, these terrorism memorials are fixed and unyielding.

Consider the text at the entrance to the Oklahoma City National Memorial, which explains why the memorial exists and what tourists should glean from their visit:

> You are entering the area where the Alfred P. Murrah Building once stood. The granite used on this pathway was salvaged from the Murrah Building. The Field of Empty Chairs is a tribute to the 168 Americans who were killed April 19, 1995. The nine rows represent the nine floors of the former Murrah Building. Each person's chair is positioned in the row that

corresponds to the floor on which they worked or were visiting. The five westernmost Empty Chairs honor those who were killed outside the Murrah Building.

No mention is made of how and why these 168 people died, an absence of context that sustains terrorism as an inexplicable evil rather than the structural project of particular human and historical agents. Ironically, this omission of specific facts and perspectives—this depoliticization of terrorism—relates to the nation's preoccupation with security.

SECURITY NARRATIVES

Terrorism memorials are among America's top tourist attractions: the Oklahoma City National Memorial drew 345,000 people in 2007, and preliminary projections for New York's 9/11 memorial suggest that more than 6,000,000 people will visit each year. By 2008, over 1,000,000 people had visited the Flight 93 temporary memorial in Shanksville, and the permanent memorial is expected to receive some 230,000 annual pilgrims.[59] If "tragic tourism" accounts for their appeal, narratives of national unity, innocence, survival, and sacrifice shape their meaning. Fears of terrorism's looming threat to self and nation are managed in these pseudo-minimalist memorials through design elements and textual references that stress security, stability, and heroism.

Freud distinguished fear and anxiety in terms of their relation and response to danger: fear, or fright, was an affect prompted by specific physiological and psychological threats, while anxiety was the state of confusion and distress prompted by the anticipation of such threats. Such distinctions are fairly ambiguous (even Freud defined *Realangst*, or, "realistic anxiety," in terms of fear) and Silvan Tomkins later argued that "terror be recognized as the same affect" as fear and anxiety.[60] Whatever their source, fear and anxiety—as manifest in nervousness, uncertainty, excitability, blind resentment, and unreasoning hysteria—are untenable states of insecurity that neither the self nor the nation can tolerate. Such feelings are often abated or controlled in comforting and safe spaces—in the familiar setting of the home, for example, or in the routine and order of the workplace.

The violation of these safe spaces is, then, especially jarring, and efforts to restore them are quick. Less than a month after 9/11, President Bush announced the formation of the Department of Homeland Security to "coordinate the executive branch's efforts to detect, prepare for, prevent, protect against, respond to, and recover from terrorist attacks within the United States."[61] Of course, as Amy Kaplan writes, the very formation of such an agency and the terms used to describe it "work to generate forms of radical insecurity by proliferating threats of the foreign lurking within and without national borders. The notion of 'the homeland' draws on comforting images of a deeply rooted past to legitimate modern forms of imperial power."[62]

Terrorism memorials are among many security narratives that have taken hold in contemporary America, narratives that interpret and explain the dangers facing the nation and, by extension, operate within a certain logic of justification for actions taken by and on behalf of the nation. Their history and analysis is an obvious subject of political science, such as David Campbell's critical reconceptualization of U.S. foreign and domestic policies, discourses of danger, and performative dimensions of national identity.[63] Their sweeping presence suggests just how naturalized fears of danger and imperatives of security have become in contemporary America. Security guards and security alarms are commonplace today, tangible evidence of pervasive fears about safety, vulnerability, and protection. Equity International, a Washington firm engaged in "facilitating the involvement of the corporate sector in homeland and global security," estimated in 2006 that $150 billion would be spent that year alone to "thwart terrorism." Terror is a huge economic opportunity in twenty-first century America, and the "terrorism industry" is cleaning up.[64]

Fears of terrorism have persuaded many Americans to unreservedly support government measures aimed at their security—and simultaneously at curtailing their civil liberties. In 1999, an ABC / *Wall Street Journal* poll found that "loss of personal privacy" was the "Number One concern" among Americans. In 2002, after 9/11 and the climate of fear orchestrated by the departments of state, justice, transportation, and energy, among other federal agencies, 79 percent of those polled cited security as their major worry.[65]

Security narratives aimed at easing those fears are officially addressed by the Department of Homeland Security (the agency responsible for those color-coded terror alerts) and the USA Patriot Act (the acronym for the national policy hurriedly passed by Congress after 9/11 titled "Uniting and Strengthening America by Providing Appropriate Tools Required to Intercept and Obstruct Terrorism Act"). They are unofficially evident—if similarly tolerated and encouraged—in the formation of vigilante groups like the Minuteman Project, a mob of some nine hundred armed "civilian volunteers" who began patrolling the U.S.-Mexico border in 2005 determined to "secure" America from undocumented immigrants. Angry with the slow, if steady, pace of the seven hundred–mile long Border Fence that President Bush authorized in 2006, the Minuteman Project raised $1 million and built their own one-mile wall in Naco, Arizona, in 2007, outfitting it with surveillance cameras and U.S. flags.

Securing the nation's memorials has become a "major concern" of the U.S. Government Accountability Office, which issued a 52-page document on the subject in 2005 calling for actions to "better protect" monuments and federal buildings all over America, especially in Washington. Since 9/11, security "enhancements" have turned the nation's capital into a veritable fortress as hundreds of millions of dollars have been spent to safeguard Washington's "most important buildings and monuments" with armed guards, defensive weapons, concrete barriers, chain-link fences, and surveillance cameras. An antiaircraft missile is positioned atop the New Executive Office Building, across the street from the White House. Memorials on the National Mall are barricaded by concrete blocks (see fig. 4.17, p. 208). A permanent 2.5-foot-tall security wall, which serves as a vehicle barrier and provides visitor seating, circles the Washington Monument. A security barrier that the National Park Service maintains will "provide a first line of defense from the potential threat of a vehicle bomb" and "serve as a deterrent to terrorists" is planned for the Jefferson Memorial.[66] And the steps of the U.S. Capitol—long a site of democratic demonstration—are now off-limits; since 2008, public entrance into the building is through the U.S. Capitol Visitor Center, a massive 580,000-square-foot, 3-level underground space featuring theaters, cafeterias, galleries, gift shops, and 26 restrooms. It seems fitting that the entrance to the Visitor Center's Great Hall features a 19-foot model of *Statue of Freedom*, the sword-and-shield-bearing figure that tops the Capitol's dome and was originally named *Armed Liberty*.

Well before 9/11, of course, many of America's urban, postindustrial public spaces were armed—"fenced off, policed, and privatized"—because of fears of crime, race, and the underclass.[67] Yet today's sweeping fears about terrorism especially delimit the nation's democratic civic spaces, especially in terms of public dissent. As one writer laments, "If it is symbols we are protecting, then what have we lost when older people can no longer stop in at the Jefferson Memorial to read the inscriptions on its curved walls, when every 'people's' monument is walled off by deadened streets and armed militia and long lines of tourists waiting to be wanded?"[68] Like other national capitols and urban centers, Washington is full of surveillance cameras. The Metropolitan Police Department monitors closed-circuit televisions at Union Station and Dupont Circle, and the United States Park Police (a division of the National Park Service) operates surveillance cameras at all of the city's major memorials and throughout the National Mall. Terrorism's possible threat to America's national treasures is used to justify the expense of these and many other "security measures": the U.S. Capitol Visitor Center, jibed "The Big Debt Dig" by the *New York Times*, cost over $621 million, some $150 million of which was spent on security.[69]

Implicit within the narrative of security is the notion that the self and nation are in danger and at risk. Compared to the risk of dying in a car accident in America (until recently, 43,000 annual deaths), from a drug overdose (20,000), or from a firearm (29,000), death by terrorism is negligible. One 2008 report showed that the risk of the average American dying "at the hands of international terrorists [is] comparable to the risk of dying from eating peanuts, being struck by an asteroid, or drowning in a toilet."[70] Yet fear of terrorism persists. As Ulrich Beck explains, fear is a binding agent in today's "risk society," and consensus is shaped in terms of which risks are permissable and which are not. Cars, drugs, and guns are all risks that contemporary Americans will tolerate, perhaps because their use is voluntary and familiar and their impact is perceived on individual terms.[71] But the risk of terrorism, however remote and unlikely, is considered untenable.

Security narratives constitute efforts to control the risk of terrorism, to prevent its repetition, and to restore harmony and order—to "work through" the trauma of terror, among other national insecurities, and generate closure. While anchored in specific historic realities—like the attacks of 9/11—the security narratives implicit in contemporary terrorism memorials focus on explaining and resolving danger through discourses of national unity and order, innocence, survival, and heroic sacrifice. Paradoxically, they also depend on *generating* fear, on feeding crisis and perpetuating national insecurities.

NAMING

Naming is typically used in contemporary memorials to secure understandings of national unity. "Names constitute the first level of the ideology of a civil society organized on the basis of patrilineal descent," Daniel Sherman observes in his study of memory and memorials in interwar France. "The inscription of a name attests to an individual's place in that society, without which a place in history would be literally unthinkable."[72] Naming is an act of claiming, an assertion of inclusion; to be named is to be acknowledged. Modern memorials are thick with names and with other texts. This is testimony to increased levels of public literacy, the bureaucratization of information, and the heightened importance granted to individuals—not just generals and presidents—in the making and meaning of modern history. As Thomas Laqueur recounts, European efforts to mark the graves of soldier dead during World

War I "witnessed the most dramatic explosion of names on a landscape in world history." The Thiepval Memorial to the Missing of the Somme, a massive stone cenotaph designed by Sir Edwin Lutyens, dominates a French battlefield where more than one million soldiers died in 1916. These included some seventy-three thousand British and Allied troops whose bodies were never recovered and whose names are inscribed on the monument's walls.[73]

Names are the building blocks of modern historical narrative, Michel de Certeau argued; indeed, steadily utilized in American commemorative cultures since the Civil War as "democratizing" symbols, names have become absolutely *de rigeur* in memorial mania.[74] Listing the names of America's soldier dead was required in the design competition for the Vietnam Veterans Memorial (for which Lin cites the Thiepval memorial as "the prime inspiration"), and was similarly mandated for the Lockerbie Memorial Cairn, the Oklahoma City National Memorial, and the nation's three major 9/11 memorials. The chronological listing of the names on the Wall was "the heart of the memorial," Lin recalled. Practices of "renaming" are equally prevalent: 40 percent of laws passed by New York's City Council from 2001 to 2003 dealt with renaming various streets (or portions of streets) in homage to 9/11 victims.[75]

Naming is a focal point in contemporary commemoration if also a subject of considerable controversy as questions of who counts (victims *and* perpetrators?), who counts where and when (victims killed immediately on site? those who die later?), and who counts the most (World Trade Center employees? rescue workers?) are hashed out during the design process and even later. The Vietnam Veterans Memorial, for instance, originally listed Dale Buis as that war's first U.S. soldier dead (killed July 8, 1959). But after the memorial was dedicated, the names of U.S. military advisors Harry Cramer (killed in 1957) and Richard B. Fitzgibbon, Jr. (killed in 1956) were added, effectively redating the start of America's historical, if never officially acknowledged, engagement in that military conflict.[76] Naming is one of many points of contention at New York's 9/11 memorial. Plans to randomly list the names of victims on the lower parapets of the monument's pools—in a design Michael Arad called "meaningful adjacencies"—were abandoned after complaints by those who felt that rescue workers should be accorded separate, special status, and by still others who insisted that victims be distinguished according to kinship and company affiliation.

Names are familiar, comforting, and recognizable signs of real people, literal evidence of humanity. As the widow of an airline passenger killed on 9/11 remarked about the Pentagon's memorial, "We will have something that you can touch, something that you can sit on and reflect, something that will just touch your heart because you will want to rub it and feel it and sit there and be able to see the sky. I think it is just one of the most memorable things you can do, just sit on a bench that has my husband's name on it."[77] Naming practices in memorial services, such as reading the names of the dead during a display of the NAMES Project Foundation's AIDS Memorial Quilt, or at anniversary ceremonies of the Vietnam Veterans Memorial (a reading in 2002 took over sixty-five hours), are similarly affective. The visual language of naming in contemporary terrorism memorials counters the shattering disorder of trauma and its silencing pain: names bear witness.

Yet naming is also annalistic, a mechanical practice of notation whereby individuals are counted and collected into groups. Lin remarks about the American soldier dead listed on the Vietnam Veterans Memorial, "These names, seemingly infinite in number, convey the sense of overwhelming numbers, while unifying those individuals into a whole"; Kimmelman describes them as "One nation. One family."[78] Individuality may be partially noted in some memorials: some names on the Wall are preceded by a diamond connoting confirmed dead or a cross designating missing in action. Likewise, each bench in the Pentagon Memorial notes the name and age of its subject. But the methodical collection and inscription of these names, like the formulaic codes of mourning used in the *New York Times*' "Portraits of Grief," speaks to social and political unity. And when names are a memorial's only script, standing alone without the benefit of plot (the story of "how") or moral (the story of "why"), they can be reduced to a deceitful narrative of national consensus—which is how Ronald Reagan read the names on the Wall in 1988.

First individualizing and then unifying, first describing the dead as persons to be mourned and then claiming them as a national body, naming's two-step narrative depoliticizes (or evades) issues of responsibility and simultaneously justifies national imperatives of resolve and retribution. In his discussion of political violence, security narratives, and national identity, Michael Shapiro argues that "by ignoring various forms of disorder within the national imaginary—that is, perpetuating the fantasy of an untroubled and unitary order—practices of violence maintain their ontological function. They operate to protect boundaries between the 'American people' and a dangerous world 'outside,' while the inside is depluralized as a unitary citizen body."[79] Rather than reckoning with the intentionality of terrorism, which aims to violently destabilize political and economic systems deemed exploitative by its perpetrators, naming practices in America's 9/11 memorials frame a unifying narrative of national innocence.

INNOCENCE

Assumptions of innocence have long been central in American national consciousness, guiding self and national imperatives of escape, isolation, and independence. From nineteenth-century narratives of America as the New Eden and Americans as the New Adams to twentieth- and twenty-first-century perceptions of America and Americans as purer, better, and simply more exceptional than anywhere and anyone else, convictions of innocence have prevailed. Such convictions legitimize American blamelessness, liberating the nation and its citizens from a legacy of historical and moral misdeeds, and sustain a state of blissful ignorance, what Lauren Berlant terms "infantile citizenship."[80]

Americans are not unaware of the strained circumstances of their seemingly Adamic character, especially as threats to and attacks on the nation have been repetitiously likened as the "loss" or "end" of American innocence throughout its history. Yet tropes of national innocence persist, permitting a lack of culpability in matters requiring adult moral agency, encouraging a self-righteous consensus that pits American exceptionalism against the rest of the world, and elevating American militarism at the expense of international law and diplomacy. "Nothing in nature is more remarkable, or dangerous, than the recuperative power of innocence in a liberal society," George F. Will cautioned in 1993.[81]

There is, of course, an enormous difference between the persistent trope of national innocence and the actual murder of innocents. The people who died in the bombing of the World Trade Center in 1993 and the Murrah Federal Building in 1995 and the people who were killed in the attacks of 9/11 were absolutely innocent victims of horrific acts of terrorism. Yet, from the moment of their murders, their deaths were manipulated to sustain politicized assumptions of American national innocence and to legitimate national security narratives of revenge and retribution—from the hastily conceived USA Patriot Act to the prolonged war on terror.

Consider, for example, the temporary memorial to Flight 93 (fig. 3.19). Metal railings are covered in handwritten slogans and bumper stickers stating "United We Stand," "America No. 1, Thank God," and "It's Not Just a Flag, It's a Way of Life." Trucks and cars in the parking lot feature magnetic decals stencilled with yellow "remembrance ribbons" and the words "Support Our Troops." As Michael Billig observes, these familiar forms of "banal nationalism" prompt the presence and power of the American state: "daily, the nation is indicated, or 'flagged,' in the lives of its citizenry. Nationalism, far from being an intermittent mood . . .

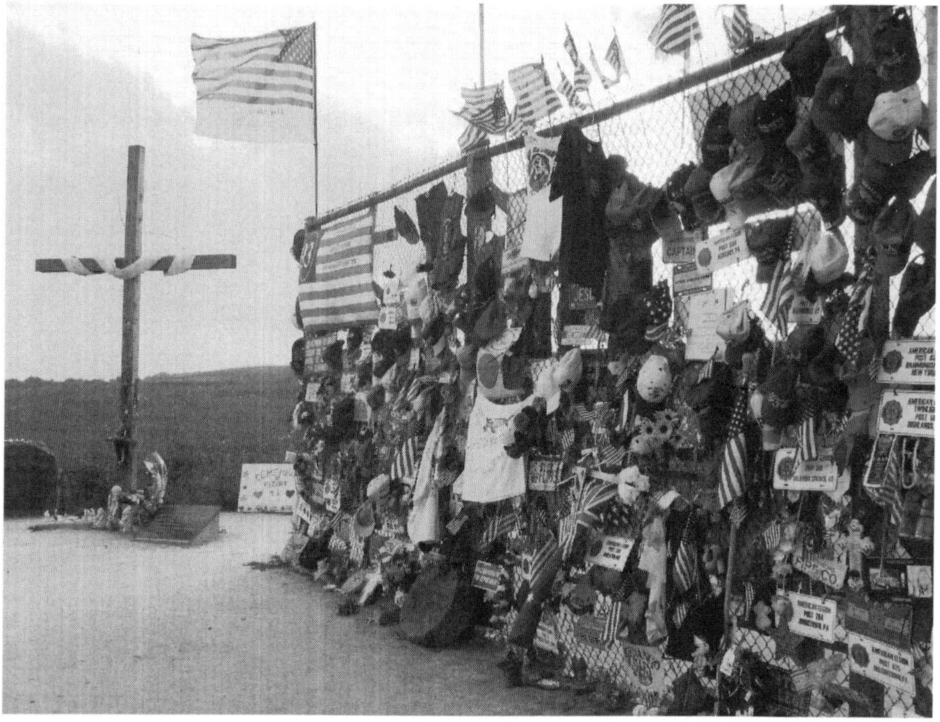

3.19. Temporary memorial dedicated to Flight 93, Shanksville, Pennsylvania, October 2005. (Photo by the author.)

is the endemic condition."[82] At Shanksville, tragic death is remembered in terms of patriotic vengeance, political self-righteousness, and fundamentalist Christianity. Other signs at the site include "Red State Insurgency," "Guns Don't Kill People, Abortion Clinics Kill People," and "Back to the Bible Or . . . Back to the Jungle!" The temporary memorial itself features a large wooden cross flanked by American flags, Christian mementos, and stuffed animals.

Teddy bears—stuffed animals symbolizing comfort and solace—are common motifs at temporary memorials, and Edward Linenthal recounts the many proposals for "teddy bear monuments, teddy bear walls, [and] teddy bear parks" that were submitted for the Oklahoma City National Memorial design competition. In 1995, less than twenty-four hours after the Murrah Federal Building was bombed, rescue workers at the site painted "God bless the children and the innocent" on a concrete slab and surrounded it with flowers, pacifiers, poems, and teddy bears. Daniel Harris similarly noted the "kitschification of September 11" in "the overkill of ribbons and commemorative quilts, haloed seraphim perched on top of the burning towers and teddy bears in firefighter helmets waving flags." Teddy bears are toys, playthings for children, and their use in contemporary American memorials intimates a condescending infantilization of the dead. While nineteen children died in the terrorist attack in Oklahoma City, the majority of those who were murdered were adults. Likewise, the median age of those killed in New York on 9/11 was thirty-seven years (only three children under the age of five years were counted among the dead). Makeshift memorials featuring teddy bears and balloons trivialized their deaths, shielded the public from the ugly horror of how (and why) they died, and perpetuated notions of an inexplicably defiled American innocence. As Harris observes, "The strident sentimentality of kitsch makes the unsaid impermissible and silences dissenting opinions, which cannot withstand the emotional vehemence of its rhetoric."[83]

Permanent terrorism memorials reiterate this by emphasizing narratives of rescue and relief. Survivors and families of victims involved with Oklahoma's memorial and the three major 9/11 memorials insisted, for example, that they address responses to the attacks: the unflagging recovery efforts of firemen and the tremendous generosity of those who donated blood and offered other forms of aid in the days following the attacks. The Flight 93 National Memorial is shaped around a story, mandated in its mission statement and competition guidelines, of "the collective acts of courage and sacrifice of the passengers and crew," who many believe thwarted a planned terrorist attack on the nation's capital.

Preference for these "progressive" narratives is not surprising; commemorating civic generosity and courage is considered a viable means of "working through" the trauma of terrorism and, as Linenthal remarks, "invites people to focus on possibility, opportunity, healing, rebuilding."[84] Yet such narratives rarely acknowledge the specifics of trauma itself, which means that their psychic impact on "working through" is superficial. Some families of those who died on 9/11, for instance, "were adamant" that New York's 9/11 memorial "should not be a 'blow by blow' of what happened on September 11," and "should not be devoted to terrorists or terrorism in general, since they felt that even mentioning the terrorists would dignify their acts."[85] Silencing the agents and actions of terror, terrorism memorials like "Reflecting Absence" substantiate notions of American innocence, absolving the nation from admissions of responsibility and veiling the disordering trauma of terror itself.

Presumptions of national innocence stem from those of national victimization. The United States was repeatedly described as an "innocent victim" following the hijacker bombings of September 11, an interpretation that conflated the murder of innocents with a myth of national innocence. As Noam Chomsky puts it, "we can think of the United States as an 'innocent victim' only if we adopt the convenient path of ignoring the record of its actions and those of its allies."[86] Victimization implies both blamelessness and authenticity; victims are typically understood as unculpable targets whose personal, subjective suffering cannot be questioned. Yet as Allen Feldman observes, "in the realm of political terror, an irony marks the contemporary ontology of victimage: rarely does a pure victim face off with a pure aggressor on the world historical stage." Likewise, Ian Buruma notes that it is "questionable when a cultural, ethnic, religious, or national community bases its communal identity almost entirely on the sentimental solidarity of remembered victimhood. For that way lies historical myopia and, in extreme circustances, even vendetta."[87] The mission statement for New York's 9/11 memorial closes with this directive: "And inspire an end to hatred, ignorance and intolerance." Yet how can a terrorism memorial steeped in historical denial and metaphors of absence, and mastered by motives of rebuilding and revenge, actually inspire these noble objectives?

SURVIVAL

Echoing themes of national unanimity and innocence, a third security narrative operative in today's terrorism memorials is survival. Many memorials are explicitly understood as "safe spaces" created by and on behalf of survivors. Each Memorial Day since the late 1980s, for example, thousands of motorcyclists with the national veterans' group Rolling Thunder, Inc., have traveled to the Vietnam Veterans Memorial to demand a full accounting of U.S. POW/MIA (prisoners of war and soldiers still missing in action) and to address issues of veterans' health care. Their annual pilgrimage has redefined Memorial Day—a national ritual that emerged in both the North and the South after the Civil War and became a federally mandated holiday in 1876—in the nation's capital. While the National Symphony Orchestra typically plays a free concert near the U.S. Capitol, the other end of the National Mall now features Rolling Thunder's deafening engines.

Rolling Thunder's rallies are collective rituals of healing for many Vietnam War veterans.[88] The group has also substantially altered public feelings about the war itself, shifting sentiments of shame, disgust, and humiliation to those of heroism, sacrifice, and survival. Rolling Thunder's name, after all, comes from the brazenly dubbed "Operation Rolling Thunder," the sustained carpet bombing of North Vietnam that the U.S. military began in the mid-1960s. Many POW/MIA booths near the Vietnam Veterans Memorial proclaim America and its soldiers as honorable and innocent victims of that war, selling items that range from the board game Vietnam Survival Tour–365 (which invites players to "experience the emotions and obstacles of the Vietnam foot soldier as you take your men on patrol thru the bush of Vietnam!") to T-shirts that declare, "I Survived the Tet Offensive."

Themes of survival are present, too, at the Oklahoma City National Memorial, whose grounds include the Survivor Tree, an American elm that weathered the 1995 bombing and has since become a symbolic totem of endurance, albeit one that is now encased inside a stone fence. Survival is a defining motif in many terrorism memorials, and many families of survivors insist that they, not just their lost kin, should also be acknowledged. Assumptions of entitlement and ownership are, of course, central to memorial mania, but these demands for recognition suggest how survival—or being a survivor—is increasingly understood as a primary facet of personal identity.

Survival is the core theme, for example, in the multiple memorials funded by the R. A. Bloch Cancer Foundation, each featuring eight life-sized bronze figures navigating a metallic maze that symbolizes "cancer treatments and success" (fig. 3.20; see also fig. 0.7, p. 4). Scattered across the country (the first Bloch Cancer Survivors Park was built in Kansas City, Missouri, in 1989; others are located in Tampa, Baltimore, Cleveland, Omaha, Dallas, Tucson, and San Diego) each memorial occupies about two acres and promotes the foundation's mission of "help[ing] all cancer patients in the process to successfully conquer their disease." Diagnosed with lung cancer in 1978, Richard Bloch (cofounder of the tax preparation outfit H&R Block) devised the parks as testimonials to his own survival (Bloch lived until 2004) and as inspirational places for others. In recent years, Bloch's foundation has funded twenty-eight of the memorials at an average cost of $1 million each. According to the foundation's administrator, funds exist to build at least fifty-two cancer survivor memorials, one in every state of the nation.[89]

Loved by some, detested by others—one critic calls them "McSculptures" for a "sappy, feel-good, über-positive America"—cancer survivor memorials embody the same prevalent, if conflicted, public desires to manage death and dying as embodied in temporary memorials and roadside shrines.[90] As Barbara Ehrenreich argues, cheerful exhortations on surviving cancer circumvent larger and angrier considerations of the multiple environmental conditions that actually cause cancer.[91]

Survival narratives are championed throughout contemporary America—in popular culture (TV shows like *Survivor* and anthems like Reba McEntire's "I'm a Survivor"), in the daily patois of personal life (talking about "surviving divorce"), and in terrorism memorials. If such narratives reify a national ethos of "survival of the fittest," they are rarely

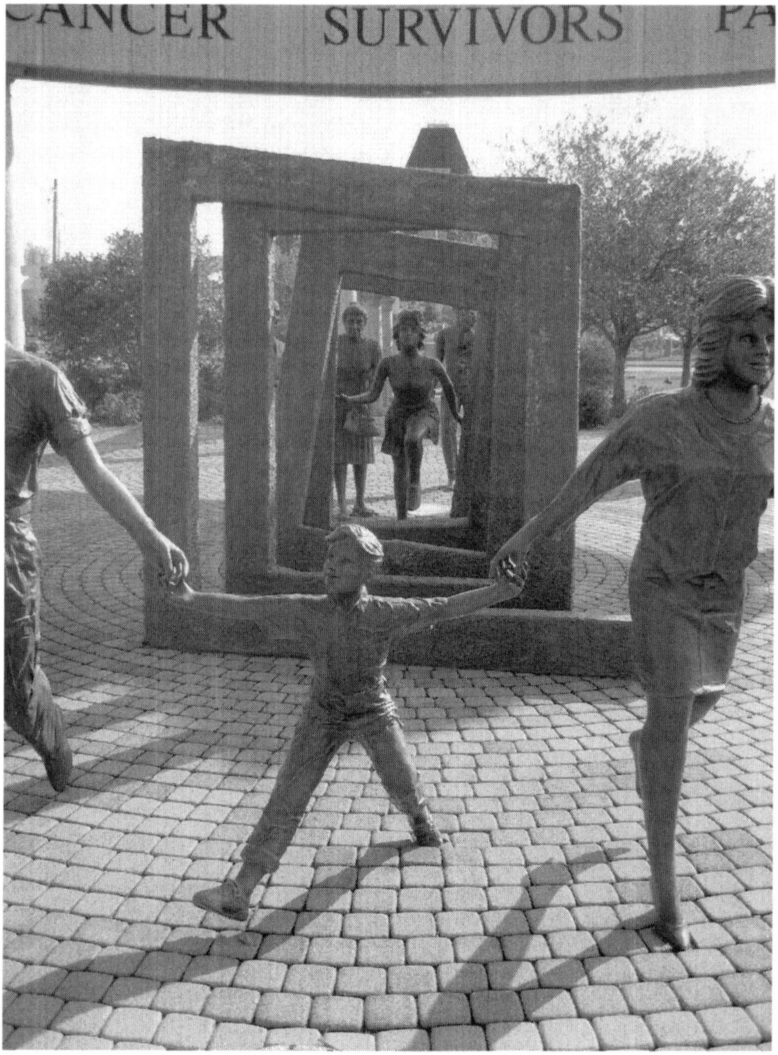

3.20. Victor Salmones, *Cancer . . . There's Hope*, detail, Richard & Annette Bloch Cancer Survivors Park, Indianapolis, Indiana, dedicated 1997. (Courtesy of Lesley A. Sharp.)

inflected by critical considerations of the circumstances that require survival—and the frequently damaging consequences of survival struggles. Rather, survivors are envied and admired for having withstood trauma and victimhood, and survival itself is praised as heroic achievement. Profound distinctions between, for example, surviving the Holocaust, cancer, divorce, a bad job, and a bad romance are conflated as equally triumphant narratives. Most significantly, narratives of heroic endurance affirm the ahistorical incoherence of statements like the one made by President Bush a year after 9/11: "The murder of innocents cannot be explained, only endured." Deliberately obfuscatory, survival rhetoric not only aggravates national anxieties about terrorism but also justifies the repetitious retribution of an "innocent" nation blindly determined to secure itself.

HEROIC SACRIFICE

Hundreds of 9/11 memorials have been built in the United States (and elsewhere, from Christchurch, New Zealand, to São Paulo, Brazil).[92] If stylistically diverse, they share a fourth related security narrative of heroic sacrifice: remembering and honoring the victims of 9/11—and those who endeavored to rescue them—as national heroes. Commemorating the trauma of 9/11 is perplexing in America, because there is no particular memorial vocabulary for the subject of trauma (except perhaps that recently realized in Holocaust memorials). As a result, many 9/11 memorials appropriate the commemorative codes of twentieth-century American war memorials—the U.S. Marine Corps War Memorial, for example—and remember the trauma of terrorism on heroic terms. Memorial mania is overrun with references to heroism—to heroic firefighters, heroic soldiers, heroic national landscapes.

Admittedly, some 9/11 memorials are more modest: plaques that list the names of the dead or groves of trees planted through the Living Memorials Project, an initiative of the U.S. Department of Agriculture Forest Service. But many, especially those that feature pieces of the World Trade Center, focus on national strength, survival, revenge, and sacrifice. New York gave away tons of steel I beams and metal scraps to at least 150 towns, fire departments, churches, and museums anxious to acquire genuine artifacts from Ground Zero. Justifying his city's request for a piece of the Twin Towers, the mayor of Lake Charles, Louisiana, remarked, "Why wouldn't we? 9/11 didn't just happen in New York, it happened to America," adding that "these pieces of history are visible reminders of the tragedy of 9/11" and that his city would "use them as symbols of the strength, determination, and resolve which unites us as one nation, and of our dedication to the principles of liberty and justice for all people."[93] The 9/11 memorial in Naperville, Illinois, similarly features a twisted I beam from the World Trade Center, as well as rubble from the Pentagon and rocks from Shanksville (fig. 3.21). Titled *Freedom Isn't Free*, the memorial honors a Naperville native who died at the Pentagon on 9/11.

For many Americans, the mangled remains of the Twin Towers are potent cultural touchstones that embody national pain and sacrifice, and thereby assume the sacrosanct dimensions of holy relics. "Sometimes

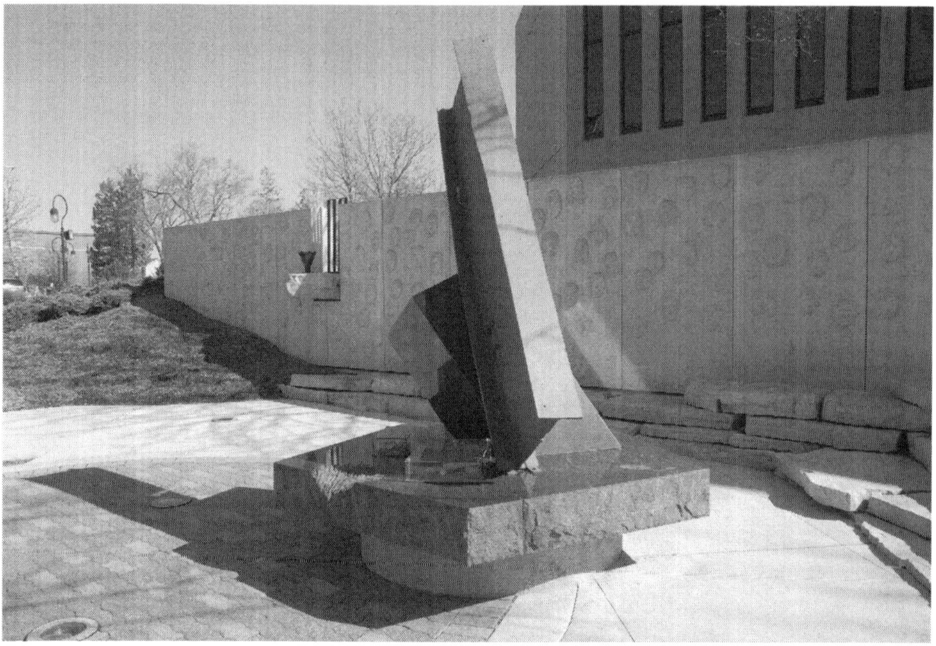

3.21. *Freedom Isn't Free*, 9/11 memorial, Naperville, Illinois, dedicated 2005. (Courtesy of Jonathan Doss.)

it takes a physical reminder to convey the spiritual feeling you have for an incident," said the mayor of Martinez, California, who scored a few pieces of Ground Zero steel for his small town. "It speaks to your soul," he added. Some 9/11 relics have been expressly consecrated: I beams acquired by Sacred Heart Church in Albuquerque were blessed with sacred oil by its Roman Catholic bishop; a two hundred–pound piece of the World Trade Center was installed in the narthex of St. Luke Orthodox Church in Palos Hills, Illinois. In 2007, an exhibition at the New-York Historical Society featured sections of the landing gear from one of the planes that hit the Twin Towers. Positioned on an elegant steel mount, the battered remains looked "like reliquaries," remarked one of the museum's curators.[94]

Sacred symbols of loss and sorrow, elevated from the ordinary to the special, 9/11's venerated relics are further informed by feelings of rage and revenge. As the designers of the Texas State Cemetery September 11 Memorial in Austin forcefully put it: "We want people to feel the relics that were washed in the blood of the innocents. We want people to recognize the horror, understand the sorrow, the righteous wrath, the resolve and remembrance." Plaques supplementing the memorial, which consists of two iron girders salvaged from Ground Zero, feature George W.

Bush's presidential address of October 7, 2001, when he announced the start of Operation Enduring Freedom and stated, "We will not waiver, we will not tire, we will not falter, and we will not fail. Peace and freedom will prevail."[95]

In Austin and elsewhere, 9/11's sacred remains sanction the war on terror. At a Kid Rock concert for U.S. troops in Iraq in 2003, for example, a piece of "recovered metal" from the World Trade Center was passed among soldiers who, one observer relates, "lunged at the opportunity to touch the steel that symbolized what so many of them felt was the purpose of their mission."[96] Likewise, at a pro-war rally held near Ground Zero a month after U.S. Marines toppled the statue of Saddam Hussein in Baghdad (see fig. 0.14, p. 9), New York governor George Pataki admonished the crowd, "Let's melt it down. Let's bring it to New York and let's put it in one of the girders that's going to rise over here as a symbol of the rebuilding of New York and the rebuilding of America." Pataki declared: "The war started here on September 11, 2001."[97] Fusing 9/11 relics with national security imperatives of unity, innocence, survival, and heroic sacrifice, many terrorism memorials blatantly frame 9/11 on militaristic terms.

Some local 9/11 memorials employ a redefined minimalist aesthetic (fig. 3.22). The September 11, 2001 Memorial in Green Bay, Wisconsin, features two thirty-foot stainless steel towers mounted on a pentagon-shaped base inscribed with the names of 9/11 dead, a map of Wisconsin, and the phrases "Peace Through Strength," "Spirit of America," United We Stand," and "Land of the Free, Home of the Brave" (fig. 3.23). Dedicated in 2005, "in loving memory of the known and the unknown, the found and the unfound," the memorial replaced a twenty-two-foot statue of a Green Bay Packer receiver (which was moved down the road to a local brewery). September 11 memorials in places ranging from Belen, New Mexico, to Freehold Township, New Jersey, similarly consist of unmodulated geometrical forms—vertical shafts of marble, quintets of granite—that emulate the Twin Towers and the Pentagon, albeit at miniscule scale..

Still other 9/11 memorials are figurative, couched in an aesthetic of verisimilitude that legitimates their reverential narratives as authentic history. Liza Todd-Tivey's sculpture of a 9/11 rescue dog features a dramatically posed German shepherd on an I-beam, outfitted in protective vest and booties and intently searching for survivors in World Trade Center rubble (fig. 3.24). Erected on the campus of New York's Farmingdale State University in 2005, the eight-foot sculpture includes recovered materials from Ground Zero and commemorates the heroic "willingness and loyalty" of 9/11 rescue personnel, human and animal.

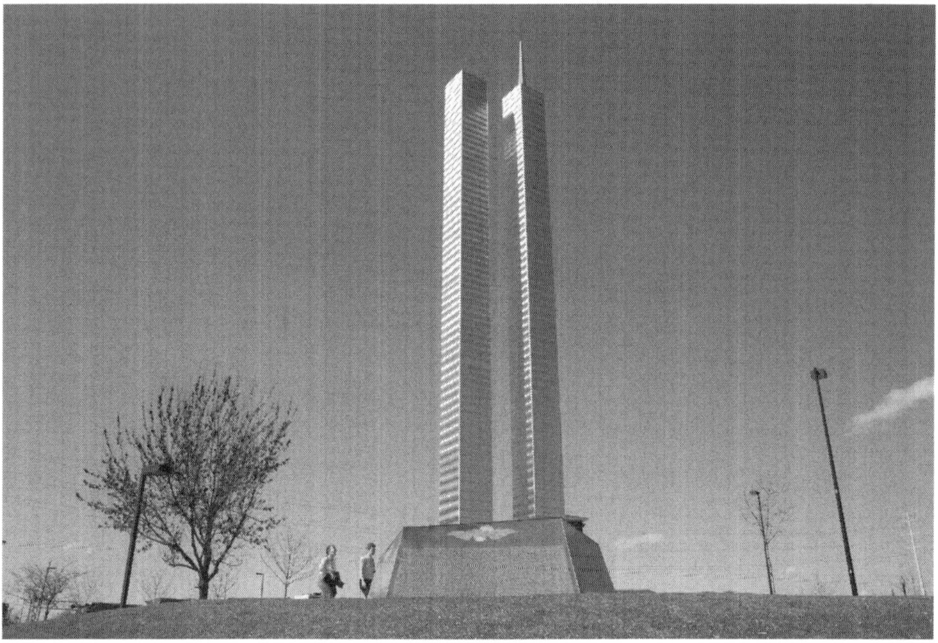

3.22. September 11, 2001 Memorial, Green Bay, Wisconsin, dedicated 2006. (Photo by the author.)

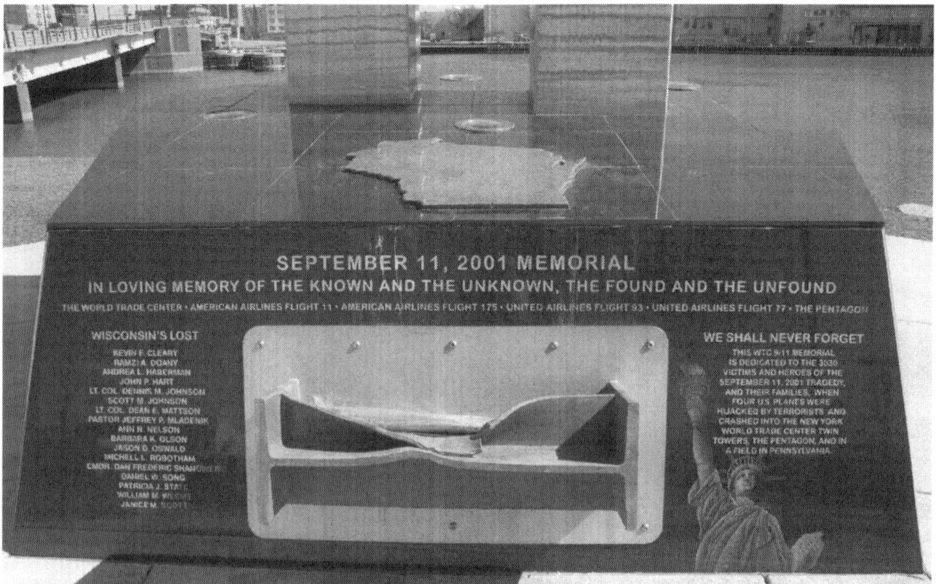

3.23. September 11, 2001 Memorial, detail. (Photo by the author.)

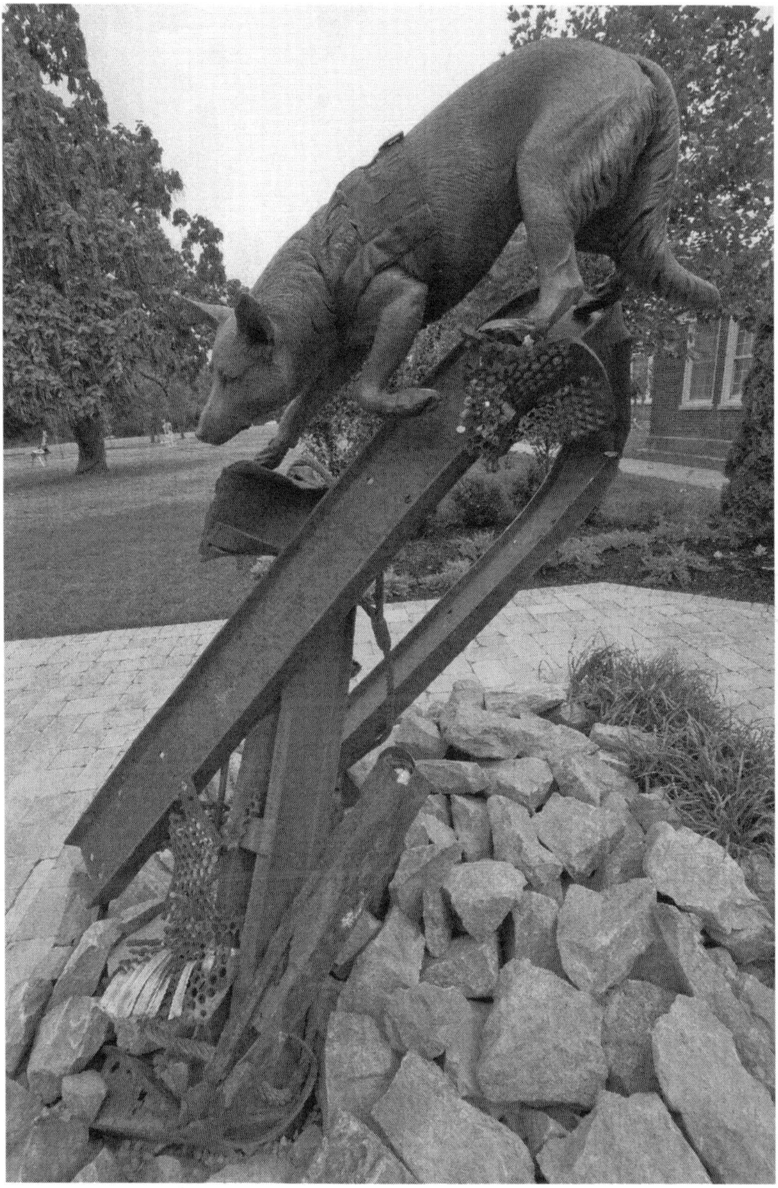

3.24. Liza Todd-Tivey, sculpture in the SUNY Farmingdale 9/11 Memorial Garden, Farmingdale, New York, dedicated 2005. (Courtesy of Liza Todd-Tivey.)

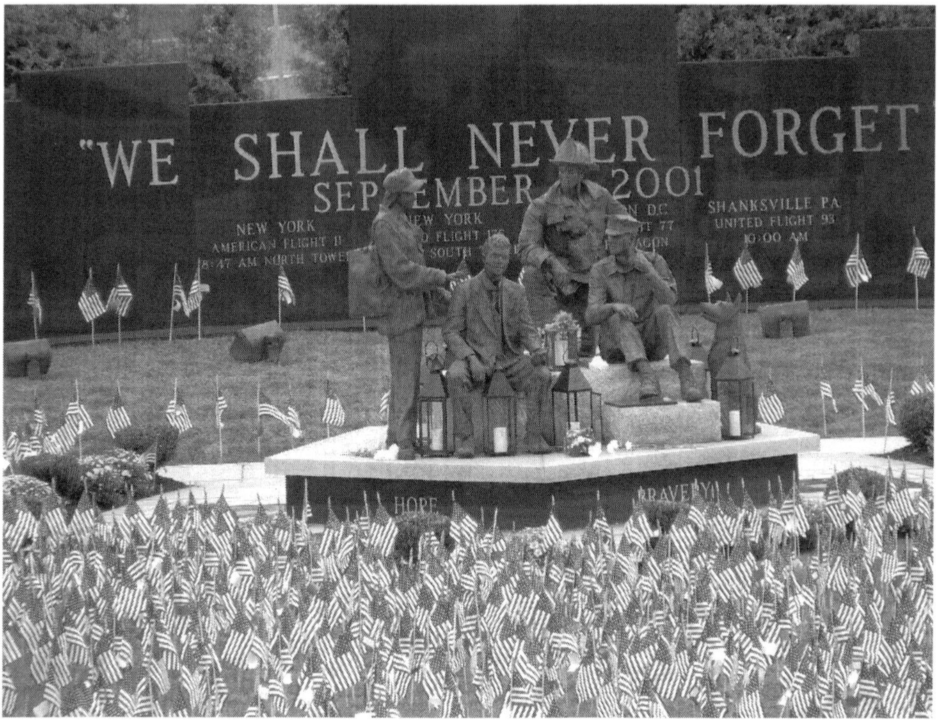

3.25. Brian Hanlon, *We Shall Never Forget*, Pennsauken, New Jersey, dedicated 2004. The flags were placed around the memorial during a 9/11 remembrance ceremony, 2008. (Courtesy of Pennsauken Township.)

Likewise, Brian Hanlon's bronze sculpture *We Shall Never Forget*, dedicated in Pennsauken, New Jersey in 2004, features life-sized figures of a stockbroker on a cell phone, a fireman, police officer, emergency medical technician, and rescue dog, all posed on a pedestal featuring the words "Hope," "Bravery," and "Peace" (fig. 3.25). Hanlon calls the piece a "tribute" rather than a memorial, a portrait of "heroism rather than grief." Nearby walkways are made of "signature pavers" ($95 each), which provide "an opportunity for you to express your respect and love not only for all those who gave their lives on September 11, 2001, but also for those heroes in your life, family or town who have displayed exceptional caring and courage."[98]

These sorts of terrorism memorials suggest that figurative commemorations of 9/11 are firmly attached to themes of heroism, courage, and survival. By contrast, consider *Tumbling Woman* (fig. 3.26), a large bronze of a naked woman in perpetual free fall that Eric Fischl sculpted to honor a friend who worked on the North Tower's 106th floor. Intended for temporary public display on Rockefeller Center's lower level,

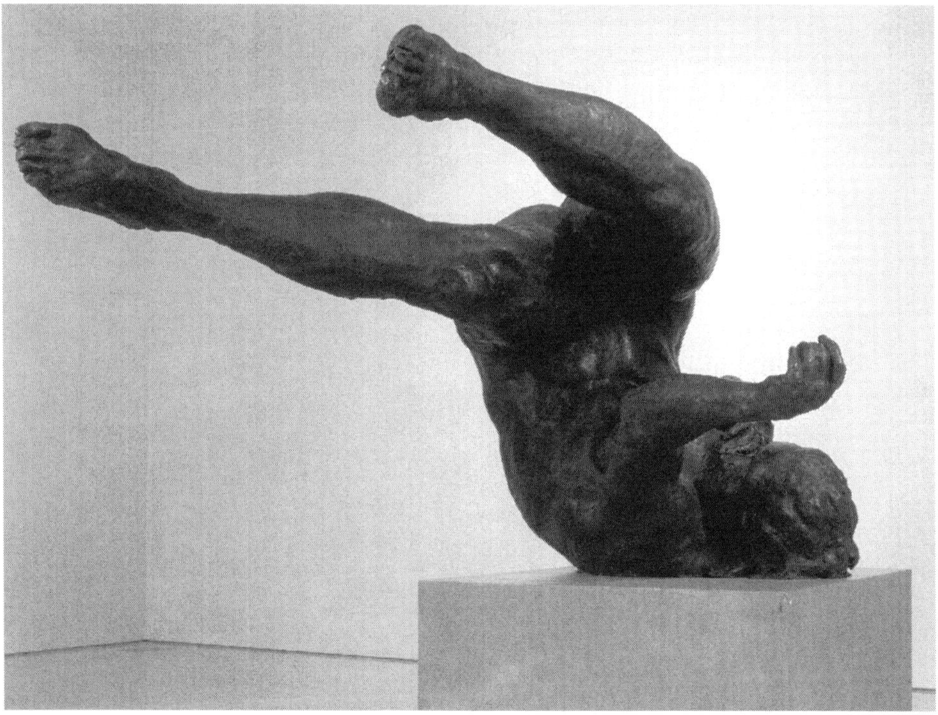

3.26. Eric Fischl, *Tumbling Woman*, 2001–2002. (Courtesy of Eric Fischl Studio.)

Tumbling Woman was seen for just eight days (in September 2002) before it was screened off and then removed for being what one tabloid journalist called "shameful" and "exploitative." In a *New York Times* op-ed titled "A Memorial That's True to 9/11," Fischl observed, "The experience [of 9/11] led me to think about what constitutes an appropriate expression for tragedy. As an artist and an American, one question still preoccupies me: if we cannot face what happened, how can we move past it?" Yet his portrait of vulnerability and loss—and the actual circumstances of death for hundreds of people who fell or jumped from the Twin Towers—was deemed aberrant in a post-9/11 America that prefers narratives of heroic rescue and survival.[99]

Some terrorism memorials eulogize 9/11's "first responders," as police, firefighters, and emergency medical workers are now called. As Elaine Tyler May observes, contemporary anxieties about national security have not only "created new heroes among fire fighters and law enforcement officials" but have revitalized cold war gender constructions of "heroic men and dependent women." One-third of those who died in the World Trade Center were female, a number which includes several female first responders. But most 9/11 memorials reify "an image of reinvigorated manhood."[100] In a time of war on terror, that image is hardly surprising; like the "standing soldier" memorials produced in the latter decades of the nineteenth century, 9/11 memorials starring all-male first responders help bang the drums of war and inspire patriotic fervor. Like the national memorial to the *Titanic* erected in Washington in 1931, they discount the gendered facts and figures of victimization in deference to ennobling themes of heroic male sacrifice.

Many 9/11 memorials promote an American civil religion of blood sacrifice, whereby patriotic sacrificial imperatives (such as dying for the flag) are naturalized as key elements of national unity. Sacrifice is typically understood in terms of bonding and cleansing, as a way to both create community and flush it of sin and trauma.[101] Consider the mission statement for Freedom's Flame, a 9/11 memorial proposed in Rancho Cucamonga, California: "The character of a nation is defined by the combined strength of her people; a strength forged and tempered in freedom's flame. The supreme sacrifice of the men and women dedicated to public safety and the victims of the World Trade Center Attack, when consumed by freedom's flame only serve to steel the resolve and strengthen the character of America."[102] Likewise, Flight 93's temporary memorial resonates with blood sacrifice sentiment—bumper stickers declaring "God Bless the Heroes of Flight 93" and signs stating "93: You Made Us Believe in Heroes." Other offerings at the site include a wooden plaque left by the Sandberg family of Elyria, Ohio, that proclaimed "We Will Never Forget Your Sacrifice So That Others May Live" and an image of an airplane framed by the words "The Heroes of Flight 93 Will Never Be Forgotten! Pennsylvania is Proud of Its 40 New Residents" (see fig. 3.19, above).

Turning victims into heroes and martyrs is a long-standing national practice—as the popular narrative of Davy Crockett's demise at the Alamo illustrates—and victims of terrorism are remembered today on similar terms.[103] On September 11, 2003, the House of Representatives passed the True American Heroes Act, posthumously awarding Congressional medals to every government employee who died in the World Trade Center and the Pentagon on 9/11, as well as to every passenger and crew member who died aboard Flight 93. In 2005, Rep. Mark Kirk (R-IL) introduced the American Heroes Act, authorizing a national Flight 93 statue and fifty additional "American hero statues," one from every state in the nation, to be displayed in the new underground U.S. Capitol Visitor Center.

This veneration of American victims as American heroes and sacrifice as a means to unite the country and purge it of trauma is problematic not just because it diminishes truly heroic acts but because it denies the historical realities of victimization. In both political and memorial cultures, those killed by terrorism are not remembered as murder victims but as freedom fighters and national martyrs, as the price all Americans must pay to defend the American way of life. Blood sacrifice is understood as an essential component of American citizenship and belonging.

The mission statement for Flight 93's permanent memorial sustains the theme of heroic national sacrifice: "May all who visit this place remember the collective acts of courage and sacrifice of the passengers and crew, revere this hallowed ground as the final resting place of those heroes, and reflect on the power of individuals who choose to make a difference."[104] So do books like *Hero of Flight 93* and *Among the Heroes: United Flight 93 and the Passengers and Crew Who Fought Back* (both published in 2002), and movies like *Let's Roll: The Story of Flight 93* (2002) and *United 93* (2006). Speaking at Shanksville on September 11, 2002, Department of Homeland Security head Tom Ridge said "America is grateful" to the forty victims who "won the first battle" in the war on terror, adding, "Faced with the most frightening circumstances one could possibly imagine, they met the challenge like citizen soldiers, like Americans."[105]

Flight recordings suggest that the passengers and crew of Flight 93 did band together to foil the terrorists who had seized their plane. Yet, "Let's roll," the legendary call to arms announced by one passenger and later used by President Bush to justify U.S. bombing in Afghanistan, was probably, the 9/11 Commission later found, the phrase "roll it," referring to moving an aisle-blocking airplane service cart. Not all of those murdered on Flight 93 were American citizens (one passenger was from Germany, another was from Japan). Yet Ridge's phrase "citizen soldiers" aligned them with the U.S. troops celebrated in Steven Ambrose's popular history of World War II (*Citizen Soldiers*, 1997), and, framing the war on terror as a similarly "good" war, collectively cast them as American heroes.[106]

To be sure, heroic response to danger—rather than passive acceptance—is a preferred personal and national narrative. As John J. Reynolds, the chairman of the Flight 93 National Memorial Advisory Commission, stated in 2005, "The most important lesson we can learn from the passengers and crew of Flight 93 is that positive action must be taken in the face of adversity."[107] Or as the Department of Homeland Security announced in its extensive "Ready" campaign in 2002: "Terrorism forces us to make a choice. Don't be afraid . . . Be ready."[108] Yet sweeping assumptions of collective courage undermine the actual heroic acts of individuals and reinforce assumptions of blameless national innocence. There is nothing heroic about being murdered in a terrorist bombing or aboard a hijacked airplane. To suggest otherwise is to spin the murder of innocents and victims into the martyrdom of self-sacrificing citizens and to justify their deaths as the highest call of American patriotism.

This, of course, is how terrorism memorials operate. Still, heated public debates about these memorials, evident in competing notions of their political, social, and psychological efficacy, suggest the unresolved terms of national identity and purpose they presumably embody.

MANAGING TERROR'S MEMORY

The first World Trade Center memorial was erected less than two years after the building was attacked in 1993. The Oklahoma City National Memorial was dedicated five years after the 1995 bombing of the Murrah Federal Building. The Pentagon Memorial was dedicated on September 11, 2008. Today, the United States is dotted with hundreds of 9/11 memorials, with many more in the works. This urgency to commemorate the victims of terrorism stems from pressure to control the meaning of terrorism and to manage its traumatic memory. Like Congressional authorization just three days after 9/11 permitting presidential use of "all necessary and appropriate force" against terrorism and swiftly approved security narratives such as the USA Patriot Act, terrorism memorials reproduce the rapid assertion, or reassertion, of national authority following the extremist acts that threaten that authority.[109] Yet managing terrorism's memory is beset by competing claims over its meaning, and its commemoration.

Today, the National Park Service is charged with managing many of America's memorials, a task that has evolved from the federal agency's original, if conflicted, mandate to both preserve and make public the nation's "spectacular nature," such as Yellowstone and the Grand Canyon.[110] Created in 1916 (after the U.S. Department of the Interior had already designated 14 national parks and 21 national monuments), the NPS now oversees 392 "units," including national parks, monuments, nature preserves, historical parks, historic sites, historic trails, battlefields, military parks, cemeteries, and national memorials. (It also manages 2,500 National Historic Landmarks and 79,000 properties listed on the National Register of Historic Places.) The NPS's "Proud Partnerships" with corporations including American Airlines, Kodak, and Ford (which helped fund the Rosie the Riveter / World War II Home Front National Historical Park in Richmond, California) illustrates the fluidity of public and private modes of cultural management today. Its management of a particular memorial guarantees the national importance of its story.

NPS rangers manage the Oklahoma City National Memorial almost every day of the year, and the memorial itself is accessible, free of charge,

24 hours a day. The site includes a 30,000 square-foot Memorial Museum (owned and operated by the Oklahoma City National Memorial Foundation), which charges a $10 admission fee and features hundreds of artifacts and photographs, interactive computers, lecture halls, a Memorial Store, and the 4,000 square-foot climate-controlled Memorial Archives containing items culled from Memory Fence. The museum's 10-chapter "storyline," which runs from "Confusion" and "Chaos" to "Remembrance and Rebuilding" and "Hope," narrates the physical devastation of Timothy McVeigh's act of terrorism (although he and his partner Terry Nichols are mentioned only briefly in exhibition text panels) and the 16 days of rescue and recovery operations that followed. The museum also features a Gallery of Honor, which displays photographs and personal belongings of those killed in the bombing. The memorial's third component is the Memorial Institute for the Prevention of Terrorism, a nonprofit "counterterrorism center focused on training, analysis and information sharing in the prevention of terrorist attacks."[111] The Institute's library features the Terrorism Memorial Flag, a 60-foot-by-35-foot banner made from 4,000 cross-stitched squares listing the names of Americans killed in "acts of terrorism" during the last 30 years.

By most accounts, the making of Oklahoma City's memorial was an inclusive grassroots effort; indeed, Linenthal describes it as an "ingeniously designed model of community consensus building." Within weeks of the bombing, mayor Ron Norick appointed a 350-member Memorial Task Force that included survivors, families of victims, and "volunteers with expertise in areas ranging from mental health, law, and the arts, to fund-raising, business, communications, and government." In 1996, the group adopted the memorial's mission statement. "Our process is not like other memorial processes," the chairman of the Oklahoma City Memorial Foundation declared in 1997. "This is one that has transcended that and become intentionally part of the healing process."[112] Kathleen Treanor, whose four-year old daughter and in-laws were killed in the bombing, writes that she was initially skeptical about a memorial: "At that time I did not believe that a memorial should be built and if one was built how could they know how to best honor the memory of people they did not know. I knew that Luther and LaRue [her in-laws] would not have wanted a conspicuous statue erected in their honor. They weren't that kind of people."[113] Eventually, Treanor became involved with the memorial, co-chairing its Family and Survivors Committee and helping to draft its mission statement.

The consensus that was reached framed the memorial within select narratives of morality, national unity, and civic revitalization. McVeigh's problematic status as a decorated Gulf War veteran-turned-terrorist was deflected by the commemoration of Oklahoma City's "good" citizens, such as its first responders. As Oklahoma governor Brad Henry stated on the eleventh anniversary of the bombing: "The legacy of April 19, 1995, is goodness overcoming evil. That's what we must remember."[114] Likewise, local interests in healing were largely absorbed by the memorial's overtures to national unanimity. Its dedication ceremony on April 19, 2000, included the Pledge of Allegiance, "God Bless America," and other ritualistic evocations of national fealty. President Clinton intoned in his dedication address, "There are places in our national landscape so scarred by freedom's sacrifice that they shape forever the soul of America—Valley Forge, Gettysburg, Selma. This place is such sacred ground."[115]

Television helped to orchestrate the sacred national meaning of Oklahoma City's terrorist bombing; CNN's coverage of this media event massaged public feelings, generated consensus about what happened, and manipulated feelings of national kinship. Concurrently, business leaders and politicians agreed to promote Oklahoma City as a national tourist destination. The evening after the bombing, "We Will Be Back" was spray painted on a nearby building—a sentiment that inspired the exhibition We Will Be Back: Oklahoma City Rebuilds at the National Building Museum in Washington, D.C., later that year. Within weeks of the bombing, urban design professionals began tackling the town's dingy central business district with an ambitious plan of historic preservation, civic renewal, and $52 million in federal funding. Despite protests about closing Fifth Street, a key thoroughfare for locals, the street was shut to vehicle traffic in deference to new assumptions (especially among the families of victims) of the area as sacred national ground—and to allow for an anticipated increase in tourism.[116]

Oklahoma City's memorial is clean and well-ordered, much like the "new" Oklahoma City that has formed, phoenixlike, from the ashes of McVeigh's bomb. Its 168 chairs are generally empty, a common symbol of loss and honor. In Christian religious cultures an empty chair signifies both Christ's absence and the possibility of his return "in the person of an unexpected guest." In funeral parades a riderless horse pays tribute to fallen leaders—in 1870, Traveller followed the caisson bearing Robert E. Lee's casket, his saddle draped with black crepe. In other ceremonies a vacant seat honors missing loved ones and / or dead comrades. In 1993, Karen Finley performed *The Vacant Chair*, a memorial to friends dead from AIDS that featured two chairs, one empty and one covered in flowers.[117] In 2003, President Bush's State of the Union address featured an empty chair in the presidential box, a symbol, according to the White House, of "the empty place many Americans will always have at their tables and in their lives because of the attacks on Sept. 11, 2001."

The chairs in the Oklahoma City National Memorial are usually roped off, preventing visitors from leaving offerings or even touching them; they are also made of materials that hardly invite visitors to sit. If their emptiness evokes loss, it also intimates silence. Chairs are generally sites of spontaneous, animated discourse—grouped around dinner or seminar tables, for example—but this memorial's seats are lined up in nine immutable rows. Avoiding contact with one another, they fail to evoke conversations among those who visit; facing a reflecting pool, they gaze upon themselves in an unending loop. The memory of terrorism is managed in this memorial through a narcotizing narrative of "comfort, strength, peace, hope and serenity," the words inscribed on its Gates of Time. Searching for more intimate forms of meaning, some visitors dip their fingers in the reflecting pool and leave their handprints on the metallic surfaces of its monumental gates.

Managing memory at the nation's major 9/11 memorials has been more contentious. Debra Burlingame's fury about "turning ground zero into a playground for culture and art" inspired Take Back the Memorial, an alliance of 9/11 family members. In a petition signed by forty-nine thousand people and sent to Governor Pataki, Mayor Bloomberg, and the Lower Manhattan Development Corporation, the group proclaimed: "We, the undersigned, believe that the World Trade Center Memorial should stand as a solemn remembrance of those who died on September 11th, 2001, and not as a journey of history's "failures" or as a debate about domestic and foreign policy in the post-9/11 world. Political discussions have no place at the World Trade Center September 11th Memorial."[118]

In 2004, the Lower Manhattan Development Corporation invited arts organizations to compete for inclusion at the new World Trade Center site; in 2005 it selected 4 groups (from 113 submissions) including the Drawing Center (a graphic arts gallery) and the International Freedom Center, a proposed museum which envisioned itself as a "living memorial" to "worldwide struggles for freedom." But when angry criticism arose about the International Freedom Center —namely, that its geopolitical ambitions might undermine 9/11's heroic national narrative, as Burlingame put it, "of decency triumphing over depravity," Governor Pataki evicted it from the memorial's sacred ground. (Facing similar attacks, the Drawing Center withdrew from the site in August 2005.) Although he admitted that freedom was "not inconsistent with the goals of memorializing our nearly 3,000 lost heroes," Pataki nevertheless found a museum focused on freedom inappropriate for Ground Zero. Less convinced, Mayor Bloomberg expressed disappointment that developers, designers, politicians, and citizens "were not able to find a way to

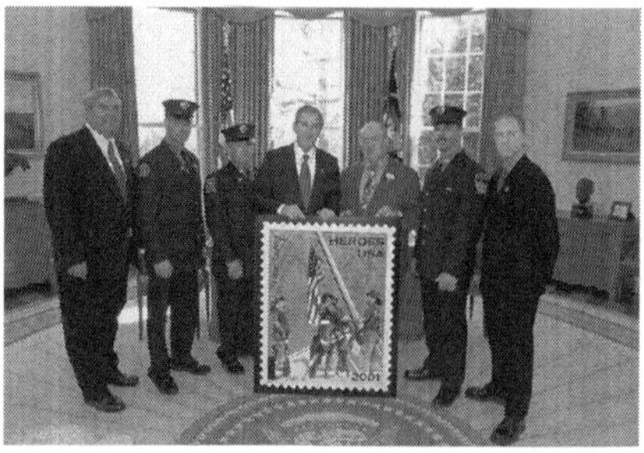

3.27. This stamp unveiling on March 11, 2002, reunited the firefighters who raised the flag with the photographer who took the photo. (Courtesy of the U.S. White House.)

reconcile the freedoms we hold so dear with the sanctity of the site." Emboldened by victory, Take Back the Memorial (the "Grief Police," as *New York* magazine called them) vowed to take back *all* of the memorial and "preserve as much of Ground Zero as possible as a battlefield."[119]

Battles over New York's 9/11 memorial have raged since 9/11 and are, of course, deeply politicized by competing notions of who and what to remember. Initially, 9/11 generated a sweeping sense of national unity; glued to their TVs and their computers, Americans were unable to stop looking at repeatedly visualized images of crashing planes and dark clouds of smoke. Such images shaped a national narrative of fear that cast all Americans as traumatized participants in a three-act performance: first, as the victims and / or survivors of an attack on the nation; second, as rescuers responding to the tragedy through collective demonstrations of help and generosity (offers of aid, money, blood); and finally, as flag-waving patriots vowing revenge. Yet even as the third act was being staged, national unity began to disintegrate as some Americans began to ask why 9/11 had happened and questioned the government's response—such as the quick manufacture of the USA Patriot Act. Today, while the shocking imagery of 9/11 remains fixed (and festishized) in American national consciousness, there is no shared narrative about 9/11 itself, which means that its representation is contested.

Consider the conflict over representing New York's first responders. Early plans involved commemorating the 343 firefighters who died at the World Trade Center with a monumental bronze statue based on newspaper journalist Thomas E. Franklin's photo of three of them hoisting an American flag: 9/11's version of Iwo Jima's iconic flag-planting moment (fig. 3.27). But these plans were scuttled because the proposed $180,000 statue showed them on multiracial terms (white, Hispanic, and black), rather than the all-white guys they really were (like 94 percent of New York's Fire Department). Bombarded with complaints of "political correctness" and "rewriting history," the FDNY and donor / developer Bruce Ratner, who had said he wanted to pay tribute to *all* the firefighters who died on 9/11 (including 24 people of color), withdrew the commission. The heroic trio said they were "disappointed" that the memorial had "become something that is political as opposed to historical."[120]

Becoming something crassly commercial, however, was just fine: the vast merchandizing of Franklin's photo drew little to no debate, save that among lawyers for the three firefighters and for Franklin's newspaper haggling over issues of intellectual property and profit. Reproduced on T-shirts, teddy bears, snowboards, Christmas ornaments, humidors, pocket watches, pocket knives, bank checks, jigsaw puzzles, pajamas, phone cards, and a 45-cent U.S. postage stamp, the image was also recreated by Madame Tussaud's Wax Museum in a multimedia extravaganza called Tribute to the Heroes of 9/11, which opened in 2002 in Times Square and then traveled to several theme parks. For high-end customers, forty-inch bronzes of the flag-hoisting firefighters, $10,000 each and titled *To Lift a Nation*, were available from sculptor Stan Watts—who also made a Firefighters Memorial Monument for the city of Brockport, New York, and designed a "colossal bronze monument" of the same subject for the National Fallen Firefighters Foundation Memorial in Emmitsburg, Maryland.[121]

As Marita Sturken observes, the attacks of 9/11 "produced a frenzied consumer response to the fear of terrorism, enabling a widespread consumerism of security." Endlessly commodified, Franklin's photo was the "unrivalled icon of 9-11," remarks Kari Andén-Papadopoulus, celebrating "the victorious resurrection of the American nation, born again, innocent but hard. The flag-raising by men in uniform gives notice to the world that Americans stand united and eternally ready to ensure their hegemony—by force of arms, if necessary."[122] Yet controversy over an all-white representation of that "hegemony" reveals the unsettled terms of how 9/11 is remembered and managed.

Since it was selected in 2004, "Reflecting Absence" has been deeply controversial among some 9/11 families and survivors who feel that the memorial's soothing design ignores their personal trauma. "Family members desire a memorial that incorporates the iconic elements of the fallen towers: the twisted metal beams that resembled a crucifix and the jagged skin of the north tower," one journalist observes. Former Metropolitan Museum of Art director Philippe de Montebello suggested that New York's 9/11 memorial feature the bent ruins of the World Trade Center's façade: "Already an icon, it should stand forever as a sculptural memorial." Yet ruins have never held much of a presence in America. Typically seen as symbols of loss and defeat, ruins do not cohere, J. B. Jackson observed, in a national landscape informed by notions of progress and reinvention.[123] Even local 9/11 memorials that incorporate sacred debris from the World Trade Center and the Pentagon supplement these ruined bits of steel and stone with visual and textual references to national strength, solidarity, and endurance. However much the members of Take Back the Memorial want New York's 9/11 monument to commemorate their personal pain, "Reflecting Absence" is anchored to a national narrative of triumph.

Yet the hegemony of that narrative, like American nationalism itself, is never fixed, and the design of New York's 9/11 memorial has been repeatedly altered. In 2006, protests about the random naming of 9/11 victims led to a new design separating firefighters and police officers from Twin Towers employees and partitioning the names of the dead at Shanksville and the Pentagon. Some still found this arrangement lacking; as the manager of a relief fund established for financial firm Cantor Fitzgerald, which lost 685 employees on 9/11, stated, "You'll know from this memorial who died at the Pentagon, who died on Flight 175, and who was a firefighter. Why do civilians not deserve the same respect and remembrance?" Others demanded the commemoration of post-9/11 employees and rescue workers who died because of dust exposure at the site.[124]

Still others protested the subterranean design of "Reflecting Absence." "This does total dishonor to the lives and deaths of these people by burying this under the ground. It's so insulting," declared Sally Regenhard, mother of a firefighter killed on 9/11. "We ask that the memorial see the light of day and not be hidden in the shadows," demanded the president of the Patrolmen's Benevolent Association at a February 2006 rally. "Those who made the ultimate sacrifice should be raised up," reiterated the president of the Detectives' Endowment Association. Issues of security were also, rather predictably, raised. The fact that New York's 9/11 memorial is intended as a huge public gathering space makes it vulnerable to terrorism, stated Governor Pataki's senior advisor for counterterrorism, who subsequently urged memorial designers to add "elements that significantly reduce the opportunity for a satchel charge explosive or airborne contaminant dissemination device."[125]

Anxieties about New York's memorial are heightened by the huge financial stakes in its design, construction, and operation. While the nation's three major 9/11 memorials are partially funded by federal dollars, they all depend on substantial private donations. The Pentagon memorial was sponsored in part by Anheuser Busch ($1 million), Boeing ($500,000), and Wal-Mart ($500,000), and the Flight 93 memorial is supported by donors including Outback Steakhouse ($2 million), Federal Express ($1 million), and 10 percent of the opening weekend gross for Universal Pictures' *United 93* (which came to $1.6 million). Funding for

New York's 9/11 memorial is promised by the Starr Foundation ($25 million), Deutsche Bank ($15 million), American Express, Bank of America, Cantor Fitzgerald, Con Edison, Merrill Lynch, and J.P. Morgan Chase Foundation ($10 million each), Bear Stearns, General Electric, and the Walt Disney Company Foundation ($5 million each), among others. The Port Authority of New York and New Jersey (which owned the Twin Towers) is charged with supporting infrastructure costs at the site. And H&R Block, sued by New York's attorney general in 2006 for fraudulent business practices in its management of retirement accounts, teamed up with New York's 9/11 memorial to promote state tax contributions. Fundraising has not been helped, memorial staffers allow, by the acrimonious protests of groups like Take Back the Memorial. Indeed, the enormous cost of New York's 9/11 memorial has led to the likelihood of an admission fee akin to those paid at some other memorials and at New York museums ($20 per adult at the Museum of Modern Art). This has prompted angry charges by some 9/11 families and survivors that the public will have to "pay to grieve."[126]

The public has already, of course, paid plenty. By 2004, the federal Victim Compensation Fund had delivered $7 billion to the families of those killed or injured on September 11, at an average of more than $2 million tax-free per person.[127] Other victims of terrorism—at the World Trade Center in 1993 and at Oklahoma City in 1995, for example—did not receive such public awards. Yet for some 9/11 families, monetary compensation is only a portion of what they feel they are entitled to at Ground Zero. In an April 2006 *New York Times* op-ed, for example, former firefighter Dennis Smith demanded the immediate "confiscation of the World Trade Center site under the eminent domain clause," adding: "It is our property. We should get it back." Discounting the site's role in New York's economy and its symbolic meaning in the nation, such demands are typical among Take Back the Memorial stakeholders—a small handful of people, actually—who insist that their personal trauma privileges their management of 9/11's memory and memorialization.[128]

If politicians have yielded to these rights claims, they have also generated critical backlash, including Michael Kimmelman's assertion that Ground Zero's "only hope" is to "give the populist experiment a rest." David Stanke angrily writes, "Enough is enough. It is time to erect a firewall around the ground zero memorial quadrant. Whatever else happens on that land, the rest of the WTC site must be free of any control randomly selected by victims' families." By 2007, "9/11 fatigue," growing public weariness with the cost and commitment of commemorating September 11, was reported. Challenges to 9/11's national dominance, especially after

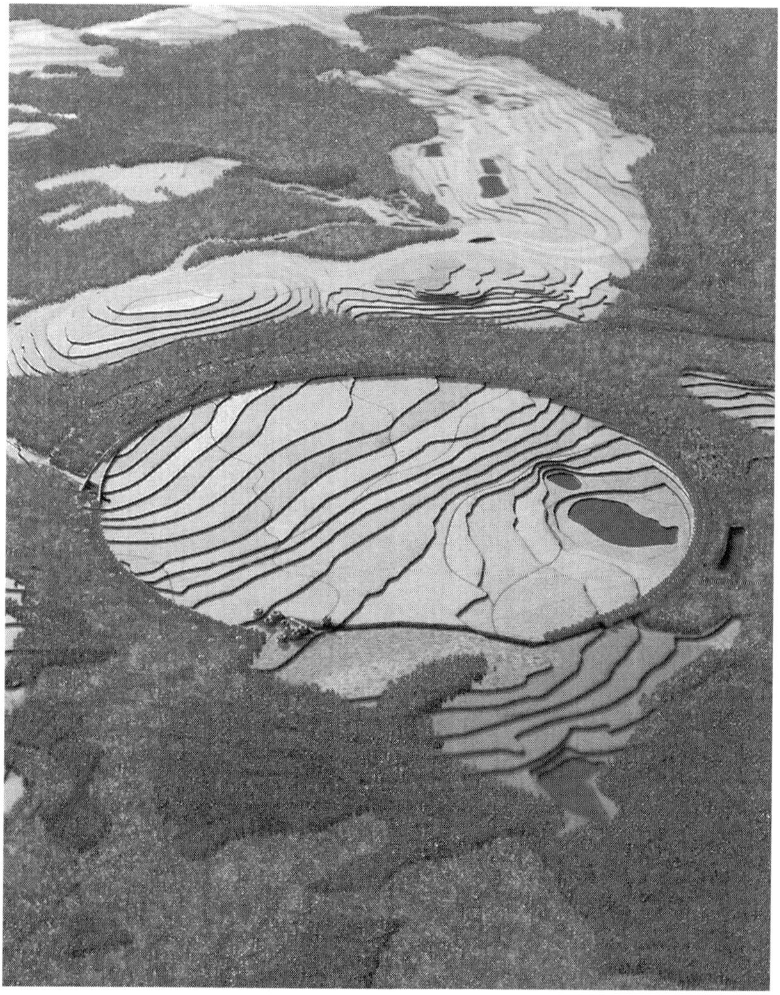

3.28. The Field of Honor, Flight 93 National Memorial. This was originally called the Crescent of Embrace. (Drawing courtesy of Paul Murdoch Architects and Aleksander Novak-Zemplinski.)

other national traumas like Hurricane Katrina, were also noted.[129] Even before the economic downturn of 2007–2008, funds raised for the nation's major 9/11 memorials began to decline.

In Pennsylvania, terrorism memorial management has also been fraught. Paul Murdoch's original plans for the Flight 93 National Memorial included the Crescent of Embrace, a grove of red maples planted in a bowl-shaped vale (fig. 3.28). Some paranoid blogospherists however, said the design was a "jihadist" symbol of "Islamo-fascist religious ideology" and called the entire memorial a "terrorist memorial mosque."

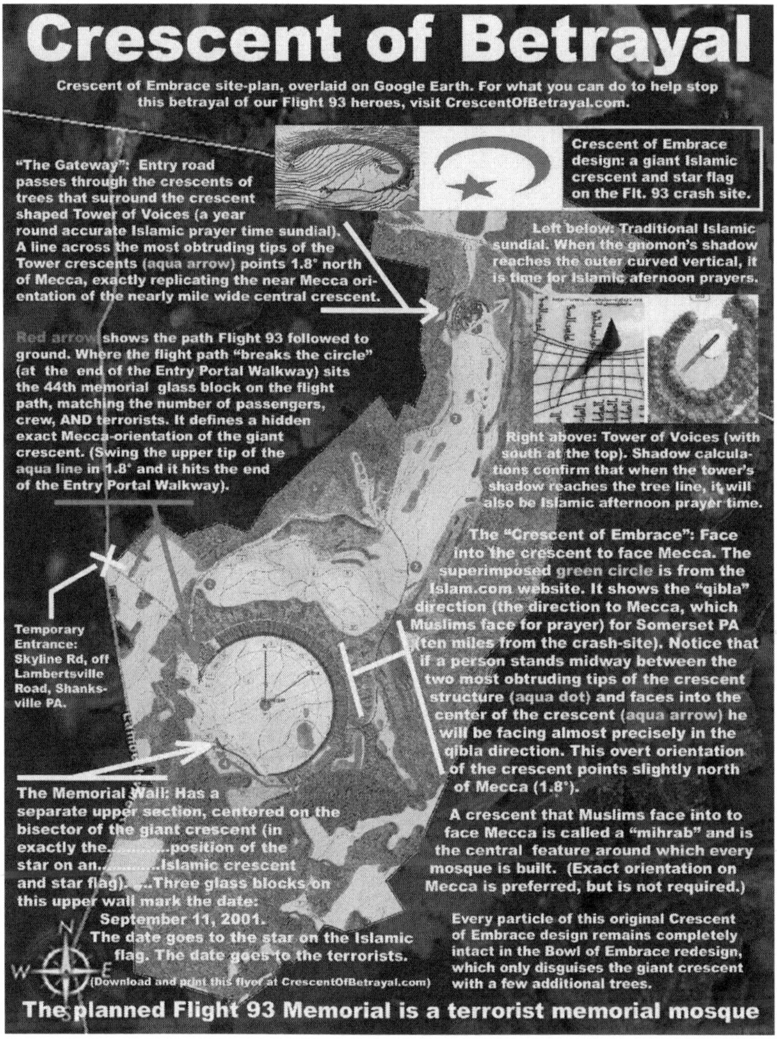

3.29. Alec Rawls, "Crescent of Betrayal," 2007. This flyer protesting the Flight 93 National Memorial can be found at http://www.crescentofbetrayal.com/.

At Error Theory, Alec Rawls posted topographical maps and polar coordinates "proving" that the Crescent of Embrace was "pointed toward Mecca" and the memorial's Tower of Voices was, in fact, an "Islamic prayer sundial" (fig. 3.29). "Someone at Paul Murdoch's architecture firm is trying to plant an Islamic flag on the bodies of our dead heroes," said Rawls, calling Murdoch a "terrorist memorializing scum" and "secretly festering Ayatollah Khomeini." Rawls proposed, instead, a "Let's Roll!" rollercoaster: "Enough with these sit-on-your-ass-and-ponder-murder-in-quietude memorials . . . Flight 93 is not about pondering what to do, it's about knowing what to do, and doing it. What better memorial than that dramatic piece of Americana, the roller-coaster, with a design as unique and thematic as the site calls for."[130]

Whether or not this Islamophobia was rather cynically overdetermined (Rawls, son of philosopher John Rawls, is described by some as the "Mark David Chapman of the blogosphere"), it fueled a memorial firestorm. Much of it raged over what kind of memorial was actually being built in Shanksville: a memorial to the victims of terrorism or a memorial to the war on terror? As one blogger remarked, "I'm the old fashioned type. I don't want to visit 'remembrance ponds,' 'reflection areas,' 'hope & healing centers,' or anything of that sort. I want huge bronze statues and flags." Another said, "We have had enough of this panty-waisted, new age-y, pop psychology-y 'healing' nonsense. We're at war. It's a time for anger and vengeance. 'Healing' is never appropriate for a war memorial."[131] Encouraged by national security narratives insisting that Flight 93 be remembered as the "first battle" in the war on terror, it is hardly surprising that some Americans expect its commemoration as a war memorial. Soothing groves of trees and a melodic Tower of Voices hardly jibe with their memorial expectations—and even seem traitorous.

Other Islamo-conspiracy–obsessed theorists jumped into the fray, including right-wing commentator Michelle Malkin and Constitutional Conservative blogger Mark McMorrow, who likened the memorial's design to "figuring swastikas into a Holocaust memorial." Pittsburgh street preacher Ron McRae vowed to block the project with a legal injunction, saying, "This is a memorial to the terrorists who killed those people, not a memorial to the folks who died there innocently. It's a slap in the face." And Congressman Tom Tancredo (R-CO), who in 2005 said "nuking Mecca" was a justifiable form of U.S. foreign policy in the war on terror, criticized the Flight 93 memorial for its "invocation of a Muslim symbol" and advised the National Park Service to reopen the competition.[132]

Never mind that these critiques completely discount how Flight 93 families themselves chose Murdoch's design as "a lasting tribute to our loved ones' heroism" and view the memorial as "a healing place" for "all people, regardless of race and religion." Never mind that the crescent is an emblem of the Greek goddess Diana and appears on the state flag of South Carolina, or that no Islamic representative has called Crescent of Embrace a "Muslim symbol" or has condemned the memorial—in the way, for example, that the Council on American-Islamic Relations demanded in the late 1990s that Nike cancel a line of sneakers featuring a logo akin to Arabic script for Allah. (Nike complied.)

Instead, a snarly handful of bloggers hijacked Flight 93 a second time, circumventing an above-board public memorial competition involving 9/11 families, local residents, design professionals, and government representatives. Within a few weeks of the online antimemorial outbreak, the National Park Service and Murdoch announced that the crescent of red maples would be replaced with a circle of trees and renamed The Field of Honor. "We think the entry is stronger now," Murdoch diplomatically stated at a press conference. "It more fully embraces the site so the focus is that much stronger on the sacred ground."[133]

However revised, Shankville's memorial still stirred paranoia about an Islamo-fascist conspiracy. The father of one man who died on Flight 93 vowed to withhold his son's name rather than have it "bastardized" at the memorial. At a public meeting organized by the memorial's advisory commission in 2006, one protester distributed flyers linking Murdoch's design with "extensive Islamic symbolism." Members of the commission listened politely and then unanimously voted to reaffirm their backing for the memorial. As one Flight 93 family member said at the meeting, "It is time for this process to move forward."[134] He received a standing ovation.

EMPATHY AND HOPE

The conspiratorial hackles raised over Flight 93's permanent memorial, the rights claims staked by Take Back the Memorial, and the fact that many Americans believe that 9/11 was an inside job ordered by the Bush administration indicate a larger national pathology about 9/11 itself. Suspicions about 9/11 memorials stem from haunting uncertainties about what 9/11 actually means in America. As George E. Marcus relates, many contemporary societies are rife with a "paranoid structure of feeling" inherited from the cold war's conspiratorial mindset and hastened by a postmodern "crisis of representation" that simultaneously reconfigured multiple bodies of knowledge and raised questions about the nature of knowledge itself. Conspiracy theory "is not confined to the marginal and excluded," adds Jodi Dean, but embodies a "paranoid style" in contemporary American political culture: a style seen in both the war on terror and the contentious management of 9/11's memory.[135]

The war on terror, explains Sean Wilentz, is a war "against a tactic, not a specific nation or political entity, which could last as long as any president deems the tactic a threat to national security."[136] As a war of ideas waged with both bombs and weapons of information (such as television and the Internet), terrorism is neither a traditional nor predictable mode of modern warfare. Targeting relatively small numbers of people and yet generating tremendous public response, terrorist acts are symbolic, shocking, and sensational, a form of political theater focused on mass fear. Given terrorism's long-standing history in America, its unpredictable and seemingly endless global trajectory, and the manner in which American security narratives work to reinscribe national fears and anxieties, it is hardly surprising that the nation's terrorism memorials especially embody public suspicion and paranoia.

Americans do want to visibly mourn the victims of terrorism. One 2005 survey showed that 94 percent of those polled felt that a 9/11 memorial should be built at the site of the World Trade Center, and 65 percent felt every American should visit it once it was built.[137] Yet memorials steeped in reproducing fear are untenable. Can the terms of terrorism's trauma and loss become transformative social and political agents? Can American memorials "hold a presence" for victims of terrorism without reifying tropes of national innocence, blood sacrifice, and violent reprisal? Several recent public art projects suggest ways in which commemoration can bear witness to the trauma of terrorism without perpetuating fear and anxiety, and without colonizing terrorism's victims for retributory ends.

During the morning rush hour of July 7, 2005, terrorist bombings of several trains and a bus in London killed fifty-two commuters (and four perpetrators), wounded more than seven hundred people, and crippled the city's public transportation system. Within minutes of the attacks, a virtual memorial that came to be called "We're Not Afraid" was up and running on a site managed by Alfie Dennen, a London-based Web developer.[138] Dennen started the memorial by posting a camera phone picture taken inside a smoke-filled Tube station, sent to him by a friend who wanted to show that he was relatively safe. By midday on what is now called 7/7, the picture was being repeatedly broadcast by the BBC and other mainstream news agencies.

Recognizing its appeal and determined to prevent the photograph's easy political manipulation via a mass-mediated campaign of fear and revenge, Dennen and friends posted a few more images: pictures of themselves holding hand-lettered signs reading "We're NOT Afraid!!" Inviting others to participate—"Show the world that we're not afraid of what happened today, that the world is a better place without fear!"—Dennen's Web site soon featured thousands of pictures ranging from cleverly Photoshopped images of the iconic London Underground sign to somber declarations of solidarity, like the picture of a man standing in front of the Oklahoma City National Memorial holding a sign stating "We Are Not Afraid" (fig. 3.30). Within a few days, the site had received four million hits. By September 2005, it was hosting thousands of im-

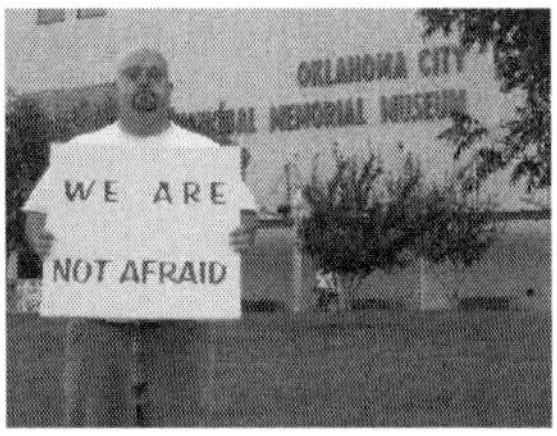

3.30. Photograph from the virtual memorial "We Are Not Afraid," July 2005 (http://www.werenot afraid.com/).

ages, had received over thirty-three million hits, and had become an electronic forum for shared response to the trauma of terrorism.

Appropriating a line from Franklin Delano Roosevelt's first inaugural address on March 4, 1933, when the president announced, "Let me assert my firm belief that the only thing we have to fear is fear itself," Dennen's virtual memorial also drew on the words "We are not afraid today" from the popular civil rights anthem "We Shall Overcome."[139] Some criticized the campaign for its naïve assertion of defiant optimism and common humanity and its political ambivalence. As one man wrote, "Well, I live in the UK and I am afraid. I'm also scared that sites like 'We're Not Afraid' encourage an unhealthy solidarity of superiority, nationalism, and xenophobia—perpetuating a 'we're good' and 'they're evil' mentality that avoids the big picture questions of how we got here." Yet as Jolyon Mitchell argues, "We Are Not Afraid" was a creative critical space of nonviolent resistance against terrorism: a virtual memorial of "global pictorial discourse" that shared feelings of dread and panic and simultaneously resisted their destructive affectivity.[140] Instead of appropriating terrorism's residual anxieties for purposes of revenge, or manipulating them for the profitable new economy of security—as did American mass media and political pundits following 9/11—"We Are Not Afraid" acknowledged the visceral pain of suffering and loss and attempted to generate a counternarrative of empathy and hope.

Growing numbers of contemporary artists respond to the fear that terrorism generates with works that critique the ideologies that foster it and simultaneously call for ethical and aesthetic strategies that refuse its reiteration. Performance artist Laurie Anderson's *Happiness* (2002), for example, centered on loss and memory in 9/11's aftermath. Countering the flood of traumatic images and bellicose invectives that deluged post-9/11 America, Anderson kept her stage bare and intimate; as she explained, *Happiness* focused on "the things that both interest and trouble me: the evolution of behavior, how we learn and what we remember, expectations, the meaning of justice, and the effects of increasing speed—colored by the darker elements of doubt and fear." If her quiet performance invited audiences to reflect on their own feelings about terrorism's trauma, it did not resolve them: *Happiness* ended with Anderson posing the question "Now what—what happens next?"[141]

Cai Guo-Qiang's *Transparent Monument* (2006), a temporary installation featuring periodic bursts of gunpowder, a pair of life-sized plastic crocodiles pierced with knives and scissors confiscated by airport security, a tall glass plank with replicas of dead birds lying at its base, and a thirty-foot limestone wall carved with various twenty-first-century vignettes, similarly engaged the affective complexities of life in post-9/11 America.[142] Situated on the rooftop of New York's Metropolitan Museum of Art, *Transparent Monument* mediated terrorism's spectacular violence—represented by clouds of smoke, lifeless birds, and angry dragons—within a visual timeline of global events that have taken place in the five years since 9/11, thus evoking both chaos and continuity.

Attentive to the affective and critical operations of trauma, this sort of art engages what Jill Bennett terms "empathic vision," an interpretive mode of seeing and feeling that acknowledges pain and suffering and encourages their sustained contemplation, but does not resolve (or cure) them.[143] Arguing that trauma cannot, in fact, be represented—not because it is beyond the scope of representation but because to do so is to colonize it for any number of purposes—Bennett calls for generative, dynamic, and transformative art practices engaged in trauma's affective contexts and consequences. Trauma is relational; it exists within a nexus of historical, political, social, and spatial experiences. Art that grapples with this generative sensibility rather than attempting to narrowly define and resolve trauma itself complicates narratives of suffering and healing and raises questions about blame and responsibility. Through understanding trauma as "a foundation for creating counterpublic spheres rather than evacuating them," as Ann Cvetkovich argues, such art has transgressive possibilities.[144]

It might seem odd, then, to consider *The Gates*—that much-hyped event in February 2005 when bright orange fabric sculptures appeared in New York's Central Park—as a terrorism memorial (fig. 3.31). Yet in its brief, ephemeral appearance, *The Gates* generated new views of a city park that has long been taken for granted and encouraged new ways of thinking about the affective disruptions of space, movement, history, and time—the sorts of disruptions that the trauma of terrorism incurred in New York on 9/11. *The Gates* was not, of course, intended as a 9/11 memorial or as a memorial to the victims of terrorism or even as a memorial per se. But for many New Yorkers—and for many of the more than four million people who visited *The Gates* during its two-week run—it was experienced and understood on those terms.

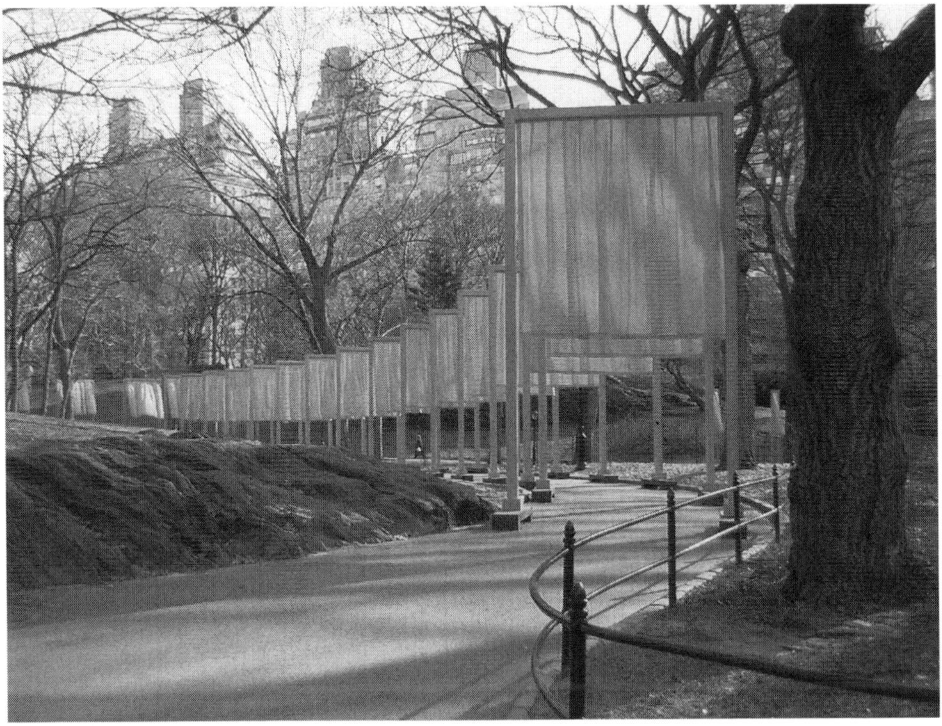

3.31. Christo and Jeanne-Claude, *The Gates*, Central Park, New York, New York, February 2005. (Photo by the author.)

The Gates was conceived by Christo and Jeanne-Claude, best known for eighteen other similarly short-term projects realized over the past three decades, from *Running Fence* (1976), a 24-mile "fence" of white nylon cloth about 18 feet tall that "ran" through sections of Sonoma and Marin Counties in California, to *Surrounded Islands* (1983), a series of floating fabric skirts that circled several uninhabited islands in Biscayne Bay, Florida. *The Gates* was similarly gigantic, featuring 7,503 individual sculptures, each approximately 16 feet high and 6 to 18 feet long, placed along 23 miles of pedestrian pathways in Central Park. Like other projects organized by Christo and Jeanne-Claude, *The Gates* questioned issues of monumentality and, by extension, relationships of space, power, and memory. While it (temporarily) occupied an immense space, *The Gates* did not dominate the park but radiated within it; while thousands of fluttering saffron sculptures lined the park's pathways there was no particular start or finish to their design, such that visitors meandered around Central Park for hours, often in freezing temperatures (fig. 3.32). Brian Massumi argues that "uncertainty can actually be empowering," encouraging "the feeling that there is always an opening to experiment, to try

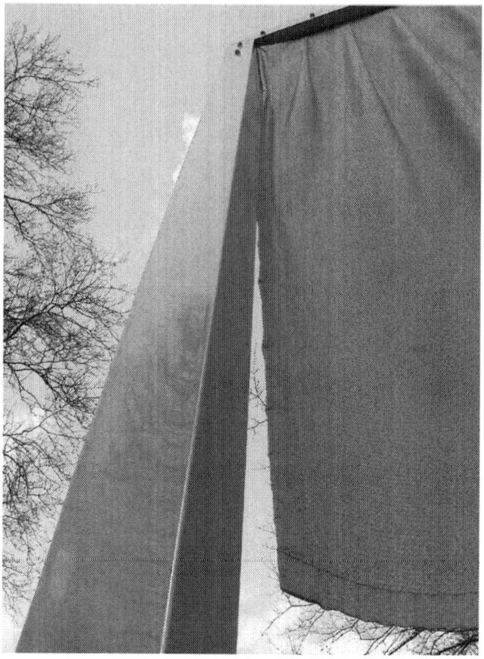

3.32. *The Gates*, detail. (Photo by the author.)

and see."[145] For the millions who navigated *The Gates* on these terms, the experience was profoundly hopeful. Like Christo and Jeanne-Claude's wrapping of the Reichstag in 1995, which Andreas Huyssen described as a "monument to democratic culture instead of a demonstration of state power," *The Gates* sparked innumerable conversations about the nature of public art and the politics of persuasion, about freedom of expression, tolerance, and memory.[146]

Some criticized *The Gates* expense ($21 million, all privately funded); some condemned its popularizing of avant-garde art practices; some dismissed it as nothing more than a spectacular civic improvement campaign orchestrated by New York City's tourism bureau. And *The Gates* was a tremendous economic boon, generating an estimated $254 million in hotel, restaurant, and retail income for the city in a generally slow midwinter month. Writing for the *New York Observer,* Hilton Kramer charged *The Gates* with being "nothing less than an unforgivable defacement of a public treasure." Jed Perl called it "public art for the cocooning generation" and, echoing Michael Fried's worries about minimalism some forty year earlier, snarled: "Just because you're being bombarded by sensations doesn't mean that you're in the presence of major art—or even mediocre art. When all feelings are regarded as aesthetic experiences, art is at risk. What Christo and Jeanne-Claude have brought to New York is their own brand of late-modern philistinism."[147]

Such critiques failed to grasp the critical dimensions of *The Gates* and how and why its transgressive possibilities held the attention of millions of people. Describing *The Gates* as "a golden river appearing and disappearing through the bare branches of the trees," Christo articulated his personal aesthetic interests. Yet he also remarked, "The project is ceremonial, it is festive, it is very invitational, and in the same way very private."[148] In stark contrast to Ground Zero and the contentious claims on that site's materiality and meaning, *The Gates* was sublime—an intimate and empathic project in which visitors were invited to reimagine the spatial and visual dynamics of the park and the city. Perhaps the most oft-repeated comment among them was not the color or the size of *The Gates* but how they *felt*—and how their feelings helped them find a way to "believe in the world" again.[149] As such, *The Gates* fed the emotional cravings of an American public traumatized by 9/11 and hopefully unconvinced by repeated efforts to frame it—and the nation—within security narratives of survival, sacrifice, and retribution.

4 GRATITUDE

Memorializing World War II and the "Greatest Generation"

One February night in 1987, during the annual fish fry in Jerusalem Township, Ohio, Rep. Marcy Kaptur (D-OH) was buttonholed by an elderly constituent: "Hey, Congresswoman Kaptur! Why is there no World War II memorial in Washington?" Somewhat taken aback, Kaptur replied that the Iwo Jima statue, the large bronze sculpture installed next to Arlington National Cemetery in 1954, might be considered such a memorial (fig. 4.1). But her questioner quickly replied "Wrong!" and informed her that "officially" the Iwo Jima memorial only paid tribute to one military service unit: the U.S. Marine Corps.[1]

Kaptur's constituent, rural mailman Roger Durbin, considered himself a bit of an expert on World War II memorials. A veteran of the Battle of the Bulge, a tank mechanic with the 10th Armored Division, Durbin had visited Washington in the early 1960s and was "astonished," he later said, to discover that in a national capital full of memorials, World War II was seemingly unrepresented. Returning to Belgium for a military reunion in 1966, Durbin was impressed by the Mardasson Memorial, a huge monument built atop the highest hill of Bastogne, where American troops held the German army in check from December 1944 to January 1945. Dedicated in 1950, the sprawling memorial features forty-foot-tall granite pillars inscribed with the names of the U.S. states and the badges of the U.S. battalions that fought in the region, as well as three altars, a crypt (designed by French artist Fernand Léger), and a series of bronze plaques narrating the siege of Bastogne. Long after his visit, Durbin recalled, "Five years after the end of World War II the small liberated nation of Belgium had a memorial built and paid for in memory of the American Army that liberated their nation. After seeing that memorial, I thought, Why can't the greatest nation in the world do that for the 16 million men and women who served America during World War II?"[2]

Inspired by Durbin's question, Congresswoman Kaptur spearheaded federal legislation authorizing the National World War II Memorial,

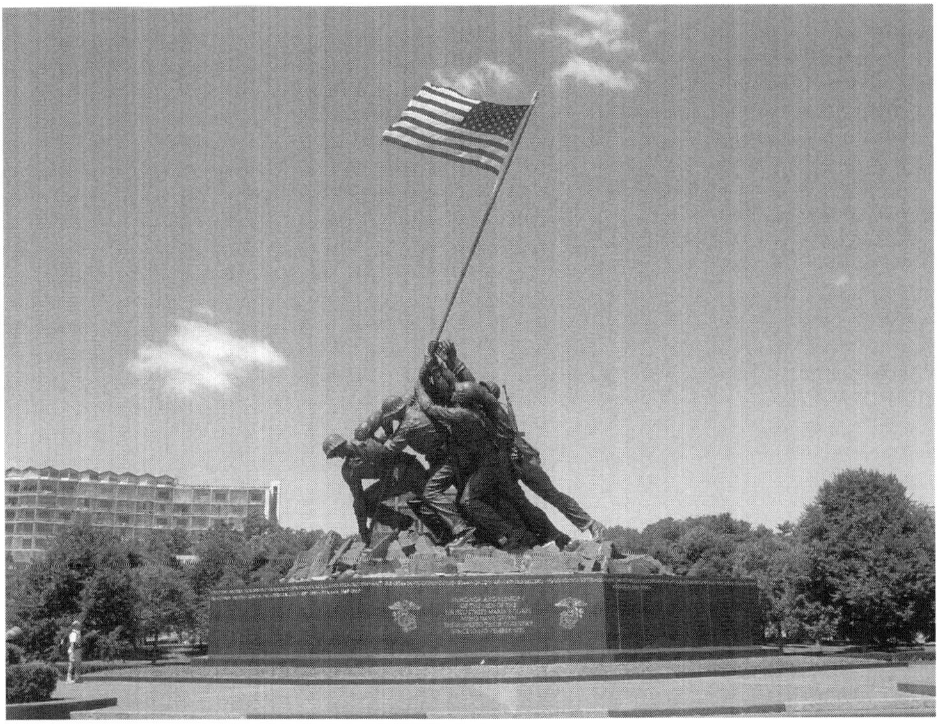

4.1. Felix de Weldon, U.S. Marine Corps War Memorial, Arlington, Virginia, dedicated 1954. (Courtesy of Christopher Hollis for Wdwic Pictures.)

which looks something like Bastogne's war memorial, only bigger (fig. 4.2). "It's time to say thank you," said movie star Tom Hanks in numerous public service ads soliciting funds for the massive 7.4-acre, $182 million monument installed on the National Mall in 2004, in between the Washington Monument and the Lincoln Memorial. "It's the right time. It's the right place. Help say 'thank you' to the World War II generation," echoed the History Channel, working in tandem with the National World War II Memorial Campaign and its chairman, former senator Bob Dole. Or as President George W. Bush put it in 2001, when he signed into law a bill expediting the memorial's construction, and overriding all legal resistance to its development: "It's time to give them the memorial they deserve."[3]

War memorials and "war memory" are flourishing in contemporary America.[4] If Memorial Day and Veterans Day observances faded in the post-Vietnam era—New York City cancelled its Memorial Day Parade in 1994 and 1995 due to public disinterest, and Milwaukee cancelled its Veterans Day Parade in 2000 for similar reasons—they have roared back since 9/11. In 2004, Washington held its first Memorial Day parade in

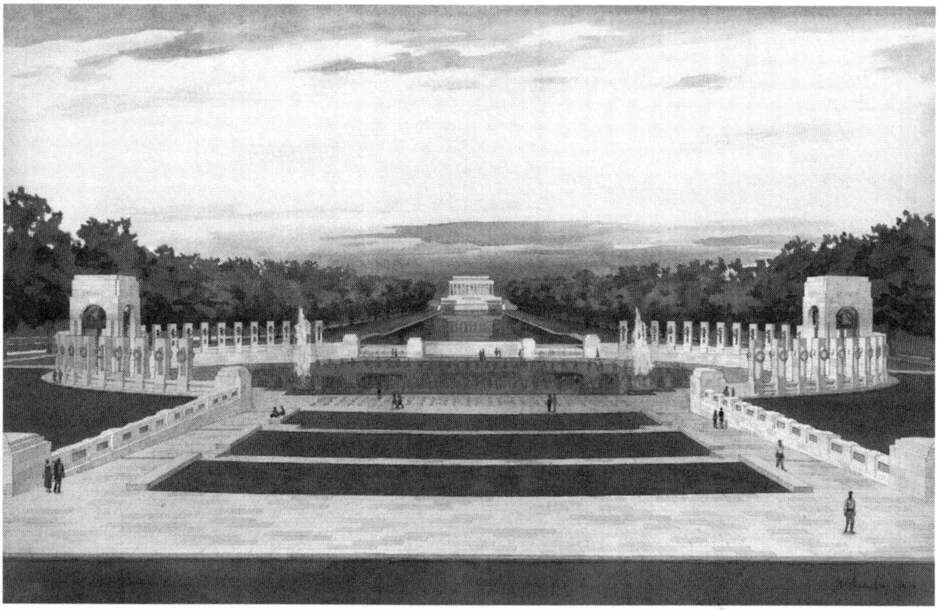

4.2. Friedrich St. Florian, National World War II Memorial, Washington, D.C., dedicated 2004. (Rendering by Joe McKendry, 2000. Courtesy of Arlington Economic Development.)

sixty years, synchronized with the unveiling of the national capital's new World War II memorial.

Scores of other World War II memorials and museums have also appeared in the past decade, from the National D-Day Memorial in Bedford, Virginia (2001) and the Rosie the Riveter / World War II Home Front National Historical Park in Richmond, California (see fig. 0.8, p. 5), to the Aleutian World War II National Historic Area in Dutch Harbor, Alaska, which the National Park Service opened in 2002. The list goes on: the South Dakota World War II Memorial (Pierre, 2001; fig. 4.3), New York State World War II Memorial (Albany, 2002), Minnesota World War II Veterans Memorial (St. Paul, 2007), Florida World War II Monument (Tallahassee, 2005), State of Maine Monument to World War II (Bangor, 1997), National World War II Museum (New Orleans, 2000), Richard I. Bong World War II Heritage Center (Superior, Wisconsin, 2002), World War II Freedom Memorial (Des Moines, 1997), Uniontown World War II Memorial (Uniontown, Pennsylvania, 2006). In Las Cruces, New Mexico, the Bataan Death March Memorial Monument (2002) features an annual 26.2-mile reenactment through the nearby deserts of the White Sands Missile Range.

Saying "thank you" to the "greatest generation" has obviously become

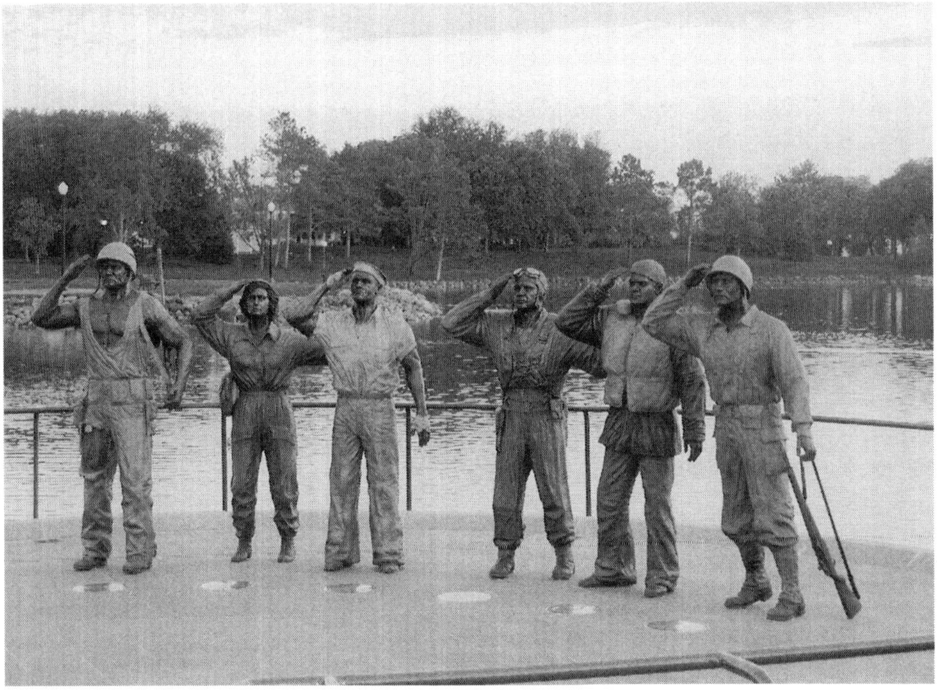

4.3. South Dakota World War II Memorial, Pierre, South Dakota, dedicated 2001. (Photo by the author.)

a popular commemorative project in contemporary America. This chapter considers why such gratitude is so urgently expressed today, more than sixty years after the end of World War II. The purpose of war memorials is to honor soldier dead and to acknowledge social debt: thanks are expressed to those who died for a nation, on behalf of a cause. Yet is gratitude an appropriate affect in the culture of war memory? What are the psychological conditions, moral functions, and political obligations of such gratitude?

LIVING MEMORIALS

Today's new memorials to an old war are animated, in part, by statistics showing that World War II veterans are dying at a rate of over a thousand a day—and thanks must be expressed "before they're all gone." They are inspired, too, by movies like *Saving Private Ryan* (1998) and *Pearl Harbor* (2001) and by books like Tom Brokaw's *The Greatest Generation* (1998). Many follow the National World War II Memorial's mission: to pay tribute to "the 16 million who served in the armed forces of the U.S. during

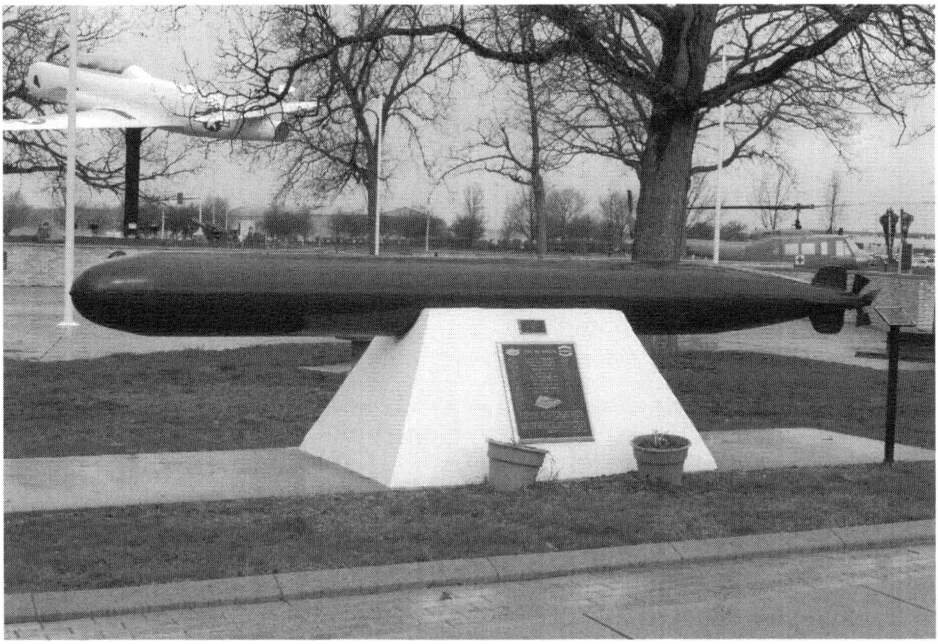

4.4. Mark 14 torpedo (standard World War II submarine torpedo) on display at the Military Honor Park, South Bend, Indiana. (Courtesy of Geoffrey Thrumston.)

World War II, the more than 400,000 who died, and the millions who supported the war effort from home."[5] Today, assumptions are widespread that these millions have never been honored in American memorial culture. "They honored Vietnam. They honored everyone else but World War II," said one Navy veteran at the dedication of the National World War II Memorial. "So I thought we deserved something." Another veteran concurred, "It's about time that memorial came into being. Finally, those who fought in World War II will be recognized."[6]

Yet World War II was commemorated—immediately and profusely, locally and nationally. The war's copious matériel became the stuff of countless memorials. Battleships and submarines were saved from scrap piles and turned into tourist attractions; Hellcats and Helldivers were refurbished and restaged in mock battles at air shows; thousands of American towns obtained tanks, B-17 bombers, and other icons of World War II weaponry and displayed them in city halls and public parks (fig. 4.4). In 1945, less than a month after the surrender of Japan, the National Park Service made plans for an Atomic Bomb National Monument in New Mexico; in 1946, Congress authorized a National Air Museum to commemorate the war's strategic reliance on airpower. After the war ended, the American Battle Monuments Commission (ABMC), a group authorized by Congress in 1923 to commemorate U.S. soldiers overseas, built fourteen military cemeteries—meticulously landscaped burial grounds embellished with chapels, statues, and walls listing the names of U.S. soldier dead—in Europe, the Philippines, and Hawaii. The ABMC also built two World War II memorials in the continental United States: the East Coast Memorial (New York, 1963, designed by Albino Manca) and the West Coast Memorial (San Francisco, 1960, designed by Lawrence Halprin), each paying tribute to servicemen killed in the Atlantic and Pacific theaters of war.[7]

World War II servicemen were similarly honored by two major national monuments: the USS *Arizona* Memorial (authorized in 1958; dedicated in Pearl Harbor in 1962), and the U.S. Marine Corps War Memorial (authorized by Congress in 1946). The seventy-eight-foot-tall Iwo Jima statue may "officially" only honor the Marines, but its epic scale and prime location by Arlington National Cemetery have made it the nation's most familiar World War II memorial since it was erected. Inspired by a photograph by Joe Rosenthal which ran in U.S. newspapers and *Life* magazine shortly after it was shot (February 23, 1945), the Iwo Jima memorial is a national icon. As Vice President Richard Nixon observed at the memorial's dedication on Veterans Day 1954, "This statue symbolizes the hopes and dreams of America."[8]

Above all, World War II was honored with "living memorials." "The memory of war," Susan Sontag argued, "is mostly local," and postwar Americans especially remembered World War II in nativist and utilitarian terms.[9] In 1946, the U.S. Commission of Fine Arts issued a *Report on War Memorials*. Explaining their "threefold purpose"—gratitude, remembrance, and inspiration—the report emphasized civic process and utility: "Since war memorials are generally the product of community effort, constructed with local funds and materials, the community itself has the responsibility of determining the form of memorial best adapted to its needs." Standing-soldier statues and piles of cannon balls were to be avoided, warned the commission, which recommended instead memorial bridges, fountains, and flagpoles. Communities were encouraged to "provide an effective setting for an annual meeting or act or remembrance, such as the placing of a wreath on Memorial or other commemorative days."[10]

"Rather than overpopulate their parks with bad statuary, many communities are planning new kinds of war memorials—for the living," Edith Stern noted in *Coronet* in 1945. "People are calling for memorials that are community-usable," reported the *Toledo City Journal* in 1946.

A 1948 survey showed that 265 American cities had built or were planning to build World War II memorials that followed the living memorial model: 42 auditoriums, 29 parks, 20 stadiums, 19 hospitals, and a variety of airports, art centers, libraries, museums, and recreation centers. "The whole country became, in a sense, a living memorial to World War II," notes Kristin Hass, explaining how building projects deferred by the Great Depression and the war—highways, bridges, auditoriums—were realized in the later 1940s and 1950s as functional and symbolic testimonials to why the war was fought.[11]

Lewis Mumford, whose son Geddes died in combat in 1944, thought living memorials were phony. "They are rather a complacent way of getting benefits for ourselves and at the same time flattering ourselves that we are spending large sums of money to commemorate our heroes. That is too easy," he wrote in 1945.[12] But most postwar Americans disagreed. Living memorials embodied changed postwar ideas about war's commemoration, now understood on socially progressive terms as a blend of gratitude, usefulness, and civic improvement. "Statues of guys in jeeps," as Stern wryly put it, were irrelevant. Or as one sentimental poet waxed: "Dead monuments are but idle toys—/ Give living things for our noble boys!"[13]

Milwaukee's War Memorial Center (1957), designed by Finnish architect Eero Saarinen and situated on the city's lakefront, personifies the useful post–World War II memorial (fig. 4.5). Guided by the motto "Honor the Dead. Serve the Living," inscribed in Latin on its granite walls, Milwaukee's memorial is basically a modern building that houses various cultural and civic organizations. A modest bronze plaque on the south façade pays homage to the city's World War II soldier dead. Sharing faith in an improved national future, other living memorials like Omaha's Memorial Park (1948), Little Rock's War Memorial Stadium (1948), and Des Moines' Veterans Memorial Auditorium (1956) further resonated with notions of "better living," a slogan coined by DuPont and broadly adopted by advertising agents, manufacturers, and urban planners anxious to affirm and renew the postwar nation's cultural, social, and economic possibilities.[14]

Although many local, national, and living memorials were raised to the war, Congress authorized the National World War II Memorial in 1993. Today, the memory work performed by the nation's original World War II memorials is no longer considered adequate,or even recalled. Ahistorical assumptions of postwar ingratitude, along with contemporary feelings of indebtedness regarding more recent wars, drive today's mania to memorialize the "greatest generation."

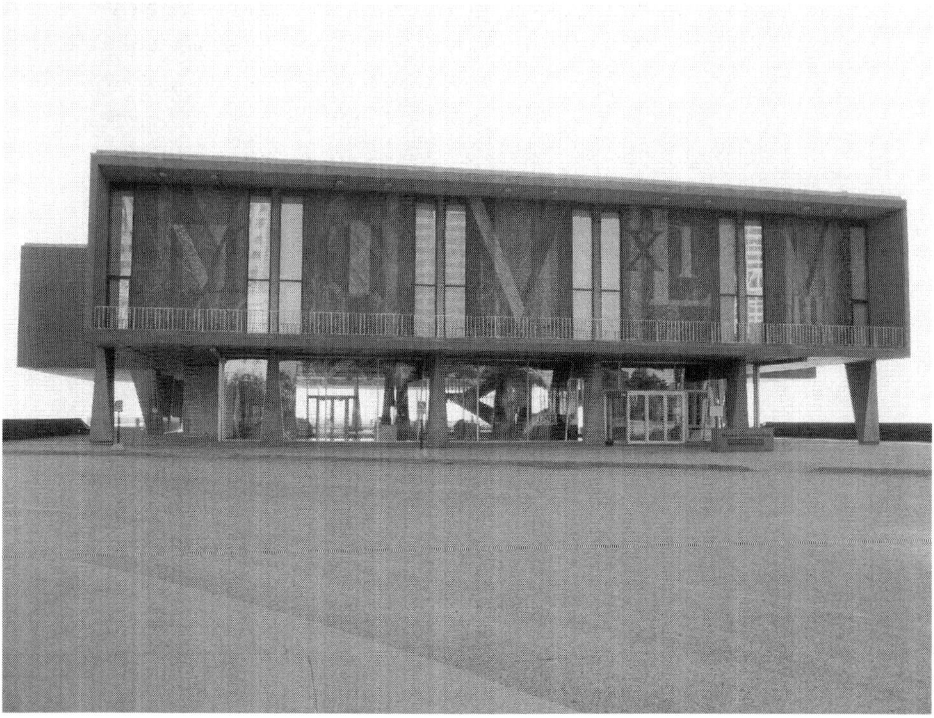

4.5. Eero Saarinen, War Memorial Center, Milwaukee, Wisconsin, dedicated 1957. (Photo by the author.)

GRATITUDE

Gratitude is typically understood as a gesture of appreciation, an expression of thankfulness. Both a psychological and social phenomenon, gratitude is a major element in multiple religious traditions; "Augustine's use of the term *gratia*," one writer observes, "was almost always in terms of divine grace rather than human obligation."[15] In a modern era of capitalist market economics and nation-states, however, gratitude is especially understood as a fundamental condition of the social contract, an important agent in social goodwill and civil order. Gratitude is thus perceived within relationships of reciprocity: of benefits given and received. As Adam Smith explained in *The Theory of Moral Sentiments* (1759), feelings of gratitude are crucial to the operation of stable, modern, and moral societies. Likewise, in the early twentieth century, sociologist Georg Simmel argued that gratitude was the "moral memory of mankind" and as such was a key component of personal and social character. Subsequent theorists have similarly posited gratitude as a positive affect with attached obligations; Terrance McConnell, for example, argues that gratitude is a moral requirement. In the past decade, gratitude has been enthusiastically embraced as an attitudinal and behavioral cure-all in the positive psychology movement, whose adherents are encouraged to keep "gratitude journals" and practice "good things" in order to transcend misery and depression and "make the world a happier place."[16]

Gratitude is motivational and inspirational. Thanks are given in anticipation of benefits, and mutual giving presumably reinforces social cohesion and goodwill. Concomitant with assumptions or expectations of reciprocity are questions of obligation and power, of the duties and abuses of gratitude. What are the circumstances under which gratitude is owed? What are the social and political requirements of gratitude? How long before a debt can be discharged? Can gratitude become pathological if a society is expected to perform acts of thanksgiving that are basically hollow? Some political theorists argue that gratitude is a problematic source of duty and obligation, primarily because it is too vague and too coercive. Forced virtue, in other words, is inauthentic and despotic; thanks should be expressed because one can express them, not because one is expected—or required—to do so. Others note the contingencies between gratitude and humility: authentic gestures of thanksgiving stem from individual and / or collective feelings of inferiority.[17]

Notwithstanding these philosophical and political concerns, public expressions of thanks have been consistent throughout American history, from the mythic "First Thanksgiving" of 1621 when Pilgrims and Wampanoag Indians feasted together in Plymouth, Massachusetts, to the "Day of Public Thanksgiving" declared in 1676 following the Puritan defeat of the Wampanoag in the bloody King Philip's War. (Since 1970, Native Americans have gathered at Cole's Hill overlooking Plymouth Rock to participate in a National Day of Mourning.) In September 1741, a "Day of Thanksgiving" was held in New York City after a slave uprising was brought to an end; in December 1777, George Washington proclaimed a "Day of Thanksgiving" to celebrate the Continental Army's defeat of the British at the Battle of Saratoga.[18] Such special days were "solidarity rituals," designed to "celebrate and rectify the society's relationship with God, to define and legitimate their social and political order, and to control internal conflict." In 1863, in the midst of the Civil War, Abraham Lincoln established the national holiday of Thanksgiving to honor all "sufferers in the lamentable civil strife" and to cultivate sectional reconciliation.[19]

Giving thanks in America, in other words, is historically associated with social consensus and political obligation. By extension, national expressions of thanksgiving have typically followed outbreaks of social conflict and episodes of war. Grounded in gratitude, the National World

War II Memorial continues this tradition. One of the inscriptions carved onto its granite blocks features these words from President Harry Truman: "Our debt to the heroic men and valiant women in the service of our country can never be repaid. They have earned our undying gratitude. America will never forget their sacrifices."

Solicitations of gratitude—saying "thank you" to the "greatest generation" with money—generated impressive buy-in for the National World War II Memorial. More than $197 million was raised from corporations and foundations ($14 million from Wal-Mart; more than $2 million each from Federal Express and the Lilly Endowment), veterans organizations ($6 million from Veterans of Foreign Wars; $4.5 million from the American Legion), various civic and fraternal clubs ($2 million from the National Funeral Directors Association; $500,000 from the Knights of Columbus), public schools ($859,000), and the federal government ($16 million). In 1999, the year that Tom Hanks's "thank you" ads first ran, memorial fundraising took in more than $42 million. Objections to such obligation were met with accusations of ingratitude. One CEO who questioned why his company should financially support the memorial was bullied by Bob Dole: "Well, World War II didn't fit my plans or sixteen million other plans, but because we were there, you're making a lot of money." Congressional management of the memorial was similarly strong-armed; when faced with public and legal protests about its design and its prime location on the National Mall, Congress hurriedly voted 400–15 to silence further opposition, and President Bush signed the memorial into law five days later, on Memorial Day, 2001.[20] Saying "no thank you" to the "greatest generation" was not an option.

Architect Friedrich St. Florian was chosen to design the memorial in 1996, after a hasty (and repeatedly revised) competition organized by the ABMC.[21] At the unveiling of the design at the White House in 1997, during which Dole was awarded the Presidential Medal of Freedom, President Bill Clinton remarked that he found the model for the new memorial "very impressive":

> The World War II Memorial will commemorate one of the great defining passages in our Nation's history. Fittingly, it will be flanked by the Washington Monument and the Lincoln Memorial. For if the Revolutionary War marks the birth of our republic, and the Civil War its greatest trial, then surely America's triumph in World War II will forever signal our coming of age . . . This memorial will stand as a lasting tribute to what Americans can achieve when they work together.[22]

Clinton's comments evoke a nation forged, tested, and united by war; war is America's "defining" identity. Deliberately wedged between two

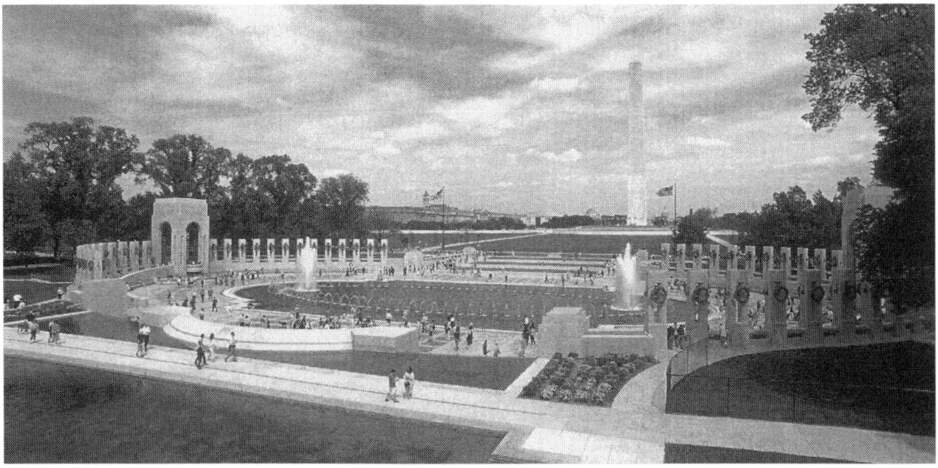

4.6. Richard Latoff, "National World War II Memorial Plaza Facing the Lincoln Memorial." Washington, D.C., 2004. (© Richard Latoff / Latoff.com.)

other national monuments, both redefined—and reduced—as war memorials, the National World War II Memorial serves to reinforce assumptions of America's historic and habitual militarism.

GRATITUDE'S MEMORIAL

Sprawled over 7.4 acres, the National World War II Memorial is primarily a huge stone plaza ceremonially framed by two 70-foot flagpoles whose bases are decorated with the seals of the Army, Navy, Marine Corps, Army Air Forces, Coast Guard, and Merchant Marine (fig. 4.6). It is ceremonially entered on 17th Street through two long stone walkways framed by balustrades, the one on the north side—the side closest to the White House—inscribed with the words "World War II Memorial / George W. Bush / President of the United States" and the names of the design architect and ABMC.

The walls are decorated with 24 small bronze bas-relief panels depicting the "all-out mobilization of America's agricultural, industrial, and military and human resources" during the war; scenes of the Atlantic theater are on one side, the Pacific on the other (fig. 4.7). Each panel is based on a montage of photographs from the Office of War Information and on drawings of reenactors dressed in World War II uniforms. Sculptor Raymond Kaskey explains, "The whole idea behind this was not to tell the story of World War II but to depict the transformation of America caused by World War II."[23] Cluttered and hard to see, the recessed panels have no captions or inscriptions. Still, they feature the only figurative

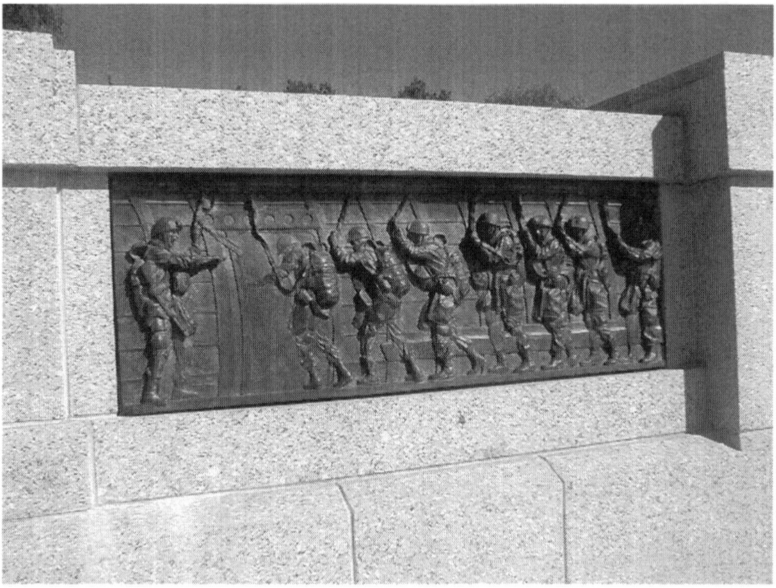

4.7. Raymond Kaskey, bas-relief panel on north balustrade wall / Atlantic front depicting paratroopers, National World War II Memorial. (Photo by the author.)

elements in the entire memorial and some visitors try to decipher their narrative before walking any further inside the memorial.

The memorial's plaza (lowered about six feet from preexisting ground level) is an immense stone crater larger than a football field (fig. 4.8). It is partially filled by an oblong pool framed by geysers and water jets that reflect and refract the light. St. Florian intended the pool as the memorial's most compelling feature. Yet it is stone—bulky blocks of smooth-faced rock, stiff arms of gray-flecked granite, monumental archways, vast expanses of blinding pavement, some 17,000 pieces of heavy stone totaling 1.1 million cubic feet—that dominates. Stone, not water, constitutes a memorial marked by strength, force, and permanence.

The vast stone plaza is flanked by two 43-foot-tall triumphal arches: one representing victory in the Atlantic, the other in the Pacific (fig. 4.9). Each contains a bronze baldacchino—a ceremonial canopy—featuring a gigantic eagle clutching a flowing ribbon connected to a victory laurel in its beak (fig. 4.10). Inlaid on the floor is a replica of the World War II victory medal (depicting a female figure subduing Mars, the Roman god of war) and the words "Victory on Land," "Victory at Sea," and "Victory in the Air." Each arch also features a small balcony overlooking the memorial, at the base of which are tiered fountains and crescent-shaped pools inscribed with the names of battles particular to each hemispherical theater of war (fig. 4.11).

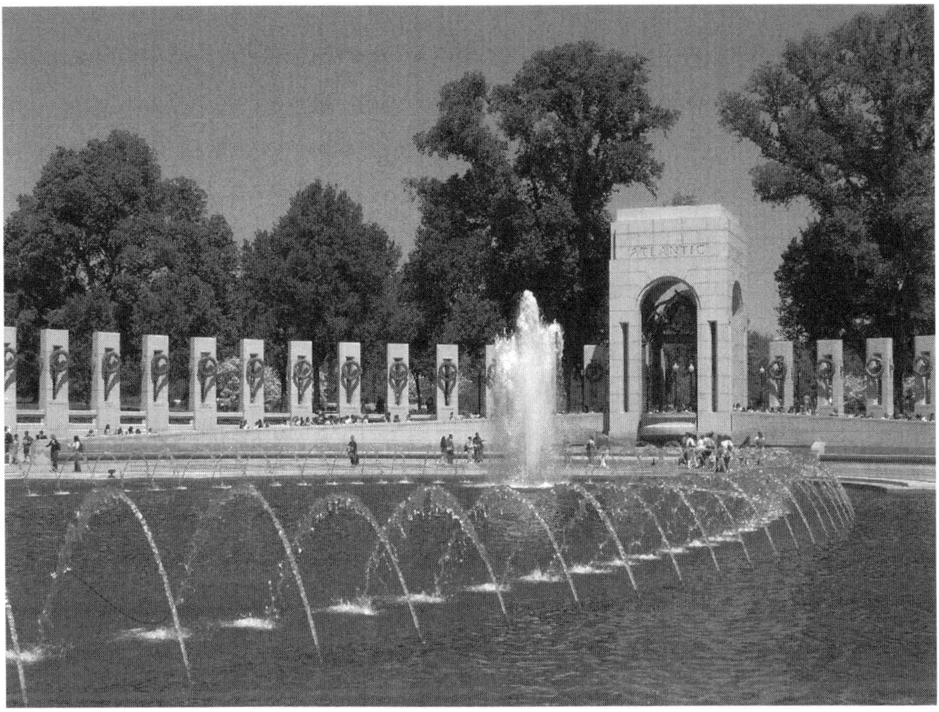

4.8. Plaza and columns, National World War II Memorial. (Photo by the author.)

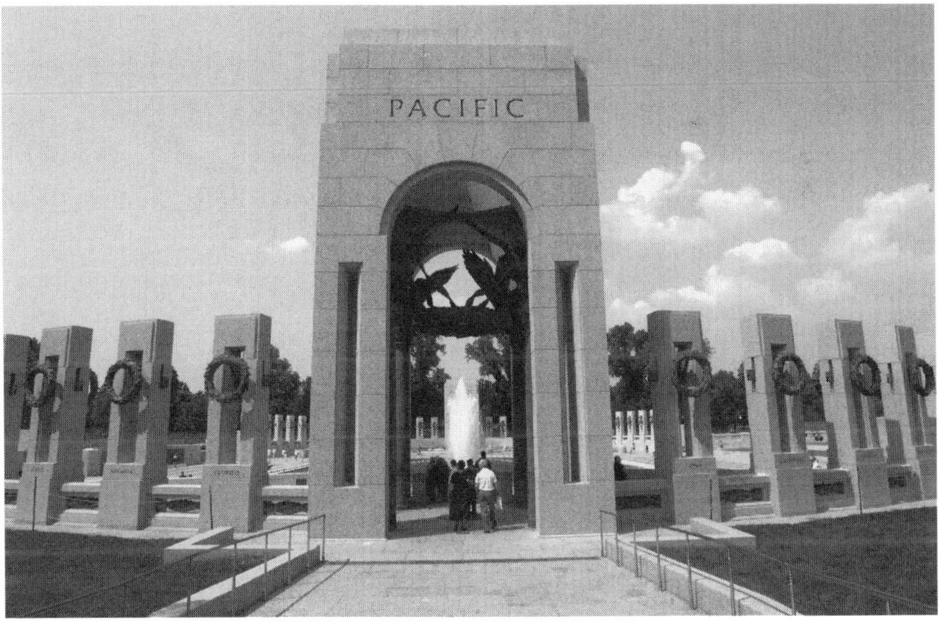

4.9. Pacific Arch, National World War II Memorial. (Photo by Master Sgt. Jim Varhegyi. Courtesy of the U.S. Air Force.)

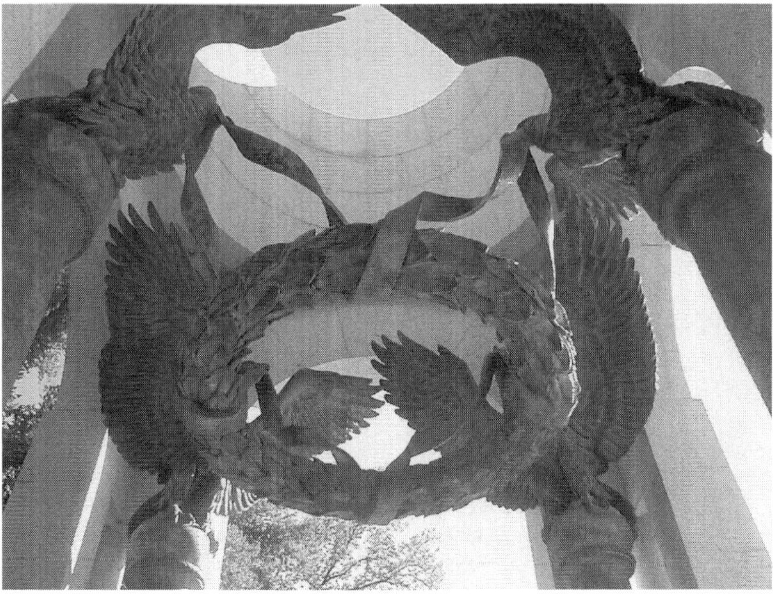

4.10. Bronze baldacchino, National World War II Memorial. Each wreath is ten feet in diameter. (Photo by the author.)

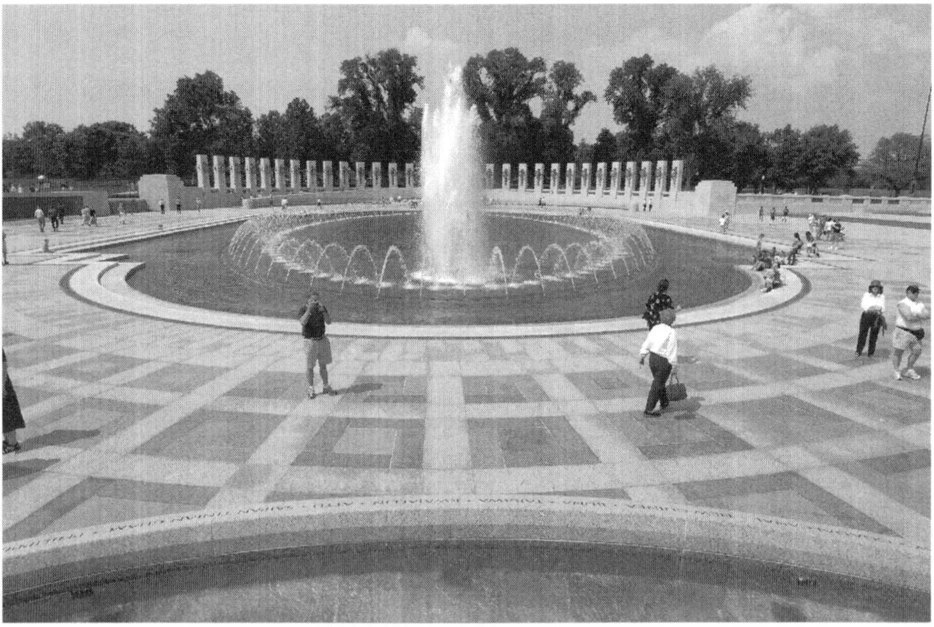

4.11. Plaza overview, National World War II Memorial. (Photo by Master Sgt. Jim Varhegyi. Courtesy of the U.S. Air Force.)

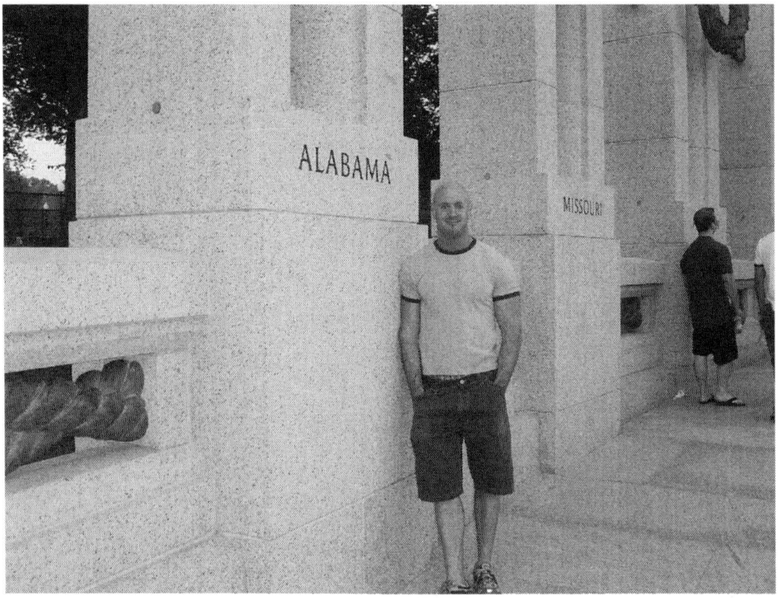

4.12. Tourists posing by home-state columns, National World War II Memorial. (Courtesy of Webshots.)

Linking the two arches and surrounding the 338-foot-long plaza is a semicircular colonnade of 56 granite stelae, each 17 feet tall, representing the 48 states, the District of Columbia, and the seven U.S. territories that comprised the nation during World War II (fig. 4.12). Their order follows the entrance of each state into the Union, Michigan standing next to Texas, West Virginia next to Nebraska; the territories are grouped together near the Pacific arch. Each pillar is draped with bronze wreaths whose designs alternate between oak leaves (traditional Western symbols of military strength and endurance) and wheat spears (agricultural abundance and power). Each stele is connected to the next by a thick bronze rope "that reinforces the idea of the states and territories closing ranks and binding the nation together." Obviously beholden to the architectural currency of Greco-Roman classicism, St. Florian explains that he designed the National World War II Memorial as a "timeless Olympus . . . where America can find its roots."[24]

At the center of the plaza, on the side nearest the Lincoln Memorial, is Freedom Wall, an 8-foot-tall, 85-foot-long curvilinear stone cenotaph flanked by waterfalls and decorated with 4,048 gold stars, one for every hundred American soldiers who died in military service during the war (fig. 4.13). The nation's 405,973 soldier dead are unnamed; instead, the National World War II Memorial collapses them into an anonymous

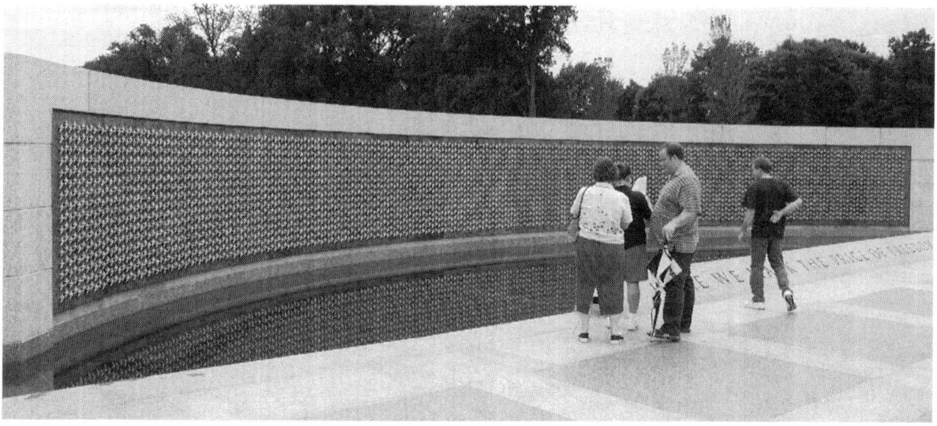

4.13. Freedom Wall, National World War II Memorial. (Photo by the author.)

patriotic mass. The stars reference the popular home front ritual of displaying a gold star in a living room window or on a front door to show a family's military loss. Freedom Wall resembles Memorial Wall at the headquarters of the CIA in Langley, Virginia, which features a field of black stars and the inscription "In honor of those members of the Central Intelligence Agency who gave their lives in the service of their country."[25] The inscription in front of Freedom Wall similarly honors World War II's soldier dead with the pat phrase "Here we mark the price of freedom."

The National World War II Memorial is sprinkled throughout with words that evoke the collective patriotism of its subject (the anonymous "they" of the "greatest generation") and its audience ("we"). Read together, they designate the sacrificial national body (fig. 4.14). The enormous Announcement Stone at the memorial's entrance, for example, reads:

> Here in the presence of Washington and Lincoln, one the eighteenth century father and the other the nineteenth century preserver of our nation, we honor those twentieth century Americans who took up the struggle during the Second World War and made the sacrifices to perpetuate the gift our forefathers entrusted to us: a nation conceived in liberty and justice.

Other inscriptions (eighteen in all) feature phrases such as "They Fought Together," "We Are Determined," and "The Eyes Of The World Are Upon You." Engraved in a commanding and familiar font that is "just a little bit blocky, like *Life* magazine," explains stone carver Nicholas Benson, because "here at home, World War II was pretty much seen through *Life*," these words reinforce the memorial's focus on collective

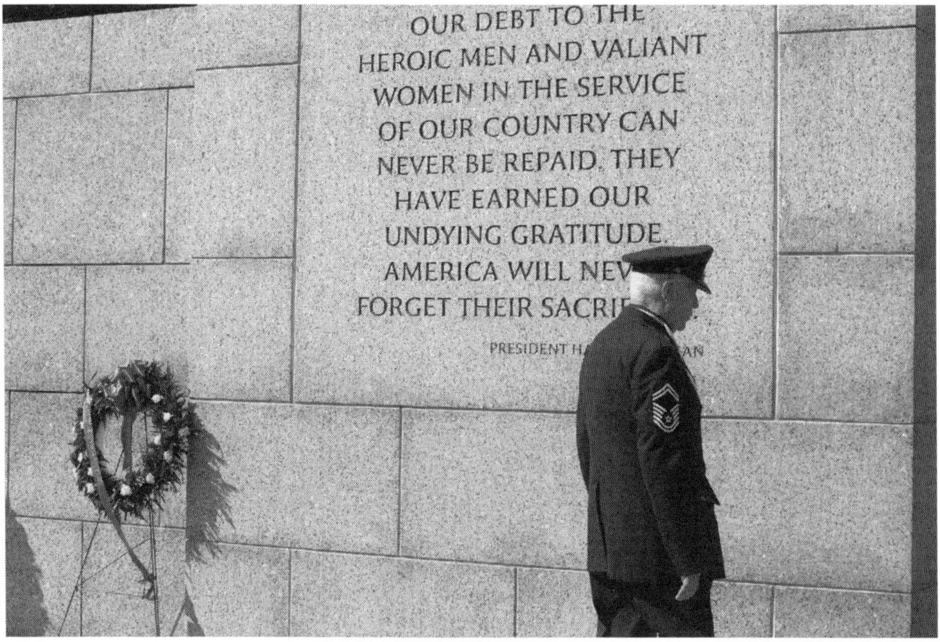

4.14. Retired Senior Master Sergeant Billy Neil reads a quote by President Harry Truman at the National World War II Memorial, September 15, 2007. (Photo by Staff Sgt. Suzanne Day. Courtesy of the U.S. Air Force.)

effort and national unity.[26] They were also uttered by "great men" like General Dwight D. Eisenhower, General Douglas MacArthur, General George C. Marshall, Admiral Chester Nimitz, President Franklin Delano Roosevelt, and President Harry Truman (and one woman, Colonel Oveta Culp Hobby), each of whom is named. Their words legitimate the National World War II Memorial's historical authority and direct its display of national unity; their names are read and remembered by visitors. The war's nameless soldier dead, by contrast, are lumped together on an unlettered wall and reduced to a monolithic national body of golden stars. As one journalist observes, visitors are "given no explanation of the awful math behind the flashy display."[27]

Indeed, audiences struggle for meaning at the National World War II Memorial. Few have the classical vocabulary to decipher the symbology of oak leaves and laurel wreaths; few equate the gold stars with soldier dead; few know that the pillars are arranged in order of admission to the union. Some search for narrative clues in the smallish bas-reliefs. Some stop at the Visitor Information Station on Home Front Drive, where the National Park Service distributes brochures and offers touch-screen computers linked to a database with the names of World War II vets. Some

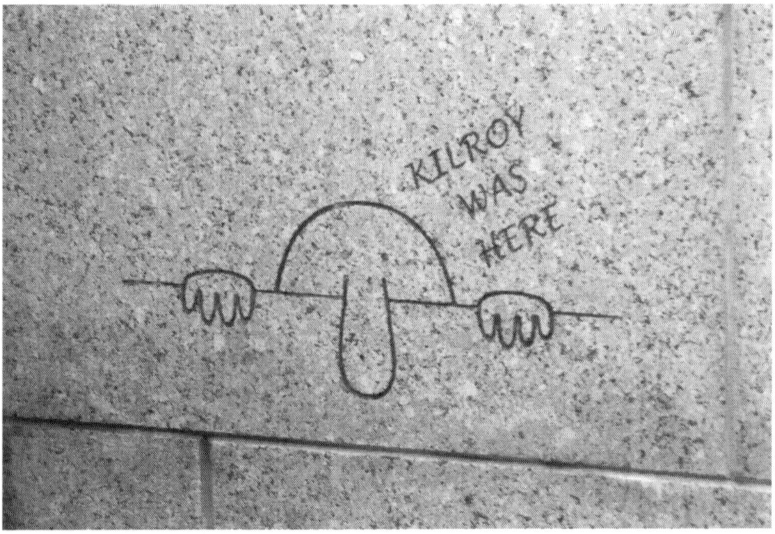

4.15. "Kilroy Was Here," engraved graffiti on the back wall of the National World War II Memorial. (Photo by the author.)

pose for pictures in front of the pillars, finding some level of identity in the names of their home states. Some search for the memorial's single bit of whimsy: a tiny "Kilroy Was Here" graffito engraved on its back wall (fig. 4.15). Some splash in the water or toss Roosevelt dimes into the fountains—despite numerous wooden signs that state "Please respect the memorial. No wading, No coins."

Nor does the National Park Service encourage visitors to leave gifts and offerings, as they do at the nearby Vietnam Veterans Memorial. This memorial "doesn't need stuff," explains the site's NPS superintendent, because it provides a "complete record" of World War II in and of itself.[28] Some visitors disagree and leave things tucked into the narrow crevices of the memorial's granite blocks: photos of soldier dead, or medals, letters, poems, and coins (fig. 4.16). Likewise, some leave floral wreaths in front of Freedom Wall. Informed by popular affective practices at other contemporary American memorials, many visitors search for ways to express their feelings at this one.

Most, however, seem simultaneously overwhelmed and unimpressed by the huge memorial—which, apparently, could have been even bigger: initial designs featuring taller granite pillars (35 feet high), a 400-seat underground auditorium, and a monumental sculpture called *The Light of Freedom* were all axed as "overbuild" by the U.S. Commission of Fine Arts.[29] Some visitors say the memorial is still "too big, too much"; others don't say much of anything. Most walk hurriedly through the memorial,

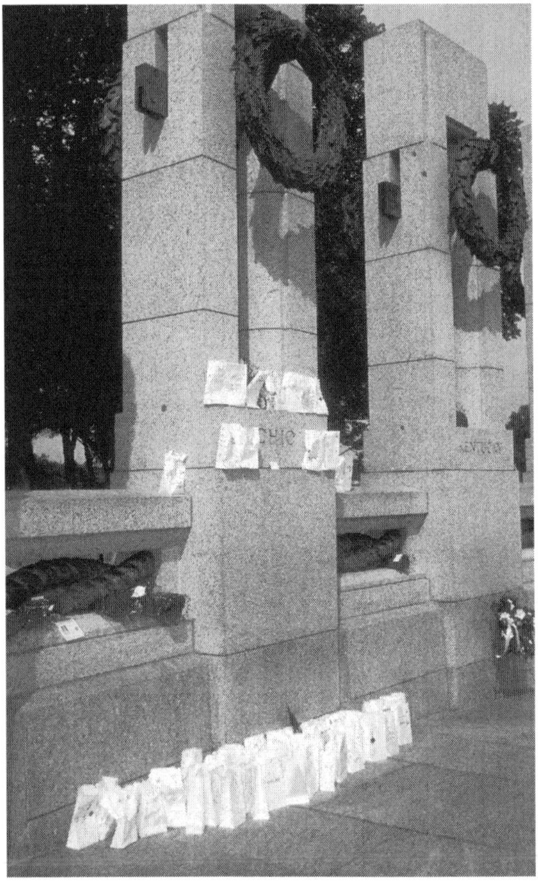

4.16. Items left at Ohio and Kentucky columns in memory of World War II veterans, Memorial Day 2009. The white bags contained medals, photos, letters, and other personal items. (Photo by Richard Latoff. © Richard Latoff/Latoff.com.)

glancing at its carved wartime homilies and its pillars and gold stars, and then moving on—and out—of its overbearing granite plaza. It is not an inviting or contemplative space; despite the use of flecked granite to reduce glare, the expansive stonework blasts white and bright. Likewise, while fountains help muffle the sounds of nearby street traffic and overhead jets, they also manufacture a kind of numbing white noise, a dull drone.

Nor is it an especially instructive memorial, one that might leave visitors with a sense of why World War II occurred, why more than 405,000 Americans died, and why this particular memorial was built. As one student told a reporter, the memorial "is really cool." When asked why the war was fought, he replied: "I don't know. No idea."[30] Deemed obtuse and uninspiring and—despite its size—inconsequential by many visitors, the memorial has been blasted by critics as a "triumphal act of hubris in stone and bronze," "bland and backward-looking," and "purest banality, an inert plaza dressed with off-the-shelf symbols of grief and glory."[31]

Friedrich St. Florian argues that "the essence" of the memorial is for "future generations": "What we want to tell young people now—and a hundred years and two hundred years from now—is that there was a generation of Americans that stood up and defended our ideals and principles when challenged. When they stand in front of that field of stars, we want them to shiver and say, 'If that happens again, I will do the same thing.'"[32]Speakers at its dedication—a ceremony titled "Tribute to a Generation" that was held on Memorial Day 2004, televised on C-Span and the History Channel, and attended by a crowd of more than a hundred thousand people—also addressed the memorial's future role. Bob Dole intoned that it was "only fitting" that its earliest visitors were school children, for "in the end, they are the ones for whom we built this shrine and to whom we now hand the baton." Each speaker—Tom Brokaw, Tom Hanks, Frederick W. Smith (CEO of Federal Express), and President George W. Bush—gave thanks to the "greatest generation"; expressions of gratitude that were couched in expectations of reciprocity from the nation's future (and current) generations. Bush made this explicit in a statement included in the dedication ceremony's printed program: "Today, as we fight a war against terrorism, we remember our veterans' commitment to our country and their legacy of patriotism. By answering the call of duty and risking their lives to protect their fellow citizens, these patriots continue to inspire all Americans."[33]

Memorials are, of course, presentist in their aims and ambitions. However much the National World War II Memorial is framed as a tribute to that war's veterans and soldier dead, another agenda is obviously at work. Consider its mission statement:

> Symbolic of the defining event of the 20th Century, the memorial is a monument to the spirit, sacrifice, and commitment of the American people to the common defense of the nation and to the broader causes of peace and freedom from tyranny throughout the world. It will inspire future generations of Americans, deepening their appreciation of what the World War II generation accomplished in securing freedom and democracy. Above all, the memorial stands as an important symbol of American national unity, a timeless reminder of the moral strength and awesome power that can flow when a free people are at once united and bonded together in a common and just cause.

As this manifesto suggests, the aim of the National World War II Memorial is not simply to say "thank you" the "greatest generation" but to dramatically reconfigure contemporary understandings of national purpose and identity. Its privileged location on the National Mall—the monumental core of America's capital city—helps promote its cause.

IMPERIAL AMERICA

Located on the National Mall's central axis, a strip of lawn stretching about two miles from the steps of the U.S. Capitol to those of the Lincoln Memorial, the National World War II Memorial occupies prime American real estate—what one author calls "the single most important public space in the country" and another likens as "our most sacred space." The Mall's national significance corresponds to its long-standing use as an open space for democratic discourse; as Lucy Barber argues, the Mall has functioned since the end of the nineteenth century to forge an "American political tradition" of active, and activist, citizenship.[34] It has repeatedly been the site of public gatherings and protests, from the 1894 march of "Coxey's Army" (a group of unemployed workers led by populist Jacob Coxey) to the 1963 March on Washington For Jobs and Freedom. In 1969, hundreds of thousands of antiwar protestors rallied at the Washington Monument; between 1987 and 1996, the NAMES Project Foundation's AIDS Memorial Quilt was displayed five times on the Mall. Now this nationally symbolic space features the National World War II Memorial.

It is one of four national memorials along the Mall's center strip, joining the Grant Memorial (dedicated in 1922) at the east end, the Lincoln Memorial (1922) at the west, and the Washington Monument (1885) in the middle (fig. 4.17). And its celebrated purpose as a war memorial has helped shift shared popular understandings of what these other national memorials now mean. While the Grant Memorial—a large sculptural ensemble featuring an equestrian statue of Union General Ulysses S. Grant flanked by full-scale figures of artillery and cavalry soldiers—is obviously a Civil War memorial, the Washington Monument and the Lincoln Memorial have never been typically viewed as memorials to the nation's Revolutionary or Civil wars. Now, however, they serve as militarized monumental bookends to a war deemed "the defining event of the 20th Century." Their neoclassical references to republican citizenship and pious national leadership have been eclipsed by the National World War II Memorial's overtures to an imperial America.

Washington was originally planned, of course, as an imperial city: in 1791, Pierre Charles L'Enfant imagined it as "the Capital of a powerful Empire" that would "extend over a large surface of ground."[35] A French-born architect and engineer, L'Enfant served with George Washington during the Revolutionary War and was appointed by the president to design the nation's new capital. Inspired by antique Roman and French

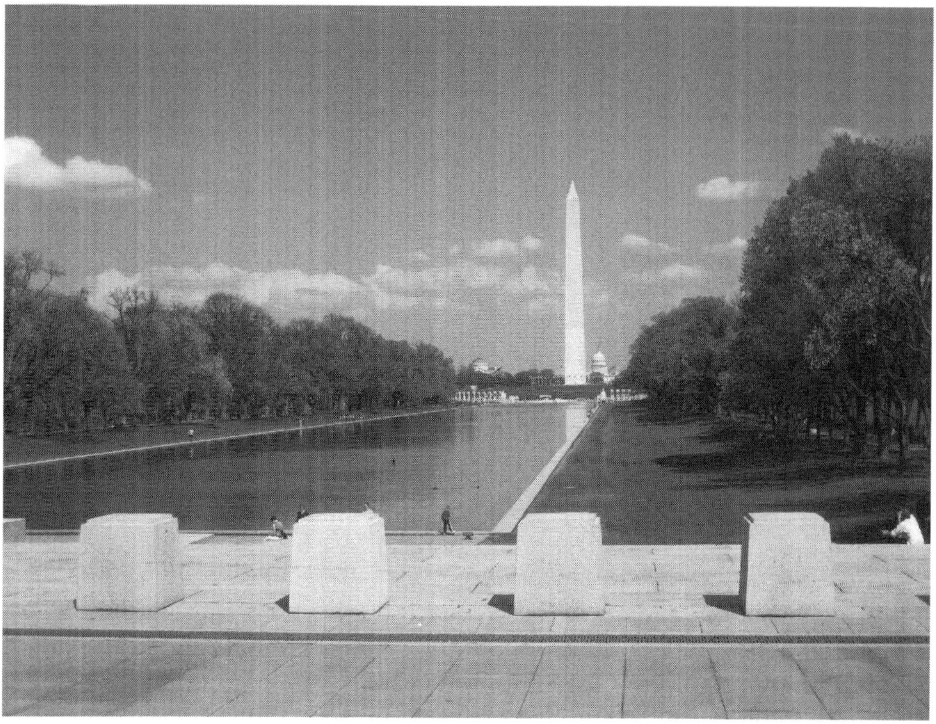

4.17. Washington Monument and Reflecting Pool, National Mall, Washington, D.C. (Courtesy of Heather Bowling.)

baroque designs, L'Enfant mapped an impressive federal city of broad radiating boulevards, spacious parks, and significant national buildings situated atop the area's highest hills: the house of Congress on one; the house of the president on the other. He imagined memorials, too, such as a sculptural group at the base of Capitol Hill to be called *Liberty Hailing Nature Out of Its Slumber*, an allegorical nod to the new nation and its federal government as the dynamic agents of a New World, a new modern civilization. Extending from the western axis of the capitol building, L'Enfant proposed a four hundred-foot-wide "Grand Avenue"—the National Mall—at the end of which he planned, as he wrote, an "equestrian figure of GEORGE WASHINGTON, a Monument voted in 1783, by the late Continental Congress."[36]

Despite near bankruptcy at the end of the war, one of the new nation's first acts was to authorize a bronze statue of General Washington in "Roman dress, holding a truncheon in his right hand" and posed atop a marble base featuring, in "basso relievo, the principal events of the war."[37] Notwithstanding the contested history of public art in America, symbols of national authority have been highly regarded right from the start—if slowly realized. It took over a century, for example, to actually erect a memorial to America's first president on the National Mall, and the 555-foot-tall obelisk that was finally raised paid homage to him as the nation's First Father, not its Supreme Commander.[38] Casting its great shadow across the national landscape, the blank shaft seemingly conferred early nineteenth-century American republican ideals of pious, self-made men and a democratic, peace-loving nation.

Of course obelisks, and where they stand, are hardly void of imperial allusions. In 1881, four years before the Washington Monument was dedicated, Cleopatra's Needle was erected in Central Park. An ancient monolith (ca. 1500 BCE) that once commemorated Ramses II's military victories over the Hittites, the obelisk was subsequently claimed by the Romans during the reign of Augustus Caesar and wound up in New York as a gift affirming Europe's colonization of Africa—and an invitation to the United States to share in the spoils. In 1885, Washington's colossal obelisk similarly tapped a vein of martial imperialism. Much like the ancient Egyptian obelisk erected in Paris's Place de la Concorde in 1836, raising the Washington Monument on the National Mall evoked America's "real, historical, ongoing, and potentially future imperial role" in the world.[39] In his presidential farewell address in 1796, Washington himself cautioned against "those overgrown military establishments which, under any form of government, are inauspicious to liberty, and which are to be regarded as particularly hostile to republican liberty." A century later, Washington's warnings were largely ignored as themes of "militaristic empire" dominated the American imaginary.[40]

The United States has long identified with ancient Rome: in the late eighteenth century, the political ideals of the new nation were modeled in part on the Roman Republic and George Washington was celebrated as its virtuous republican exemplar. Yet Rome's other face—its imperial other, the Rome of the Caesars—has also repeatedly surfaced as an American national paradigm. Indeed, to differentiate between America's imagined identity as "republic" or "empire" is to obscure its origins as a continental landmass violently seized from others, deliberately colonized, and hugely expanded and exploited through the actions of manifest destiny. America has always been beholden to imperialist pretensions, although it has often elected to deny them or to muddy their dynamics by identifying itself as the republican ideal. As Amy Kaplan argues, "disavowal of empire has long served as the ideological cornerstone of U.S. imperialism and a key component of American exceptionalism."[41] Controversy, for example, over the 1991 exhibition The West as America: Reinterpreting Images of the Frontier, 1820–1920, organized by the National Museum of American Art, largely hinged on objections to curatorial reassessment

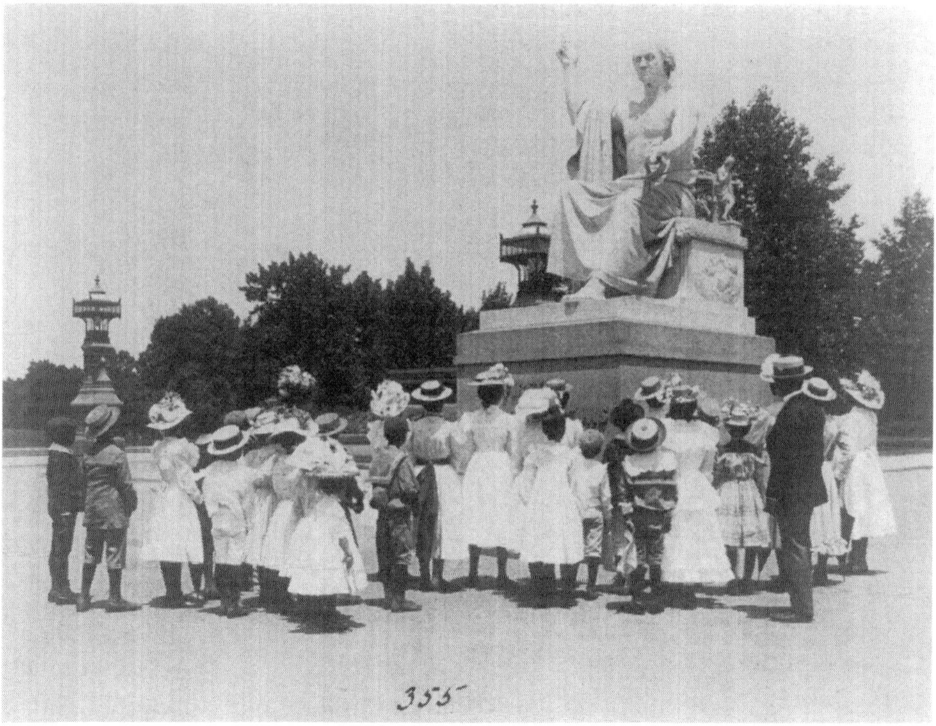

4.18. Frances Benjamin Johnson, African American schoolchildren facing the Horatio Greenough statue of George Washington at the U.S. Capitol, [1899?]. (Library of Congress, Prints and Photographs Division [digital ID no. cph 3a24897].)

of nineteenth-century American paintings in terms of racism and imperialism.[42] Visions of empire trouble national consciousness, even if they are inextricable from the nation's persistent sense of itself as special, boundless, benign, and better.

Such troubles were at the core of controversy over one of the nation's earlier memorials to George Washington: a $20,000 marble sculpture commissioned by Congress in 1832 that depicted the First Father as a neoclassical god seated on an imperial throne, holding a sheathed gladius (Roman sword), clothed in a toga and sandals, and displaying an impressively well-toned and completely bare chest (fig. 4.18). At the time, both the nudity and the imperial allusions of the twelve-ton colossus were ridiculed. Former New York mayor Philip Hone called Horatio Greenough's sculpture "a grand martial Magog, undressed, with a napkin lying in his lap." Nathaniel Hawthorne jested, "Did anyone ever see Washington naked? It is inconceivable." And U.S. congressman Leonard Jarvis insisted that the "emblematical Statue . . . is not *our* Washington." Intended for the rotunda of the U.S. Capitol, the memorial was moved outside to the building's less prominent east lawn.[43]

By the end of the nineteenth century, however, when the nation had become an industrial power with far reaching global authority, symbols of imperial Rome were widely employed to loudly pronounce—and legitimate—American imperialism. Examples include the 1893 Chicago World's Fair and the 1899 Dewey Arch, a temporary triumphal arch, one hundred feet tall and eighty feet wide, erected in New York at the intersection of Broadway and Fifth Avenue (briefly renamed the Appian Way) for an elaborate three-day tribute to Admiral George Dewey's victory over the Spanish fleet in Manila Bay. "The intention of the Arch is to symbolize the power of the U.S. as a maritime nation," the tribute's official program pronounced. "The Romans were masters in their temporary and permanent commemoration of triumphs; other nations have only followed their example."[44]

Roman styles were deemed especially suitable in the jingoistic era of the early twentieth century; their arrogant appeal to militarism and empire segued with America's own, especially after the Spanish-American War (1898) and U.S. territorial acquisition of Cuba, Puerto Rico, Hawaii, Guam, and the Philippines. Outfitted with triumphal arches, Corinthian columns, towering vaults, and colonnaded courts, public spaces ranging from train stations and libraries to museums, theaters, and parks were designed as the fabric of imperial America. "The twenty years between 1890 and 1910 saw the complete rehabilitation of the Roman mode, as the very cloak and costume of imperial enterprise," Lewis Mumford observed, adding "the architecture impresses and awes a populace that shares vicariously in its glories." Likewise, as one Gilded Age architect described New York's Pennsylvania Station (1910), whose monumental grandeur was modeled on the Roman Baths of Caracalla and the Coliseum: "The conditions of modern American life, in which undertakings of magnitude and scale are carried through, involving interests in all parts of the world, are more clearly akin to the life of the Roman Empire than that of any other civilization."[45] The official values promoted by the era's City Beautiful aesthetic, in other words, not only included national self-confidence, unity, and patriotism but global saber rattling, gunboat diplomacy, and neocolonialism.

The imperial national capital imagined by L'Enfant was finally realized in the twentieth century. Under the McMillan Plan (1901–1902), Washington was revisualized as a triumphal federal capital, with the National Mall its most symbolic centerpiece.[46] Extended by more than a mile (as acres of swampy marshland were filled in), L'Enfant's "Grand

Avenue" was relandscaped with waterworks (like the Reflecting Pool), walkways, formal gardens, and groves of trees. Its west end was anchored by the Lincoln Memorial, a giant white shrine to the nation's sixteenth president that architect Henry Bacon intended as a stoic statement of national unity, although audiences at its dedication in 1922 were segregated. Surrounded by thirty-six columns (the states of the union at the time of Lincoln's death) and housing Daniel Chester French's monumental marble statue of the seated (and fully clothed) president, Bacon's Doric temple was modeled on the colonnaded Parthenon, which once housed an immense statue of Athena. Yet raised high on a podium, approached by a steep flight of steps, and featuring a statue whose giant hands rest on an imposing white throne inscribed with fasces, symbols of imperial authority, the Lincoln Memorial also alludes to Roman architectural sources, and hence to early twentieth-century visions "of the nation-state and the federal government under the providential oversight of an imperial presidency."[47]

Critics viewed the Lincoln Memorial on exactly these imperialist terms. As Mumford observed in 1924, "Who lives in that shrine, I wonder—Lincoln, or the men who conceived it: the leader who beheld the mournful victory of the Civil War, or the generation that took pleasure in the mean triumph of the Spanish-American exploit, and placed the imperial standard in the Philippines and the Caribbean?"[48] Even if subsequent generations of Americans chose different meanings for the Lincoln Memorial—claiming it as an icon of emancipation and civil rights, for example, at the Marian Anderson protest concert held on its grounds in 1939, and at the March on Washington For Jobs and Freedom rally in 1963—its neoclassical aesthetics permit its easy use as a symbol of American imperialism. On January 17, 1993, "An American Reunion" concert was held at the Lincoln Memorial as the principal public event of President Bill Clinton's first inauguration. Some three hundred thousand people listened to Ray Charles sing "America the Beautiful" and Bob Dylan sing "Chimes of Freedom." Many watched clips of Martin Luther King, Jr.'s "I Have a Dream" speech, aired on giant video screens set up in nearby Potomac Park. Four days later, Clinton announced that the United States would maintain the former Bush administration's policy on Iraq, and U.S. military aircraft fired at multiple targets in Iraq.[49]

Memorials are made because they correspond to immediate social and political needs; the "very essence of the monument," Françoise Choay remarks, "lies in its relationship to lived time and to memory." Most of America's Civil War memorials, for example, were built in the late nineteenth and early twentieth centuries, when the nation was dominated by the racism of Jim Crow and engaged in imperialist exploits like the

Spanish-American War. Such monuments explained the Civil War as a conflict over states rights—"The War Of Northern Aggression," as some Southern Confederate memorials are inscribed—and banished the nation's history of slavery to visual purgatory. In the South, especially, "standing-soldier" memorials became masculine recovery projects for white men: material culture manifestations of the heroic white male body that helped recuperate socially constructed masculine attributes such as power, strength, militarism, and control, and thereby restore the white South's lost manhood. As Kirk Savage observes, Richmond's 1890 dedication of the Robert E. Lee Monument (see fig. 0.16, p. 12) was a "brilliant effort to re-present white mastery in the postwar world."[50]

Such war memorials inspired patriotic chauvinism at a moment of burgeoning American imperialism—at home, as the last surviving population of American Indians was incarcerated on federal reservations, and overseas, in the Philippines, Cuba, Panama, Nicaragua, Haiti (which the United States invaded in 1915), the Dominican Republic, and elsewhere. "We cannot fly from our world duties; it is ours to execute the purpose of a fate that has driven us to be greater than our small intentions," insisted Senator Albert J. Beveridge (R-IN) in 1898, adding, "What does all this mean for every one of us? It means opportunity for all the glorious young manhood of the republic—the most virile, ambitious, impatient, militant manhood the world has ever seen."[51] "Hiker statues" and "fighting doughboy" sculptures erected in the first few decades of the twentieth century further celebrated the nation's bellicose ambitions.

Imperialism, militarism, and hyper-masculinity are all key to the National World War II Memorial, with its Roman Empire motifs, its acres of bright white stone, its multiple quotes from "great men," and its blatant emphasis in both design and mission statement on the "awesome power" of the United States. Its neoclassical style is seen all over the nation's capital, in federal buildings like the Capitol and Supreme Court, as well as major memorials. Washington's World War I Memorial (1931), Jefferson Memorial (1943), and Women in Military Service for America Memorial (1997) all adopted neoclassical styles to signify permanence and power and evoke democratic veneration. Somewhat ironically, an imperial aesthetic featuring columned plazas, triumphal arches, and granite memorials, an aesthetic employed in numerous European capitals where it "most often glorified the military triumphs of absolute monarchs, rarely acknowledging the sacrifice of those unwillingly conscripted to fight wasteful and futile military adventures," became the preferred architectural currency of the modern capital of the democratic United States.[52]

Neoclassicism is an elastic aesthetic—consider its appropriation at

Caesars Palace in Las Vegas—but is typically employed to glorify its subjects.[53] Moreover, it is a style most often used when the eminence of those subjects is generally unquestioned. It was unabashedly appropriated for the National World War II Memorial because, today, World War II is celebrated as an intrinsically "good war" of unambiguous virtue. As St. Florian remarked in 2001, "during World War II there was a high sense of purpose. The country had a very clear vision of its own standing, of its own morality. It was not an ambiguous time." He added. "The most important thing for the memorial was really to make it timeless. The architecture will fit splendidly into Washington. It has that timeless quality that the other memorials have. The memorial plaza will be the most beautiful public space in our capital city."[54]

St. Florian's appropriation of the "timeless" imperial aesthetic of monumental Washington has not gone uncensored, but less because critics object to the memorial's overtures to American Empire than to empires elsewhere, at other historical times. "That colonnade? Il Duce would have loved it," groused *Time* magazine's Richard Lacey, noting that the memorial's "clean-lined take on neoclassicism" followed the Fascist style "favored by Mussolini." Marc Fisher of the *Washington Post* similarly described it as a "hodgepodge of cliché and Soviet-style pomposity." Others likened its refined classicism and stupendous size to the authoritarian aesthetics of the Third Reich. Paul Goldberger called it "watered-down Albert Speer," referencing the monumental building projects of Hitler's favorite architect; Paul Greenberg of the *Arkansas Democrat-Gazette* called it "the kind of thing the Axis might have built if they'd won the war"; and one angry World War II vet simply stated, "It looks like Hitler won the war." An editorial cartoon by Paul Conrad in the *Los Angeles Times* showed GIs Willie and Joe, the dogface mainstays of wartime cartoonist Bill Mauldin, standing inside the memorial's imperial plaza and muttering, "Looks like an officers' club . . . a German officers' club."[55]

Few memorials are installed without protest, especially in the nation's capital. Even the Jefferson Memorial met opposition; in 1938, protesters chained themselves to trees in the Tidal Basin after learning that the proposed memorial threatened cherry trees planted there in 1912 (a gift from Japan after President Teddy Roosevelt mediated in their favor during the Sino-Japanese War).[56] In 2000, a group of World War II GIs formed Veterans to Save the Mall to protest the National World War II Memorial. Disgruntled with its audacious design and the way it was "muscled through" Congress, they were also disheartened with its glorification of the war and their own participation. "We don't like anything as grandiose in the center of America's front yard," explained ex-Army corporal John Graves, the group's cochairman, during a protest rally organized a day before groundbreaking ceremonies for the memorial. "I get a $175.10 check every month, and I got a really good college education from the GI Bill," he added, implying that he hardly needed an "empty pile of stone" as his legacy. Challenging the "thank you" campaign led by Bob Dole and Tom Hanks, Graves's group launched its own public service advertisements: TV spots featuring Graves sternly addressing the camera and stating, "Some people want to pave over our National Mall . . . to build a grandiose World War II memorial. Destroying our National Mall should not be our legacy."[57]

Other World War II veterans echoed his sentiments. "I'm not arrogant enough to think any one of us has the same right to be memorialized on this Mall as Abraham Lincoln or George Washington," said one; "I would gladly give up my Purple Heart for doing away with that horrible desecration," said another. Invited to speak on a panel called "War Stories," one of many events sponsored by the Smithsonian Institution during the dedication of the National World War II Memorial, historian Howard Zinn—who was a bombardier in the Army Air Corps and flew combat missions over Europe in the last months of the war—told the audience, "I certainly don't want our government to use the triumphal excitement surrounding World War II to cover up the horrors now taking place in Iraq."[58]

Zinn's assessment of the presentist dimensions of the National World War II Memorial is shared by other veterans. "This is just a glorified cheer for modern day America," observes serviceman Charles Cassel, a Washington architect and founding member of the National Coalition to Save Our Mall, a group of World War II veterans, architects, urban planners, and concerned citizens that formed in 2000 "to defend our national gathering place and symbol of Constitutional principles against threats posed by recent and ongoing proposals—for new memorials, security barriers, service buildings and roads." Save Our Mall chairperson Judy Scott Feldman angrily testified before the U.S. Commission of Fine Arts, denouncing the new war memorial's "imperial and triumphal design" as "unacceptably reminiscent of Fascist and Nazi regimes." Ignoring such criticism, the commission unanimously approved it.[59]

The National World War II Memorial location, scale, style, and intentions are aligned with the nation's long-standing and recently revitalized reputation as a militaristic empire. It is deliberately positioned in the middle of a highly symbolic national landscape, a sacred civic space where the nation's memory is transcribed in stone. Its prominent size punctuates this monumental core and naturalizes its imperialist image, suggesting that the quest for empire has been the nation's "defining" purpose all along. And despite the mutable dynamics of both American nationalism and American memorials, this imperial image may be permanent. In 2003, Congress and the president approved legislation prohibiting further development on the National Mall's central strip, claiming that with the addition of the National World War II Memorial, the Mall's core was now a "substantially completed work of civic art."[60] Such a mandate confines the nation's "front yard" and, by extension, the nation itself, within a highly prescribed identity.

Some fear that the memorial's booming assertion of homogenous and unwavering patriotism might restrict public gatherings and demonstrations on the National Mall. "By digging the World War II Memorial into the space between Lincoln and Washington," one reporter predicts, "we will no longer see masses of Americans celebrating or protesting at Lincoln's feet. The empowering walk from George to Abe is no more." Or as Lisa Benton-Short argues, the new memorial transforms the National Mall "from an active space of civic participation and engagement to a space that encourages a more passive consumption of commemoration."[61] While the National World War II Memorial occupies an immense public space seemingly open to public debate, its imperial aesthetic hardly encourages democratic dissent—not that the current conditions of the national security state do either.

Those conditions, of course, contextualize why it was built and what it means in America today. As Herbert Muschamp argued, the memorial essentializes World War II as "an age of moral certainty, a time innocent of complexity, irony, or ambiguity."[62] Embracing bloodless victory, it elides why and how so many died. Fixed on national unity, it discounts the facts of racial segregation among U.S. troops and the forced relocation of Japanese Americans under Executive Order 9066. It erases the global dimensions of the war: framed by the states of the Union and its territorial acquisitions, inscribed with the names of Asian and European battles but not those of America's allies or its foes, the National World War II Memorial implies that the U.S. single-handedly won a war against some unknown enemy. While it includes the inscription "Americans came to liberate, not to conquer; to restore freedom and to end tyranny" (etched on the base of each bronze flagpole), its vainglorious aesthetic suggests otherwise. Its brazen celebration of the virtues of war speaks to a dominant martial ethos.

WAR PORN

Bursts of machine-gun fire sting the water; soldiers stumble out of landing craft and struggle to shore; bodies litter the beach (fig. 4.19). Welcome to the National D-Day Memorial in Bedford, Virginia, a nine-acre, $25 million tribute to "the sacrifices of the Allied Armed Forces who landed in Normandy, France on June 6, 1944."[63] Located in the southwestern part of the state, about ten miles from the Blue Ridge Mountains, the memorial features a gigantic triumphal arch, symbolically forty-four feet and six inches tall. Inscribed on its polished granite entablature is the word "OVERLORD": the code name of the military operation commanded by General Dwight D. Eisenhower (fig. 4.20). The sprawling site also showcases sculptures, war materiel (anchors, propellers, and a restored Aeronca L-3 "Grasshopper" aircraft), formal gardens (including one planted in the design and colors of the Supreme Headquarters Allied Expeditionary Force shoulder patch), flags representing the twelve Allied nations, and a Necrology Wall listing the names of U.S. servicemen killed on D day.

Most visitors are drawn to the memorial's interior plaza, where the action on Omaha Beach is dramatically restaged—albeit reduced to a frozen tableau of life-sized bronze action figures slogging their way through a six-inch-deep pool toward a simulated beach made of aggregate concrete (fig. 4.21). Every few seconds, jets of water shoot up in sync with a soundtrack of pattering machine guns. One fallen GI lies crumpled on the shore, his head resting near a waterlogged Bible. Another screams in anguish while scaling a twenty-foot metal wall standing in for the cliffs at Pointe-du-Hoc. Occasionally, the memorial is open at night and the grounds are flooded in red, white, and blue lights. Every Father's Day in June, it hosts the "World War II in Miniature Show and Contest," sponsored by the Roanoke Valley Chapter of the International Plastic Modelers Society. "This monument pays tribute to those who died on D day but also to those who lived to secure the beachhead and carry freedom inland," reads the memorial's entrance plaque. "Treasure it."

While framed as an international memorial to Allied forces, the National D-Day Memorial is clearly beholden to the obligations and demands of American war memory. Authorized by Congress in 1997, it is located in Bedford because the town claims more losses on D day than any other American town: nineteen of its thirty-five citizen soldiers died during the invasion, two more during the fighting in Normandy. However appalling this hokey memorial, which has all the commemorative decorum of a water park, "the order of the day is gratitude," intoned President George W. Bush at its dedication in 2001, held on the 57th anniversary of D day and attended by some twenty-four thousand people. "Today we give thanks for all that was gained on the beaches of Normandy," he stated. "We remember what was lost, with respect, admiration, and love."[64]

Americans certainly love D day: more than eight hundred thousand

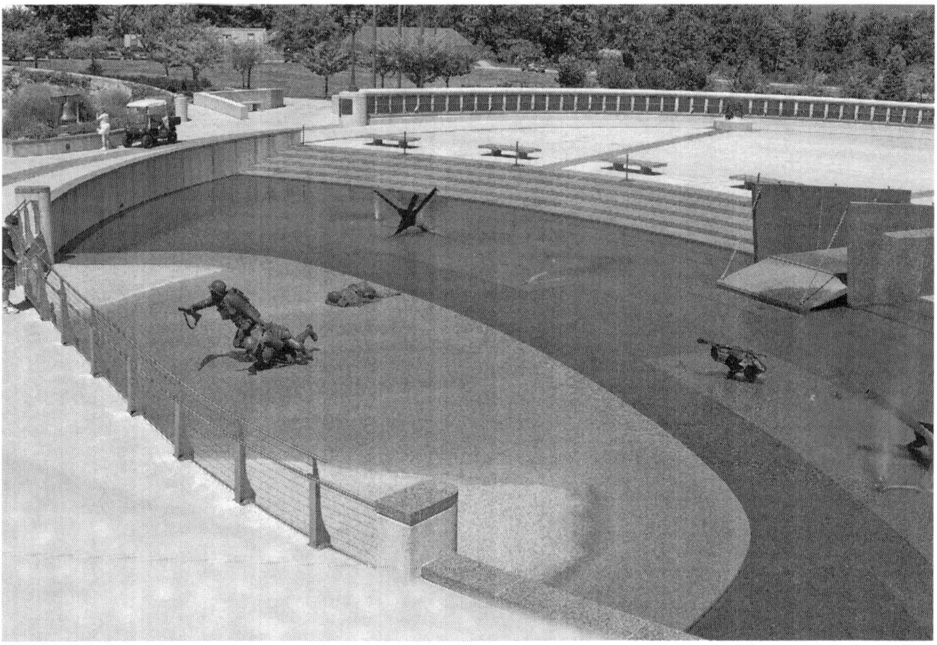

4.19. Landing beach tableau, National D-Day Memorial, Bedford, Virginia, dedicated 2001. (© 2009 SmugMug, Inc.)

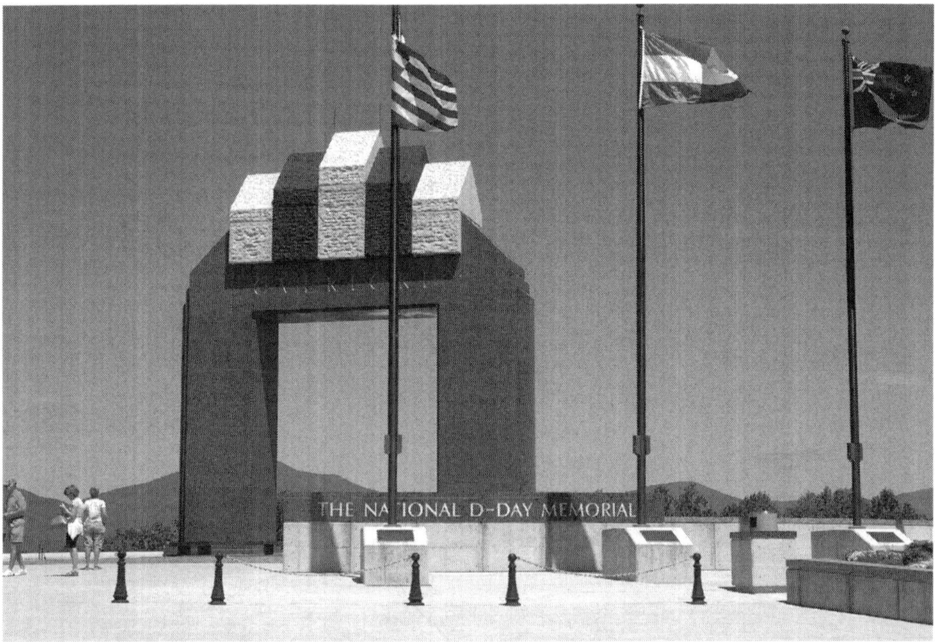

4.20. Overlord Arch, National D-Day Memorial, Bedford, Virginia. (© 2009 SmugMug, Inc.)

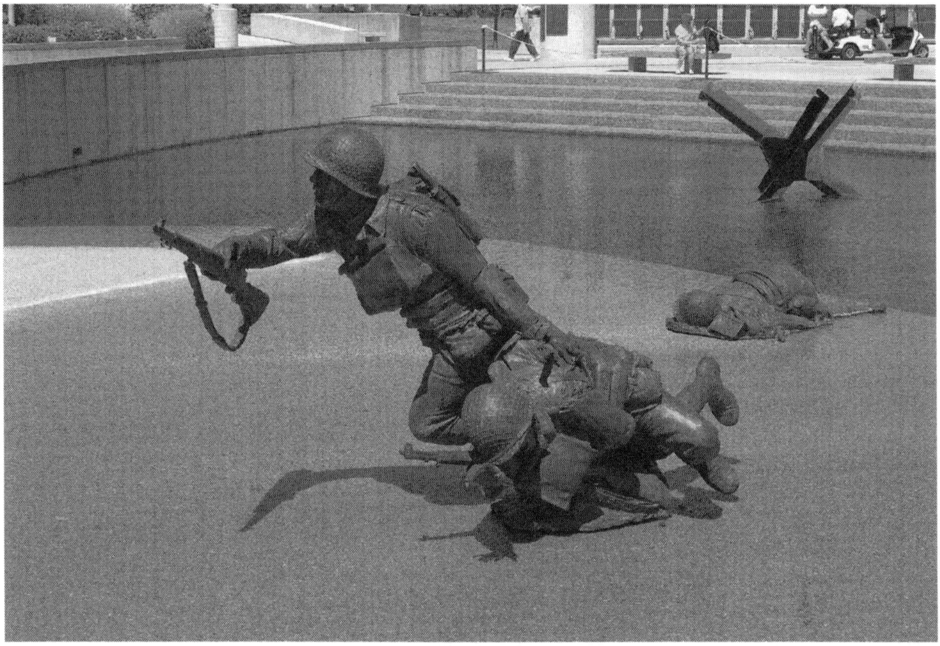

4.21. Landing beach tableau, detail, National D-Day Memorial. (© 2009 SmugMug, Inc.)

visited the National D-Day Memorial in its first five years of operation. It has become a ritualized stopover for Rolling Thunder riders heading to Washington (240 miles northeast) for their annual Memorial Day rally. When they reach Bedford, the veterans circle the memorial and lay a wreath at Overlord Arch. Likewise, the National D-Day Museum in New Orleans, which opened in 2000 and was renamed the National World War II Museum in 2006, attracted some three hundred thousand visitors a year before Hurricane Katrina, which put it in the top 10 percent of museum attendance nationwide. *Saving Private Ryan*, a $70 million blockbuster that included a carnage-strewn twenty-five minute D day sequence that critics and movie goers couldn't stop talking about, was the most popular Hollywood release of 1998, generating a domestic gross alone of over $216 million and winning Steven Spielberg an Oscar for best director. Among the plethora of World War II computer and video games, titles like *Close Combat: Invasion Normandy* (2000), *Medal of Honor: Allied Assault* (2002), *Call of Duty* (2003), and *Brothers in Arms: D-Day* (2006) attest to D day's resonance in the gaming industry.[65] More than sixty years later, D day continues to loom large in the American national imagination.

So does Pearl Harbor, which is repeatedly circulated in America's political rhetoric and culture industries in order to shore up various national scenarios. In the early 1980s, for example, Pearl Harbor's fortieth anniversary prompted much media hype about America's "trade war" with Japan being induced by an "economic Pearl Harbor." A decade later, Pearl Harbor's fiftieth anniversary was commemorated by a host of books, TV shows, and museum exhibitions that effectively crystallized December 7, 1941, as *the* day the war started for America. This downplays competing (or revisionist) narratives that consider increased defense industry production in the late 1930s or prior U.S. knowledge of the Japanese attack. As Emily Rosenberg argues, Pearl Harbor's legacy has been to reinforce American beliefs that war is "event-driven"—that Americans only go to war when attacked by the forces of evil, and that the United States is essentially an innocent and peace-loving nation.[66]

The $135 million movie *Pearl Harbor*, a three-hour epic that opened in May 2001, reaffirmed these cause-and-effect, good-versus-evil understandings of World War II (and war in general) for many Americans. So did its blitz of marketing tie-ins, which ranged from Hasbro's Pearl Harbor GI Joe collection and ASAP's video game *Pearl Harbor: Zero Hour*, to military history books, war movie re-releases (such as a refurbished version of the 1970 film *Tora! Tora! Tora!*), and numerous TV specials (like MSNBC's "Pearl Harbor: Attack on America," hosted by General Norman Schwarzkopf). It is hardly surprising, then, that four months after the movie was released, Pearl Harbor became the most "enduring analogy" to 9/11. On September 11, 2001, George W. Bush wrote, "The Pearl Harbor of the 21st century took place today" in his presidential diary; the next day, the *New York Times* included thirteen articles mentioning Pearl Harbor. Banners screaming "DAY OF INFAMY," echoing FDR's description of Pearl Harbor as "a date which will live in infamy," headlined many U.S. newspapers.[67]

Long before 9/11, of course, Americans had been pining for the glory days of World War II and, more generally, pursuing a giddy romance with all things war: the "war on drugs," "the war on AIDS," "the war to control the legal culture," as Robert Bork described his unsuccessful bid for the Supreme Court in 1987. However contradictory the uses of these multiple war metaphors, war itself is ingrained in American national consciousness because of abiding assumptions that war alone is "the best way to mobilize Americans and to capture their problems and conflicts."[68] War is the great American distraction: mythologized as a patriotic project, articulated as an economic linchpin, desired for its explicit, stimulating, visceral, and authenticating capacities. And war porn is the great American cultural expression, not as a form of sexual fantasy and social transgression but as an instrument of national consensus, conformity, and normalcy.

Jean Baudrillard likened war porn to the titillation derived from Abu-Ghraib's atrocity snapshots. Staff at *Adbusters* used the term to describe *Time*'s "Person of the Year" cover in 2003, which featured a group of young, good-looking GIs dressed in desert khakis and body armor, cradling M-16s. Inside, the magazine described them as "the face of America, its might and good will."[69] Constituting both the subjects and objects of the nation's martial authority, war porn characterizes the contemporary American lust for war, evinced not only in war movies, war games, war toys, and war memorials but in the general fetishization of war itself on every conceivable level of American society. Americans today are utterly seduced by war, argues Andrew Bacevich, and are especially swayed by a "new American militarism" manifest in "a romanticized view of soldiers, a tendency to see military power as the truest measure of national greatness, and outsized expectations regarding the efficacy of force." He adds: "To a degree without precedent in U.S. history, Americans have come to define the nation's strength and well-being in terms of military preparedness, military action, and the fostering of (or nostalgia for) military ideals."[70]

Whether or not this "new American militarism" is all that new—many scholars have discussed the nation's prevailing martial ethos at the turn of the twentieth century—it is central to contemporary American identity.[71] It is increasingly realized in America's growing body of war memorials, which are, without doubt, memorial mania's largest body (along with 9/11 memorials, many of which are conceived as war memorials). Their burgeoning numbers, which range from abstract monuments and figurative memorials to benches, flagpoles, and street signs (in Yuma, Arizona, new city streets are named after U.S. soldier dead), speak to a generally unquestioned American faith in militarism, and accommodate the nation's sense of itself as a military presence and power, as a force to be reckoned with.

HONORING SOLDIER DEAD

The dedication of the Vietnam Veterans Memorial in 1982 spurred the making of hundreds of similar memorials across the country—over five hundred, estimates one author—and shows no sign of abating. In 2009 alone, Vietnam War memorials were dedicated in Clinton, Ohio, Laton, California, Iowa City, Iowa, and Carlisle, Pennsylvania; in recent years they have been erected in Coventry, Connecticut (2008), Cedar City, Utah (2008), New Bedford, Massachusetts (2006), Pierre, South Dakota (2006), Chicago (2005), and Port St. Lucie, Florida (2003). Several mobile versions of the Vietnam Veterans Memorial regularly tour the country,

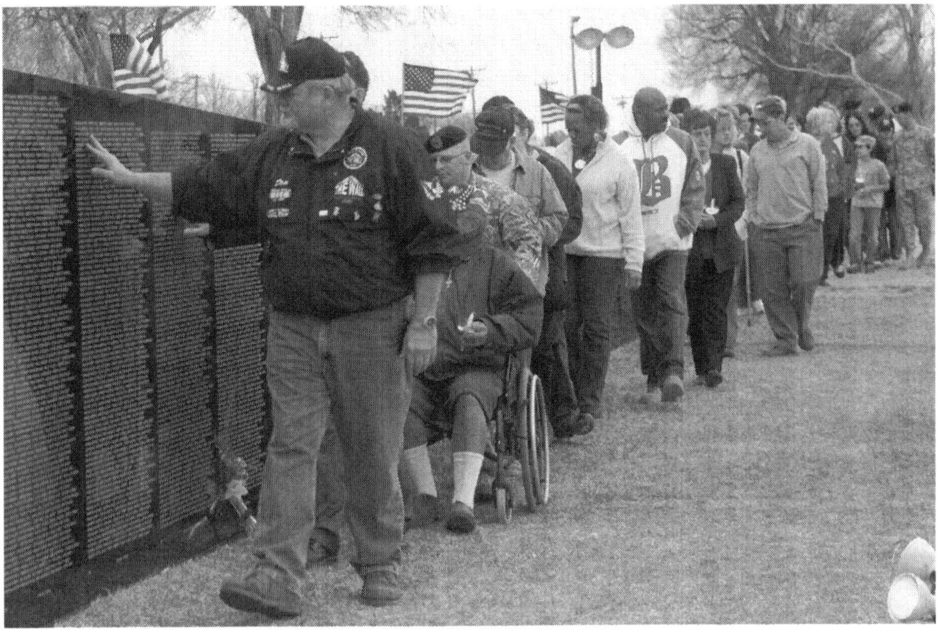

4.22. The Traveling Wall, March 2008. Veterans and others in Clovis, New Mexico, tour a scaled-down version of the Vietnam Veterans Memorial organized by the American Veterans Traveling Tribute. (Photo by Airman First Class Liliana Moreno. Courtesy of the U.S. Air Force.)

including the Moving Wall (a half-size replica, sponsored by Vietnam Combat Veterans, Ltd., since 1984), the Wall That Heals (also half-size, sponsored by the Vietnam Veterans Memorial Foundation since 1996), the Vietnam Traveling Memorial Wall (a three-fifths scale version), and the American Veterans Traveling Tribute (a four-fifths scale replica).[72] Towns typically pay more than $4,000 a week to rent these temporary versions of the Wall (fig. 4.22).

Likewise, much as the commemorative subjectivity of the Wall was expanded by the addition of two figurative bronze sculptures installed nearby—Frederick Hart's *Three Fighting Men* (1982) and Glenna Goodacre's Vietnam Women's Memorial (1993)—a number of memorials are dedicated to Vietnam's "dogs of war": in Riverside, California (2000), Fort Benning, Georgia (2000), Streamwood, Illinois (2001, fig. 4.23), and Holmdel, New Jersey (2006, fig. 4.24). A campaign to build a national war dog memorial is underway, and a bill authorizing such a monument was introduced in 2006 by Rep. Walter B. Jones (R-NC), who declared, "Over the course of our Nation's military history, those who have bravely served our country in battle have been recognized and remembered for their loyalty and service. In that tradition, one breed of hero has been too

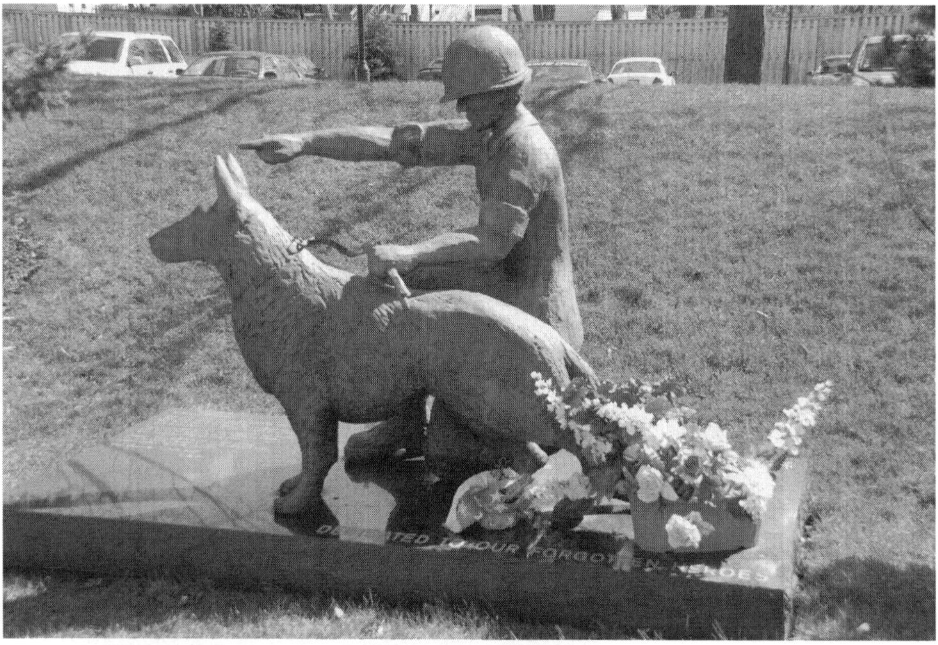

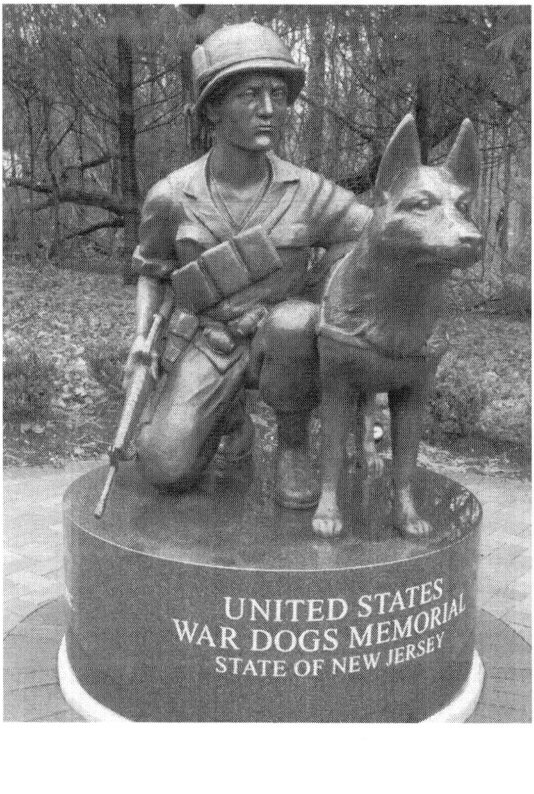

4.23. Anthony Quickle, *Guardians*, War Dog Memorial, Streamwood, Illinois, dedicated 2001. (Courtesy of Jonathan Doss.)

4.24. Brian Lindsay, United States War Dogs Memorial, Holmdel, New Jersey, dedicated 2006. (Photo by Scott Lindsay. © Brian Lindsay and USWDA.)

often overlooked . . . The National War Dog Monument will honor the loyalty, courage and sacrifices [they] made."[73]

Memorials to America's military engagement in Vietnam have influenced many other war memory projects. The Korean War Veterans Memorial was dedicated in Washington in 1995 and similar memorials were raised more recently in Toledo, Ohio (2006), Lawrence, Kansas (2005), Baton Rouge, Louisiana (2004), Lake County, Indiana (2003), Philadelphia (2002), Wichita, Kansas (2001), and Wilsonville, Oregon (2000). Memorials to the cold war, such as the Victims of Communism Memorial (see fig. 1.1, p. 18), and to the Gulf War, including Operation Desert Shield / Desert Storm memorials erected in Greensburg, Pennsylvania (1992), Evansville, Indiana (1993), and Lincoln City, Oregon (1994) also dot the American landscape. Memorials to current wars in Iraq and Afghanistan have already been built in Rapid River, Michigan (2009), Kingsport, Tennessee (2008), Lewiston, Maine (2006), Willington, Connecticut (2005), and Blanca, Colorado (2004). In 2004, the Middle East Conflicts War Memorial was dedicated in Marseilles, Illinois, where each summer thousands participate in an Illinois Motorcycle Freedom Run "to Honor Fallen Heroes."[74] In 2006, the Veterans of Foreign Wars proposed a shared Middle Eastern Veterans Memorial for the nation's capital, aimed at honoring all U.S. soldiers involved in all of America's military incursions in the region since 1990.

Memorials to U.S. soldier dead are a windfall in today's commercial monument industry. Increasingly common are memorial benches to soldiers killed in Iraq, simple granite seats inscribed with names, birth and death dates, and epithets of remembrance that retail for $200. So are "fallen soldier" statues marketed by companies like Large Art, a custom sculpture firm in Baltimore (fig. 4.25). Also called *Battlefield Crosses*, these bronze arrangements of boots, helmets, and rifles cost $4,400 and are among the most popular items from Large Art; as of 2007, over seventy had been sold, including five erected in Iraq. As company owner and artist Richard Rist remarks, "I sense an eagerness to almost overcompensate in honoring our war dead."[75]

The Vietnam Veterans Memorial has had a big impact, too, on how this growing body of war memorials is defined and understood. Typically, today's war memorials are cast as "service" memorials: tributes to veterans rather than the wars they fought in. Such distinctions are specious; the nation builds memorials to combat soldiers, not peacetime clerk typists.[76] Whatever they are called, memorials that commemorate the nation's soldiers are war memorials.

And today they are both copious and historically sweeping. In 2004, a memorial to the "Army of Occupation," the U.S. troops commanded by

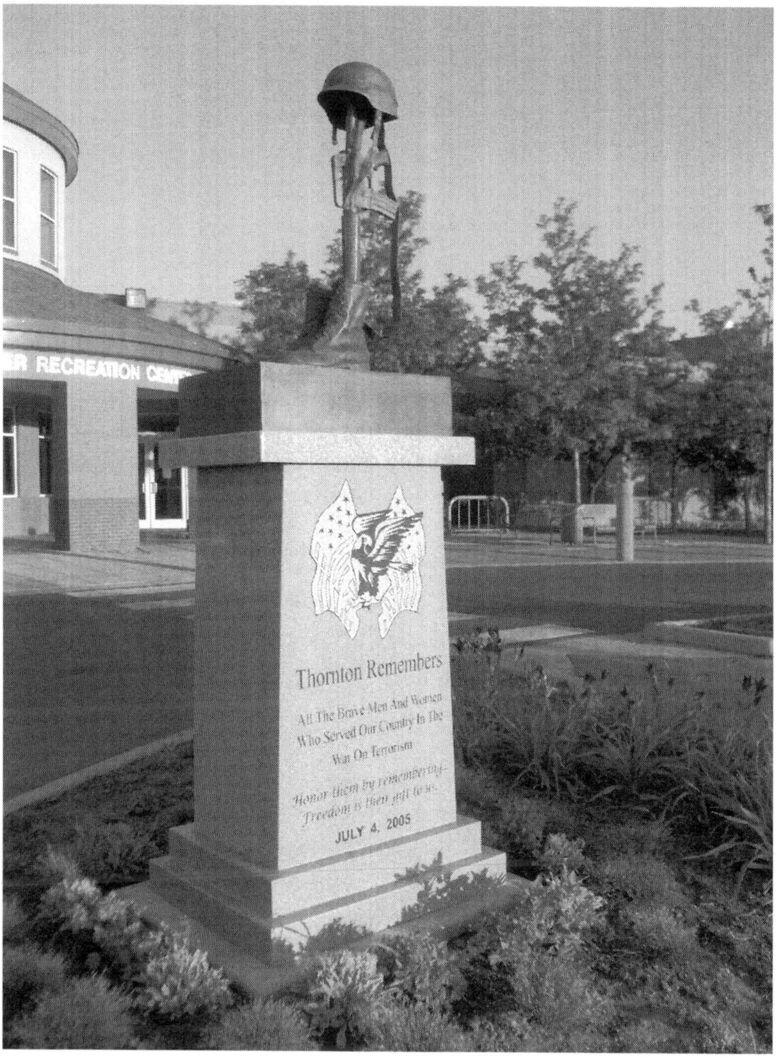

4.25. Richard Rist, Fallen Soldier Memorial, Thornton, Colorado, dedicated 2005. (Photo by the author.)

General Zachary Taylor during the Mexican-American War, was dedicated in Corpus Christi, Texas. In 2006 in Kansas City, the Liberty Memorial—a World War I memorial originally dedicated in 1926—was refurbished and expanded to include the National World War I Memorial Museum. In San Francisco, plans are in place for the Abraham Lincoln Brigade Monument, the first national memorial to the three thousand Americans who fought in the Spanish Civil War from 1936 to 1938. In 2004 in Iowa, a $10 million Memorial Park & Education Center was dedicated at Fort

Des Moines, where the first Officer Candidate School opened to African American men in 1917 and where the Women's Army Auxiliary Corps trained during World War II. In 1999, Congress authorized memorials honoring Medal of Honor recipients in Riverside, California, and Indianapolis (and a National Medal of Honor Museum in Mount Pleasant, South Carolina).

Also common are "additive" memorials, such as bronze plaques tacked on to already extant war memorials in order to list the names of subsequent generations of soldier dead. Recognizing the time-consuming and costly efforts of repeatedly raising new war memorials to commemorate the nation's nonstop history of combat, some communities have opted for "all-war" memorials that collectively remember all of America's soldiers and wars—and leave plenty of room for future war memory. These include the Veterans Walk of Honor in Ripon, Wisconsin (dedicated 2001), the "All Wars" Veterans Memorial in Scottsburg, Indiana (2008), and a forthcoming memorial in Picatinny, New Jersey, "for the bygone, ongoing, and future sacrifices made by all New Jersey fallen soldiers."

The Community Veterans Memorial (2003) in Munster, Indiana, commemorates Americans "who participated in the great wars of the 20th century—World Wars I and II, Korea, Vietnam, Desert Storm."[77] Designed by Julie Rotblatt and Omri Amrany, perhaps best known for their oversized statue of a slam-dunking Michael Jordan in front of Chicago's United Center, Munster's $3.2 million memorial is located next to a landfill on the outskirts of town. The seven-acre site features sculptures and "actual war memorabilia" (a P-51 Mustang fighter plane, 75mm Airborne Pack Howitzer, and Huey helicopter) sprinkled among landscapes meant to depict "the terrains of the countries in which the conflicts took place." World War II is represented by a recreation of Omaha Beach; Vietnam by a ruined Buddhist temple, bas-reliefs of jungle scenes, and a menacing Green Beret aiming a 40-mm grenade launcher at anyone in his way (and standing near the partial remains of another GI whose body was exploded by a booby trap, fig. 4.26). The Gulf War is recreated in piles of pea gravel simulating sand dunes and a billowing ten-foot bronze cloud that mimics the burning oil wells of Kuwait (fig. 4.27). Nearby, in a closing vignette called *The Emptiness of War*, a small boy clutching his father's dog tags surveys the entire combat tableau from the vantage of his bombed-out house.

Like the National D-Day Memorial, Munster's memorial is an interactive space filled with dramatic (and disturbing) images, text panels, and audio guides describing each wartime scene. It is also shamelessly contrived as an all-war theme park modeled on a miniature golf course. Spiraling walkways made of memorial bricks—which patrons are encour-

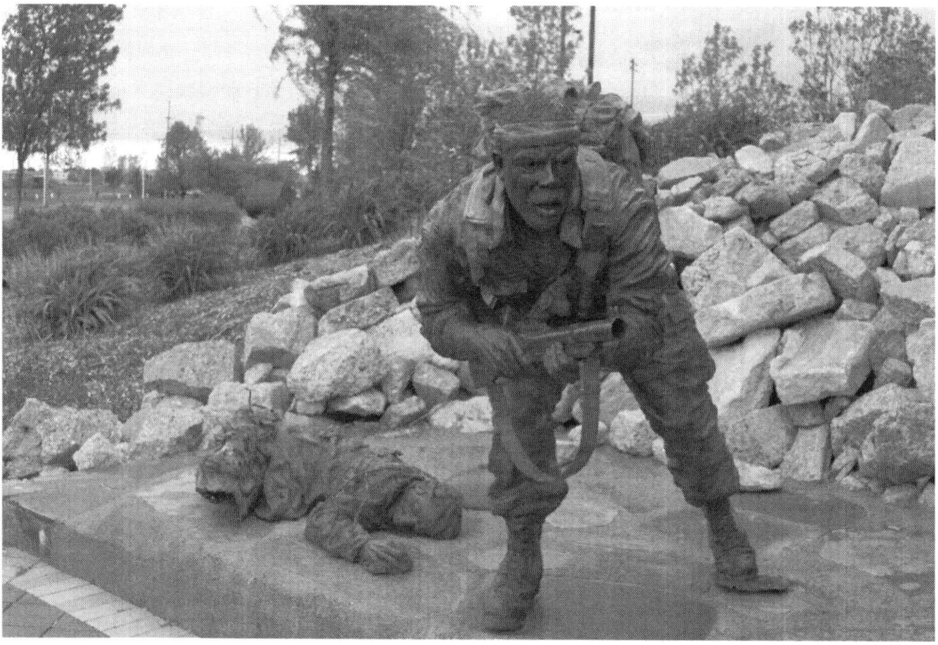

4.26. Julie Rotblatt and Omri Amrany, Community Veterans Memorial, detail of Vietnam scene, Munster, Indiana, dedicated 2003. (Courtesy of Geoffrey Thrumston.)

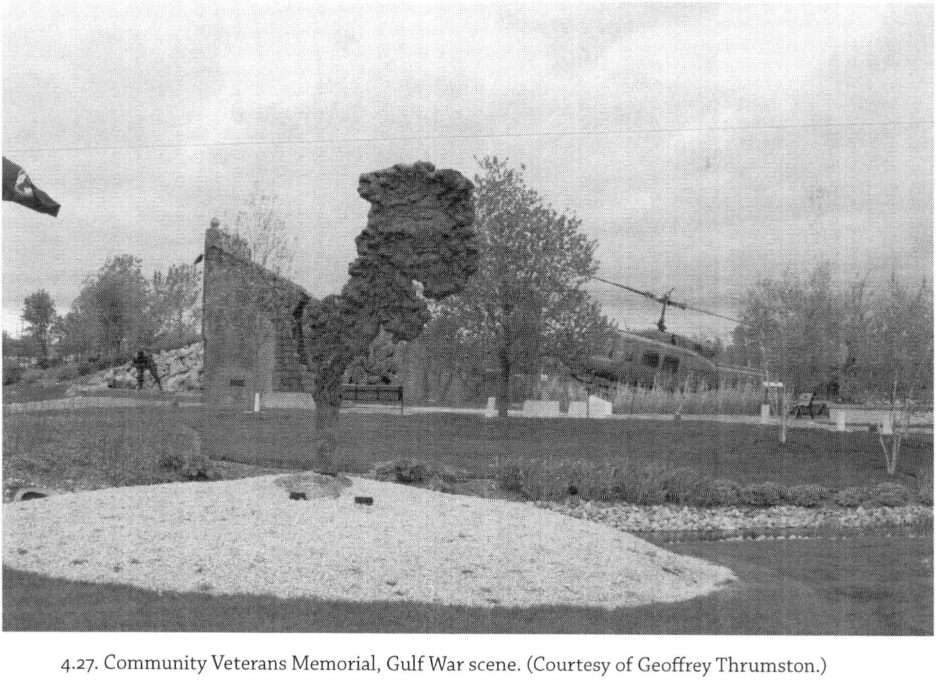

4.27. Community Veterans Memorial, Gulf War scene. (Courtesy of Geoffrey Thrumston.)

aged to purchase as "a permanent tribute to loved ones who fought to preserve our freedoms"—link all wars in an endless loop. Winding their way through the memorial's vast space, walking from one park attraction to the next, visitors perpetually reanimate national war memory. Benches, ponds, and landscaped lawns lend a recreational air to the site, inviting visitors to throw Frisbees and have a picnic while they also look at the bodies of dead soldiers and stroll past wartime dioramas. And visitors are enthusiastic: children crawl through the ruined buildings and climb on the Howitzer while their parents exclaim about the "lifelike" qualities of the bronze statues.

Although Rotblatt says Munster's memorial addresses the "horrors of war" and "how we hope to evolve as a species to break the cycle of war," its spectacular sets, battle-ready cast of characters, heroizing script ("in the bush, without a helmet, he moves swiftly and silently" is the audio guide description of the Special Forces soldier), and dizzying theme park dynamics hardly inspire antiwar sentiment.[78] Rather, as one visitor observed, "Anybody that's an American that's in this country, that sits there and wants to pick at this and that, maybe they should come and look at this thing and see what the veterans are doing. They had a job to do and they did it." Each September, Munster's war memorial hosts Freedom Walk, one of more than forty such walks organized by the Department of Defense to pay tribute to the victims of 9/11 and rally support for U.S. troops. In 2005, participants in Washington donned free Freedom Walk T-shirts and marched from the Pentagon to the National Mall, viewing war memorials that Secretary of Defense Donald Rumsfeld said serve to remind Americans of "the sacrifices of this generation and of each previous generation that has so successfully defended our freedoms."[79]

Some of the nation's newer war memorials follow the minimalist style of the Vietnam Veterans Memorial; others include images and expressions that romanticize American soldiers and celebrate American militarism. Phoenix's Vietnam War Memorial combines highly polished black blocks featuring the names of soldier dead with figurative bronze sculptures (see fig. 0.9, p. 5). Likewise, the Korean War Monument in New Bedford, Massachusetts (2001), features a black wall etched with the names of soldier dead, photographs of tanks, aircraft carriers, Corsair fighter bombers, and the inscription "Korean War, 1950–1953, Freedom Is Not Free."

That adage, engraved on a wall of the Korean War Veterans Memorial (and above the entrance to the American Legion headquarters) in Washington, D.C., has been widely adopted in contemporary American war memorials. References to "freedom" range from the inscription "Here We Mark the Price of Freedom" at the National World War II Memorial to the words carved on the World War II Freedom Memorial in Des Moines, Iowa: "For those who labored, fought, and died for freedom." Freedom is also, of course, the ostensible objective of the war on terror. America's military is "working for the spread of freedom" worldwide, said President Bush in November 2003, adding, "The advance of freedom is the calling of our time; the calling of our country."[80] Freedom, in other words, is a national allegory that justifies why wars are fought and why soldiers die. It is embraced as a uniquely American attribute that defines the terms of national citizenship, blood sacrifice, and politics alike; it holds so much authority in the national imagination that it generally goes unquestioned. But the slogan "Freedom Is Not Free" is exceptionally Orwellian, implying that freedom requires debt, entails costs, and demands sacrifices. By virtue of being inscribed on war memorials (and generally nowhere else), such a slogan declares that war is the price of freedom and, in fact, requires the sacrifice of freedom: that freedom must be sacrificed to be free. It is an adage beholden to the problematic culture of gratitude that informs contemporary American war memorials.

WE ARE ALL WARRIORS

New Bedford, a port city about sixty miles south of Boston, is typical in terms of its growing body of war memorials and their expansive expressions of gratitude: thanks are given to multiple American publics for their participation in multiple wars. The city hosts a fair number of statues and monuments like *The Whaleman* (1913) by Bela Pratt and a memorial dedicated in 1996 to Frederick Douglass (who lived in New Bedford from 1838 to 1841), and most of them are war memorials. New Bedford's Department of Veterans' Services lists over sixty war memorials, ranging from single soldier memorials such as the stone dedicated in 2006 to Staff Sergeant Joseph Camara, killed in Iraq in 2003, to mass memorials like the New Bedford Merchant Marines Memorial, dedicated in 2004 to local mariners who lost their lives in World War II. The city's Soldiers and Sailors Monument dates to 1866, and a handful of World War I memorials were dedicated in the 1920s, but most of New Bedford's war memorials were raised after 1950 and in tribute to specific soldier publics: the American Portuguese War Veterans Memorial (1950), the Franco-American War Veterans Square (1950, which features an M26 Pershing tank), the Italian-American War Memorial (1950), the Jewish War Veterans Memorial (1962), the American Lebanese Veterans Memorial (1965), the Cape Verdean American Veterans Memorial (1970), the Black American War Memorial (1980), and the Polish American Veterans War Memorial (1995). In 1999, the 54th Volunteer Regiment Plaza was dedicated in downtown New Bedford, in tribute to black troops who enlisted in the Union army.

Until recently, minority military representation was minimal in American commemorative cultures, save for notable exceptions like the Shaw Memorial (Boston, 1897), the World War Black Soldiers Memorial (also known as the Victory Monument, Chicago, 1928), and the All Wars Memorial to Colored Soldiers and Sailors (Philadelphia, 1934). In 1948, army officers strongly resisted President Truman's executive order to desegregate the military.[81] Today, however, the U.S. military is a leading minority employer—and soldiers of color are the subjects of multiple memorials to multiple wars. The Haitian Memorial Monument, a $500,000 bronze sculpture that pays homage to the Chasseurs-Volontaires de Saint-Domingue, a regiment of five hundred Haitian soldiers who fought against the British along coastal Georgia in 1779, was dedicated in Savannah in 2007. The African-American World War II Navy Memorial was dedicated in North Chicago in 2006.

New memorials paying tribute to the Civil War's black soldiers are especially prevalent. In 1998, the African American Civil War Memorial, featuring Ed Hamilton's *Spirit of Freedom*, was unveiled in Washington, D.C. (fig. 4.28). In 2004, Kim Sessums's African American Monument, a $300,000 sculpture that depicts black contraband and commemorates "the service of the 1st and 3rd Mississippi Infantry Regiments, African Descent," was dedicated at Vicksburg National Military Park.[82] Aimed at cultivating minority membership in the national imaginary, none of these war memorials reference the slavery economics that led to and fed the Civil War, nor do they address the demeaning conditions for black troops in a segregated American military. Focused on gratitude, they pay tribute to the service of black soldiers without critiquing the originating conditions of their servitude.

In recent decades, enormous efforts have been expended to include all Americans in national war memory. In 2000, Congress authorized the $65 million American Veterans Disabled for Life Memorial on a site near the U.S. Capitol. A memorial to honor Latino veterans is being built in Avondale, Colorado. Native American soldiers are commemorated by projects including the Indian Memorial, the 2003 addition to the Little Bighorn National Battlefield Monument near Crow Agency, Montana; the National Native American Vietnam Veterans Memorial (1995) at The Highground, a 140-acre veterans memorial park near Neillsville, Wisconsin; and the Cherokee Warrior Memorial (2005) in Tahelquah, Oklahoma, which features two 105-mm cannons and 2,000 brick pavers honoring Cherokee veterans. In 1996, the American Indian Veterans Memorial Organization initiated plans for Warrior's Path, a $2.5 million

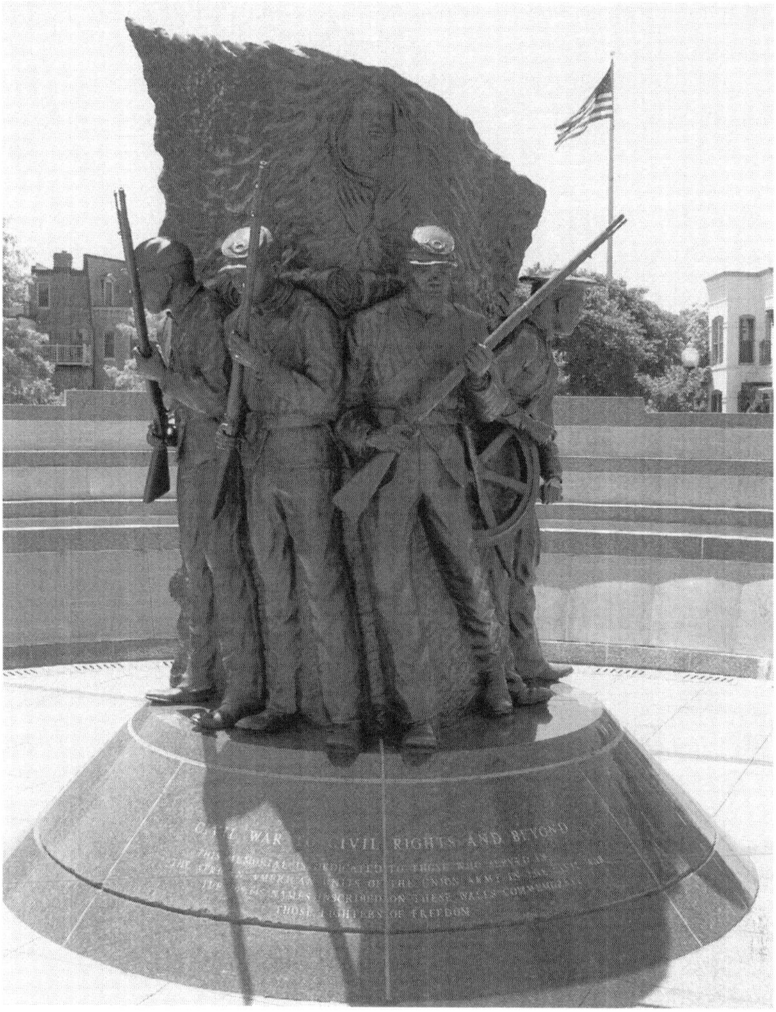

4.28. Ed Hamilton, *Spirit of Freedom*, African American Civil War Memorial, Washington, D.C., dedicated 1998. (Photo by the author.)

memorial in Phoenix dedicated to all American Indian veterans. The "Go for Broke" Monument (Los Angeles, 1999), National Japanese American Memorial (Washington, D.C., 2000; see fig. 5.15, p. 300), and 100th Infantry Battalion Memorial (Fort Benning, Georgia, 1999), all pay tribute to Japanese Americans who served in the U.S. armed forces during World War II, despite being forcibly interned in wartime relocation camps and accused of national disloyalty.

Women soldiers are commemorated by the Vietnam Women's Memorial, Women in Military Service for America Memorial, New York State

Women Veterans Memorial (Albany, 1998), and Women's War Memorial (Broken Arrow, Oklahoma, 2007). Women are woefully underrepresented in American memorial culture; none of the forty-four national memorials managed by or affiliated with the NPS, for example, specifically focus on women, and fewer than 4 percent of the seventy thousand sites listed in the National Register of Historic Places are associated with women. While the Vietnam Women's Memorial honors the 265,000 American women who served during that war (10,000 in uniform), it is designated a component of the Vietnam Veterans Memorial, located a short distance away. Yet women have played leading roles in national war memory, from organizing Civil War memorials at the turn of the twentieth century to orchestrating the recovery and return of soldier dead to U.S. soil after World War I.[83] The Daughters of the Republic of Texas have been the guardians of the Alamo since the early 1900s, maintaining it as a shrine to Texan heroes. Daughters of World War II Veterans were instrumental in creating the Rosie the Riveter / World War II Home Front National Historical Park (see fig. 0.8, p. 5), which pays tribute to female wartime industrial workers and replicates the frame of the Liberty cargo ships they produced at Kaiser Shipyards in Richmond, California. In 1999, a memorial to the women veterans of Berks County, Pennsylvania, was dedicated, and other women warrior monuments are on the books in Hemet, California, and Augusta, Maine.

Women's war memorials are often praised for their grassroots public processes and inclusionary ambitions—for challenging memorial culture's mostly male domain, historically recovering the two million women who have served in the U.S. armed forces since the nation's beginnings, and depicting American women as powerful martial figures.[84] At first glance, women soldier memorials, like women soldiers, would seem to complicate traditional assumptions about gender roles and militarism while expanding the subjectivity of national citizenship. Yet none of these memorials effectively reckon with the dominant masculinity in America's armed forces or consider the processes by which women are actually "included" in the U.S. military.

In Charleston, West Virginia, for example, an eight-foot bronze statue of a woman soldier was commissioned for inclusion in the Veterans Memorial, a $3.8 million monument on state capitol grounds that features similarly oversized statues of male soldiers. Dressed in a contemporary uniform of fatigues, T-shirt, and combat boots, the female figure was deemed "too masculine" by a review panel of female veterans, and the women's memorial was cancelled. Although sculptor P. Joseph Mullins followed a commemorative directive to depict a "modern woman" soldier, the panel of women vets said they wanted something that "looked more like a lady" instead of statues that "just look like another male."[85] Given mainstream stereotypes of female soldiers as hypermuscled control freaks, it is not surprising that women warrior memorials are the focus of heated debate among women soldiers themselves, especially regarding the representation of femininity and gendered respectability. But membership in the American military body is predicated on incorporation within an especially macho culture; as Heather Höpfl argues, "one must become a man in order to demonstrate [the] discipline and commitment" that defines the modern military.[86] That view is often at odds with those held by female veterans.

Assumptions, in fact, that contemporary war memorials especially or only pay tribute to particular soldiers—women soldiers or black soldiers, for instance—and not a national military, are misleading. As Bryan Turner observes, today's war memorials are seemingly "more concerned with the forgotten soldier, the mistreated, the disappeared . . . Individuals, not states, get memorialized as, for example, in Maya Lin's Vietnam Veterans Memorial." Yet these memorials are made because their backers insist that they, too, are entitled to a place in American historical memory. Even if they are individualized and localized, they are components of *national* war memory; however much they pay tribute to and maybe even mourn America's soldier dead, they exist because of the larger context of American militarism and the nation's infatuation with "warrior charisma."[87]

Individualism is actually a driving force behind American nationalism; as Oscar Campomanes remarks, representations of individual soldiers are often "the common sign in which a whole nation must recognize itself."[88] Although the U.S. military confusingly marketed itself as an "Army of One" from 2000 to 2005, military membership for *all* soldier bodies is predicated on their uniformity in a national military body that adheres to imperatives of strength, bravery, heroism, and authority. These imperatives have been traditionally associated with masculinity but as Judith Butler argues, gender is not what we are but what we perform, and in the U.S. military, performance is geared toward the protection of fellow soldiers and the completion of mission.[89] In this light, particular soldier memorials like women's war memorials perform the same role as other American war memorials: framing their subjects and their audiences in a militarized national narrative.

BLOODLESS SACRIFICE

"Monuments to veterans are popular again," headlined one 2006 story on the war memorial "binge" in Southern California's Riverside County, where tributes to Vietnam veterans, Native American soldiers, women soldiers, and Medal of Honor recipients are underway, and memorials like *Letters Home* are already in place (fig. 4.29). Dedicated in 2004 in Temecula, twenty miles from Camp Pendleton (one of the largest military bases in America), the $558,000 memorial features a semicircular bench and the lifelike figure of a buff and battle-ready soldier, helmet on his knee, M-16 at his side. He sits on sandbags as he pens a letter, using his helmet as a writing table. A wall at his back is embellished with the texts of sixteen other letters written by American soldiers over the course of the nation's wartime history, from the Revolutionary War to the War in Iraq; a Path of Honor leading to the bench consists of memorial pavers ($65 each) engraved with the names of local soldiers. Sculptor Christopher Pardell calls *Letters Home* a "service memorial," not a war memorial. "These are your neighbors, your friends," he explains. "The ordinary people who have always gone off to defend freedom."[90]

Located by the Temecula Duck Pond, a quiet park laid out like a golf course, *Letters Home* naturalizes war as an everyday part of American life: civilians and soldiers sit together in a pastoral setting and "communicate." "I think Chris'[s] vision is extraordinary. It's a great tribute to these men and women because it humanizes them," remarks Andrew Carroll, author of the 2001 bestseller *War Letters: Extraordinary Correspondence from American Wars* (a source for many of the memorial's letters). "It keeps us mindful of the thousands who have served and for the principles for which they served. Their service pays us dividends every single day," adds Temecula mayor Mike Naggar.[91] "Tomorrow I may see if four years at West Point and $250,000 of taxpayer money has produced an effective leader," reads one of the memorial's letters—an excerpt from a note that twenty-three-year-old Second Lieutenant Todd J. Bryant wrote to his wife on September 19, 2003. A month later he was killed in Fallujah.

Memorials like *Letters Home* are obviously nostalgic, geared toward audiences who harbor fantasies of other, mythical American wars. Today's soldiers don't write letters; they text message—and send photos of Abu Ghraib on their cell phones. But this contemporary wartime reality does not mesh with preferred images like the soldier depicted in Pardell's sculpture.[92] While such memorials humanize American GIs, they remember them on sentimental terms that gloss over their lives and deaths as modern soldiers. This is not, of course, peculiarly American; as Jay Winter explains, modern European publics reckoned with the shock and horror of World War I by turning to "traditional" memory tropes like patriotism, valor, and glory to mediate their deep bereavement.[93] As a

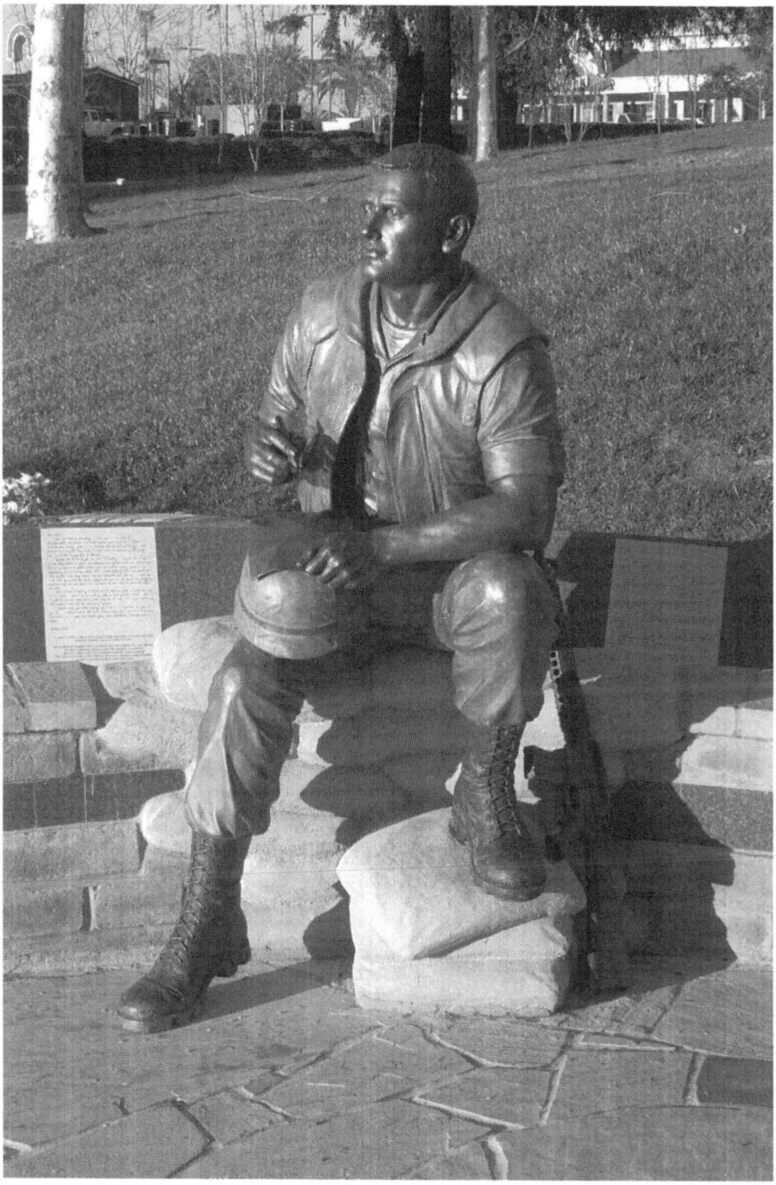

4.29. Christopher Pardell, *Letters Home*, a veterans' memorial designed for the City of Temecula, California, dedicated 2004. (Courtesy of Christopher Pardell.)

typical site of contemporary American war memory, Temecula's *Letters Home* similarly mediates war's loss and devastation with formal and iconographic devices—such as authenticating life-size statues and metaphorical references to "freedom"—that normalize and justify war.

Like the "Support Our Troops" bumper stickers that decorate American cars and trucks, war memorials like *Letters Home* define contemporary war memory in terms of the sacrifices of the nation's citizen soldiers—not the national security interests that dictate why wars are fought.[94] However carefully these "sacrificing soldier" memorials list the names of soldier dead on their walls and in their sidewalk pavers, they conceal the histories of why and how they died. They also perpetuate a national narrative of bloodless sacrifice.

With occasional exceptions like the dead GI on the beach in the National D-Day Memorial and the disfigured corpses in Munster's all-war theme park, most of today's war memorials are utterly bloodless. Few feature the abject soldier body; most focus on strong physical types. Even memorials that depict vulnerable soldiers do so on inspirational terms. As Susan Sontag observed, in the "current political mood" of patriotism and war porn, "pictures of wretched hollow-eyed GIs that once seemed subversive of militarism and imperialism" are re-viewed and revised as images of "ordinary American young men doing their unpleasant, ennobling duty." War memorial bodies are depicted as normal, natural, and national bodies, as stoic soldier subjects who perform to social and political expectations, for which the nation gratefully receives and accepts "dividends." They conform to popular modern assumptions about a strong body politic and an able-bodied masculinity that, as David Serlin argues, helps to articulate a heroizing and consensual "rhetoric of Americanism."[95]

Images of abject soldiers are largely prohibited today anyway: the U.S. Department of Defense has banned media images of U.S. soldier dead since the Gulf War, ostensibly to honor and protect their privacy and that of their families. In 2006, President Bush authorized the Respect for America's Fallen Heroes Act, which bars demonstrators at military funerals.[96] Wrenching images of wounded soldiers are equally problematic. Since 2007, embedded photojournalists covering the war on terror have been constrained by military regulations requiring that they obtain "the service member's prior written consent" in order to depict casualties. Publishing the names or unit of the wounded is strictly prohibited. This "disappearance of the dead" in contemporary war coverage, David Campbell observes, is not just the result of military dictates but mass media's own policing of wartime images deemed problematic. Public complaints about being "forced" to look at horrible images of soldier dead in newspapers or on TV are powerful incentives to avoid such images in a commercially driven media industry.[97]

Not surprisingly, these sorts of visual restrictions and regulations, coupled with the horrific conditions of the war itself, have dramatically eroded mass media presence in the Middle East, and subsequently, public information about the war. Coverage of the severe physical consequences of the war on terror, in which "limb-loss has occurred twice as often as in any other conflict of the past century," is minimal and has mostly focused on the injuries of male soldiers, although women comprise 15 percent of active duty forces.[98] When a lead character lost his leg in the syndicated cartoon *Doonesbury*, Garry Trudeau (who drew George W. Bush as an empty Roman helmet) was commended by the U.S. Department of Defense for raising public awareness about the grim injuries to large numbers of U.S. soldiers in the Iraq War. However, when Trudeau began listing the names of U.S. soldiers killed in the war, many papers dropped his cartoon.[99]

Shielding the public from the realities of contemporary American militarism took an especially ridiculous turn in early 2003, when a tapestry copy of Picasso's *Guernica* (a 1937 painting depicting the horrors of the Spanish Civil War), which has been on display at United Nations headquarters in New York since 1985, was covered up by a blue cloth during press conferences given by Secretary of State Colin Powell and other government officials announcing U.S. military intentions in Iraq. As Maureen Dowd cynically observed, "Mr. Powell can't very well seduce the world into bombing Iraq surrounded on camera by shrieking and mutilated women, men, children, bulls, and horses."[100]

Images of war may be banned, but Powell, like many Americans, embraces the nation's culture of war memorials. "Paying homage to the fallen holds a deeply personal meaning for me and for anyone who ever wore a uniform," Powell stated in a 2004 article titled "Why Memorials Matter," published by USA *Weekend Magazine* and marketed to coincide with the dedication of the National World War II Memorial. Reminiscing about visiting the graves of family members on Memorial Day as a child, and later touring Washington's memorials with foreign dignitaries, Powell observed that America's memorials "teach us much about the ideas that unite us in our diversity, the values that sustain us in times of trial, and the dream that inspires generation after generation of ordinary Americans to perform extraordinary acts of service."[101]

The multiple generations recalled in America's many war memorials testify to the nation's prevalent culture of militarism. As a significant and expanding body of war porn, war memorials cue Americans to concepts of citizenship, patriotism, and unity as they simultaneously whet national appetites for further martial adventures. The "awesome power" referenced in the National World War II Memorial's mission statement equates American militarism with similarly awesome and all-powerful forces like hurricanes, tsunamis, and volcanic eruptions. American militarism is naturalized as inevitable and unstoppable, and the nation's war memorials are the prominent bearer of an American military sublime.

Yet war porn encompasses two affective dimensions—pleasure and anxiety—and the trauma of the nation's nonstop warring certainly generates fear and panic among some American publics. While Americans romanticize soldiers, war itself is profoundly destabilizing. Memorials that reference the abject soldier body and the trauma of war may, if only tentatively, hint at deep anxieties regarding the nation's militarism. Yet they are few in number. Most contemporary American war memorials, like the National World War II Memorial, dwell on a fantasy of triumphant militarism that is shaped in part by the problematic narrative of the Vietnam War.

ERASING VIETNAM

At 7.4 acres, the National World War II Memorial is one of the largest memorials on the National Mall; the Vietnam Veterans Memorial and Korean War Veterans Memorial, by contrast, take up just 2 and 2.5 acres, respectively. The new war memorial was originally slated for a location near the Vietnam Veterans Memorial, in Constitution Gardens. But J. Carter Brown, chairman of the U.S. Commission of Fine Arts—which had blanket authority to approve or reject the new memorial's location and its final design—said "no" to this site choice, saying it was "unacceptable" to "tuck [the memorial] away in the woods." As Brown declared in 2001: "In the twentieth century, World War II was our finest hour, the moment when this country emerged as the leading nation of the world." Locating the memorial by the Wall would be like "burying" it "into this little ghetto," Brown added, and would make it "a kind of postage stamp footnote to the Vietnam Memorial." Basically arguing that World War II was a bigger and more important war, Brown insisted that the new memorial be granted a "larger space"—and more significant one—on the National Mall's central strip.[102] His insistence articulates the National World War II Memorial's defining purpose: to erase the conflicted meaning of the Vietnam War in American national consciousness and replace it with a simpler and unambiguous narrative of World War II, the "good war."

World War II is remembered today as the "good war," and its participants as the "greatest generation," in part because of bestselling books like Tom Brokaw's *The Greatest Generation*, which celebrates the "true patriotism" and noble sacrifice of various Americans who came of age between the Great Depression and World War II.[103] This is not how the war and that generation were originally framed by writers and veterans like James Jones, Norman Mailer, Joseph Heller, and Kurt Vonnegut, whose wartime narratives shared darker and more skeptical themes of alienation, futility, and insanity. In *From Here to Eternity* (1951), Jones provided a scathing critique of military hierarchy and the cruelty of combat; in *Catch-22* (1961), Heller spoofed the war's bureaucracy and bureaucrats, including a certain General Peckem who required "all tents in the Mediterranean theater of operations to be pitched along parallel lines with entrances facing proudly toward the Washington Monument." Postwar manifestations of World War II's trauma and waste were similarly embodied in the web-like paintings of abstract expressionist artist Jackson Pollock, the gloomy movies of film noir, the creepy tones of science fiction, and the cynical literature of the Beat generation.[104]

Since the 1980s, however, and especially since its fiftieth anniversary in the mid-1990s, World War II's reputation as a "good war" has firmly taken hold in America. Its contemporary currency of goodness and greatness is driven by the lingering national nightmare of Vietnam. As a much-hated war of defeat, Vietnam does not settle well in a standard "American historical metanarrative" of popular and triumphant militarism. Vietnam is a "dangerous history" which dredges memories of other fraught moments in the 1960s, like battles over civil rights. Vietnam was and remains despised—"public opinion polls from 1969 onward have revealed that a *majority* of the American population condemned U.S. intervention in Vietnam as a tragic mistake"—which raises questions about assumptions of national consensus and commitment during wartime. Vietnam was "bad," most Americans agree, and the war's soldiers were badly treated: spat upon by antiwar activists, or left behind as POW/MIA in south Asian jungles—or so many Americans believe.[105] Vietnam evinced humiliation, embarrassment, and deep national divisions; Vietnam was when America "lost its way." Most importantly, "Vietnam won't go away. Its ghosts still haunt the American psyche," conservative analysts like Ernest Lefever bemoan, arguing that Vietnam's legacy (the "Vietnam syndrome") has produced an insecure national culture of "shame, guilt, and self-flagellation" that has "erupted in flag-burning and other attacks on traditional institutions."[106]

In recent years, America's strategy of exorcism has been to retreat to a (seemingly) less haunting history, to repeatedly articulate it on positive terms, and to mobilize various forms of popular memory that permit the silencing of Vietnam. World War II dominates American war memory today: a "good war" whose romantic reimagination and "emotional and moral capital" is crucial to the nation's current military exploits.[107] Situating the National World War II Memorial in the middle of the National Mall was entirely deliberate—a concerted effort to challenge the memory and symbolic authority of the Vietnam Veterans Memorial. Attendance figures suggest some degree of success. In 2008, the National Park Service counted 4,153,749 people at the National World War II Memorial, and 4,243,573 at the Vietnam Veterans Memorial.[108]

Among the most visited memorials in the nation's capital, the Vietnam Veterans Memorial is also prestigious in architectural circles; it was honored in 2007, for example, with the Twenty-Five Year Award by the American Institute of Architects, a prize given for particularly respected modernist design. The memorial's popular and critical appeal centers, quite literally, on its conversational and reflective capacities (see fig. 3.7, p. 129). Visitors remember and honor the fallen on particularly affective terms as their bodies are reflected in its highly polished black marble, and thus blended with the names of over fifty-eight thousand soldier dead. Some touch the names engraved on its walls and leave gifts and offerings, further imprinting its memory and meaning on kinesthetic terms. Levels of interpretation vary. Many embrace it on curative terms, as a therapeutic vehicle of national recovery. In 1982, J. Carter Brown used the word "healing" to describe the memorial, saying, "we want to heal the wound."[109] Others argue that the memorial's somber black walls evoke the enduring wounds of the Vietnam War, "with its lack of a singular, historical narrative defining a clear-cut purpose and outcome." In this view, the Vietnam Veterans Memorial, like the Vietnam War itself, remains a subject of national debate, a form of "national pedagogy" where Americans may consider, question, and mourn themselves, their actions, their histories.[110]

The National World War II Memorial, by contrast, replaces dialogue with dogma, and recasts war on triumphal terms. Its dominating presence on the National Mall, neoclassical style, and all-white aesthetic aim to erase the discursive, countercultural, and counter-memorial ethos of the all-black Vietnam Veterans Memorial. Its primary purpose is to cure the country of any lingering doubts about its course of imperialism and militarism; its therapy is one of bluster and bravado. If Maya Lin's memorial commemorates human loss on a monumental scale, Friedrich St. Florian's memorial commemorates national consensus on a monumental scale. Somewhat ironically in an era that professes opposition to Big Government, the National World War II Memorial evokes the authority of the state. Rather than listing the names of soldier dead, its rhetoric and aesthetic speak to the clout of the military's supreme commanders, generals and statesmen alike.. Rather than encouraging experiential modes of knowledge, it returns to notions of commemoration predicated on unblinking reverence. Indeed, the National World War II Memorial represents a new, or restored, cultural nationalism deeply embedded in historical amnesia, one that essentializes World War II as a virtuous and uncomplicated war of victory and certainty, an "epochal hinge moment in history," writes James Wolcott, "that was morally unambiguous, a Manichean struggle of good versus evil, democracy versus tyranny, William Holden versus Otto Preminger."[111]

World War II veterans and their progeny have together helped craft these simplistic narratives of the "good war" and the "greatest generation." In 1995, veterans (and their congressional representatives) forced the Smithsonian Institution's National Air and Space Museum to abandon the exhibit The Last Act: The Atomic Bomb and the End of World War II, which aimed to contextualize modern-era military bombing of civilian targets and the use of atomic weapons. Their fury that the Smithsonian's exhibit might prompt national debate about the ethics of such bombing and call into question selective accounts of the "good war" itself compelled curators to substitute a show titled The *Enola Gay*: Something More Than an Airplane (dubbed "Enola Lite" by more sarcastic critics).[112]

And while the group Veterans to Save the Mall fought against the National World War II Memorial, other World War II veterans such as Roger Durbin and Bob Dole gained congressional and popular support by arguing that the "greatest generation" had not been properly thanked in American memorial culture. The memorial they raised was a tribute to themselves—"the citizen soldiers who answered liberty's call"—and the virtuous war they fought. As Dole remarked at the memorial's unveiling in 2004: "What we dedicate today is not a memorial to war, rather it's a tribute to the physical and moral courage that makes heroes out of farm and city boys and that inspires Americans in every generation to lay down their lives for people they will never meet, for ideals that make life itself worth living."

Tom Brokaw, son of a veteran stationed during the war at a South Dakota army ammunition depot, extends this lofty piety in *The Greatest Generation*, inspired by a visit to the battlefields of Normandy and a sense that he "had failed to appreciate what they had been through and what they had accomplished." "I am in awe of them," Brokaw concludes. "This is the greatest generation any society has produced." If his book prompted a virtual industry of "greatest generation" product, Brokaw's awe was echoed in Stephen Ambrose's bestselling books *Band of Brothers* (1992) and *Citizen Soldiers* (1997), and Steven Spielberg's *Saving Private*

Ryan. All are popular culture texts by men who came of age during the Vietnam era; all provide similarly congratulatory accounts of the social cohesion and patriotic citizenship of the generation of their fathers, the "greatest generation."[113]

Along with the National World War II Memorial, these texts are not only or merely about that generation, of course, but about modeling that generation's exalted "virtues [of] self-reliance, self-discipline, and self-sacrifice" for contemporary American publics still haunted by the "bad" and "dangerous" specter of Vietnam. Rendering invisible the waste and trauma of both wars, these celebratory narratives reek of self-loathing as the progeny of the "greatest generation" wrestle with their own equally stereotypical reputations as dishonorable war losers, and look to their elders for approval, guidance, and atonement. "What makes Brokaw's species of generational hagiography so repugnant," argues Thomas Hawley, "is its refusal to acknowledge anywhere the slaughter in Vietnam as an event conceived in support of the 'greatest generation's' most cherished ideals, in particular, mindless anticommunism, evangelical patriotism, and childlike faith in the superiority of the American Way."[114]

Today, World War II is celebrated as the national path to recovery—a journey backward to go forward. And if Vietnam has not been erased in American national memory, it has been revised and reinvented. Some of its myths persist. Bruce Franklin argues that the Nixon administration (and Ross Perot in particular) orchestrated the POW/MIA myth of American soldiers abandoned in Vietnam in order to shore up declining public support for the war. Jerry Lembcke has dissected the myth of the spat-upon Vietnam vet and calls it an urban legend.[115] Yet both linger, feeding conspiracy theories about U.S. government cover-ups and encouraging expectations of entitlement among Vietnam veterans.

Movies like *Rambo: First Blood Part* II (1985), in which former Special Forces soldier John Rambo (Sylvester Stallone) mutters "Do we get to win this time?" and TV shows like *Magnum, P.I.* (1980–1988), which featured a former marine turned private detective, helped reinvent the Vietnam vet as a "warrior hero" and faithful American patriot.[116] Organizations like Rolling Thunder have been instrumental in revising public and political understandings of the Vietnam War and its U.S. soldiers, shifting popular perceptions of defeat and victimization to courage and bravery. The United States continues to spend over $100 million a year to recover POW/MIA soldier dead in Southeast Asia— "slightly over $1.2 million per identified remains" estimates one author. Such recovery efforts are perceived as modes of national reckoning with the war (what Rolling Thunder and POW/MIA groups call "full accounting").[117] So is the POW/MIA Memorial Flag Act of 2002, a public law enacted by the 107th Congress that requires the display of this flag at the Vietnam Veterans Memorial, the Korean War Veterans Memorial, and the National World War II Memorial. The notable number of Vietnam memorials that have been raised in recent years and the ways in which growing numbers of Vietnam vets today proudly display their service medals in their living rooms and their offices also attest to the war's reinvention in contemporary American memory. "I think now it's almost become prestigious to say that you're a Vietnam veteran," remarks one fifty-seven-year old soldier who had thrown away his Purple Heart in 1967 and reclaimed it in 2005.[118]

The most significant symbol of rehabilitation is the Vietnam Veterans Memorial Visitor Center, a $100 million museum just north of the Wall near the Lincoln Memorial. Built underground, the 35,000-square-foot center will "transform the Memorial into a profound learning experience for America's youth and others," says Jan Scruggs, the former U.S. infantry corporal who initiated the Vietnam Veterans Memorial in the late 1970s. The museum will house thousands of artifacts left at the memorial and feature a cafeteria and bookstore along with a movie theater, dioramas of major battles, interpretive wall panels, and photos and personal mementos of soldier dead (including a digital display marking veterans' birthdays). "This addition to the Memorial is a tribute to the three million men and women who served in the Vietnam War and will transform The Wall that heals into The Wall that educates," Scruggs declared in 2003, when President Bush signed the center into law.[119] Time Warner has donated $10 million to the museum, and backers expect it to draw 1.5 million visitors each year.

If criticized by some for its underground "bunker or tunnel" aesthetics ("it will be more a tribute to the Viet Cong," grumbled one vet) and for its "mauling of the National Mall" by others, the new museum is geared toward Vietnam's reinvention as a war of valor, if not exactly victory, in the national narrative. The comments of one congressional backer, Rep. John E. Peterson (R-PA), spell out its projected "learning experience": "When we decide to have a conflict, we win. When we made a decision to fight, we win. Don't repeat the mistake made in the Vietnam War."[120] In light of such pronouncements, it is doubtful that the Gulf of Tonkin affair, the My Lai Massacre, the killings at Kent State, and the anti–Vietnam War movement will be covered in this museum. Unlike the Vietnam Veterans Memorial, the new museum is intended as an unwavering expression of national gratitude to America's soldiers. As Colin Powell, honorary chairman of the center's fund raising campaign, notes,

"This will be a center that is about those who fought and those who died, so we don't forget their sacrifice. And it will have no statement to make about the war other than the gallantry and the heroism of those who answered the call of their country."[121]

When anti–Iraq War protesters gathered at the Vietnam Veterans Memorial in March 2007, members of Rolling Thunder and a veterans group that calls itself Gathering of Eagles (GoE), showed up to defend "their" memorial. Forming a gauntlet on the sidewalks near the Wall, the vets carried signs reading, "This time we choose not to lose" and "War There or War Here," and shouted "If you don't like America, get out!" and "Jihadists! You're brain-dead!" As one man insisted: "The anti-war / anti-America group cannot be allowed to use the Vietnam Memorial Wall as a back-drop to their anti-America venom and stain the hallowed ground that virtually cries out with blood at the thought of this proposed desecration . . . it must not happen." On its Web site, the GoE calls itself "non-partisan, non-violent, and non-confrontational" and states: "We believe that war memorials are sacred ground; as such, we will not allow them to be desecrated, used as props for political statements, or treated with anything less than the solemn and heartfelt respect they—and the heroes they honor—deserve."[122] Apparently, GoE's support for the Iraq War is not considered a "political statement."

These new interpretations of the Vietnam War stem from beliefs that national episodes of loss and defeat, as well as those of mass resistance and public protest, are untenable in today's America. As Robert McMahon observed in 2002, "The comments of top public officials, former officials, and vindicationists from the media, right-wing think tanks, and certain sectors of academe betray a palpable frustration with their failure to erase societal memories of Vietnam as the lost, pointless, morally repugnant war." Such frustrations relate less to Vietnam itself, of course, than to sustaining public support for the nation's current wars, and for America's unrestrained ambitions as a militaristic empire. National anxieties that Iraq is the "new Vietnam" do not bode well for the war on terror's continuance. Worries that "key elements of the antiwar paradigm still reign within the nation's collective memory," and that they might continue to disturb the nation's military interests, inform the urgent installation of both the Vietnam Veterans Memorial Visitor Center and the National World War II Memorial.[123]

REVISUALIZING THE SEDUCTION OF WAR

In 1995, in a column titled "The Monument Glut," James Reston, Jr., questioned the avalanche of war memorials in Washington, D.C.:

> As the soul of the nation, the nation's capital should reflect the breadth of the society's achievements. But coming to Washington is turning into a martial experience: a contemplation of wars won, lost and stalemated. The remaining 70 acres of the Washington Mall may be on the road toward the cluttered look of the Gettysburg battlefield. It is as if America recognizes only one type of hero. What happened to the American hero as scientist? As religious leader? As artist or musician? Shouldn't a memorial to the Rev. Martin Luther King, Jr. take precedence over black Revolutionary War veterans on the mall?

In 2003, reflecting on the "determining influence" of war photography, Susan Sontag was even more direct, asking: "Is there an antidote to the perennial seductiveness of war? Could one be mobilized actively to oppose war by an image (or a group of images)?"[124]

Such questions grapple with the dilemma of war memory, with how the representation and commemoration of war sustains and perpetuates war itself. Some war memorials, like the Vietnam Veterans Memorial, attempt to shift the subject of commemoration from the valorization of war to the loss of soldier dead. Some, like *Letters Home*, attempt to humanize the ordinary American soldier. All war memorials are driven by social obligations of debt and public feelings of thanks, and are beholden to sociopolitical expectations of reciprocity. But is gratitude an appropriate affect in war memory? If so, can gratitude be mobilized differently: can the nation pay tribute to soldiers without reproducing war?

Consider Arlington West: first created on Veterans Day 2003 in Santa Barbara, California, when Stephen Sherrill raised 340 small white wooden crosses on a beach in front of Stearns Wharf, the city's highly touristed waterfront (figs. 4.30 and 4.31). Neatly lined up in rows like the gravestones in the national cemetery it imitates, Arlington West's crosses represent the numbers of U.S. soldiers killed in Iraq and Afghanistan during the war on terror. "The motivation was to bring people's attention to the terrible price we're paying for the invasion and occupation of Iraq," said Sherrill, a member of the national organization Veterans for Peace. The memorial became a weekly event, going up and coming down every weekend, and was enlarged to include coffins draped with American flags, a portable wall with the names and head shots of U.S. soldier dead, and a sign that stated: "If we were to honor the Iraqi dead, it would cover the entire beach."

Located in an area frequented by surfers and sunbathers, Arlington West was intentionally unexpected and jarring: a "cemetery in the sand." Sherrill explained, "The Bush administration has banned television cameras from filming the caskets returning from Iraq . . . because they don't

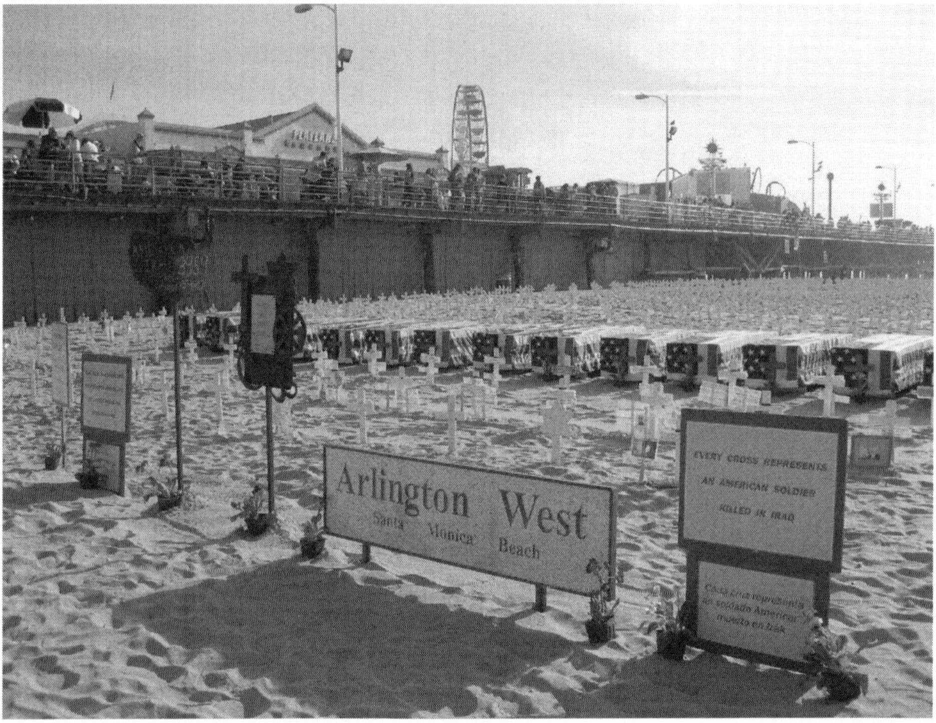

4.30. Arlington West, Santa Monica, California, February 2008. (Photo by the author.)

want the people to see what this is costing us. So we're making it visible."[125] In 2004, other California chapters of Veterans for Peace began raising versions of the memorial on beaches in Santa Monica and Oceanside. Every weekend the fields of crosses grew larger: 512 in late January 2004; 3,444 on Memorial Day 2007; 4,081 on Memorial Day 2008.

A similar memorial is Eyes Wide Open, first displayed in January 2004 at Chicago's Federal Plaza, where it featured 504 pairs of combat boots regimented into long rows, each pair bearing the name of a U.S. soldier killed in Iraq. Organized by the American Friends Service Committee, a Quaker-affiliated group dedicated to peace and social justice, the memorial was officially called Eyes Wide Open / Beyond Fear, Toward Hope / An Exhibition of the Human Cost of the Iraq War, and, like Arlington West, was envisioned as a way to show Americans "the true costs of the war." Also intended to "go on until the war stops," the memorial moved from city to city. On Memorial Day 2004, when the National World War II Memorial was dedicated at the west end of the National Mall, Eyes Wide Open—now with 804 pairs of boots—was displayed on the Mall's other side, in a park near the U.S. Capitol.

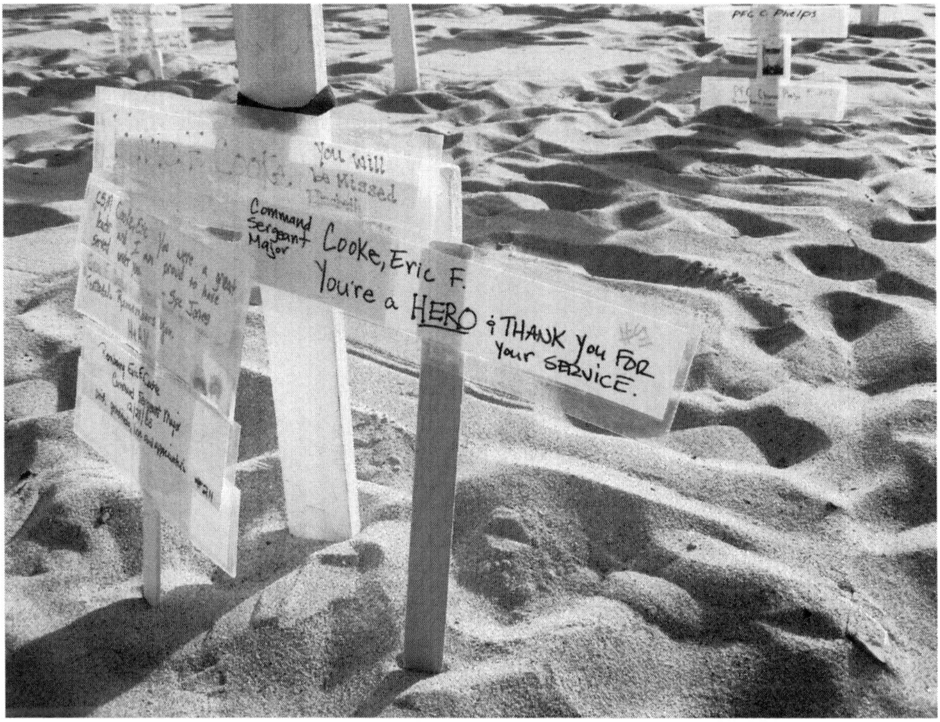

4.31. Arlington West, detail. (Photo by the author.)

Arranged in alphabetical order, many of the boots were accompanied by photographs, letters, postcards, teddy bears, American flags, dog tags, and other items left by families and visitors. Most of the boots were purchased in Army / Navy stores but at least nine pairs were donated by the families of soldier dead. From 2004 to 2007, Eyes Wide Open was displayed in over a hundred cities, growing larger each time: 1,490 pairs of boots in Dallas' City Hall Plaza in February 2005; 2,748 pairs in Denver's Civic Center in October 2006 (figs. 4.32 and 4.33). By March 2007, Eyes Wide Open had grown to over 3,400 pairs of boots. After May 2007, the memorial became too big to be shown in its entirety and, like the NAMES Project Foundation's AIDS Memorial Quilt, was divided into smaller displays around the nation.[126]

A third memorial, begun in Lafayette, California, on Veterans Day 2006, featured a field of white crosses and a billboard reading: "In Memory of 2,867 U.S. Troops Killed in Iraq." Erected on a hillside facing the city's light rail station and Highway 24, a major thoroughfare running from the East Bay suburb to San Francisco, Lafayette's memorial was created by local building contractor Jeff Heaton to "remind people there

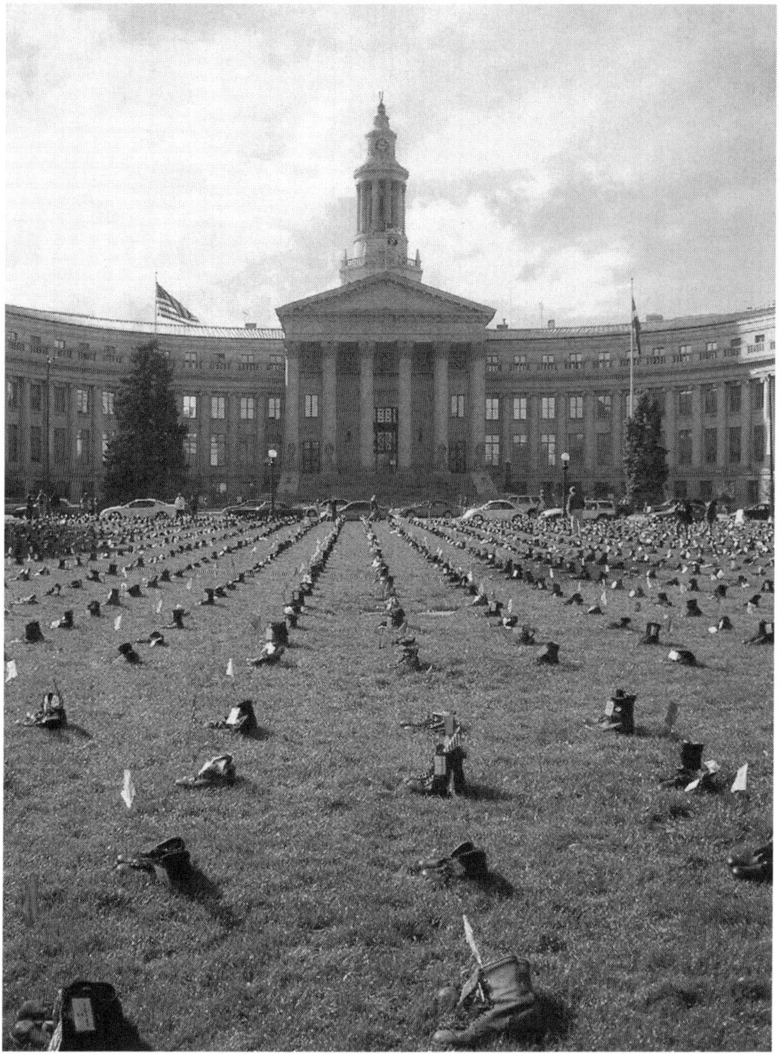

4.32. Eyes Wide Open Memorial, Denver, Colorado, October 2006. (Photo by the author.)

are lives being lost, families being devastated." Inspired by a visit to the Vietnam Veterans Memorial in 2003, Heaton returned to his hometown determined to make his own memorial, but each time he planted crosses they were torn down or stolen. In November 2006 he tried again, raising about three hundred crosses, and found a more sympathetic audience. "Anyone who tried to do something like this three years ago was called un-American, unpatriotic," said Heaton in 2007. "But now it's completely changed." Within a few months, what came to be called the Lafayette Hillside Memorial included thousands of crosses erected by a growing

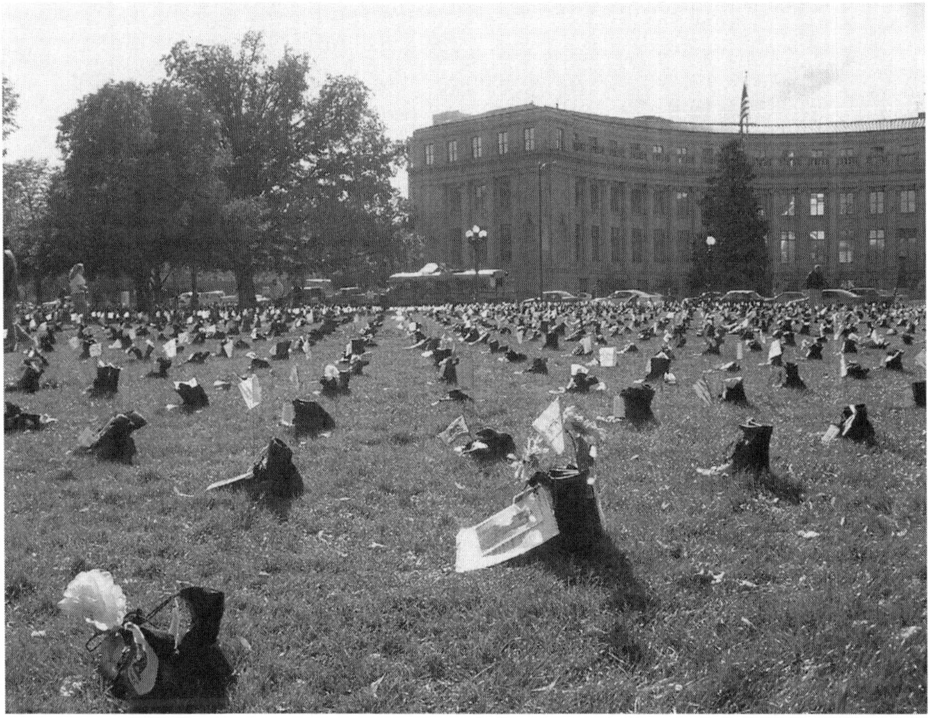

4.33. Eyes Wide Open, detail. (Photo by the author.)

pool of volunteers, a neon sign illuminating the numbers of U.S. soldier dead, and candlelight vigils organized by the antiwar group MoveOn. In March 2009, on the sixth anniversary of the war, the memorial's central sign read: "In Memory of Our Troops, 4,925." Like Arlington West, Lafayette's memorial also included a handful of Jewish Stars of David and Islamic crescents, referencing the multiple faith communities of U.S. soldiers. "It's a living memorial," Heaton remarked in 2007. "It's going on as the war goes on."[127]

Each of these memorials follow the experiential model of the Vietnam Veterans Memorial, encouraging visitors to touch their symbolic markers—boots, crosses, flags—and add their own personal offerings. Each has become a pilgrimage site, a destination for the memory and mourning of the nation's soldier dead. "It's my little way of paying tribute," explains one Santa Barbara resident who visits Arlington West every weekend. Each memorial is keyed to public feeling: many people cry at these memorials, while others angrily denounce them as treasonous. "That's the most disrespectful, ugly, liberal, goddamned thing I've ever seen and I'm a veteran, OK?" shouted one man, caught on local TV at Lafayette's memorial in November 2006. Likewise, at an Eyes Wide Open display in Escondido, California, in 2005, a woman whose twenty-year old son had died a year earlier in Iraq told a reporter, "This road back from hell is hard enough without having to defend my son's name in a political arena." Her son, she added, "made the ultimate sacrifice" and "did it for the American way of life and not for some political view."[128] Some families have asked Eyes Wide Open to remove the names of their dead soldier kin from the memorial, and memorial staffers comply by tagging their boots with a label that says "name removed request of family." They still read all of the names of U.S. soldier dead at Eyes Wide Open memorial services.

Driven by desires to remember and grieve, each of these memorials is also directed toward "speaking truth" about the war in Iraq, and, in the case of Eyes Wide Open, "speaking truth to power," an integral component of Quaker faith. Each presumes that by visualizing the numbers of U.S. soldier dead on highly symbolic and affective terms, the trauma of war itself will be exposed to multiple American publics. Arlington West and Eyes Wide Open also reference Iraqi dead: the latter's memorial includes Dreams and Nightmares, an exhibit featuring the names, photographs, and personal narratives of Iraqi civilians, and piles of shoes representing just a fraction of the thousands of Iraqis who have died since the U.S. invasion in March 2003.[129] In 2007, Eyes Wide Open also featured a Cost of War exhibition, with a billboard stating, "One Day of the Iraq War = $720 million. How would you spend it?"

Yet each of these memorials is conflicted by the problematic obligations of gratitude. None of their makers, for example, describe them as "antiwar" memorials, believing that this might imply disrespect for U.S. troops. Heaton, in fact, sees the Lafayette memorial as a way of "showing gratitude and honoring our soldiers." When antiwar protesters added signs to the memorial that stated "Bush Lied, Troops Died," he removed them, explaining, "I'm trying to keep it from becoming too politicized." In March 2007, members of the pro-war group Move America Forward staged a rally at the Lafayette memorial, their first stop on a cross-country campaign aimed at generating public support for the war in Iraq. "We need to support our troops, and I thank you for being out here to do that," one speaker told the crowd.[130]

Arlington West's sponsors also frame their beachfront memorials on honorific terms, as tributes to U.S. military killed in Iraq. "They are our protectors, and we are stewards of them," explains one member of Veterans for Peace in a documentary film made about the memorial. Some of the memorial's crosses include handwritten notes that read, "Thank you for fighting for our country," and its sponsors discuss the "ingratitude" of a federal veterans administration that has failed to meet the health care needs of Iraq War veterans.[131] Expectations of gratitude are linked with those of heroism and veneration; as Stacy Menusa, the widow of a gunnery sergeant killed in an Iraqi ambush in 2003 told a reporter when she made the pilgrimage to see her husband's cross at Arlington West in Santa Barbara, "I see heroes." A cross dedicated to Command Sergeant Major Eric F. Cooke included a note reading, "You're a *HERO* & thank you for your service." After viewing Eyes Wide Open in Austin in 2005, one woman wrote, "I saw respect being bestowed to unknown lives that have been lost. I didn't see it as an anti-war movement. I saw it as it was intended—as a memorial."[132]

Refusal to contextualize or "politicize" these memorials extends to how they are generally understood as "Iraq war dead memorials," not *war* memorials. They "stand for the warriors, not the war," said one reporter, overlooking their reference to dead Iraqi civilians.[133] As a spokesman for Eyes Wide Open explained, "The biggest criticism leveled at the peace movement during Vietnam was that we did not welcome back the troops. They became the enemy. Not this time. More and more people understand that we can support the troops while condemning the war. Many joined the military because they faced either dead-end jobs or no jobs at all."[134] Amidst already prevalent public anxieties that Iraq is "the new Vietnam," Iraq War dissidents and proponents alike distance themselves from Vietnam's perceived mistakes by saying "thank you" to today's soldiers.

War memorials weld feelings of gratitude with national imperatives, cultivating affective modes of citizenship and patriotism and persuading publics of the necessity of war itself. Whether they pay tribute to U.S. soldiers individually and experientially according to the commemorative model established by the Vietnam Veterans Memorial or anonymously and gloriously as in the imperial setting of the National World War II Memorial, contemporary American war memorials are agents of national thanksgiving and cannot transcend the limitations and obligations of gratitude. While Arlington West, Eyes Wide Open, and the Lafayette Hillside Memorial mourn today's soldier dead by naming and picturing them, they also honor them as soldiers. They do not question the huge economic and political appeal of militarism in today's America; they do not consider why military service is often the only job option for some Americans or how armed conflict and imperialism largely define American national purpose today.[135]

Consider how different the National Mall would be today if the Martin Luther King, Jr. National Memorial had been raised where the National World War II Memorial now stands.[136] Such a memorial might have disrupted the nation's celebration of militaristic empire with a narrative, instead, of its aspirations toward civil rights and racial justice, thereby proposing an alternative course of American national and self-consciousness. Elsewhere in America, memorials shaped by public feelings of shame aspire to such alternatives, which is the subject of the next chapter.

5 SHAME

Duluth's Lynching Memorial and Issues of National Morality

In October 2003, a lynching memorial was dedicated in Duluth, Minnesota, a port city in the northeastern corner of the state (fig. 5.1). Located downtown, a few blocks from Lake Superior, the memorial recalls the June 15, 1920, murders of three African American men employed with the John Robinson Circus, which had stopped in Duluth for a single day of performances. Falsely accused of sexually assaulting a local white woman, the men—and three other black men who also worked for the circus—were arrested and incarcerated in Duluth's jail, located in the heart of the city's business district.

That night, the jail was stormed by a mob of some ten thousand people (about one-tenth of the city's population) who overpowered the police with bricks and battering rams and grabbed three of the prisoners from their cells. Dragged up a steep hill, past a crowd of onlookers including children, women, and a group of Shriners attending a local meeting, the three young men were viciously beaten and then lynched from the crook of an electric light pole next to Duluth's Shrine Auditorium, a few blocks from the jail. After they were murdered, several carefully staged photographs were taken of their battered bodies, illuminated by the headlights of automobiles and framed by dozens of well-dressed white men leaning into the center, some on tiptoe, all in the act of posing with their human trophies (fig. 5.2). As author Michael Fedo describes one of these photographs, which was widely sold in Duluth area stores as a ten-cent postcard titled "Picture of a Lynching," "These are not people who are ashamed to be seen here. This is 'I want to be in this picture.'"[1]

Built directly across the street from the site of the lynchings, at the intersection of First Street and Second Avenue East, Duluth's memorial is a small courtyard plaza with a curving sidewalk and beige-colored walls. Incised with patterned designs at their base, the angled walls feature epithets by authors including Albert Einstein, Mahatma Gandhi, and Oscar Wilde. They are bordered by a quote from eighteenth-century Brit-

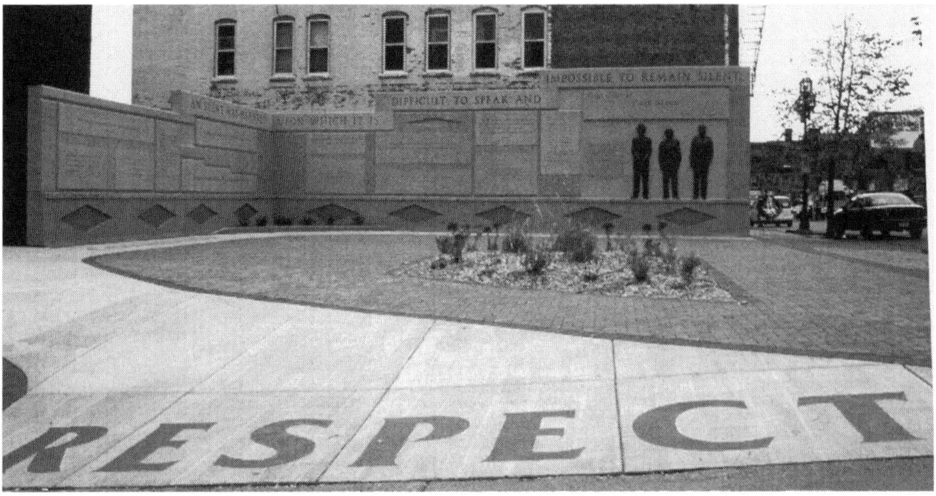

5.1. Carla Stetson, Clayton Jackson McGhie Memorial, Duluth, Minnesota, dedicated 2003. Text for the memorial was chosen by Anthony Peyton Porter. (Courtesy of Carla Stetson.)

ish philosopher and statesman Edmund Burke: "An event has happened upon which it is difficult to speak and impossible to remain silent."[2]

The memorial's sidewalks are embedded with three words: respect, compassion, and atonement. Somewhat ironically, the brick wall in back of the memorial features fading signage for Duluth's Union Gospel Mission (established in 1922 and still located next door) and a passage from Psalms 46:1: "God is our refuge, strength, a very present help in trouble." Below this is a paragraph describing the events that occurred on June 15, 1920, and the memorial's main iconographic element: three life-size bronze figures dedicated to the three men who were murdered in Duluth: Elias Clayton (age 19), Elmer Jackson (age 22), and Isaac McGhie (age 20) (fig. 5.3). The memorial's official name, in fact, is the Clayton Jackson McGhie Memorial. It is the first large-scale memorial in America dedicated to lynching, to what the NAACP in November 1920 declared "the greatest shame in the United States."[3]

Whereas lynching and pictures of lynching once fed a rapacious American appetite for sadistic racism, today's commemoration of lynching suggests growing recognition of the nation's historical legacy of racist violence. This legacy, this national inheritance, is a "memory stain," and it is shameful.[4] Like other lynching recovery projects, Duluth's lynching memorial animates this shame and redirects the dehumanizing spectacle of lynching to a project focused on "bearing witness" to its victims.

Growing numbers of shame-based memorials, including those that

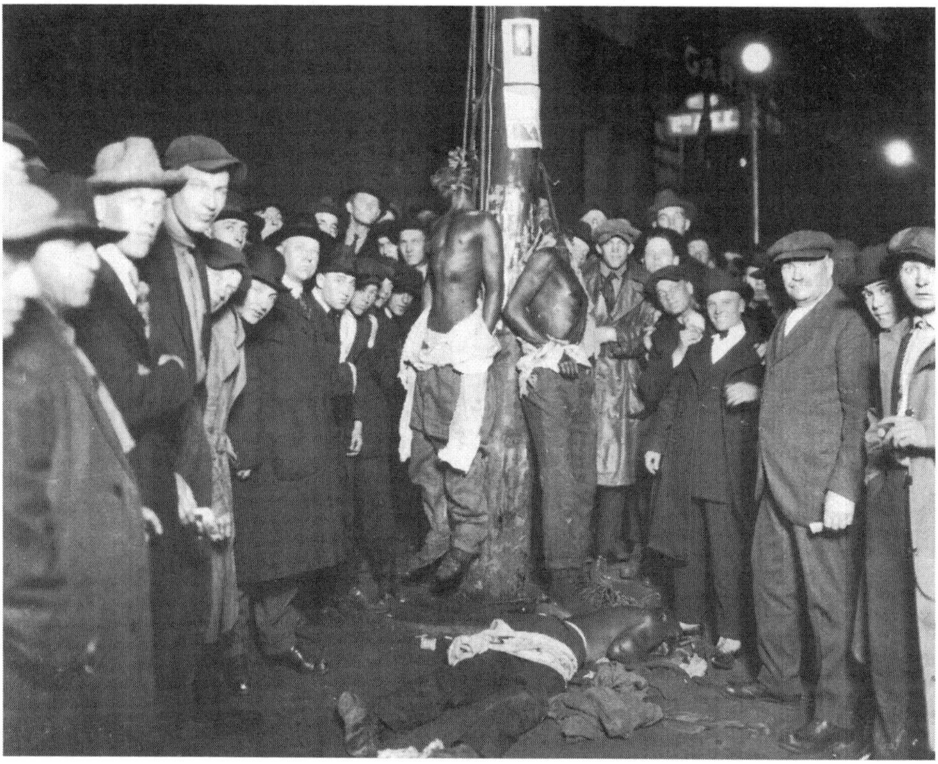

5.2. Ralph Greenfield, "Picture of a Lynching," 1920. Photograph of the lynching of Elias Clayton, Elmer Jackson, and Isaac McGhie in Duluth, Minnesota. (Courtesy of the Minnesota Historical Society.)

recall the subjects of racial terrorism, slavery, and war relocation during World War II, are being raised in America today. "Sites of shame" are increasingly considered places worthy of commemoration and have become pedagogical imperatives of both local communities and federal agencies like the National Park Service. This chapter considers the contemporary cultural, political, and social dimensions of these shame-based memorials. What does shame mean in America today? Who is shaming, and who is ashamed? What are the affective possibilities of shame?

SITES OF SHAME

Unlike affects such as grief, gratitude, fear, and anger, shame's currency in contemporary America is shadowy. Shame might have had more shared social meaning in the nation's past: in 1954, for example, when lawyer Joseph Welch beseeched Senator Joe McCarthy during the televised Army-McCarthy hearings, "Have you no sense of decency, sir, at

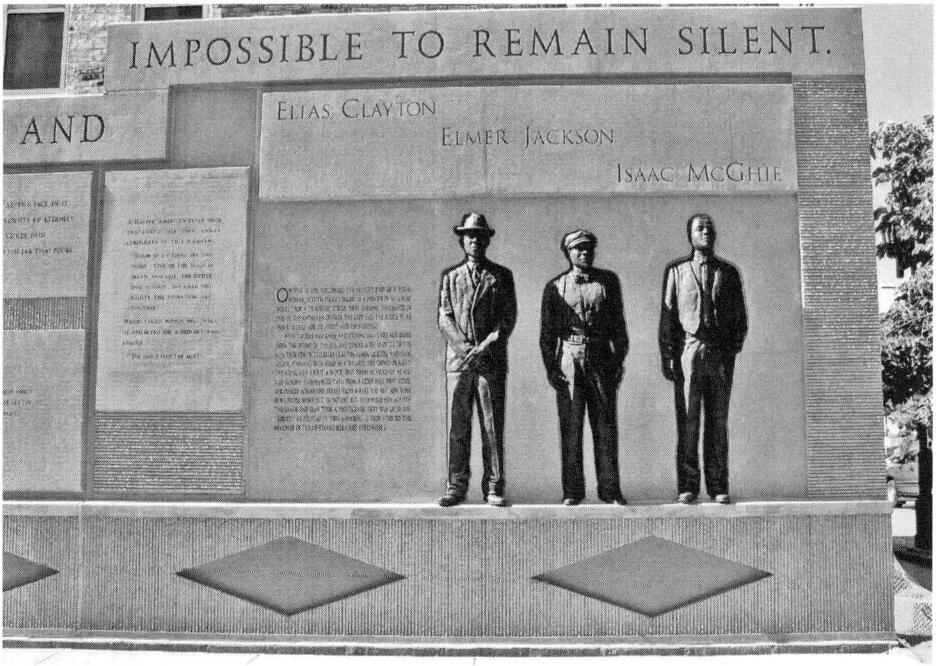

5.3. Clayton Jackson McGhie Memorial, detail. (Courtesy of Carla Stetson.)

long last?" or in 1963, when President John F. Kennedy admonished Congress to enact civil rights legislation with the words "Those who do nothing are inviting shame."[5] In the mid-1960s, poverty was called "the shame of a nation," and its eradication—"one of the most urgent endeavors in which America is engaged," declared Vice President Hubert Humphrey in 1965—was considered the political obligation of a Great Society.[6]

Today, shame about the nation's transgressions is generally absent in terms of how most Americans think about themselves and the nation. This is hardly surprising: recalling shameful episodes and histories is fraught with struggles over their very admission in the national narrative. To acknowledge shame, after all, is to admit that there is something to be ashamed about. And for many Americans, shameful moments in the nation's past are just that—in the past and therefore removed from presentist personal and / or collective understandings of relevance and responsibility. "I didn't live then, so it's not my problem," is one response; "Why bring that all up again, it's too painful," is another. Or as Virginia legislator Frank D. Hargrove rather callously put it in 2007, during debates calling for a state resolution officially apologizing for slavery in America: "black citizens should get over it." As cultural geographer Ken

Foote observes, "shame can be a powerful motive to obliterate all reminders of tragedy and violence," to the degree that stigmatized places often become invisible in the national landscape.[7]

Recently, however, reckoning with the nation's shameful transgressions has become an agenda in American memorial culture. Contemporary memorials to executed witches, for example, dedicated in Salem and Danvers, Massachusetts, in 1992, commemorate the mostly female victims of a pathological public culture of superstition and religious intolerance in the late seventeenth century (see fig. 0.3, p. 3). The inscription on the Danvers memorial reads: "In memory of those innocents who died during the Salem Village witchcraft hysteria of 1692." Memorials commemorating the mass murders of Native Indians, the chattel slavery of Africans in the Americas, the forced internment of Japanese Americans during World War II, and the victims of lynching similarly remember shameful American histories. Doing so, Dolores Hayden cautions, involves more than simply adding previously ignored or avoided subjects to the national memorial landscape.[8] It requires a conceptual reassessment of shame's diversity, its necessity in a just society, and its affective potential as a mode of redemption.

The United States is not unique in its recent recovery of shameful national histories. Germany has made substantial efforts to address its responsibility in the Holocaust, including dedicating the Memorial to the Murdered Jews of Europe in 2005 (see fig. 3.8, p. 134). Belgium has mounted public exhibitions such as Memory of Congo (2005) to address King Leopold's bloody colonization of Central Africa from 1885 to 1908—and the deaths of an estimated ten million Africans. In 1996, South Africa formed the Truth and Reconciliation Committee to detail the violations of human rights in that country from 1960 to 1994. In 2000, Spain's Association for the Recovery of Historical Memory initiated the exhumation of some thirty thousand Spaniards killed during the Spanish Civil War and under the dictatorship of General Francisco Franco; issues of apology and reparation have also emerged in Spain's national conversation.[9] In 2007, the Monument to the Victims of State Terrorism was dedicated in Buenos Aires, one of several new memorials raised to the "disappeared" murdered during Argentina's military dictatorship of 1976–1983. And in France, artists Julian Bonder and Krzysztof Wodiczko are designing a memorial to the abolition of slavery, a project commemorating the port city of Nantes's ignoble role in the transatlantic slave trade and the global dimensions of human trafficking today.

In Russia the Memorial to the Victims of the Gulag was erected in Moscow's Lubyanka Square in 1990 (across the street from KGB headquarters); and in 1998, the Gulag Museum opened at Perm-36, a forced labor camp where many of the Soviet Union's most prominent political dissidents were imprisoned. In 2006, the National Park Service partnered with Perm-36 and organized a traveling exhibition on the Soviet Gulag at several of the American memorials it manages, including the Manzanar National Historic Site.[10]

The NPS, in fact, has taken a leadership role in commemorating shameful episodes in American history. "Sites of shame," as one of its advisory board members recommended in 1994, "should be included in the park system to present a complete picture of our history."[11] If the Smithsonian's various museums have had a more difficult time representing the complexities of national memory—as seen in battles over exhibiting the "dilemmas of nuclear strategy" at the National Air and Space Museum and in discussing revisionist interpretations of American Western paintings at the National Museum of American Art—the NPS has successfully developed new sites and redeveloped older ones that complicate standard sagas of a progressive and heroic national history. Beginning in the 1990s, the NPS—with Congressional authorization—initiated a series of new monuments, parks, and historic sites that, as its chief historian remarked in 2005, "require that we understand the past, not simply celebrate it." It also developed a number of "civic engagement" initiatives aimed at preserving sites that address issues of social injustice and raise consciousness about their contemporary relevance. As participants in this NPS program stated in 1999, "We hold in common the belief that it is the obligation of historic sites to assist the public in drawing connections between the history of our site and its contemporary implications. We view stimulating dialogue on pressing social issues and promoting humanitarian and democratic values as a primary function."[12]

New understandings of the complicated "obligations" of American history strongly influence who and what the NPS deems memorable today. In 1995, Senator Tom Daschle (D-SD) introduced a bill authorizing the Wounded Knee National Tribal Park on the Pine Ridge Indian Reservation in southwestern South Dakota. The NPS-affiliated park, yet to be built, would commemorate the December 29, 1890, massacre of more than 300 Lakota Indians by the U.S. Army's 7th Cavalry.[13] In 2001, the Minidoka Internment National Monument in south-central Idaho, where over 9,300 Americans of Japanese ancestry were forced to relocate during World War II, became the NPS's 385th unit. In 2007, the Sand Creek Massacre National Historic Site was dedicated in southeastern Colorado, on the site where in November 1864, more than 200 Cheyenne and Arapaho Indians, mostly women, children, and older men, were murdered by Colorado militia and U.S. volunteer soldiers.

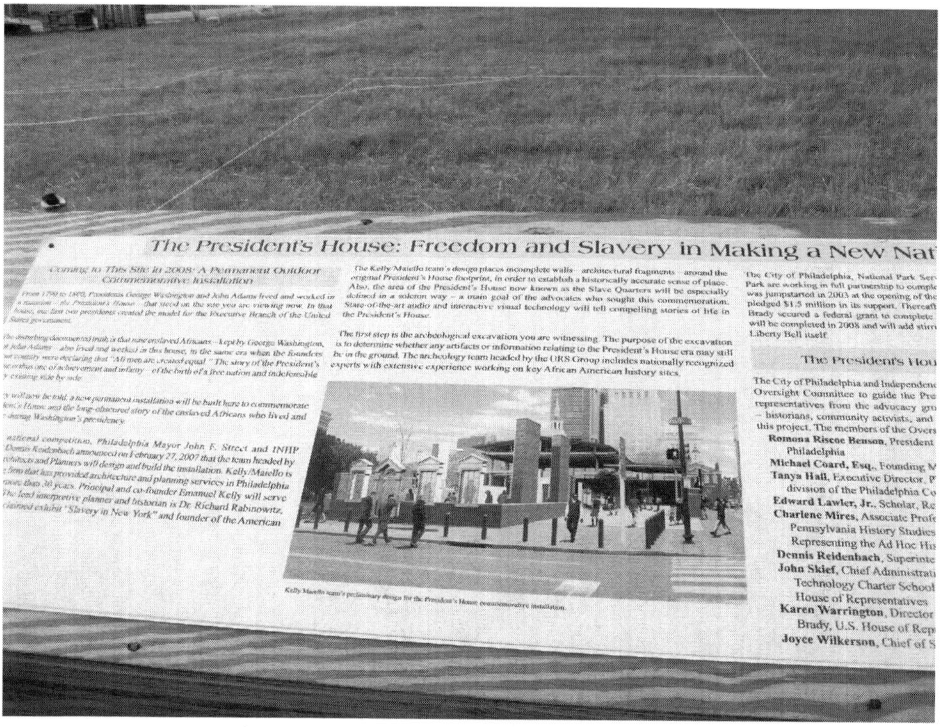

5.4. Temporary signage for the President's House, an outdoor memorial to be built next to the Liberty Bell Center and Independence Hall, Philadelphia, Pennsylvania. Note the ropes marking the location of house's original rooms in the background. (Photo by the author.)

Since 2002, the NPS has also been reckoning with the remains of the President's House in Philadelphia, where George Washington and John Adams lived during their presidencies—with at least nine African slaves—from 1790 to 1800 (fig. 5.4). Located one block from Independence Hall, the house's former slave quarters are less than five feet from the entrance to the redesigned Liberty Bell Center, where the nation's premiere icon of freedom is on public display. Although most of the house was demolished in the 1830s, the NPS launched an archaeological dig at the site in 2007 and has committed several million dollars (as has the city of Philadelphia) toward its commemoration. When completed, the site will feature a permanent outdoor installation of architectural fragments framing the footprint of the original brick house and an interpretive program of images, text, and sound recordings centering on "freedom and slavery in making a new nation." "It will give us an opportunity to talk about the heroic and the shameful that took place on this site," observes the NPS's acting superintendent of Independence

National Historical Park. "'We the People' applies to everyone who was part of what made this nation."[14]

Other new NPS units include the Brown v. Board of Education National Historic Site (dedicated in Topeka, Kansas, 2004), the Little Rock Central High School National Historic Site (Arkansas, 2002), and the Selma to Montgomery National Historic Trail (a fifty-four-mile trail that follows Alabama's Highway 80 and was authorized by Congress in 1996). Each articulates the racial geographies of twentieth-century struggles for civil rights in accordance with the agency's recent assessment that the national narrative "is often noble, but sometimes shameful and sad."[15] While the nation's history is full of shameful moments of religious intolerance, labor exploitation, gender discrimination, and environmental abuse, among others, racial injustice is the primary subject of today's shame-based memorials. Although some might argue that the nation cannot tolerate "self-accusing centers of memory," these sites and others, including Duluth's lynching memorial and slavery memorials and museums recently erected or underway in Georgia, North Carolina, Ohio, and Virginia, suggest otherwise.[16]

Yet what does the recovery of these shameful sites reveal, and how do these shame-based memorials help Americans "understand" the past? How is shame itself understood, and how does its admission in the national narrative shape and direct ideas about citizenship? Most significantly in a discussion of visual and material cultures, what are the ethics of remembering and representing abject images and histories? What are the responsibilities of acknowledging shame in the national narrative?

SHAME

Shame is understood as an uncomfortable or painful emotion due to impropriety, disgrace, disapproval, or regret. Its linguistic roots and cognate meanings are intimately attached to feelings about the body and rules regarding its public display. In English, for example, the word "shame" relates to the German *Scham*, which refers to descriptions of genitalia and modesty.[17]

Various accounts detail how feelings of shame relate to personal and social anxieties about the body and sexuality. Consider Augustine's explanation that shame's origination in the Garden of Eden stemmed from Adam's and Eve's "self-conscious and ashamed" recognition of their nakedness and lust, or Freud's thesis that shame functions to leash and inhibit sexual excess. Canonical "shame dramas" such as the Italian artist Masaccio's fifteenth-century fresco *Expulsion of Adam and Eve from the Garden of Eden*, writes Martha Hollander, crystallize the "sexual anxiety, social embarrassment, humiliation, and ostracism" of shame.[18] Contemporary shame narratives such as Duluth's lynching memorial similarly stem from the acknowledgement of impropriety and regret but, importantly, also critique standard visual articulations and social assumptions of shame's often uncomfortably corporeal dimensions.

Shame is, of course, intensely body based. Triggered by desire and arousal, shame is manifest in heated physiological responses like blushing. Sociologist Norbert Elias argued that shame was fundamental to Western modernity's "civilizing" of the body: modern manners and notions of physical self-control arose from shared social acknowledgement that certain bodily behaviors (like spitting in public) were shameful. By extension, decreased shame thresholds may be found when mannered behaviors are socially unrestrained—at mob lynchings, for example.[19]

In his work on affect, clinical psychologist Silvan Tomkins asserted that shame "operates ordinarily only after interest or enjoyment has been activated, and inhibits one or the other or both. The innate activator of shame is the incomplete reduction of interest or joy. Hence any barrier to further exploration which partially reduces interest or the smile of enjoyment will activate the lowering of the head and eyes in shame." Shame, in other words, is that which we find painful or humiliating to talk about or to look at, that which (as Elias argued) we are socially motivated to repress. And yet shame is also that which is compelling: shame follows the "incomplete reduction" of our attention.[20]

More than an uncomfortable physical sensation, shame is a marker of self and social interests. If we—individually or collectively, personally or nationally—are not interested or don't care, we are not ashamed. We are not born ashamed; we learn shame. Public expressions and representations of shame—like Duluth's lynching memorial—derive from consensual agreements to shift from the pleasure of looking to the pain and vulnerability of critical knowledge. As Tomkins noted, shame "generates the torment of self-consciousness."[21]

Freud, whose later work linked shame with narcissism, argued that "the force which opposes scopophilia [literally, the love of looking], but which may be overridden by it . . . is *shame*." Jean-Paul Sartre's model of shame in *Being and Nothingness* similarly centered on visuality; in his well-known example of the peeper crouching at the keyhole—who, suddenly realizing that he himself is being watched, is struck by burning feelings of embarrassment and humiliation—Sartre posited shame as the degradation of the gaze, the indignity of being viewed as an other, as an object, by another.[22] If Sartre's theoretical motive was to establish the embodied conditions of human consciousness and subjectivity and Freud's was to stress shame's role as a regulator of psycho-sexual excess, their perceptions similarly rested on shame's physical—and particularly visual—affective conditions: on how shame renders vulnerability through acts of seeing and being seen. Likewise, Tomkins's extensive analysis of shame especially emphasized "the enactment of shame in practices of looking."[23]

Importantly, however, and contra Freud, shame does not require the negation of looking; rather, seeing and being seen are often significant factors in shaming and being ashamed. Understanding how shame works in contemporary commemoration means being attentive to the dynamics of visual perception: of watching and being watched, of witnessing, of being the subject or the object of the gaze. But sight is not the only sensual pathway to understanding how shame operates. As Mark Smith argues, shameful feelings about slavery in antebellum America were mediated in part by hapticity (or touch), and by understanding "the skin of the enslaved in terms of interiority, emotion, and humanitarianism."[24] Thus, while shame may generate intense self-analysis, it is also inherently social and has moral and public possibilities. As Tomkins argued, "the nature of the experience of shame guarantees a perpetual sensitivity to any violation of the dignity of man." As Elspeth Probyn similarly contends, "shame is intensely productive politically and conceptually in advancing a project of everyday ethics."[25]

This is not to argue that shame is an intrinsic social or national trait, as various post–World War II scholars asserted in their hierarchical accounts of "shame cultures" and "guilt cultures." Anthropologists like Ruth Benedict, for example, went to great lengths to profile the United States as a "guilt" culture and Japan as a "shame" culture, with the implication that Western guilt—as opposed to Eastern shame—was the more "mature" affect in terms of social (and political) evolution.[26] Such concepts are largely abandoned today, mostly because of their essentialist underpinnings and their impossible premises of cultural and social homogeneity, if also because of their imperialist presumptions of Western, and especially American, evolutionary superiority. (Concurrent with the war on terror, however, these ideas have reemerged among some xenophobic bloggers and talk show pundits determined to divide what they perceive as the shame-based tribal cultures of "Islamo-fascism" from a guilt-ridden Judeo-Christian United States.)

By extension, the words "shame" and "guilt" are often used interchangeably today, which muddies their social and cultural distinctions. Still, however much shame is confounded with guilt, there are subtle differences. Guilt results from a violation of rules and from individual obligations of responsibility, whereas shame is more inherently social:

however much we are personally and self-consciously ashamed, such feelings are generally triggered by our relationships with others. Shame's affective potential, its usefulness, turns on these social interactions.

Shame's usefulness has been a subject of interest since at least the mid-1990s, when rants about the nation's social problems turned noticeably toward topics like personal morality, homosexuality, "common decency," and vulgarity. "Americans are fed up with everything from teen pregnancy to drunk drivers. How do we restore a sense of right and wrong?" asked the editors of *Newsweek* in a 1995 cover story headlined "The Return of Shame." In 1996, radio therapist Dr. Laura (Laura Schlesinger) published *How Could You Do That?! The Abdication of Character, Courage, and Conscience*, a self-help bestseller that shrilly demanded a return to heterosexual marriage in order to restore national order. In his 1997 memoir *My American Journey*, Colin Powell wrote that, "a sense of shame is not a bad moral compass," and reminisced that he "would have preferred a beating" to hearing his mother say, "I'm ashamed of you. You embarrassed the family." As one author remarks, this contemporary "cry for traditional family values is in some ways a cry of 'come back, shame, come back.'"[27]

At the same time, a flourishing "anti-shame" discourse has emerged, ranging from pop psychology bestsellers like *Healing the Shame That Binds You* (1988) and *Letting Go of Shame* (1989), to philosopher Martha Nussbaum's *Hiding from Humanity: Disgust, Shame, and the Law* (2004), which makes the case against an increasing trend toward shaming penalties in American law.[28] As a means of regulating social norms, shame may work to vilify those who do not or cannot live according to shame's rules: moralizing standards of shaming stigmatize difference and do not reckon with the pain of unearned shame—the shame of being raped, for example. Or the shame of "being identified with a people who could with impunity be treated worse than animals," as the narrator of James Weldon Johnson's novel *The Autobiography of an Ex-Colored Man* (1912) painfully describes his "unbearable shame" of racial identification with the thousands of black Americans who were regularly being lynched when this novel was first published. Although shame may play a "positive role in development and social life, in connection with valuable ideals and aspirations," Nussbaum cautions that "a liberal society has particular reasons to inhibit shame and to protect its citizens from shaming."[29]

Considerations of shame's stigmatizing vicissitudes have been especially central in queer theory, not surprising given contemporary political and religious invectives regarding the purported shame of homosexuality. In contrast with the social consensus of "gay pride," concepts of "gay shame" are grounded in opposition and resistance. As Eve Kosofsky Sedgwick explained in her writings on affect and queer performativity, "The forms taken by shame are not distinct 'toxic' parts of a group of individual identity that can be excised; they are instead integral to and residual in the process in which identity is formed. They are available for the work of metamorphosis, reframing, refiguration, *trans*figuration." Shame, in other words, is a key affect in identity formation and as such has enormous potential in terms of self, and social, *trans*formation. By "interrupting" identity, shame may recalibrate it; by embracing shame on reparative rather than suspicious or threatening terms, self and social identities may be remade along more promising lines.[30]

José Esteban Muñoz elaborates on shame's transformational possibilities in his theory of "disidentification," or the ways in which queers of color, among others, negotiate "politically dubious or shameful components" to rework—to work "on and against," not to assimilate within—dominant cultures. "*Queer* itself is a taking back of the shaming epithet," Muñoz writes, and queer practices (including queer theory) can serve to reanimate "shame as an inhabitable and potentially enabling identity site." He concludes, "The promises made by disidentification's performances are deep. Our charge as spectators and actors is to continue disidentifying with this world until we achieve new ones."[31]

Shame is profoundly paradoxical: a combination of looking at and looking away, a "negative" affect, as Tomkins termed it, which may offer positive social and political possibilities. Shame, he argued, "is the affect of dignity."[32] Its cultural usefulness begins with understanding its disabling and diminishing of human potential, and then shifts and expands to urgent expectations of change, of social and political transformation, of human rights. Public expressions of shame—including memorials that recall the nation's history of slavery and lynching—derive from public feelings of moral responsibility.

Shame's absence in American memorial cultures, at least until relatively recently, is not surprising. Traditionally, public monuments and memorials in the United States—the Washington Monument, for example, or the Marine Corps War Memorial—commemorate triumphant historical moments and/or heroic individuals. Contemporary memorials such as Duluth's embody new approaches in commemorative culture and new understanding of public citizenship. Challenging monolithic and mythologizing accounts of a virtuous American history, the Clayton Jackson McGhie Memorial posits a counternarrative of racial violence, civic trauma, and sociopolitical complicity. And it visibly engages the scopophilic dilemma of representing racial terrorism and trauma without voyeurism and dehumanization.

Archives compiled by the Tuskegee Institute (now Tuskegee University) show a record of 4,742 lynchings in the United States between 1882 and 1968; an estimated 3,445 of the victims were black. Conservatively based only on reported murders, these figures are undoubtedly much too low. Yet even if complete statistics can never be calculated epidemic proportions of racially motivated lynchings were reached, and thousands were recorded. As Dora Apel explains in *Imagery of Lynching* (2004), Jim Crow America was a nation obsessed with lynching—and with looking at lynching.[33]

Following the Civil War and throughout the twentieth century, American racists made full use of acts and images of racial terrorism to extend the dehumanizing inequities of slavery and to sustain assumptions of white racial superiority. Lynching rituals—barbaric public performances which involved stabbing, shooting, dragging, hanging, burning, and cutting human bodies—included visual documentation. New technologies of visual communication, such as Kodak's affordable and accessible pocket cameras (Kodak sold more than 150,000 of its one-dollar Brownie cameras in 1900), and the simultaneous surge of amateur or snapshot photography at the turn of the last century, enabled a mass pictorial discourse of racist violence.[34] As one observer noted, "hundreds of [K]odaks clicked all morning" at the site where Thomas Brooks was lynched in Somerville, Tennessee, in April 1915:

> People in automobiles and carriages came from miles around to view the corpse hanging from the end of a rope . . . Picture card photographers installed a portable printing plant at the bridge and reaped a harvest in selling postcards showing a photograph of the lynched Negro. Women and children were there by the score. At a number of country schools the day's routine was delayed until boy and girl pupils could get back from viewing the lynched man.[35]

Lynching may have peaked in the United States during the 1890s, when ritualized spectacles of racial terrorism occurred as often as every other day.[36] But lynching's brutal eruption at many other historical moments—during certain years of the Progressive Era, immediately after World War I, at the start of the Great Depression, at the end of World War II, during the era of civil rights—was a festering sore throughout the course of American modernity. This is not to argue that lynching was either a "natural" phenomenon like a volcanic eruption or a pathogenic disease beyond human control; rather, lynching was the intentional project of particular groups of people, and its cancerous metastasis in modern America was the result of pervasive and oppressive racism. Understanding lynching on metaphoric terms as an epidemiological course of racial terrorism calls attention to its endemic conditions in the national narrative.[37]

Nor has lynching disappeared in America, as the detestable 1998 murder of James Byrd, Jr., a black man from Jasper, Texas, makes clear. Byrd was dragged in chains from a pickup truck, his body ripped to shreds, his head and limbs torn from his torso. The truck was driven by three white men, one of them a white supremacist whose numerous tattoos included a Nazi swastika, the words "Aryan Pride," and the image of a black man hanging from a tree. In recent years, lynching nooses have resurfaced with alarming regularity in America: at post offices, on college campuses, in fire stations, draped around the neck of a bronze statue of Tupac Shakur located in a public garden named after him in Stone Mountain, Georgia. In September 2007, the appearance of several nooses on the White Tree, a segregated spot next to a high school in Jena, Louisiana, sparked one of the largest civil rights protests in decades. A month later, a noose found hanging on the office door of an African American professor at Columbia University Teachers College prompted a similar rally and an FBI hate-crime investigation.[38]

The looming specter and realized performance of lynching was—is—a deliberate and largely unchecked restraint on the autonomy and citizenship of the black body, or any other "body" that threatens white, heteronormative power—as with the lynching of Matthew Shepard, a queer college student, in Laramie, Wyoming, in 1998. Scholarship on lynching, from foundational histories to cultural studies, contextualizes it as a means of maintaining white elite patriarchy, and as a symptomatic rebuke to both New Negro and New Woman movements in the early twentieth century.[39] If the history and memory of lynching troubles a progressive national narrative, so too does its representation, and the commemoration of its victims. Memorials such as Duluth's admit to a shameful history of racist violence in the United States, and simultaneously raise questions about its disturbing contemporary presence.

"The United States of Lyncherdom," as Mark Twain put it in a vitriolic essay written in 1901 (first published in 1923), was a nation caught up in an "epidemic of bloody insanities," an "advancing disease" that was, Twain asserted, a "mania." Horrified by a newspaper story about the lynching of a black man in his home state of Missouri, Twain elaborated on lynching's national significance as an imitative "spectacle" of "public infamy" and "moral cowardice." Lynching was not only, Twain underlined, a sadistic peculiarity of the Deep South—although Cotton Belt states such as Alabama, Georgia, Louisiana, Mississippi, and

Texas surpassed all others in terms of numbers of lynchings and acts of racial terrorism. Searching for "California's hang trees," for example, contemporary photographer Ken Gonzales-Day discovered 352 instances of lynching in the Golden State between 1850 and 1935, most of them perpetrated against people of color.[40]

Other scholars similarly recount how spectacle lynching was a national—and modern—phenomenon. As Jacqueline Goldsby argues, lynching's "cultural logic" was a "networked, systemic phenomenon" triggered by widespread anxieties about the nation's shift to corporate-monopoly capitalism after the Civil War, and modernism's threat to established codes of gender, race, and class.[41] As those anxieties escalated after World War I, Duluth's outbreak of racial violence was preceded and followed by many others: in Green River, Wyoming (December 1918), Tuscaloosa, Alabama (March 1919), Chicago (July 1919), Washington, D.C. (July 1919), Omaha, Nebraska (September 1919), Center, Texas (August 1920), Ocoee, Florida (November 1920), Athens, Georgia (February 1921), and Tulsa, Oklahoma (May–June 1921). During the "Red Summer" of 1919, race riots erupted in more than twenty-five American cities. In Chicago, a five-day riot that began when a black youth was killed while swimming at a whites-only beach resulted in thirty-eight deaths and left more than a thousand black families homeless.[42]

Lynching's endemic terror was rooted in multiple and interlinked cultures, beliefs, and acts of racism. Its cancerous spread in the New South at the turn of the last century was simultaneous with a "passionate emotional style" resonant as much in southern political and social behaviors as in visual and material cultures. This style was central to ritualized and highly affective modes of white Christian evangelicalism practiced in the South, and some scholars argue that racial terrorism was, in essence, "a performative affirmation of fundamentalist Christian faith in a white supremacist national community."[43]

Yet throughout the nation, and throughout the twentieth century, fear and anger about a dangerous and deviant black race, and especially black masculinity, were whipped up on numerous fronts: in newspaper articles warning about lawless black men, in cartoons depicting black men as oversexed devils and rapists, in political speeches describing black men as brute savages. The primary aim of these assertions was to instigate white mob violence against black men; the contagion of spectacle lynching, as René Girard argues in his writing on ritual violence and human sacrifice, functioned to create cohesion and community among those who felt menaced by outsiders and others. In 1922, for example, Mississippi congressman Thomas Upton Sisson denounced the Dyer Anti-Lynching Bill by declaring that he "would rather the whole black race of this world were lynched than for one of the fair daughters of the South to be ravished and torn by one of these black brutes."[44]

Like the sex panics of the 1980s and 1990s, when hysteria about homosexuality set off spasms of outrage among a seemingly heteronormative (and apparently threatened) moralizing majority, the emotional dynamics of twentieth-century spectacle lynching spun on the worries that transgressions of race and gender posed to modern American patriarchy. In protecting white women from black men, elite white men maintained their own power and authority. That is not to say that some white women did not accept and advance this "protection." As Grace Hale writes, many white women "actively participated" in mass public lynchings, and did so "as more than the passive alleged victims that fueled white men's fury." In Duluth, for example, as Elias Clayton, Elmer Jackson, and Isaac McGhie were dragged up Second Avenue East and lynched, "women in high heels kicked and stomped" at their bodies.[45]

These acts of racial violence were fixedly modern: emotional public performances that were specific to the destabilizing dynamics wrought by industrialization, urbanization, corporate capitalism, the enlarged terrain of mass media, and the sustained growth of multiple publics. Lynchings, Hale explains, were "modern public spectacles." They often featured mobs—casts—of thousands: spectator-participants who viewed lynching on instrumental terms and were utterly complicit in its devastating effects. Lynchings were eagerly consumed by even larger audiences as they were repeatedly revisualized and replayed in various forms of American mass media: newspapers, photographs, postcards, magazines, radio programs, movies, and phonographic records. Racial terrorism, as Paul Gilroy argues, was fundamental to the circulation of Western modernity.[46]

RACIAL TERRORISM IN DULUTH

Duluth's eruption of racial violence in June 1920 was no less passionate and no less modern. It corresponded, in fact, to the most emotionally volatile and most modern of circumstances: modern-day labor. In 1915, U.S. Steel opened a $20 million, 600-acre "monster plant" outside of Duluth. It became the city's single largest employer, with some 3,000 workers producing 540,000 tons of steel ingots per year by 1920.[47] Duluth was also a hotbed of organized labor, both craft and industrial, and the nerve center of the Industrial Workers of the World in the 1910s. Strikes, walkouts, and violence were not uncommon; in 1918, a Duluth group called the Knights of Liberty lynched a Finnish dockworker because of his antiwar beliefs.[48] U.S. Steel's virulent antiunion tactics compounded fraught labor conditions. The company's complete rout of a national steel strike in 1919, for example, left workers in Duluth and across the country vulnerable and bitter.

Duluth's factory required a permanent, full-time, year-round labor pool, which U.S. Steel staffed by importing workers from its other plants in Pennsylvania and Indiana. It maintained them inside Morgan Park, a company town built near the factory, named after financier J. P. Morgan and modeled on City Beautiful ideals. Complete with its own stores, schools, churches, parks, and a community center (the Good Fellowship Clubhouse) that featured a swimming pool, movie theater, bowling alley, and gym, Morgan Park was a carefully engineered industrial village that, like most early modern company towns, "embodied illusions of social unity and coherence during periods of dramatic social and economic change." Illusions, indeed: Morgan Park was completely segregated. Although all workers in the Duluth plant were required to pay dues to support Morgan Park's multiple community resources, African American employees were not allowed to use them.[49] Racism informed the hierarchy of Duluth's civic and spatial organization as much as it dictated its social, political, and cultural landscapes.

During World War I, U.S. Steel's Duluth plant employed around a hundred black workers, most of whom had left the rural south during the Great Migration for economic opportunities in the urban north. Earning around $3.00 a day, blacks were typically paid less than whites and were often hired as scabs. Most of Duluth's black population—around five hundred in 1920—lived in the Gary neighborhood on the far west side of town, and African American parents warned their children, "never get off the streetcar in Morgan Park." While their numbers were small, their presence was noticed, especially among white military veterans who coveted the jobs that African Americans held in a time of postwar recession (in 1920, for example, eighteen blacks worked in Duluth's downtown post office).

Race relations in post–World War I Duluth were marked by "an uneasy tension," one author notes, so much so that when the John Robinson Circus arrived in the city on June 13, 1920, Duluth police chief John Murphy paid a visit to the circus manager and informed him that it would be best if its 120 black laborers "avoided going downtown or hanging around the West Duluth streets."[50] They apparently took his advice, sequestering themselves on the outskirts of town during the circus's short 35-hour stay. Folks from Duluth, of course, streamed to the site, attracted by what they saw in the free circus parade on the morning of June 14, and by the color posters pasted all over town advertising "Herds of Performing Elephants," "Droves of Camels," "Congo the Hippopotamus," and

"Madame X the Incredible Snake Handler." Veteran showman John Robinson had started his circus in the middle of the nineteenth century, and his family kept it solvent in the twentieth century by continually upgrading its exotic and erotic appeal. An ad in the *Duluth Herald* promoted it as "America's First and Foremost Circus, Now the Finest in the World."[51]

Circuses like this were the epitome of modernity: mobile, mysterious, and artificial spectacles ("specs") that were also highly routinized, controlled, and competitive forms of modern capitalism. In 1929, John Ringling bought out the American Circus Corporation (which included the John Robinson Circus), thereby monopolizing all major "traveling shows" in the United States. Typically organized by canny and conservative businessmen (like Robinson and Ringling), the traveling circus "was a powerful cultural icon of a new, modern nation-state" argues Janet Davis, a peripatetic form of amusement that was structured by, and simultaneously helped structure, "normative tropes about labor, racial inequality, separate spheres, and U.S. hegemony." Business-first and antiunion, "the big shows marketed themselves as exemplars of a burgeoning industrial America, incorporating, and sometimes even introducing, the latest in consumerism, advertising, transportation, and management theory."[52]

If formerly bawdier, more spontaneous, and carnivalesque, what Mikail Bakhtin lauded as a counterhegemonic folk culture, modern circuses were Big Top outfits featuring highly rehearsed trapeze acts and prancing animals, all expertly coordinated by authoritative ringmasters. Modern specs were also subject to legal regulations like taxation and licensing and to strict codes of conduct aimed at protecting locals from the potential "menace" posed by amoral outsiders (the bunco artists and hoochie koochie dancers of circus sideshows) and dark-skinned others; hence, Chief Murphy's visit to the manager of the John Robinson Circus.[53]

Murphy's visit wasn't entirely necessary, since modern circuses themselves regulated race and policed racial differences on terms ranging from hiring practices and performances to ticket sales and seating. Most black circus workers were employed as manual laborers, cooks, and roustabouts. A few appeared in specs set in antebellum plantations or pseudo-African villages, where they wore exotic robes and accessories that were gradually removed during performances so that their fetishized bodies were practically naked—a circus version of what Anne McClintock calls "porno-tropics." Circus clowns adopted a metaphorical blackface that featured a "huge red mouth, lolling, paint-encircled eyes," and a "big, fake nose," and circus showmen, Davis notes, "played upon this visual connection by arguing that African American men literally *were* clowns because of their supposed affinity for clowning and the circus." Many

Duluth residents would have understood these racist implications long before the John Robinson Circus showed up. In 1920 alone, for example, five different blackface minstrel shows played in Duluth.[54]

Consider the script for "The Plantation Darkey at the Circus," performed during the 1895–1896 season of the Ringling Brothers' Circus:

> [T]he great American "nigger" has a laugh not only his own but one that owns him as well. In the presence of the clown he and the laugh are firmly bound together. They can't get away from one another; not the nigger and the laugh! Oh, no! It is with him under every inch of his black skin, in every nerve, muscle, sinew, even in his bones. Every atom in his body responds to it . . . At times it leaps out of his capacious mouth, like a flame of fire.[55]

Racist performances like these, backed by beliefs that black men were essentially corporeal and childlike—or, primitive and premodern—helped "make" a derogatory blackness as much as they perpetuated assumptions of white supremacy. They were deliberately contrasted with other acts like "The Terrific Roman 4-Horse Chariot Race," which was staged by Sells Brothers Circus in 1893 and featured white male acrobats controlling powerful animals. Jim Crow similarly managed modern circus audiences; in Duluth, as elsewhere in early twentieth-century America, black and white circus fans sat separately.

Modern circuses were exciting venues where half-naked girls rode bareback, exotic animals and people paraded and performed, and multiple arenas were jammed with nonstop action and surprise. Circuses were crowded, colorful, and confusing spaces that permitted—albeit briefly—some subversion of normative tropes of class, gender, and race. A *circus*, after all, implies frenzy, abandon, chaos, and excess: some thing and some place out of the ordinary. And modernity was marked as much by capitalist imperatives of order, control, and management as it was by the sabotage of those mechanisms in order to generate new markets and increased profits. American modernism was, above all else, "profoundly paradoxical."[56]

Thus, even as the modern circus was a site of codes and rules, it was also a temporal public space where social and cultural boundaries were somewhat looser, and perhaps less restrained, than in "real life." Like other forms of modern popular entertainment in the early twentieth century, most notably vaudeville and motion pictures, circuses catered to crowds and centered on thrills, on dynamic displays of sexuality and spectacular performances of physical abandon. After the John Robinson Circus played its final show in Duluth, two local teenagers ventured to the back of the Big Top and performed their own physical "acts." Twenty-four hours later, a frenzied mob convinced that a white female had been sexually assaulted lynched three black circus workers.

Traveling specs were often a "signal for local young men to run riot;" sites where fights broke out between hometown rubes who felt suckered and circus workers who became their targets. Black workers were especially vulnerable, and Duluth's lynching was not the only attack. In 1890, a white man killed a black man at the Sells Brothers' sideshow in Navasota, Texas, "after supposedly being insulted by him"; in 1898, "there was talk of lynching the negro" after a fight between a white man and a black man at a circus in Falls City, Nebraska; in 1926, a riot and near lynching took place near Melville, Saskatchewan, a small-town railroad hub in eastern central Canada, "after a black circus worker allegedly made advances to a white woman."[57]

The racial violence that surged in Duluth in mid-June 1920 similarly stemmed from sexual allegations, from claims by a young white couple—James Sullivan (age eighteen) and Irene Tusken (age nineteen)—that they had been attacked on the evening of June 14 by black circus workers and that Tusken had been raped. No matter that the claims were unfounded, backed by neither witnesses nor physical evidence: by 7:00 a.m. on June 15, six black men were in custody in Duluth's downtown jail. By noon, angry crowds demanding vengeance were circulating on the city's streets. By early evening, a green truck driven by a thirty-eight-year-old delivery man named Louis Dondino was ambling through Duluth's neighborhoods with a cab full of other white men holding lengths of rope over their heads and inciting the gathering mob with shouts like "Come on! Show what kind of men you are! The niggers raped that girl, and she might be dead . . . What if she was your sister or daughter? Join the neck-tie party!" By 9:30 p.m. the mob had broken into Duluth's downtown jail. By 11:30, they had lynched three black men. Posing for pictures while McGhie's and Jackson's brutalized bodies were still hanging from the utility pole, and Clayton's body had been dumped onto the bloody pavement to fit within the visual range of the camera, one man shouted: "Send them pictures to Alabama. Tell 'em to keep their niggers."[58]

LYNCHING AS VISUAL SPECTACLE

Duluth's lynching was a public performance and became part of the public record; like other modern spectacles of racial terrorism, lynching received considerable national media coverage. In November 1922, pressing for passage of the Dyer Anti-Lynching Bill in the U.S. Senate, the NAACP placed a full-page ad in the *New York Times* and eight other national dailies that was headlined, "The Shame of America. Do you know that the *United States* is the *Only Land on Earth* where human beings are *BURNED AT THE STAKE*?"[59] In June 1920, Duluth's lynching was reported in the *Times* and the *Chicago Daily Tribune*, and in regional newspapers like the *Duluth Herald*, the *Ely Miner*, and the *Mankato Daily Free Press*. It was covered in detail in the *National Advocate* and the *Appeal*, black newspapers in St. Paul. It was denounced by some: the *Minneapolis Journal* said Duluth's lynch mob had "put an ineffaceable stain on the name of Minnesota," the *Chicago Evening Post* said Duluth was now "condemned in the eyes of the nation," and the *Duluth News-Tribune* printed an editorial titled "Duluth's Disgrace" that blatantly stated: "Duluth has suffered a disgrace, a horrible blot upon its name that it can never outlive."[60]

But other papers praised the lynching: "The city of Duluth is not disgraced," said the *Mankato Daily Free Press*. "The city of Duluth can recover from any stigma that may be attached to the quick hanging of the negroes. A few years hence people will have forgotten the incident—but the unfortunate girl—what of her? She is the one to be considered. Her fate is far worse than that which has befallen the city." And the *Ely Miner* declared: "The lynchings in Duluth will have a wholesome effect on the class of help carried by ordinary circus and carnival troupes. The chances are that no colored help with a carnival attraction or circus in the county will be tolerated hereafter." Sure enough, two days after the lynching, the police chief of Superior, Wisconsin (across the bridge from Duluth) announced: "We are going to run all idle negroes out of Superior and they're going to stay out." Black workers with a carnival in Superior were fired and "told to get out of the city," and the carnival was forced, somewhat ironically, to employ "whites to do the work formerly done by the negroes" in a spec depicting "plantation days."[61]

The *Duluth Ripsaw*, a muckraking weekly responsible for ousting several crooked police officers in 1917, was the only local paper to expose the accusations against the three murdered circus workers as outrageous lies and to damn the lynchings as "the crowning tragedy of a generation . . . conceived in a lawless resort, carried out by hoodlums, and permitted by a weak and incompetent police department." Declaring the lynchings a "travesty on humanity, law, order, and justice," the paper stated, "After investigation and a careful analysis of allegations, the *Ripsaw* is forced to the conclusion that six Negroes did not rape Miss Irene Tusken at West Duluth on the night of Monday, June 14."[62]

The *Ripsaw* was also the only paper to report on legal action against "mercenary photographer" Ralph Greenfield, who was fined $25 for displaying "obscene" and "debasing" photographs of the Duluth lynching in his storefront window in Superior. Reporters described sales of the pictures—which ranged from a dime for a postcard to a dollar for a large photograph and were "peddled up and down the streets of Duluth" by "little boys"—as "a ghoulish act, sordidly done, solely for money, and aggregating thousands of dollars in receipts."[63]

Like the lynchings, the photographs of the abject bodies of Clayton, Jackson, and McGhie were mobile public spectacles: atrocity images that circulated from one American city to the next. Duluth's "Picture of a Lynching" is practically identical to a postcard made a year earlier in Omaha of the lynching of forty-one-year-old packinghouse laborer Will Brown. Both images show crowds of white men consciously posing for an off-frame photographer; both show the tortured bodies of black men on display. Both are night shots, made possible by new technologies of flash photography and street and car lights. And both were sold as cheap souvenirs, affordable and widely consumed objects that, as Susan Stewart argues, work to normalize the unfamiliar and make it an acceptable, and owned, part of everyday life.[64]

In 1912, a Unitarian minister in New York who condemned lynching opened his mail to find a postcard "depicting a crowd in Alabama posing for a photographer next to the body of a black man dangling by a rope." On the back was this message: "This is the way we do them down here. The last lynching has not been put on card yet. Will put you on our regular mailing list. Expect one a month on the average." Other lynching postcards featured more casually horrifying comments. On the reverse of a postcard depicting the charred corpse of seventeen-year-old Jesse Washington, a black man lynched in Robinson, Texas in 1916, one member of the lynch mob wrote, "This is the Barbecue we had last night. My picture is to the left with a cross over it, your son Joe."[65]

Lynching postcards, in other words, did more than simply record racial terrorism; they familiarized its horror by "habituating Americans," Goldsby observes, "to see the deaths and sufferings of African American people as a disturbing but tolerable sight." Other widely circulated atrocity postcards performed similar roles, including those made by commercial photographer George Trager of the aftermath of the 1890 Wounded Knee massacre. Trager's pictures of frozen Lakota corpses, U.S. soldiers posing with the heaped bodies of Indian dead, and a trench that served as a mass grave, justified the slaughter of Native Americans as the inevitable outcome in the struggle of a superior white "civilization" against Indian "savagery." One contemporary ad for these postcards described them as "just the thing to send to your friends back east." Business was brisk, and an extra half-dozen people were hired to print the cards in Trager's nearby studio in Nebraska.[66]

Mixed in with millions of other postcards—the Curt Teich Company of Chicago, for example, one of the largest postcard manufacturers in the

United States, kept up to forty million cards in its active stocks in the early twentieth century—these pictures of murdered African Americans and massacred American Indians legitimated racial terrorism within other acceptable forms of visual, material, and performative cultures. Even though beginning in 1908 the U.S. Post Office forbade the mailing of items "tending to incite arson, murder, or assassination," such postcards still circulated. Decades after Wounded Knee, souvenir postcards of the Indians murdered there could still be purchased at the Wounded Knee Trading Post on the Pine Ridge Reservation, which advertised its stock on highway billboards that commanded: "See the Wounded Knee Massacre Site, Visit the Mass Grave. Postcards, Curios, Don't Miss It!"[67]

Photographs of Duluth's lynching (see fig. 5.2, above) show a filthy pavement littered with trash and matches, as if the crowd considered burning the bodies of the men they had just murdered, as they did in Omaha. Some hold scraps of cloth torn from the shirts of their victims; some are splattered with the blood that poured from the bodies of their victims. At other lynchings, perpetrators often cut off body parts as curios and souvenirs, not just to further dehumanize their victims but because these corporeal keepsakes embodied the undying authority, and constant presence, of racism in American national consciousness.[68]

Lynching photos and body parts are the visual and material vestiges—memory stains—of white supremacy and racial terrorism. If spectacle lynching had focused only on erasing black presence, these memory traces would not have been produced and preserved. But they were, because however despised and degraded, black bodies possessed powers that white bodies felt compelled to control; because demonstrations of black inferiority determined the terms of white superiority. By posing with the men they murdered, by *dismembering* them in public displays, white lynch mobs reenacted and *remembered* a national mandate of racial hierarchy. Their rituals of racial terrorism aimed at maintaining that hierarchy, and perpetuating whiteness in terms of power, privilege, and violence.

Duluth's lynching pictures are even more disturbing because despite the horror of what they had just done, these white men acted like regular guys mugging for a group photo at a company picnic, not like the participants in a lynch mob. Leaning forward into the camera's range, some holding up lynching trinkets and smiling, they denied their membership in the *mob* by beckoning the photographer to represent them, instead, as *individual* actors in a standard American drama. "I want to be in this picture," Fedo imagines these men saying. Or as one Minnesota newspaper reported, a "noticeable feature of the [Duluth lynching] mob was that despite the grim work in which it was engaged, good humor and comparative order pervaded."[69] Leon Litwack writes that the most "ordinary and respectable people," the good Americans of a supposedly civilized society, carried out the eruptive mania of racial terrorism. They are "our best citizens, who are foremost in all works of public and private good," stated one Georgia newspaper. These are "not men who flout law but men who sincerely believe they have the best interests of their fellow men and women at heart," reported another newspaper in Mississippi.[70]

Some believe that the representation of trauma helps to evacuate it, that visualizing atrocity exposes its causes and consequences and compels viewers to think of ways to prevent it from happening again. Pictures of Emmett Till's tortured body performed this sort of national consciousness raising in the mid-1950s, during the era of civil rights. Yet as Saidiya Hartman remarks in a discussion of slavery narratives: "Are we witnesses who confirm the truth . . . Or are we voyeurs fascinated with and repelled by exhibitions of terror and suffering?"[71] The voyeuristic dimensions of lynching photography exemplify these problems—especially when they stand alone as visual evidence. Duluth's lynching photos, for example, are the only known pictures of Clayton, Jackson, and McGhie; no photographs from when they were alive appear to exist. Photos that feature debased black bodies and triumphant white perpetrators embody the cultural codes of racism. However revelatory, these images repeatedly dehumanize their victims as they simultaneously reanimate the power of their murderers. Their evidentiary terms—how they are seen, and by whom—are equally problematic.

Images of spectacle lynching have a long modern history, and particular contemporary resonance due to the popularity of the exhibition Without Sanctuary: Lynching Photography in America. Based on a cache of 130 lynching postcards and photos collected by James Allen and John Littlefield, Without Sanctuary opened at the New-York Historical Society in 2000, and then traveled to the Martin Luther King, Jr. National Historic Site in Atlanta, the Andy Warhol Museum in Pittsburgh, the Chicago History Museum, and the Charles H. Wright Museum of African American History in Detroit, among other venues.[72] The show's catalogue featured 98 of the photographs and went into several printings. As an exhibition, catalogue, and Web site, Without Sanctuary was seen by tens of thousands of people (50,000 at the New York venue alone) and garnered a huge amount of critical attention. Writing for the *Nation*, for example, Patricia Williams observed, "It's a difficult task, this re-viewing of violence, this striving for reflection rather than spectacle, for vision rather than voyeurism, for study rather than exposure."[73] Many critics noted the irony that horrible photos originally made to confirm white supremacy were now, no less horrible, being used to confirm racial terrorism in American history. Many presumed that this functional alteration seemed to suggest a changed national sensitivity regarding race and racism.

These assumptions rest on those of a shared national gaze, on assumptions that today, lynching and lynching photos are commonly understood and elicit similarly felt responses. Yet lynching's recurrence as a threat and action in places like Jena, Louisiana, and Jasper, Texas, and the malleability of lynching images elsewhere in contemporary America suggest otherwise. John Williams King, for instance, one of the men who killed James Byrd in 1998, sported a tattoo of a black man being lynched. In 1992, the rap group Public Enemy reproduced a photo of a lynching on the cover of "Hazy Shade of Criminal" to protest what band frontman Chuck D called the legal "lynching" of black boxer Mike Tyson (convicted in 1992 of rape). And the group Justice For All juxtaposes lynching photos with pictures of Jews murdered in the Holocaust, Indians murdered at Wounded Knee, Cambodians murdered by the Khmer Rouge, and aborted fetuses in the large panels it displays at antiabortion rallies—uniting all of these graphically violent images under the headline "What is it called when the victims have no choice?" As these examples suggest, the visual evidence of lynching photographs, or photography in general, is "neither univocal nor fixed" because, as Shawn Michelle Smith observes, "photographic *meaning* is always shaped by context and circulation, and determined by viewers."[74]

Assumptions that lynching photos command shared meanings and feelings discount, for example, who is looking, and how different viewers understand visual discourses of violence and trauma differently. Many critics assumed that the audiences who attended Without Sanctuary, or those who visited the exhibition's Web site or perused its catalogue, shared the view that lynching was—is—abhorrent. But seeing atrocity images does not necessarily teach anything about them. Visibility alone hardly guarantees meaning. Moreover, there are profound differences between how images of lynched men and women of color are seen and understood by people of color, and what they may mean to white viewers. "Who, in fact, is the 'we' imagined by all these interconnected venues for viewing," Grace Hale asks, speculating that white viewers may look at lynching photographs to "experience the trauma of race" without acknowledging the role that whiteness has played in the performance of racial terrorism. "Why do we learn very little about the people who participated in the tortures, took the photographs, and sent the postcards? Why do we learn nothing about the people who saved the images down through the years?" she further queried in her review of Without Sanctuary, challenging the project and its organizers to move beyond the visual spectacle of lynching's victims to the more critically engaged history of lynching's perpetrators, and the particular terms of racialized violence that have defined the hierarchies of race in modern America.[75]

Images of pain and death demand self and national scrutiny. Who is looking, and why? Do people look at lynching photographs to bear witness to national shame? To confirm lynching's role as a regulating instrument of racialized difference? To sadistically champion the effects of racial terrorism? In the ideal ethical scenario, photographs of lynching might be considered agents of mourning and outrage: images that permit insights into the terms of human degradation, urge empathy with the dead, and prompt action against their reoccurrence. But critically vacuous fascination with wound culture—with the trauma and pain of others, without the necessary interrogation of our own desires to look at that trauma and pain—discounts these possibilities. Importantly, photographs of the debased bodies of Clayton, Jackson, and McGhie, or the mob that killed them, were not included in Duluth's lynching memorial. As Susan Crane argues in a discussion of Holocaust photography, "choosing not to look" at atrocity images may be the only ethical alternative to unmediated and uncritical use of such images.[76]

Photography is, of course, a dominant feature in many contemporary memorials. The Korean War Veterans Memorial features 2,400 photos of that war's support personnel sandblasted onto its polished granite walls. Patriots Park, a memorial in Portsmouth, Rhode Island that pays tribute to an infantry unit of black slaves and freemen authorized in 1775, features photographs of Revolutionary War reenactors dressed in period costumes, holding period weapons. The Desert Holocaust Memorial in Palm Desert, California features a series of bronze plaques reproducing photographs of Nazi concentration camps. "Image ladders" in the Rosie the Riveter/World War II National Historical Park feature photographs of female defense industry workers (see fig. 0.8, p. 5). Growing numbers of American gravestones feature etched photos of the dead and pictures of their favorite things (pets, snowboards, Corvettes). And many memorials—from the Marine Corps War Memorial to the 9/11 sculptures modeled on Thomas Franklin's snapshot of three firemen at Ground Zero—are basically three-dimensional replicas of the photographs that originally deemed these places and people meaningful and hence memorable.

As these examples suggest, memorials that aim to secure and stabilize historical narratives often turn to photographs to imply authenticity and infallibility. While there is no ontological basis for photography's privileged status as "a direct transcription of the real," particularly since photos (like all images) can be manipulated and can manipulate their viewers, photos are still generally and uncritically perceived as inherently "truthful." Although Roland Barthes concluded in *Camera Lucida* that photography is an exceptionally affective medium that "completely de-realizes the human world of conflicts and desires, under cover of illustrating it," photo-memory is cemented in modern minds as proof, or "intractable reality."[77]

Photography's authority, in other words, dominates modern memory. For memorials like the Clayton Jackson McGhie Memorial, for commemorative projects that aim to jar memory and raise questions about shameful civic and national histories, photo-vision—especially images that depict white mob violence and black victimization—is *too* authoritative. Refusing the voyeuristic photo-spectacle of human degradation, Duluth's memorial recalls the racial terrorism of lynching with a different narrative of human dignity and social responsibility.

SHAME'S MEMORIAL

Racial terrorism's extralegal spectacle continued long after 1920. Despite declarations of civic shame by the NAACP and growing public protest, lynching in America continued.[78] The federal government repeatedly failed to enact anti-lynching legislation: the Dyer Anti-Lynching Bill passed in the Senate in 1922, but was overturned by the House. In Duluth, a special grand jury condemned the city's commissioner of public safety, stating: "That there were innocent bystanders and onlookers, as claimed by the police, is no grounds for their utter lack of organized attempt to stop the mob."[79] Yet only eight men from Duluth's ten thousand–member lynch mob were tried and only three—including Louis Dondino—were convicted on charges of rioting, each serving less than fifteen months in prison. No one was ever convicted for the murders of Clayton, Jackson, and McGhie. However, seven black workers with the John Robinson Circus were indicted for rape, and two were tried. One man was acquitted and the other, Max Mason, a cook from Decatur, Alabama, who had been with the Robinson outfit since 1910, was sentenced to thirty years in Stillwater State Prison. Mason served four years and in 1925 his sentence was unexpectedly commuted, with the proviso that he leave the state of Minnesota and never return.[80]

Memories of Duluth's 1920 lynchings faded, although black residents of Duluth never forgot. Many left: while Duluth's overall population grew by 2,000 from 1920–1930, its black population dropped by 16 percent.[81] The few hundred who stayed kept Duluth's history of racial terrorism current in conversations with their children, and in warnings to black newcomers. They also organized a local chapter of the NAACP, inviting W. E. B. Du Bois as their first speaker in March 1921, and pressed for a statewide anti-lynching bill that was signed into law by Minnesota legislators in April 1921. Minnesota was the first U.S. state to pass an anti-lynching law. Yet a year later, the KKK met for its first Minnesota gathering in a park outside Minneapolis. And racism in Duluth became more oppressive; black workers were passed over for jobs, black families were redlined from buying or renting in certain neighborhoods, and black teachers were not allowed to teach in Duluth's public schools.[82]

Some Minnesota natives retained the historical memory of Duluth's lynchings. Sinclair Lewis, born in Sauk Center, Minnesota in 1885, moved to Duluth in the mid-1940s to work on *Kingsblood Royal* (1947), a wrenching novel that traces the emergent racial consciousness of a white World War II hero. Doing some genealogical research and discovering that he is not, in fact, descended from British royalty but is the heir of a "full-blooded Negro," middle-class banker Neil Kingsblood announces his racial ancestry to his friends and fellow citizens and experiences—along with his wife and family—full-blown racial terrorism, including an attempted lynching. Lewis set his story in a mythical Minnesota city he named "Grand Republic," located near Duluth. Random House advertised his novel as "a blazing story with a theme that will jolt the nation." If controversial when it was first published because of its radical critique of racism and prescient take on the privileges of whiteness in modern middle-class America, *Kingsblood Royal* quickly went out of print.[83]

Bob Dylan, who was born in Duluth in 1941 and whose father lived in an apartment in downtown Duluth at the time of the 1920 lynchings, opened his 1965 song "Desolation Row" with several obvious allusions to his hometown's shameful history:

> They're selling postcards of the hanging
> They're painting the passports brown
> The beauty parlor is filled with sailors
> The circus is in town
> Here comes the blind commissioner
> They've got him in a trance
> One hand is tied to the tight-rope walker
> The other is in his pants
> And the riot squad they're restless
> They need somewhere to go
> As Lady and I look out tonight
> From Desolation Row.

Lynching postcards influenced other American artists, too, including Dylan's folk music predecessor and idol, Woody Guthrie. Pictures of a 1911 mob lynching of a black woman and her son in Guthrie's hometown of Okemah, Oklahoma, a lynching that his father attended, were published in the local newspaper and later figured in ballads such as "Bloody Poll Tax Chain" and "Slipknot."[84]

Official local histories like *Duluth: Sketches of the Past* (1976) ignored the city's notorious lynching.[85] The first full account appeared in Michael Fedo's *They Was Just Niggers* (1979), which took its title from a comment made by one of the spectator-participants in Duluth's 1920 lynch mob. Fedo's book compelled Craig Grau, a professor at the University of Minnesota–Duluth, to track down the unmarked graves of Clayton, Jackson, and McGhie in the local Lutheran cemetery. In 1991, Duluth's chapter of the NAACP erected a grave marker in the cemetery with the names of the three murdered men and the inscription "Deterred But Not Defeated." Further reconsideration of Duluth's lynchings gained momentum a few years later, after local journalist Heidi Bakk-Hansen read a copy of Fedo's book and discovered that the street corner she walked past every day on her way to work was where Clayton, Jackson, and McGhie had been lynched. On June 7, 2000, she published the article "Duluth's Lingering Shame" for Duluth's *Ripsaw News*; a week later, on the eightieth anniversary of the lynchings, a community vigil was held at the intersection of First Street and Second Avenue East.[86]

Shortly thereafter, the Clayton Jackson McGhie Memorial Committee was formed. Spearheaded by Bakk-Hansen, community activist Henry Banks, and high school teacher Catherine Ostos, committee membership expanded to many "old guard" Duluth residents who had ties to the community dating to the lynching. These included Melissa Taylor, an African American woman whose family has lived in Duluth for several generations; Perry Kennedy, who joined an all-black unit of the Army Air Corps in the 1940s; and Bob Grytdahl, a white man who was the city's deputy police chief in 2001. All were dismayed by Duluth's lack of historical knowledge regarding its racist past, disturbed by recurrent episodes of racism in its present, and "determined to infuse the 1920 deaths into the consciousness of the[ir] community." As Taylor observed, "all the undercurrent of emotion and hate and fear that drove this community to do that in 1920 still exists."[87]

Duluth's racial configuration in terms of black and white citizens has changed little since 1920; in 2000, only about 1,400 blacks were counted among the city's total population of 86,000. Yet in recent years, more than a few racist incidents have occurred. As Grytdahl remarked, "This isn't just a project to raise money to build a memorial. This is a project to get our community thinking about the future of racial equality in Duluth."[88] Challenging northern—and national—assumptions that spectacle lynching was a "strictly southern" phenomenon, something that happened "somewhere else," the Clayton Jackson McGhie Memorial Committee placed racial terrorism squarely in Duluth's purview and considered strategies for both its historical commemoration and contemporary condemnation.

One of their first initiatives was a city-wide reading of Fedo's book (reissued in 2000 as *The Lynchings in Duluth*). Critical conversations about the 1920 lynchings sparked interests in their commemoration; initial ideas about doing so with a plaque or historical marker expanded to a large-scale memorial. In 2002, the committee persuaded the city to permit the construction of a memorial on an empty lot across the street from the site of the lynchings, on land donated by a local firm (Lamar Outdoor Advertising). As the project unfolded, the committee collaborated with the Duluth Public Arts Commission and the Minnesota Historical Society, and raised $267,000 from local churches, law firms, banks, and schools, as well as an undisclosed amount from Bill Berry, formerly a drummer for the band R.E.M., who was born in Duluth in 1958. One local woman, preferring to remain anonymous, donated $10,000. "The most poignant contribution," recalls the memorial's designer, Carla Stetson, "came from a woman whose grandfather had been working at the jail that night and while watching the memorial being built told her: 'Those boys were innocent.'"[89] Memorial fundraising included benefit concerts, poetry readings, lectures, and a screening of *Strange Fruit*, a documentary about the haunting song recorded by Billie Holiday in 1939 that was inspired by photos of two black men lynched in Marion, Indiana in 1930.[90]

Over a three-year period, the Clayton Jackson McGhie Memorial Committee revived civic remembrance of Duluth's lynchings and simultaneously constructed civic support for the commemoration of its victims. As Bakk-Hansen later remarked, "many people came forward" after the memorial project was announced, including "people who were descendants of perpetrators and people who hid in their homes that night in fear for their lives."[91] A call for entries drew seventeen proposals, including an oversized bronze sculpture of a black man pleading for his life, a statue of a black man tossing a pair of dice, and other projects featuring broken columns (a traditional funerary symbol of a life cut short) and weeping willows. Stetson's proposal was deemed more specific to the site, the community, and the memorial committee's aspirations regarding "a just and equitable future for all."[92] Minneapolis writer Anthony

Peyton Porter was chosen to organize textual materials addressing the memorial's context.

Occupying a corner less than fifty feet from the lamppost where Clayton, Jackson, and McGhie were hung in 1920, Duluth's memorial is an unassuming pocket-park framed by the Kozy Bar, the Carter Hotel, First Street Exchange Pawn, Union Gospel Mission, and Gene's Auto Body (fig. 5.5). Located in a gritty neighborhood that is slowly being gentrified, the memorial encloses a small garden and a few benches. It is quiet and inviting, a contemplative space where visitors can reflect on the moral and ethical implications of the thirteen quotes etched on its walls (fig. 5.6). These range from Oscar Wilde's "The truth is rarely pure, and never simple" and James Baldwin's "We are responsible for the world in which we find ourselves, if only because we are the only sentient force that can change it" to Albert Einstein's "The world is a dangerous place, not because of those who do evil, but because of those who look on and do nothing" and Elie Wiesel's "There may be times when we are powerless to prevent injustice, but there must never be a time when we fail to protest." Other quotes from Euripides, Siddhartha, Marian Wright Edelman (founder of the Children's Defense Fund), and Thich Nhat Hanh (a Vietnamese Buddhist monk), are similarly attuned to the memorial committee's goal of "facing head-on the worst of our collective past," and cultivating those shameful memories to generate social change and political transformation.[93]

Like many shame-based projects today, Duluth's memorial is framed by "bearing witness," which, as Shoshana Felman explains, is "not merely to narrate, but to commit oneself and . . . the narrative to others: to take responsibility for history or for the truth of the occurrence." Bearing witness liberates the victims of trauma from historical amnesia and restores their humanity. It "connects us, and obligates us, to each other," adds Kelly Oliver, who argues that witnessing is the basis of human subjectivity and as such is "an ethical and social responsibility."[94]

Duluth's memorial recalls the city's 1920 lynching, restores the subjectivity of the three men who were murdered, and calls on viewers to recognize their own, and the nation's, complicity in racial violence. Since its beginnings, the United States has struggled with the seemingly contradictory impulses of two currents: shared assumptions of national purpose manifest in "a purifying drive for morality," and personal ambitions of self-reliance and independence evident in a "liberating drive for individualism."[95] Utilizing a visual vocabulary of shame, Duluth's memorial reckons with both: with the shame of the *nation's* immoral acts of racist violence, and with the shameful recognition of *individual* participation

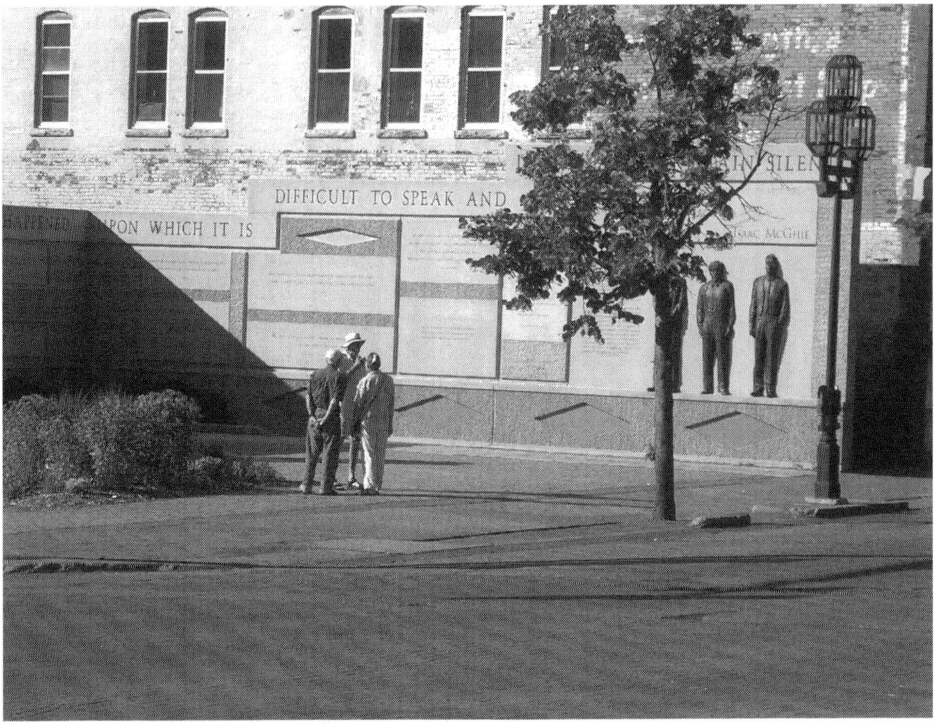

5.5. Clayton Jackson McGhie Memorial. (Photo by the author.)

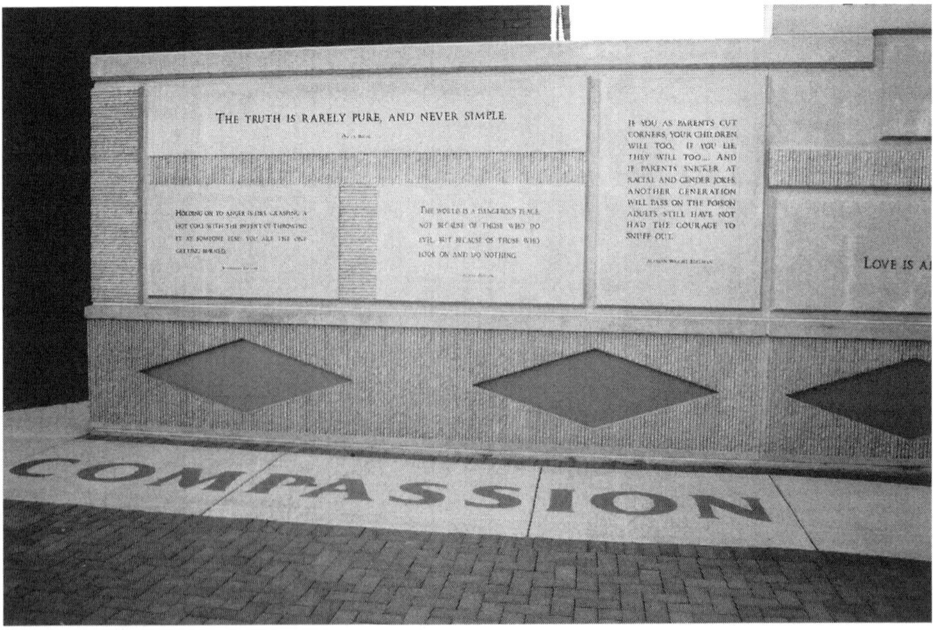

5.6. Clayton Jackson McGhie Memorial, detail. (Courtesy of Carla Stetson.)

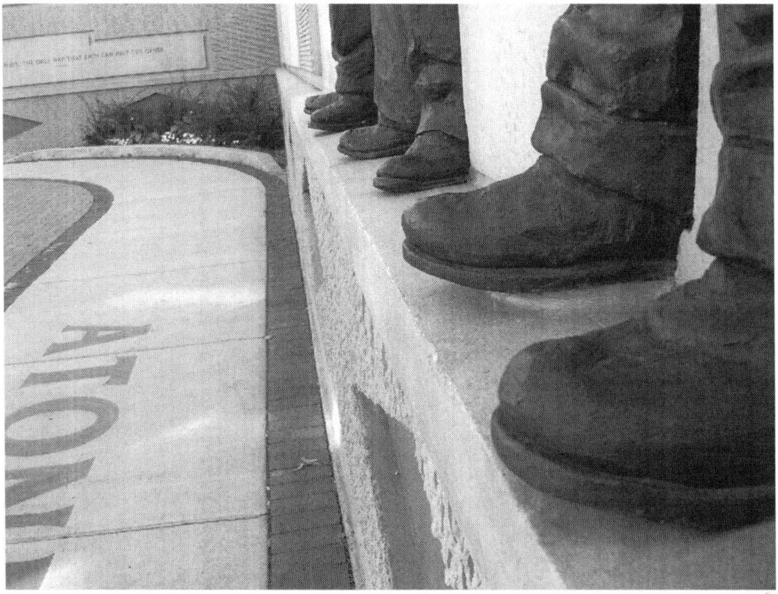

5.7. Clayton Jackson McGhie Memorial, detail. (Courtesy of Carla Stetson.)

in the objectification and dehumanization of other human beings. Its design deliberately encourages this recognition (fig. 5.7). "Most people 'read' the memorial from left to right," Stetson observes. "By the time they get to the information about the lynching and see the bronze figures, the word 'you' has been used three times in the various quotes."

While trauma "undermines subjectivity and witnessing restores it, the process of witnessing is not reduced to the effects of trauma," Oliver argues.[96] Rather than reproducing images of white mob violence and black victimization, Duluth's memorial focuses on the individuality of three wrongly accused men, and on bearing witness to issues of moral accountability. Since pictures of Clayton, Jackson, or McGhie while alive have not been found, Stetson modeled the memorial's seven-foot figures on three local high school and college students. Each young man is dressed in period clothing: vests, suspenders, narrow belts, button down shirts, caps, hats, jackets, heavy shoes. And each stands with confident self-assurance, his eyes cast slightly upward, glancing across the street to where he was murdered (fig. 5.8). "His look forces *you* to look," Stetson remarks.[97] An account of their deaths is sandblasted into the wall nearest their sculpted torsos; the words "impossible to remain silent" and their names are incised above their heads; the word "atonement" is writ large directly under their feet. This appeal to voice, name, and agency segues with the nation's emphasis on individualism and the unique self; the

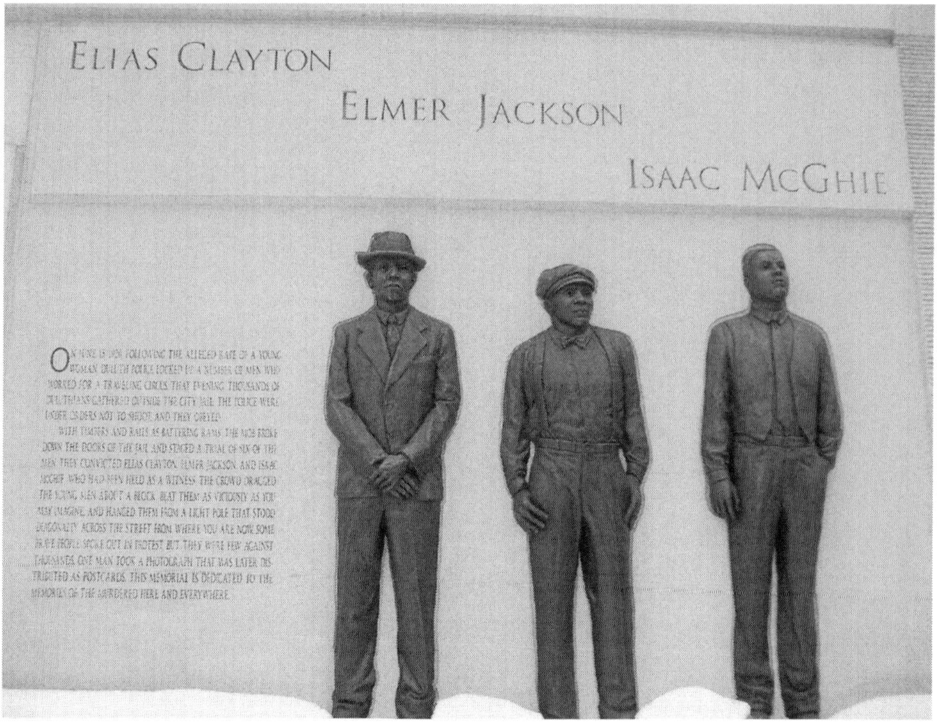

5.8. Clayton Jackson McGhie Memorial, detail. (Courtesy of Carla Stetson.)

appeal to reparations meshes with national directives to build a better, more democratic, and more inclusive America: consider, for example, the democratizing impulses of civil rights, and other rights-based models of citizenship today.

Importantly, the Clayton Jackson McGhie Memorial refuses to engage in the curative cliché of absence common in contemporary American memorial culture. As Dominick LaCapra observes in his discussion of trauma, absence, and loss, "When loss is converted into (or encrypted in an indiscriminately generalized rhetoric of) absence, one faces the impasse of endless melancholy, impossible mourning, and interminable aporia in which any process of working through the past and its historical losses is foreclosed or prematurely aborted."[98] Duluth's memorial avoids this impasse by emphasizing loss, not absence: by retaining an emphasis on the individual figure, it remembers the three men who were murdered in 1920. Their subjectivity is emphasized; they are not represented as corporeal circus workers or battered lynching victims, but as men. Importantly, too, Duluth's memorial does not heroize these men or make them into martyrs, categories of risk, bravery, and sacrifice that they did not choose. Rather, it casts them as ordinary Americans to whom shameful things were done. Highlighting their individuality and shaming the complicity of Duluth's lynch mob, this memorial appeals to contemporary notions of social justice.

SLAVERY MEMORIALS

Other contemporary American publics have also taken up the ideals of a democratic nation—and have turned to shame-based memorials and shaming speeches to reanimate those ideals in the present day. These include slavery memorials, museums, and apologies, as well as commemorative projects centered on Japanese American internment during World War II.

In 2002, the African American Monument was dedicated in Savannah, Georgia, along the city's heavily touristed riverfront and at the site of disembarkation for hundreds of thousands of enslaved Africans during the eighteenth century (fig. 5.9). In a city that features over fifty memorials and a 55 percent black population, this was Savannah's first memorial focused on African Americans. (In 2007, the Haitian Memorial Monument was dedicated in the city's Franklin Square.) It is also one of the nation's few public sculptures dedicated to slavery; another is *Reconciliation*, a bronze statue erected in 2007 in Richmond that contextualizes that city's role in the slave trade.[99] Orchestrated by a retired schoolteacher and designed by a local artist, Savannah's slavery memorial depicts life-size figures of a modern middle-class black family (man, woman, two children) standing closely together and dressed in gender specific clothing (the man wears a suit and tie, the woman a long skirt).[100] A link of chains circles their feet. The family faces the Savannah River, whose navigable proximity to the Atlantic Ocean facilitated the city's central role and steady profits in slave trafficking.

The memorial's granite pedestal features a quote from Maya Angelou that reads, in part: "We were stolen, sold and bought together from the African Continent. We got on the slave ships together. We lay back to belly in the holds of the slave ships in each other's excrement and urine together, sometimes died together, and our lifeless bodies thrown overboard together" (fig. 5.10). Approved by the city in 1992, Savannah's slavery memorial stalled over Angelou's brutal description of the Middle Passage's racial terrorism. Floyd Adams, Savannah's first African American mayor, argued that Angelou's words were "too graphic" for a public memorial. City alderman David Jones agreed, saying: "This inscription is ugly. Even though it was true, it can make one bitter. We're moving forward. I want my children to know about it, but I don't want them to live in yesterday."[101] After being asked for a more "optimistic" inscrip-

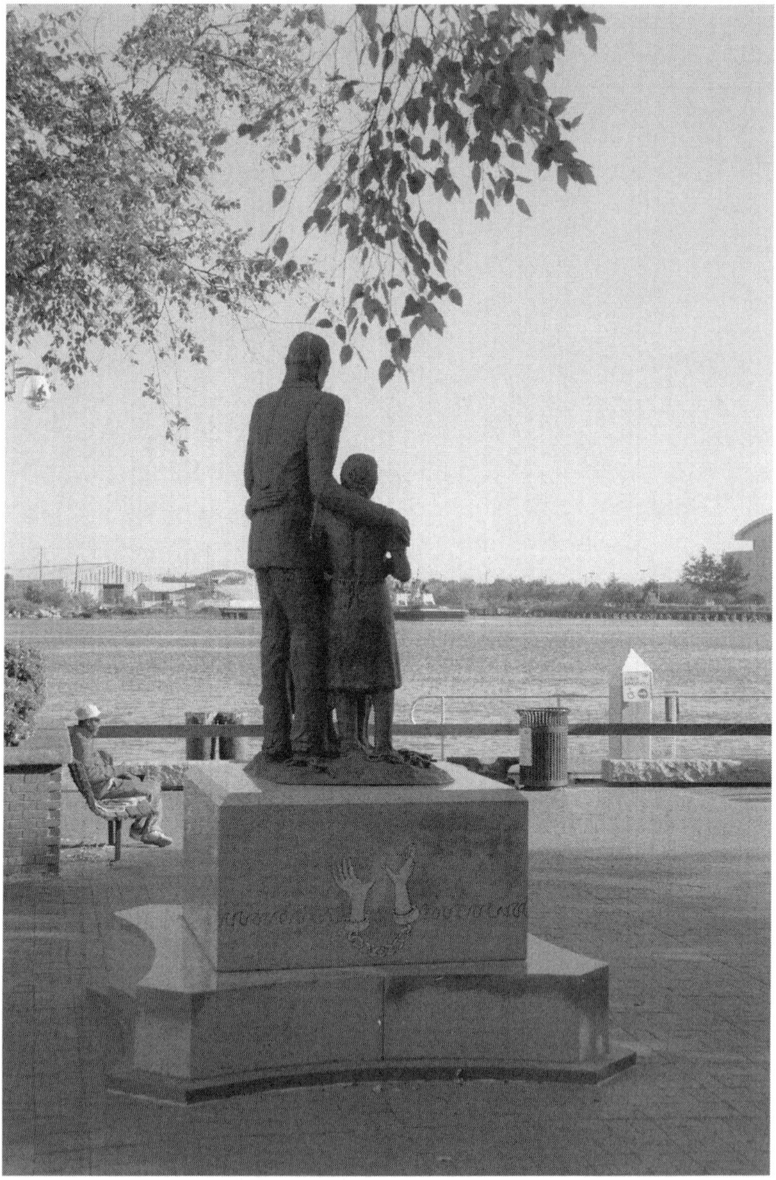

5.9. Dorothy Spradley, African American Monument, Savannah, Georgia, dedicated 2002. (Courtesy of Darlene Bordwell, Acclaim Images.)

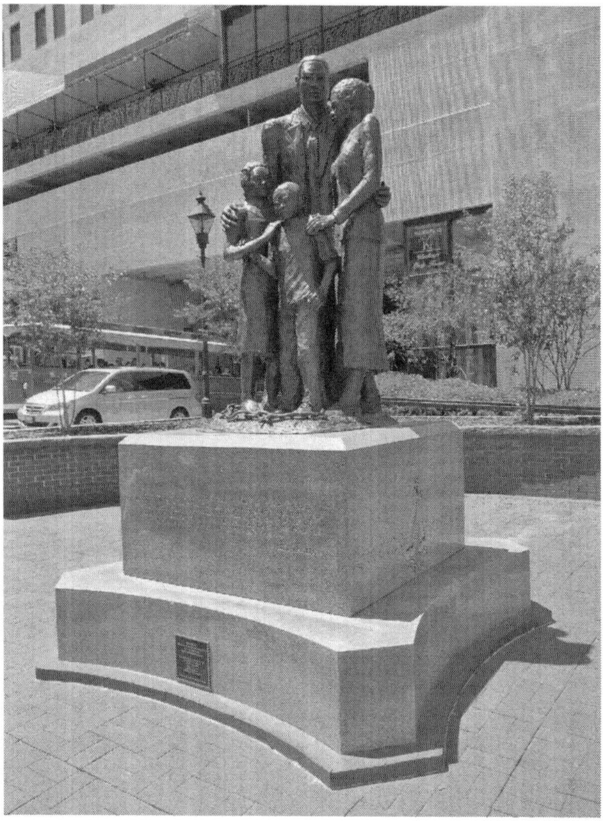

5.10. African American Monument. (Photo by the author.)

tion, Angelou added the following sentence: "Today, we are standing up together, with faith and even some joy." Even with these heartening words, one protester showed up at the memorial's dedication ceremonies carrying a sign demanding "Wipe the 'Excrement' Off of Savannah's Monuments" on one side, and "We refuse to sit upon your stool of everlasting repentance" on the other. Obviously, this was not someone for whom either the historical realities of slavery or the ethical demands of its shaming carried much weight.

Local newspapers published a number of responses after the memorial's dedication. One man wrote to the *Savannah Morning News*: "The monument, with its inscription describing lying in excrement and urine, is bound to wipe the smile off the face of the giddiest tourist, and I suspect that many will follow my example and avoid River Street in the future." His letter prompted this one: "Slaves did lie in urine and filth. Does he expect big grins on their faces? Monuments like the one on River Street are to educate the public about the horrific torment and cruelty that has been repeated over centuries to human beings . . . The name of the game is human compassion."[102]

Slavery memorials are framed by the same ethical dilemmas as lynching memorials: how do you commemorate tragic and traumatic histories without perpetuating their causes (the white supremacist presumptions that refused black subjectivity) or reanimating their effects (the pain and victimization of others)? Although, as Dell Upton writes, many Southern cities now feature both Confederate memorials and civil rights memorials, slavery is only tentatively represented in American memorial culture.[103]Slavery's historical recovery, as represented in the President's House in Philadelphia, is one form of commemoration; its admission in the form of apologies is another.

In 2008, New Jersey—the last northern state to abolish slavery, in 1846—became the first northern state to formally apologize for slavery. Stating that "for many African-Americans the scars left behind are unbearable, haunting their psyches and clouding their vision of the future," New Jersey legislators passed a resolution expressing "profound regret for the State's role in slavery" and apologizing "for the wrongs inflicted by slavery and its after effects." In 2007, Alabama, Maryland, North Carolina, and Virginia issued equally official slavery apologies, and in recent years, legislators have considered similar resolutions in Connecticut, Delaware, Georgia, Massachusetts, Missouri, New York, Tennessee, and Vermont. In July 2008, Congress passed a resolution apologizing for the "fundamental injustice, cruelty, brutality and inhumanity of slavery and Jim Crow." Earlier, in June 2005, the Senate approved a resolution apologizing for its historical failure to enact federal anti-lynching laws throughout the twentieth century.[104]

Slavery apologies have also been expressed by various companies and colleges. In 2005, Wachovia Corporation and J. P. Morgan Chase, two of the biggest banks in the country, issued apologies for past profits gained through slave transactions. In 2006, Brown University issued the results of a three-year study documenting its historic ties to slavery and calling for, among other amends, a slavery memorial on its campus.[105]

Public apologies are motivated by several related needs: explanations and acknowledgements of offense, expressions of shame and remorse to those who have been offended, and assurances that such offenses will not be repeated. If issued to restore humanity and dignity to those who have been offended, apologies may also be offered to avoid future grievances. Apologies do not, however, entitle forgiveness. An apology is not a pardon, a reprieve, or a form of amnesty. Rather, apologies follow from acknowledgements of complicity and decisions to take responsibility, while forgiveness is the discretionary option of those who have been harmed.

Apologies, like shame, are inherently social and depend on assumptions of shared values; their role in the nation's recovery and review of its historical legacy of slavery and racial terrorism hinges on socially shared notions of shame. Aaron Lazare explains, "People are not guilty for actions in which they did not participate. But just as people take pride in things for which they had no responsibility (such as famous ancestors . . . and great accomplishments of their nation), so, too, must these people accept the shame (but not the guilt) of their family . . . and their nations. Accepting national pride must include willingness to accept national shame when one's country has not measured up . . . . this accountability is what we mean when we speak of having a national identity." Likewise, as Ali Mazrui, a member of the Organization of African Unity, observed in the mid-1990s, "If Americans of the 20th and 21st century [*sic*] are prepared to inherit the intellectual and moral assets of the Founding Fathers, should they not also accept the moral debt of the Founding Fathers?"[106] Successful national apologies are contingent on understanding American nationalism as an ongoing project, and on shared desires for an improved national future.

Contemporary memorials commemorating the nation's history of slavery are implicitly engaged in issues of apology, if often inadequately. In 2005, for example, the University of North Carolina at Chapel Hill unveiled a memorial commemorating slavery's role in the making of the university: a $106,000 sculpture by Do-Ho Suh titled *Unsung Founders, Bond and Free* (fig. 5.11). The sculpture consists of a low and highly polished stone table supported by the uplifted arms of dozens of bronze figures, male and female, each about one foot tall. Located near Silent Sam, a Civil War memorial erected on campus in 1913 by the United Daughters of the Confederacy, Suh's sculpture is circled by four roughhewn stools, each modeled on fieldstone grave markers in Chapel Hill's African American cemetery. The memorial's tabletop is inscribed with this text: "The Class of 2002 honors the University's unsung founders, the people of color bond and free, who helped build the Carolina that we cherish today."

Response has been mixed. Some protest Suh's "midgetization" of slave labor, some object to a slavery memorial being designed by a Korean-born artist, and some are angry that African American students and faculty were not involved in the memorial process. Still others find the university's slavery memorial "powerful, beautiful, and provocative." Suh modeled it on *Public Figures* (2003), a temporary sculpture installed in the lobby of New York's City Hall that consisted of a monumental granite pedestal without a sculpture or statue mounted on its base. Instead, the pedestal itself was supported by tiny rows of anonymous male and female

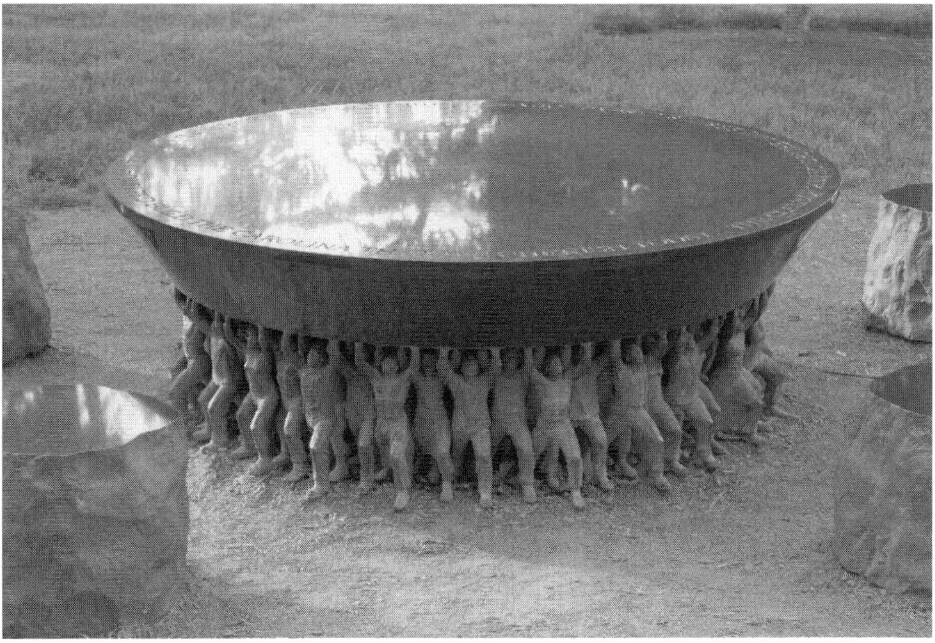

5.11. Do-Ho Suh, *Unsung Founders, Bond and Free*, University of North Carolina, Chapel Hill, dedicated 2005. (Courtesy of Jim Hirschfield.)

figures, all collectively carrying the weight of the heavy stone with their upraised arms. Turning the rationale of the traditional monument—like the school's Confederate memorial—upside down, Suh said *Public Figures* aimed to challenge "the established notion of the common citizen revering a monument to an important figure."[107] Transferred, however, to the American South, and to the historical context of a people of color long denied citizenship, let alone subjectivity, Suh's memorial concept on the Chapel Hill campus was more than a little problematic.

However much the nation may now want to apologize for its shameful history of chattel slavery, slavery's representation itself remains limited and highly contested. White supremacy, by contrast, is highly visible in America's memorial cultures. According to James Loewen, at least fifty monuments, markers, and historic sites scattered across the country commemorate the post–Civil War genesis of racist extremists like the Ku Klux Klan, and only a few do so in a negative light. Slavery, Kirk Savage explains, was rarely represented in nineteenth-century American public art and when it was, slaves were shown as complacent servants devoted to their benevolent masters and their own submission—as seen in the Confederate Monument at Arlington National Cemetery (see fig. 0.18, p. 14).[108] During statue mania, slavery was only vaguely referenced in abolition memorials that typically depicted Abraham Lincoln as the Great Emancipator and cast black Americans on subservient terms.

African American artists struggled with these representations, challenging both demeaning stereotypes and derogatory rescue narratives that reproduced black American passivity and dependence and reinforced white American power and paternalism. In her series of historical tableaux designed for the Negro Building at the 1907 Jamestown Tercentennial Exposition, African American sculptor Meta Warrick Fuller made several scenes depicting the landing of the first African slaves at Jamestown, Virginia, in 1619, and the labor of black slaves two hundred years later on antebellum plantations. But most of her fourteen dioramas centered on narratives of post–Civil War racial uplift and performances of black middle-class respectability. Despite her interest in representing the historical experiences of black Americans, Fuller's allegorical scenes of black families, farms, churches, and schools made no reference to the racial terrorism of Jim Crow.[109]

Contemporary representations of slavery tend to follow similarly limiting narratives of race betterment. Emphasizing the triumph of survival, many slavery memorials imply that racial ownership and oppression in America were "curious abnormalities—aberrations—historical accidents," as Nathan Huggins put it, "to be countered in the progressive upward reach of the nation's destiny."[110] *Freedom* remains the dominant trope in today's commemoration of slavery, and freedom typically trumps slavery, against which it is pitted, not paired, in American historical memory.

Yet slavery, Ira Berlin observed in 2004, "has a greater presence in American life now than at any time since the Civil War ended."[111] Movies like *Amistad* (1997) and *Beloved* (1998), documentaries such as *Unchained Memories: Readings from the Slave Narratives* (2002) and *Slavery and the Making of America* (2004), and bestselling books like Toni Morrison's *Beloved* (1987) and Edward Ball's *Slaves in the Family* (1998) demonstrate the extent of slavery's historical recovery in the national narrative. So do slavery-centered memorials, museums, and exhibitions like Slavery in New York at the New-York Historical Society in 2005—which proved to be the museum's most popular show in its two hundred-year history. The "slavery heritage" industry, which offers tours of slave routes and plantations where slaves worked, is also booming.[112] Capitalizing on this new national attention to slavery, in January 2003, the National Slavery Memorial Act was introduced in Congress by a bipartisan group including Congressman Cliff Stearns (R-FL) and Senator Trent Lott (R-MS). In 2009, the United Nations announced plans for a $3.5 million slavery memorial to be built on the grounds of UN headquarters in New York.

Clearly, slavery haunts the American national narrative and continues to disturb national consciousness. When Jesse Jackson visited the Hurricane Katrina evacuation center in New Orleans in September 2005 he reportedly said, "It's like looking at the hull of a slave ship." Likewise, Barack Obama's March 2008 speech in Philadelphia, delivered in the shadow of Independence Hall and titled "A More Perfect Union," repeatedly referenced slavery as the nation's original sin and called on Americans to confront and overcome its legacy. As Ron Eyerman argues, slavery remains a dominant site of national memory, a marker of trauma not just for black Americans but for all Americans.[113]

Yet in terms of contemporary memorials, slavery's foundational role in the making of the nation—along *with* freedom—is downplayed in favor of upbeat chronicles of self and social success since, or despite, slavery. This is exemplified in the two-part international Underground Railroad Memorial designed by Ed Dwight (2001). The first section, *Gateway to Freedom*, features slaves standing on the banks of the Detroit River and facing Canada; the second section depicts a group of emancipated African Americans, including a man with his arms raised up in thanks, standing on the banks of Windsor, Ontario, in front of the twenty-two-foot-tall *Tower of Freedom* (fig. 5.12). Likewise, figurative works by Ed Hamilton including the Amistad Memorial (New Haven, 1992) and *York* (Louisville, 2003) depict black slaves on heroic terms and slavery itself as a narrative of endurance and overcoming. *York*, an eight-foot-tall bronze statue of the slave who traveled with the Lewis and Clark Expedition of 1804–1806 (he was owned by William Clark), features a strong-bodied black man holding a rifle in one hand and a dead bird in the other (fig. 5.13). Standing on a chunk of rock representing the banks of the Ohio River, York scans the skies. The irony of his westward gaze, and of the fact that Clark refused to free him until long after the expedition had ended (York's emancipation is dated sometime between 1815 and 1832), is inescapable.

Museums that aspire to tell the story of slavery in America include the Old Slave Mart in Charleston, South Carolina, and the Slave Relic Museum in Walterboro, South Carolina, both mostly focused on displays of African American arts and crafts. The United States National Slavery Museum, the brainchild of former Virginia governor Douglas Wilder, has a more ambitious agenda of "helping America in commemorating, understanding, and overcoming slavery." Designed by Chien Chung Pei, the projected $200 million museum will feature a hundred thousand square feet of exhibition space (along with classrooms, archives, and a library) on a thirty-eight-acre site outside Fredericksburg, Virginia.[114] Like slavery memorials, American slavery museums tend to skirt slavery's

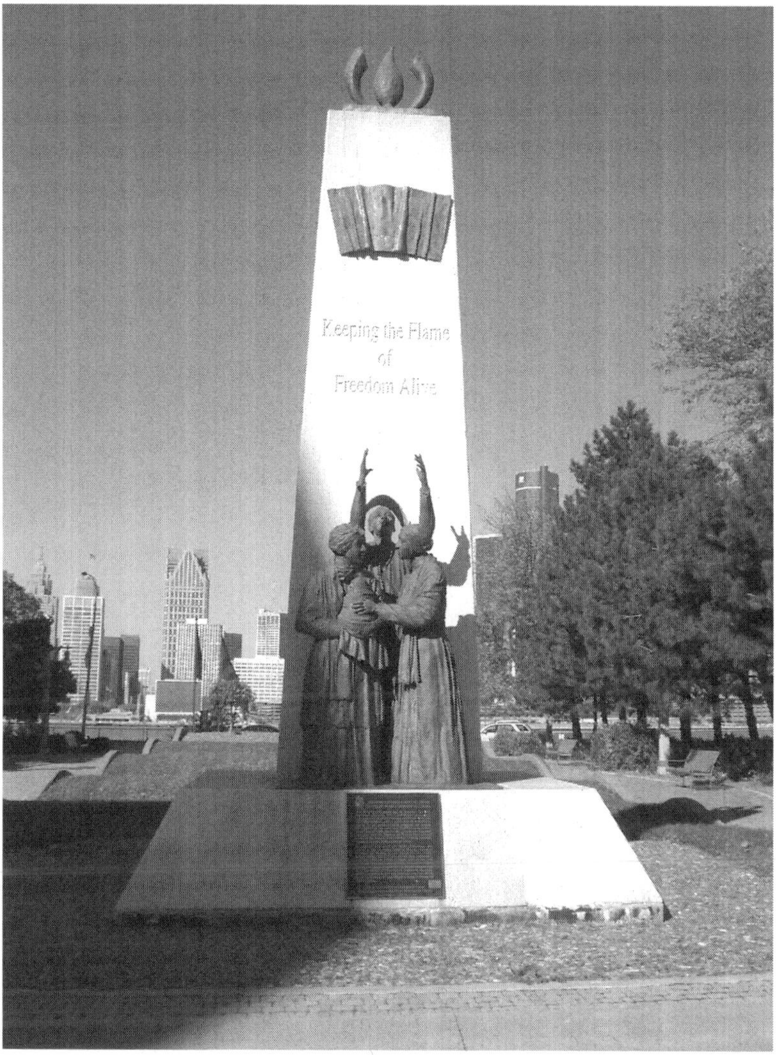

5.12. Ed Dwight, *Tower of Freedom*, Underground Railroad Memorial, Windsor, Ontario, dedicated 2001. (Photo by the author.)

trauma in their exhibitions and even their names: the stated mission of the $110 million National Underground Railroad Freedom Center, for example, which opened in Cincinnati in 2004, is to reveal "stories about freedom's heroes, past and present, challenging and inspiring everyone to take courageous steps for freedom today." While the museum's centerpiece is a reconstructed slave holding pen from Kentucky dating to 1834, its major pavilions are called the Pavilion of Perseverance and the Pavilion of Courage.

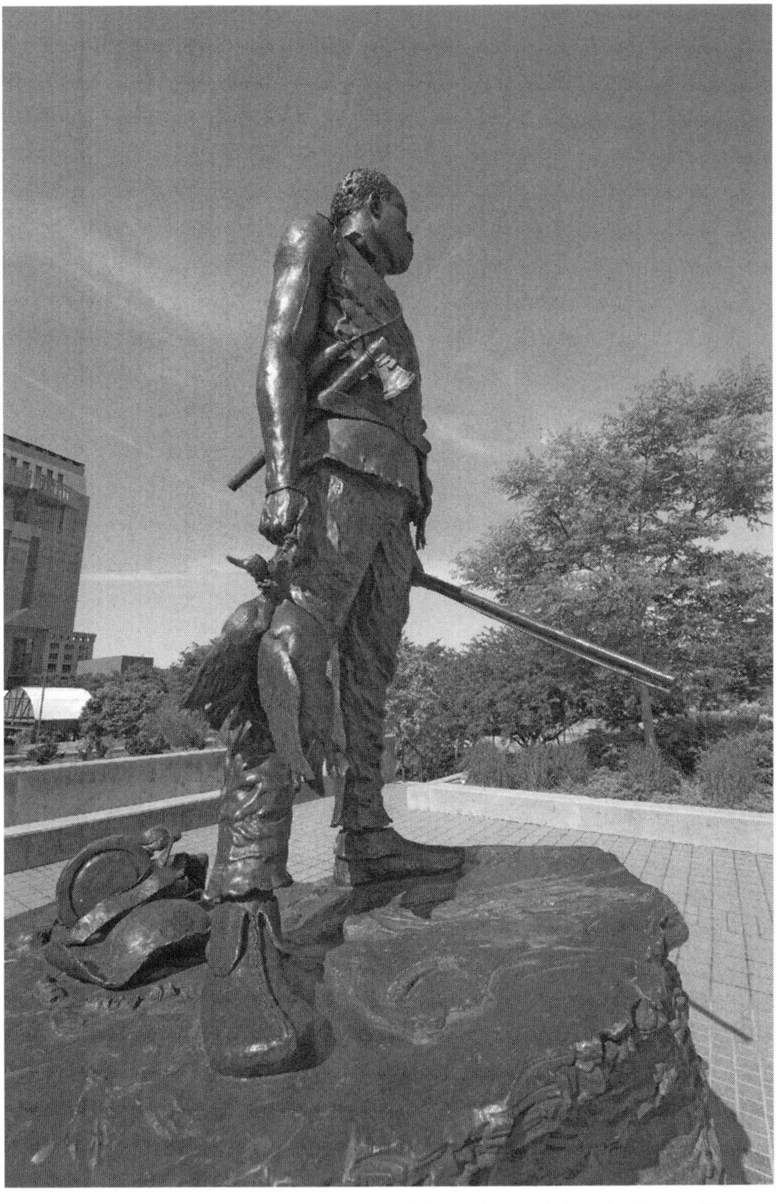

5.13. Ed Hamilton, *York*, Louisville, Kentucky, dedicated 2003. (Photo by Dennis MacDonald. Courtesy of World of Stock.)

With its broken chains, focus on the family, and uplifting text of togetherness, faith, and joy, Savannah's African American Monument similarly embodies a simplistic narrative of triumph over adversity. While it ostensibly commemorates the nation's shameful history of slavery—referenced only in Angelou's words and in the largely decorative chains at the feet of its four figures—it focuses more specifically on a presentist ideal of a heteronormative, middle-class American family. On the one hand, this depiction of domesticity calls attention to what chattel slavery wrecked and ripped apart. But depicting only those to whom shameful things were done, rather than those who did shameful things, is inadequate. Casting the black body alone—here depicted as a black family body—as both the problem and the solution to slavery's national memory is untenable. The slaveholders who violated human rights and profited from slavery's obscene violence are rendered invisible in this memorial, written out of local and national history. Slavery's institutional underpinnings, its fundamental role in the economic and cultural success of the early nation, its legacy in terms of racial terrorism, its political and social resonance today in terms of abiding national assumptions about racial difference, and, especially, its resurfacing in contemporary debates about apologies and reparations "as a litmus test for public morality," are muffled in deference to this memorial's banal representation of a mainstream black family.[115]

There is, of course, a profound difference between remembering slavery in a majority African American community like Savannah and remembering lynching in a mostly white city like Duluth. Shared recognition that these acts of racial terrorism are shameful does not translate into shared representational strategies or shared notions of self and/or collective complicity, or even shared ideas about what is shameful. Assumptions that Americans share a single collective memory of racial terrorism, like essentialized notions of black or white identity, are fallacious. Michael Eric Dyson argues, "While it is true that our common history of slavery and racial oppression signifies a common goal of freedom from oppression for black people, broadened horizons of racial experience and more sophisticated conceptions of racial identity make the articulation of a single, unitary, racial goal highly problematic."[116] Despite the popularity of the slavery heritage industry, many Americans whose ancestry includes being victimized by racial terrorism may be loath to see those atrocities represented because of the pain and shame that these memory stains continue to evoke. Further, such anxieties stem from slavery's abiding injustices—despite contemporary rhetoric about freedom and equity in the United States, racial bias has not disappeared.

In *Accused/Blowtorch/Padlock* (1986), artist Pat Ward Williams appropriated a photograph of a lynched black man that originally appeared in *Life* magazine in 1937, mounted it inside a panel of weathered window frames, and centered it on black tarpaper. She filled the margins with this anguished handwritten text:

> Can you be black and look at this without fear? Life mag. published this photo. Could Hitler show pics of the Holocaust to keep the JEWS in line? WHO took this picture? Couldn't he just as easily let the man go? Did he take his camera home and bring back a BLOWTORCH? HOW can this photograph EXIST?[117]

The ethics of trauma's representation relate to the persistent dangers of re-victimization. Resolving these problems, and coming to terms with how to commemorate the nation's shameful history of racial dehumanization, begins with the nation's acknowledgement of—and apology for—racial terrorism.

REMEMBERING INTERNMENT

Apologies have been pivotal to the commemoration of other shameful national histories, such as the internment during World War II of some 112,000 Japanese Americans in 10 internment camps managed by the U.S. Justice Department's War Relocation Authority. "Here we admit a wrong. Here we affirm our commitment as a nation to equal justice under the law," reads the focal quote in the National Japanese American Memorial, designed by Davis Buckley and dedicated in Washington, D.C., in 2000 (fig. 5.14). Located on a small plot of land just north of the U.S. Capitol, the $10.8 million memorial is bordered by cherry trees and a curved granite wall listing the names and locations of the camps, the numbers of people who were detained in each, and quotes recounting their experiences. Featured within the enclosed space is a shallow pool emulating a Zen garden, a sculpture designed by Nina Akamu of two cranes struggling to break free from lengths of barbed wire, and an interactive Memorial Bell with a bronze chime designed by Paul Matisse.

The memorial was originally commissioned to "honor Japanese American patriotism in World War II," most notably the 26,000 Japanese American men and women who volunteered to serve in the U.S. armed forces and the 800 who were killed in action. But it evolved into a more complicated memory project. Its central quote, for example, comes from President Ronald Reagan during the signing of the 1988 Civil Liberties Act, by which the U.S. government officially apologized for the historical injustice of Japanese American internment and agreed to provide

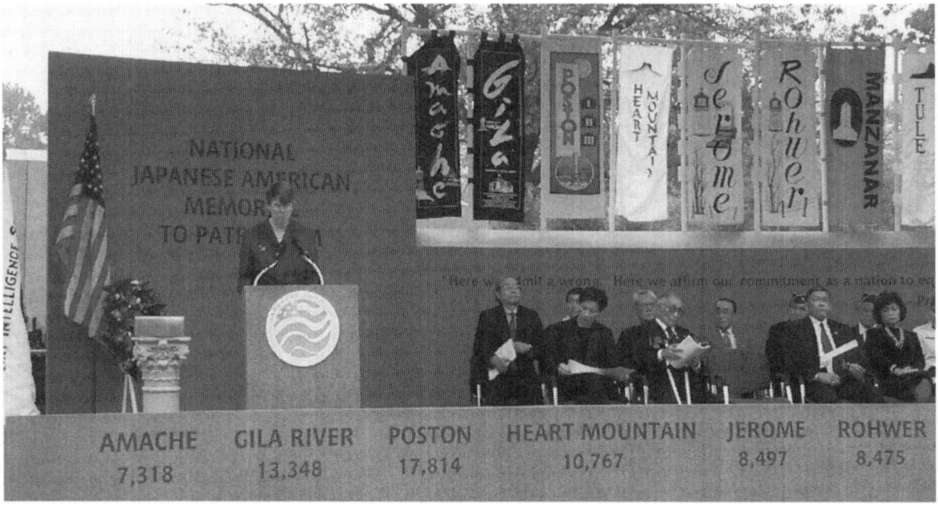

5.14. Then attorney general Janet Reno at the dedication ceremony for the National Japanese American Memorial, November 15, 2000. The memorial was designed by Davis Buckley Architects and Planners. (Photo by Rudi Williams. Courtesy of the Department of Defense.)

monetary compensation to those who had been imprisoned. Its main wall features a statement by Mike Masaoka, a wartime spokesman for the Japanese American Citizens League who some consider a traitor for acquiescing to, rather than protesting against, government demands for ethnic evacuation and internment.[118] Further, while the memorial's central wall lists the names of the war's Japanese American soldier dead, the area immediately beneath Reagan's words features an unmarked vault containing earth collected from the 10 internment camps. "The memorial goes to the issue of who we are as a democracy," Buckley observes. "That is the underlying thought here, and I was deeply committed to it." President Bill Clinton remarked: "We are diminished when any American is targeted unfairly because of his or her heritage. This memorial and the internment sites are powerful reminders that stereotyping, discrimination, hatred, and racism have no place in this country."[119]

Internment memorials negotiate the fraught dimensions of American national identity. First, they *remember* the shameful history of Japanese American internment: a history of American concentration camps benevolently renamed "relocation" centers; a history of people imprisoned without due process or legal hearings; a history silenced after the war. Acts of remembrance reinsert this shameful history into the national narrative. A California Historical Landmark plaque placed at the entrance

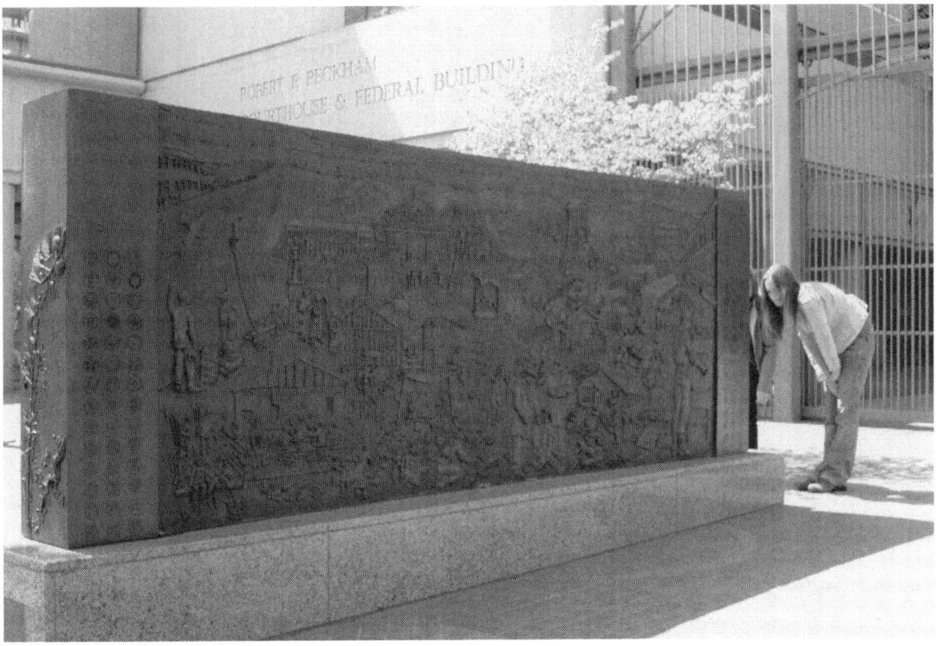

5.15. Ruth Asawa, Japanese American Internment Memorial, San Jose, California, dedicated 1994. (Courtesy of Geoffrey Thrumston.)

to Manzanar in 1973, for example, calls the site a concentration camp, not an internment camp, and reads: "May the injustices and humiliation suffered here as a result of hysteria, racism, and economic exploitation never emerge again." Second, rather than projecting idealized narratives of the triumphant survival of internment's victims or focusing only on traumatic accounts of their degradation, these memorials articulate an interaction among victims and their perpetrators that, as Elazar Barkan writes in his discussion of political restitution, "enables the rewriting of memory and historical identity in ways that both can share."[120]

Consider San Jose's Japanese American Internment Memorial, a $217,000 project commissioned by the city's Public Art Program and funded in part through percent-for-art dollars (fig. 5.15). The memorial's eighteen-foot bronze wall narrates the nineteenth-century arrival of Japanese immigrants to the region, their work as farm laborers and shop owners, and their forced internment during World War II. Juxtaposing the text of Executive Order 9066 (FDR's authorization of ethnic internment, signed in February 1942) with the *mon* (family crests) of the Japanese Americans who were interned, it includes this statement: "This memorial is dedicated to the Japanese-American men, women, and children whose Constitutional rights were denied solely because of their ancestry. Let their story remind us of our shared responsibility to uphold the moral rights of all individuals at all times." Located a half-block from the War Relocation Authority building where San Jose's ethnic evacuees were ordered to gather in 1942, the memorial was erected in front of the Robert Peckham Federal Building in 1994. Highlighting the failures of the national ideal in scenes of trauma and shame, this memorial's specific location recalls restitution and justice as constitutive elements in American national identity.

At the Manzanar National Historic Site, where 10,000 Japanese Americans were imprisoned from 1942 to 1945 in a 540-acre camp confined by a barbed wire fence, guarded by military police, and monitored by eight armed watchtowers, the National Park Service similarly negotiates a shameful national history of perpetrators and their victims through a shared discourse of civil rights and restitution. Documenting the humiliating public roundup of Japanese American citizens, their lives inside the camps, and the paranoid political culture that devised their imprisonment, the site's Interpretive Center includes a memorial wall listing the names of Manzanar's internees, a scale model of the camp, and exhibits on apology and redress. Informational panels include provocative questions like "What does Manzanar mean to history?" and "What does Manzanar mean to me?" A memorial in the camp cemetery is the site of annual remembrance ceremonies (fig. 5.16).

Over 86,000 people visit Manzanar each year, including one retired Navy man who wrote in the museum's comments book, "Proud to be an American, ashamed of this little piece of American history." We might quibble over his use of "little," but he joins many other Americans who are drawn to these unsettling sites and moments of national shame. In 2006, Congress authorized an additional $38 million to preserve and "maintain the memory" of the nation's nine other Japanese American internment camps, including Heart Mountain in Wyoming and Amache in Colorado.[121] Development of the Issei Memorial at the Minidoka Internment National Monument in Idaho, and the $5 million Bainbridge Island Japanese American Memorial in Washington is also underway. Yet why are contemporary Americans so interested in unsettling reminders of national shame? What does this interest, and the recovery of these histories, suggest about current understandings of national and self identity?

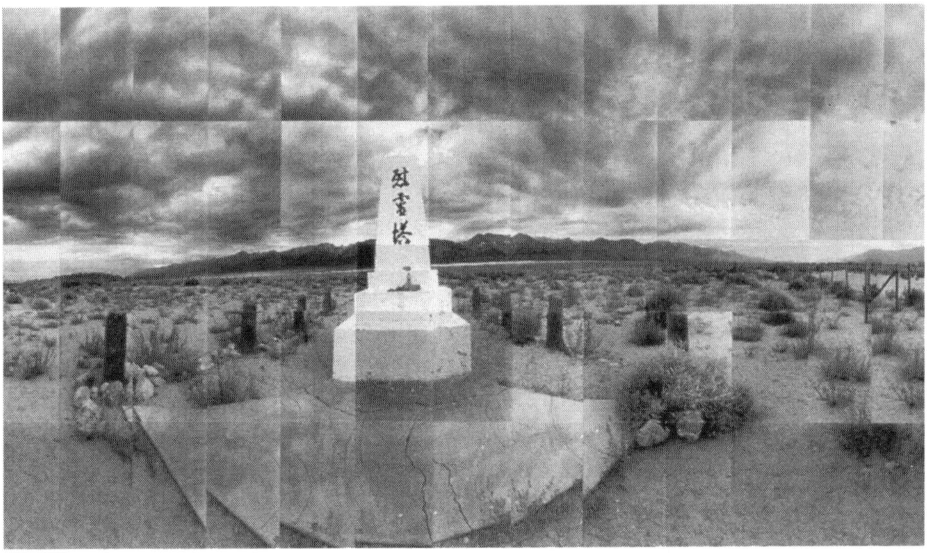

5.16. Masumi Hayashi, "Manzanar Relocation Camp, Monument (Version 1), Inyo, California," 1995. Panoramic photo collage with Fuji Crystal Archive prints. The words on the monument, erected in 1943 by camp prisoners, read "*i rei to*," or, "soul consoling tower." (Courtesy of Dean Keesey.)

THE AFFECTIVE POSSIBILITIES OF SHAME

In 1989, lamenting slavery's commemorative neglect in America and explaining why she wrote the novel *Beloved*, Toni Morrison observed, "There is no place you or I can go, to think about or not think about, to summon the presences of, or recollect the absences of slaves . . . There is no suitable memorial or plaque or wreath or wall, or park or skyscraper lobby. There's no 300-foot tower. There's no small bench by the road." In 2008, the Toni Morrison Society dedicated its first (of a projected ten) Bench by the Road memorials at Fort Moultrie on Sullivan's Island, South Carolina, near the point of entry into North America for about 40 percent of the millions of Africans who were enslaved in this country.[122] Maintained by the National Park Service, the memorial consists of a six-foot-long metal bench that faces the Intracoastal Waterway and a historical plaque that concludes: "Nearly half of all African Americans have ancestors who passed through Sullivan's Island."

Mandating "sites of shame" as important sites of national memory clearly broadens the scope of national membership. The cliché that history belongs to the winners doesn't apply when a nation's memorials are especially attuned to slavery, lynching, and racial profiling. Histories that include victims in the national narrative, and thereby critique its imperfections, are central to today's memorial cultures because contemporary Americans like Morrison and millions of others want those histories commemorated—and are not intimidated by how they challenge standard accounts of American history. Rather than adhering to stories of national progress, these histories admit the complications, contradictions, and obligations of American national identity. Doing so often involves reckoning with the nation's ghosts, with the specters from the past who continue to haunt the national imaginary.

The African Burial Ground National Monument, located in Lower Manhattan and dedicated in 2007, is a prime example (fig. 5.17). The small site (about a third of an acre) features an outdoor memorial and an indoor visitor center commemorating the once much larger grounds (6.6 acres) where an estimated 20,000 enslaved Africans were interred between the late seventeenth century and the late eighteenth century. As New York expanded in the nineteenth century, sacred space in what had been the outskirts of the city became prime office space in the heart of downtown Manhattan, and the burial ground was paved over and filled in with courthouses and civic centers. The labor and lives of New York's significant slave public—in the mid-seventeenth century, 25 percent of Manhattan's Dutch colony was comprised of enslaved Africans; in 1737, 20 percent of the city's residents were slaves—were largely forgotten.[123]

In 1991, during the preconstruction survey for a $276 million, thirty-four-story federal office building to be located at 290 Broadway, just north of New York's City Hall, archaeologists discovered the human remains of over four hundred African slaves, many ritually interred in hexagonal wooden coffins pointing east, and some accompanied by symbolic funerary artifacts such as coins, cowrie shells, buttons, beads, and pieces of coral. One coffin lid featured a heart-shaped design made from ninety-three iron nails, interpreted as either the West African symbol *Sankofa* (meaning "going backward to go forward") or *Akoma* ("patience and tolerance"). The General Services Administration, the federal agency charged with overseeing government projects like office buildings, deemed the discovery significant but was lax in following archaeological and preservation standards, such that some of the burial findings were destroyed. African American historians, citizen activists, and politicians were incensed, and New York mayor David Dinkins (the city's first black mayor) called on William Diamond, the GSA's regional administrator, to halt the excavation and adhere to specific federal mandates regarding the recovery and preservation of human remains.

Diamond, a Reagan appointee who authorized the destruction of *Tilted Arc*, a minimalist sculpture by Richard Serra that was commissioned by the GSA and located in New York's Foley Square until 1989 (when Dia-

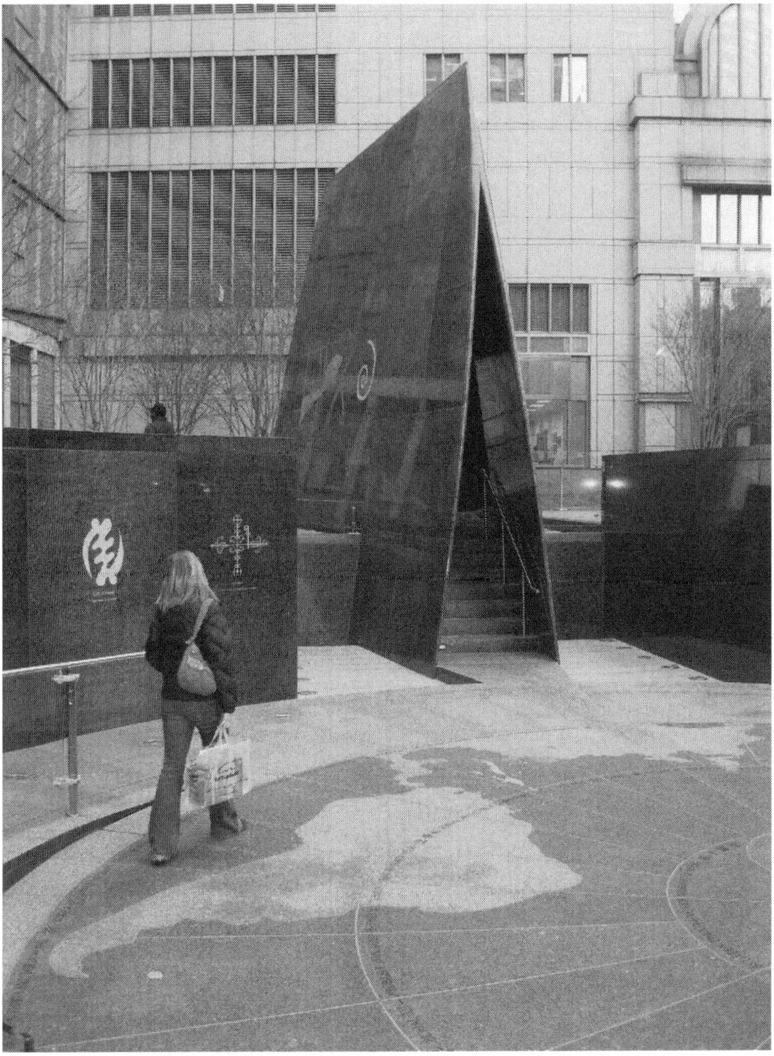

5.17. Rodney Léon, Ancestral Chamber, African Burial Ground National Monument, New York, New York, dedicated 2007. (Photo by the author.)

mond orchestrated its midnight-hour removal), rejected the mayor's request, stating that he "would not be put in a position of abrogating important government contracts because of political pressure."[124] Diamond was overruled, however, by federal representatives who recognized the African burial ground's historic value, and in 1993, Congress designated the site a National Historic Landmark. Recommendations were further made that the new federal office building feature "a world-class memorial museum and research center of African-American history and culture,"

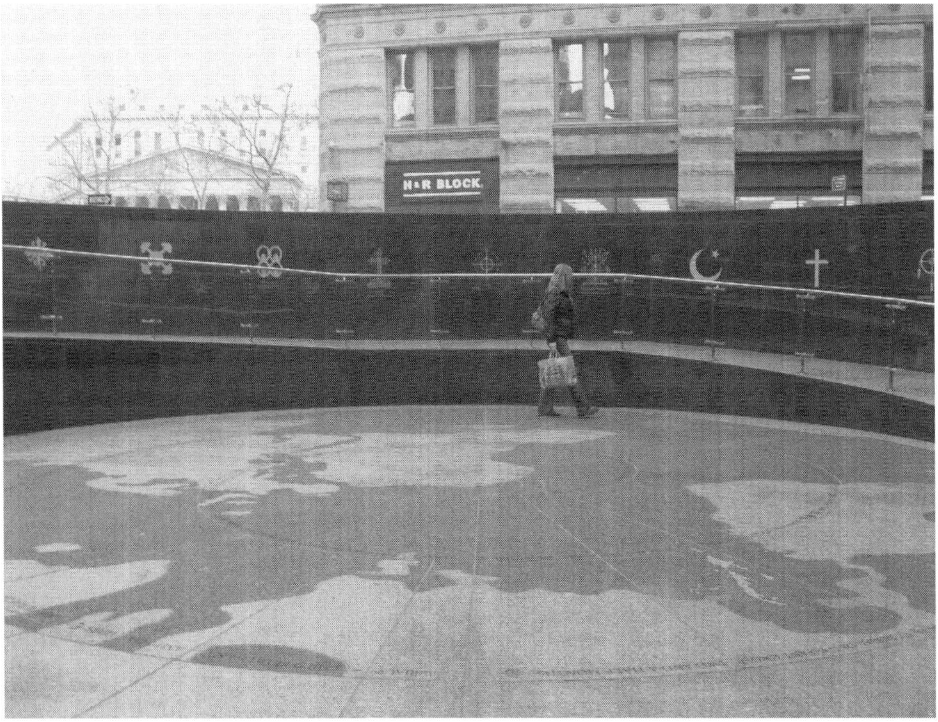

5.18. Ancestral Libation Court, African Burial Ground National Monument. (Photo by the author.)

including public artwork in its first floor lobby and a permanent outdoor memorial. Also mandated was the "ceremonial reinterment" of the 425 excavated human remains found on the site.[125]

In October 2003, elaborate Rites of Ancestral Return were held, during which human remains and burial artifacts were reinterred at the site in seven specially designed wooden crypts. Maya Angelou addressed a large crowd with these words: "You may bury me in the bottom of Manhattan. I will rise. My people will get me. I will rise out of the huts of history's shame."[126] At dedication ceremonies four years later, thousands of people listened to speeches by Angelou and New York mayor Michael Bloomberg and watched performances of African musicians and dancers. They were the first to walk through the memorial's Ancestral Chamber, a narrow, twenty-five-foot-tall, highly polished granite room intimating both the interior of a slave fort and a slave ship. The memorial also includes an Ancestral Libation Court, a similarly walled and sunken space, four-feet below street level, embellished with symbols of the African Diaspora (fig. 5.18).

The court's stone floor depicts a map of the world, with West Africa

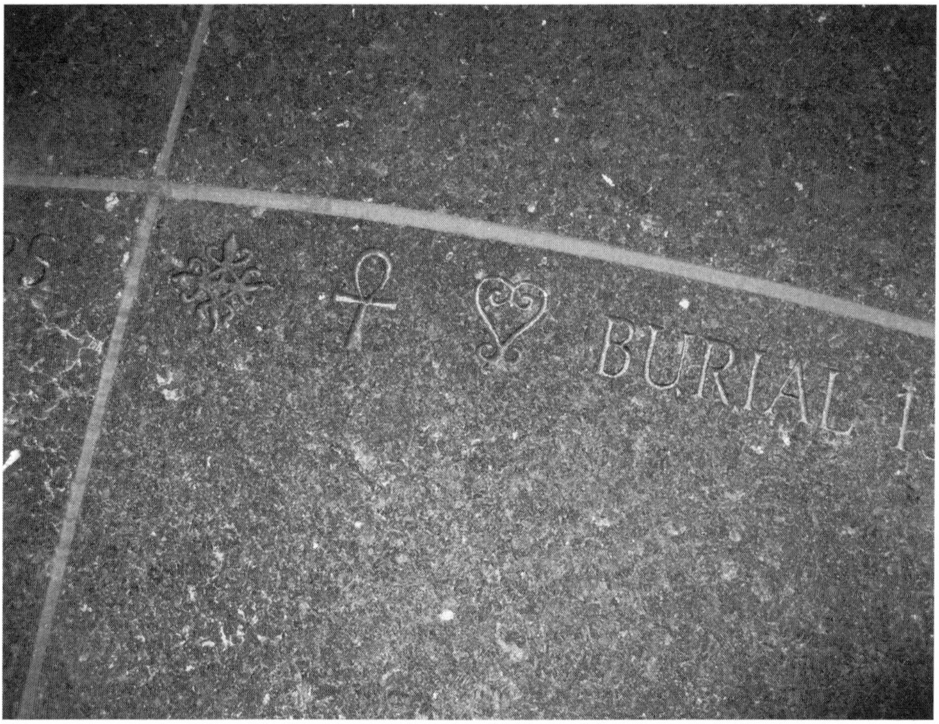

5.19. African Burial Ground National Monument, stone floor detail. (Photo by the author.)

at its center, and a small hole where libations may be offered during ceremonial rituals. Words engraved on the floor reference the thousands of slaves buried below: "Burial 205 woman between eighteen and twenty years," "Burial 75 newborn or stillborn baby" (fig. 5.19). Designed by Rodney Léon, the $5 million monument also features a Memorial Wall illustrating the physical boundaries of the original burial ground and an Ancestral Re-Interment Grove marked by seven grassy mounds and a grove of trees. A Wall of Remembrance facing the public street bordering the memorial reads: "For all those who were lost, For all those who were stolen, For all those who were left behind, For all those who were not forgotten."

On this tiny plot of land—less than a fraction of the acreage occupied by the National September 11 Memorial & Museum at the World Trade Center, located a few blocks south—slavery's shameful history in New York is visibly confronted and commemorated. That history is acknowledged on terms that downplay victimization and appeal, especially, to the ethics of work. Rather than explicitly referencing the pain and trauma of forced human bondage, or rendering that bondage on heroic terms, the African Burial Ground National Monument reminds visitors of the tens of thousands of enslaved Africans who built New York and enabled enormous colonial, and eventually national, profits. Work, and notions of a moralizing work ethic, have long been central to American understandings of self and national identity; as Frederick Douglass remarked in 1853, "Men are not valued in this country, or in any country, for what they *are*; they are valued for what they do."[127] Work, a value and a sentiment that has repeatedly granted legitimacy and enabled citizenship in the national narrative, is employed in this memorial to shame visitors about slavery's erasure in American history: indeed, the shame of slavery related here is the shame of forgetting how slavery literally made the nation. In a memorial that is simultaneously a cemetery and a ceremonial center, America's haunted legacy of slavery is revealed and remembered, and the scope of national subjectivity is expanded, via the inclusionary terms of labor.

In 2006, when the African Burial Ground was designated a national monument (becoming the NPS's 390th unit), Department of the Interior secretary Gale Norton remarked, "After facing this painful past, we come together to preserve this sacred ground. This burial ground teaches slavery's shame. It also teaches that repentance and remembrance lead to renewal."[128] As Lazare argues, the accountability of American national identity involves both pride and shame. Indeed, one explanation for shame's surfacing in contemporary memorial cultures is heightened attention to issues of moral accountability: to recognizing, for example, the dual terms of slavery and freedom in the national narrative. Skeptics might have it that "holding the moral high ground has become a good investment" for certain corporations, colleges, and governments. But as Barkan observes, expectations that nations in particular "act morally and acknowledge their own gross historical injustices" emerge from shared public feelings that nations have shamefully failed to live up to their ideals and can, with apologies, reparations, and memorials, work to right those wrongs. Shame has enormous potential as a revitalizing instrument of shared national purpose centered on redeeming the past.[129]

Admittedly, redemption is a paradoxical proposition: the idea of slavery and lynching—or any kind of violence and terrorism—being appropriated in American memorial culture in order to redeem these histories (or permit them again) is horrifying and cynical. Writing about 9/11's commemoration, for example, Marita Sturken observes that redemption narratives "tend to be politically regressive in that they are attempts to mediate loss through finding the good—a newfound patriotism, feelings of community—that has come from pain. As such, they have been used throughout history to justify political agendas." Likewise, LaCapra warns against recovering past traumas in order to redeem the present, cautioning, "The meaning that is redeemed is typically that which is desired for the present, and figures in the past tend to become vehicles or mouthpieces for contemporary values."[130] This is certainly the case with Savannah's slavery memorial, which redeems the nation's shameful past in terms of today's socially desired American family.

Yet redemption does not have to be solely bound to national narratives of domination and denial; rather, redemption may also engage a national imaginary of liberation and freedom. Redemption has multiple meanings: to buy back, to free from harm, to repair, to make good, to atone. George Shulman argues that a way to engage redemption as a moral and politically progressive project is to focus on "redemption of," not "redemption from": to both recover and to make good on that which is flawed. Criticism of redemptory art, Maeve Cooke observes, disregards its "cognitive dimension—its claim to offer insight" and to convey "ethical knowledge." Redemption, she adds, is also an irresolvable aporia, an "ethical idea that is at once impossible and indispensable": impossible because it can never be completely achieved; indispensable because "it fulfils regulative functions" and "guides our ethical thinking, giving points to our criticism of history and society."[131]

Redemption on these terms is neither comfortable nor casual and is certainly not a vehicle by which the nation's shameful histories may be ignored or justified for presentist purposes. The nation cannot be freed from its traumatic past, nor should it. But notions of redemption may be used to disturb a national narrative steeped in indignant claims of innocence and denial. Redemption can be an affective strategy through which social and moral obligations can be recast, and made meaningful. Redemption can make history meaningful and liberate its subjects from historical amnesia. To redeem is to claim what has been forgotten or ignored as something worthy of remembrance. Importantly, redemption's meaning-making necessitates a grasp of its responsibilities and limits, from an accounting of the shameful and traumatic histories that require redemption, to the recognition that we cannot know, or identify with, or own, the pain and suffering of others. LaCapra describes this as "empathic unsettlement" or "emotional response [that] comes with respect for the other and the realization that the experience of the other is not one's own."[132] Redemption is not, then, a limiting form of progressive history focused on "healing" history's wounds and coming to some sort of closure, but a critically and affectively engaged narrative that acknowledges failure, defeat, and damage as it simultaneously aims to bear witness, right wrongs, and imagine a better future. Such empathic response is ongoing and never complete, and centers on critically reckoning with the past on particularly unsettling affective terms, like shame.

Tomkins argued that shame is a form of social or group cohesion: "the fact that the other identifies sufficiently with others to be ashamed rather than to show contempt strengthens any social group and its sense of community. Just as contempt strengthens the boundaries and barriers between individuals and groups and is the instrument par excellence for the preservation of hierarchical, caste, and class relationships, so is shared shame a prime instrument for strengthening the sense of mutuality and community whether it be between parent and child, friend and friend, or citizen and citizen."[133] As such, shame can mobilize shared understandings of civic morality.

This is certainly the case in Duluth, where multiple publics deeply ashamed of their city's failure to curtail racial violence in June 1920, and determined that such shameful acts of racial terrorism never be repeated, came together to build the Clayton Jackson McGhie Memorial. This memorial not only admits the lynching of these three young men into Duluth's civic history but also admits the culpability—and responsibility—of Duluth's citizens. As such, it raises issues of ongoing social and moral obligations.

Duluth's memorial has generated a host of local initiatives aimed at improving race relations, and more generally, raising consciousness about related issues of local and national responsibility. The history of the 1920 lynching, for example, has become an integral part of Duluth's public school curriculum, and students regularly take field trips to the site. The original memorial committee has evolved into the Clayton Jackson McGhie Memorial Board, a nonprofit group that maintains a Web site, offers college scholarships to local high school students, and networks "with other communities around the nation who are likewise working to confront historic wrongs and create a present and future where a true and deep racial reconciliation is achieved."[134]

Their work has encouraged other American towns to confront their own shameful histories of racial terrorism. In Scottsboro, Alabama, a historical marker commemorating the trial and incarceration of the Scottsboro Boys, a group of nine young black men falsely accused of rape in 1931, was formally dedicated in front of the Jackson County Courthouse in 2004. In Monroe, Georgia, the Moore's Ford Memorial Committee has organized to develop a memorial park at the site of Moore's Ford Bridge, where two black couples (one of them pregnant) were lynched in 1946 by a mob of around fifty-five men, many of them members of the KKK. Although President Harry Truman demanded a federal investigation into the Moore's Ford Bridge murders and the FBI compiled a five hundred-page report, no one was indicted. In 1998, a memorial service was held at the bridge; in 1999, a historical marker was placed on Highway 78 (about two and a half miles east of the site). In July 2005, on the fifty-ninth anniversary of the murders, Georgia state representative Tyrone Brooks organized a reenactment of the lynchings to press for prosecution of the perpetrators (several of whom were believed to still be alive). About two hundred people (and several television crews) watched the performance, which was staged by an all-black cast who (except for the four actors depicting the lynching victims) wore white masks (some marked KKK) and screamed race-baiting epithets. "This is a stain on our history, and a burden on our soil," said Brooks. "We cannot find closure until there is prosecution. We cannot find reconciliation until there is prosecution."[135] The lynching reenactment at Moore's Ford Bridge has since become an annual event.

Duluth's lynching memorial was formally dedicated on October 10, 2003, in a public ceremony attended by about three thousand people. A funeral march led by a six-piece New Orleans style jazz band retraced the route the lynch mob had taken through downtown Duluth on the evening of June 15, 1920. March participants included Duluth mayor Gary Doty, members of the city council, local clergy, police, school children, and hundreds of other local residents; the dedication featured prayers, poems (one read by Eddie Glenn, the student who posed for the memorial's likeness of Elias Clayton), and musical performances. It also included a speech from Warren Read, a fourth-grade teacher from Kingston, Washington, who was horrified to learn while researching his family's history that his great-grandfather, Louis Dondino, had been one of the leaders of Duluth's lynch mob. His voice choking with emotion, Read apologized to Clayton, Jackson, and McGhie during his remarks and observed that "true shame is not in the discovery of a terrible event such as this, but in the refusal to acknowledge and learn from that event." Read added, "I think that one of the things that adds to a sense of no resolution, of being trapped within the horrible postcard of that night, is that it has for so long existed in a snapshot . . . I stand here as a representative of [my great-grandfather's] legacy, and I willingly place that responsibility upon my shoulders."[136]

Not everyone is willing to shoulder that responsibility. In a *New York Times* article on Duluth's lynching memorial, a fifty-six-year-old Duluth local complained, "Why should we spend the money on that? The kids in our schools are still going without, and I don't know what it's going to do to give those people this, eighty years after. Besides, those men wouldn't have been killed if they hadn't done nothing, would they? Come on."

Likewise, following the lynching reenactment at Moore's Ford Bridge in 2005, a commenter calling themselves "mikemason" posted the following on the Web site for American Renaissance, a white separatist blog that bills itself as "America's premiere [*sic*] publication of racial-realist thought": "Can whites reenact the 50k whites killed by blacks in the past 50 yrs? Can 1 million white females reenact the rapes by black males the past 100 yrs? What about the 100 million violent crimes against whites the past 50 yrs? Stupid blacks cant [*sic*] make it in white society so they only whine and lie to try to get more welfare trillions." Another blogger, "betty," posted a similar rant on the same site: "Let's have re-enactments of the millions of Black on White crimes since the phoney [*sic*] civil rights laws and integration!"[137]

Recognizing and interpreting the shameful history of Japanese American incarceration is also contested. In California, some Owens Valley residents and local veterans groups strongly opposed Manzanar's memorialization, and the Historical Landmark plaque placed at the camp's entrance has been repeatedly vandalized (and repeatedly reinstalled). Others have pressured state and federal agencies to more broadly contextualize Manzanar in terms of its multiple histories and publics—its Native American, ranching, agricultural, and pioneer histories, and its key role in California's water wars.[138]

What the nation's Japanese American internment camps should be called, and how they are remembered, is also subject to debate. As Robert Hayashi observes, "The National Park Service declared that 'concentration camp,' the term most commonly used by *Nikkei* organizations such as the JACL, the Manzanar Committee, and the Japanese American National Museum, was unacceptable."[139] In 2006, the NPS asked Congress to remove the word "internment" from the Minidoka camp's name and requested that the park be renamed the Minidoka National Historical Site. Some of those who were imprisoned there strongly object. As James Azumano remarks, "It is a real dilemma and a constant challenge: how politically correct do you want to be over what at the time was a civil rights atrocity? It's a struggle with terminology that continues today. What are you going to call Guantánamo 50 years from now?" Commemorating—or even naming—the "traumascapes" of American shame, the places "marked by traumatic legacies of violence, suffering, and loss," is neither easy nor comfortable.[140]

Shame can be reparative when individuals, communities, and nations recognize that injustices have been committed against others, that those injustices continue to have power, and that current understandings of self and national identity are complicit with those injustices. Shame is relational; it hinges on the social contract. Shame's redemptive potential depends on the affirmation of others—those to whom shameful things were done—being perceived as legitimate members of society. It is further contingent on "failure to live up to a social ideal," and the urgent desire to take up that ideal now; as Sara Ahmed argues, shame "can construct a collective ideal even when it announces the failure of that ideal to be translated into action."[141] Duluth's lynching memorial emerged from this collective ideal and animates how a flawed civic and national past can be redeemed and made meaningful.

6 ANGER

Contesting American Identity in Contemporary Memorial Culture

Sometime in January 1998, in Alcalde, New Mexico, someone chopped off the right foot of a statue of Juan de Oñate (fig. 6.1). A sixteenth-century Spanish conquistador, Oñate is remembered by New Mexican Hispanics as a heroic founding father, the leader of an expedition of six hundred Spanish soldiers and their families who in 1598 established the first European settlement in what became the United States. The first territorial governor of New Mexico, Oñate is further revered for forging a trade route between Mexico City and Santa Fe and introducing Catholicism and the horse to the region.

Among New Mexico's Native Americans, however, who make up 10 percent of the state's population, Oñate is remembered as a brutal conqueror. In 1599, the Acoma Pueblo who fought against encroaching Spanish authority were captured and enslaved. Their village and ceremonial buildings were razed, and two dozen of their warriors were punished by having one of their feet amputated. Four centuries later, those claiming responsibility for mutilating Oñate's memorial sent the following note to local media:

> We took the liberty of removing Oñate's right foot on behalf of our brothers and sisters of Acoma Pueblo. This was done in commemoration of his 400th year anniversary acknowledging his unasked for exploitation of our land. We see no glory in celebrating Oñate's fourth centennial, and we do not want our faces rubbed in it. If you must speak of his expedition, speak the truth in all its entirety. We will be melting his foot down and casting small medallions to be sold to those who are historically ignorant.[1]

Dedicated in 1994, the twelve-foot bronze statue is located in front of the Oñate Monument Resource and Visitor Center in Rio Arriba County, north of Espanola. The pet project of political boss Emilio Naranjo, longtime Democratic state senator in a county with the nation's highest per capita rate of heroin overdoses and where 20 percent of locals live below

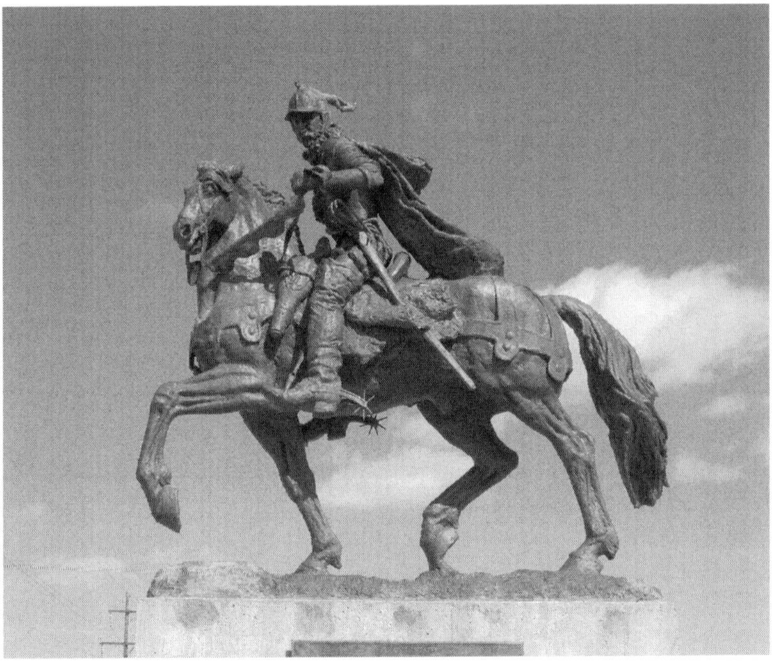

6.1. Reynaldo Rivera, Juan de Oñate Monument, Alcalde, New Mexico, dedicated 1994. (Photo by the author.)

the federal poverty line, the cultural center cost $1.5 million.[2] Designed by Renaldo ("Sonny") Rivera, the $108,000 sculpture was modeled after an equestrian statue of Marcus Aurelius and depicts the Spanish conquistador decked out in battle armor. Shortly after it was installed, "people dressed as clowns" delivered a comically counterfeit "war shield" to the visitor center: a fringed circular hide titled the "Enchanted Taxpayer Award" that was decorated with feathers and little clay feet and inscribed "The Agony of Defeet." Smaller text in the middle of the shield criticized the center as "the most inappropriate use of taxpayers' money . . . to build the most incorrect monument possible. Way to go, guys."[3]

Punning and trickster play are trademarks of Native American humor and contemporary art: witty, ironic, and politically engaged performances typically aimed at subverting conventional symbols of power and authority.[4] Given Oñate's brutality toward New Mexico's indigenous peoples and the fact that his name, translated from its Basque origins, means "at the foot of the mountain pass," it comes as no surprise that a group claiming to speak for the Acoma Pueblo chopped off the conquistador's right foot as a wry gesture of retaliation. The humor was lost, however, among many New Mexican Hispanics.

Angry letters and newspaper columns followed the memorial's mutilation. "It's typical of the mindlessness that goes on these days," stormed historian Marc Simmons, author of numerous accounts of colonial New Mexico, including a biography of Oñate. "These things are always done by people who have never read a history book and know nothing of what they're talking about." Elsewhere, Simmons called Oñate "the George Washington of New Mexico," adding, "It was because of him and his courage and his perseverance that we have New Mexico." Tom Chávez, director of the New Mexico History Museum, located in Santa Fe's seventeenth-century Palace of the Governors, described the statue's vandalism as "a trend of pan-Indianism" and declared, "We're suffering the fallout of political correctness and the ethnic chauvinism of the '60s." And Santa Fe artist Irene Brandtner de Martinez bluntly stated, "Cutting off the right foot of the Oñate statue is but another manifestation of the cultural and historical rape of indigenous Hispanic New Mexico. This hatred of everything Spanish and Spanish-American must stop."[5]

Other New Mexicans saw things differently. "I couldn't control a rather loud affirmative cheer for those good people who whacked off the foot of the statue of Juan de Oñate in Alcalde recently. Anyone who reads the history of Oñate's crimes of humanity inflicted on the Acomas . . . would fully support this meaningful act," Cindy Bogert Bibo Lamm wrote in a letter to the *Santa Fe New Mexican*. "I'm part of the Acoma Pueblo, a descendant of those who were dishonored those many years ago . . . If taking the foot off a statue was needed to make sure the whole story of Oñate was heard than [*sic*] so be it," wrote P. J. Lopez. "Oñate was a ruthless killer, a man motivated by greed," wrote Andrew Lauriano, former governor of the Sandia Pueblo. The All-Indian Council, a group representing New Mexico's nineteen Pueblo tribes, joined Lauriano in opposing any state-funded memorials to Oñate. Likewise, Acoma artist Maurus Chino, who credits the controversy over Alcalde's Oñate statue with sparking his political activism, chastised Congressman Manuel Luján (R-NM) for helping to orchestrate funding for "such a racist and offensive statue."[6] Finally, local journalist Richard McCord suggested, "Perhaps Oñate's bronze foot should be left off, and a plaque installed to explain its absence. Then pilgrims to his shrine can absorb his grandeur and his horror, in some form of truth."[7] Notwithstanding such advice, the statue was repaired with a new foot. The old one, according to local legend, is hidden somewhere on Acoma Pueblo.

The "Oñate foot-chopping incident," as this tale of memorial vandalism is sometimes called, has become an inspirational metaphor for any number of critics interested in unraveling the fraught dynamics of contemporary New Mexican cultural politics.[8] Here is a tale of iconoclasm and bitterly contested memories. Here is a tale of contentious claims to regional—and ultimately national—origins and highly factionalized disputes regarding historical causes and consequences. Here is a tale of anger—perhaps the most pervasive and certainly the most performative of memorial mania's affective conditions. Mania, after all, is especially understood in terms of furor and frenzy, agitation and excessive passion. Memorials are not, in and of themselves, "angry"; there is no particular "anger" memorial. But their making and meaning often embodies and induces anger, especially when memorials are understood as the public symbols of disputed narratives of American ownership, legitimacy, belonging, and control. This chapter considers how feelings are mobilized in today's memorial cultures to express the rights-claims of particular publics, including previously disenfranchised peoples whose histories have been only recently deemed memorable in America.

MEMORIAL MANIA AND REVISIONIST HISTORY TODAY

The affective conditions of anger in contemporary American memorial cultures relate in particular to the shifting dynamics of the national narrative, of who "counts" in the unfolding of American history, whose story is most important, who is telling the tale. Rancor over recent forms of American historical revisionism, over the perceived slights of political correctness and multiculturalism and their tainting of a supposedly more truthful or more authentic American past, stems from both an unwillingness to admit to the fundamentally fluid terms of American nationalism and intolerance for its ever-expanding cast of characters. Anger about Juan de Oñate's celebrated status in southwestern history—the four hundredth anniversary of his founding of the Spanish colony was marked by 185 different forms of commemoration, from statues and stamps to songs and parades—induced an act of defacement intent on exposing the flaws in that historical memory, and destabilizing its authority. Anger about that act induced heated reactions from pro-Hispano adherents intent on reconfiguring American history on their own terms: on gaining recognition for the Catholic Spanish founders of America, and thereby contesting the still prevalent privileging of Puritan New England in American memory.

Anger is rife in today's memorial culture, particularly in response to conflicted claims over American war memory, hero worship, and foundational histories. In Richmond, Virginia, a memorial to Abraham Lincoln raised the ire of Confederate sympathizers when it was installed at the National Park Service Civil War Visitors Center at Tredegar Iron Works in 2003 (fig. 6.2); indeed, the park's superintendent received more

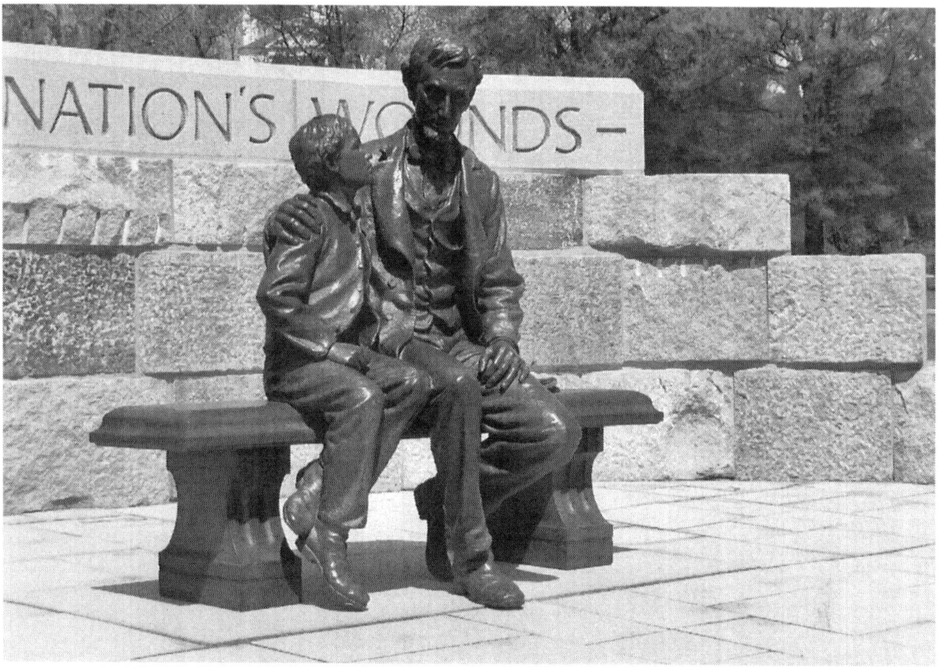

6.2. David Frech, *Lincoln and Tad*, Richmond, Virginia, dedicated 2003. (© David Frech.)

than a thousand angry anti-statue emails. Unveiled on the 138th anniversary of Lincoln's visit to the former Confederate capital during the waning days of the Civil War, the memorial depicts Lincoln with his arm draped around his twelve-year-old son Tad and the words "To Bind Up the Nation's Wounds" written on the wall in back of them. During the memorial's dedication ceremonies, a small plane buzzed overhead pulling a red banner inscribed with the state motto of Virginia, "Sic Semper Tyrannis" ("thus always to tyrants"), which John Wilkes Booth purportedly shouted from the stage of Ford Theater after assassinating Lincoln in 1865. Protesters also unfurled rebel battle flags in Richmond's Hollywood Cemetery. "They have no concept of history and how it might be the wrong place to put the statue," fumed Bragdon Bowling, the Virginia commander of the Sons of Confederate Veterans. "As a Southerner, I'm offended. You wouldn't put a statue of Winston Churchill in downtown Berlin, would you? What's next, a statue of Sherman in Atlanta?"[9] Since it was dedicated, the memorial has been under constant surveillance by strategically placed security cameras.

Contemporary war memory is similarly charged in Phoenix. Soon after it was dedicated in September 2006, Arizona's official 9/11 memorial became the subject of rancorous debate between Len Munsil, Republican candidate for governor, and Democratic incumbent Janet Napolitano. The memorial, a large concrete and steel sculpture titled *Moving Memories*, included fifty-four different inscriptions ranging from "216 Arizona firefighters respond to WTC" and "Must Bomb Back" to "Erroneous U.S. air strike kills 46 Uruzgan civilians" and "You don't win battles of terrorism with more battles." Munsil, a conservative Christian, chided the piece as an unpatriotic "tribute to moral relativism" and demanded that it be torn down, while Governor Napolitano defended the $500,000 project (paid for with private funds) as a "bold, dynamic, educational, and unforgettable learning tool." While Napolitano handily won the 2006 election, furor over *Moving Memories* raged for several years until an agreement was reached to remove several phrases found offensive to some right-wing politicians and to add those they approved of, such as "United We Stand," "Let's Roll," and "God Bless America." Even this wasn't enough for Arizona state representative John Kavanagh, a Republican who introduced legislation to remove all of the inscriptions and replace them with a 9/11 timeline. As Kavanagh explained, the designers of *Moving Memories* "wanted to provoke thought and discussion, where most Arizona residents expected a straight memorial where you come to remember, meditate, to pray. There lies the root of the problem."[10]

Arguments about what memorials are supposed to be—"straight" versus provocative, implicit versus deliberative—are at the source of memorial mania's angriest outbursts. So are issues of subjectivity: the "problem" of who constitutes American historical memory and the terms of their representation. These issues have embroiled commemorations of Martin Luther King, Jr., for decades, from acrimonious debates over establishing a national holiday in his honor and renaming city streets and highways in his memory to aggrieved claims on his image and legacy.[11] Anger about King's place in America's national narrative, both literally and metaphorically, has erupted in numerous acts of vandalism. In Kansas in 1993, vandals defaced a bronze sculpture of King on the campus of Wichita State University, painting the face white and writing "KKK" on the pedestal. In Tampa in 2002, a bust of King was vandalized on the University of South Florida campus; in Austin in 2004, a statue of King at the University of Texas was sprayed with silver paint; in Chico, California, in 2008, a statue of King in a city park was vandalized.

Anger often erupts over how King should be depicted: as a man of the people, dressed in a suit, or a man of faith, dressed in clerical robes. (Suits usually win.) Debates over his status as a passionate political radical are practically nonexistent; since the 1990s, King's public image as the provocative leader of a civil rights revolution has been replaced by that of a nonthreatening political moderate. In 2008, the U.S. Commission of

Fine Arts criticized the twenty-eight-foot-tall statue of King that is the centerpiece of the four-acre, $100 million Martin Luther King, Jr. National Memorial, located on the northeast corner of the National Mall's Tidal Basin, as too "confrontational" (fig. 6.3). The statue, called *Stone of Hope*, depicts King standing with his arms crossed, looming from a huge pillar of carved granite. "My image of Dr. King is of him leaning forward in anticipation, holding his chin or raising his arm," complained one commissioner, while others urged a more "subtle" approach that avoided the "colossal monumentalization" associated with "a genre of political sculpture that has recently been pulled down in other countries." Obviously referencing the social realist styles of the Soviet Union, Saddam's Iraq, and other recently fallen states—and overlooking popular American memorial colossi like Mount Rushmore and Crazy Horse—the commission was seemingly worried that King might come off as too commanding, too influential. The project's artist consultants shot back that they viewed King as a powerful and inspirational figure: "We see him as a warrior . . . a warrior for peace . . . not as some pacifist, placid, kind of vanilla, but really a man of great conviction and strength." Still, they reshaped their design and satisfied the commission by adding "a hint of a smile" to King's face and making him a softer, gentler American warrior.[12]

Anxieties about King's critical position in American history help account for the battles waged over his memory and image; questions about his commemoration suggest reluctance to accept the profound changes he helped generate in America. The King family itself has fueled bitter litigation over his commemoration, including aggressive lawsuits filed against historians and journalists for violating the family's copyright of King's 1963 "I Have a Dream" speech, squabbles with the National Park Service over its management of the Martin Luther King, Jr. National Historic Site in Atlanta, and disputes dating to the 1980s over the conceptual, geographic, aesthetic, and financial terms of King's national memorial in Washington. As Dexter King stated in 1995, "We feel strongly that the heritage of the civil rights movement is too important to be controlled by a Government agency that has only superficial familiarity with the internal dynamics of our freedom struggle." In 2007, the King family charged the foundation building his national memorial in Washington $800,000 for the use of his words and his image.[13]

Bruising arguments over what King should look like and who is entitled to his representation are ubiquitous. In 2005, black citizens in Rocky Mount, North Carolina, who constitute 56 percent of the town's thirty thousand residents, orchestrated the removal of a King memorial that they deemed too "arrogant" and not "realistic" enough, and because the sculptor, Erik Blome, was not black (fig. 6.4). "We need an artist who

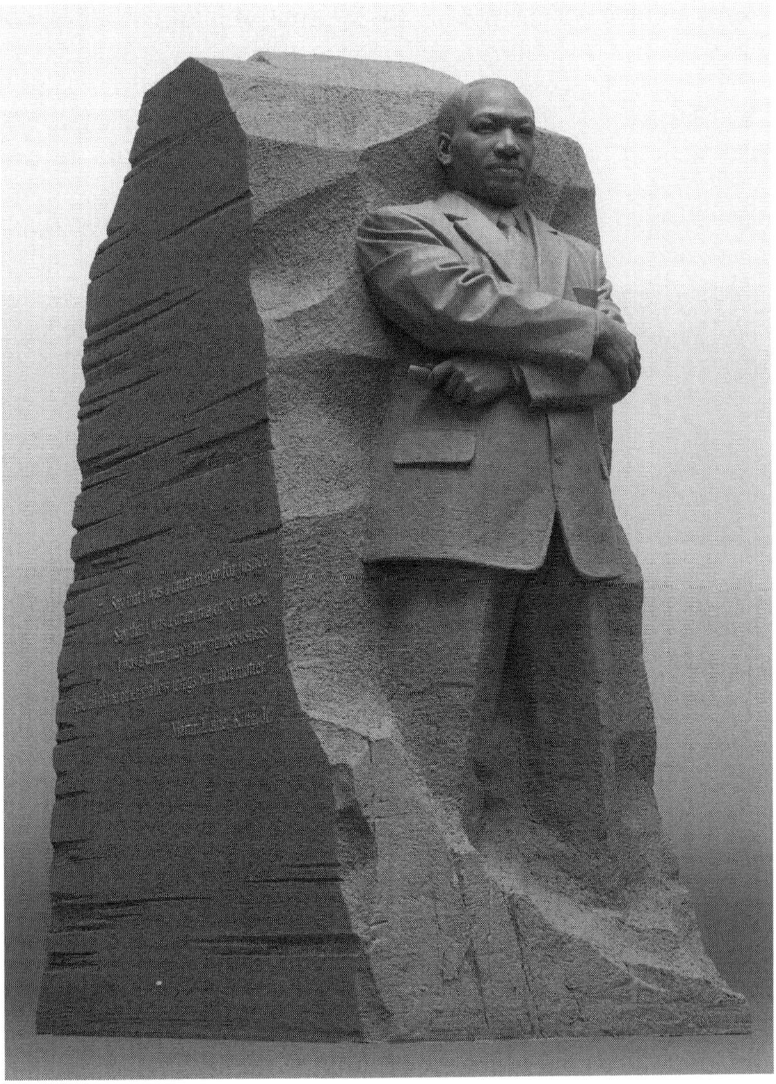

6.3. Lei Yixin, *Stone of Hope*, Martin Luther King, Jr. National Memorial, Washington, D.C. (© 2007. Property of the Washington, D.C., Martin Luther King, Jr. National Memorial Project Foundation, Inc. Washington, D.C., USA. All rights reserved. Reproduced under license for limited use.)

can relate," said one local resident in the city where King gave an early version of his "I Have a Dream" speech. Others protested that the $56,000 statue, originally installed in 2003, "looked like a white man painted black." Eventually, after spending another $71,000 on alternative memorial proposals and finding nothing that Rocky Mount residents seemed to like, the town's City Council voted to reinstall Blome's statue—and

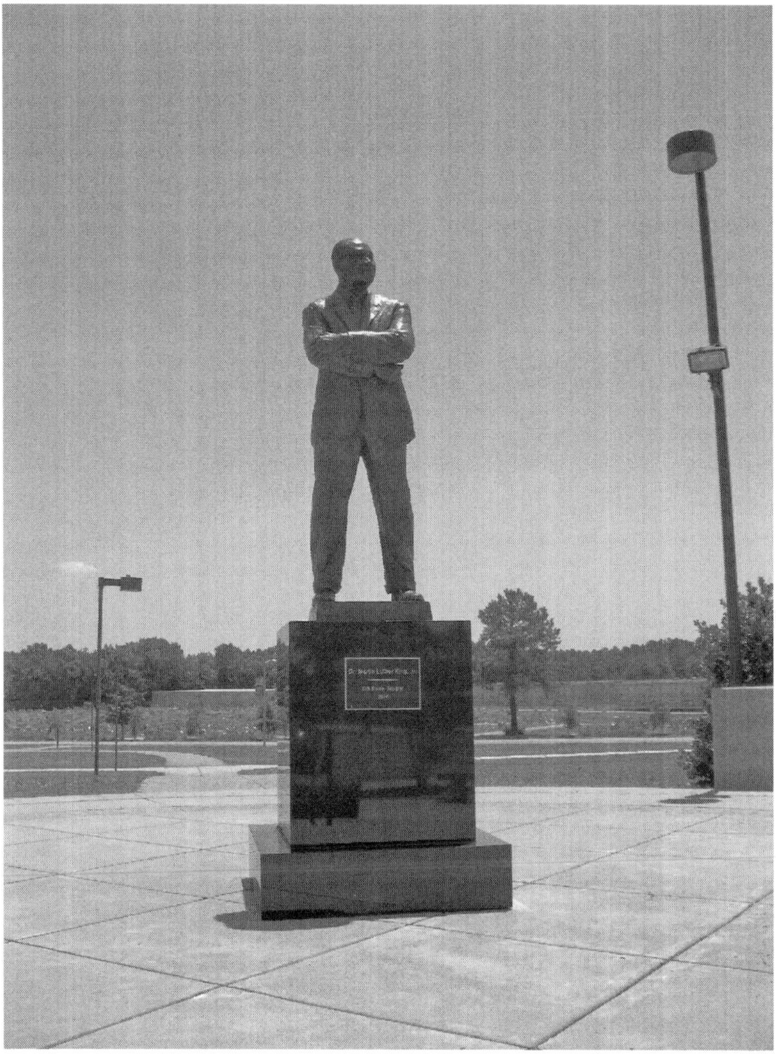

6.4. Erik Blome, *Dr. Martin Luther King, Jr.*, Rocky Mount, North Carolina, dedicated 2003. (Courtesy of Leigh Ann Hallberg.)

to repair damage caused when it was crudely sawed off its pedestal and stored in a city warehouse. Today it stands in the center of Rocky Mount's Martin Luther King, Jr., Park, a flat and mostly treeless field flanked by an electrical substation and a cemetery. For Ed Dwight, who has designed scores of monuments focused on African American subjects, including the Underground Railroad Memorial (see fig. 5.12, p. 295) and a statue of King commissioned by the City of Denver, Blome's sculpture of King is simply not satisfactory. "White people don't look at us as we look at ourselves," says Dwight. "I compete with many white artists all over the country, and they bring their maquettes in and they don't look anything like the subject. It's a cultural thing, a very, very spiritual thing."[14]

Similar protests surfaced when Chinese artist Lei Yixin was selected to carve *Stone of Hope* for the King national memorial, a project many African American artists felt they should control. "I believe that black artists have the right to interpret ourselves first," declared Gilbert Young, an Atlanta painter who organized the Web site King Is Ours to challenge the "outsourcing" of the memorial to a sculptor best known for his statues of Communist Party leaders like Mao Zedong. "We've been sold out; our culture has been sold out," Young raged. "I don't know how we can give this job to someone who doesn't even believe in our form of government." Ed Dwight, who was hired as an artistic consultant for the King national memorial, also objected to Lei's selection, saying "he doesn't know how black people walk, how they stand, how their shoulders slope." Dwight called Lei's statue a "shrinking, shriveled inadequate personage."[15]

Members of the King National Memorial Foundation, however, ten out of twelve of whom are African American, say Lei was chosen because of his talent with a chisel. "This is no different than the Houston Rockets working with Yao Ming, or Jackie Chan in Hollywood movies," explained the president of the foundation. "We don't want to take the stand to say African Americans can only work on this project. We appreciate the diversity we have." As the coproducer of the Sino-American play *Passages of Martin Luther King* (which opened in Beijing in 2007) observes, "Those who insist that only an African American should sculpt the bust of the Rev. Martin Luther King, Jr. forget what the great civil rights leader said about the importance of being judged by 'the content of (one's) character.' I'm a white American, born 12 years after a sniper's bullet cut down King in Memphis, but I suspect that if King heard the suggestion that a Chinese artist was incapable of portraying an African American, he'd roll over in his grave."[16]

Anger over the subject of America's discovery has been especially rancorous, and protests against Christopher Columbus have regularly erupted since the 1980s. At the turn of the last century, Columbus was honored in hundreds of statues, sculptures, busts, fountains, plaques, plazas, parks, and streets all over America, and championed as the most important actor in the drama of national discovery (see fig. 1.3, p. 23). Today his prestige is much diminished. In 1990, the National Council of Churches passed a resolution stating that "Columbus's invasion marked the beginning of slavery" and "eventual genocide" for indigenous Americans. In 1992, the five hundredth anniversary of the explorer's Caribbean landfall was marked by protests in Boston, Philadelphia, New York, Dallas, Denver, and Columbus, and generated a growing movement to replace Columbus Day, a designated U.S. national holiday since 1968, with Indigenous Peoples Day. Since 1990, South Dakota has celebrated Native American Day instead of Columbus Day. While a 2005 survey found that Columbus is still a respected, if not exactly heroic, figure among many Americans, it also found that his lingering presence in the nation's historical memory is mostly one of intellectual inertia: many Americans continue to imagine Columbus on positive terms because they are unaware of alternative interpretations. In the 1950s, for example, most American school children were taught a "simplified laudatory view of Columbus in the lower grades, and very little thereafter."[17]

Today, Columbus is debunked in American history textbooks, and his unexamined presence in American memorial cultures is vehemently contested. Calling Columbus a mass murderer, Indian activist Russell Means poured blood on a Columbus memorial in Denver's Civic Center Park in 1989, stating: "We don't want to destroy this monument to the Columbus legacy. We only want to add to it. The truth. The true Columbus." In 1991, Washington's Columbus Memorial Fountain was splashed with red paint; in 2002, the memorial was targeted again and inscribed with the message "510 years oppression, 510 years resistance" (fig. 6.5). In 1997, a statue of Columbus in Pittsburgh's Schenley Park was spray painted with the words "murderer" and "stolen lands." In 1998, a woman defaced a bust of Columbus (and one of Amerigo Vespucci) during a tour of the White House. In March 2001, a man smashed a statue of Columbus in San Jose's City Hall with a sledgehammer, shouting "Genocide!" and "This man murdered us!"[18] A few months later, a Columbus statue in Santa Barbara was beheaded and spray painted with the words "Tell children the truth." In 2004, a Columbus statue in Boston's Christopher Columbus Waterfront Park was marked with the word "MURDERER" in red paint; in 2006, the same statue was decapitated.

Columbus iconoclasm is not confined to the United States. In 1992, statues of Columbus were vandalized in Mexico City and El Salvador, and a statue of Queen Isabella of Spain, Columbus's patron, was bombed in La Paz, Bolivia. In Tegucigalpa, Honduras, in 1997, protestors smashed a statue of the explorer in the city's Columbus Plaza, and painted its head and hands red. In Caracas in 2004, demonstrators toppled a Columbus statue and dragged it through the streets to the Teresa Carreño Theater, where thousands of people celebrated the Day of Indigenous Resistance, a Venezuelan national holiday since 2002. "Just like the statue of Saddam in Baghdad," one local Web site reported, "that of Columbus the tyrant also fell this October 12, 2004 in Caracas."[19]

"Monuments are mortal," Robert Nelson and Margaret Olin remind

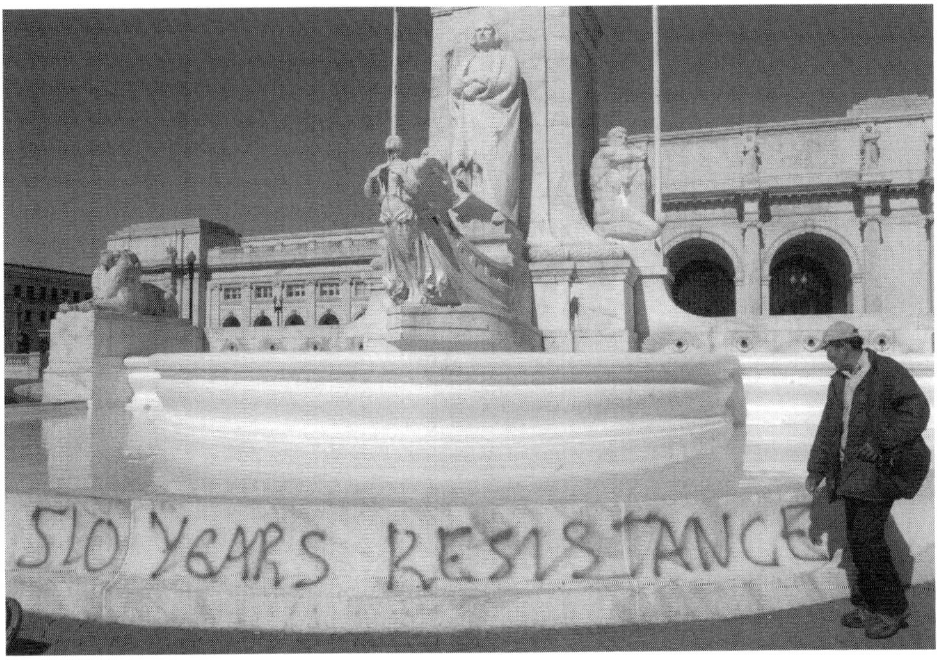

6.5. Mark Wilson, "Christopher Columbus Statue Vandalized." Washington, D.C., October 14, 2002. (© 2002 Getty Images.)

us, and their damage and destruction are integral to their states of being.[20] The typical memorial runs a course from creation to decline, although occasionally, like a human body, it may have its existence extended—and altered—with the addition or substitution of some new part. Or it may fade away and be appropriated later for an entirely different commemorative purpose: Stonehenge becoming a must-see site of modern British tourism, or the Vietnam Veterans Memorial becoming the staging ground for pro-war rallies. Deeply symbolic monuments may be destroyed in times of profound identity transformation. The toppling of Columbus statues in Honduras and Venezuela, like the toppling of Lenin and Stalin statues in Russia in the 1990s, the bulldozing of Muslim mosques during the Bosnian war, the Taliban's obliteration of the monumental rock-cut Bamiyan Buddhas in March 2001, and Al Qaeda's attacks on the World Trade Center on 9/11, occurred at times of significant political and social change. Likewise, American assaults on statues of King George in the 1770s and on memorials to Oñate, King, and Columbus today, embody struggles over self and state redefinition during critically transformative moments of independence, civil rights, and multiculturalism. Memorials are often altered or replaced at such times; the revisionist terms of new politics and new regimes demand new or at least modified symbolic identities.

Memorial mania's most acrimonious conditions often correspond to revisionist terms. Despite the variable dimensions of the national imaginary in America (and elsewhere), anger about the violation of certain precepts, the invalidation of long held beliefs, being forced to change, or feeling victimized, surfaces again and again in contemporary memorial cultures. Charged with negotiating the fluctuating demands of citizenship, nationalism, and other facets of American identity, memorials are often the target—and the source—of public anger.

ANGER

Motivated by fear, anxiety, irresolution, uncertainty, loss of confidence, lack of trust, provocation, and a sense of slight, among other things, anger is an especially performative affect. Manifest in impatience, frustration, conflict, aggression, and violence, and in feelings of rage and hatred, anger is dramatic, dynamic, and heated. We talk about "boiling over" and "blowing up" in anger, about "striking back" in anger, about "seeing red" when we're angry. Anger is varied—there are differences between feeling annoyed and exploding in rage. Anger is reactive: a defensive response to perceptions of wrongdoing, a way to vent feelings of helplessness or victimization. And anger is seemingly ubiquitous in contemporary America, prevalent in political, popular, and memorial cultures alike.

In Greek mythology, anger was understood as "heroic mania," a kind of heightened emotional frenzy that the female deities of madness—Lyssa and Mania—used to goad warriors into appalling acts of savagery and violence (for example, the "wrath of Achilles").[21] Although the Stoic philosopher Seneca despised anger as greedy self-indulgence, calling it the "most hideous" of the emotions, both the Greeks and the Romans valued anger as a legitimate and even obligatory means of revenge, of righting wrongs and settling scores. For them, anger was a form of manly self-assertion, an affirmation of pride, a code of honor. Yet its volatility, its seeming contagion ("only fury plagues whole communities at once," said Seneca), and its threat to social and political order, especially by slaves, women, and lower classes who might upset the status quo, also prompted a discourse of anger management in the Greco-Roman world.[22] In Christian mythology, anger is one of the seven deadly sins, although in the Bible, anger is less clear-cut: God is a figure of wrath and anger is encouraged as a "righteous" demonstration of faith (Samuel 11:6, Exodus 4:14), but anger also "lodges in the bosom of fools" (Ecclesiastes 7:9) and

Christ instructed his followers to keep their anger in check by turning the other cheek and doing "good to those who hate you" (Luke 6:28).

Anger's role in contemporary American psychic, social, and political health is similarly contradictory. Anger is the subject of an immense therapeutic industry concerned with its control at the same time that anger has gained widespread popular and political currency. Bestselling books like *The Anger Advantage: The Surprising Benefits of Anger and How It Can Change a Woman's Life* (2003), new expressions like "going postal" (coined in 1983 after a U.S. Post Office employee opened fire on his boss in Anniston, Alabama), furious blogs like Error Theory (and the "flame wars" they encourage), and hit songs like Toby Keith's "Courtesy of the Red, White, and Blue (The Angry American)," which, written just after 9/11, features the defiantly patriotic lyrics "This big dog will fight / When you rattle his cage / And you'll be sorry that you messed with / The U. S. of A. / 'Cause we'll put a boot in your ass / It's the American Way," all suggest anger's prevalence today. So does road rage, a relatively recent term for "the epidemic" of aggressive driving supposedly plaguing America's roads. As *Time* magazine put it in 1998, "It's high noon on the country's streets and highways. This is road recklessness, auto anarchy, an epidemic of wanton carmanship."[23]

Anger is endemic in today's mass media, an affect that reporters obsessively sniff out and sensationalize. It's the modus operandi of rant-filled talk radio programs like *The Rush Limbaugh Show* and *The Savage Nation*, and equally shrill cable TV "news" shows like *The O'Reilly Factor*. Some of this media-anger is occasionally tempered; in 2003, shock-jock Michael Savage was fired from hosting a weekend show on MSNBC after shouting at one caller "You should only get AIDS and die, you pig." Also in 2003, Rush Limbaugh was fired from ESPN's *Sunday NFL Countdown* after making race-baiting comments about a Philadelphia Eagles quarterback. In 2007, Don Imus was suspended from his morning talk radio show after calling players on the Rutgers University women's basketball team "nappy-headed hos." But these slap downs are relatively rare. More typically, the media that many Americans rely on for their daily and breaking news is dominated by loud-mouthed innuendo, confrontational interviews, politically motivated smears, racist and sexist rants, pugnacious outbursts, a tendency to spin facts, and a general pattern of quarrelsome drivel that veers more toward screaming than informed conversation. In 2007, over two million Americans watched Bill O'Reilly's show on Fox News every night, making *The O'Reilly Factor* the most watched cable TV news program for the sixth year in a row.[24]

If this culture of "angry talk" informs Americans about news, it also shapes understandings about how to talk and what to talk about.

Grounded in perceptions of offense and harm, the angry tones of today's mass media segue with widespread worries about the status and security of the nation. And while some of this flame-throwing prattle is purely theatrical and geared toward increased ratings, much of it is fed by unsettling fears about "what's happening" in (and to) America. Anger is not an isolated affect: as Tomkins theorized, anger is dependent on fear and often becomes the affective response to fears of powerlessness, insignificance, and disrespect. Writing about "large-scale, culturally motivated violence in our times," Arjun Appadurai argues that post-9/11 America—and much of the rest of the world—inhabits a "geography of anger" sparked by "uncertainty about the enemy within and the anxiety about the always incomplete project of national purity."[25] The contentious dynamics of American public culture, including the angry tones of memorial mania, are squarely situated in this affective geography.

Those dynamics are fueled by contemporary opinions that anger is a legitimate and justifiable response by citizens and nation alike. However much anger may be the product of an overactive and highly manipulative "news" industry—Michael Fumento calls road rage a media invention, and Barry Glassner points out that the odds of being killed by someone who "goes postal" in the workplace are less than one in two million—anger is often encouraged and even celebrated in America today. Anger is increasingly understood as a demonstration of real feelings, of authenticity. It is also held as a sign of agency, as a way that those who feel marginalized may seek representation and gain rights. "The notion that anger is good," writes Peter Wood, "that it empowers the oppressed, inspires the timid, and unleashes creativity—compels a lot of contemporary Americans," whereas holding back, or repressing anger, is perceived as a sign of weakness, a failure of conviction, an indicator of low self-esteem.[26]

Anger is further commended today as the socially and politically appropriate response to perceptions of national injustice, damages, and slights. As a means to right wrongs, "anger seeks revenge," observes Philip Fisher. Consider what President George W. Bush said in his "Address to a Joint Session of Congress and the American People" nine days after 9/11: "Tonight we are a country awakened to danger and called to defend freedom. Our grief has turned to anger, and anger to resolution. Whether we bring our enemies to justice, or bring justice to our enemies, justice will be done." Bush reiterated this angry vow of revenge in his 2004 State of the Union address, declaring, "After the chaos and carnage of September the 11th, it is not enough to serve our enemies with legal papers. The terrorists and their supporters declared war on the United States, and war is what they got."[27] His remarks received hearty applause, arguably suggesting that the reactive response of American anger as manifest in the war on terror, and the implication that American anger trumps legal recourse or adherence to an international code of law are widely shared. In a post-9/11 America where outrage is condoned, belligerence is exalted, and furor is encouraged, anger commands respect and unifies the nation.

This unanimity of anger informs the nation's contemporary culture wars, especially battles over rights, representation, and revisionist histories. This is not particularly new; angry disputes and disagreements have played a role throughout the course of the nation's deliberative democracy, from debates over slavery and suffrage in the nineteenth century to those over abortion and immigration today. Conflict is inevitable in democratic politics, argue Amy Gutmann and Dennis Thompson, and civic debates facilitate the conditions that allow for the contestation and reformulation of national ideals and values.[28] The problem is how some kinds of anger circumvent these critically constructive national conversations and projects; there are profound differences between the types of anger that lead a nation to abolish slavery, unite a nation in wartime, or excoriate a nation's diverse citizenry on talk radio and cable TV.

Anger, Carol Tavris observes, is an emotion "without social rules of containment." Controlling it, particularly as anger is widely recognized as a menace to mental health, has become a central focus of the nation's personal therapy industry. Managing anger is also recognized as a strategy of social and political influence. While anger is pervasive in contemporary America, there are still certain assumptions about who can get angry: angry men are often rewarded, whereas angry women are often perceived as hysterics and bitches who are "out of control"; angry whites are often respected as important political allies, whereas angry blacks are perceived as dangerous threats to social order.[29] Likewise, there are certain assumptions about what to be angry about. The hostility that erupts when legendary figures like Oñate are contested, or when public stewards like the National Park Service revamp long-standing interpretive traditions, suggests that revisionist histories are particular sources of anger in memorial mania.

REVISING LITTLE BIGHORN

In 1991, President George H. W. Bush signed legislation changing the name of the Custer Battlefield National Monument to the Little Bighorn Battlefield National Monument. He also authorized the development of an Indian memorial at the site in southeastern Montana where, in late June 1876, Lieutenant Colonel George Armstrong Custer and 210 soldiers, scouts, and civilians attached to the U.S. 7th Cavalry were an-

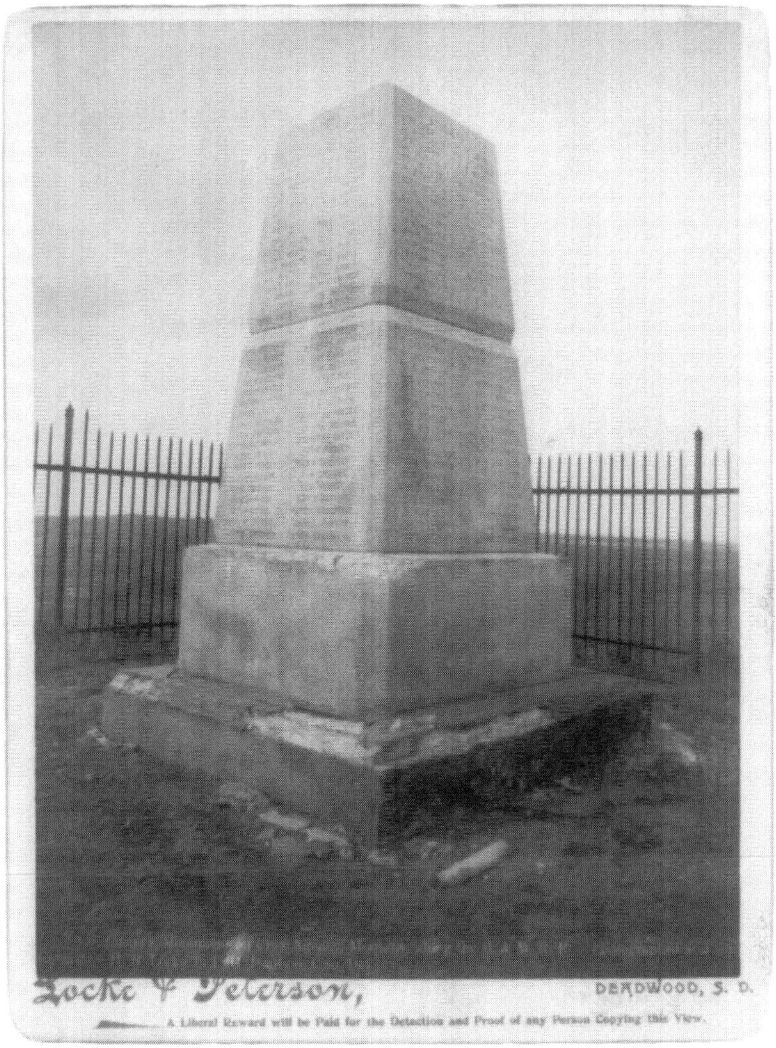

6.6. 7th U.S. Cavalry Monument, Crow Agency, Montana, dedicated 1881. (Photo by H.R. Locke, 1894. Library of Congress, Prints and Photographs Division, digital ID no. cph 3b38596.)

nihilated by a force of several thousand Arapaho, Cheyenne, and Lakota. While a clear military victory for the Indians, led by chiefs such as Sitting Bull and Crazy Horse, this seminal battle over the course of the American West was subsequently remembered on Custer's terms, as "Custer's Last Stand." The site of the battle was dominated by memorials to Custer and his men, including the 7th U.S. Cavalry Monument, an imposing granite edifice dedicated in 1881 (fig. 6.6). Commissioned and paid for by the federal government, the eleven-foot monument was inscribed with the names of Custer's slain army and erected atop the battlefield's highest hill, where Custer and his men were buried in a mass grave.[30]

Three years after the battle, the site was designated a national military cemetery. Placed under the jurisdiction of the U.S. War Department and eventually interring the remains of some five thousand soldier dead, Little Bighorn thus came under the control of an army that lost the battle but won ownership of the land where it was fought, along with its historical interpretation and cultural management. In 1940, the National Park Service took over the site; in 1946, it became a National Monument. As Edward Linenthal relates, Little Bighorn has long been hallowed ground in the American national imaginary, a venerated place where "patriotic orthodoxy" went "essentially unchallenged" for over a century. Almost immediately after the battle, Little Bighorn—and especially Last Stand Hill—was deemed a sacred shrine to Custer and the 7th Cavalry, defeated soldiers revered as national martyrs whose blood sacrifice "made possible the 'opening' of the American West for Anglo-American civilization."[31] Even today, southeastern Montana is hailed as "Custer Country" by the state's tourism bureau. Battlefield reenactments, which have been performed in the area since the early twentieth century, are staged each June and draw thousands of spectators.

Few episodes have occupied such a central—and controversial—place in the American national narrative as Custer's Last Stand. Disbelief that a band of "savages" defeated a modern army led by a decorated Civil War hero and that historical memory of the 1876 battle depended on the accounts of American Indians who were its only survivors fostered lingering disputes about what "really" happened at Little Bighorn and why. Heated debates over whether Custer and his men fought valiantly or turned tail (the claim of recent archaeological analysis), the chronology of the battle, and Custer's character as a soldier have fueled Custer's mythos since the man's demise. Nor does "Custerology," as Michael Elliott calls the historical interpretation and commemoration of the Battle of Little Bighorn, show any sign of fading.[32] At least forty-five movies (including the 1941 Hollywood western *They Died With Their Boots On*), three thousand books, thousands of Web sites, multiple monuments (such as a statue of Custer at a roadside park near New Rumley, Ohio, where he was born, and one in Monroe, Michigan, where he lived as a boy), and numerous American towns (Custer City, Texas; Custer, Idaho; Custer, Wisconsin), counties, and courthouses have claimed Custer.

Custer's defeat holds particular allure. In 2003, Senegalese artist Ousmane Sow recreated Custer's Last Stand in a tableau of life-sized bronze figures for the American Effect exhibition at the Whitney Museum. One hundred and twenty years earlier, Buffalo Bill Cody used the Last Stand as a closing act in his Wild West shows. In the late 1890s, the Anheuser-Busch Brewing Company popularized sales of Budweiser with *Custer's Last Fight*, a color lithograph mass-distributed to saloons all over the country that depicted a saber-swinging Custer outfitted in a snazzy red scarf, brawling with menacing Indians. These visual and performative fabrications, Joy Kasson writes, helped many Americans imagine a Wild West that "blurred the lines between fiction and fact, entertainment and education." Although Native American participants in the Battle of the Little Bighorn produced ample visual documentation, including ledger book drawings by Minniconjou Lakota artist Red Horse, operatic inventions like *Custer's Last Fight* dominated American memory until relatively recently.[33]

Ignored were the larger issues of the nation's imperialist claims on Native American lands and the manner in which Custer's defeat was avenged in the subsequent slaughter of American Indians and the seizure of their territories throughout the rest of the nineteenth century: the grim "legacy of conquest" that Patty Limerick chronicles in her history of the American West.[34] Only with movies like *Little Big Man* (1970), and books like Dee Brown's *Bury My Heart at Wounded Knee* (1970) and Vine Deloria's *Custer Died for Your Sins* (1969), which look at Western history from the "Indian point of view," did reconsideration of Custer's mythological status in American national consciousness begin to emerge in popular culture and critical theory.

Reconsidering Custer's commemoration and the social and political authority of the Custer myth has a much older history among American Indians. Just a few years after its erection, the 7th U.S. Cavalry Monument was fenced off to prevent vandalism by visitors intent on pocketing a piece of history, and/or contesting its commemoration. In 1925, the daughter of a Cheyenne chief killed at Little Bighorn (an estimated one hundred Indians were killed during the 1876 battle) wrote to the site's military superintendent requesting a marker in her father's memory. Her letter was never answered and the battlefield remained attached to "the symbolic dominance of Custer" until the Red Power movement refocused attention on American Indian history and civil rights. In June 1976, several hundred members of the American Indian Movement (AIM) "interrupted" the Custer Battlefield's centennial anniversary with their own memorial services, which included parading the American flag upside down (an international signal of distress). Threatening to set fire to the battlefield's museum, which had opened in 1952 and featured one exhibit called The Hostile Indians and another displaying Custer's military uniforms, AIM spokesman Russell Means delivered an angry speech demanding an Indian memorial at the site and invoking contemporary atrocities against people of color, observing, "I can't imagine a Lt. Calley National Monument in Vietnam."[35]

In 1988, AIM again interrupted battlefield anniversary ceremonies by digging a hole near the 7th U.S. Cavalry Monument, filling it with cement, and erecting a four-foot metal plaque that read: "In honor of our Indian Patriots who fought and defeated the U.S. Calvary [*sic*]. In order to save our women and children from mass-murder. In doing so, preserving rights to our Homelands, Treaties and sovereignty." During the ceremony, Means threatened, "You remove our monument, and we'll remove yours." The plaque remained at the base of the monument for several months until the NPS put it on display in the battlefield's museum, accompanied by a note from the park's superintendent explaining that it was a "temporary symbol of our intent to develop a memorial that will represent the shared perspectives of the tribes involved in the battle."[36] If some were deeply offended by AIM's symbolic defacement of the battlefield's dominating monument, it motivated the National Park Service to reckon with issues of Native American history, memory, and representation.

Change began in 1991, with the renaming of the battlefield. (Custer National Cemetery retained its name.) It did not come easily. Angry accusations of political correctness were lobbed at the historians, park rangers, and politicians—including Congressman Ron Marlenee (R-MT), Senator Ben Nighthorse Campbell (D-CO, and Northern Cheyenne), and Senator John McCain (R-AZ)—who had urged reconsideration of the historic site. The upshot was a compromise; while Congress mandated that the battlefield be redesignated and a memorial "to honor the Indian participants in the battle" be established, the new memorial was also expected to "encourage peace among people of all races" and "be compatible" with the original 7th U.S. Cavalry Monument, which could not be moved, removed, or altered in any way.[37] Revising or contesting the "patriotic orthodoxy" of Custerology was mediated by notions of reconciliation.

In 1996, the NPS conducted a design competition for the Indian Memorial with the guidance of the Little Bighorn Battlefield National Monument Advisory Committee, an eleven-member group of historians, artists, landscape architects, and representatives of the Indian Nations involved in the original battle. The committee's task was to select "a living memorial to the Plains Indian women, children, and men who took part in the battle and whose spirit and culture survive." Some 554 proposals were received in the competition, many featuring "traditional" Indian symbols such as eagles, peace pipes, buffalo horns, medicine lodges, and tepees. One entry, more attuned to AIM's spirit of anarchy, proposed the "voluntary destruction of the monstrous symbol of white domination that is Mount Rushmore" and hauling the rocks and debris from the destroyed national monument to the Little Bighorn site for use in building the new Indian Memorial.[38] It was not a contender.

The new memorial was mandated to "express the theme 'Peace Through Unity.'" Developed by two tribal elders whose ancestors fought at Little Bighorn—Austin Two Moons (Northern Cheyenne) and Enos Poor Bear, Sr. (Oglala Lakota)—this theme was metaphorically intended to unite still-contentious Plains Indian tribes and the nation as a whole.[39] It significantly impacted the design and meaning of the new memorial: if originally commissioned to honor the Indian victors of the Battle of Little Bighorn and thus revise prevailing assumptions of Custer's defeat cum victory, the Indian Memorial was simultaneously beholden to presentist provisos regarding national unity. The contextual details of a nineteenth-century battle over human survival, property rights, and national destiny were marginalized in favor of a seamless contemporary narrative of once warring tribes—Arapaho, Arikara, Cheyenne, Crow, Lakota, and the armies of the United States—now reconciled as all Americans.

In 1997, landscape architects John R. Collins and Alison J. Towers, based in Philadelphia, were selected to design the Indian Memorial. In 2002 (more than a decade after the memorial was originally commissioned), $2.3 million in federal funds were authorized to build the new memorial and revamp the battlefield's visitor center, entry signs, and trailheads. Also in 2002, Colleen Cutschall, an Oglala Lakota artist originally from Pine Ridge, South Dakota, was chosen to design a sculptural component for the memorial titled *Spirit Warriors*.

The Indian Memorial is sited along a gradually curving ridgeline that originates at Last Stand Hill and the 7th U.S. Cavalry Monument, which remains the most visible and most visually imposing marker at the battlefield (fig. 6.7). Located about seventy-five yards northeast along the same bluff as the monument, but at a lower level, the Indian Memorial is a circular berm about thirty-five feet in diameter. Carved into the prairie in a configuration inspired by Plains Indian medicine wheel designs, the memorial also resembles minimalist earthworks by Robert Smithson and Robert Morris. Its inner walls, about ten feet in height, are made of rough granite blocks occasionally faced with polished stone tablets, on which are inscribed information about the various tribes involved in the Battle of Little Bighorn, the names of Indians who died, and reproductions of Native American pictographs and ledger drawings depicting the fight (fig. 6.8). Included among the panels are references

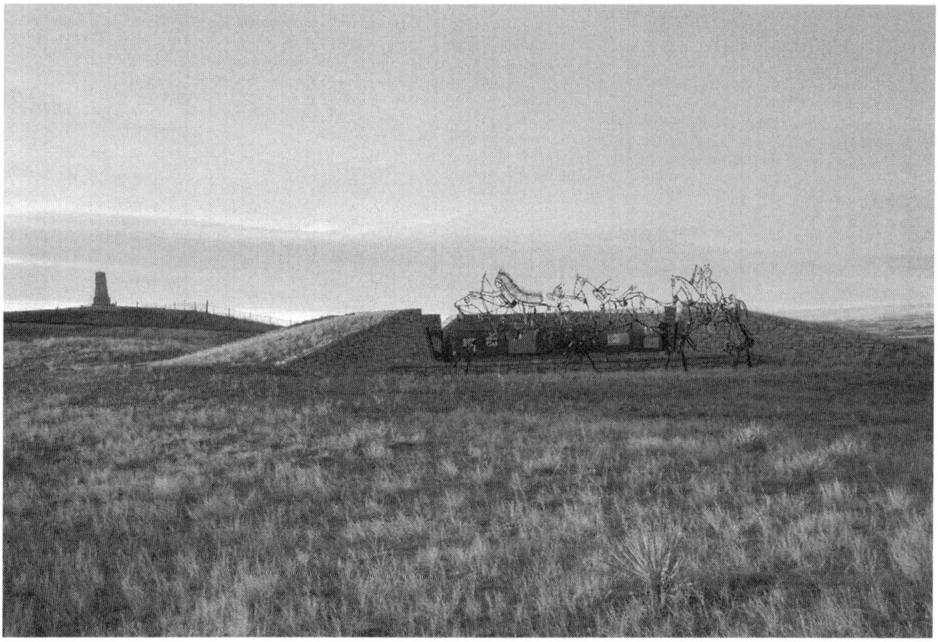

6.7. Overview of Indian Memorial, Little Bighorn National Battlefield Monument, Crow Agency, MT, dedicated 2003. Designed by John R. Collins and Allison J. Towers, Philadelphia. (©2005 Bob Reece. All rights reserved.)

to Crow and Arikara scouts who aided the 7th U.S. Cavalry and fought against the Arapaho, Cheyenne, and Lakota.

The north side of the memorial features Cutschall's *Spirit Warriors*, a sculpture based on Plains pictographs depicting three Indian warriors on horseback and a Native American woman handing one of them a war shield (fig. 6.9; see also fig. 0.10, p. 5). Cutschall remarks, "The figures are meant to possess a certain ethereal quality in contrast to the weight and substance of the earthen and stone mound form, as the sculpture must be respectful of the memorial design and of the battlefield as a whole."[40] The sculpture has become a focal point for battlefield visitors, some of whom attach tokens of remembrance such as flowers, ribbons, small bundles of sage or tobacco, dollar bills, and "Native Pride" caps (fig. 6.10). As with the National World War II Memorial, the NPS does not collect or save these memorial offerings.

Inside the Indian Memorial, opposite *Spirit Warriors*, is the Spirit Gate, a narrow passageway that visually frames the 7th Cavalry obelisk and Last Stand Hill (fig. 6.11). Described by the memorial's design team as a "cut in the earth" and a "symbol of the wound that this battle created between cultures," the Spirit Gate's stone-lined corridor includes

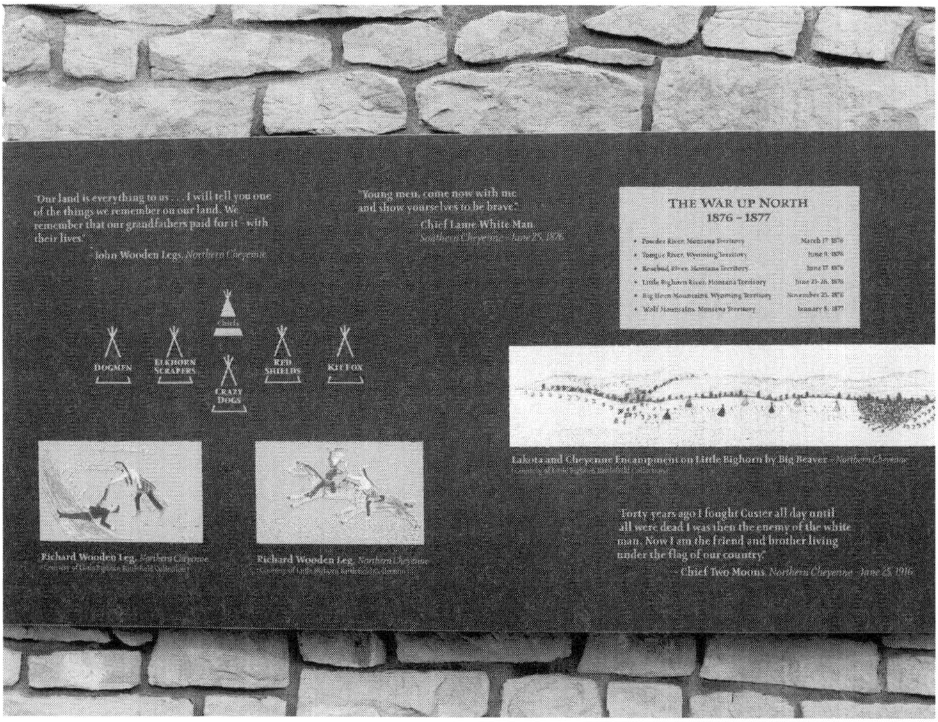

6.8. Indian Memorial, detail of text panels inside the monument. (Photo by the author.)

such emblematic features as the Pool of Tears and the Weeping Wall. As the artists explain, the rough-hewn walls of this "metaphorical gateway" trickle with water, thereby becoming "a weeping wall" which "remembers the humanity and culture that was lost long ago." Intended as a "visual dialogue" between the 7th U.S. Cavalry Monument and the Indian Memorial, the Spirit Gate serves to welcome the souls of "the Cavalry dead symbolically into the [Indian] memorial's circle" and to "symbolize the mutual understanding of the infinite all the dead possess."[41] This symbolic invitation clearly resonates with the memorial's "Peace Through Unity" theme, and its emphasis on reconciliation.

The Little Bighorn Battlefield National Monument drew about 295,000 visitors in 2007, many listening to park rangers describe the 1876 battle as a "clash of cultures" between Euro Americans and Native Americans who came together on the Montana prairie to defend their ways of life. Rangers also point out the "clash of cultures" among tribes of Plains Sioux who were historical enemies. The battle took place on Crow territory, through which Arapaho, Cheyenne, and Lakota were migrating, defying federal orders of reservation confinement and searching for grasslands and water for their horses. Sitting Bull, chief of the

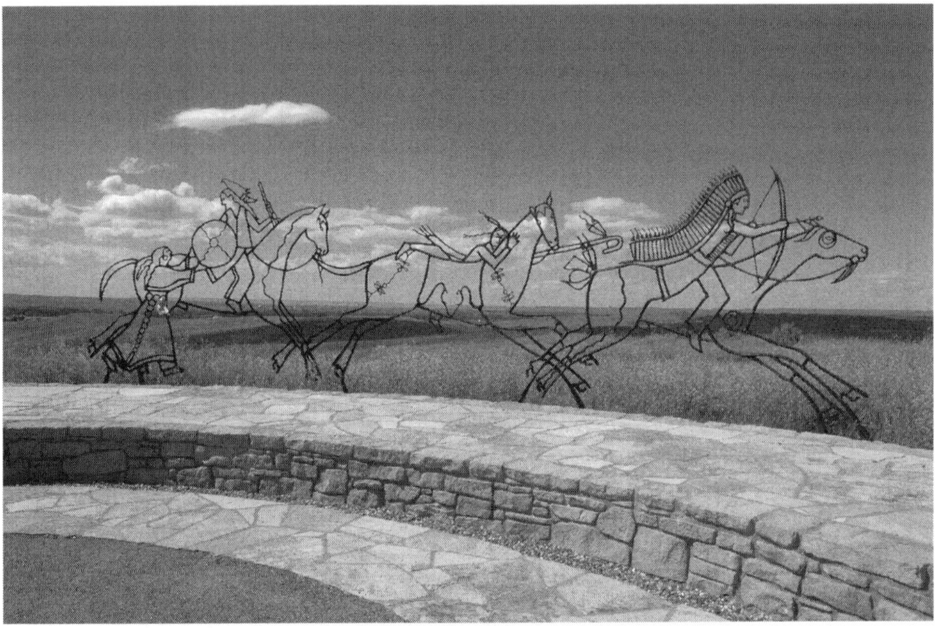

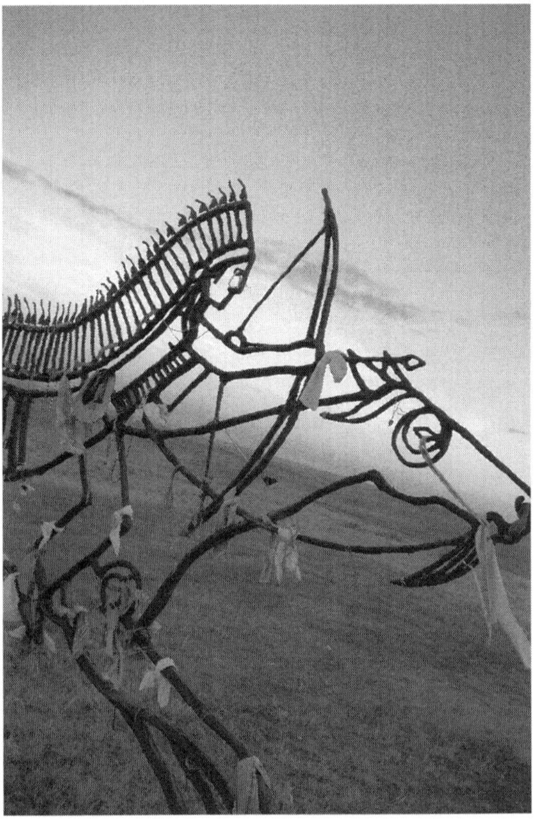

6.9. Colleen Cutschall, *Spirit Warriors*, 2003. Metal armature sculpted of bronzed steel rods. Indian Memorial, Little Bighorn National Battlefield Monument. (© 2005 Bob Reece. All rights reserved.)

6.10. Colleen Cutschall, *Spirit Warriors*, detail of items attached to the sculpture. (© 2005 Bob Reece. All rights reserved.)

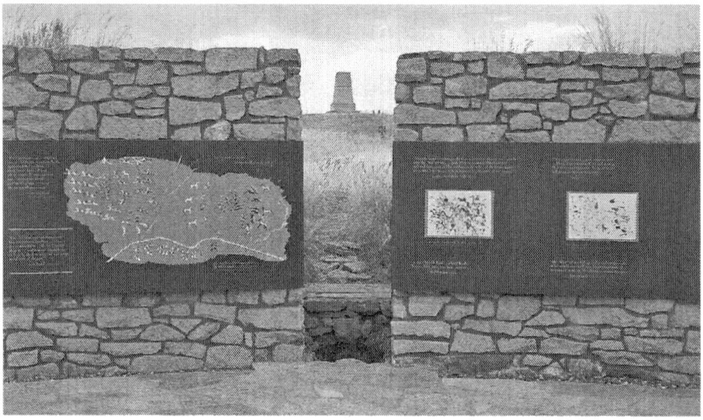

6.11. Spirit Gate, Indian Memorial. (Photo by the author.)

Hunkpapa Lakota, convinced the tribes to meet at Little Bighorn River (also called Greasy Grass) in a demonstration of mass force against the U.S. cavalry. Over the decades, the showdown at Little Bighorn took on mythical dimensions for both sides; for Native Americans, as Richard Slotkin observes, Little Bighorn symbolizes a unifying historical experience "whether their ancestors fought Custer or not, and despite the differences in their cultures, histories, and geographical homelands."[42] In recent years, the NPS's historical agenda has been to provide Little Bighorn visitors with the nuances of American Western conflict, rather than accommodating a standard narrative of good versus evil. In 2008, the battlefield's museum opened a new exhibit on Sitting Bull, featuring several personal items donated by his relatives.

But narratives of unity and patriotism help perpetuate Little Bighorn's mythological status in the national imaginary. While the Indian Memorial honors Native American warriors, it does not radically alter entrenched assumptions about the history of the American West and American Indians. Revising Little Bighorn's dominant symbolic resonance as a shrine to Custer is complicated by a larger national inability to reckon with the experiences of loss and defeat. The vanquished U.S. armies at the Alamo and Little Bighorn, for example, were long regarded as the moral victors in battles that actually advanced the nineteenth-century nation's territorial and political powers; such "defeat empathy," Wolfgang Schivelbusch contends, relieved losers from social humility and paved the way toward national recovery and renewal. This was especially true when the vanquished held moral authority on racial terms and the battles they lost were remembered as sites of racial difference: as sites where valiant Euro American martyrs fought to the finish against uncivilized and eventually displaced Mexicans and Indians.[43]

These racialized memories linger in certain memorials. The Indian Memorial's original design, for example, included two thirty-foot timber poles framing the Spirit Gate, each displaying colorful pennants. But this towering feature was eliminated, presumably because it challenged the 7th U.S. Cavalry Monument's dominating claim on American Western history. That is, while Custer "lost" the battle of Little Bighorn, he "gained" the West for the nation; while Plains Sioux "won" the battle of Little Bighorn, they soon lost their nomadic way of life and were incarcerated on federal reservations. Response to Indian victory at Little Bighorn was swift and U.S. military retaliation was brutal. The 1890 massacre at Wounded Knee, for example, was led by 500 troops attached to the 7th Cavalry, Custer's old outfit victorious in bloody revenge.[44] By 1900, the nation's indigenous population numbered less than 250,000 (compared with an estimated 8 to 12 million in the pre-contact Americas), and Custer and his men were celebrated as the moral heroes of Little Bighorn.

This is what the granite monument erected to them on Last Stand Hill was originally meant to convey. If the Indian Memorial challenges that meaning by celebrating the military victory of Native American warriors at Little Bighorn, it does not account for the loss of tribal autonomy and land rights that followed the battle. Forced to "be compatible" with the 7th U.S. Cavalry Monument, the new memorial is conflated with longstanding assumptions of national unity through violence and militarism. Restricted by the theme "Peace Through Unity," it fails to reckon with the myth of the Western frontier, and stereotypes about American Indians.

PICTURING INDIANS

Despite insistence that the 7th U.S. Cavalry Monument remain firmly planted on Last Stand Hill, memorials do get moved—and removed—in America. Fleeting fame plays some part: in 2006, California legislators voted to remove a statue of nineteenth-century Unitarian minister Thomas Starr King, one of two memorials representing the state in the U.S. Capitol's National Statuary Hall Collection (the other one depicts Father Junipero Serra), and replace it with a seven-foot bronze of Ronald Reagan. Likewise, Michigan's statue of Zachariah Chandler (a onetime mayor of Detroit) was replaced with one of Gerald Ford, and Kansas substituted a memorial to Samuel Glick (a former governor) with one to Dwight Eisenhower. "When kids come, they want somebody they recognize," remarks Barbara Wolanin, U.S. Capitol curator. "Some of the 19th-century people might have had a lot of pull in the state at the time, but people don't really know them much now."[45]

Perceptions of historical irrelevance parallel those of historical offense. In recent years, a San Francisco memorial to California pioneers has been repeatedly splashed with gallons of paint and targeted with rocks and bottles. Dedicated on Thanksgiving Day 1894, the eight hundred-ton, forty-seven-foot tall Pioneer Monument is protested today for its patriarchal history of the state—from its focus on white male founders (including land baron James Lick, who commissioned the memorial) to its scenes of Franciscan priests converting Native Americans. In 1995, the San Francisco Arts Commission received a letter from a representative of the American Indian Movement Confederation requesting "the removal of a monument which symbolizes the humiliation, degradation, genocide and sorrow inflicted upon this country's indigenous people by a foreign invader, through religious persecution and ethnic prejudice."[46] After considerable public debate, the commission countered by adding a plaque to the Pioneer Monument that reads, in part:

> At least 300,000 Native people—and perhaps far more—lived in California at the time of the first settlement in 1769. During contact with colonizers from Europe and the United States, the Native population of California was devastated by disease, malnutrition, and armed attacks. The most dramatic decline of the Native population occurred in the years following the discovery of gold in 1848.

Other memorials deemed similarly inappropriate in terms of Native American history and representation include a nineteenth-century statue in Mystic, Connecticut, commemorating the "heroic achievement" of John Mason, who led a 1637 massacre against the Pequot Indians. It was removed in 1995, although reinstalled a year later in nearby Windsor with a new plaque describing Mason's virtues as a colonial governor. In 1997, a nineteenth-century obelisk in Milford, Pennsylvania, erected to honor local Indian killer Tom Quick was attacked with a sledgehammer and reduced to rubble. In 2007, a ninety-foot obelisk commemorating the 1811 Battle of Tippecanoe in Indiana Territory, during which U.S. forces defeated a large confederation of Indians organized by Tecumseh and wiped out the Shawnee village of Prophet's Town, was spray painted with the messages "Justice will be served," "Give us back our spiritual capital," and "America Repent!" If stigmatized as vandalism, such acts of memorial defacement clearly aim at dismantling mainstream assumptions about American history.

Historical revision is most evident in memorial culture's additive strategies; indeed, today's heightened urge to memorialize certainly stems from vastly expanded understandings of who counts in American history. Challenging the "whites only" history of Richmond's Monument

Avenue, for example, a memorial to African American tennis star Arthur Ashe (born in Richmond in 1943) was added in 1996. Challenging the male-centric history of Yale University and of American memorial culture in general, Maya Lin's *Woman's Table*, a polished stone circle inscribed with a timeline of female enrollment at the university (lots of zeroes followed by gaining numbers), was dedicated on the campus in 1993, twenty-four years after the school began admitting female undergraduates.

Name changing is also an act of historical revision. In 1988, Nichols Hall, a student dorm at the University of Colorado, Boulder, named after a lieutenant governor who participated in the 1864 Sand Creek Massacre, was renamed Cheyenne-Arapaho Hall. In 2002, West Side Park in Modesto, California, was renamed Cesar E. Chavez Park. In 2003, Vanderbilt University dropped the word "Confederate" from its Confederate Memorial Hall (also a dorm), despite heated objections (and a legal battle) by the United Daughters of the Confederacy, which had originally funded the building in 1935.[47] In 2004, "Jap Rock," a popular diving spot near Boca Raton, Florida, was renamed Yamato Rock. By 2003, at least 730 streets in 39 states and Washington, D.C., had been named, or renamed, for Martin Luther King, Jr.[48]

These revisionist practices—changing names, adding plaques, moving memorials, adding new memorials—tend to occur when "traditional" forms of commemoration are found lacking or demeaning. Beginning in the 1970s, many American colleges and universities renamed their sports teams because of growing public perception that Indian stereotypes like "braves," "savages," "warriors," and "redskins" were derogatory. Birds and animals became the substitutes: in 1972, the Stanford Indians became the Stanford Cardinals; in 1994, the Ripon College Redmen became the Red Hawks; in 2006, the West Georgia Braves became the West Georgia Wolves. Professional sports teams downplayed the controversy, disingenuously claiming that their mock-Indian names, mascots, tomahawk chops, and war chants actually "honored" Native Americans. In a 1991 statement, the Washington Redskins declared that their name has long "reflected positive attributes of the American Indian, such as dedication, courage, and pride."[49] By extension, Little Bighorn's Indian Memorial remains similarly attached to stereotypes of Native Americans as fierce and formidable warriors. This stems of course from the memorial's battlefield context. But it also stems from the fraught dynamics of Native American representation.

Picturing Indians has historically been problematic in America. Whether represented as noble savages, courageous warriors, ethnographic exotics, spiritual seers, and / or—especially today—eco-guardians

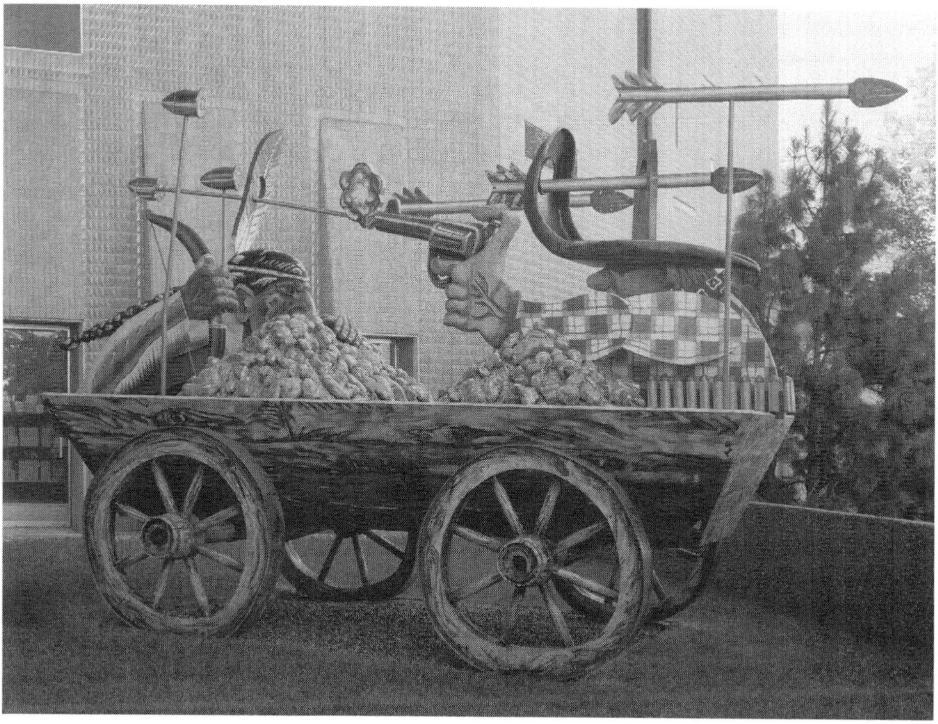
6.12. Red Grooms, *Shoot Out*, 1982. Painted aluminum. Denver Art Museum, Denver, Colorado. (© 2010 Red Grooms / Artists Rights Society [ARS], New York.)

of a troubled national landscape, American Indians have repeatedly been stereotyped to fit the changing needs, and as Phil Deloria explains, the "expectations" of non-Indians throughout American history.[50] In Denver in 1911, expectations that Indians were "savage redskins" forced Frederick MacMonnies to revise his Pioneer Monument, substituting a statue of Kit Carson for a Native American (see fig. 1.2, p. 21). In Denver in 1982, expectations that Indians are proud and serious warriors led to the removal of the satirical sculpture *Shoot Out* from a tract of land owned by the University of Colorado (fig. 6.12). Designed by pop artist Red Grooms, *Shoot Out* features the outlandish and oversized figures (actually torsos) of a cowboy and an Indian, battling atop a ramshackle wagon filled with gold-colored rocks (literally, fool's gold). The painted aluminum diorama is clearly a caricature: an irreverent lampoon of a B-grade Hollywood Western, a pop art version of Mel Brooks's 1974 Western spoof, *Blazing Saddles*. But to the one hundred people who attended a demonstration demanding its removal, some saying they would "paint it black" if the sculpture weren't removed, others saying they would use dynamite to get rid of it, *Shoot Out* was perceived as a disrespectful affront to Native Americans. As Shawnee Indian and political science professor Glenn Morris stated at the rally, "The winning of the West is not humorous, and resulted in a near genocide of the Native Americans."[51]

Contemporary expectations that Native Americans be remembered and represented as esteemed warriors are widespread; evident, for example, in the annual Crazy Horse Ride, a four-day horseback tribute to military veterans that mostly includes Oglala Lakota teens and adults and that organizers describe as "a way to say thank you to our warrior culture." Warrior expectations are found, too, in an art exhibition that the Native American Rights Fund sponsored in Boulder in 2007, titled Modern Day Warriors: Empowering the Young Voices of Native America, and in the speech that Mount Rushmore National Park Service superintendent Gerard Baker, a Mandan-Hidatsa, gave in 2008 encouraging Native American high school students with interests in journalism to become the "warriors" of a new information age.[52] While the United State's current wars and martial identity certainly inform a national vocabulary of warrior speech, they also accommodate assumptions that American Indians are especially, innately, warlike. Even today's weapons of war like Black Hawk and Apache helicopters, Tomahawk missiles, and the fictional "Winnebagos of Death" (mobile biological weapons facilities) that were the supposed harbingers of Iraq's weapons of mass destruction, are informed by these stereotypes.

Warrior expectations also explain any number of contemporary—and contested—memorials representing Native Americans. In 2004, several high school students in Rapid City, South Dakota, protested the public display of a ten-foot bronze sculpture of a dejected Indian male, dressed in buckskin leggings and standing with his hands tied behind his back, saying that the statue misrepresented Native Americans as "defeated people" (fig. 6.13). Located for twelve years in front of Prairie Edge, a popular Rapid City art gallery, *He Is, They Are* was designed by Glenna Goodacre in 1991, who later observed: "I'm not big on social messages in my art, but my thoughts back then were that the Native American experience was characterized first by being kicked off the land, followed by having their hands tied."[53]

Today, however, tropes of Native American victimization, and notions of an Indian subjectivity defined in terms of pain, suffering, loss, and defeat, are perceived as insults, especially among Indians and especially when pitted against tropes of national authority and masculine influence. Today, strength and steely anger are expected Indian tropes. Beginning in 2000, for example, Rapid City renamed itself "The City of Presidents" and began erecting dozens of memorials to the nation's chief executives on its downtown streets: a folksy nod on every corner to

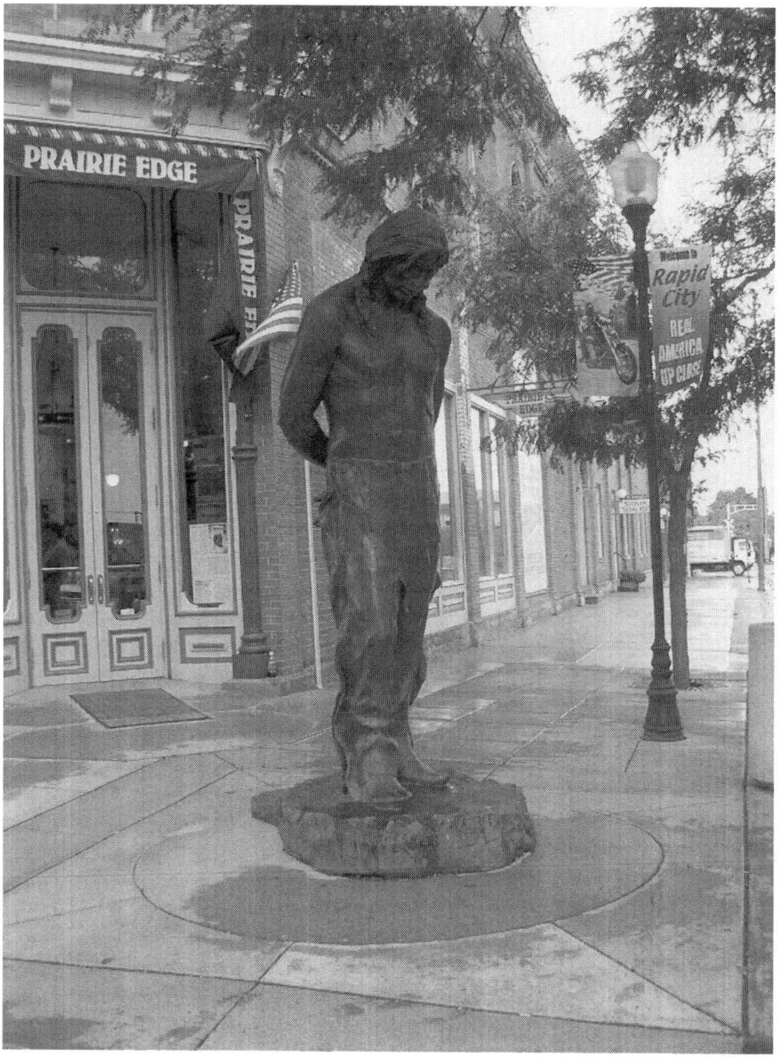

6.13. Glenna Goodacre, *He Is, They Are*, Rapid City, South Dakota, original design 1977. (Photo by the author.)

Mount Rushmore's colossal patriarchs, located about twenty-two miles away. Each June, Rapid City hosts the Festival of Presidents, a "two-day patriotic civic event" with a parade, free concerts, and "an official salute to our American heroes." Including a figure of a bound and dejected American Indian amidst lifelike bronzes of mighty national leaders like Andrew Jackson and Ronald Reagan incensed more than a few Rapid City residents. In 2008, store owners replaced *He Is, They Are* with a different statue representing a Lakota naming ceremony, explaining, "Some

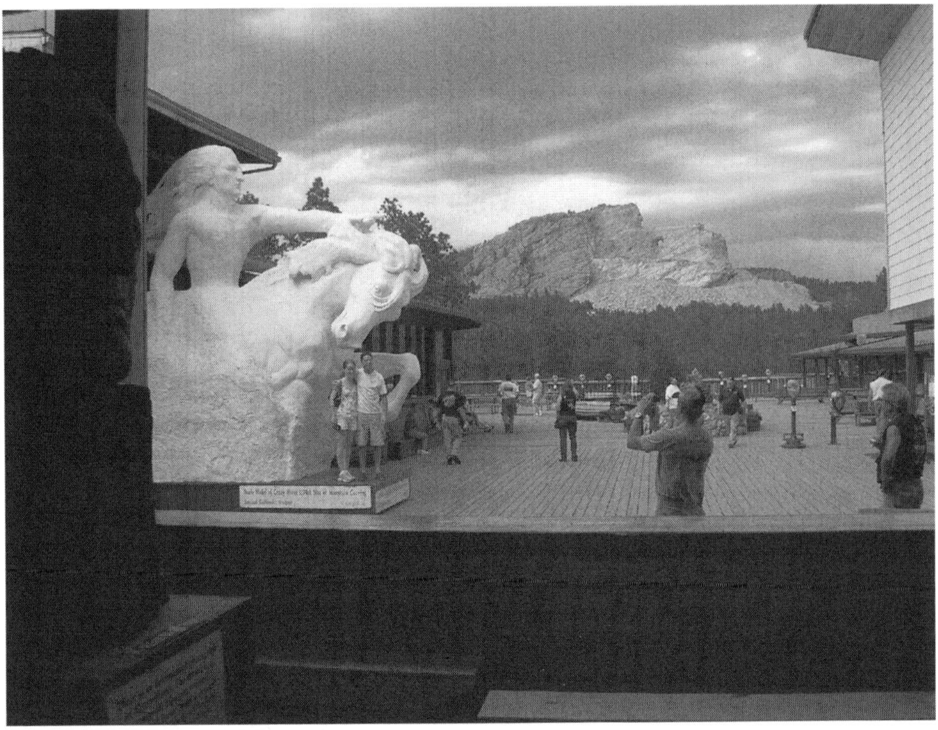

6.14. Korczak Ziolkowski, Crazy Horse Memorial, Crazy Horse, South Dakota, begun 1948. (Photo by the author.)

people in the area Native American community felt this statue was degrading to Native Americans. We regret that."[54]

The Crazy Horse Memorial is perhaps the best example, and certainly the biggest, of today's expected Indian-as-warrior image (fig. 6.14). Located in the Black Hills of South Dakota, about forty miles from Rapid City, seventeen miles from Mount Rushmore, and close to the town of Custer, the memorial was designed by Korczak Ziolkowski, who worked on Mount Rushmore in the late 1930s. It was inspired by Oglala Lakota Chief Henry Standing Bear, who originally asked Gutzon Borglum to add Crazy Horse's head to Mount Rushmore. After Borglum refused, he asked Ziolkowski to carve a separate mountain monument to the charismatic nineteenth-century Indian who helped win the Battle of Little Bighorn and is revered by Lakota as the guardian of the Black Hills. As Standing Bear reportedly said, "My fellow chiefs and I would like the White Man to know the Red Man has great heroes, too."[55]

Ziolkowski acquired the rights to the selected mountain and surrounding property through a mining claim—the exact sort of land grab and treaty violation that Crazy Horse and Plains Sioux fought against—

and began sculpting an image of the esteemed warrior who was killed in 1877. When several Lakota elders present at the memorial's opening ceremony (held after the mountain was first blasted with dynamite, in June 1948) protested that Ziolkowski's model didn't look anything like the Indian warrior they had fought aside at Little Bighorn, the artist replied that his memorial was meant to be a "symbolic" representation of "all Indians."[56] Far from finished (to date, only the eighty-seven-foot tall sculpted face of Crazy Horse has been carved), the memorial is basically an equestrian statue of a bare-chested Indian warrior astride an animated stallion: his long, unbraided hair and his horse's mane blowing in the wind, his left arm pointing across the landscape. It's an ironic gesture, really, since Crazy Horse is depicted pointing east—toward the Midwestern plains and away from the Black Hills (*Paha Sapa*) that the Lakota Sioux revere as sacred lands.

Visitors—more than one million in 2007—don't seem to notice. They pay $10 each (or $27 per carload) to tour the Crazy Horse Memorial Complex, which features a seventeen-foot (1/34th scale) model of the memorial, a box of rocks blasted from the mountain (one free per customer), and a big wooden deck with a magisterial view of Crazy Horse's carved head. Inside the complex are exhibitions of Native American art, displays of Ziolkowski's tools and early sculptures, a restaurant, and a gift shop. Tours start in the Orientation Center Theater with the twenty-minute video *Crazy Horse: Dynamite and Dreams*, which dramatizes Ziolkowski's risk-taking art practices, impressive engineering skills, mountain man persona, hyper-virility (father of ten), and particular American Dream: carving a huge mountain memorial that while ostensibly a generic symbol of an Indian warrior who represents "all" Native Americans, is, above all, a grandiose testimonial to Korczak Ziolkowski.

Crazy Horse, in fact, is fairly ephemeral at the Crazy Horse Memorial, and so are the Native Americans that the memorial claims to honor. The memorial is supposed to include a University of the American Indian, complete with a medical training center, sports complex, museum, and airport, although none of these facilities have been built. While some Indians display their artwork in the memorial's exhibition halls, relatively few Native Americans work at, or choose to visit, the Crazy Horse Memorial. When South Dakota held its twentieth annual Native American Day ceremonies at the memorial in October 2009, which included native dance and drum teams, the event was capped by a dynamite blast on the mountain. Indeed, the memorial especially serves as a shrine to Ziolkowski and his patronizing attitudes about Native Americans. "By carving Crazy Horse," he once explained, "If I can give back to the Indian some of his pride and create the means to keep alive his culture and heritage, my life will have been worthwhile."[57] Visitors are encouraged to "catch the vision—join the dream" by enrolling in the memorial's Blaster's Club ($500) or Crazy Horse League ($10,000). Much is made of Ziolkowski's do-it-yourself attitude, of how this "Storyteller in Stone" repeatedly refused offers of federal and state funding in order to maintain "personal control" over his "Crazy Horse Dream." Although Ziolkowski died in 1982 (and is buried in a tomb below the head of Crazy Horse's stallion), many of his children have resolved to see their father's dream come true.

Seemingly a counter-memorial to Mount Rushmore's tribute to America's elite, male, Anglo European leadership, Crazy Horse actually confirms what Carole Blair and Neil Michel call the "Rushmore effect" by repeating and reinforcing that popular memorial's national ethos of masculinity, militarism, and gigantism (fig. 6.15).[58] At an anticipated 563 feet tall and 641 feet long, the Crazy Horse Memorial is much touted for its massive scale: taller than the Washington Monument (555 feet), taller than the Statue of Liberty (305 feet), and so big that all four of Mount Rushmore's presidential heads could be lined up inside Crazy Horse's forehead (a weird statistic casually included in the memorial's publicity materials). Its audacious size reinforces Gutzon Borglum's self-promoting assertion that bigness equals greatness, and that his style of "colossal art," evident in big-scale memorials like Stone Mountain and Mount Rushmore, should become the standard "in all National expression." As Borglum declared in 1927, "we in America are developing in dimensions out of all proportions to the civilizations that inspired and freed us, but which long have cramped our style."[59]

If today's U.S. Commission of Fine Arts objects to rendering Martin Luther King, Jr., on "colossal art" terms, Ziolkowski enthusiastically adopted this "bigger is better" mantra. And someday his sculpture of the Lakota warrior who fought and defeated Custer may become the world's largest carved mountain memorial. In the meantime, Crazy Horse—like Mount Rushmore—privileges the personal striving and technological might of its memorial maker, perpetuating a romantic national narrative of hardworking and fiercely independent white men on the Western frontier, and their paternalistic habit of "speaking for" American Indians. "Interest in Indian culture," Vine Deloria commented in 1987, "has escalated beyond anyone's wildest imaginings," but "public attitudes toward Indians, sadly, have changed very little."[60]

Not everyone, of course, shares Ziolkowski's and Borglum's big-scale version of the American Deam. "We all hate Mount Rushmore," says Charmaine White Face, the Oglala Lakota chairperson of the Defenders of the Black Hills, a group dedicated to seeing that the provisions of the

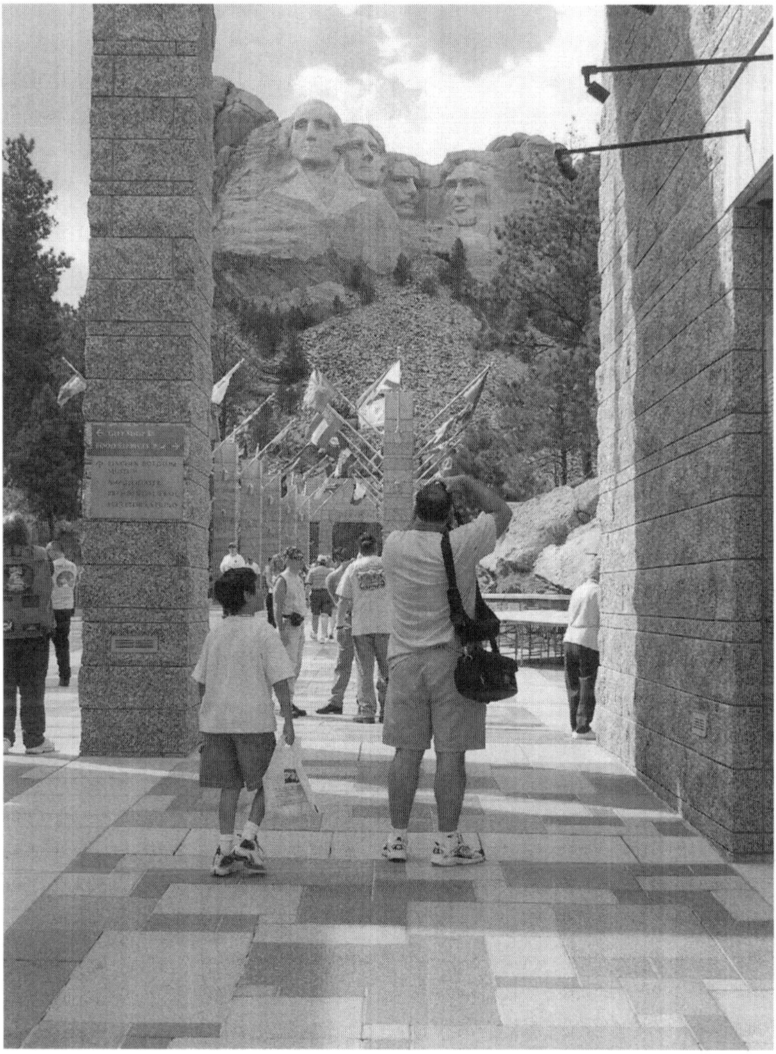

6.15. Gutzon Borglum, Mount Rushmore, Keystone, South Dakota, dedicated 1941. (Photo by the author.)

Fort Laramie Treaties of 1851 and 1868 (treaties that originally protected the Black Hills for exclusive use by the Lakota) are upheld by the federal government of the United States. "It's a sacred mountain that has been desecrated," she adds. "It's like a slap in the face to us—salt in the wounds—as if a statue of Adolf Hitler was put up in the middle of Jerusalem." Indian activist Charlotte Black Elk says much the same about the Crazy Horse Memorial: "The Lakota view, and my personal view, is the Black Hills are sacred and all should be treated in a respectful manner. Using dyamite to blast the mountain to bits to create the likeness of Crazy Horse is an endeavor the great warrior himself would have condemned." And Gerard Baker, the NPS head at Mount Rushmore, relates, "A lot of Indian people look at Mount Rushmore as a symbol of what white people did to this country when they arrived—took the land from the Indians and desecrated it . . . Indians are always telling me to blow up Mount Rushmore."[61]

Blowing up Mount Rushmore—as concise an expression of anger as any—has been a recurrent theme, and scheme, for decades. In 1972, the NPS received a threat that someone planned "to blow the Mount Rushmore Sculpture off the mountainside"; in 1975, a bomb destroyed a section of the national memorial's visitor center. (In 2005, the NPS spent $3 million on Homeland Security measures designed to protect the memorial from terrorism.) It's a subject with some popular culture currency, too: in Dan O'Brien's novel *Spirit of the Hills* (1986), Indian activists deliberate the pros and cons of bombing Mount Rushmore; in the movie *Skins* (2002), Pine Ridge Indian Reservation police officer Rudy Yellow Lodge honors his dying brother's last request by dumping gallons of pink paint on George Washington's chiseled face. The memorial gets obliterated in movies like *The Peacekeeper* (1997) and *10.5: Apocalypse* (2006).

Borglum and Ziolkowski made mountain memorials that are meant to be looked at, and revered, from a distance. Their defacement is, in part, an act of reclamation, or repossession. In the early 1970s, for example, members of AIM claimed Mount Rushmore and renamed it "Mount Crazy Horse." Camping near Teddy Roosevelt's head, they protested the federal government's treaty violations, "the faces of 4 white men on our land," and the changed status of the Black Hills as "a National Park for the 'white people.'" In 1987, members of Greenpeace and Earth First! similarly trespassed on Mount Rushmore, unfurling a hundred-foot banner stating "We the People Say No to Acid Rain" under George Washington's chin.[62] In 2009, Greenpeace returned to the memorial and draped a sixty-five-foot banner with a picture of Barack Obama and the words "America Honors Leaders, Not Politicians: Stop Global Warming" at the side of Lincoln's face.

These performances (or "symbolic occupations," as AIM called their takeover of Mount Rushmore) are deliberately kinesthetic: acts aimed at physically reclaiming an untouchable national memorial and revising its remote symbolism with supplemental meanings. AIM's actions were also iconoclastic, grounded in a refusal to venerate sacred national property by questioning the terms of its existence and demanding its return as sacred tribal landscape. For Plains Sioux for whom the Black Hills are hallowed ground, the locus of Lakota foundational memory and the embodiment of Lakota spirituality, both Mount Rushmore and the Crazy Horse Memorial are sacrilege and contesting their geo-spiritual violation is an act of faith. Yet for millions who visit these South Dakota memorials each year, faith is found in carved icons of national leaders and awesome acts of big-scale engineering. While the National Park Service maintains that Mount Rushmore represents "all Americans . . . our courage, dreams, freedom, and greatness," and the Crazy Horse Memorial is touted on similarly democraticizing terms, some publics disagree with what counts as sacred ground in America, and who and what defines national identity.

PEACE THROUGH UNITY

Native American anger about Mount Rushmore and the Crazy Horse Memorial relates to questions of representation and agency, and disagreements over dominant cultural assumptions that all Americans share the same understandings of public history and public space. Opposition to these memorials stems from perceptions of their inappropriate violation of sacred lands, and inauthentic assertions of national consensus. Native American resistance to a Wounded Knee memorial similarly stems from the fraught terms of cultural heritage, including conflicts about land ownership and the sanctity of space, and disputes over the interpretation of a past that for many indigenous Americans is very much a part of the present.

Establishment of a memorial at the site of the Wounded Knee Massacre has languished since it was approved by Congress in 1995. Anger among various Indian publics about federal government control of the site and surrounding lands and about being excluded from the proposed memorial's narrative and management, combined with suspicions that NPS obligations toward national consensus might eliminate references to Wounded Knee II (AIM's seventy-one-day siege at the site in 1973) or ban Lakota religious rituals that are regularly held at Wounded Knee, doom the memorial to failure. The fact that the U.S. government has never officially apologized for the 1890 massacre and continues to call it an "incident," is seen as further evidence of bad faith.

There are also fundamental disagreements over what constitutes cultural heritage and who is entitled to it. The establishment of national parks throughout the American West, Mark Spence explains, often entailed "the exclusion or removal of native peoples." The creation of Glacier National Park in Montana in 1910, for example, terminated Blackfeet (Siksika) rights to lands where they had hunted, fished, logged, and held religious ceremonies for several hundred years.[63] In 1995, members of the Wounded Knee Landowners Association dismissed Wounded Knee's authorization as a national park as a *wasichu* ("white man's") memorial that "got the story wrong" and threatened to turn "sacred ground into a tourist destination." As Mary Nolan observes in a discussion of the politics of memory in post-World War II Germany, "Building a monument to victims in the land of the perpetrators does not alter the irreconcilable differences between their pasts and the memories of them."[64]

The Sand Creek Massacre National Historic Site, on the other hand, dedicated in Kiowa County, Colorado, in 2007, demonstrates a contemporary NPS "commitment to cross-cultural integrity and cooperation."[65] Focused on the preservation and interpretation of the area's cultural and natural resources, the site includes a granite monument erected in 1960, visitor center, and hiking trails. Cheyenne and Arapaho are involved in the site's management plan, and certain sacred spaces and ceremonial areas, including a cemetery, are dedicated to Indian visitors. In 2008, the Colorado legislature issued a formal apology for the Sand Creek Massacre, which it compared to the Jewish Holocaust, and the United Methodist Church donated $50,000 to the development of a Sand Creek research and learning center as a gesture of atonement for the actions of Methodist pastor Colonel John Chivington, the "fighting preacher" who led the November 1864 massacre. Today, the 2,400-acre site hosts an annual Spiritual Healing Run during which Indian sprinters, some of them descendents of the Cheyenne and Arapaho who were murdered at Sand Creek, trek the 100-mile distance to Denver. The run ends at *Wheel*, a memorial designed by Cheyenne-Arapaho artist Edgar Heap of Birds that utilizes ten metal trees to form a modern day medicine wheel, and features the Cheyenne words "NAH-KEV-HO-EYEA-ZIM," or "We are always returning back home again" on a nearby wall (fig. 6.16).

How should Americans remember the nation's violent dispossession of indigenous peoples? Native American genocide is still largely a taboo subject in America: repressed in the historical narrative, and overlooked when contemporary mass killings like those at Virginia Tech in 2007 are called the "worst" in U.S. history. It is not entirely invisible. "Spectral Indians" haunt American literature from Nathaniel Hawthorne to Stephen King, Renée Bergland argues, unsettling conventional ideas about national purpose, citizenship, and belonging.[66] Likewise, America's commemorative cultures are increasingly attuned to the nation's bloody history of Indian removal; in recent years, roadside signs and granite memorials have been erected tracing the forced dispossession of Potawatomi from Indiana to Kansas in 1838 (fig. 6.17).

America's Indian memorials are similarly haunted and ultimately subverted or sustained by the contradictions of American nationhood.

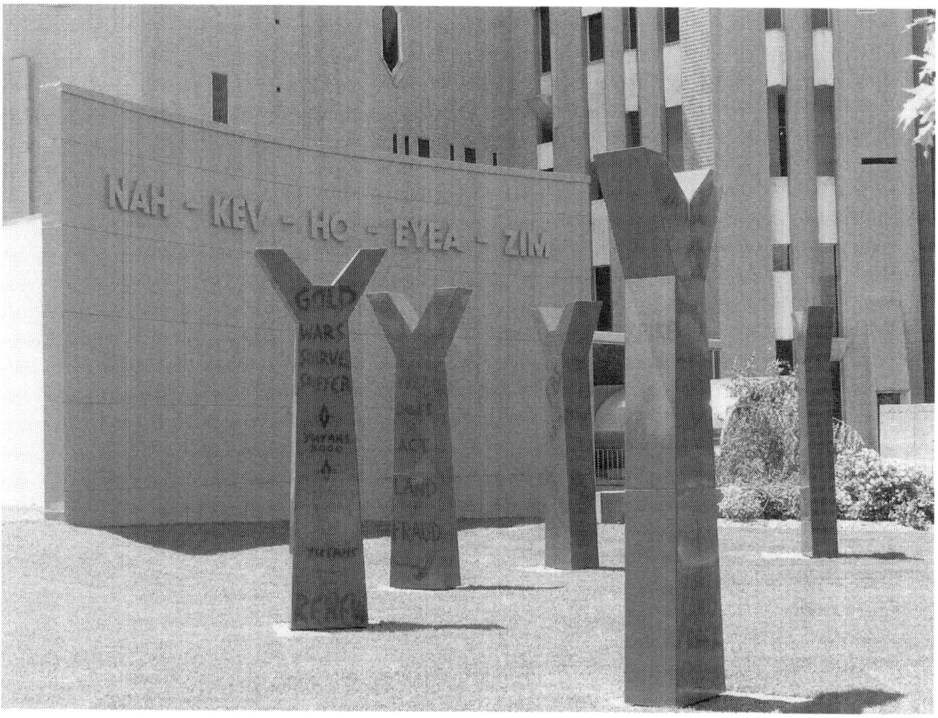

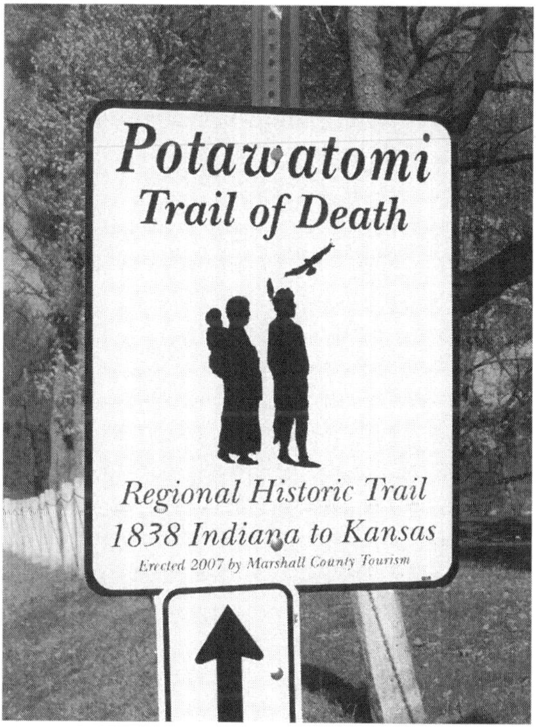

6.16. Edgar Heap of Birds, *Wheel*, 2007. Denver Art Museum, Denver, Colorado. (Photo by the author.)

6.17. Roadside marker for the Potawatomi Trail of Death at U.S. Highway 31 and Peach Road, Marshall County, Indiana. Marker erected 2007. (Photo by the author.)

Wounded Knee's commemoration is unlikely because of seemingly irreconcilable differences over what to remember (a massacre or an "incident") and who is remembering. Sand Creek's commemoration resulted from alliances among multiple publics including tribal representatives, NPS staffers, landowners, and politicians. At the Little Bighorn Battlefield National Monument, an admittedly different, if bittersweet, site of indigenous victory, the Indian Memorial was created to pay tribute to Indian warriors, "to give equal honor and equal dignity to all the warriors who were involved," Senator Ben Nighthorse Campbell declared at dedication ceremonies in 2003.[67] Following the theme "Peace Through Unity," it commemorates an historical moment of nineteenth-century harmony among different American Indian tribes. As Oglala Lakota Enos Poor Bear, Sr. stated:

> During the time of our elders, things were better for our Indian people than they are today. The way that our elders made things better was through unity. Unity of purpose; unity of dedication; and unity of effort. When we look back over the pages of time, we observe that all the major accomplishments of Indian people were brought about when unity was present. The major victory that our people enjoyed here at this very battlefield was the result of a unified effort among Indian people . . . If this Indian memorial is to serve its total purpose, it must not only be a tribute to the dead; it must contain a message for the living.[68]

"Peace Through Unity" is an odd theme for a war memorial. It fails to explain what prompted the huge demonstration of tribal unity at Little Bighorn in June 1876, and it paints a picture of tribal togetherness that overlooks a long history of Plains Indian rivalry—and North American territoriality in general. The recent placement, for example, of headstones marking where Cheyenne and Lakota warriors fell on the battlefield, which are inscribed "Died in Defense of His Homeland," enrages some Crow whose "homeland" was Little Bighorn and who view other Indians as invaders.[69] While the Indian Memorial aims to countenance such bad feeling it also feeds a false consciousness of a Native American rainbow coalition that lumps all Indians together, much like Ziolkowski's sculpture of Crazy Horse. This manufactured unification and assumption of indigenous consensus serves to reinforce the separation, and distinction, of the Indian Memorial and the 7th U.S. Cavalry Monument—Native Americans on one side, "real" Americans on the other. Despite its laudable goals of "equal honor and equal dignity," the Indian Memorial is a prime example of how, as Wendy Brown argues, "well-intentioned contemporary political projects and theoretical postures inadvertently redraw the very configurations and effects of power that they seek to vanquish."[70]

Memorial mania is especially marked by rights claims and demands for respect: the Indian Memorial at Little Bighorn, like many contemporary memorials, was created in order to confer recognition to previously ignored or underconsidered historical subjects. Recognition plays a major role in contemporary American political culture and is central to understandings of both personal and collective identity. Indeed, the politics of recognition at Little Bighorn, which included changing the name of the battlefield and building a memorial to those who won the battle, center on granting and/or restoring dignity and respect to Native Americans who were, in the destructive unfolding of American Western colonization and exploitation, stripped of both. Recognition and respect accommodate rights-claims; Little Bighorn and Sand Creek are claimed as sacred sites by American Indians, and their memorial management today by the National Park Service indicates that these claims are now honored in the national narrative.

While this is necessary, it is not sufficient; the problem with rights discourse, Brown observes, is that it may simply be a "regulatory discourse, a means of obstructing or coopting more radical political demands." Indeed, the making of the Indian Memorial, as the rangers at the Little Bighorn site remark, has "really taken the pressure off" public demands over the past few decades that the National Park Service "do something that tells the other side of the story." While the new memorial tells the "other side" it is limited by a mandate of all-American unity, especially expressed in post-9/11 America in terms of national allegiance and patriotism.[71] While Indians are now included in Little Bighorn's story, their struggle for tribal self-determination has become consumed by a dominating national narrative of heroic nineteenth-century all-American frontier warfare. There is no hint, save the occasional button left at the *Spirit Warriors* sculpture reading "The Black Hills are NOT FOR SALE," that land rights and civil rights remain key political priorities for contemporary Native Americans.

In 1996, Gerard Baker, then NPS superintendent at Little Bighorn, said the site needed to be more visibly attuned to the emotional and experiential needs of Native American visitors. (Visitation increased 21 percent following the monument's renaming in 1991.) "When Indian people come here, they cry and they get mad for the loss of that way of life, that freedom. It's something we'll never get back. That's what this place is for," Baker remarked, adding that he felt that the newly commissioned Indian Memorial should be located on the same hill as the 7th U.S.

Cavalry Monument. For the site as a whole, Baker imagined a "much-improved infrastructure" including "a better library, a better interpretive program. I want to leave behind me a better all-around environment for everybody who visits here, one that shows what happened before those two days in June."[72] On the battle's 120th anniversary, Baker organized an "Attack at Dawn" ceremony, during which Indians rode horses to the 7th U.S. Cavalry Monument and "counted coup" by hitting it with a stick, symbolically reenacting a traditional battlefield ritual of bravery.

Custerphiles were outraged and demanded that the NPS fire Baker. "Gerard has a crusade going, the Indianization of the battlefield," bristled Bob Wells, editor of The Custer / Little Bighorn Battlefield Advocate, a blog dedicated to "fighting grave desecration, 'political correctness,' racism, and overdevelopment at the Little Bighorn (formerly Custer) Battlefield National Monument." "He's gone way overboard," Wells added. "It would be a serious mistake to plant the Indian Memorial anywhere near the memorial of the 7th Cavalry. The magnetism and dignity of that monument is that it occupies the hill."[73]

Today, the 7th U.S. Cavalry Monument maintains its "magnetism" atop Last Stand Hill, and the Indian Memorial is sited on a lower register seventy-five yards away. If this compromise satisfied some Custer buffs (including Wells), others blast the new memorial as a radically politicized affront to their canonical histories of the American West. "They're trying to make this over into an Indian battleground," one park visitor, a retiree from Florida, fumed after the site was renamed. "You can't change history, which is what they're trying to do! These people were savages!"[74]

Nor are all American Indians pleased with the Indian Memorial. Some don't want any federally managed narratives of their history; it is "a dishonor and even sacrilegious to put an Indian memorial in the invaders' graveyard," contends Indian activist Richard Williams.[75] Others oppose the inclusion of references to Arikara and Crow scouts who sided with the 7th Cavalry, or the use of the term "Sioux" rather than "Lakota" in the memorial's reference panels and publicity materials. Some protest its design by non-Indians; still others are "disappointed" by its inauthenticity. "They glamorized the whole thing," complained Dennis King, vice chairman of the Oglala tribe in Pine Ridge, South Dakota, at the 2003 dedication ceremonies. "They took away our finest hour and put up a monument that isn't us." He added, "If you didn't know about our culture, you'd think this memorial reflects us spiritually; you'd think this is some sacred design of the Sioux nation, the Cheyenne, the Arapaho, which it ain't. They just Hollywood-ized it."[76] Likewise, Rosalie Little Thunder, a Lakota teacher from Rapid City, observes: "We always believe in honoring the ancestors and the sacrifices they made. However, we had extreme racism and genocide in those times, and that remains. To ignore the oppression somehow gives me a feeling that the memorial is very superficial."[77]

And Russell Means, who helped jumpstart the Indian Memorial with AIM's guerrilla theater performances in the 1970s, called the new memorial "absolutely disrespectful" because of the role that the Spirit Gate plays in welcoming the souls of the 7th Cavalry's fallen soldiers.[78] True to form, Means disrupted the new memorial's dedication ceremonies, which were attended by four thousand people and featured speeches by dignitaries such as interior secretary Gale Norton, Montana governor Judy Martz, Ben Nighthorse Campbell, and tribal leaders. Aimed at honoring veterans of "all wars," the dedication included a flyover by two Black Hawk helicopters, a color guard from a 7th Cavalry unit stationed at Ford Hood, Texas, and a tribute to Private Lori Piestewa, a Hopi woman who was the first American Indian killed in the Iraq War. The ceremony opened with a Crow woman singing "God Bless the U.S.A.," the patriotic Lee Greenwood song that filled the airwaves after 9/11 with the lyrics "I'm proud to be an American / where at least I know I'm free / And, I won't forget the men who died / who gave that right to me." Seizing the podium during a ceremonial lull, Means delivered a rambling fifteen-minute speech to a largely receptive crowd, saying "I want to tell you a little of the history here before the government revises it" and lampooning the 7th U.S. Cavalry Monument as "the phallic symbol up on the hill." But Means also used the occasion to proclaim the fundamental "American-ness" of American Indians, saying that in contrast to Irish Americans, Japanese Americans, and Latino Americans, "We put 'American' before our ethnicity," adding, "Americans have to put America first. That's when we develop a culture together."[79]

To a large extent, the Indian Memorial embodies the sentiment that in today's America "we" are all warriors. The unified culture that Means, the National Park Service, and many visitors to the Little Bighorn Battlefield National Monument collectively embrace is a culture of conflict and hostility, oddly articulated as "Peace Through Unity." When the design for the Indian Memorial was first announced, Patty Limerick wrote that she "imagine[d] a different kind of memorial—one in which no point of view dominates." Responses to her op-ed were heated: "I look forward to future proposals from revisionist historians on the construction of memorials to the Mexican dead at the Alamo and the Japanese at Iwo Jima," groused Dan Pollak of New Jersey, while Eric Cheyfitz, a professor at Cornell, chided Limerick for downplaying the "complexity" of American Western history by characterizing the Battle of Little Bighorn as an "event" that "was not the least bit coherent or clear."[80] However much it has been mythologized, Little Bighorn was an explicit demonstration of the imperialist agenda of manifest destiny, an act of war against an indigenous population that fought back and "won" this particular battle. The key to its commemoration is not to relinquish a point of view, but to articulate the dynamics of nineteenth-century American Western warfare, to recognize the devastating consequences of its violence for victims and victors alike, and to imagine the transformative possibilities of historical memory.

COUNTER-MEMORIALS, ICONOCLASM, AND HISTORICAL REVISION

How can memorials inform multiple American publics about the nuanced trajectories of American history and prepare them for revised understandings of national identity and purpose? Indeed, *can* memorials do this? Critics such as James Young and Annie Coombes, and artists including Sam Durant and Edgar Heap of Birds, offer "counter-memorials" that posit new ways of thinking about memory and history. Young coined the term "counter-monument" in his writing on modern commemoration in Germany, defining projects aimed at reckoning with Germany's twentieth-century past, including the Holocaust and Fascism, as "brazen, painfully self-conscious memorial spaces conceived to challenge the very premise of their being." Counter-monuments like Jochen Gerz and Esther Shalav-Gerz's *Harburg Monument Against Fascism*, a twelve-meter lead-plated stele that was erected near Hamburg in 1986 and then slowly sank and disappeared into the ground over the next five years, not only challenged assumptions of the traditional monument's presence and permanence but insisted that commemorative meaning be determined by—instead of for—the public. Engaged in what Michel Foucault defined as an oppositional "counter-memory," the counter-monument ideally encourages public agency and articulates the complexities of modern history. The Gerzes' project, for example, invited visitors to write their names and anything else they wanted on the monument before it disappeared, and thus "commit" themselves "to remain vigilant" in remembering the German experience of Fascism.[81]

We may question how—or if—a disappeared, or invisible, monument can prompt public memory, although ephemeral and impermanent memorials play strategic roles in some non-Western societies.[82] But the processual and discursive terms that define the counter-monument are pertinent in memorial mania. A discursive—meaning multifocal and deliberative—sensibility certainly shaped Juan de Oñate's contentious commemoration in Albuquerque during four hundredth anniversary

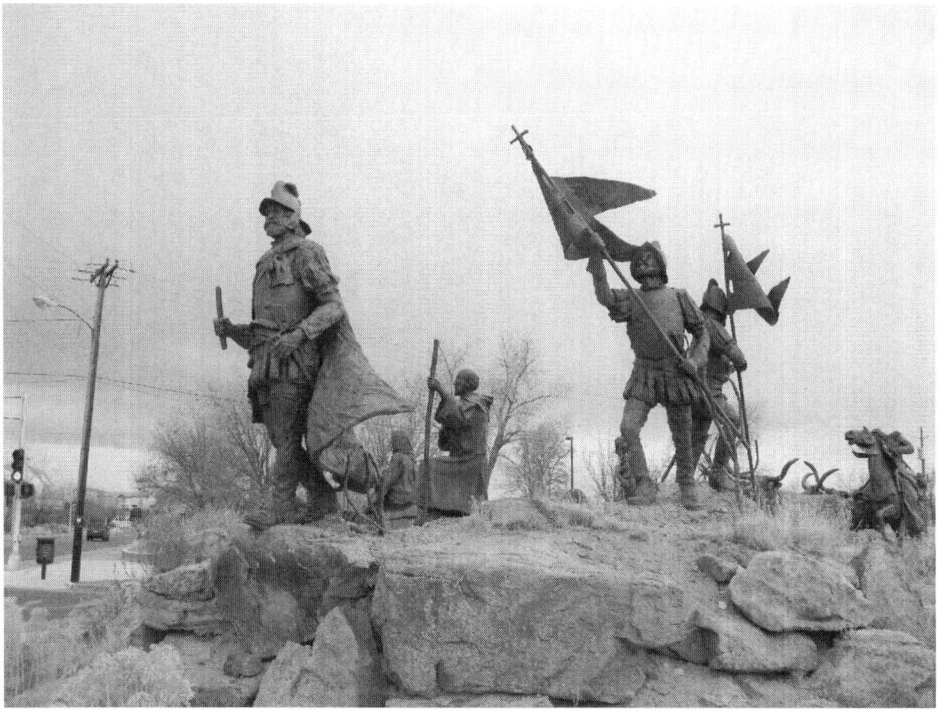

6.18. Betty Sabo and Reynaldo Rivera, *La Jornada*, Cuarto Centenario Memorial, Albuquerque, New Mexico, dedicated 2005. (Photo by the author.)

celebrations of his "discovery" of New Mexico. In May 1997, the Albuquerque Arts Board was asked to honor Oñate with a modest $10,000 bronze bust; nine years later, the city unveiled a much more elaborate and expensive $600,000 project featuring sixteen life-sized bronze figures, various animal sculptures, a sixty-foot earthwork, and detailed text panels (fig. 6.18).[83] The memorial's extensive nine-year process involved heated public debate—including angry protests by Pueblo Indians attending Albuquerque City Council hearings with signs reading "Oñate? My foot!"—and the collaboration of three different artists representing the region's dominant ethnic groups: Sonny Rivera (Hispanic), Betty Sabo (white), and Nora Narajo-Morse (Tewa, Santa Clara Pueblo). Civic deliberation eventually determined that if the sixteenth-century conquistador was to be honored at all, a revised story must be told: one that shifted from a worshipful focus on Oñate to the consequences of Spanish colonization.

Installed in 2005 in front of the Albuquerque Museum, close to the city's Old Town district, the Cuarto Centenario Memorial occupies 33,500 square feet and consists of two related narratives: *La Jornada* (The

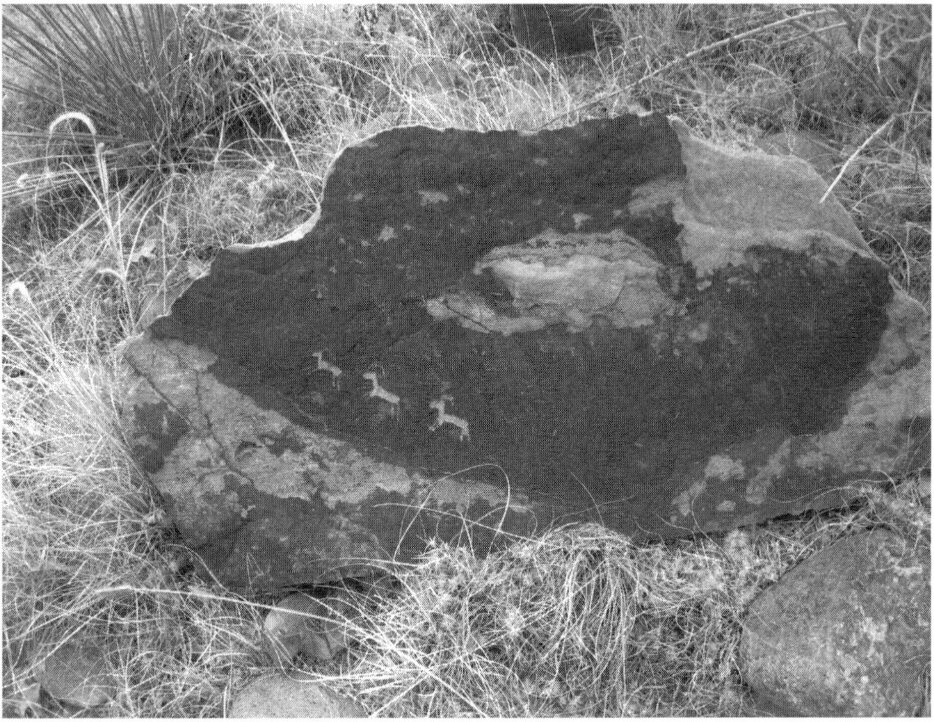

6.19. Nora Naranjo-Morse, *Numbe Whageh*, Cuarto Centenario Memorial, Albuquerque, New Mexico. (Photo by the author.)

Journey) and *Numbe Whageh* (Our Center Place, or The Environment). The first story details Oñate's trek through Nuevo Mexico with soldiers, priests, horses, longhorn cattle, and sheep; while a bronze statue of Oñate leads the group, the entire section is contained within a low retaining wall displaying bronze plaques naming the Spanish families that accompanied him in 1598. The second story consists of a spiral earthwork landscaped with local plants and rocks, some featuring pictographs significant to the Acoma, Hopi, Santa Clara, and Taos Pueblo Indians of New Mexico (fig. 6.19).

While linked, the two stories are stylistic opposites.. If the project recounts the founding of sixteenth-century New Mexico, it does not resolve New Mexico's subsequent four hundred years of historical trauma. Indeed, the memorial's oppositional narratives frame the state's contentious history of racial and religious relationships, and allude to the angry dynamics of its current sociocultural politics. The lengthy, controversial process of making the memorial generated "useful dialogue among citizens," observes Arturo Sandoval, a key player in Albuquerque's Cuarto

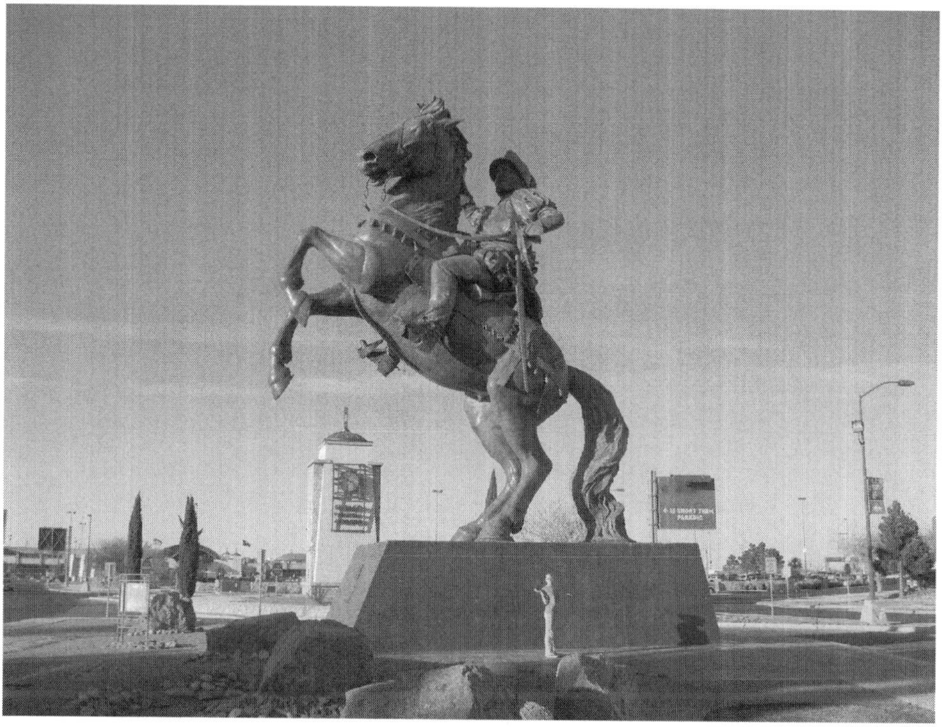

6.20. John Houser, *The Equestrian*, El Paso, Texas, dedicated 2007. (Photo by the author.)

Centenario Planning Committee.[84] Today, teachers use it as a starting point to discuss New Mexico's saga of ethnic and racial conflict; the memorial also lends itself to informed conversations about the state of contemporary race and economic relations in the American Southwest and especially along the U.S-Mexico border.

The discursive potential of other Oñate memorials, on the other hand, is less evident, mostly because they are honorific statues, not counter-memorials. In April 2007, *The Equestrian* was dedicated in El Paso: a monumental bronze of Oñate decked out in full conquistador regalia and waving a copy of *La Toma*, the legal document by which Spain justified its seizure of lands north of the Rio Grande (fig. 6.20). Commissioned by the Twelve Travelers Foundation (a local history booster club), the statue was designed by John Houser, whose father (Ivan Houser) was an assistant on Mount Rushmore. Like Borglum's grandiose memorials, El Paso's 34,000-pound, 36-foot-tall sculpture (45 feet counting its painted cement base) is celebrated for its size ("the biggest equestrian bronze in the world") and impressive display of technical skill. "I think it's the culminating dream of every sculptor to do a really important equestrian statue," Houser asserts, adding, "It's one of the most difficult things that can be done."[85] Originally meant for installation on the U.S.-Mexico border—the artist apparently envisioned it as a southwestern version of the Statue of Liberty—and then in downtown El Paso near the city's library and history museum, the $2 million statue now stands in front of El Paso International Airport. Originally named after Oñate, it was renamed *The Equestrian* by the El Paso City Council in 2003 after heated public protests that the memorial glorified a "war criminal and butcher" who "caused so much grief, pain, and destruction."[86]

Naïvely assuming that a colossal statue of Oñate would be universally—let alone regionally—admired, Houser and his patrons were taken aback by the controversy. "It's like saying Columbus didn't discover America," one backer complained. New Mexico historian Marc Simmons took an angrier approach, calling the El Paso City Council "utterly spineless" for erasing Oñate's name from the memorial. "They absolutely capitulated and collapsed in the face of opposition," Simmons said, adding: "History isn't for sissies. If you made statues only of saints, you'd have no statues." Removing Oñate's name may relinquish *The Equestrian* of critical historical perception and responsibility, but Acoma artist Maurus Chino and other regional residents say they easily glean "the savagery and brutality that is part of our history" in its dominating presence. Chino wants the memorial removed and wants a public apology from Houser, who he says "has never taken responsibility for glorifying such a violent act." Filmmakers John Valdez and Christina Ibarra, whose documentary *The Last Conquistador* (2008) charts the memorial's fraught development, agree: "Houser was so focused on making his own place in history that he was blind to the social implications of his work," remarks Ibarra. And Valdez observes, "This statue has certainly gotten people talking. No, it hasn't gotten them talking: it's created a situation where people are yelling, where people are angry, screaming at each other, crying."[87]

Worried about a repeat of the contentious nine-year battle over Albuquerque's Oñate memorial or the vandalism of Alcalde's Oñate memorial in 1998, El Paso politicos renamed and relocated *The Equestrian* to downplay its disruptive potential. Rather than canceling the project (which several city council members advocated) or reworking the laudatory statue into something more productive in terms of civic memory, El Paso hid its big bronze elephant out by the airport. Dedicated as an anonymous horseman (none of the memorial's explanatory texts even mention Oñate's name), and protected by the airport's forces of Homeland Security, *The Equestrian* is simply a huge statue of "some Spanish guy on a horse," some locals say. Originally intended as an affirming marker of civic identity and an El Paso tourist hook, the memorial is usually deserted.

Neither *The Equestrian* nor Alcalde's Oñate statue reckon with the sociopolitical and cultural dynamics of American southwestern history in ways that might "challenge the very premise of their being," although chopping off Oñate's foot might be considered a counter-memorial act. Indeed, vandalism is a kind of discourse—if a form of "semiotic disobedience" that has never been viewed as "legitimate speech under the laws of property, intellectual property, or First Amendment theory" in the United States.[88] (Defacing the American flag, on the other hand, is protected by the Supreme Court as a symbol of constitutionally protected free speech.) As iconoclasm (literally, breaking images), and hence as assaults on images considered offensive and inappropriate, acts of vandalism have occurred throughout the history of America's statue and memorial mania. In the 1880s, various parties vandalized a granite monument erected at the site where British spy Major John André was hung in 1780 in Tappan, New Jersey. In 1900, unknown parties defaced an elaborate granite canopy housing Plymouth Rock, the venerated (and entirely fabricated) landfall of the Mayflower pilgrims in Massachusetts. In 1970, members of AIM and Native Americans from twenty-five different tribes painted Plymouth Rock red then buried it in several inches of sand.[89] In 2007–2008, 9/11 memorials in San Francisco; Staten Island; New York; Freehold Township, New Jersey; Arcadia, Wisconsin; and Emmett, Idaho, and an Iraq War memorial in Mount Pleasant, Michigan, were vandalized.

In recent decades, a number of Confederate monuments have been defaced: in 2004, the Lee Memorial on Richmond's Monument Avenue was spray painted with the words "Death to Nazis" and "Happy Birthday MLK;" also in 2004, a Confederate memorial in Charleston was spray painted with the words "Kill Whitey" and "genocidal" and marked with anarchy symbols. In 2006, a standing-soldier memorial in Brunswick, Georgia, was targeted with bricks; in 2007, the faces and hands of the soldiers depicted on Alabama's Confederate Memorial, located on the grounds of the state capitol in Montgomery, were painted black and the letters and numbers "N.T. 11 11 31" were painted on the monument's base (referencing the execution of Nat Turner, who was hung on November 11, 1831, for his leadership in a slave rebellion). Dixie defenders like the Sons of Confederate Veterans call such vandalism "heritage violation" and demand that it be prosecuted as a hate crime against white southerners—although in Montgomery, the vandals were three white teenagers. Yet as David Lowenthal explains, the "creed of heritage" is a historical fiction that "thrives on ignorance and error" and "falsified legacies."[90] Contemporary neo-Confederates who argue that rebel memorials (and rebel battle flags) represent "heritage not hate," and should be venerated as historically neutral symbols of southern cultural identity, deny the secessionist South's unforgivable defense of slavery: which is why these memorials were made and what they mean.

Memorials are defaced and despoiled when the histories and ideologies they embody, such as the Southern Confederacy's violation of human rights, are deemed illegitimate and invalid. Vandalism might be seen as purposeful anger, a sign of revisionist intentions; indeed, Alfred Gell theorized that iconoclasm was a form of artistic agency. Likewise, Michael Taussig sees defacement as vengeful truth telling, as a way of unmasking the secrets that lie at the core of power. "Defacement is like Enlightenment," he writes. "It brings insides out, unearthing knowledge, and revealing mystery."[91] For these critics, iconoclasm is a transgressive act aimed at unveiling and destabilizing fundamental narratives of state and/or religious power: chopping off Oñate's foot, for example, in order to challenge Spanish colonial land claims and foundation myths in the American Southwest.

Vandalism is also, of course, an act of intolerance and can become the performance of political authority whereby the ideologically charged monuments, memorials, and sacred spaces that represent the "other" are attacked and destroyed in order to forge new, or different, regional and/or national identities: razing Native American *kivas*, for example, in order to repudiate Pueblo Indian religious and cultural authority, and replacing them with Spanish colonial missions. In this regard, "cultural cleansing" and ethnic cleansing are intrinsically related, as Robert Bevan explains in a discussion of Germany's 1938 Kristallnacht and other highly calculated, highly symbolic, acts of material/memorial destruction. "The link between erasing any physical reminder of a people and its collective memory and the killing of the people themselves is ineluctable," he writes. "The continued fragility of civilized society and decency is echoed in the fragility of its monuments."[92]

Translation, rather than erasure, is the focus of Annie Coombes's consideration of "monuments erected to commemorate regimes that have since been discredited and disgraced." These include the Voortrekker Monument in Pretoria, South Africa, which was dedicated in 1949. Rather than being torn down after the country's first democratic elections in 1994, this foundational icon of Afrikaner nationalism and apartheid was retooled as a focal point of South Africa's post-apartheid remaking, providing "the stage upon which new identities and challenges have been launched."[93] If a somewhat tenuous symbol of South Africa's new multiculturalism, Pretoria's fortress-like granite monument seems to have been especially remade on ecofriendly terms as a nature reserve and bird watching center, landscaped with indigenous plants and replete with regional game and hiking and mountain biking trails. Bypassing racial politics for nature's supposedly neutral turf, this problematic memorial has become a leading icon in South Africa's new economy of cultural tourism.

Other "disgraced monuments" are disavowed and relocated. In Zimbabwe (formerly Rhodesia), memorials to Cecil Rhodes and Lord Salisbury that once dominated public squares now stand in national museums. In Hungary, Budapest's Statue Park Museum hosts a number of exiled memorials of former Communist leaders; in Russia, Moscow's Park of Arts Museon (formerly known as Fallen Monument Park or the Park of Totalitarian Art) features similarly demoted Soviet icons. In Tallinn, Estonia, in 2007, a Red Army war memorial was removed from the capital city's center and rededicated in a military cemetery three kilometers away.[94]

Still other ignominious memorials are contested and reinterpreted with the addition of alternative histories—such as erecting a statue of Arthur Ashe in Richmond. In 2006, the University of Mississippi dedicated a life-size bronze memorial of James Meredith, the first black student to attend the school (in 1962) about a hundred yards from a nineteenth-century standing-soldier statue of a Confederate infantryman. If this sort of commemorative accrual permits a discourse of racialized memory—imagine the two statues talking to one another across Ole Miss's leafy lawns, or Arthur Ashe and Robert E. Lee exchanging words (or volleys) down Richmond's Monument Avenue—it also marks the passage from one belief system to another by disrupting the monolithic symbolic capital of Southern white supremacy and asserting the doctrine of civil rights. Simply adding more memorials isn't adequate, of course: commemorative accrual must be accompanied by a critical reconsideration of historical memory itself.

Moreover, while counter-memorials aim to negotiate the complexities of history and permit the agency of multiple publics, they also need to posit new, or revised, understandings of commemoration and produce new discourses of representation: this is their transformative potential. Sam Durant's *Proposal for White and Indian Dead Monument Transpositions, Washington, D.C.*, reconsiders the plethora of memorials that mark the nation's Indian Wars and reconfigures the National Mall as a necropolis (fig. 6.21). Durant's project was originally devised for the 2005 Monuments for the USA exhibition at the Wattis Institute for Contemporary

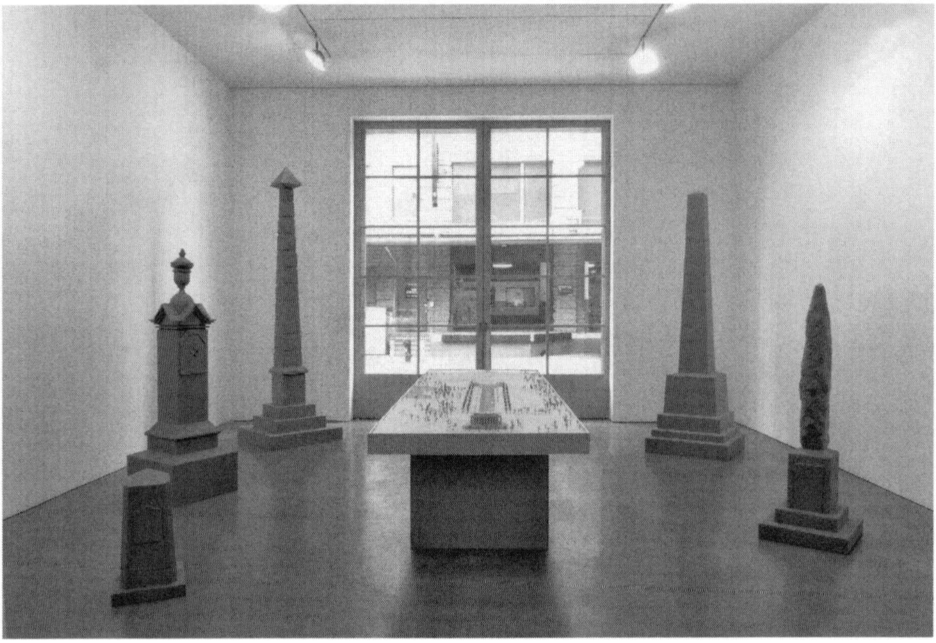

6.21. Sam Durant, *Proposal for White and Indian Dead Monument Transpositions*, 2005. Installation view, Paula Cooper Gallery, New York. (Photo by Ellen Wilson. Courtesy of Sam Durant and Paula Cooper Gallery, New York.)

Art in San Francisco, an ambitious show of hypothetical memorials inspired by curator Ralph Rugoff's hopeful vision of a "monumental America" that may "reactivate our critical imagination." *Proposal* transfers hundreds of nineteenth-century obelisks and vertical shafts erected all over America to the core of the nation's capital, and tackles their shared ideological precept: the United States' persistent use of war as an instrument of national policy. Positioning monuments to "White dead" around the Reflecting Pool, all of them "nonfigurative permanent markers commemorating White settlers killed by Indians," and similar memorials to "Indian dead" in front of the Washington Monument, Durant exposes the Indian Wars as the staging ground of indigenous genocide.[95]

The literal markers of historical memory, the official signs that history museums and historic sites erect to explain their existence and guide visitor expectations, are the stylistic and narrative sources for Edgar Heap of Birds's temporary public memorials. *Building Minnesota* (1990, fig. 6.22) featured forty aluminum signs lettered in the same Helvetica typeface used on highway signs, each with the names of the forty Native Americans who were executed in the 1860s (from a group of over three hundred who were sentenced to death) for their participation in

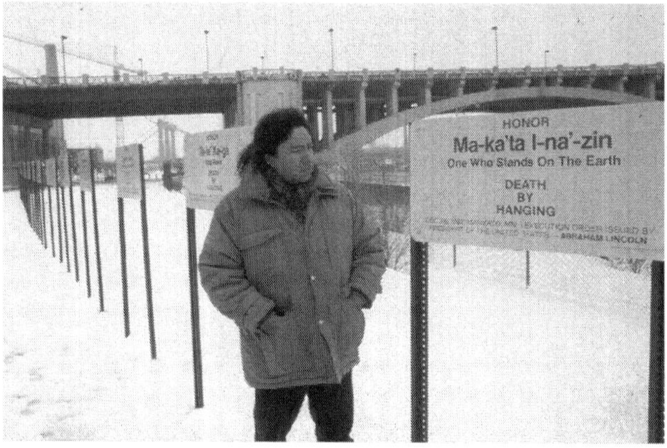

6.22. Edgar Heap of Birds, *Building Minnesota*, temporary installation, Minneapolis, Minnesota, 1990. (Courtesy of Edgar Heap of Birds.)

the 1862 Sioux Uprising: a rebellion brought on by Indian starvation on federal reservations in Minnesota when promised food allotments were withheld. *Who Owns History?* (1992) juxtaposed a bronze plaque that celebrated an eighteenth-century Pittsburgh fort for shaping "the destiny of the great west" and establishing "Anglo-Saxon supremacy in the United States" with a sign devised by the artist that read: "Fort Pitt / Victory / Destiny / Anglo Saxon / Supremacy / Who Owns History?" *Wheel* (see fig. 6.16, above) references nineteenth-century Indian Wars, territorial maps, symbols from various indigenous cosmologies, and contemporary appeals to Native American political activism. "This modern day *Wheel*," the artist explains, "seeks to educate the diverse citizens and visitors of Colorado. An enlightenment can occur if a truthful view of Native American experience of destruction, evolution and a rebuilding of cultural identity is realized."[96]

Describing Heap of Birds's public art projects as "counter-monuments," Rebecca Solnit observes, "They speak to excluded people of erased history; they revise, but they don't reconcile or conciliate."[97] Interrogating the look and content of historical memory, and mixing "official" narratives with those that have been forgotten or denied, Heap of Birds reclaims and transforms American history and indigenous art on discursive terms. His critical and often uncomfortable memory work is a far remove from the conciliatory tones of the Indian Memorial, which glosses the nation's legacy of violence and militarism in a paean to a shared warrior identity. While the Indian Memorial importantly adds the story of indigenous victory to Little Bighorn's narrative, it fails to reckon with the tensions that led to its making, and thus perpetuates their angry dialectical opposition.

George E. Marcus maintains that "the solution to good citizenship is located in our capacity to feel." Can feelings of anger cultivate good citizenship? Can anger play a productive role in democratic public culture? Anger, after all, is the directive of the war on terror: "I was lifted up by a wave of vengeance and testosterone and anger, I could feel it," President George W. Bush told a filmmaker in 2003, explaining how he led the nation to war after 9/11. But anger can also prompt social and political activism: "My response to racism is anger," Audre Lorde wrote in 1981. "Women responding to racism means women responding to anger; the anger of exclusion, of unquestioned privilege, of racial distortions, of silence, ill-use, stereotyping, defensiveness, misnaming, betrayal, and co-optation . . . Anger expressed and translated into action in the service of our vision and our future is a liberating and strengthening act."[98] Anger's different affective dimensions, from misdirected rage to transformative potential, is at the core of controversy surrounding *Danzas Indigenas* (Indigenous Dances), a memorial gateway in Baldwin Park, California (fig. 6.23).

In 1993, Judith Baca was commissioned by the Los Angeles County Metropolitan Transportation Authority and the City of Baldwin Park to create *Danzas Indigenas* for the Baldwin Park Commuter Rail Station. Baca, a public artist and the director of SPARC, the Social and Public Art Resource Center in Venice, California, is perhaps best known for her 2,500-foot mural *The Great Wall of Los Angeles* (1976–1983), located on the walls of the Tujunga Wash Flood Control Channel in Van Nuys. Baldwin Park's modest $56,000 Metrolink project consists of a twenty-foot entry arch, small plaza, and train platform embellished with floor tiles, planters, kiosk shelters, and benches. *Danzas Indigenas* centers on historic and cultural details specific to Baldwin Park, a quiet working-class town with a predominantly Latino population of about eighty thousand people nestled in the central San Gabriel Valley, about twenty miles east of Los Angeles. Commemorating the histories and hopes of its residents, *Danzas Indigenas* is a democratizing model of community-based public art—and was recognized as such for more than twelve years.

Detailed floor patterns in the train platform, for instance, trace the site plans for several eighteenth-century Franciscan missions that were built near Baldwin Park, an area that once consisted of ranches, small farms, and vineyards and was nicknamed "Pleasant View." In 1906, the town was named after Elias "Lucky" Baldwin, a wealthy landowner whose estate figures in Helen Hunt Jackson's classic California tale *Ramona* (1884). Interwoven with historic details of the missions are abstracted designs

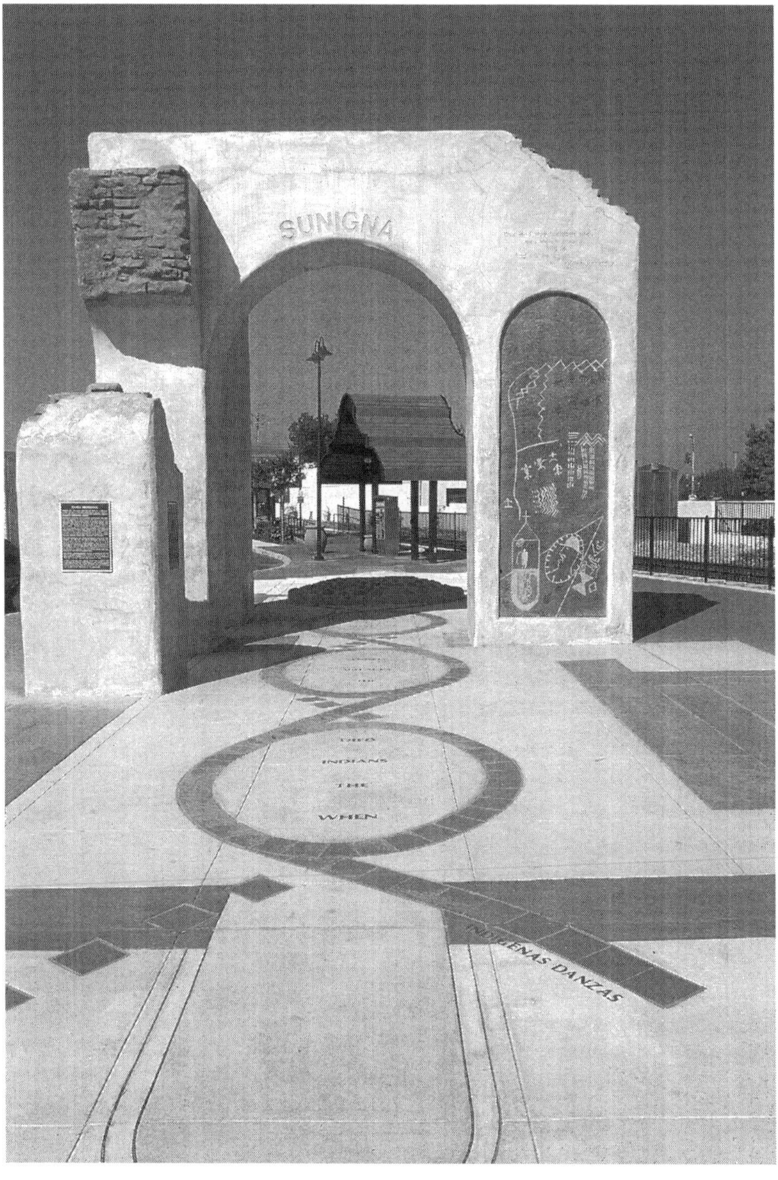

6.23. Judy Baca, *Danzas Indigenas*, Baldwin Park, California, dedicated 1993. (Courtesy of Judy Baca.)

representing two lines of dancers from the Gabrielinos (or Tongva) and Chumash tribes. These elliptical designs reference the region's original inhabitants and provide the memorial's name. Floor text in brass lettering features five different languages—Gabrielino, Chumash, Luiseno, Spanish, and English—and speaks to the waves of immigrants and layers

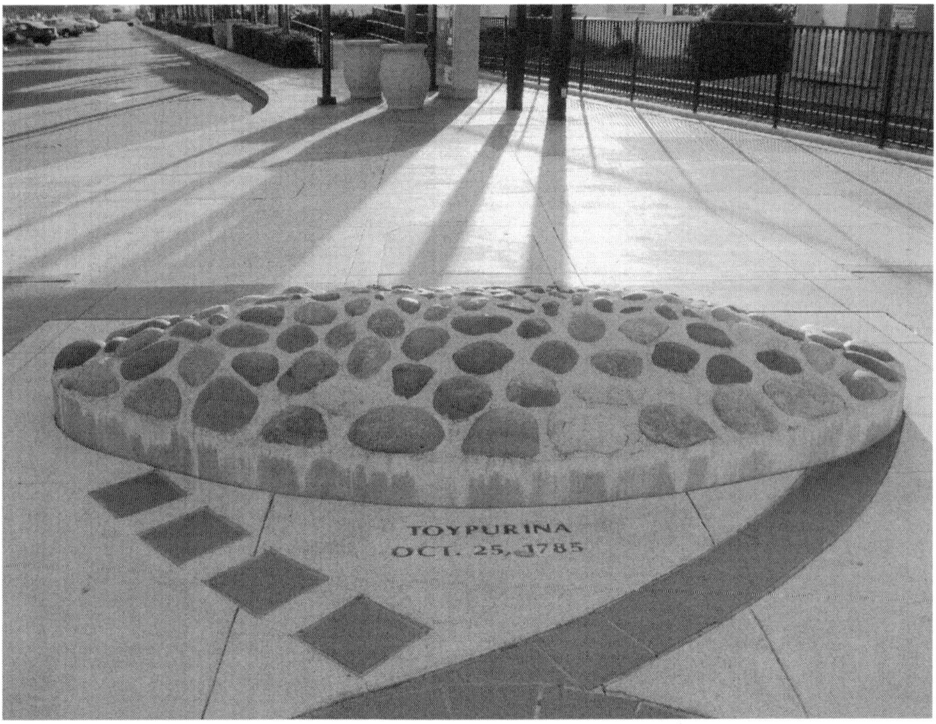

6.24. Judy Baca, *Danzas Indigenas*, detail of the prayer mound. (Photo by the author.)

of history that make up this typical Southern California town. Statistics on the numbers of cattle raised at nearby missions, and the numbers of grape vines that were planted, are juxtaposed with the numbers of indigenous peoples who were forced to labor at the missions, and the numbers who died.

The roofs of the kiosk shelters and the entry arch, which is made of stucco and exposed adobe brick, allude to the Spanish colonial architecture of the San Gabriel Mission, established in 1771 and located about one mile from the Baldwin Park Metrolink station. A stone prayer mound in front of the arch, placed where the altar would be located in the outline of the San Gabriel Mission's floor plan, is dedicated to Toypurina, a twenty-three-year-old Tongva medicine woman who led a revolt against the mission in 1785 (fig. 6.24). As Baca remarks, "I was interested in why the San Gabriel Mission looked like a fortress, and as I did research I discovered its dark history as a place where indigenous people were literally worked to death."[99] Inscribed in tile underneath the arch are the words "When the Indians died, the villages ended," the comments of a Tongva elder who was a consultant on the memorial.

The two sides of the arch further historicize the region, past and present. Refuting a sanitized Taco Bell aesthetic, the arch is fragmented in partial ruins to suggest the enduring presence of Spanish colonialism in California's historical memory and to show how colonialism was, and is, contested. One side of the arch, the side exiting into the city, is sandblasted with the words "Baldwin Park" and is etched with comments that Baca collected from local residents talking about their town's general character and their hopes for the future. These include, "A small town feeling," "Not just adults leading but youth leading too," "Use your brain before you make up your mind" (the observation of Baldwin Park's mayor), and "The kind of community that people dream of, rich and poor, brown, yellow, red, white, all living together." These optimistic words are countered by another statement, tucked into a corner of the arch, which reads: "It was better before *they* came." The comment was made by a longtime local white politician discussing Mexican immigration after World War II, but Baca left it unexplained and ambiguous, inviting viewers to imagine for themselves who "they" might be.

The other side of the memorial arch, the side that leads to the trains, is marked *Sunigna*, the original Tongva name for the area. It features drawings based on indigenous pictographs and a fragment of a poem by Chicana author Gloria Anzaldúa, which reads, "This land was Mexican once, was Indian always and is. And will be again." The poem, which opens Anzaldúa's 1987 collection *Borderlands/La Frontera*, reflects on the precarious circumstances of bordered cultures and contested lands, and speaks to the Southwest's—and all of America's—complex historical mosaic.[100] In 1770, just before the Franciscans arrived, the Tongva numbered about ten thousand and covered a territory of some 1,500 square miles in the greater Los Angeles Basin. Until 1848, Baldwin Park, like all of Southern California, was owned by Mexico. Today, only about three hundred Tongva people remain and only a handful speak the language. As Baca remarks, "I wanted to put memory into a piece of land once owned by the American Indian cultures—memory and willpower are what any culture, the ones living then and those living now, has to have to preserve itself."

Imagining Baldwin Park as a layered site of memory, *Danzas Indigenas* recollects the process of Spanish conquest and colonization that aimed to erase the history of indigenous California. It simultaneously remembers the history of indigenous resistance that refused that erasure by including, for example, Toypurina's story. "The missions were the first sweat shops of California," Baca remarks. "My hope was to bring Toypurina's spirit back to the site so she would be an inspiration to young women today, to show them they can organize and lead." The memorial is scattered with other subtly subversive historical referents, from the entry arch's ruined façade to the inclusion of bronze seals on the stone seats in the train shelters—so that when commuters sit down they are "branded" like the Indians and animals that were enslaved in nearby missions. Ironically, these defiant historical and aesthetic particulars were completely overlooked in the angry protests that erupted over the memorial in the spring of 2005, more than a decade after it was originally dedicated.

Controversy began when the "anti–illegal immigrant" group SOS (Save Our State), demanded the removal of some of the quotes on the memorial arch. The group especially objected to Anzaldúa's words, which they declared "offensive and seditious" and "anti-American."[101] Taking the poem out of context, SOS accused Baca of creating a memorial advocating "reconquista," a concept advanced by Chicano nationalists in the 1970s and popularized by the Mexica Movement in the 1990s that demands the return of parts of the American Southwest to Mexico in order to restore the Aztec homeland of Aztlán. Baca laughs at SOS's suggestion: "I was never engaged in 'reconquista'—someone had to explain to me what it is all about. I couldn't believe that SOS was hung up on this—and didn't seem to notice the monument's historical details." SOS also attacked the quote "It was better before *they* came," mistakenly assuming that *they* referred to white Americans and that the quote came from a person of color. In a specious lawsuit, SOS charged the city with promoting racism, separatism, and "treasonous sentiments" in a "tax-supported monument."

SOS was not really interested in the memorial, of course, and targeted *Danzas Indigenas* and the mostly Latino population of Baldwin Park to gain publicity for its political platform. Fronted by the motto "Save Our State: Home to Real Grassroots Activists Fighting Illegal Immigration," SOS was founded in 2004 by Joe Turner, a former stock trader from Ventura (about eighty-five miles northwest of Baldwin Park) who describes himself as "an aggressive person" who "like[s] to be in control." Named after California's Proposition 187, the "Save Our State" initiative that denied health care and education benefits to undocumented immigrants, Turner's group assumed that "our" state, and by extension their version of the nation, was mostly white. Linked to the Minuteman Project (the vigilantes that police the U.S.-Mexican border), various white supremacist and neo-Nazi groups like National Vanguard (whose members joined SOS in protesting against *Danzas Indigenas*), and the United American Committee (an anti-Islam hate group), SOS was aggressively racist.[102]

Preying especially on contemporary fears that undocumented immigrants are a threat to national security and a financial burden on "citizen taxpayers," Turner saw himself as the movement's white knight: "People who feel the way we do on this issue are hungering for someone who is going to take charge. What I'm trying to do is send up a flag, to tell people, 'I know you're angry and I know you want to get involved, and here's a way to do it.'" In 2005, he told a reporter, "Deep down, I feel like I've been called to greatness."[103] In 2006, Turner was hired by the lobbying group FAIR (Federation for American Immigration Reform) and drafted an "Illegal Immigrant Relief Act" aimed at revoking the license of any business that hires or helps undocumented workers, and prohibiting towns from conducting business in any language except English. Within a few months the initiative had been embraced by ten cities across the country; by summer 2006, inflammatory billboards stating "Stop the Invasion: Save Our Border" sponsored by Grassfire.org had sprung up in Los Angeles, Dallas, Chicago, Atlanta, and New York. In 2008, the Southern Poverty Law Center counted 888 hate groups in its annual "The Year in Hate" tally (up from 602 in 2000) and linked the rise to an increasingly angry anti-immigration movement. "The immigration debate has turned ugly and the result has been a growth in white supremacist hate groups and anti-Latino hate crime," a center representative observed. "I believe in the superiority of America and American culture," Turner rebutted, certain that "America" means a monocultural Anglo European identity.[104]

SOS's initial Web site clearly stated its poisonous race baiting: "Californians are tired of radical revisionist history and militant separatist rhetoric . . . Californians are tired of watching their communities turn into Third World cesspools as a result of a massive invasion of illegal aliens." It also featured a link to a "Hall of Shame" that vilified Latino leaders. SOS's initial actions included boycotting Home Depot's sponsorship of day labor hiring centers, and pressuring a Los Angeles TV station to remove billboards that read "Los Angeles, Mexico" and featured Mexico City's landmark *Angel of Independence* above the LA skyline. "Enough is enough," Turner proclaimed in 2005. "We have reached the point where we can no longer sit back and allow our government to aid and abet the illegal alien invasion. We must respond as our founding fathers would have responded. We must refresh the tree of liberty." Arrested several times for assault and battery during various SOS "actions," Turner said his group's underlying philosophy was the "transference of pain," which "means that if you do not make it painful enough for an organization or entity to continue doing what they're doing, then they're simply going to keep doing it."[105] Probably unaware of its theoretical debt to Wittgenstein and Freud, SOS's "transference of pain" translated into forcing groups and communities to pay for their political and moral values to the point of bankruptcy. SOS's goal in Baldwin Park was the city's financial devastation.

In 2005, Turner organized two protests at *Danzas Indigenas*, each held with permits obtained from the city and each met by strong opposition. He announced the protests on the *John & Ken Show*, the most-listened to local talk radio show in the nation whose right-wing hosts regularly vilify "no-good illegal immigrants" and demand "political human sacrifice" of politicians who oppose "illegal alien" roundups.[106] "Baldwin Park 1" took place on May 14, 2005, and featured about sixty SOS supporters and some five hundred counter-protesters, each group separated by a line of seventy riot police hired from area law enforcement departments. A police helicopter circled above the memorial during the entire rally. SOS supporters waved signs reading "Stop Illegal Immigration" and "You Have the *Right* to Be Deported!" while members of Aztlán Mexica Nation, ANSWER (Act Now to Stop War and End Racism), and Mexicanos Unidos held placards that said "Stop Embarrassing White People," and "Just Say No to Racism."

Both sides were angry; each group taunted the other. One member of Turner's group was hit in the head with a water bottle, which prompted SOS to file a legal claim seeking $1 million in damages from the City of Baldwin Park, and further demand that the city "eliminate the racist comments set forth in the challenged monument." (The suit was thrown out of court.) Playing the provocateur, Turner tried crossing the police line several times and sneered "bring it" at his opponents. "I love it. It's great," he told a *Los Angeles Times* reporter covering the rally as he smiled at the large crowd of furious protesters. "They're communicating my message better than I could." Discussing SOS's small numbers, Turner later remarked: "I don't measure success or victory by the size of the crowd turnout. I'm looking to inflict economic damage and I'm also looking to use the size of the crowd that opposes us to our propaganda advantage, with respect to showing the public all of the Mexican flags waving, the American flags they're kicking, their violence against us, the epithets they hurl."[107]

"Baldwin Park 2," held on June 25, 2005, was even more emotionally charged. While SOS intended to simply restage its anti-immigration politics and garner further publicity by piggy-backing off the anger of its opponents, the second protest prompted a significant reconsideration of protest itself among *Danzas Indigenas*'s defenders. "I was surprised at the absence of nonviolent protest in the first rally, the style of protest that was used during the civil rights and farmworkers' movements," Baca recalled. "And along with others I decided we needed to rethink our whole approach to activism." Rather than fueling SOS's "dualistic, binary" anger, Baca and SPARC encouraged counter-demonstrations to provide "a third space for a plurality of voices" and to articulate issues of freedom of expression, creative integrity, and anti-racism. As Baca explained on SPARC's Web site: "The groups who oppose us welcome confrontation so that they can broadcast their message of fear to others through the media. We will not succumb to their tactics . . . They will offer cynicism and we will offer ceremony. They will raise criticism and we will offer culture. They will condemn art and we will simply make more of it. They will paint a picture of weakness and we will celebrate our strength, for in our eyes, the law protects us, our creativity dignifies us."[108] Promoting the second rally as "The Reconquest of Justice, Peace, Liberty and Love," Baca and SPARC designed posters advertising the protest as a "celebratory festival to confront this latest incarnation of terrorism by disarming its violence with love, humor, dignity, compassion, understanding, indigenous spirituality, inclusivity, and resistance."

SOS was represented by about fifty supporters at "Baldwin Park 2," including members of the Aryan supremacist group White Pride World Wide (also known as Stormfront). Over one thousand Baldwin Park residents, including high school and college students and city politicians, as well as musicians, poets, dancers, performance artists, guerrilla theater groups, and peace organization activists defended *Danzas Indigenas*. Drawing on the "innovative tactical repertoire" successfully employed in many labor-organizing drives and anti-racism rallies held in Southern California since the 1990s, the memorial's backers constituted a highly creative multi-ethnic coalition.[109]

Baca and members of SPARC organized a ninety-foot mobile memorial titled *You Are My Other Me* that featured placards with images and quotes on both sides (fig. 6.25). Held by about thirty people and flipped back and forth during the three hour rally, the signs read "Good art confuses racists," "The land does not belong to us, we belong to the land," and "America turns its back on hate groups." The day of the second protest, the Baldwin Park City Council issued a resolution honoring Baca and *Danzas Indigenas* that read, in part: "The strong sentiments expressed by people who make various interpretations of its meaning after 12 years, is a testament to its value as an artwork." As Baldwin Park's mayor, Manuel Lozano, declared, "This monument represents our city, our people, and all America. And we support it." Unlike the first rally, "Baldwin Park 2" saw few angry outbursts from counter-demonstrators, although Turner did his best to provoke them.

Agitation over *Danzas Indigenas* tested the terms of memorial mania. The defense of Baldwin Park's memorial was neither cheap nor effortless:

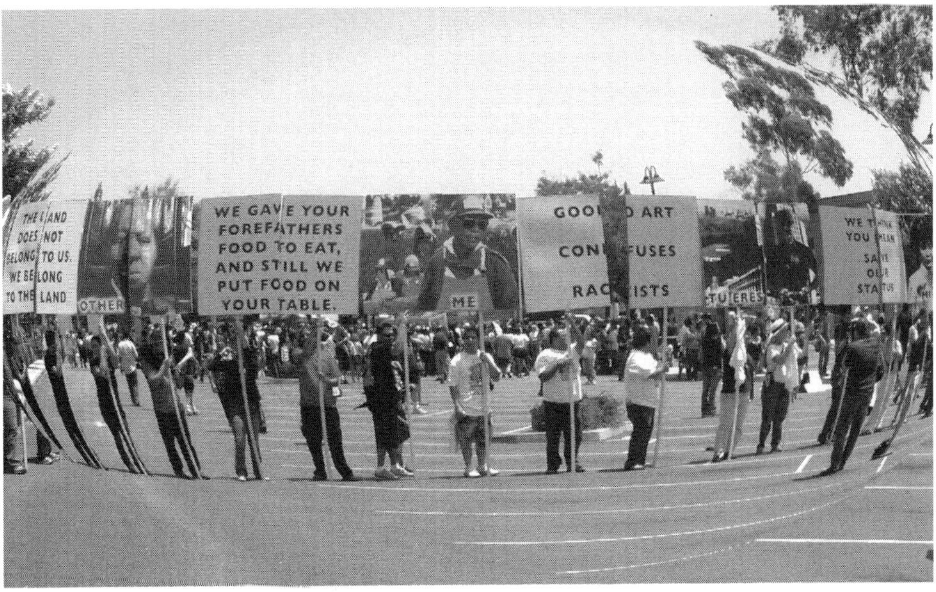

6.25. *You Are My Other Me*, mobile mural at "Baldwin Park 2" protest, June 25, 2005, Baldwin Park, California. (Courtesy of Judy Baca.)

the city spent more than $40,000 on security during the two rallies and Baca and SPARC, along with other arts and activist groups, spent hundreds of hours devising strategies to combat SOS's immigrant-bashing agenda. There were other damages, too: Baldwin Park city administrators and Baca were besieged by racist emails and death threats during the two-month time span of the two rallies. SOS's targeting of *Danzas Indigenas*, which amounted to the racial profiling of an entire community, forced multiple publics to rethink the point and purpose of commemoration—and to determine the depth of their commitment to the issues and histories that memorials embody. "Hate groups want to waste our time," Baca observes. "Public culture is forced to be defensive, always defending itself against hate and intolerance."

Like the contested memorials to Oñate in Texas and New Mexico, controversy over *Danzas Indigenas* was grounded in the dynamics of American citizenship and national memory: of who "counts" as an American today and what America itself means and represents. Such dynamics are particularly charged by today's immigration policies and southwestern border politics: "the No. 1 issue facing America," anti-immigration politicos argue.[110] The U.S.-Mexico border has long played a symbolic role in constituting U.S. territoriality and concepts of nationalism. Because it is porous—quite literally: much of the border is unfenced and sandy soil makes any stable wall unlikely—and because the nation has historically depended on immigration, the border is physically and practically virtual. While the Border Fence, like growing numbers of armed walls being built around the world to separate nations and territories (for example, Israel and Palestine, India and Pakistan, and Botswana and Zimbabwe), aims to project lasting power it actually symbolizes the "ungovernability of globalism" as Wendy Brown puts it, and the crumbling authority of sovereign states.[111]

The U.S.-Mexico border is also, of course, very real on legal and military terms: a line that delimits the land claims of two different nations, a space that in 2006 President George W. Bush demanded be defended, if not with an impenetrable fence, then with high-tech tools "like motion sensors, drones and satellites." The border is, in fact, hyper-real: not just a two thousand–mile line separating Mexico and the United States but a looming presence in every town in America; a "third border," Mike Davis explains, that polices Latino populations wherever they live.[112] Whether Nebraska, Georgia, Maine, or California, the politics of the border are performed each time U.S. Immigration and Customs Enforcement raids an American workplace or community.

Porous but rigid, unstable yet constant, the border is perhaps the most obvious metaphor for America today: a nation that while fundamentally shaped by multiculturalism and repeatedly engaged in its own reinvention is also occupied by certain publics who resent and angrily contest its variable dimensions and fluctuating terms. Immigration—because it represents a threat to understandings of an Anglo European homeland and history—is their primary target; the impotent deterrent of the U.S.-Mexico Border Fence their final solution. No wonder a memorial gateway like *Danzas Indigenas*—not a wall, but an inviting doorway—raised such ire. In June 2005, comments on SOS's Web site included "We are angry! We are seething with anger and boiling with rage," followed by, "The monument in Baldwin Park is not just a rock, it is a disgusting testament to how pathetically apathetic Americans have grown in response to the hostile takeover attempt by the Mechistas [Chicano separatists] and the massive illegal alien invasion. It is a slap in the face to all Americans and an insult to us all." SOS's rage was, of course, utterly misdirected. Rather than targeting *Danzas Indigenas*, and arguing that Mexico represents a threat to American national identity, SOS might have considered the broader scope of neoliberal policies aimed at recreating the globe—not just the United States—"in the interests of the unimpeded operations of capitalist 'free' markets."[113] But that would have required a post-nationalist political alignment across racial and ethnic lines that SOS, whose paranoid anti-immigration platform mostly amounted to declarations of white supremacy, racist nativism, and zealous isolationism, could not fathom.

At "Baldwin Park 2," anger's transformative potential, its capacity to raise consciousness rather than fuel further conflict, was realized in the mobile memorial *You Are My Other Me.* Striving for creative cultural discourse, the second rally's counter-demonstrations were thoughtful, productive, and politicaly progessive. As artist Suzanne Lacy put it in an online forum organized by SPARC: "Maybe this is what art is supposed to do. Maybe this is how art becomes something more than concrete and steel, paint on a canvas."[114] Baca similarly observes:

> Our capacity as a democracy to disagree and to coexist is precisely the point of this work. No single statement can be seen without the whole, nor can it be removed without destroying the diversity of Baldwin Park's voices. Silencing every voice with which we disagree, especially while taking quotes out of context, either through ignorance or malice, is profoundly un-American.

A year later, in May 2006, more than two million people took to the streets in Los Angeles to support immigrant rights (as did millions more throughout the nation). In May 2007, a third SOS protest against *Danza Indigenas* was met with a similar display of support from Baldwin Park residents, community activists, and artists.

The affective possibilities of anger lie in ameliorating its negative effects—in practicing self-restraint in the interest of democratic politics and social reform, in channeling fury into something passionate and progressive. As the struggle over *Danzas Indigenas* suggests, memorials have the capacity to unleash anger's productivity by providing the spaces and subjects that permit cultural and political creativity and prompt acts of "good" citizenship. Whether or not today's Americans are up to the demands of emotionally productive politics remains to be seen.

Notes

Introduction

1. See the scrapbook at http://www.nhstateparks.org/state-parks/alphabetical-order/franconia-notch-state-park/old-man-of-the-mountain-historic-site/old-man-scrap book/; see also Karen Halttunen, "'That great natural curiosity': The Old Man of the Mountain as *Lusus Naturae*," *Common-Place* 4, no. 2 (January 2004), http://www.common-place.org/vol-04/no-02/halttunen/ (accessed September 3, 2008).

2. "Old Man of the Mountain Memorial Design Unveiled," February 7, 2007, at: http://www.nhparks.state.nh.us/ParksPages/parknews/parknews07 (accessed September 3, 2008).

3. Deborah Solomon, "From the Rubble, Ideas for Rebirth," *New York Times*, September 30, 2001.

4. These numbers reference only the victims of the September 11, 2001, attacks and do not include 9/11's nineteen perpetrators.

5. Philip Nobel, "The Downtown Culture Derby Begins," *New York Times*, August 31, 2003; Robin Pogrebin, "The Incredible Shrinking Daniel Libeskind," *New York Times*, June 20, 2004; Edward Wyatt, "Six Plans for Ground Zero, All Seen as Starting Point," *New York Times*, July 17, 2002. In 2009, Freedom Tower was renamed One World Trade Center.

6. Robert Bevan, *The Destruction of Memory: Architecture at War* (London: Reaktion Books, 2006), 188; George Mosse, *Fallen Soldiers: Reshaping the Memory of the World Wars* (Oxford: Oxford University Press, 1990), 212.

7. David Zucchino, "Army Stage-Managed Fall of Hussein Statue," *Los Angeles Times*, July 3, 2004.

8. Pierre Bourdieu, *Outline of a Theory of Practice* (Cambridge: Cambridge University Press, 1977), 114–20.

9. Wayne Craven, *Sculpture in America*, rev. ed. (Newark, NJ: University of Delaware Press, 1984), 46–47; David Hackett Fischer, *Liberty and Freedom* (New York: Oxford University Press, 2005), 176; Arthur S. Marks, "The Statue of King George III in New York and the Iconography of Regicide," *American Art Journal* 13, no. 3 (Summer 1981): 61–82.

10. Albert Boime, *The Unveiling of the National Icons: A Plea for Patriotic Iconoclasm in a Nationalist Era* (Cambridge: Cambridge University Press, 1998), 141–43; see also Carole Blair and Neil Michel, "The Rushmore Effect: Ethos and National Collective Identity," in *The Ethos of Rhetoric*, ed. Michael J. Hyde (Columbia: University of South Carolina Press, 2004), 160–63.

11. Karen L. Cox, "The Confederate Monument at Arlington: A Token of Reconcilia-

tion," in *Monuments to the Lost Cause: Women, Art, and the Landscapes of Southern Memory*, ed. Cynthia Mills and Pamela H. Simpson (Knoxville: University of Tennessee Press, 2003), 158.

12. For a history of presidential wreath-giving at the Confederate Monument and protest against it, see Edward Sebesta and James Loewen, "Dear President Obama: Please Don't Honor the Arlington Confederate Monument," May 18, 2009, http://hnn.us/articles/85884.html (accessed October 13, 2009).

13. Tony Horwitz, *Confederates in the Attic: Dispatches from the Unfinished Civil War* (New York: Vintage, 1998); see also Sanford Levinson, *Written in Stone: Public Monuments in Changing Societies* (Durham, NC: Duke University Press, 1998), 61.

14. Here I paraphrase Ann Cvetkovich, *An Archive of Feelings: Trauma, Sexuality, and Lesbian Public Cultures* (Durham, NC: Duke University Press, 2003), 7.

15. Teresa Brennan, *The Transmission of Affect* (Ithaca, NY: Cornell University Press, 2004). For other accounts of affect in multiple disciplines see, for example, Antonio Damasio, *Descartes' Error: Emotion, Reason, and the Human Brain* (New York: Avon Books, 1994); Silvan Tomkins, "Affect, Imagery, Consciousness," in *Shame and Its Sisters: A Silvan Tomkins Reader*, ed. Eve Kosofsky Sedgwick and Adam Frank (Durham, NC: Duke University Press, 1995), Brian Massumi, *Parables for the Virtual: Movement, Affect, Sensation* (Durham, NC: Duke University Press, 2002); Eve Kosofsky Sedgwick, *Touching Feeling: Affect, Pedagogy, Performativity* (Durham, NC: Duke University Press, 2003); Jill Bennett, *Empathic Vision: Affect, Trauma, and Contemporary Art* (Palo Alto, CA: Stanford University Press, 2005); Sianne Ngai, *Ugly Feelings* (Cambridge, MA: Harvard University Press, 2005); Jane F. Thrailkill, *Affecting Fictions: Mind, Body, and Emotion in American Literary Realism* (Cambridge, MA: Harvard University Press, 2007); and Amanda Wise and Selvaraj Velayutham, "Towards a Typology of Transnational Affect" (Working Paper 4, Centre for Research on Social Inclusion, Macquarie University, Australia, 2006).

16. See Jameson's discussion of "the waning of affect" in *Postmodernism, or, The Cultural Logic of Late Capitalism* (Durham, NC: Duke University Press, 1991), 10. In his influential book *The Structural Transformation of the Public Sphere: An Inquiry into a Category of Bourgeois Society*, trans. Thomas Burger (1962; Cambridge, MA: MIT Press, 1989), philosopher Jurgen Habermas discussed an ideal public sphere invested in collective democratic action and informed by "public reason."

Chapter 1

1. Andreas Huyssen, "Monumental Seduction," in *Act of Memory: Cultural Recall in the Present*, ed. Mieke Bal, Jonathan Crewe, and Leo Spitzer, (Hanover, NH: Dartmouth College / University Press of New England, 1999), 191; idem, *Twilight Memories: Marking Time in a Culture of Amnesia* (New York: Routledge, 1995), 3.

2. James M. Goode observes that 325 outdoor sculptures were counted in Washington in 1974 and 625 in 2008; see Goode, *Washington Sculpture: A Cultural History of Outdoor Sculpture in the Nation's Capital* (Baltimore, MD: The Johns Hopkins University Press, 2008), 9.

3. This list does not include memorials recently erected at embassies, including statues of Mustafa Kemal Atatürk (2004) and Crown Princess Märtha of Norway (2005).

4. A similar statue was erected in Freedom Park in Rosslyn, Virginia, in 1996, which also displayed parts of the Berlin Wall, stones from the Warsaw Ghetto, a toppled statue of

Lenin, a replica of Thomas Crawford's *Statue of Freedom* (placed on top of the U.S. Capitol in 1863), and a bronze replica of Martin Luther King, Jr.'s Birmingham jail-cell door.

5. Carole Blair, "Contemporary U.S. Memorial Sites as Exemplars of Rhetoric's Materiality," in *Rhetorical Bodies*, ed. Jack Selzer and Sharon Crowley (Madison: University of Wisconsin Press, 1999), 36, 52n13; Felicity Barringer, "A City of Memorials Finds Itself Filling Up," *New York Times*, December 30, 2006.

6. Martha Norkunas, *Monuments and Memory: History and Representation in Lowell, Massachusetts* (Washington DC: Smithsonian Institution Press, 2002), 13; see also Cathy Stanton, *The Lowell Experiment: Public History in a Postindustrial City* (Amherst: University of Massachusetts Press, 2006).

7. Maurice Agulhon, "La 'statueomanie' et l'histoire," *Ethnologie française* 8, no. 1 (1978): 145–72; idem, *Marianne Into Battle: Republican Imagery and Symbolism in France, 1789–1880*, trans. Janet Lloyd (Cambridge: Cambridge University Press, 1981), 70, 132, 138; June Hargrove, *The Statues of Paris, An Open-Air Pantheon: The History of Statues to Great Men* (New York: Vendome Press, 1990), 125; Jean Adhémar, "Les statues parisiennes de grandes homes," *Gazette des Beaux-Arts* 83, no. 6 (March 1974): 149–52.

8. Benedict Anderson, *Imagined Communities: Reflections on the Origin and Spread of Nationalism* (New York: Verso, 1983), 64. For examples, see Michele H. Bogart, *Public Sculpture and the Civic Ideal in New York City, 1890–1930* (Chicago: University of Chicago Press, 1989); Wayne Craven, *Sculpture in America*, rev. ed. (Newark, NJ: University of Delaware Press, 1984), 372–553; Melissa Dabakis, *Visualizing Labor in American Sculpture: Monuments, Manliness, and the Work Ethic, 1880–1935* (Cambridge: Cambridge University Press, 1999); Daniel Robbins, "Statues to Sculpture: From the Nineties to the Thirties," in *200 Years of American Sculpture* (New York: Whitney Museum of American Art, 1976), 112–59; and Lorado Taft, *The History of American Sculpture*, rev. ed. (New York: MacMillan Co., 1924).

9. Greg Esser, "Hazardous Trail to a Lasting Legacy," *Public Art Review* 13, no. 1 (Fall / Winter 2001): 29–33.

10. Benton, quoted in Gilbert Fite, *Mount Rushmore* (Norman: University of Oklahoma Press, 1964), 34–35; see also Albert Boime, "Patriarchy Fixed in Stone: Gutzon Borglum's Mount Rushmore," *American Art* 5, nos.1–2 (Winter / Spring 1991): 153.

11. "Columbus Eulogized at Statue Unveiling," *New York Times*, June 9, 1912.

12. Mitch Kachun, *Festivals of Freedom: Memory and Meaning in African American Emancipation Celebrations, 1808–1915* (Amherst: University of Massachusetts Press, 2003), 161, 156–57. The *Bee* was published in Washington, D.C., between 1882 and 1922. See also Freeman Henry Morris Murray, *Emancipation and the Freed in American Sculpture* (Washington DC, 1916), 102–9.

13. Kirk Savage, *Standing Soldiers, Kneeling Slaves: Race, War, and Monument in Nineteenth-Century America* (Princeton, NJ: Princeton University Press, 1997), 162–64; Kachun, *Festivals of Freedom*, 156. The 1870 Philadelphia memorial was never built, although in 1934 the city dedicated the All War Memorial to Colored Soldiers and Sailors, designed by J. Otto Schweizer. On the postbellum monument industry see Lewis Waldron Williams II, "Commercially Produced Forms of American Civil War Monuments" (MA thesis, University of Illinois, 1948), as noted in Savage, *Standing Soldiers, Kneeling Slaves*, 248–49nn1, 5.

14. On origins of the term "doughboy," see Jennifer Keene, *Doughboys, the Great War, and the Remaking of America* (Baltimore, MD: The Johns Hopkins University Press, 2001), 3.

15. Advertisement for "American Doughboy Art Lamp," *American Legion Weekly*, May 26, 1922. For more on doughboy memorials, see Jennifer Wingate, "Over the Top: The Doughboy in World War I Memorials and Visual Culture," *American Art* 19, no. 2 (Summer 2005): 26–47.

16. Michele Bogart, *The Politics of Urban Beauty: New York and Its Art Commission* (Chicago: University of Chicago Press, 2006), 16; John Bodnar, *Remaking America: Public Memory, Commemoration, and Patriotism in the Twentieth Century* (Princeton, NJ: Princeton University Press, 1992), 13–14, 245.

17. John Bodnar, "Public Memory in an American City: Commemoration in Cleveland," in *Commemorations: The Politics of National Identity*, ed. John Gillis (Princeton, NJ: Princeton University Press, 1994), 79.

18. David Glassberg, *American Historical Pageantry: The Uses of Tradition in the Early Twentieth Century* (Chapel Hill: University of North Carolina Press, 1990), 191; see also Neil Harris, "Festival Culture, American Style," in *The Arts of Democracy: Art, Public Culture, and the State*, ed. Casey Nelson Blake (Philadelphia: University of Pennsylvania Press, 2007), 11–30.

19. Adelia Belle Beard, "The American Pageant," *American Homes and Gardens*, July 1912, 239, as noted in Sarah J. Moore, "Making a Spectacle of Suffrage: The National Woman Suffrage Pageant, 1913," *Journal of American Culture* 20 (Spring 1997): 89.

20. Paul A. Pickering and Alex Tyrrell, eds., *Contested Sites: Commemoration, Memorials and Popular Politics in Nineteenth-Century Britain* (London: Ashgate, 2004), 12–13.

21. German E. Berrios, "Of Mania: Introduction," *History of Psychiatry* 15, no. 1 (2004): 105–24.

22. Sergiusz Michalski, *Public Monuments: Art in Political Bondage 1870–1997* (London: Reaktion Books, 1998), 45; "To Stop Statue Mania," *New York Times*, July 23, 1911; Hargrove, *The Statues of Paris*, 254–60.

23. "Deformities in Sculpture" and "Inartistic Public Monuments," *Leslie's Weekly*, June 1, 1893, 350–51, 356, as noted in Timothy J. Garvey, *Public Sculptor: Lorado Taft and the Beautification of Chicago* (Urbana: University of Illinois Press, 1988), 81, 88; Charles Moore, "Memorials of the Great War," *The American Magazine of Art* 10, no. 7 (May 1919): 233.

24. "Sculptural Art in Decadence: Display of Statuary at Chicago Shows a Painful Lack of Originality," *New York Herald*, May 29, 1893; see also the discussion of "Statuemania" in Penelope Curtis, *Sculpture 1900–1945* (Oxford: Oxford University Press, 1999), 38–39.

25. Michele H. Bogart, "The Ordinary Hero Monument in Greater New York: Samuel J. Tilden's Memorial and the Politics of Place," *Journal of Urban History* 28, no. 3 (March 2002): 268. Tilden won the popular vote for the presidency in 1876 but was overruled by Electoral College votes. See also Bogart's discussion of the fate of a monument by Frederick MacMonnies: "The Rise and Demise of *Civic Virtue*," in *Critical Issues in Public Art: Content, Context, and Controversy*, ed. Harriet F. Senie and Sally Webster (New York: Icon Editions, 1992), 175–88.

26. Janet Scudder, *Modeling My Life* (New York: Harcourt, Brace, and Co. 1925), 155.

27. Lee Friedlander, *The American Monument* (New York: Eakins Press, 1976).

28. Grace Glueck, "Art in Public Places Stirs Widening Debate," *New York Times*, May 23, 1982. For financial data see "Executive Summary," *Public Art Programs Fiscal Year 2001: A Detailed Statistical Report on the Budgets and Programming of the Nation's Public Art Programs During Fiscal Year 2001* (Washington DC: Americans for the Arts, 2003), 3.

29. Miwon Kwon, *One Place After Another: Site-Specific Art and Locational Identity* (Cambridge, MA: MIT Press, 2002), 8, 52–55.

30. Allen Weller, "Lorado Taft, the Ferguson Fund, and the Advent of Modernism," in *The Old Guard and the Avant-Garde: Modernism in Chicago, 1910–1940*, ed. Sue Ann Prince (Chicago: University of Chicago Press, 1990), 41.

31. Jeff Huebner, "The Art Institute's Ferguson Fund Must Always Be for Public Sculpture," *Chicago Art Critics Association Review* 5, no. 1 (April 2004), http://www.chicagoart criticsassociation.org/P/n04.html (accessed June 26, 2004). On Taft's fountain see also Garvey, *Public Sculptor*, 2–6, 150–51.

32. Gary Garrels, *Beyond the Monument*, exhibition catalog (Cambridge, MA: MIT Hayden Corridor Gallery, 1983), n.p.

33. Arlene Raven, introduction to *Art in the Public Interest* (Ann Arbor, MI: UMI Research Press, 1989), 1; Douglas McGill, "Sculpture Goes Public," *New York Times Magazine*, April 27, 1986, 42–45, 66–67, 85–87.

34. Rosalind Krauss, *Passages in Modern Sculpture* (New York: Viking, 1977), 270.

35. Rosalyn Deutsche, *Evictions: Art and Spatial Politics* (Cambridge, MA: MIT Press, 1996), xiv; Erika Doss, *Spirit Poles and Flying Pigs: Public Art and Cultural Democracy in American Communities* (Washington DC: Smithsonian Institution Press, 1995).

36. Michael Warner, *Publics and Counterpublics* (New York: Zone Books, 2002), 182; see also Mary Kupiec Cayton, "What is Public Culture? Agency and Contested Meaning in American Culture—An Introduction," in *Public Culture: Diversity, Democracy, and Community in the United States*, ed. Marguerite S. Shaffer (Philadelphia: University of Pennsylvania Press, 2008), 1–25, 316–18.

37. Sally Stein, "The President's Two Bodies: Stagings and Restagings of FDR and the New Deal Body Politic," *American Art* 18, no. 1 (Spring 2004): 32–57. It is now believed that Roosevelt contracted Guillain-Barré syndrome in 1921, not polio.

38. David W. Houck and Amos Kiewe, *FDR's Body Politics: The Rhetoric of Disability* (College Station: Texas A&M University Press, 2003).

39. Justice Felix Frankfurter, "The Memorial to F.D.R.: What the President Wanted," *Atlantic Monthly*, March 1961, 39–40. Such a stone was, in fact, placed in front of the National Archives in April 1965.

40. Michael Schudson, *The Good Citizen: A History of American Civil Life* (New York: Free Press, 1998), 239, 242, 288; Lawrence Halprin, "Halprin on the FDR Memorial," *Landscape Architecture*, June 2001, 7.

41. H. W. Janson, *The Rise and Fall of the Public Monument* (New Orleans, LA: The Graduate School, Tulane University, 1976), 1; Rosalind E. Krauss, "Sculpture in the Expanded Field," in *The Originality of the Avant-Garde and Other Modernist Myths* (1979; Cambridge, MA: MIT Press, 1985, 279.

42. Alois Riegl, "The Modern Cult of Monuments: Its Character and Its Origin," trans. Kurt W. Forster and Diane Ghirardo, *Oppositions: A Journal for Ideas and Criticism in Architecture* 25 (Fall 1982): 21; Françoise Choay, *The Invention of the Historic Monument*, trans. Lauren M. O'Connell (1992; New York: Cambridge University Press, 2001), 6; Eric Hobsbawm, foreword, to Dawn Ades et al., *Art and Power: Europe Under the Dictators 1930–1945* (London: Thames & Hudson, 1995), 13; Marvin Trachtenberg, *The Statue of Liberty* (New York: Viking, 1976), 15.

43. Marita Sturken, "Monuments: Historical Overview," in *Encyclopedia of Aesthetics*, ed. Michael Kelly (New York: Oxford University Press, 1998), 3:274; Wilbur Zelinsky, *Nation into State: The Shifting Symbolic Foundations of American Nationalism* (Chapel Hill: University of North Carolina Press, 1988), 181. See also Choay, *The Invention of the Historic Monument*, 6–8.

44. Maya Lin, untitled essay in *Grounds for Remembering: Monuments, Memorials, Texts* (Berkeley: Doreen B. Townsend Center for the Humanities, University of California, 1995), 13; James Ingo Freed, "The United States Holocaust Memorial Museum," in *The Art of Memory: Holocaust Memorials in History*, ed. James E. Young (New York: Prestel-Verlag, 1994), 89.

45. Lewis Mumford, *The Culture of Cities* (New York: Harcourt, Brace, Jovanovich, 1938), 434; Krauss, "Sculpture in the Expanded Field," 279–80.

46. Hansen's design was crafted in collaboration with his wife, artist Zofia Hansen, and with Jerzy Jarnuszkiewicz and Julian Palka; see his description of the proposal in Oskar Hansen, "'The Road' Monument Design," in *Towards Open Form* (Warsaw: Fundacja Galerii Foksal, 2005), n.p. Henry Moore, "Auschwitz Monument," in *Henry Moore: Writings and Conversations*, ed. Alan Wilkinson (Berkeley: University of California Press, 2002), 134–35; Roger Berthoud, *The Life of Henry Moore* (New York: E. P. Dutton, 1987), 271–73; Katarzyna Murawska-Muthesius, "Oskar Hansen, Henry Moore, and the Auschwitz Memorial Debates in Poland, 1958–59," in *Figuration/Abstraction: Strategies for Public Sculpture in Europe 1945–1968*, ed. Charlotte Benton (Aldershot, UK: Ashgate, 2004), 193–211; and James Young, *The Texture of Memory: Holocaust Memorials and Meaning* (New Haven, CT: Yale University Press, 1993),133–41.

47. Theodor Adorno, "Cultural Criticism and Society," in *Prisms*, trans. Samuel and Shierry Weber (Cambridge, MA: MIT Press, 1981), 34.

48. Elvira Slack, "No Victory Arches Wanted," *New York Times*, June 24, 1943), 20; Kenneth Reid, "Memorials? Yes—but No Monuments!" *Pencil Points* 25 (May 1944): 35; Joseph Hudnut, "The Monument Does Not Remember," *Atlantic Monthly*, September 1945, 55–59.

49. Andrew M. Shanken, "Planning Memory: Living Memorials in the United States During World War II," *Art Bulletin* 84, no. 1 (March 2002): 130–47; see G. Kurt Piehler, *Remembering War the American Way* (Washington DC: Smithsonian Institution Press, 1995), 109–11, for a discussion of "living memorials" after World War I.

50. Ann Maria Torres, *Isamu Noguchi: A Study of Space* (New York: Monacelli Press, 2000), 47–48, 54.

51. Robert Burstow, "Butler's Competition Project for a Monument to 'The Unknown Political Prisoner': Abstraction and Cold War Politics," *Art History* 12, no. 4 (December 1989): 472–96; Harriet Senie, *Contemporary Public Sculpture: Tradition, Transformation, and Controversy* (New York: Oxford University Press, 1992), 23–24; and "Big Row For Big Prize," *Life*, June 1, 1953, 39–42.

52. Claes Oldenburg, *Proposals for Monuments and Buildings, 1965–1969* (Chicago: Big Table Publishing Company, 1969), 166.

53. Janson, *The Rise and Fall of the Public Monument*, 1; James Wines, "De-Architecturalization," in *Esthetics Contemporary*, ed. Richard Kostelanetz (Buffalo, NY: Prometheus Books, 1978), 278; see also Nicholas J. Capasso, "The Death of the Monument" in "The National Vietnam Veterans Memorial in Context: Commemorative Public Art in America, 1960–1997" (PhD dissertation, Rutgers, the State University of New Jersey, 1998), 16–77.

54. Oldenburg, quoted in 1968 interview with Paul Carroll, "The Poetry of Scale," in *Proposals for Monuments and Buildings*, 20, 24–26.

55. Oldenburg, quoted in Suzaan Boettger, *Earthworks: Art and the Landscape of the Sixties* (Berkeley: University of California Press, 2002), 21, and in Paul Cummings, *In-*

terview with Claes Oldenburg (Washington DC: Archives of American Art / Smithsonian Institution, 1973), 286.

56. As noted in Labib Habachi, *The Obelisk of Egypt* (New York: Charles Scribner's Sons, 1977), 183.

57. Teresa Brennan, *The Transmission of Affect* (Ithaca, NY: Cornell University Press, 2004).

58. Tammy Fonce-Olivas, "City Finances 'Equestrian' Project," *El Paso Times*, August 28, 2006; see also chapter 6 of this book.

59. Spiro Kostof, *America By Design* (New York: Oxford University Press, 1987), 265.

60. Maurice Halbwachs, *On Collective Memory*, ed. and trans. Lewis A. Coser (Chicago: University of Chicago Press, 1992), 38, 182–83; this includes an English translation of Halbwach's *The Social Frameworks of Memory*, originally published in1925.

61. Michael North, "The Public as Sculpture: From Heavenly City to Mass Ornament," *Critical Inquiry* 16, no. 4 (Summer 1990): 876–77.

62. Kirk Savage, "The Past in the Present: The Life of Memorials," *Harvard Design Magazine* 9 (Fall 1999): 14, 16; idem, "Trauma, Healing, and the Therapeutic Monument," in *Terror, Culture, Politics: Rethinking 9/11*, ed. Daniel J. Sherman and Terry Nardin (Bloomington: Indiana University Press, 2006), 104.

63. Michael Kammen, *Mystic Chords of Memory: The Transformation of Tradition in American Culture* (New York: Vintage, 1991), 33.

64. Kerwin Lee Klein, "On the Emergence of *Memory* in Historical Discourse," *Representations* 69 (Winter 2000): 127–50; Barbie Zelizer, "Reading the Past Against the Grain: The Shape of Memory Studies," *Critical Studies in Mass Communication* 12, no. 2 (June 1995): 215–16; Jay Winter, "The Generation of Memory: Reflections on the 'Memory Boom' in Contemporary Historical Studies," *GHI Bulletin* 27 (Fall 2000): 69–92. In an earlier essay, Charles Maier used the phrase "memory industry" to describe Holocaust commemoration; see Maier, "A Surfeit of Memory? Reflections on History, Melancholy and Denial," *History and Memory* 5, no. 2 (1993): 136–52.

65. Pierre Nora, *Les Lieux de mémoire* (Paris: Gallimard, 1984–92); Marita Sturken, "The Remembering of Forgetting: Recovered Memory and the Question of Experience," *Social Text* 57, no. 4 (Winter 1998): 103–25.

66. Pierre Nora, "Between Memory and History: *Les Lieux de mémoire*," *Representations* 26 (Spring 1989): 13; Juliet Mitchell, "Memory and Psychoanalysis," in *Memory*, ed. Patricia Fara and Karalyn Patterson (Cambridge: Cambridge University Press, 1998), 99. See also the influential work of cognitive psychologist Endel Tulving, such as *Elements of Episodic Memory* (Oxford: Oxford University Press, 1983).

67. Klein, "On the Emergence of *Memory* in Historical Discourse," 146.

68. Nora, "Between Memory and History," 8–9, 12.

69. Paul Ricoeur, *Memory, History, Forgetting*, trans. Kathleen Blamey and David Pellauer, (2000; Chicago: University of Chicago Press, 2004).

70. Roy Rosenzweig and David Thelen, *The Presence of the Past: Popular Uses of History in American Life* (New York: Columbia University Press, 1998).

71. Alfred Gell, *Art and Agency: An Anthropological Theory* (Oxford: Clarendon Press, 1998), 100.

72. Not quite: the room where King actually stayed was demolished and then reconfigured in order to facilitate maximum museum visitor access; see Mabel O. Wilson, "Between Rooms 307: Spaces of Memory at the National Civil Rights Museum," in *Sites of*

Memory: Perspectives on Architecture and Race, ed. Craig Evan Barton (New York: Princeton Architectural Press, 2001), 23–24.

73. Lin, *Grounds for Remembering*, 13; Lawrence Halprin, *The Franklin Delano Roosevelt Memorial* (San Francisco: Chronicle Books, 1997), 7.

74. Guiliani quoted in "Public Viewing Platform Opens at Ground Zero," CNN.com, December 30, 2001, http://archives.cnn.com/2001/US/12/30/rec.viewing.platforms/ (accessed November, 23, 2005); and Diane Cardwell, "First Viewing Platform Opens to Public," *New York Times*, December 30, 2001.

75. Alison Landsberg, *Prosthetic Memory: The Transformation of American Remembrance in the Age of Mass Culture* (New York: Columbia University Press, 2004), 2.

76. W. J. T. Mitchell, "There Are No Visual Media," *Journal of Visual Culture* 4, no. 2 (2005): 265; idem, *Picture Theory: Essays on Verbal and Visual Representation* (Chicago: University of Chicago Press, 1994), 2; Caroline A Jones, *Eyesight Alone: Clement Greenberg's Modernism and the Bureaucratization of the Senses* (Chicago: University of Chicago Press, 2005), 390.

77. Mark M. Smith, "Still Coming to 'Our' Senses: An Introduction," *Journal of American History* 95, no. 2 (September 2008): 379; see also articles under the heading "The Senses in American History: A Round Table" *Journal of American History* 95, no. 2 (September 2008): 378–451 and Mark M. Smith, *Sensory History* (New York: Oxford 2007).

78. Joan W. Scott, "The Evidence of Experience," *Critical Inquiry* 17, no. 4 (Summer 1991): 779; Joan W. Scott, "Experience," in *Feminists Theorize the Political*, ed. Judith Butler and Joan W. Scott (New York: Routledge, 1992), 37.

79. Rosenzweig and Thelen, *The Presence of the Past*, 126.

80. T. Fujitani, Geoffrey M. White, and Lisa Yoneyama, introduction to *Perilous Memories: The Asia-Pacific War(s)* (Durham, NC: Duke University Press, 2001), 5.

81. Anderson, *Imagined Communities*, 3, 6; Ernest Renan, "What is a Nation?" in *Becoming National: A Reader*, ed. Geoff Eley and Ronald Grigor Suny (New York: Oxford University Press, 1996), 52–54; John Breuilly, *Nationalism and the State* (Chicago: University of Chicago Press, 1985), 3; and Miroslav Hroch, "From National Movement to the Fully-formed Nation: The Nation-building Process in Europe," in *Mapping the Nation*, ed. Gopal Balakrishnan (New York: Verso, 1996), 79.

82. See, for example, David W. Noble, *Death of a Nation: American Culture and the End of Exceptionalism* (Minneapolis: University of Minnesota Press, 2002).

83. Anthony D. Smith, *Nations and Nationalism in the Global Era* (Cambridge: Polity Press, 1995), 1–18.

84. Prasenjit Duara, *Rescuing History from the Nation: Questioning Narratives of Modern China* (Chicago: University of Chicago Press, 1995), 8, 15–16; Thomas Scheff, "Emotions and Identity: A Theory of Ethnic Nationalism," in *Social Theory and the Politics of Identity*, ed. Craig Calhoun (Cambridge, MA: Blackwell Publishers, 1994), 277–303; George E. Marcus, *The Sentimental Citizen: Emotion in Democratic Politics* (University Park: Pennsylvania State University Press, 2002).

85. David Harvey, *A Brief History of Neoliberalism* (Oxford: Oxford University Press, 2005), 85.

86. Simon Schama, *Landscape and Memory* (New York: Alfred A. Knopf, 1995), 385–99; see also Albert Boime, *The Unveiling of the National Icons: A Plea for Patriotic Iconoclasm in a Nationalist Era* (Cambridge: Cambridge University Press, 1998), 142–67, and Carole Blair and Neil Michel, "The Rushmore Effect: Ethos and National Collective Identity," in

The Ethos of Rhetoric, ed. Michael J. Hyde (Columbia: University of South Carolina Press, 2004), 156–96.

87. National Park Service Web site on Mount Rushmore: http://www.nps.gov/moru (accessed March 22, 2005). These words paraphrase Borglum's own; see also Matthew Glass's discussion of the video shown at the Mount Rushmore visitors center that is narrated by NBC news anchor Tom Brokaw, in "Producing Patriotic Inspiration at Mount Rushmore," *Journal of the American Academy of Religion* 62, no. 2 (Summer 1994): 267–68.

88. In January 2009, Bush also authorized three areas of the Pacific Ocean as national monuments and protected marine sanctuaries: the Marianas Trench Marine National Monument, the Rose Atoll Marine National Monument, and the Pacific Remote Islands Marine National Monument.

89. Miranda J. Banks, "Monumental Fictions: National Monument as a Science Fiction Space," *Journal of Popular Film and Television* 30, no. 3 (2003): 136–45.

90. Nora, "Between Memory and History," 19.

91. "History," National AIDS Memorial Grove Web site, http://www.aidsmemorial.org/history.

92. These include Casey Nelson Blake, ed., *The Arts of Democracy: Art, Public Culture, and the State* (Philadelphia: University of Pennsylvania Press, 2007); Bogart, *Public Sculpture and the Civic Ideal*; Bogart, *The Politics of Urban Beauty*; Deutsche, *Evictions*; Doss, *Spirit Poles and Flying Pigs*; Cher Krause Knight, *Public Art: Theory, Practice, and Populism* (Malden, MA: Blackwell Publishing, 2008); Kwon, *One Place After Another*; Suzanne Lacy, ed., *Mapping the Terrain: New Genre Public Art* (Seattle, WA: Bay Press, 1995); Lawrence J. Prelli, ed., *Rhetorics of Display* (Columbia: University of South Carolina Press, 2006); Raven, *Art in the Public Interest*; Senie and Webster, *Critical Issues in Public Art;* and Sarah Schrank, *Art and the City: Civic Imagination and Cultural Authority in Los Angeles* (Philadelphia: University of Pennsylvania Press, 2009). See also Linda Cunningham, *The Memorial Redefined: Reconsideration of a Major Public Art Form* (New York: College Art Association, 1989).

93. See, for example, Marita Sturken, *Tangled Memories: The Vietnam War, the AIDS Epidemic, and the Politics of Remembering* (Berkeley: University of California Press, 1997); Kristin Ann Hass, *Carried to the Wall: American Memory and the Vietnam Veterans Memorial* (Berkeley: University of California Press, 1998); Halprin, *The Franklin Delano Roosevelt Memorial*; and Edward T. Linenthal, *The Unfinished Bombing: Oklahoma City in American Memory* (New York: Oxford University Press, 2001). On Holocaust memorials, see James Young's many contributions, including *The Texture of Memory*, *The Art of Memory*, and *At Memory's Edge: After-Images of the Holocaust in Contemporary Art and Architecture* (New Haven, CT: Yale University Press, 2000).

94. See, for example, Martha Nussbaum, *Upheavals of Thought: The Intelligence of Emotions* (Cambridge: Cambridge University Press, 2001); William M. Reddy, *The Navigation of Feeling: A Framework for the History of Emotions* (Cambridge: Cambridge University Press, 2001); Peter N. Stearns and Carol Z. Stearns, "Emotionology: Clarifying the History of Emotions and Emotional Standards," *The American Historical Review* 90, no. 4 (October 1985): 813–36; and Peter N. Stearns and Jan Lewis, eds., *An Emotional History of the United States* (New York: New York University Press, 1998). A cognate field is "sensory history," or the history of the senses; see note 76.

95. Henry Rousso, *The Vichy Syndrome: History and Memory in France Since 1944*, trans. Arthur Goldhammer (Cambridge, MA: Harvard University Press, 1991); James Wilkin-

son, "A Choice of Fictions: Historians, Memory, and Evidence," *PMLA* 111, no. 1 (January 1996): 87.

96. Barbara H. Rosenwein, *Emotional Communities in the Early Middle Ages* (Ithaca, NY: Cornell University Press, 2006), 2; see also Barbara H. Rosenwein, "Worrying About Emotions in History," *The American Historical Review* 107, no. 3 (June 2002): 821–45; Thomas J. Ferraro, *Feeling Italian: The Art of Ethnicity in America* (New York: New York University Press, 2005), 204); Barry Shank, *A Token of My Affection: Greeting Cards and American Business Culture* (New York: Columbia University Press, 2004), 7.

97. Lauren Berlant, "Critical Inquiry, Affirmative Culture," *Critical Inquiry* 30 (Winter 2004): 446.

Chapter 2

1. Matt Bai, "Anatomy of a Massacre," *Newsweek*, May 3, 1999, 25–31.

2. Christopher Cooper and Robert Tomsho, "Aftermath: In Littleton, Companies Walk a Fine Line," *Wall Street Journal*, May 5, 1999; Julie Cart, "Shrine and Its Removal are Balms to Columbine," *Los Angeles Times*, May 6, 1999. Other area businesses responded to the Columbine murders with full-page newspaper ads, banners, and marquees: a huge blue ribbon inscribed with the word "Columbine" was hung outside Denver's Mile High Stadium, and a sign reading "Our prayers are with you, CHS" was erected outside the Hooters restaurant on Colorado Boulevard.

3. Mary V. Chandler, "Heartbreak, Mystery Shroud Shrine," *Rocky Mountain News*, May 2, 1999.

4. See, for example, *Descansos: An Interrupted Journey*, with text by Rudolfo Anaya, Denise Chávez, and Juan Estevan Arellano (Albuquerque, NM: El Norte Publications, 1995); and James Griffith, *Beliefs and Holy Places: A Spiritual Geography of the Pimería Alta* (Tucson: University of Arizona Press, 1992).

5. Henry S. Peters, "Sidewalk Roses Mark Strikers' Death Spot," *San Francisco Call-Bulletin*, July 6, 1934), as cited on the Virtual Museum of the City of San Francisco Web site, http://www.sfmuseum.org/hist4/maritime23.html (accessed September 1, 2005).

6. Lloyd Lewis, *Myths After Lincoln* (New York: Harcourt, 1929), 120; Carl Sandburg, *Abraham Lincoln: The War Years*, vol. 4 (New York: Harcourt, 1939), 401.

7. Erika Doss, *Elvis Culture: Fans, Faith, and Image* (Lawrence: University Press of Kansas, 1999), 97–105.

8. Vickie Chachere, "Remembering Carlie: Home of Florida Slaying Victim Becomes Memorial," *Denver Post*, February 8, 2004; Hudson Sangree, "Grief Overflows for Slain Tracy Girl," *Modesto (CA) Bee*, April 17, 2009.

9. For an overview of terminology see Peter Jan Margry and Christina Sánchez-Carretero, "Memorializing Traumatic Death," *Anthropology Today* 23, no. 3 (June 2007): 1–2.

10. Peter Jan Margry, "Performative Memorials: Arenas on Political Resentment in Dutch Society," in *Reforming Dutch Culture*, ed. Peter Jan Margry and H. Roodenburg (Aldershot, UK: Ashgate, 2008): 109–33.

11. This is similarly argued in *Disaster Ritual*, a study of contemporary ritual dynamics in Dutch and international contexts, whose authors observe that the memorials, marches, and services that follow many disasters are "strikingly coherent and orderly"; see Paulus G. J. Post et al., eds., *Disaster Ritual: Explorations of an Emerging Ritual Repertoire* (Leuven, Belgium: Peeters Publishers, 2003), 246.

12. See, for example, Bob Bednar, "Making Space on the Side of the Road: Towards a Cultural Study of Roadside Memorials" (2004), at http://people.southwestern.edu/~bednarb/roadsidememorials/ (accessed October 13, 2009); Erika Doss, *The Emotional Life of Contemporary Public Memorials: Towards a Theory of Temporary Memorials*, Meertens Ethnology Cahier 3 (Amsterdam: Amsterdam University Press, 2008); idem, "Death, Art, and Memory in the Public Sphere: The Visual and Material Culture of Grief in Contemporary America," *Mortality* 7, no. 1 (2002): 63–82; Sylvia Grider, "Public Grief and the Politics of Memorial," *Anthropology Today* 23, no. 3 (June 2007): 3–7; C. Allen Haney, Christina Leimar, and Juliann Lowery, "Spontaneous Memorialization: Violent Death and Emerging Mourning Ritual," *Omega* 35, no. 2 (1997): 159–71; Cheryl R. Jorgensen-Earp and Lori A. Lanzilotti, "Public Memory and Private Grief: The Construction of Shrines at Sites of Public Tragedy," *Quarterly Journal of Speech* 84 (1998): 150–70; Rebecca M. Kennerly, "Getting Messy: In the Field and at the Crossroads with Roadside Shrines," *Text and Performance Quarterly* 22, no. 4 (October 2002): 229–260; Peter Jan Margry, "The Murder of Pim Fortuyn and Collective Emotions: Hype, Hysteria, and Holiness in The Netherlands?" *Etnofoor: Antropologisch Tijdschrift* 16, no. 2 (2003): 106–31; and Irene Stengs, "Ephemeral Memorials Against 'Senseless Violence': Materialisations of Public Outcry" in *Etnofoor: Antropologisch Tijdschrift* 16, no. 2 (2003): 26–40, 106–31.

13. Jack Santino, "Not An Unimportant Failure: Rituals of Death and Politics in Northern Ireland," in *Displayed in Mortal Light*, ed. Michael McCaughan (Antrim, Northern Ireland: Antrim Arts Council, 1992), n.p.

14. Jack Santino, "Performative Commemoratives: Spontaneous Shrines and the Public Memorialization of Death," in *Spontaneous Shrines and the Public Memorialization of Death*, ed. Jack Santino (New York: Palgrave MacMillan, 2006), 13. See also Margry, "Performative Memorials."

15. Harriet F. Senie, "Mourning in Protest: Spontaneous Memorials and the Sacralization of Public Space," in Santino, *Spontaneous Shrines and the Public Memorialization of Death*, 45.

16. Jack Santino, *Signs of War and Peace: Social Conflict and the Use of Public Symbols in Northern Ireland* (New York: Palgrave, 2001), 103; Susanne Greenhalgh, "Our Lady of Flowers: The Ambiguous Politics of Diana's Floral Revolution," in *Mourning Diana: Nation, Culture, and the Performance of Grief*, ed. Adrian Kear and Deborah Lynn Steinberg (New York: Routledge, 1999), 40–59; and George Monger and Jennifer Chandler, "Pilgrimage to Kensington Palace," *Folklore* 109 (1998): 104–8. For other discussions see *Planet Diana: Cultural Studies and Global Mourning*, ed. Ien Agn et al. (Kingswood, Australia: Research Centre in Intercommunal Studies, University of Western Sydney, 1997), and Tony Walter, ed., *The Mourning for Diana* (London: Berg, 1999).

On the other hand, surveys conducted shortly after Diana's death asking informants to record their "reflections, feelings, opinions, [and] observations" about the media hype surrounding her demise found ambiguous responses that counter notions that Diana's death was collectively or critically mourned. See the detailed analysis compiled by James Thomas in *Diana's Mourning: A People's History* (Cardiff: University of Wales Press, 2002).

17. See, for example, Jennifer Clark, ed., *Roadside Memorials: A Multidisciplinary Approach* (Armidale, Australia: EMU Press, 2007); Holly Everett, *Roadside Crosses in Contemporary Memorial Culture* (Denton: University of North Texas Press, 2002); George Monger, "Modern Wayside Shrines," *Folklore* 108 (1997): 113–14; and John Wolffe, "Royalty and Public Grief in Britain: An Historical Perspective 1819–1997," in Walter, *The Mourning for Diana*, 53–64.

18. P. West, *Conspicuous Compassion: Why Sometimes It Is Really Cruel to Be Kind* (London: Civitas, 2004), as noted in Mervi Pantti, "Masculine Tears, Feminine Tears—and Crocodile Tears: Mourning Olof Palme and Anna Lindh in Finnish Newspapers," *Journalism* 6, no. 3 (2005): 357.

19. Jules Prown, *Art as Evidence: Writings on Art and Material Culture* (New Haven, CT: Yale University Press, 2002); Daniel Miller, ed., *Material Cultures: Why Some Things Matter* (Chicago: University of Chicago Press, 1998), 6.

20. Pierre Nora, "Between Memory and History," *Representations* 26 (Spring 1989): 13.

21. Doss, "Death, Art, and Memory in the Public Sphere," 66–67; Edward T. Linenthal, *The Unfinished Bombing: Oklahoma City in American Memory* (New York: Oxford University Press, 2001), 165–69. Kristin Hass suggests that as many as "a million objects were carried to (and stuffed into)" Memory Fence in the first year after the bombing; see Hass, *Carried to the Wall: American Memory and the Vietnam Veterans Memorial* (Berkeley: University of California Press, 1998), 126. Jane Thomas, curator of the Oklahoma City Memorial Foundation, says that this archive contains a collection of around three hundred thousand items; see Linenthal, *The Unfinished Bombing*, 167, 282–83n77.

22. Elizabeth Hallam and Jenny Hockey, *Death, Memory and Material Culture* (New York: Berg, 2001), 129–54; Jay Ruby, *Secure the Shadow: Death and Photography in America* (Cambridge, MA: MIT Press, 1995).

23. Emily Yellin, "New Orleans Epitaph: Dead Man Shirts," *New York Times*, April 17, 2000; Allison Engel, "In the Rear Window, Tributes to the Dead," *New York Times*, December 11, 2005.

24. Bruno Latour, "Introduction: From *Realpolitik* to *Dingpolitik* or How to Make Things Public," *Making Things Public: Atmospheres of Democracy*, ed. Bruno Latour and Peter Weibel (Cambridge, MA: MIT Press, 2005), 16.

25. Arjun Appadurai, *Modernity at Large: Cultural Dimensions of Globalization* (Minneapolis: University of Minnesota Press, 1996), 84; Rudi Colloredo-Mansfeld, "Matter Unbound," *The Journal of Material Culture* 8, no. 3 (November 2003): 252.

26. Hallam and Hockey, *Death, Memory and Material Culture*, 8.

27. By 1993, some 250,000 objects collected at the Vietnam Veterans Memorial had been collected and catalogued; see Hass, *Carried to the Wall*; and Thomas Allen, *Offerings at the Wall: Artifacts from the Vietnam Veterans Memorial Collection* (Atlanta, GA: Turner Publishing, 1995). On Oklahoma City's collection, see Carol Brown, "'Out of the Rubble': Building a Contemporary History Archive—The Oklahoma City National Memorial Archives," *Perspectives* (October 1999), http://www.historians.org/Perspectives/issues/1999/9910/9910EIP.CFM (accessed September 8, 2006).

28. Colorado Historical Society, "Columbine Memorial Recovery Strategy Meeting, May 6, 1999," memo, Decorative and Fine Arts Division, Colorado Historical Society, Denver, File Copy, Box 2000.130. By contrast, materials left on private grounds, such as Elvis's gravesite at Graceland, are generally not saved; see Doss, *Elvis Culture*, 102–4.

29. See, for example, Dana Heller, ed., *The Selling of 9/11: How a National Tragedy Became a Commodity* (New York: Palgrave, 2005); and Marita Sturken, *Tourists of History: Memory, Kitsch, and Consumerism from Oklahoma City to Ground Zero* (Durham, NC: Duke University Press, 2007).

30. Bill Brown, "Commodity, Nationalism, and the Lost Object" (lecture delivered at The Pathos of Authenticity: American Passions of the Real conference, John F. Kennedy-Institut für Nordamerikastudien, Berlin, June 21, 2007).

31. Bond quoted in Tara Burghart, "Sept. 11 Artifacts in Demand," *Denver Post*, December 13, 2001.

32. Ekaterina Haskins, "Between Archive and Participation: Public Memory in a Digital Age," *Rhetoric Society Quarterly* 37, no. 4 (2007): 414. For the Web site of the September 11 Digital Archive, see http://911digitalarchive.org/.

33. Clay Shirky, "Private, Public, and the Collapse of the Personal," in Michael Connor et al., *The New Normal* (New York: Independent Curators International, 2009), 53.

34. Haskins, "Between Archive and Participation," 415.

35. Valerie Neal, "Mourning Our Astronauts: Public Commemoration after the Space Shuttle Tragedies" (paper presented at the American Studies Association Annual Meeting, November 4, 2005, Washington, D.C.).

36. For insights on the challenges that temporary memorials pose for public institutions see James B. Gardner and Sarah M. Henry, "September 11 and the Mourning After: Reflections on Collecting and Interpreting the History of Tragedy," *The Public Historian* 24, no. 3 (Summer 2002): 37–52; and Michele V. Cloonan, "Monumental Preservation: A Call to Action," *American Libraries* (September 2004): 34–38. European museums are also facing these issues; see Margry, "The Murder of Pim Fortuyn and Collective Emotions," 113–4.

37. Carole Blair, "Contemporary U.S. Memorial Sites as Exemplar's of Rhetoric's Materiality," in *Rhetorical Bodies*, ed. Jack Selzer and Sharon Crowley (Madison: University of Wisconsin Press, 1999), 46.

38. C. Nadia Seremetakis, ed., *The Senses Still: Perception and Memory As Material Culture in Modernity* (Chicago: The University of Chicago Press, 1994), 9; see also Paul Connerton, *How Societies Remember* (Cambridge: Cambridge University Press, 1989) and Christopher Pinney's discussion of "corpothetics," or "the sensory embrace of images" in *Beyond Aesthetics: Art and the Technologies of Enchantment*, ed. Christopher Pinney and Nicholas Thomas (Oxford: Berg, 2001), 158.

39. Alicia C. Shepard, "The Columbine Shooting: Live Television Coverage," in *Thinking Clearly: Cases in Journalistic Decision-Making*, ed. Tom Rosenstiel and Amy Mitchell (New York: Columbia University Press, 2003), 57–81.

40. Daniel Dayan and Elihu Katz, *Media Events: The Live Broadcasting of History* (Cambridge, MA: Harvard University Press, 1994), 1; see also Nick Couldry, *Media Rituals: A Critical Approach* (New York: Routledge, 2003).

41. Justin Watson, *The Martyrs of Columbine: Faith and the Politics of Tragedy* (New York: Palgrave Macmillan, 2002), 1; Howard Kurtz, "Media Blitz Raises Coverage Questions," *Washington Post*, April 22, 1999.

42. Jessica Seigel, "Hugging the Spotlight: The Media at Columbine," *Brill's Content*, July–August 1999, http://jessicasiegel.com/articles/columbine.shtml (accessed January 17, 2008); Mindy Sink, "Small Town Propelled to World Stage," *New York Times*, April 25, 1999.

43. Josef Adalian, "School Tragedy Adds Eyes to Mags," *Variety*, April 26–May 2, 1999): 26; Janna Malamud Smith, "Telling Our Terrible Stories to the Tube," *New York Times*, April 25, 1999; Sink, "Small Town Propelled to World Stage."

44. S. Dunwoody, "Scientists, Journalists, and the Meaning of Uncertainty," in *Communicating Uncertainty: Media Coverage of New and Controversial Science*, ed. S. M. Friedman, S. Dunwoody, and C. L. Rogers (Mawah, NJ: Lawrence Erlbaum, 1999), 61; Mary Ann Doane, "Information, Crisis, Catastrophe," in *Logics of Television: Essays in Cultural Criticism*, ed. Patricia Mellencamp (Bloomington: Indiana University Press, 1990), 222.

45. Josh Rymes, senior Broadcast News major at the University of Colorado, Boulder, quoted in Tara McLain, "Tragedy 101," *Bylines* [University of Colorado, Boulder, School of Journalism and Mass Communication Alumni Newsletter] (Spring 1999): 16. On the ethical dimensions of documenting trauma see Ronald L. Grimes, "Shooting Rites," in *Colloquium: Music, Worship, Arts* 2 (Autumn 2005): 1–10. Author Dave Cullen asserts that Harris and Klebold were not, in fact, outcasts but sadists and psychopaths; see his book *Columbine* (New York: Twelve, 2009).

It is noted that the Media Research Center, dedicated to "documenting, exposing, and neutralizing liberal media bias," views TV coverage of Columbine and other school shootings quite differently; see, for example, Geoffrey Dickens, "Outgunned: How the Network News Media Are Spinning the Gun Control Debate," *Media Research Center Special Report*, January 5, 2000, http://www.fulton-armory.com/MRC2.htm (accessed June 21, 2005).

46. Michael Roberts, "Anniversary Post-Mortem," *Westword* (April 27, 2000): 19; Dusty Saunders, "Columbine Coverage More than Just a Story for Couric," *Rocky Mountain News*, April 17, 2004.

47. Patricia Mellencamp, "TV Time and Catastrophe, Or *Beyond the Pleasure Principle* of Television," in Mellencamp, *Logics of Television*, 253.

48. Sigmund Freud, "Mourning and Melancholia," The Standard Edition of the Complete Psychological Works of Sigmund Freud, trans. James Strachey (London: Hogarth Press, 1974): 14: 243–58 (quote, 245).

49. George Hagman, "Mourning: A Review and Reconsideration," International Journal of Psychoanalysis 76 (October 1995): 909–25; Tammy Clewell, "Mourning Beyond Melancholia: Freud's Psychoanalysis of Loss," Journal of the American Psychoanalytic Association 52, no. 1 (Spring 2004): 43–67.

50. José E. Muñoz, "Photographies of Mourning: Melancholia and Ambivalence in Van Der Zee, Mapplethorpe, and Looking for Langston," in Race and the Subject of Masculinities, ed. Harry Stecopoulos and Michael Uebel (Durham, NC: Duke University Press, 1997), 355–56. See also Michael Moon, "Memorial Rags," in Professions of Desire: Lesbian and Gay Studies in Literature, ed. George E. Haggerty and Bonnie Zimmerman (New York: Modern Language Association, 1995), 233–40; Philip Novak, "Circles and Circles of Sorrow: In the Wake of Morrison's Sula," PMLA 114 (1999): 184–93; and Greg Forter, "Against Melancholia: Contemporary Mourning Theory, Fitzgerald's The Great Gatsby, and the Politics of Unfinished Grief," differences 14, no. 2 (2003): 134–70.

51. Phyllis R. Silverman and Dennis Klass, "Introduction: What's the Problem?" in Continuing Bonds: New Understandings of Grief, ed. Dennis Klass, Phyllis Silverman, and Steven L. Nickman (Washington DC: Taylor & Francis, 1996), 3–30 (quote, 19).

52. The "stage" or phase model stems from Elizabeth Kübler-Ross, who theorized the grieving process in terms of a progression from anger to bitterness and finally to acceptance; see On Death and Dying (New York: Macmillan, 1969); and Linenthal, The Unfinished Bombing, 94.

53. Larry Beresford, "Looking Back at Columbine," in Living With Grief, Coping with Public Tragedy, ed. Marcia Lattanzi-Licht and Kenneth J. Doka (New York: Brunner-Routledge, 2003), 46–47; Karen Daly, principal, Martin Park Elementary School, Boulder, Colorado, memo to parents, April 22, 1999; David Brown, "Some Question Value of Trauma Sessions," Washington Post, May 3, 1999.

54. Jerome Groopman, "The Grief Industry," New Yorker, January 26, 2004, 30–38; on CISM, see Louis A. Gamino, "Critical Incident Stress Management and Other Crisis Counseling Approaches," in Lattanzi-Licht and Doka, Living With Grief, 123–38.

55. John R. Jordan and Robert A. Neimeyer, "Does Grief Counseling Work?" Death Studies 27 (2003): 778; Marcia Lattanzi-Licht, quoted in Beresford, "Looking Back at Columbine," 47; Christina Hoff Sommers and Sally Satel, One Nation Under Therapy: How the Helping Culture is Eroding Self-Reliance (New York: St. Martin's Press, 2005).

56. National Education Association, Crisis Communications Guide and Toolkit (Washington DC: NEA Communications, 2000), Book 3: 10; "Paying Tribute to Deceased School Community Members," ERCM Express [a newsletter of the U.S. Department of Justice Emergency Response and Crisis Management Technical Assistance Center] 3, no. 3 (2007): 5.

57. Arellano, "Alma mia de tu alma," in Descansos, 97

58. "Safety Week Opens with 'No Death Day,'" New York Times, October 9, 1922; "Unveil Monuments to Traffic Accidents," New York Times, May 2, 1926. A second similar memorial was erected at Broadway and 64th Street on the same day.

59. Graham Underwood, "Crosses Caution Drivers," Boulder Daily Camera, May 10, 2004; Bert Morgan, "Letter to the Editor," Life, May 19, 1941, 140; Robert Penn Warren, All the King's Men (New York: Harcourt, Brace, and Company, 1946), 3. Beginning in 1945, various garden clubs and civic organizations sponsored roadside signs in conjunction with the Blue Star Memorial Highway Marker program, which was designed to honor veterans of the U.S. armed services.

60. Michael Warner, Publics and Counterpublics (New York: Zone Books, 2002), 177.

61. The First International Symposium on Roadside Memorials was held at the University of New England, Armidale, New South Wales, Australia, in June 2004. Publications include those listed in notes 12 and 15; see also Jon K. Reid and Cynthia L. Reid, "A Cross Marks the Spot: A Study of Roadside Death Memorials in Texas and Oklahoma," Death Studies 25 (2001): 341–56; and Maida Owens, "Louisiana Roadside Memorials: Negotiating an Emerging Tradition," in Santino, Spontaneous Shrines and the Public Memorialization of Death, 119–45. For online sales of roadside memorial crosses see http://www.everlifememorials.com/Roadside-Memorial-Cross-p/pv-cross.htm.

62. Jennifer Clark and Majella Franzmann, "Authority from Grief, Presence and Place in the Making of Roadside Memorials," Death Studies 30, no. 6 (July 2006): 579–99.

63. Michael D. Shear, "Roadside Memorials Banned By VDOT," Washington Post, February 21, 2003; Judy Keen, "Warning Signs May Replace Memorials," USA Today, May 2, 2007.

64. Ian Urbina, "As Roadside Memorials Multiply, A Second Look," New York Times, February 6, 2006; "Delaware Highway Memorial Garden at Smyrna Rest Area Officially Opens," press release, State of Delaware Web site, October 15, 2007, http://www.deldot.gov/public.ejs?command=PublicNewsDisplay&id=2817 (accessed January 18, 2008).

65. Ted Shaffrey, "States Weigh Highway Shrines," Denver Post, September 1, 2002; see also "Colorado Court Rules Roadside Cross 'Litter' Not 'Venerated Object,'" Freethought Today 18, no. 5 (June/July 2001): 9–13. See also John P. Ferré's discussion of roadside memorials in "Last Words: Death and Public Expression," in Quoting God: How Media Shape Ideas about Religion and Culture, ed. Claire Badaracco (Waco, TX: Baylor University Press, 2005), 133–37.

66. Shear, "Roadside Memorials Banned By VDOT"; Mike Johnson and Peter Maller, "DOT Decides to Allow 1-Year Roadside Shrines," *Milwaukee Journal-Sentinel*, August 31, 2003; Cathy Brown, Associated Press, "Law signed legalizing roadside memorials," June 19, 2003, http://alaskalegislature.com/stories/061903/roadmemorial.shtml (accessed June 26, 2005).

67. Esther B. Fein, "For Lost Pregnancies, New Rites of Mourning," *New York Times*, January 25, 1998; Linda L. Layne, "Baby Things as Fetishes? Memorial Goods, Simulacra, and the 'Realness' Problem of Pregnancy Loss," in *Ideologies and Technologies of Motherhood: Race, Class, Sexuality, Nationalism*, ed. Heléna Ragoné and France Winddance Twine (New York: Routledge, 2000): 111–38.

68. Tamar Lewis, "A Move for Birth Certificates for Stillborn Babies," *New York Times*, May 22, 2007; Lynn M. Morgan, "When Does Life Begin? A Cross-Cultural Perspective on the Personhood of Fetuses and Young Children," in *Talking About People*, ed. Haviland and Gordon, 2nd ed. (Mountain View, CA: Mayfield Publishing Co., 1996), 24–34; Linda L. Layne, *Motherhood Lost: The Cultural Construction of Pregnancy Loss in the United States* (New York: Routledge, 2002); see also Lauren Berlant's discussion in *The Queen of America Goes to Washington City: Essays on Sex and Citizenship* (Durham, NC: Duke University Press, 1997), 83–144.

69. See http://www.memorialfortheunborn.org/ (accessed July 2, 2005).

70. See "Operation Save America Presents: Rachel's Park Memorial National Vision," http://operationsaveamerica.org/rpm/rachel's-park-memorial.htm (accessed September 9, 2006).

71. Brian Massumi, *Parables for the Virtual: Movement, Affect, Sensation* (Durham, NC: Duke University Press, 2002), 41.

72. "Prospectus for the Arch of Triumph of the Immaculate Heart of Mary and International Shrine of the Holy Innocents," http://www.archoftriumph.org/prospectus.html (accessed June 6, 2006); Rick Kern, "Proposed Memorial to Abortion Victims Ignites a Firestorm of Controversy," *The Word* [an evangelical Christian newspaper for Buffalo and Western New York], July 30, 2001, reprinted at http://www.archoftriumph.org/news3/html (accessed September 16, 2006). See also Michael I. Niman, "Thirteen Fools and a Golden Arch," *ArtVoice*, April 18, 2002, http://mediastudy.com/articles/av4-18-02.html (accessed June 6, 2006); and Bruce Jackson, "Our Lady of Ever-Expanding Mystery," *Buffalo Report*, May 1, 2002, http://buffaloreport.com/020501mystery.html (accessed September 9, 2006); Christopher Buckley, *Boomsday* (New York: Warner Books, 2007), 135.

73. David Kelly, "Church Plans to Bury the Ashes of Fetuses From Abortion Clinic," *Los Angeles Times*, January 22, 2005; Katie Kerwin McCrimmon, "100 Hold Vigil at Memorial Wall for Buried Fetuses," *Rocky Mountain News*, January 22, 2005; Sharon Lerner, "Shameless in Colorado," *The Nation*, February 24, 2005, 12.

Michael C. Kearl recounts a similar episode in Los Angeles in 1984, when sixteen thousand aborted fetuses were found on the premises of a defunct pathology laboratory. The Southern California chapter of the Catholic League offered to bury the remains in a religious ceremony that included the erection of a memorial plaque, and the Los Angeles District Attorney agreed. The California Court of Appeals, however, held that the district attorney's decision was in violation of the Establishment Clause of the California Constitution (which argues against state religious preference), and the remains were given a nonreligious burial. See Kearl, *Endings: A Sociology of Death and Dying* (Oxford: Oxford University Press, 1989), 323.

74. Lesley A. Sharp, "Commodified Kin: Death, Mourning, and Competing Claims on the Bodies of Organ Donors in the United States," *American Anthropologist* 103, no. 1 (March 2001): 112–33; see also Sharp, *Strange Harvest: Organ Transplants, Denatured Bodies, and the Transformed Self* (Berkeley: University of California Press, 2006).

75. "The National Donor Memorial," *Update: A News Magazine for the Transplant Community* (Richmond, VA: United Network for Organ Sharing, 2003), 1.

76. Clinton, quoted in Beresford, "Looking Back at Columbine," 42; Linenthal, quoted in J. Morgan, "Americans Leave Tokens of Grief at Murrah Building Blast Site," *Boulder Daily Camera*, April 19, 1998; Linenthal, *The Unfinished Bombing*, 111.

77. Lucy Lippard, *Off the Beaten Track: Tourism, Art, and Place* (New York: The New Press, 1999), 118–119; Sarah Vowell, *Assassination Vacation* (New York: Simon & Schuster, 2005).

78. Mark Facknitz, "Getting It Right by Getting it Wrong: Maya Lin's Misreading of Sir Edwin Luytens' Thiepval Memorial," *Crossings: A Counter-Disciplinary Journal* 7 (2004/2005): 50. On the growth of "tragic," "dark," and "death" tourism, see, for example, John Lennon and Malcolm Foley, *Dark Tourism: The Attraction of Death and Disaster* (New York: Continuum, 2000); and Graham M. S. Dann and A. V. Seaton, eds., *Slavery, Contested Heritage, and Thanatourism* (New York: Haworth Hospitality Press, 2001).

79. Sturken, *Tourists of History*, 211–18; Susan Stewart, *On Longing: Narratives of the Miniature, the Gigantic, the Souvenir, the Collection* (Baltimore, MD: The Johns Hopkins University Press, 1984); see also Paul Williams, *Memorial Museums: The Global Rush to Commemorate Atrocities* (New York: Berg, 2007). Consumption of tragedy is not unique to the United States: gift shops and souvenirs can be found at the Dachau Concentration Camp Memorial, the Cape Coast and Elmina slave fort museums in Ghana, and the Hiroshima Peace Memorial Museum, among other places.

80. Lois Romano, "Perimeter of Pain: Once a Simple Fence, Now a Heartbreaking Tribute to Bombing Victims," *Washington Post*, January 25, 1996.

81. Georges Bataille, *Oeuvres Completes*, vol. 3 (Paris: Gallimard, 1970–1988), 88.

82. David W. Dunlap, "For 9/11 Wall, A Little Support and a Permanent Place," *New York Times*, April 28, 2008; Lippard, *Off the Beaten Track*, 119; Joan W. Scott, "The Evidence of Experience," *Critical Inquiry* 17, no. 4 (Summer 1991): 773–97.

83. On the Bath School disaster, see Monty J. Ellsworth, *The Bath School Disaster* (Bath, MI: M. J. Ellsworth, 1927); Grant Parker, *Mayday: The History of a Village Holocaust* (Lansing, MI: Liberty Press, 1980); and Jeff Seidel, "Life After Terrorism," *Detroit Free Press*, December 9, 2001. On the 1958 Chicago fire, see David Cowan and John Kuenster, *To Sleep With the Angels: The Story of a Fire* (Chicago: Ivan R. Dee, 1996).

84. Lynn Riddle, "Where a Tragedy Occurred, a Coming Together," *New York Times*, January 22, 1995; "Seven Drown in Same Lake as Susan Smith's Boys," CNN.com, September 1, 1996, http://www.cnn.com/US/9609/01/drownings/index.html (accessed March 11, 2004). In 1997, the memorials were moved further away from the shore of John D. Long Lake.

85. See "Bob Fuller's Roadside Memorials," http://www.coloribus.com/adsarchive/tv-commercials/road-safety-bob-fullers-roadside-memorials-523518/ (accessed March 17, 2009).

86. "Memorial Honors Future Victims" (video), *Onion News Network*, http://www.theonion.com/content/video/preemptive_memorial_honors_future (accessed September 3, 2008); on the Buildings of Disaster collection, see http://www.boym.com/ and http://www.mossonline.com/product-exec/product_id/30435/category_id/257 (accessed September 3, 2008). Boym also has a second miniature line called Missing Monuments, consisting of replicas of memorials and buildings that have been destroyed.

87. Gail Holst-Warhaft, *The Cue for Passion: Grief and Its Political Uses* (Cambridge, MA: Harvard University Press, 2000), 2.

88. Robert Pogue Harrison, *The Dominion of the Dead* (Chicago: University of Chicago Press, 2003), 57.

89. Mary Marshall Clark, "The September 11, 2001 Oral History and Narrative Project: A First Report," *Journal of American History* 89, no. 2 (September 2002): 568. Thomson is discussed in Timothy G. Ashplant, Graham Dawson, and Michael Roper, "The Politics of War Memory and Commemoration: Contexts, Structures, and Dynamics," in *The Politics of War Memory and Commemoration*, ed. Timothy G. Ashplant, Graham Dawson, and Michael Roper (New York: Routledge, 2000), 14.

90. David Simpson, 9/11: *The Culture of Commemoration* (Chicago: University of Chicago Press, 2006), 156, 95.

91. American Psychological Association, "End-of-Life Care Issues," http://www.apa.org/pi/eol/historical.html (accessed June 17, 2003).

92. "2005 Wirthlin Report, A Study of American Attitudes Toward Ritualization and Memorialization" (Mount Sterling, OH: Funeral and Memorial Information Council, 2005).

93. On the Project on Death in America, see Robert A. Neimeyer, "Research on Grief and Bereavement: Evolution and Revolution," *Death Studies* 28, no. 6 (July–August 2004): 489.

94. Jessica Mitford, *The American Way of Death* (New York: Random House, 1963); Tony Walter, "A New Model of Grief: Bereavement and Biography," *Mortality* 1, no. 1 (1996): 7–25.

95. Cathy Caruth, introduction to *Trauma: Explorations in Memory*, (Baltimore, MD: The Johns Hopkins University Press, 1995), 4–5.

96. Georges Bataille, *Eroticism, Death and Sensuality* (San Francisco: City Light Books, 1986), 82.

97. Roland Barthes, *Camera Lucida: Reflections on Photography*, trans. Richard Howard (New York: Farrar, Straus and Giroux, 1981), 87. At Clement Park, the few objects that did reference death—such as a teddy bear smeared with ketchup that was supposed to look like blood—were quickly removed by park staff.

98. On notions of the dead remaining persistently social creatures see Sharp, *Strange Harvest*, 210.

99. Haney, Leimer, and Lowerty, "Spontaneous Memorialization," 159–60.

100. Harrison, *The Dominion of the Dead*, 143–45; Zoë Crossland, "Buried Lives: Forensic Archaeology and the Disappeared in Argentina," *Archaeological Dialogues* 7, no. 2 (2000): 146–59.

101. Anthony DePalma, "Illness Persisting in 9/11 Workers, Big Study Finds," *New York Times*, September 6, 2006.

102. Shaila Dewan, "Disasters and the Dead," *New York Times*, October 16, 2005; Suzan Clarke, "Families Remember WTC Victims, Fight for a Proper Burial," *Journal News* (Westchester, New York), October 18, 2005, http://www.voicesofsept11.0rg/artman/publish/Fresh_Kills/article_002075.php# (accessed January 9, 2006). During construction and rebuilding at the World Trade Center site, hundreds of human remains, mostly bone fragments, continued to be recovered; see David W. Dunlap, "Road at Trade Center Site to Be Excavated for Remains," *New York Times*, December 30, 2006.

103. C. J. Chivers, "Lost at Sea Isn't What It Used to Be," *New York Times*, November 14, 1999.

104. Michael Sledge, *Soldier Dead: How We Recover, Identity, Bury, and Honor Our Military Fallen* (New York: Columbia University Press, 2005), 33; James P. Delgado, "Memorials, Myths and Symbols: The Significance of the ARIZONA Memorial," *Valley Forge Journal*

5, no. 4 (1991): 310–26; Edward Linenthal, *Sacred Ground: Americans and Their Battlefields*, 2nd ed. (Urbana: University of Illinois Press, 1993), 173–212.

105. Katherine Verdery, *The Political Lives of Dead Bodies: Reburial and Postsocialist Change* (New York: Columbia University Press, 1999), 31, 35.

106. Franny Nudelman, *John Brown's Body: Slavery, Violence, and the Culture of War* (Chapel Hill: University of North Carolina Press, 2004), 4, 175.

107. On Wells and *Crisis*, see Anne P. Rice, ed., *Witnessing Lynching: American Writers Respond*, (New Brunswick, NJ: Rutgers University Press, 2003), 46–60, 141–50. On Emmett Till, see Shaila Dewan, "How Photos Became Icon of Civil Rights Movement," *New York Times*, August 28, 2005; Karla F.C. Holloway, *Passed On: African American Mourning Stories* (Durham, NC: Duke University Press, 2002), 129–33, 136–38; and Christine Harold and Kevin Michael DeLuca, "Behold the Corpse: Violent Images and the Case of Emmett Till," *Rhetoric & Public Affairs* 8, no. 2 (2005): 263–86. Ernest Wither's photograph of Till's body appeared in *Jet* on September 15, 1955. Earlier, in 1949, the *Chicago Defender* published pictures of Caleb Hill, lynched in Irwinton, Georgia; see "Think This Picture Ugly? Well, So Is Lynching!" *Chicago Defender*, June 11, 1949.

108. "Statement by the President on the Death of Abu Musad al-Zarqawi," June 8, 2006, http://www.whitehouse.gov/news/releases/2006/06/20060608.html (accessed June 20, 2006. In February 2009, the Obama administration lifted the media ban on photographs of flag-draped coffins of U.S. soldiers.

109. Watson, *The Martyrs of Columbine*, 4–6.

110. Dave Cullen, "From Solace to 'Satan': Do Columbine-area evangelists soothe or fuel kids' alienation?" *Denver Post*, May 30, 1999; Andrew Walsh, "Preaching the Word in Littleton," *Religion in the News* 2, no. 2 (Summer 1999), http://www.trincoll.edu/depts/csrpl/RINVol2No2/littleton.htm (accessed July 7, 2005). Other area evangelical organizations include the Promise Keepers, headquartered ten miles from Columbine High School, and Focus on the Family, located in Colorado Springs.

111. "United in Prayer," *Rocky Mountain News*, April 22, 1999.

112. Amy Goldstein, "Deaths Seen in Christian Context," *Washington Post*, April 27, 1999.

113. Cullen, "From Solace to 'Satan'"; Walsh, "Preaching the Word in Littleton."

114. Cullen, "From Solace to 'Satan'"' Rev. Bruce Porter, quoted in "Out of Control? Columbine Religious Service Outrage Minority Faiths, Spur Accusations of Proselytizing," *American Atheists*, April 30, 1999, http://www.mailarchive.com/ctrl@listserv.aol.com/msg12113.html (accessed July 7, 2005).

115. Diane Carman, "And Still They Come to the Tear-Stained, Hallowed Ground," *Denver Post*, April 25, 1999; J. Bottum, "Awakening at Littleton," *First Things* 95 (August/September 1999): 29.

116. Bill Duryea, "Seeking Solace in Religion," *St. Petersburg Times*, April 25, 1999.

117. Lisa Miller, "Site of Tragedy Attracts Samaritans, Zealots," *Wall Street Journal*, May 5, 1999; Walsh, "Preaching the Word in Littleton."

118. Christian Smith, *American Evangelicalism: Embattled and Thriving* (Chicago: University of Chicago Press, 1998), 121.

119. Quoted in Bottum, "Awakening at Littleton," 31.

120. Zanis, quoted in Joni Hannigan, "Columbine Crosses Prompt Baptist Youths' Reflections" (Southern Baptist Convention '99 Newsroom, June 12, 1999), http://www.sbcannualmeeting.org/sbc99/news6.htm (accessed January 18, 2008). See also Peggy Lowe,

"Killers' Kin Thanked Cross-Builder," *Denver Post*, May 27, 1999; and Tom McNamee, "Staking His Ministry on 'Crosses for Losses,'" *Chicago Sun-Times*, May 23, 2005.

121. Helen T. Gray, "Carpenter's Memorial to Slain Students Thrusts Spotlight Upon Him," *Kansas City Star*, September 10, 1999; Wendy Murray Zoba, "'Do You Believe in God?' Columbine and the Stirring of America's Soul," *Christianity Today Magazine*, October 4, 1999, http://www.christianitytoday.com/ct/1999/october4/9tb032.html (accessed January 18, 2008).

122. Zoba, "'Do You Believe in God?'"; Peggy Lowe and Andrew Guy, Jr., "Clement Park Begins Slow Return to Normalcy," *Denver Post*, May 5, 1999. See also Lorraine Adams, "Columbine Crosses Can't Bear Weight of Discord," *Washington Post*, May 3, 1999; and Grider, "Public Grief and the Politics of Memorial."

123. Adams, "Columbine Crosses Can't Bear Weight of Discord." The crosses were reinstalled at Clement Park several times over the course of a few weeks.

124. Sandra Fish, "Gun Control Strife," *Daily Camera* (Boulder), May 2, 1999.

125. Charlton Heston, opening comments (NRA Annual Meeting, Denver, Colorado, May 1, 1999), http://www.nracentral.com/annual_meeting_denver_heston_opening.ph (accessed August 3, 2005).

126. "Deaths: Final Data for 1999," *National Vital Statistics Reports* 49 (2001): 8.

127. Kieran Nicholson, "Father Plans Vigil on Memorial Day," *Denver Post*, May 29, 1999; Dan Haley, "Protesters Chop Down Trees," *Denver Post*, September 27, 1999.

128. Kate V. Hartig and Kevin M. Dunn, "Roadside Memorials: Interpreting New Deathscapes in Newcastle, New South Wales," *Australian Geographical Studies* 36, no. 1 (March 1998): 5–20.

129. Douglas Crimp, "Mourning and Militancy," *October* 51 (Winter 1989): 18. By 2005, the quilt featured over forty-six thousand panels and weighed over fifty-four tons, and the NAMES Project Foundation had evolved into an international foundation centered on AIDS awareness and eradication; see the foundation Web site, http://www.aidsquilt.org/index.htm; and Jesse McKinley, "A Changing Battle on AIDS is Reflected in a Quilt," *New York Times*, January 31, 2007.

130. John Seabrook, "The AIDS Philosopher," *Vanity Fair*, December 1990, 111, as noted in Peter S. Hawkins, "Naming Names: The Art of Memory and the NAMES Project AIDS Quilt," *Critical Inquiry* 19 (Summer 1993): 764–65.

131. Christopher Capozzola, "A Very American Epidemic: Memory Politics and Identity Politics in the AIDS Memorial Quilt, 1985–1993," *Radical History Review* 82 (Winter 2002): 92; Ann Cvetkovich, *An Archive of Feeling: Trauma, Sexuality, and Lesbian Public Cultures* (Durham, NC: Duke University Press, 2003), 163.

132. See http://www.agentorangequiltoftears.com.

Chapter 3

1. President Bill Clinton, "Remarks at Pan Am 103 Event," December 21, 1993, http://www.clintonfoundation.org/legacy/122193-speech-by-president-at-pan-am10393-speech-by-event.htm (accessed January 2, 2006); and idem, "Remarks of Dedication of Cairn for Pan Am," November 3, 1995, http://www.clintonfoundation.org/legacy/110395-remarks-by-president-at-dedication-of-cairn-for-pan-am.htm (accessed January 2, 2006).

2. President Bill Clinton, "Speech at Oklahoma City National Memorial," April 19, 2000, http://www.clintonfoundation.org/legacy/041900-speech-by-president-at-oklahoma-city-national-memorial.htm (accessed January 2, 2006).

3. Glenn Collins, "Design Selected for a Memorial at Ground Zero," *New York Times*, January 7, 2004; Amy Westfeldt, "'Reflecting Absence' to Fill Space," *Daily Camera* (Boulder), January 7, 2004.

4. Debra Burlingame, "The Great Ground Zero Heist," *Wall Street Journal*, June 7, 2005, and quoted in Robin Finn, "Fighting for the Underlying Meaning of Ground Zero," *New York Times*, August 12, 2005.

5. United States Department of Justice, "Strategic Goal One," http://www.usdoj.gov/ag/annualreports/pr2001/pdf/Section01.pdf (accessed January 2, 2006).

6. See Tydnall Report Web site, http://www.tyndallreport.com/; see also Lori Robertson, "High Anxiety," *American Journalism Review* 25, no. 3 (April 2003): 18–25; Brian Massumi, "Fear (The Spectrum Said)," *Positions: East Asia Cultures Critique* 13, no. 1 (Spring 2005): 31.

7. National Center for Disaster Preparedness, *Snapshot 2005: Where the American Public Stands on Terrorism and Preparedness Four Years After September 11: Confusion, Loss of Confidence, and Unmet Challenges* (New York: Columbia University Mailman School of Public Health, 2005), 2; Thomas Hargrove and Guido H. Stempel III, "Some Think Feds Involved in 9/11," *Daily Camera* (Boulder), August 3, 2006.

8. Lauren Berlant, *The Anatomy of National Fantasy: Hawthorne, Utopia, and Everyday Life* (Chicago: University of Chicago Press, 1991), 20. As of 2009, the death toll for the victims of September 11 was 2,976, of which 236 people were non–U.S. citizens.

9. Quoted in information distributed by the Oklahoma City Memorial Foundation, 1997.

10. Christopher Hewitt, *Understanding Terrorism in America: From the Klan to Al Queda* (New York: Routledge, 2002).

11. Courtney C. Radsch, "Star-Spangled Fear, Across Two Centuries; Exhibition Looks at Response to Threats on U.S. Soil," *New York Times*, August 5, 2004.

12. Jean Baudrillard, *The Spirit of Terrorism and Requiem for the Twin Towers*, trans. Chris Turner (London: Verso, 2002), 4.

13. President George W. Bush, "Remarks at the Pentagon," September 11, 2002, http://www.whitehouse.gov/news/releases/2002/09/20020911.html (accessed January 2, 2006).

14. Peter Sloterdijk, *Critique of Cynical Reason*, trans. Michael Eldred (Minneapolis: University of Minnesota Press, 1987), 5–6; Thomas Foster, "Cynical Nationalism," in *The Selling of 9/11: How a National Tragedy Became a Commodity*, ed. Dana Heller (New York: Palgrave Macmillan, 2005), 255.

15. Michael Kimmelman, "Out of Minimalism, Monuments to Memory," *New York Times*, January 13, 2002.

16. Omar Sacirbey, "Berlin Struggles to Pick a Memorial to Holocaust," *Christian Science Monitor*, January 27, 1998, international edition.

17. Andrew Shanken, "Planning Memory: Living Memorials in the United States During World War II," *Art Bulletin* 84, no. 1 (March 2002): 132.

18. Erika Doss, *Benton, Pollock, and the Politics of Modernism: From Regionalism to Abstract Expressionism* (Chicago: University of Chicago Press, 1991), 363–423.

19. Jean-François Lyotard, "Answering the Question: What is Postmodernism?" in *The Postmodern Condition*, trans. Geoff Bennington and Brian Massumi (Minneapolis: University of Minnesota Press, 1984), 81.

20. Anna Chave, "Minimalism and Biography," *Art Bulletin* 82, no. 1 (March 2000): 149. See also Ann Goldstein and Lisa Mark, eds., *A Minimal Future? Art as Object 1958–1968*

(Cambridge, MA: MIT Press, 2004); and in particular, James Meyer's essay on East and West Coast Minimalists, "Another Minimalism," 33–50.

21. E. C. Goossen, "Two Exhibitions," in *Minimal Art*, ed. Gregory Battcock (1968; repr., Berkeley: University of California Press, 1995), 168–69.

22. Battcock, *Minimal Art*, 32, 36; Robert Morris, "Notes on Sculpture," *Artforum* (February 1966); reprinted in Battcock, *Minimal Art*, 232, 235.

23. Hal Foster, "The Crux of Minimalism," in *The Return of the Real: The Avant-Garde at the End of the Century* (Cambridge, MA: MIT Press, 1996), 38.

24. Robert Smithson, "Cultural Confinement," *Artforum* (October 1972); reprinted in Nancy Holt, ed., *The Writings of Robert Smithson* (New York, 1979): 132–33.

25. Chave, "Minimalism and Biography," 150; Alex Potts, *The Sculptural Imagination: Figurative, Modernist, Minimalist* (New Haven: Yale University Press, 2001), 190.

26. Francis Frascina, *Art, Politics, and Dissent: Aspects of the Art Left in Sixties America* (Manchester: Manchester University Press, 1999); see also David Raskin, "Specific Opposition: Judd's Art and Politics," *Art History* 24, no. 5 (November 2001): 682–706.

27. Michael Fried, "Art and Objecthood," *Artforum* 5 (June 1967): 12–23.

28. Carole Pateman, *Participation and Democratic Theory* (Cambridge: Cambridge University Press, 1970).

29. Kimmelman, "Out of Minimalism, Monuments to Memory."

30. Paul Goldberger, "Requiem: Memorializing Terrorism's Victims in Oklahoma," *New Yorker*, January 14, 2002, 90–91; Michael Kimmelman, "Finding Comfort in the Safety of Names," *New York Times*, August 31, 2003.

31. Lin, quoted in "Vietnam Veterans Memorial: America Remembers," *National Geographic*, May 1985, 557, and in the film *Maya Lin: A Strong Clear Vision*, directed by Freida Lee Mock (1995; American Film Foundation, DVD). The number of names on the wall reached 58,253 in 2006.

32. Daniel Abramson, "Maya Lin and the 1960s: Monuments, Time Lines, and Minimalism," *Critical Inquiry* 22, no. 4 (Summer 1996): 708.

33. "The Vietnam Veterans Memorial Design Competition: Design Program" (1980), as noted in Abramson, "Maya Lin and the 1960s," 685–87, 701.

34. Anonymous Vietnam War veteran quoted in Robert K. Brigham, "Monument or Memorial? The Wall and the Politics of Memory," *Historical Reflections / Reflexions Historiques* 25, no. 1 (1999): 166; Scruggs, quoted in Robin Wagner-Pacifici and Barry Schwartz, "The Vietnam Veterans Memorial: Commemorating a Difficult Past," *American Journal of Sociology* 97, no. 2 (September 1991): 394.

35. Kimmelman, "Out of Minimalism, Monuments to Memory"; Marita Sturken, *Tangled Memories: The Vietnam War, the* AIDS *Epidemic, and the Politics of Remembering* (Berkeley: University of California Press, 1997), 75; W. J. T. Mitchell, "The Violence of Public Art: *Do the Right Thing*," in *Picture Theory: Essays on Verbal and Visual Representation* (Chicago: University of Chicago Press, 1994), 381.

36. Ronald Reagan, "Remarks at the Veterans Day Ceremony at the Vietnam Veterans Memorial," November 11, 1988; at: http://www.reagan.utexas.edu/archives/speeches/1988/111188b.htm (accessed January 25, 2006).

37. Nancy K. Miller and Jason Tougaw, eds., *Extremities: Trauma, Testimony, and Community* (Urbana: University of Illinois Press, 2002), 1.

38. Mark Seltzer, "Wound Culture: Trauma in the Pathological Public Sphere," *October* 80 (Spring 1997): 3–26; see also Seltzer, *Serial Killers: Death and Life in America's Wound Culture* (New York: Routledge, 1998). *CSI: Crime Scene Investigation* was the top-rated show

in 2002–2003 and 2003–2004, and *NCIS: Naval Criminal Investigative Service* topped the Nielsen ratings in December 2006.

39. See, for example, Ruth Leys, *Trauma: A Genealogy* (Chicago: University of Chicago Press, 2000).

40. On the Vietnam War as "national trauma," see Michael Anderegg, ed., *Inventing Vietnam: The War in Film and Television* (Philadelphia: Temple University Press, 1991). On trauma's medicalization on psychiatric terms, see Richard J. McNally, *Remembering Trauma* (Cambridge, MA: Harvard University Press, 2003), 4–9.

41. Cathy Caruth, *Unclaimed Experience: Trauma, Narrative, and History* (Baltimore, MD: The Johns Hopkins University Press, 1996); Caruth, ed., *Trauma: Explorations in Memory* (Baltimore, MD: The Johns Hopkins University Press, 1995); Shoshana Felman, *The Juridical Unconscious: Trials and Traumas in the Twentieth Century* (Cambridge, MA: Harvard University Press, 2002); and Shoshana Felman and Dori Laub, *Testimony: Crises of Witnessing in Literature Psychoanalysis and History* (New York: Routledge, 1992); Dominick LaCapra, *Writing History, Writing Trauma* (Baltimore, MD: The Johns Hopkins University Press, 2001); and idem, *Representing the Holocaust: History, Theory, Trauma* (Ithaca, NY: Cornell University Press, 1994).

42. Caruth, *Unclaimed Experience*, 24; Fritz Breithaupt, "Rituals of Trauma: How the Media Fabricated September 11," in *Media Representations of September 11*, ed. Steven Chermak, Frankie Y. Bailey, and Michelle Brown (Westport, CT: Praeger, 2003), 69.

43. Tom Toremans, "Trauma: Theory-Reading (and) Literary Theory in the Wake of Trauma," *European Journal of English Studies* 7, no. 3 (2003): 333–51; Caruth, introduction to *Trauma*, 3–4. See also Wulf Kansteiner, "Geneaology of a Category Mistake: A Critical Intellectual History of the Cultural Trauma Metaphor," *Rethinking History* 8, no. 2 (June 2004): 193–221.

44. Elaine Scarry, *The Body in Pain: The Making and Unmaking of the World* (New York: Oxford University Press, 1985).

45. Saitowitz quoted in James Young, *The Texture of Memory: Holocaust Memorials and Meaning* (New Haven, CT: Yale University Press, 1993), 334.

46. Edward T. Linenthal, *The Unfinished Bombing: Oklahoma City in American Memory* (New York: Oxford, 2001), 184.

47. Hans-Ekkehard Butzer and Torrey Butzer, "The Oklahoma City Memorial," original design proposal to Oklahoma City Memorial Design Competition, 1997, files, The Oklahoma City Memorial Foundation, Oklahoma City (capitalization in the original

48. The "common field" slogan was written by Captain Stephen Ruda of the Los Angeles City Fire Department and adopted by the Flight 93 National Memorial Commission.

49. Sewall Chan, " A New, Longer Name for the 9/11 Memorial," *New York Times*, August 17, 2007. Bloomberg, quoted in Sean D. Hamill, "Bloomberg Visits Flight 93 Crash Site on 9/11 Trip," *New York Times*, September 24, 2007.

50. Nicolai Ouroussof, "The Ground Zero Memorial, Revised but Not Improved," *New York Times*, June 22, 2006; Charles V. Bagli and David W. Dunlap, "Memorial Cost at Ground Zero Nears $1 Billion," *New York Times*, May 5, 2006; Douglas Feiden, "Cost of 9/11 Memorial and Museum at Ground Zero Expected to Hit $1 Billion," *New York Daily News*, August 15, 2008.

51. Kimmelman, "Out of Minimalism, Monuments to Memory"; Harriet F. Senie, "Absence Versus Presence: The 9/11 Memorial Design," *Sculpture* 23, no. 4 (May 2004): 10–11. On proposals submitted to the World Trade Center Memorial competition, see the Lower Manhattan Development Corporation's Web site: http://www.wtcsitememorial.org/

submissions.html (accessed January 24, 2006). See also Nancy Princenthal, "Absence Visible," *Art in America* (April 2004): 38–45.

52. Sam Lubell, "Inside the Jury: An Interview with James Young," *Architectural Record* 192, no. 2 (February 2004): 24; see also James E. Young, "The Stages of Memory at Ground Zero," in *Religion, Violence, Memory, and Place*, ed. Oren Baruch Stier and J. Shawn Landres (Bloomington: Indiana University Press, 2006), 214–34.

53. Marita Sturken, "Memorializing Absence," in *Understanding September 11*, ed. Craig Calhoun, Paul Price, and Ashley Timmer (New York: W. W. Norton, 2002), 374–84.

54. Julian Reid, "Architecture, Al-Qaeda, and the World Trade Center," *Space and Culture* 7, no. 4 (November 2004): 396–408; Osama bin Laden, untitled speech, October 7, 2001, Doha, Qatar: Al Jazeera TV, as noted in Reid, "Architecture, Al-Qaeda, and the World Trade Center," 397 (emphasis added).

55. Elizabeth Diller and Ricardo Scofidio, "To Rebuild or Not: Architects Respond," *New York Times Magazine*, September 21, 2001, 81; Edward Wyatt, "2 Lofty Visions for the Void at Ground Zero," *New York Times*, February 5, 2003.

56. Dominick LaCapra, "Trauma, Absence, Loss," *Critical Inquiry* 25 (Summer 1999): 698.

57. Memorial mission statement, Lower Manhattan Development Corporation, http://www.renewnyc.com/Memorial/memmission.asp (accessed January 24, 2006).

58. Maureen Dowd, "Unbearable Lightness of Memory," *New York Times*, November 30, 2003.

59. On attendance figures for the Oklahoma City National Memorial, see National Park Service statistics, http://www2.nature.nps.gov/mpur/Reports/viewreport.cfm?reportnameID=861; on projected attendance figures for the National September 11 Memorial & Museum, see David W. Dunlap, "At Ground Zero, A Place to Recall a Lost Era," *New York Times*, August 29, 2005; on the Flight 93 National Memorial, see "Kirk Swauger, "Land Use Around Flight 93 Site Debated," *Tribune-Democrat* (Johnstown, PA), April 1, 2006, and Martha T. Moore, "For Flight 93 memorial, long-waited progress," *USA Today*, September 11–13, 2009.

60. For Freud's writings on fear and anxiety see, for example, "Introduction to Psychoanalysis" (1916) and "Beyond the Pleasure Principle" (1920) in *The Standard Edition of the Complete Psychological Works of Sigmund Freud*, trans. and ed. James Strachey (London: Hogarth Press, 1959); on Tomkins's discussion, see Eve Kosofsky Sedgwick and Adam Frank, eds., *Shame and Its Sisters: A Silvan Tomkins Reader* (Durham, NC: Duke University Press, 1995), 236.

61. "Executive Order 13328 of October 8, 2001, Establishing Office of Homeland Security and the Homeland Security Council," http://www.fas.org/irp/offdocs/eo/eo-13228.htm (accessed February 1, 2006).

62. Amy Kaplan, "Homeland Insecurities: Transformations of Language and Space," in *September 11 in History: A Watershed Moment?* ed. Mary L. Dudziak (Durham, NC: Duke University Press, 2003), 64.

63. David Campbell, *Writing Security: United States Foreign Policy and the Politics of Identity*, rev. ed. (Minneapolis: University of Minnesota Press, 1998); see also Campbell, "Time Is Broken: The Return of the Past in the Response to September 11," *Theory & Event* 5, no.4, http://muse.jhu.edu/journals/theory_and_event/v005/5.4campbell.html (accessed February 2, 2006).

64. Dana Milbank, "At Homeland Security, No Money Left Behind," *Washington Post*,

April 12, 2006; John Mueller, *Overblown: How Politicians and the Terrorism Industry Inflate National Security Threats, and Why We Believe Them* (New York: Simon & Schuster, 2006).

65. Mike Butcher, "Privacy Plays on U.S. Morality Mind," *New Media Age*, November 18, 1999, 26; Gary Langer, "Poll: Broader Concern on Privacy Rights, But Terrorism Threat Still Trumps," January 10, 2006, http://www.abcnews.go.com/Politics/story?id=1490715 (accessed January 15, 2006).

66. United States Government Accountability Office, "Homeland Security: Actions Needed to Better Protect National Icons and Federal Office Buildings from Terrorism" (Washington DC: US Government Accountability Office, 2005), 19–20; Michael Janofsky, "Security Efforts Turning the Capital Into an Armed Camp," *New York Times*, February 22, 2004. See also Mark Maremont, "Elsewhere: Form and Function: Disguising Security as Something Artful," *Wall Street Journal*, June 24, 2004; and Catesby Leigh, "Balancing Security and Aesthetics," *Wall Street Journal*, June 30, 2005.

67. Setha Low, "The Memorialization of September 11: Dominant and Local Discourses on the Rebuilding of the World Trade Center Site," *American Ethnologist* 31, no. 3 (2004): 328. For further accounts of America's expanding geography of paranoia, see Low, *Behind the Gates: Life, Security, and the Pursuit of Happiness in Fortress America* (New York: Routledge, 2003); Mike Davis, *City of Quartz: Excavating the Future in Los Angeles* (New York: Vintage, 1992); and Michael Sorkin, ed., *Indefensible Space: The Architecture of the National Insecurity State* (New York: Routledge, 2007).

68. Fred Hiatt, "Jefferson Fenced In," *Washington Post*, January 10, 2005.

69. Editorial, "The Capitol's Accidental Monument," *New York Times*, February 22, 2006; editorial, "A Visit Worth the Time and Money," *New York Times*, February 23, 2007.

70. John Tierney, "Living in Fear and Paying a High Cost in Heart Risk," *New York Times*, January 15, 2008.

71. Ulrich Beck, *Risk Society: Towards a New Modernity* (London: Sage, 1992): 49; John Tulloch and Deborah Lipton, *Risk and Everyday Life* (London: Sage, 2003): 8, 34.

72. Daniel Sherman, *The Construction of Memory in Interwar France* (Chicago: University of Chicago Press, 1999), 94.

73. Thomas Laqueur, "Untitled Comments," in *Grounds for Remembering: Monuments, Memorials, Texts, Occasional Papers of the Doreen B. Townsend Center for the Humanities*, ed. Christina M. Gillis (Berkeley: Doreen B. Townsend Center for the Humanities, University of California, 1995), 3:1; Jay Winter, *Sites of Memory, Sites of Mourning: The Great War in European Cultural History* (Cambridge: Cambridge University Press, 1995), 105. See also Thomas Laqueur, "Memory and Naming in the Great War," in *Commemorations: The Politics of National Identity*, ed. John Gillis (Princeton, NJ: Princeton University Press, 1994): 150–67; and Hélene Lipstadt, "Learning from Lutyens," *Harvard Design Magazine*, Fall 1999, 66. The Thiepval memorial was dedicated in 1932.

74. Michel de Certeau, *The Practice of Everyday Life*, trans. Steven F. Randall (Berkeley: University of California Press, 1984), 131–53; Michael Kammen, "Democratizing American Commemorative Monuments," *The Virginia Quarterly Review* 77, no. 2 (Spring 2001): 280–88.

75. Lin, quoted in Gillis, *Grounds for Remembering*, 8; see also Mark Facknitz, "Getting It Right by Getting it Wrong: Maya Lin's Misreading of Sir Edwin Luytens' Thiepval Memorial," *Crossings: A Counter-Disciplinary Journal* 7 (2004/2005): 47–69; Elizabeth O'Brien, "A Street by Another Name?" *Downtown Express* 16 (October 21–27 2003), http://www.downtownexpress.com/de_26/astreetbyanother.html (accessed November 25, 2006).

76. Kim Theriault, "Re-membering Vietnam: War, Trauma, and 'Scarring Over' After 'The Wall,'" *Journal of American Culture* 26, no. 4 (December 2003): 430n8. Congressional and Defense Department reconsideration of the official dates of U.S. occupation of Vietnam have helped to shape these shifting considerations of who died first.

77. Timothy Dwyer, "For Pentagon Memorial, the Power of Touch," *Washington Post*, February 1, 2007.

78. Maya Lin, *Boundaries* (New York: Simon & Schuster, 2000), 4.5; Kimmelman, "Finding Comfort in the Safety of Names."

79. Michael J. Shapiro, *Violent Cartographies: Mapping Cultures of War* (Minneapolis: University of Minnesota Press, 1997), 30.

80. See, for example, R. W. B. Lewis, *The American Adam: Innocence, Tragedy, and Tradition in the Nineteenth Century* (Chicago: University of Chicago Press, 1955); and Lauren Berlant, *The Queen of America Goes to Washington City: Essays on Sex and Citizenship* (Durham, NC: Duke University Press, 1997), 27.

81. Will made his remarks in a review of the newly opened United States Holocaust Memorial Museum in 1993; see George F. Will, "Holocaust Museum: Antidote for Innocence," *Washington Post*, March 10, 1993.

82. Michael Billing, *Banal Nationalism* (Thousand Oaks, CA: Sage Publications, 1995), 6.

83. Linenthal, *The Unfinished Bombing*, 119–20, 127–28; Daniel Harris, "The Kitschification of September 11," Salon.com January 25, 2002, http://archive.salon.com/news/feature/2002/01/25/kitsch/print.html (accessed July 9, 2007).

84. Linenthal, *The Unfinished Bombing*, 43–53.

85. "Focus Group: Families of Victims," in *New York New Visions Memorials Process Team Briefing Book: Findings from the Outreach, Temporary Memorials & Research Working Groups, March* 2002, ed. Johannah Rodgers (New York: New York New Visions, 2002), 7.

86. Noam Chomsky, *9-11* (New York: Seven Stories Press, 2001), 35.

87. Allen Feldman, "Political Terror and the Technologies of Memory: Excuse, Sacrifice, Commodification, and Actuarial Modalities," *Radical History Review* 85 (Winter 2003): 69; Ian Buruma, "The Joys and Perils of Victimhood," *The New York Review of Books*, April 8, 1999, 4.

88. Raymond Michalowski and Jill Dubisch, *Run for the Wall: Remembering Vietnam on a Motorcycle Pilgrimage* (New Brunswick, NJ: Rutgers University Press, 2001).

89. See "Cancer Survivor Parks" at http://blochcancer.org; further information on park numbers and development is from Vangie Rich, executive director, R. A. Bloch Cancer Foundation (e-mail message to author, March 24, 2006). Some of the parks, such as those in Chicago and Tampa, have been exempted from the bronze statuary requirement.

90. Kelly Klaasmeyer, "McSculpture for America," *Art Lies* 41 (Winter 2003–2004): 11–12; for discussion of the Cancer Survivor Park's curative efficacy, see Rebecca Fish Ewan, "Prescription for Healing," *Landscape Architecture*, February 2003, 59–65, 86–88; and William Speidel, "Getting Serious About Therapeutic Practice," *Landscape Architecture*, October 2003, 49–50.

91. Barbara Ehrenreich, "Welcome to Cancerland: A Mammogram Leads to a Cult of Pink Kitsch," *Harper's Magazine*, November 2001, 43–53; idem, *Bright-Sided: How the Relentless Pursuit of Positive Thinking Has Undermined America* (New York: Metropolitan Books, 2009).

92. For one list of 9/11 memorials, see "Voices of September 11," http://www.voices

ofsept11.org/dev/memorials.php?mem_id=282 (accessed October 14, 2009); see also Cara Mia DiMassa, "Soothing Suffering with Steel," *Los Angeles Times*, April 2, 2003.

93. Roach, quoted in Peter C. Beller, "Twin Towers, USA," *New York Magazine*, November 28, 2005, 32; and "Lake Charles 9-11 Memorial," http://www.cityoflakecharles.com/aroundtown/memorial.asp (accessed October 9, 2006).

94. Glenn Collins, "On Display, the Agonized Objects and Photos of 9/11," *New York Times*, September 5, 2007.

95. Ross, quoted in DiMassa, "Soothing Suffering with Steel." On Austin's memorial, see Christy Hoppe, "State's Sept. 11 Memorial: 'You Feel It in Your Soul,'" *Dallas Morning News*, September 12, 2002; and John Shelton Lawrence, "Rituals of Mourning and National Innocence," *The Journal of American Culture* 28, no. 1 (March 2005): 35–48.

96. Christy Ferer, "A 9-11 Widow Reflects on a Visit to Troops in Iraq," U.S. Marine Corps / Public Affairs press release, September 9, 2003, as noted in Lawrence, "Rituals of Mourning and National Innocence," 37–38.

97. "NY Rallies at Ground Zero for Troops," CNN.com, April 11, 2003, http://www.cnn.com/2003/US/Northeast/04/10/sprj.irq.ny.rally/index.html (accessed November 12, 2006). Pataki "achieved his smelting fantasy, sort of" in arranging for a ruined World Trade Center girder to be recast into the hulk of the new battleship, the USS *New York*; see Devin Zuber, "Flânerie at Ground Zero: Aesthetic Countermemories in Lower Manhattan," *American Quarterly* 58, no. 2 (June 2006): 295.

98. Robert Baxter, "9/11 Remembered," *Courier Post* (Camden, NJ), September 7, 2003, http://www.courierpostonline.com/columnists/cxba090703a.htm (accessed January 2, 2006).

99. Andrea Peyser, "Sick 9/11 Art Yanked," *New York Post*, September 19, 2002; Eric Fischl, "A Memorial That's True to 9/11," *New York Times*, December 19, 2003. The sculpture was meant to be exhibited for two weeks; for a full discussion see Randall Van Schepen, "Falling / Failing 9/11: Eric Fischl's *Tumbling Woman* Debacle," *Aurora: The Journal of the History of Art* 9 (2008): 116–43. See also David Friend's discussion of how images of World Trade Center "jumpers" were suppressed in *Watching the World Change: The Stories Behind the Images of* 9/11 (New York: Farrar, Straus and Giroux, 2006), 129–41.

100. Elaine Tyler May, "Echoes of the Cold War: The Aftermath of September 11 At Home," in Dudziak, *September 11 in History*, 49–50; see also Susan Faludi, *The Terror Dream: Fear and Fantasy in Post-*9/11 *America* (New York: Metropolitan Books, 2007).

101. Carolyn Marvin and David Ingle, *Blood Sacrifice and the Nation: Totem Rituals and the American Flag* (Cambridge: Cambridge University Press, 1999); see also Nancy Jay, *Throughout Your Generations Forever: Sacrifice, Religion, and Paternity* (Chicago: University of Chicago Press, 1992).

102. Freedom's Flame designers William Lecky and Lawrence Noble, quoted at http://www.freedomsflame.us (accessed January 23, 2006).

103. Competing historical narratives challenge the popular view of Crockett's demise; see James E. Crisp. *Sleuthing the Alamo: Davy Crockett's Last Stand and Other Mysteries of the Texas Revolution* (New York: Oxford University Press, 2005).

104. "Planning for the Flight 93 Memorial," *Flight 93 National Memorial Newsletter* 4 (November 2005): 1.

105. "'America is Grateful' to Flight 93 Heroes," CNN.com, September 11, 2002, http://archives.cnn.com/2002/US/09/11/ar911.memorial.pennsylvania (accessed February 20, 2005).

106. Steven Ambrose, *Citizen Soldiers: The U.S. Army From the Normandy Beaches to the Bulge to the Surrender of Germany, June 7, 1944-May 7, 1945* (New York: Simon & Schuster, 1997).

107. John J. Reynolds, statement, September 15, 2005, originally posted on the Flight 93 National Memorial Web site.

108. Reynolds, statement; U.S. Department of Homeland Security, "Ready" campaign, http://www.ready.gov/.

109. As noted in May, "Echoes of the Cold War," 38; see also Jenny Edkins, *Trauma and the Memory of Politics* (Cambridge: Cambridge University Press, 2003), 102.

110. Hal Rothman, *The New Urban Park: Golden Gate National Recreation Area and Civic Environmentalism* (Lawrence, : University Press of Kansas, 2004), ix; see also Robin Winks, "The National Park Service Act of 1916: "A Contradictory Mandate?" *Denver University Law Review* 74, no. 3 (1997): 575–624.

111. See the Memorial Institute for the Prevention of Terrorism Web site, http://www.mipt.org/about (accessed April 2, 2009).

112. Linenthal, *The Unfinished Bombing*, 119–35, 229–30; Robert Johnson, chairman of the Oklahoma City Memorial Foundation, quoted in Maria Puente, "Bombing memorial a monument to healing," *USA Today*, June 30, 1997. For information on the making of the Oklahoma City National Memorial, see the Web site, http://www.oklahomacitynationalmemorial.org/index.php (accessed October 9, 2007).

113. Kathleen Treanor, "An Appeal from the Heart," The Oklahoma City National Memorial homepage, http://connections.oklahoman.net/memorial/appeal.html (accessed October 9, 2006).

114. Angel Riggs, "Oklahoma City Bombing, 11 Years Later," *Tulsa World*, April 20, 2006.

115. President Bill Clinton, "Speech at Oklahoma City National Memorial."

116. City of Oklahoma City, "Federal Government Provides Recovery Funds," press release, April 2000. The federal government provided $52.5 million in HUD (housing and urban development) community development block grants to fund the Murrah Recovery Program, a loan partnership between local banks and the city to restore business activity in the downtown area damaged by the bombing; for further discussion, see Jennifer Spangler, "A Memorial to Terrorism's Victims: Commemorative Public Art in the Born Again City" (master's thesis, University of California, Davis, 2004).

117. Galen Cranz, *The Chair: Rethinking Culture, Body, and Design* (New York: W. W. Norton, 1998), 29–30; Edward Lucie-Smith, *Movements in Art Since 1945*, 3rd ed. (London: Thames & Hudson, 1995), 288.

118. Burlingame, quoted in Finn, "Fighting for the Underlying Meaning of Ground Zero"; "Take Back the Memorial Petition," http://takebackthemeorial.org (accessed June 25, 2005).

119. David W. Dunlap, "Governor Bars Freedom Center at Ground Zero," *New York Times*, September 29, 2005); Robert Kolker, "The Grief Police," *New York Magazine*, November 28, 2005, 46–56.

120. Stephanie Gaskell, "Firefighters' Memorial a Statue of Liberties?" *Rocky Mountain News*, January 12, 2002; Clarence Page, "Don't Whitewash NYFD's Dismal Diversity Record," *Denver Post*, January 17, 2002.

121. Watts also made a three-foot version of his sculpture for the firehouse shared by Engine Company 325 and Ladder Company 163 in Woodside, Queens; see Jonathan

Lemire, "'Bronzed' FDNY Photo Finds Home in Woodside," *New York Daily News*, September 11, 2003.

122. Marita Sturken, *Tourists of History: Memory, Kitsch, and Consumerism in American Culture* (Durham, NC: Duke University Press, 2007), 4; Kari Andén-Papadopoulus, "The Trauma of Representation: Visual Culture, Photojournalism, and the September 11 Terrorist Attack," *Nordicon Review* 24 (2003): 98.

123. Michael Powell, "9/11 Memorial Design Selected," *Washington Post*, January 6, 2004; Philippe de Montebello, "The Iconic Power of an Artifact," *New York Times*, September 25, 2001; J. B. Jackson, *The Necessity for Ruins and Other Topics* (Amherst: University of Massachusetts Press, 1980).

124. David W. Dunlap, "Plan is Changed for Arranging Names on Trade Center Memorial," *New York Times*, December 14, 2006; David W. Dunlap, "Relatives' Groups Use TV and Internet to Call for More Details with Names on 9/11 Memorial," *New York Times*, January 25, 2007; "Bill Would Create 9/11 Memorial," *Indianapolis Star*, January 29, 2007; see also note 49, above.

125. Amy Westfeldt, "Ground Zero Memorial in Jeopardy," *Washington Post*, May 7, 2006; Glenn Collins, "Protesters Step Up Calls for 9/11 Memorial Above Ground," *New York Times*, February 28, 2006; David W. Dunlap, "Security Concerns Raised About Memorial at Ground Zero," *New York Times*, April 21, 2006.

126. David W. Dunlap, "Group Protests Plan to Charge Fee to Enter 9/11 Museum," *New York Times*, April 11, 2006.

127. David W. Chen, "Striking Details in Final Report on 9/11 Fund," *New York Times*, November 18, 2004. Total compensation for 9/11, for both businesses and individuals, topped $38 billion, and 5,553 people were deemed eligible for the Victim Compensation Fund. In 2007, New York City mayor Michael Bloomberg requested millions more in federal funding for the rising health care costs of 9/11 first responders.

128. Dennis Smith, "Take Back the Towers," *New York Times*, April 58, 2006. Kolker, in *The Grief Police*, estimates that the "hard-core activists" of Take Back the Memorial and other 9/11 groups number less than thirty people.

129. Michael Kimmelman, "Ground Zero's Only Hope: Elitism," *New York Times*, December 7, 2003; David Stanke, "Free the Rest of the WTC From the Memorial," *Downtown Express*, October 7–13, 2005, http://www.downtownexpress.com/de_126/freethe restofthewtc.html (accessed October 9, 2007); N. R. Kleinfield, "As 9/11 Draws Near, a Debate Rises: How Much Tribute is Enough?" *New York Times*, September 2, 2007.

130. Alec Rawls posted these comments between September 2005 and February 2006 on his blog Error Theory (http://errortheory.blogspot.com). See also Alec Rawls, *Crescent of Betrayal: Dishonoring the Heroes of Flight 93* (Los Angeles: World Ahead Publishing Co., 2008). Rawls's conspiratorial insights parallel similarly ludicrous post-9/11 Web sites insisting that Satan's face *can be seen* in photographs of dark clouds of smoke surrounding the Twin Towers; see, for example, "Devil Face in the Smoke of 911 at the WTC," http://www.christianmedia.us/devil-face.html (accessed April 23, 2006).

131. "Maximus delirious" [commenter 226], comment on blog post "Flight 93 Outrage," September 8, 2005, http://littlegreenfootballs.com/weblog/?entry=17441#comments; Blogger "Ex-Donkey," September 29, 2005, http://rightwingnation.com/index.php/date/2005/09 (accessed March 13, 2006).

132. McMorrow, quoted in Pamela Reed Ward, "Flight 93 Memorial Decried as Islam Symbol," *Pittsburgh Post-Gazette*, September 10, 2005; Kirk Swauger, "Flight 93 Memorial

Challenged," *Tribune-Democrat* (Johnstown, PA), September 8, 2005; Anne C. Mulkern, "Tancredo Rips Sept. 11 Memorial," *Denver Post*, September 14, 2005.

133. Paula Reed Ward, "Flight 93 Memorial Crescent Now a Circle," *Pittsburgh Post-Gazette*, December 1, 2005. Two Pennsylvania professors who competed for the Flight 93 National Memorial have argued that Murdoch's revised design drew on their motifs; see Sean D. Hamill, "Paper Revives Design Debate Over Memorial," *New York Times*, May 19, 2008.

134. Amy Worden, "Fighting to Build a 9/11 Memorial in a Violated Land," *Philadelphia Inquirer*, September 11, 2007; Kecia Bal, "Flight 93 Backers Focus on Funding," *Tribune-Democrat* (Johnstown, PA), February 18, 2006; see also Sean D. Hamill, "Critics Say Flight 93 Memorial Design Appears Islamic," *New York Times*, May 5, 2008.

135. George E. Marcus, "The Paranoid Style Now," in *Paranoia within Reason: A Casebook on Conspiracy as Explanation*, ed. George E. Marcus (Chicago: University of Chicago Press, 1999); George E. Marcus and Michael G. Powell, "From Conspiracy Theories in the Incipient New World Order of the 1990s to Regimes of Transparency Now," *Anthropological Quarterly* 76, no. 2 (2003): 323–34; Jodi Dean, "Theorizing Conspiracy Theory," *Theory and Event* 4, no. 3 (Fall 2000), http://muse.jhu.edu/journals/theory_and_event/v004/4.3r_dean.html (accessed January 2, 2006). See also Peter Knight, ed., *Conspiracy Nation: The Politics of Paranoia in Postwar America* (New York: New York University Press, 2002). For a discussion of conspiracy theories about 9/11, see Jarrett Murphy, "The Seekers: The Birth and Life of the '9-11 Truth' Movement," *Village Voice*, February 22–28, 2006, 23–28.

136. Sean Wilentz, "The Worst President in History?" *Rolling Stone*, April 21, 2006, 32–37.

137. "National Poll Shows Americans Remain Deeply Impacted by 9/11 and Believe the World Trade Center Memorial Will Help Heal the Nation," Zogby International Poll, August 17–20, 2005 (World Trade Center Memorial Foundation, September 8, 2005).

138. Jolyon Mitchell, "Posting Images on the Web: The Creative Viewer and Non-Violent Resistance Against Terrorism," *Material Religion* 2, no. 2 (July 2006): 146–73.

139. See Brian Ward, "'People Get Ready': Music and the Civil Rights Movement of the 1950s and 1960s," *History Now: American History Online* 8 (June 2006), http://www.historynow.org/06_2006/historian2.html (accessed November 1, 2006).

140. Mitchell, "Posting Images on the Web," 165, 168.

141. Krista L. May, "Laurie Anderson," *PopMatters*, May 22, 2002, http://www.popmatters.com/music/concerts/a/anderson-laurie-020511.shtml (accessed November 16, 2006); see also Emma Govan, "Witnessing Trauma: Theatrical Responses to Terrorism," in *Art in the Age of Terrorism*, ed. Graham Coulter-Smith and Maurice Owen (London: Paul Holbertson Publishing , 2005); 50–54.

142. Gary Tinerrow, *Cai Guo-Qiang: Transparent Monument* (New York: Charta, 2006). Other exhibitions, such as A Knock at the Door (2005), dealt more specifically with the impact of the Patriot Act on American civil liberties; see Caryn James, "Beyond Comforting the Afflicted," *New York Times*, September 12, 2005.

143. Jill Bennett, *Empathic Vision: Affect, Trauma, and Contemporary Art* (Palo Alto, CA: Stanford University Press, 2005).

144. Ann Cvetkovich, *An Archive of Feelings: Trauma, Sexuality, and Lesbian Public Cultures* (Durham, NC: Duke University Press, 2003), 15.

145. Brian Massumi, "Navigating Moments with Brian Massumi," in Mary Zournazi, *Hope: New Philosophies for Change* (New York: Routledge, 2003), 211.

146. Andreas Huyssen, *Present Pasts: Urban Palimpsests and the Politics of Memory* (Palo Alto, CA: Stanford University Press, 2003), 36.

147. Hilton Kramer, "Saffron Succotash! Those Absurd Gates a Blight on Art, City," *New York Observer*, February 28, 2005; Jed Perl, "Aestheticism Lite," *New Republic*, February 11, 2005, http://www.tnr.com/doc.mhtml?i=mindseye&s=perl021105 (accessed March 16, 2005).

148. Calvin Tomkins, "The Gates to the City," *New Yorker*, March 29, 2004, 75–76.

149. Massumi, paraphrasing Gilles Deleuze in "Navigating Moments with Brian Massumi," 242.

Chapter 4

1. Rick Hampson, "17 Years in the Making, WW II Shrine is a Reality," *USA Today*, April 19, 2004.

2. Nicolaus Mills, *Their Last Battle: The Fight for the National World War II Memorial* (New York: Basic Books, 2004), 6–7.

3. George W. Bush, statement by the President, May 28, 2001, http://www.whitehouse.gov/news/releases/2001/05/20010529-3.html (accessed December 7, 2006). Roger Durbin died before the memorial was built, in 2000.

4. T. G. Ashplant, Graham Dawson, and Michael Roper, *The Politics of War Memory and Commemoration* (London: Routledge, 2000), 3.

5. Statement of purpose, The National World War II Memorial, http://www.wwiimemorial.com/default.asp?page=facts.asp&subpage=intro (accessed December 7, 2006). Unless otherwise noted, information pertaining to the memorial, including its mission statement, statistics, and speeches given at its dedication in 2004, can be found at the National World War II Memorial Web site, http://www.wwiimemorial.com/default.asp?page=home.asp.

6. Susan Levine, "A Day to Celebrate the Living, Mourn the Lost," *Washington Post*, May 30, 2004; Jon Ward, "Hard-Fought: Salute in Stone Culmination of a 17-Year Campaign," *Washington Times*, May 21, 2004.

7. G. Kurt Piehler, *Remembering War the American Way* (Washington DC: Smithsonian Institution Press, 1995), 141–43. The Atomic Bomb National Monument was "derailed," writes Piehler, although the Trinity Site in Carizozo, New Mexico, was designated a National Historic Landmark in 1965. The National Air and Space Museum opened in Washington, D.C., in 1966. On the American Battle Monuments World War II military cemeteries, see James M. Mayo, *War Memorials as Political Landscape: The American Experience and Beyond* (New York: Praeger, 1988), 100–9; and James C. Cobb, "World War II Normandy: American Cemetery and Memorial," in *American Places: Encounters with History*, ed. William E. Leuchtenburg (New York: Oxford University Press, 2000), 52–65. See also Dean W. Holt, *American Military Cemeteries: A Comprehensive Illustrated Guide to the Hallowed Grounds of the United States, Including Cemeteries Overseas* (Jefferson, NC: McFarland, 1992).

8. Karal Ann Marling and John Wetenhall, *Iwo Jima: Monuments, Memories, and the American Hero* (Cambridge, MA: Harvard University Press, 1991), 17. The publication of this book, which details how Rosenthal's photo-op became a national icon, prompted protests accusing the authors of revisionist distortion and anti-Americanism; see Karal Ann Marling and John Wetenhall, "Patriotic Fervor and the Truth About Iwo Jima," *Chronicle of Higher Education*, September 26, 1993.

9. Susan Sontag, *Regarding the Pain of Others* (New York: Farrar, Straus and Giroux, 2003), 35.

10. National Commission of Fine Arts, *Report on War Memorials* (Washington DC: United States Government Printing Office, 1947), 3–6, 12. The commission is now called the U.S. Commission of Fine Arts. Thanks to Bernard Mergen for sharing this and his unpublished paper "Artifacts as Historical Documents: The Aesthetics and Politics of the Marine Corps War Memorial and the Vietnam Veterans Memorial" (1983). See also James Dahir, *Community Centers as Living War Memorials: A Selected Bibliography with Interpretative Comments* (Brattlesboro, VT: Russell Sage Foundation, 1946); and Anne Holliday Webb, *Commemoration Through Community Services* (New York: American City Magazine, 1945).

11. Edith M. Stern, "Legacy to the Living," *Coronet* 17, no. 5 (February 1945): 12; Charles B. Stevenson, "Survey of War Memorial Plans of 500 Cities and Towns, *Toledo City Journal*, February 23, 1946; "War Memorials—Planned or Completed," *American City*, February 1948, 99–100; Kristin Ann Hass, *Carried to the Wall: American Memory and the Vietnam Veterans Memorial* (Berkeley: University of California Press, 1998), 58.

12. Lewis Mumford, "Monuments and Memorials," *Good Housekeeping*, January 1945, 17.

13. Stern, "Legacy to the Living," 12; Millicent Easter, "Living Monuments," *Recreation* 39 (January 1945): 518, as noted in Andrew M. Shanken, "Planning Memory: Living Memorials in the United States During World War II," *Art Bulletin* 84, no .1 (March 2002): 141n104.

14. Andrew M. Shanken, "Better Living: Toward a Cultural History of a Business Slogan," *Enterprise & Society* 7, no. 3 (2006): 485–519.

15. Edward P. Harpham, "Gratitude in the History of Ideas," in *The Psychology of Gratitude*, ed. Robert A. Emmons and Michael E. McCullough (New York: Oxford University Press, 2004), 25.

16. Adam Smith, *The Theory of Moral Sentiments*, ed. Knut Haakonssen (1759; New York: Cambridge University Press, 2002); Georg Simmel, "Faithfulness and Gratitude," in *The Sociology of Georg Simmel*, ed. Kurt H. Wolff (1908; Glencoe, IL: Free Press, 1950), 388; Michael E. McCullough, Shelley D. Kilpatrick, Robert A. Emmons, and David B. Larson, "Is Gratitude a Moral Affect?" *Psychological Bulletin* 127, no. 2 (2001): 249–66; Terrance McConnell, *Gratitude* (Philadelphia: Temple University Press, 1993), 9 and passim; Martin Seligman, *Authentic Happiness: Using the New Positive Psychology to Realize Your Potential for Lasting Fulfillment* (New York: Free Press, 2002).

17. A. John Simmons, *Moral Principles and Political Obligations* (Princeton, NJ: Princeton University Press, 1979), 157–180; George Klosko, "Four Arguments Against Political Obligation from Gratitude," *Public Affairs Quarterly* 5 (1991): 33–48; Ross Buck, "The Gratitude of Exchange and the Gratitude of Caring: A Developmental-Interactionist Perspective of Moral Emotion," in Emmons and McCullough *The Psychology of Gratitude*, 101, 106.

18. David D. Hall, *Worlds of Wonder, Days of Judgement: Popular Religious Belief in Early New England* (New York: Alfred A. Knopf, 1989), 172; Jill Lepore, *New York Burning: Liberty, Slavery, and Conspiracy in Eighteenth-Century Manhattan* (New York: Vintage, 2005), 211.

19. Richard P. Gildrie, "The Ceremonial Pilgrim: Days of Humiliation and Thanksgiving," *New England Historical and Genealogical Register* 136 (January 1982): 3–4; Lincoln, quoted in Matthew Dennis, *Red, White, and Blue Letter Days: An American Calendar* (Ithaca, NY: Cornell University Press, 2002), 87.

20. Mills, *Their Last Battle*, 168–69, 190–91. Additional funds were placed in the National World War II Trust Fund of the U.S. Treasury.

21. The competition received 408 design proposals.

22. William J. Clinton, "Remarks on Presenting the Presidential Medal of Freedom to Former Senator Bob Dole," January 17, 1997, The American Presidency Project, http://www.presidency.ucsb.edu/ws/print.php?pid=54083 (accessed December 18, 2006). For details on the memorial competition, see Mills, *Their Last Battle*, 107–35.

23. George Gurney, "Interview: Sculpting the World War II Memorial, A Conversation with Raymond Kaskey," *American Art* 18, no. 2 (Summer 2004): 96–105.

24. Thomas B. Grooms, *World War II Memorial* (Washington DC: U.S. General Services Administration, 2004), 25; Friedrich St. Florian, remarks made at Art, Politics, and Process: Creating the National World War II Memorial symposium, Washington, D.C., April 22, 2004.

25. Thanks to David Kieran for sharing this information and his unpublished paper "Recovering from the Vietnam Syndrome at the National WWII Memorial," American Studies Department, George Washington University (2004). The CIA's Memorial Wall also includes a Book of Honor in a locked stainless steel and glass case.

26. Allen Freeman, "Room with a View," *Landscape Architecture*, July 2004, 108–17. For discussion of *Life*'s coverage of World War II, see Erika Doss, ed., *Looking at Life Magazine* (Washington DC: Smithsonian Institution Press, 2001), 12–13, 91–92, 179–81.

27. David S. Broder, "A Fitting, if Flawed, Tribute," *Washington Post*, May 27, 2004. There is no explanation for how 405, 973 soldier dead are matched to the 4,048 gold stars of Freedom Wall.

28. As noted by Kristin Ann Hass, "Inscribing Sites of Memory: Resistant? Transformative? Sacred? Tracking Public Memorial Practice on the National Mall," paper presented at the American Studies Association Annual Meeting, Washington, D.C., November 4, 2005. The National Park Service does not save items left at the National World War II Memorial.

29. Mills, *Their Last Battle*, 147; see also Christopher Shea, "The Brawl on the Mall," *Preservation* 53 (January / February 2001): 39–40.

30. Mark Fisher, "A Memorial That Doesn't Measure Up," *Washington Post*, May 4, 2004.

31. Christopher Knight, "A Memorial to Forget," *Los Angeles Times*, May 23, 2004; Blake Gopnik, "Many Words, Little Eloquence," *Washington Post*, May 23, 2004; Richard Lacayo, "A Monument to Blah," *Time*, May 3, 2004, 68.

32. Friedrich St. Florian, quoted in Grooms, *World War II Memorial*, 80.

33. George W. Bush, statement included in "The Dedication of the National World War II Memorial Tribute Program" (Washington DC: American Battle Monuments Commission, May 29, 2004).

34. Michael Bednar, *L'Enfant's Legacy: Public Open Spaces in Washington, D.C.* (Baltimore, MD: The John Hopkins University Press, 2006), 72; Joseph Ellis, "Right Time, Wrong Place," *New York Times*, March 24, 1997; Lucy Barber, *Marching on Washington: The Forging of an American Political Tradition* (Berkeley: University of California Press, 2002).

35. Pierre Charles L'Enfant site description, March 1791, as noted in Elizabeth S. Kite, *L'Enfant and Washington, 1791–1792* (Baltimore, MD: The Johns Hopkins University Press, 1929), 47–48.

36. Pamela Scott, "'This Vast Empire': The Iconography of the Mall, 1791–1848," in

The Mall in Washington, 1791–1991, ed. Richard Longstreth, 2nd ed. (New Haven, CT: Yale University Press, 2002), 42; Pierre Charles L'Enfant, "Plan of the city intended for the permanent seat of t[he] United State[s]" [map] (Washington DC: Library of Congress, 1791). The description of the George Washington monument is found in the left-hand section of the map, titled "References."

37. Worthington Chauncey Ford, Gaillard Hunt, John C. Fitzpatrick, and Roscoe R. Hill, eds., *Journals of the Continental Congress, 1774–1789*, vol. 24 (Washington DC: U.S. Government Printing Office, 1922492–95. The statue was never made.

38. Kirk Savage, "The Self-Made Monument: George Washington and the Fight to Erect a National Memorial," *Winterthur Portfolio* 22, no. 4 (Winter 1987): 225–42.

39. Todd Porterfield, *The Allure of Empire: Art in the Service of French Imperialism, 1798–1836* (Princeton, NJ: Princeton University Press, 1998), 41; see also Brian A. Curran, Anthony Grafton, Pamela O. Long, and Benjamin Weiss, *Obelisk: A History* (Cambridge, MA: MIT Press, 2009).

40. George Washington, "Farewell Address," September 17, 1796, in *Compilation of Messages and Papers of the Presidents*, ed. J. D. Richardson (Washington DC: Bureau of National Literature, 1907), 1:213; Chalmers Johnson, *The Sorrows of Empire: Militarism, Secrecy, and the End of the Republic* (New York: Metropolitan Books, 2004).

41. Amy Kaplan, "Violent Belongings and the Question of Empire Today—Presidential Address to the American Studies Association, October 17, 2003," *American Quarterly* 56, no. 1 (March 2004): 3; see also Amy Kaplan and Donald E, Pease, eds., *Cultures of United States Imperialism* (Durham, NC: Duke University Press, 1993).

42. William H. Truettner, ed., *The West as America: Reinterpreting Images of the Frontier, 1820–1920* (Washington DC: National Museum of American Art, 1991); for discussions of the controversy, see Steven C. Dubin, *Displays of Power: Memory and Amnesia in the American Museum* (New York: New York University Press, 1999), 152–85; and Alan Wallach, *Exhibiting Contradiction: Essays on the Art Museum in the United States* (Amherst: University of Massachusetts Press, 1998), 105–17. The museum is now called the Smithsonian American Art Museum.

43. Hone, quoted in Russell Lynes, *The Art-Makers* (New York: Dover Publications, 1970), 119–21; Hawthorne and Jarvis, quoted in Vivien Green Fryd, *Art and Empire: The Politics of Ethnicity in the U.S. Capitol, 1815–1860* (New Haven, CT: Yale University Press, 1992), 76. The sculpture was placed in the collection of the Smithsonian Institution in 1908 and is currently housed in the National Museum of American History, Washington, D.C.

44. Margaret Malamud, "The Imperial Metropolis: Ancient Rome in Turn-of-the-Century New York," *Arion* 7, no. 3 (2000): 64–108; on the Dewey Arch see Michele Bogart, *Public Sculpture and the Civic Ideal in New York City, 1890–1930* (Chicago: University of Chicago Press, 1983), 100–4.

45. Lewis Mumford, "The Imperial Façade," in *Sticks and Stone: A Study of American Architecture and Civilization* (1924; New York: Dover, 1954), 134; architect W. Symmes Richardson, quoted in Malamud, "The Imperial Metropolis," 69–70.

46. The McMillan Plan was drafted by Daniel Burnham, Charles McKim, Frederick Law Olmsted, and Augustus Saint-Gaudens, and subsequently became a model for many "city beautiful" designs all over America; see Thomas Hines, "The Imperial Mall: The City Beautiful Movement and the Washington Plan of 1901–1902," in Longstreth, *The Mall in Washington, 1791–1991*, 78–99.

47. Christopher A. Thomas, *The Lincoln Memorial and American Life* (Princeton, NJ: Princeton University Press, 2002), 70–71, 167.

48. Mumford, "The Imperial Façade," 141–42.

49. Likewise, President Barack Obama's 2009 inauguration ceremonies included "We Are One: The Obama Inaugural Celebration at the Lincoln Memorial," with performances by Beyoncé, Bono, Bruce Springsteen, and Stevie Wonder. The president welcomed audiences to "this celebration of American renewal" and made note of the memorials on the National Mall "that affirm our unyielding faith—a faith that anything is possible in America." Three days later, the president authorized the dramatically accelerated use of unmanned drone strikes in Pakistan. See "Obama's Speech at the Lincoln Memorial," *New York Times*, January 18, 2009, and Jane Mayer, "The Predator War," *New Yorker*, October 26, 2009, 37.

50. Françoise Choay, *The Invention of the Historic Monument*, trans. Lauren M. O'Connell (1992; New York: Cambridge University Press, 2001), 7; Kirk Savage, *Standing Soldiers, Kneeling Slaves: Race, War, and Monument in Nineteenth-Century America* (Princeton, NJ: Princeton University Press, 1997), 155.

51. Albert J. Beveridge, "March of the Flag," September 16, 1898, quoted in Thomas J. Paterson, ed., *Major Problems in American Foreign Policy: Documents and Essays*, (Lexington, MA: Heath, 1989), 1:389–91.

52. James S. Russell, "Crowding the Mall: The National Memorial Dilemma," *Harvard Design Magazine*, Fall 1999, 34–35.

53. Margaret Malamud and Donald T. McGuire, Jr., "Living Like Romans in Las Vegas: The Roman World at Caesars Palace," in *Imperial Projections: Ancient Rome in Modern Popular Culture*, ed. Sandra R. Joshel, Margaret Malamud, and Donald T. McGuire, Jr. (Baltimore, MD: The Johns Hopkins University Press, 2001), 249–269.

54. Thomas Keenan, "The Way We Live Now: Questions for Friedrich St. Florian," *New York Times Magazine*, July 1, 2001, sec. 6–23.

55. Lacayo, "A Monument to Blah"; Fisher, "A Memorial That Doesn't Measure Up"; Paul Goldberger, "Not in Our Front Yard," *New Yorker*, August 7, 2000, 27–28; Paul Greenberg, "Monumental Mistake," *Arkansas Democrat-Gazette*, May 30, 2001; Carlos Widman, "A Touch of Albert Speer," *Der Spiegel*, June 2, 2001; cartoon by Paul Conrad, *Los Angeles Times*, October 16, 2000.

56. Michael Kammen, *Visual Shock: A History of Art Controversies in American Culture* (New York: Alfred A. Knopf, 2006), 28.

57. "Battle Raging over Site, Design of U.S. World War II Memorial," CNN.com, June 5, 2000, http://archives.cnn.com/2000/US/06/05/wwii.memorial/ (accessed January 2, 2007); Marc Fisher, "A Scourge of War Not Worthy of This Battlefield," *Washington Post*, November 14, 2000; "Veteran Group is Waging Battle to Block World War II Memorial, *Wall Street Journal*, June 6, 2000.

58. Veterans, quoted in Fisher, "A Scourge of War"; and "Monumental Mistake," *Boston Globe*, May 27, 2001; Howard Zinn, "Dissent at the War Memorial," *Progressive*, August 2004, 14–15. Zinn spoke on May 27, 2004, at a session held on the national mall and sponsored by the Smithsonian Institution Center for Folklife and Cultural Heritage.

59. Cassel, quoted in Christopher Newton, "A Historic Vista Now Will Make Room for World War II Memorial," *Boston Globe*, May 27, 2001; Feldman, quoted in Irvin Molotsky, "Panel Backs World War II Memorial on Mall in Washington," *New York Times*, July 21, 2000; see also Feldman's essay "Turning Point: The Problematics of Building on the

Mall Today," in *The National Mall: Rethinking Washington's Monumental Core*, ed. Nathan Glazer and Cynthia R. Field (Baltimore, MD: The John Hopkins University Press, 2008), 134–58. On the National Coalition to Save Our Mall, see their Web site, http://www.savethemall.org/about/index.html.

60. The 2003 bill was an amendment to the 1986 Commemorative Works Act. If intended to bolster memorial development elsewhere in the nation's capital, it also made the National World War II Memorial the national mall's final addition. See Matthew T. Witt, "America's Palimpsest: Ground-Zero Democracy and the Capitol Mall," *Public Administration Review* 65, no. 5 (September 2005): 517; see also Steven Johnston, "Political Not Patriotic: Democracy, Civic Space, and the American Memorial / Monument Complex," *Theory and Event* 5, no. 2 (2001), http://muse.jhu.edu/journals/theory_and_event/v005/5.2johnston.html (accessed November 28, 2004).

61. Fisher, "A Memorial That Doesn't Measure Up"; Lisa Benton-Short, "Politics, Public Space, and Memorials: The Brawl on the Mall," *Urban Geography* 27, no. 4 (2006): 299.

62. Herbert Muschamp, "An Appraisal: New War Memorial is a Shrine to Sentiment," *New York Times*, June 7, 2001.

63. The project was originally estimated at $17 million; see Kate Bernice, "D-Day Memorial is Clouded By Scandal, Debt and Doubts," *New York Times*, April 27, 2003.

64. "Remarks by the President at the Dedication of the National D-Day Memorial," June 6, 2001, http://www.whitehouse.gov/news/releases/2001/06/20010606–2.html (accessed January 8, 2007). Bedford's claims and costs were both contested; see Zernike, "D-Day Memorial is Clouded by Scandal."

65. War games in general are the top money makers in the online computer industry: the World of Warcraft series, marketed by Blizzard Entertainment and featuring games like Burning Crusade (2007), has more than eight million subscribers who pay $15 a month to play. See Seth Schiesel, "O Brave New World That Has Such Gamers In It," *New York Times*, January 19, 2007.

66. Emily S. Rosenberg, *A Date Which Will Live: Pearl Harbor in American Memory* (Durham, NC: Duke University Press, 2003), 66–67, 130, 188. John Bodnar similarly argues that movies like *Saving Private Ryan* preserve "the World War II image of American soldiers as inherently averse to bloodshed and cruelty;" see his essay "*Saving Private Ryan* and Postwar Memory in America," *American Historical Review* 106, no. 3 (June 2001): 805.

67. David Hoogland Noon, "Operation Enduring Analogy: World War II, The War on Terror, and the Uses of Historical Memory," *Rhetoric & Public Affairs* 7, no. 3 (2004): 339; Dan Balz and Bob Woodward, "America's Chaotic Road to War," *Washington Post*, January 27, 2002; Christopher Hayes, "The Good War on Terror: How the Greatest Generation Helped Pave the Road to Baghdad," *In These Times*, September 8, 2006, 24.

68. Michael Sherry, *In the Shadow of War: The United States Since the 1930s* (New Haven, CT: Yale University Press, 1995), 460–61.

69. Jean Baudrillard, "Pornographie de la guerre," *Liberation*, May 19, 2004, reprinted as "War Porn," in *The Conspiracy of Art: Manifestos, Texts, Interviews* (Cambridge, MA: MIT Press, 2005), 205–12; "A Slap in the Face: War Porn," *Adbusters*, March–April 2004, http://adbusters.org/the_magazine/52/War_Porn.html (accessed January 10, 2007).

70. Andrew J. Bacevich, *The New American Militarism: How Americans Are Seduced by War* (New York: Oxford University Press, 2005), 2.

71. Jackson Lears discusses the "martial ideal" in turn-of-the-twentieth-century America in *No Place of Grace: Antimodernism and the Transformation of American Culture, 1880–*

1920 (New York: Pantheon, 1983), 97–102; see also Jonathan Hansen, *The Lost Promise of Patriotism: Debating American Identity, 1890–1920* (Chicago: University of Chicago Press, 2003); and Amy Kaplan, *The Anarchy of Empire in the Making of U.S. Culture* (Cambridge, MA: Harvard University Press, 2002).

72. Patrick Hagopian, "The Commemorative Landscape of the Vietnam War," in *Places of Commemoration: Search for Identity and Landscape Design*, ed. Joachim Wolschke-Bulmahn (Washington DC: Dumbarton Oaks, 2001), 312–13n1; see also Jerry L. Strait and Sandra S. Strait, *Vietnam War Memorials: An Illustrated Reference Guide to Veterans Tributes Throughout the United States* (Jefferson, NC: McFarland Publishers, 1988). On the influence of Lin's memorial, see Nicholas J. Capasso, "The National Vietnam Veterans Memorial in Context: Commemorative Public Art in America, 1960–1997" (PhD diss., Rutgers, The State University of New Jersey, 1998), 240–57. On traveling versions of the Vietnam Veterans Memorial, see Julia Bleakney, *Revisiting Vietnam: Memoirs, Memorials, Museums* (New York: Routledge, 2006), 86–87.

73. "Jones Introduces Bill to Authorize National Military Working Dog Team Monument," press release, April 7, 2006, http://jones.house.gov/text_release.cfm?id=407 (accessed January 13, 2007).

74. See the Illinois Motorcycle Freedom Run Web site, http://www.ilfreedomrun.org/index.php?option=com_content&view=frontpage&Itemid=55 (accessed October 15, 2009).

75. Richard Rist, e-mail message to author, March 21, 2007.

76. However, during the conflict in Kosovo, a number of Bronze Stars were awarded to U.S. soldiers in the Air Force and the Navy who never actually saw combat. This drew complaints from the Army and perceptive analysis from the members of Critical Art Ensemble regarding the future of the military body; see "Reimagining the War Machine," *Body & Society* 9, no. 4 (2003): 89–91.

77. For information on the memorial, see http://www.webcitynet.com/vets/index.shtml (accessed July 12, 2008).

78. Julie Rotblatt, "War Memorial, The Fine Art Studio of Rotblatt-Amrany," http://rafasculptureonline.com/commissions_part03.htm (accessed January 13, 2007).

79. Caller, quoted in "Indiana War Memorial" segment, "Hello Beautiful!! The Sunday Morning Arts Show" (Jenny Lawton, prod., Chicago Public Radio, October 17, 2004), http://www.chicagopublicradio.org/audio_library/hb_oct04.asp (accessed January 15, 2007); Rumsfeld, quoted in U.S. Department of Defense, News transcript, Defense Department briefing, August 9, 2005, http://www.defenselink.mil/transcripts/transcript.aspx?TranscriptID=3082 (accessed January 20, 2007).

80. President George W. Bush, "Remarks at the 20th Anniversary of the National Endowment for Democracy," November 6, 2003, Washington, D.C., at: http://www.whitehouse.gov/news/releases/2003/11/20031106–2.html (accessed February 3, 2008).

81. Andrew J. Bacevich, "Elusive Bargain: The Pattern of U.S. Civil-Military Relations Since World War II," in *The Long War: A New History of U.S. National Security Policy Since World War II*, ed. Andrew J. Bacevich (New York: Columbia University Press, 2007), 212.

82. "Monument Honors African Americans," *Mississippi History Newsletter* online ed., 46, no. 2 (February 2004), http://www.mdah.state.ms.us/pubs/mhn/feb04index.html (accessed January 15, 2007).

83. For statistics of women's memorials, see Martha Norkunas, *Monuments and Memory: History and Representation in Lowell, Massachusetts* (Washington DC: Smithsonian In-

stitution Press, 2002), 94; see also Eileen Eagan, "Immortalizing Women: Finding Meaning in Public Sculpture," in *Her Past Around Us: Interpreting Sites for Women's History*, ed. Katherine T. Corbett (Malabar, FL: Krieger Publishing Co., 2003), 31–68. On women and Civil War commemoration, see especially Cynthia Mills and Pamela H. Simpson, eds., *Monuments to the Lost Cause: Women, Art, and the Landscapes of Southern Memory*, (Knoxville: University of Tennessee Press, 2003); and David W. Blight, *Race and Reunion: The Civil War in American Memory* (Cambridge, MA: Harvard University Press, 2001), 255–299. On women and the recovery of military dead, see G. Kurt Piehler, "The War Dead and the Gold Star: American Commemoration of the First World War," in *Commemorations: The Politics of National Identity*, ed. John R. Gillis (Princeton, NJ: Princeton University Press, 1994), 168–85; and Michael Sledge, *Soldier Dead: How We Recover, Identify, Bury, and Honor Our Military Fallen* (New York: Columbia University Press, 2005), 136.

84. Nick Capasso, "Remember the Ladies: New Women's Memorials in Boston," *Sculpture* 19, no. 5 (June 2000): 46–51.

85. "West Virginia: Less G.I. Joe, More Barbie?" *New York Times*, March 3, 2005; Jennifer Lunden, "Women Vets Say Memorial Statue Too Masculine," "All Things Considered," National Public Radio, March 5, 2005, http://www.npr.org/templates/story/story.php?storyId=452426 (accessed January 17, 2007).

86. Heather J. Höpfl, "Becoming a (Virile) Member: Women and the Military Body," *Body & Society* 9, no. 4 (2003): 26; see also Cynthia Nantais and Martha F. Lee, "Women in the United States Military: Protectors or Protected? The Case of Prisoner of War Melisa Rathbun-Nealy," *Journal of Gender Studies* 8, no. 2 (1999): 181–91.

87. Bryan Turner, "Warrior Charisma and Spiritualization of Violence," *Body & Society* 9, no. 4 (2003): 105.

88. Oscar Campomanes, "The American Soldier in Love and War" (paper presented at the annual meeting of the Organization of American Historians, Chicago, 1992), cited in Melani McAlister, *Epic Encounters: Culture, Media, and U.S. Interests in the Middle East, 1945–2000* (Berkeley: University of California Press, 2001), 250n50.

89. Judith Butler, *Gender Trouble: Feminism and the Subversion of Identity* (New York: Routledge, 1990).

90. Joe Vargo, "Lest We Forget: Homage and Monuments to Veterans Are Popular Again," *Press Enterprise* (Riverside, CA), December 30, 2006, http://www.pe.com/localnews/inland/stories/PE_News_Local_S (accessed January 16, 2007); John Hunneman, "'Letters Home' Tells War Stories in the Words of Those Who Served," *North County Times* (San Diego, CA), November 7, 2004, http://www.nctimes.com/articles/2004/11/08/news/californian/11 (accessed January 16, 2007). The Vietnam Veterans Memorial in New York City (1985) similarly incorporates excerpts from soldier's letters on its glass blocks; see Bernard Edelman, ed., *Dear America: Letters Homes from Vietnam* (New York: W. W. Norton, 1985).

91. Carroll, quoted in Vargo, "Lest We Forget"; Naggar, quoted in Hunneman, "'Letters Home' Tells War Stories"; Andrew Carroll, *War Letters: Extraordinary Correspondence from American Wars* (New York: Simon & Schuster, 2001).

92. See also Stephen Herrero's limited edition, tabletop bronze *Letters from Home*, which retails for $375 at Wolf Creek Gallery's Web site, http://wolfcreekgallery.com.

93. Jay Winter, *Sites of Memory, Sites of Mourning: The Great War in European Cultural History* (Cambridge: Cambridge University Press, 1995), 2–5.

94. Kristen Hass elaborates on these tropes in her book, *Sacrificing Soldiers* (forthcoming, 2010).

95. Sontag, *Regarding the Pain of Others*, 38, David Serlin, *Replaceable You: Engineering the Body in Postwar America* (Chicago: University of Chicago Press, 2004), 2.

96. The bill, HR 5037, bans demonstrations within 300 feet of a military cemetery and 150 feet from any military funeral (including those at non-federal sites) within an hour of the memorial service; see Nathan Burchfiel, "Bush Signs Law to Bar Military Funeral Protests," CNSNews.com, December 27, 2006, http://www.cnsnews.com/ViewNation.asp?Page=Nation/archive/ (accessed January 20, 2007).

97. David Carr, "Not to See the Fallen Is No Favor," *New York Times*, May 28, 2007; David Campbell, "Horrific Blindness: Images of Death in Contemporary Media," *Journal for Cultural Research* 8, no. 1 (January 2004): 60.

98. Michael Weisskopf, "A Grim Milestone: 500 Amputees," *Time*, January 18, 2007, http://www.time.com/time/nation/article/0,8599,1580531,00.html (accessed March 25, 2007); Denise Grady, "Struggling Back from War's Once-Deadly Wounds," *New York Times*, January 22, 2006. One exhibition detailing the experiences of contemporary women soldiers is When Janey Comes Marching Home: Portraits of Women Combat Veterans (2008), organized by photographer Sacha Pflaeging and filmmaker and author Laura Browder.

99. Gene Weingarten, "Doonesbury's War," *Washington Post*, October 22, 2006.

100. Maureen Dowd, "Powell Without Picasso," *New York Times*, February 5, 2003.

101. Colin Powell, "Why Memorials Matter," *USA Weekend Magazine*, April 30–May 2, 2004), http://www.usaweekend.com/partners/mktpromo/040502articles/04 (accessed April 26, 2004).

102. J. Carter Brown, comments made at "Civic Design, Public Space, and the Washington Mall: A Roundtable Discussion on the National World War II Memorial," American Studies Association Annual Meeting, November 10, 2001, Washington, D.C., and as noted in Mills, *Their Last Battle*, 86.

103. Tom Brokaw, *The Greatest Generation* (New York: Random House, 1998), 152.

104. Joseph Heller, *Catch-22* (New York: Simon & Schuster, 1994), 26; Bodnar, "*Saving Private Ryan* and Postwar Memory in America," 812–15; Erika Doss, *Benton, Pollock, and the Politics of Modernism: From Regionalism to Abstract Expressionism* (Chicago: University of Chicago Press, 1991), 336–47.

105. Marilyn B. Young, "Dangerous History: Vietnam and the 'Good War,'" in *History Wars: The Enola Gay and Other Battles for the American Past*, ed. Edward T. Linenthal and Tom Engelhardt (New York: Metropolitan Books / Henry Holt and Company, 1996), 200; Robert J. McMahon, "Contested Memory: The Vietnam War and American Society, 1975–2001," *Diplomatic History* 26, no. 2 (Spring 2002): 175. A 1993 *Wall Street Journal* / NBC poll indicated that two-thirds of Americans continued to believe that US soldiers were still being held captive in Southeast Asia; see Marvin E. Gettleman, Jane M. Franklin, Marilyn Young, and H. Bruce Franklin, eds., *Vietnam and America: A Documented History*, rev. ed. (New York: Grove Press, 1995), 514.

106. Ernest W. Lefever, "Vietnam's Ghosts," *Wall Street Journal*, March 21, 1997, as noted in McMahon, 160, 174–75.

107. Zinn, "Dissent at the War Memorial," 15.

108. "Most-Visited National Memorials," *USA Today*, September 11–013, 2009. The Lincoln Memorial was the most visited memorial, with 4,678, 861 people counted in 2008.

109. J. Carter Brown, quoted in the 1994 documentary *Maya Lin: A Strong Clear Vision*, directed by Frieda Lee Mock. On similar understandings of healing and closure narratives see Patrick Hagopian, *The Vietnam War In American Memory: Veterans, Memorials,*

and the Politics of Healing (Amherst: University of Massachusetts Press, 2009), and Edward T. Linenthal, *The Unfinished Bombing: Oklahoma City in American Memory* (New York: Oxford, 2001), 94–97.

110. Marita Sturken, *Tangled Memories: The Vietnam War, the AIDS Epidemic, and the Politics of Remembering* (Berkeley: University of California Press, 1997), 44; Charles Griswold, "The Vietnam Veterans Memorial and the National Mall: Philosophical Thoughts on Political Iconography," *Critical Inquiry* 12 (Summer 1986): 688–719.

111. James Wolcott, "Color Me Khaki," *Vanity Fair*, September 2004, 230.

112. Dubin, *Displays of Power*, 186–226; Linenthal and Engelhardt, *History Wars*, 2–7.

113. Brokaw, *The Greatest Generation*, xviii–xix, xxx; for more "greatest generation" products, see Tom Brokaw, *The Greatest Generation Speaks: Letters and Reflections* (New York: Random House, 1999), and idem, *An Album of Memories: Personal Histories from the Greatest Generation* (New York: Random House, 2001). For an excellent critique of the "greatest generation" narrative, see Kenneth D. Rose, *Myth and the Greatest Generation: A Social History of Americans in World War II* (New York: Routledge, 2008), 2–5.

114. Biesecker, "Remembering World War II," 399, 401; Thomas M. Hawley, *The Remains of War: Bodies, Politics, and the Search for American Soldiers Unaccounted For in Southeast Asia* (Durham, NC: Duke University Press, 2005), 256–57.

115. H. Bruce Franklin, *MIA or Mythmaking in America: How and Why Belief in the POWs has Possessed a Nation* (New York: Lawrence Hill Books, 1992); Jerry Lembcke, *The Spitting Image: Myth, Memory, and the Legacy of Vietnam* (New York: New York University Press, 1998).

116. Harry W. Haines, "'They Were Called and They Went': The Political Rehabilitation of the Vietnam Veteran," in *From Hanoi to Hollywood: The Vietnam War in American Film*, ed. Linda Dittmar and Gene Michaud (Rutgers, NJ: Rutgers University Press, 1990), 88–90.

117. Sledge, *Soldier Dead*, 93; Hawley, *The Remains of War*, 161; Michael Allen, "Artifacts of Loss: Lost Bodies and Lost Wars in American Mourning," paper delivered at the American Studies Association Annual Meeting, Washington, D.C., November 4, 2005.

118. Eric Tucker, "Vietnam Veterans Regaining Medals, Their Sense of Pride," *Rapid City Journal*, August 8, 2005.

119. Petula Dvorak, "Vietnam Wall Visitor Center Approved," *Washington Post*, August 4, 2006; "President Bush Signs Visitor Center Bill," November 18, 2003, *Vietnam Veterans Memorial Fund* Web site, http://ww.vvmf.org/index.cfm?SectionID=298 (accessed January 24, 2007).

120. Dvorak, "Vietnam Wall Visitor Center Approved"; Peterson, quoted in Christopher Knight, "The Continued Mauling of the National Mall," *Los Angeles Times*, September 9, 2006.

121. Powell, quoted in Jan. C. Scruggs, letter to the editor, "A Memorial to an Earlier War," *New York Times*, August 18, 2006.

122. Brigid Schulte, "Veterans, Others Denounce Marchers," *Washington Post*, March 18, 2007; veteran Bud Gross, quoted in C. J. Raven, "'Gathering of Eagles' to Protect Vietnam Veterans Wall," *U.S. Veteran Dispatch*, February 7, 2007, http://www.usvetdsp.com/feb07/eagle.htm (accessed October 12, 2007); for the Gathering of Eagles Web site, see http://gatheringofeagles.org/.

123. McMahon, "Contested Memory," 182; see also Andrew Bacevich, *The Limits of Power: The End of American Exceptionalism* (New York: Metropolitan Books, 2008).

124. James Reston, Jr., "The Monument Glut," *The New York Times Magazine*, September 10, 1995, 48–49; Sontag, *Regarding the Pain of Others*, 122.

125. Dina Vainer, "Beach Crosses Stand in Honor of Dead Troops," *Daily Nexus* (University of California, Santa Barbara), January 26, 2004, http://www.dailynexus.com/article.php?a=6469 (accessed January 25, 2007).

126. See the Eyes Wide Open Web site, http://www.afsc.org/eyes/.

127. "Group Refuses to Remove Lafayette War Dead Memorial," KTVU.com, November 20, 2006, http://www.ktvu.com/print/10362819/detail.html (accessed November 25, 2006); Katharine Mieszkowski, "Peace Movement at a Crossroads," Salon.com, January 20, 2007, http://www.salon.com/news/feature/2007/01/20/lafayette_crosses/print.html (accessed January 29, 2007); Jeff Heaton, quoted in "Memorial Verite 1/7/07," http://www.youtube.com/watch?v=yy8ZpnvLCEM&mode=related&search (accessed February 3, 2007).

128. Veronica Torrejon, "Growing Santa Barbara War Memorial Sparks Range of Emotions," *Common Dreams News Center*, April 9, 2004, http://www.commondreams.org/cgi-bin/print.cgi?file=headlines0 (accessed February 3, 2007); Lafayette mock war memorial report from NBC 11 News, November 25, 2006, http://www.youtube.com/watch?v=suya8tHWwJw (accessed February 3, 2007); Seth Hettena, "Memorial Stirs Objection, Support Among Parents of Deceased," Boston.com, March 13, 2005, http://www.boston.com/news/nation/articles/2005/03/13/memorial (accessed June 7, 2006).

129. In October 2006, researchers at Johns Hopkins University in Baltimore and al-Mustansiriya University in Baghdad estimated that 655,000 Iraqi civilians had died since the United States invaded Iraq in March 2003; see David Brown, "Study Claims Iraq's 'Excess' Death Toll Has Reached 655,000," *Washington Post*, October 11, 2006. While Iraqi dead are referenced in Eyes Wide Open, represented by piles of shoes (which disconcertingly reference those collected from Nazi death camps and displayed in Holocaust museums), the memorial's visual centerpiece is its expanding field of boots commemorating U.S. soldier dead.

130. Heaton quoted in Mieszkowski, "Peace Movement at a Crossroads"; "Move America Forward" speaker quoted in video, http://lafayettecrosses.blogspot.com/ (accessed May 20, 2007).

131. Comments from *Arlington West*, directed by Peter Dudar and Sally Marr (2004, distributed by Laughing Tears Productions, DVD

132. Menusa, quoted in Torrejon, "Growing Santa Barbara War Memorial;" Christine Giles, "Letter to the Editor," *American Statesman* (Austin, TX), February 24, 2005, as noted in Ken MacLeish, "The Tense Present History of the Second Gulf War: Revelation and Repression in Memorialization," *Text, Practice, Performance* 6 (2005): 69–84.

133. Gregg Zoroya, "Modern Memorials Stand for the Warriors, Not the War," *USA Today*, May 25, 2005, http://www.usatoday.com/news/nation/2005-05-25-memorials-cover_x.htm (accessed January 9, 2007).

134. Michael McConnell, "Build War Memorial During War," in *Eyes Wide Open, Beyond Fear-Towards Hope, An Exhibition on the Iraq War* (Chicago: American Friends Service Committee, 2004), 45.

135. On the contemporary appeal of the military see, for example, Lizette Alvarez, "More Joining American Military as Jobs Dwindle," *New York Times*, January 19, 2009.

136. Kirk Savage similarly imagines placing a statue of King in front of the "great white temple" of the Lincoln Memorial; see Savage, *Standing Soldiers, Kneeling Slaves*, 212. Of

course, fierce battles are also waged over King's commemoration in contemporary America (see chapter 6 of this volume).

Chapter 5

1. Michael Fedo, quoted in Chris Julin and Stephanie Hemphill, "A Mob Lynches Three Black Men," June 2001, Minnesota Public Radio Online, http://news.minnesota.publicradio.org/projects/2001/06/lynching/page1.shtml (accessed October 24, 2004). Unless otherwise noted, references to the 1920 lynching in Duluth stem from this online resource. Fedo's book *The Lynchings in Duluth* (St. Paul: Minnesota Historical Society Press, 2000) was originally released as *They Was Just Niggers* (Ontario, CA: Brasch and Brasch, 1979).

2. Edmund Burke, "Speech on the Sixth Article of Charge, May 5, 1789," *The Works of the Right Honorable Edmund Burke*, vol. 10 (London: John C. Nimmo, 1997), 159. Burke wrote this during impeachment proceedings against Warren Hastings, a former Governor General of India accused of high crimes and corruption

3. Press Service of the NAACP, "Senator France, Representative Dyer to Urge Federal Anti-Lynching [Law]," press release, November 29, 1920, NAACP Papers, Part 7: The Anti-Lynching Campaign, 1912–1955, Series B: Anti-Lynching Legislative and Publicity Files, 1916–1955, Library of Congress (Microfilm, Reel 26, Frames 407–08).

4. Nancy K. Miller, "Memory Stains: Annie Ernaux's *Shame*," in *Extremities: Trauma, Testimony, and Community*, ed. Nancy K. Miller and Jason Tougaw (Urbana: University of Illinois Press, 2002), 211.

5. Joseph Welch asked this now-famous question on June 9, 1954, during the Army-McCarthy hearings in Washington, D.C. The quote from John F. Kennedy is from the Civil Rights Address, delivered June 11, 1963, before Congress. The contemporary press often quote Welch as asking, "Have you no sense of decency, sir, at long last? Have you no shame?" but Welch never used the word "shame" in his exchange with McCarthy.

6. See Philip M. Stern and George de Vincent, *The Shame of a Nation*, with a foreword by Hubert H. Humphrey (New York: Ivan Obolensky, Inc., 1965), a photo book on American poverty.

7. Colbert I. King, "In Virginia, More to 'Get Over' Than Slavery," *Washington Post*, January 20, 2007; Ken Foote, *Shadowed Ground: America's Landscapes of Violence and Tragedy*, rev. ed. (Austin: University of Texas Press, 2003),174.

8. Dolores Hayden, *The Power of Place: Urban Landscapes as Public History* (Cambridge, MA: MIT Press, 1995), 8.

9. See, for example, Alan Riding, "Art Show Forces Belgium to Ask Hard Questions About its Colonial Past," *New York Times*, February 9, 2005; Georgina Blakeley, "Digging Up Spain's Past: Consequences of Truth and Reconciliation," *Democratization* 12, no. 1 (February 2005): 44–59.

10. Louis Hutchins, "What Does the Soviet Gulag Have to Do with the National Park Service?" in *People, Places, and Parks: Proceedings of the 2005 George Wright Society Conference on Parks, Protected Areas, and Cultural Sites*, ed. David Harmon (Hancock, MI: George Wright Society, 2005), 119–22. For further discussion of the Gulag Memorial in Moscow, see the 1994 film *Disgraced Monuments*, directed by Mark Lewis and Laura Mulvey.

11. Robin Winks, "Sites of Shame," *National Parks*, March / April 1994, 23–24.

12. Dwight T. Pitcaithley, "National Parks and the Interpretive Message Since 1990,"

in Harmon, *People, Places, and Parks*, 444; Hutchins, "What Does the Soviet Gulag Have to Do with the National Park Service?" 119.

13. On conflicts over the memorial see chapter 6; see also Mario Gonzalez and Elizabeth Cook-Lynn, *The Politics of Hallowed Ground: Wounded Knee and the Struggle for Indian Sovereignty* (Urbana: University of Illinois Press, 1999), 132–33.

14. Acting superintendent Dennis Reidenbach quoted in Joseph A. Slobodzian, "Independence Mall Slavery Memorial Gets Federal Funding," *Philadelphia Inquirer*, September 6, 2005; and in Stephan Salisbury, "Past Imperfect Comes Alive for 'We the People'—All of Them," *Philadelphia Inquirer*, October 14, 2005.

15. National Park System Advisory Board, *Rethinking the National Parks for the 21st Century* (Washington DC: National Geographic Society, 2001), as noted in Pitcaithley, "National Parks and the Interpretive Message Since 1990," 446.

16. James E. Young, *The Texture of Memory: Holocaust Memorials and Meaning* (New Haven, CT: Yale University Press, 1993), 53.

17. Similarly related to the German word *Scham*, the French word *pudeur* derives from the Latin root *pudor*, with links to words like pudenda, or female sex organs. The standard Greek term for genitalia is *aidoia*, a derivative of *aidos*, the word for shame; see Bernard Williams, *Shame and Necessity* (Berkeley: University of California Press, 1993), 78.

18. Robert Metcalf, "Unrequited Narcissism: On the Origin of Shame," *Studies in the History of Ethics: A Peer Reviewed Electronic Journal and Research Portal* (September 2006), http://www.historyofethics.org/092006/092006Metcalf.shtml (accessed March 28, 2007); Martha Hollander, "Losses of Face: Rembrandt, Masaccio, and the Drama of Shame," *Social Research* 70, no. 4 (Winter 2003): 1343; see also Hollander's edited volume *Art and Shame* (New York: Ashgate, 2010).

19. Norbert Elias, *The Civilizing Process*, vol. 1, *The History of Manners*, trans. Edmund Jephcott (1939; New York: Pantheon, 1982), 115.

20. Silvan Tomkins, *Affect Imagery Consciousness*, vol. 2, *The Negative Affects* (New York: Springer, 1963), 123; Elspeth Probyn, *Blush: Faces of Shame* (Minneapolis: University of Minnesota Press, 2005), 13–15.

21. Silvan Tomkins, quoted in Eve Kosofsky Sedgwick and Adam Frank, eds., *Shame and Its Sisters: A Silvan Tomkins Reader* (Durham, NC: Duke University Press, 1995), 136.

22. Sigmund Freud, *The Standard Edition of the Complete Psychological Works of Sigmund Freud*, vol. 7 (1901–1905), *Three Essays on Sexuality and Other Writings*, trans. James Strachey (London: The Hogarth Press, 1953), 157; Jean-Paul Sartre, *Being and Nothingness: An Essay on Phenomenological Ontology*, trans. Hazel E. Barnes (New York: Philosophical Library, 1956), 259, as noted in Kathleen Woodward, "Traumatic Shame: Toni Morrison, Televisual Culture, and the Cultural Politics of Emotions," *Cultural Critique* 46 (Autumn 2000): 213–14.

23. David Benin and Lisa Cartwright, "Shame, Empathy, and Looking Practices: Lessons from a Disability Studies Classroom," *Journal of Visual Culture* 5, no. 2 (2006): 159.

24. Mark M. Smith, "Getting in Touch with Slavery and Freedom," *Journal of American History* 95, no. 2 (September 2008): 387; see also Mark M. Smith, *How Race is Made: Slavery, Segregation, and the Senses* (Chapel Hill: University of North Carolina Press, 2006).

25. Tomkins, quoted in Sedgwick and Frank, *Shame and Its Sisters*, 136; Elspeth Probyn, "Everyday Shame," *Cultural Studies* 18, no. 2/3 (March / May 2004): 329.

26. Ruth Benedict, *The Chrysanthemum and the Sword: Patterns of Japanese Culture* (Boston: Houghton Mifflin, 1946). Eric R. Dodds expanded on Benedict's notion of shame

cultures and guilt cultures in *The Greeks and the Irrational* (Berkeley: University of California Press, 1951).

27. Jonathan Alter, "The Return of Shame," *Newsweek*, February 6, 1995, 20–26; Laura Schlesinger, *How Could You Do That?! The Abdication of Character, Courage, and Conscience* (New York: Harper Collins, 1996); Colin Powell, *My American Journey* (New York: Random House, 1997), 610; Dov Cohen, "The American National Conversation About (Everything but) Shame," *Social Research* 70, no. 4 (Winter 2003): 1089.

28. John Bradshaw, *Healing the Shame That Binds You* (Deerfield Beach, FL: Health Communications, 1988); Ronald T. Potter-Efron and Patricia S. Potter-Efron, *Letting Go of Shame: Understanding How Shame Affects Your Life* (Minneapolis: Hazeldon Foundation, 1989); Martha C. Nussbaum, *Hiding from Humanity: Disgust, Shame, and the Law* (Princeton, NJ: Princeton University Press, 2004), 15.

29. James Weldon Johnson, *The Autobiography of an Ex-colored Man*, ed. William L. Andrews (1912; New York: Penguin, 1990), 137, as noted in Shawn Michelle Smith, *Photography on the Color Line: W. E. B Du Bois, Race, and Visual Culture* (Durham, NC: Duke University Press, 2004), 128; Nussbaum, *Hiding from Humanity*, 15.

30. Eve Kosofsky Sedgwick, *Touching Feeling: Affect, Pedagogy, Performativity* (Durham, NC: Duke University Press, 2003), 63; see also Sedgwick and Frank, "Shame in the Cybernetic Fold: Reading Silvan Tomkins," in *Shame and Its Sisters*, 22; and David M. Halperin and Valerie Traub, eds., *Gay Shame* (Chicago: University of Chicago Press, 2009).

31. José Esteban Muñoz, *Disidentifications: Queers of Color and the Performance of Politics* (Durham, NC: Duke University Press, 1999), 11–12, 194, 200.

32. Tomkins, *Affect Imagery Consciousness*, 118.

33. Statistics compiled by staff at the Archives at Tuskegee Institute (Tuskegee, Alabama), under the direction of sociologist Monroe Work, http://www.law.umkc.edu/faculty/projects/ftrials/shipp/lynchingyear.html (accessed March 7, 2006); see also Philip Dray, *At the Hands of Persons Unknown: The Lynching of Black America* (New York: Random House, 2002), vii–xi. Dora Apel, *Imagery of Lynching: Black Men, White Women, and the Mob* (New Brunswick, NJ: Rutgers University Press, 2004).

34. See Nancy Martha West, *Kodak and the Lens of Nostalgia* (Charlottesville: University Press of Virginia, 2000), for a discussion of Kodak's revolutionary role in the production of amateur photography. In my review of West's book (*Winterthur Portfolio* 35, no. 4 [Winter 2000]: 301–5) I wrote, "We rarely take photos of the nastier moment and events in our lives—the fights at the dinner table, the arguments at work, the disappointments of our jobs and relationships" (303). I was wrong—as lynching photography attests.

35. Anon., "Lynching," *Crisis* 10 (June 1915): 71, as noted in Leon F. Litwack, *Trouble in Mind: Black Southerners in the Age of Jim Crow* (New York: Vintage Books, 1998), 486–87.

36. Joel Williamson, "Wounds Not Scars: Lynching, the National Conscience, and the American Historian," *Journal of American History* 83, no. 4 (March 1997):1235.

37. See Emily Martin, "Toward an Anthropology of Immunity: The Body as Nation State," *Medical Anthropology Quarterly* 4, no. 4 (December 1990): 410–26, for a discussion of the relationships between body metaphors and national identity.

38. Leslie Fulbright, "Resurgence of Nooses Reminds African Americans of Past Horrors," *San Francisco Chronicle*, October 29, 2007; Anahad O'Connor, "Hate-Crime Investigation at Columbia," *New York Times*, October 10, 2007; Paul Vitello, "In Nooses, Many See a New Trial on Race," *New York Times*, October 21, 2007.

39. For foundational histories, see Jacqueline Dowd Hall, *Revolt Against Chivalry: Jessie Daniel Ames and the Women's Campaign Against Lynching* (New York: Columbia University

Press, 1979); Joel Williamson, *Crucible of Race: Black / White Relations in the American South Since Emancipation* (New York: Oxford University Press, 1984); W. Fitzhugh Brundage, *Lynching in the New South: Georgia and Virginia, 1880–1930* (Urbana: University of Illinois Press, 1993), Stewart E. Tolnay and E. M. Beck, *A Festival of Violence: An Analysis of Southern Lynchings, 1882–1930* (Urbana: University of Illinois Press, 1995), and Litwack, *Trouble in Mind*. See also Norton H. Moses, *Lynching and Vigilantism in the United States: An Annotated Bibliography* (Westport, CT: Greenwood, 1997). For studies that discuss lynching on expanded geographic, cultural, and theoretical terms, see Grace Elizabeth Hale, *Making Whiteness: The Culture of Segregation in the South, 1890–1940* (New York: Pantheon, 1998); William D. Carrigan, *The Making of a Lynching Culture: Violence and Vigilantism in Central Texas, 1836–1916* (Urbana: University of Illinois Press, 2004); Jonathan Markovitz, *Legacies of Lynching: Racial Violence and Memory* (Minneapolis: University of Minnesota Press, 2004); and Michael J. Pfeifer, *Rough Justice: Lynching and American Society, 1847–1947* (Urbana: University of Illinois Press, 2004).

40. Mark Twain, "The United States of Lyncherdom," in *Europe and Elsewhere*, ed. Albert Bigelow Paine (New York: Harper and Brothers,1923), 239–49; see also Terry Oggel's restoration of Twain's original essay in "Speaking Out About Race: 'The United States of Lyncherdom' Clemens Really Wrote," *Prospects: An Annual of American Cultural Studies* 25 (2000): 115–58. Ken Gonzales-Day, *Lynching in the West, 1850–1935* (Durham, NC: Duke University Press, 2006), 6n20, 240.

41. Trudier Harris, *Exorcising Blackness: Historical and Literary Lynching and Burning Rituals* (Bloomington: Indiana University Press, 1984); Jacqueline Goldsby, *A Spectacular Secret: Lynching in American Life and Literature* (Chicago: University of Chicago Press, 2006), 5 and passim.

42. James Weldon Johnson, *Along This Way* (New York: Viking Press, 1935), 341.

43. Dolores Janiewski, "The Reign of Passion: White Supremacy and the Clash Between Passionate and Progressive Emotional Styles in the New South," in *An Emotional History of the United States*, ed. Peter N. Stearns and Jan Lewis (New York: New York University Press, 1998), 127; Peter Ehrenhaus and A. Susan Owen, "Race Lynching and Christian Evangelicalism: Performances of Faith," *Text and Performance Quarterly* 24, no. 3/4 (July / October 2004): 277.

44. René Girard, *Violence and the Sacred*, trans. Patrick Gregory (Baltimore, MD: The Johns Hopkins University Press, 1977); Sisson, quoted in Markovitz, *Legacies of Lynching*, xv.

45. On contemporary sex panics, see Michael Warner, *The Trouble with Normal: Sex, Politics, and the Ethics of Queer Life* (New York: Free Press, 2000). Hale, *Making Whiteness*, 208; Fedo, *The Lynchings in Duluth*, 101.

46. On phonographic recordings of lynchings, see Goldsby, *A Spectacular Secret*, 13–15; on films, see Robert Jackson, "A Southern Sublimation: Lynching Film and the Reconstruction of American Memory," *Southern Literary Journal* 11, no. 2 (Spring 2008): 102–20; on lynchings as "modern spectacles," see Hale, *Making Whiteness*, 209. Paul Gilroy, *The Black Atlantic: Modernity and Double Consciousness* (Cambridge, MA: Harvard University Press, 1993).

47. Riled that Minnesota's natural resources were being outsourced to cities like Pittsburgh and Gary, state legislators demanded that U.S. Steel open a mill in Duluth in exchange for tax rebates on the company's major iron ore holdings in northern Minnesota's Mesabi Range. See Arnold R. Alanen, "Morgan Park: U.S. Steel and a Planned Company Town," in *Duluth: Sketches of the Past, A Bicentennial Collection*, ed. Ryck Lydecker and Law-

rence J. Sommer (Duluth, MN: American Revolution Bicentennial Commission, 1976), 111–13.

48. Chris Julin, "The Other Lynching in Duluth," June 2001, Minnesota Public Radio Online, http://news.minnesota.publicradio.org/projects/2001/06/lynching/olli.shtml (accessed April 18, 2007).

49. Margaret Crawford, "The 'New' Company Town," *Perspecta* 30 (1999): 49; Arnold R. Alanen, *Morgan Park: Duluth, U.S. Steel and the Forging of a Company Town* (Minneapolis: University of Minnesota Press, 2007), 186, 198.

50. Fedo, *The Lynchings in Duluth*, 4–5.

51. Advertisement for the John Robinson Circus, *Duluth Herald*, June 10, 1920; see also Duluth Lynchings Online Resource: Historical Documents Relating to the Tragic Events of June 15, 1920, http://collections.mnhs.org/duluthlynchings/html/purpose.htm (accessed June 15, 2006).

52. Janet M. Davis, *The Circus Age: Culture and Society Under the American Big Top* (Chapel Hill: University of North Carolina Press, 2002), 10, 25; Bluford Adams, "Book Review: *The Circus Age: Culture and Society Under the American Big Top*," *Business History Review* 77, no. 3 (Autumn 2003): 512–14.

53. Mikhail Bakhtin, *Rabelais and His World*, trans. H. Iswolsky (Bloomington: Indiana University Press, 1984); Tina Loo and Carolyn Strange, "The Traveling Show Menace: Contested Regulation in Turn-of-the-Century Ontario," *Law & Society Review* 29, no. 4 (1995): 639–40.

54. Anne McClintock, *Imperial Leather: Race, Gender, and Sexuality in the Colonial Contest* (New York: Routledge, 1995), 22; Davis, *The Circus Age*, 188; Alanen, *Morgan Park*, 198. Alanen notes, too, that Morgan Park hosted an annual minstrel show from 1925 to 1948 (283).

55. Davis, *The Circus Age*, 174–75.

56. Erika Doss, *Twentieth-Century American Art* (Oxford: Oxford University Press, 2002), 12.

57. Davis, *The Circus Age*, 224, 188–90; Loo and Strange, "The Traveling Show Menace," 643–44.

58. Fedo, *The Lynchings in Duluth*, 46–47, 110.

59. Advertisement, *New York Times*, November 23, 1922 (original emphasis); see also "The Shame of America," http://historymatters.gmu.edu/d/6786 (accessed April 14, 2007). This ad is also reproduced in Markovitz, *Legacies of Lynching*, 23.

60. "The Duluth Disgrace," *Minneapolis Journal*, June 17, 1920; editorial, *Chicago Evening Post*, quoted in *Duluth Herald*, June 19, 1920; "Duluth's Disgrace," *Duluth News Tribune*, June 17, 1920.

61. "The Duluth Tragedy," *Mankato (MN) Daily Free Press*, June 17, 1920; editorial, *Ely (MN) Miner*, June 25, 1920; "Superior Police to Deport Idle Negroes at Once," *Duluth News Tribune*, July 17, 1920.

62. "Negroes Did Not Rape Girl," *Duluth Ripsaw*, June 26, 1920.

63. "Superior Puts End to Ghoulish Trade," *Duluth Ripsaw*, June 26, 1920. The lynching photographs were apparently taken by staffers with the *Duluth News Tribune*.

64. See Gonzales-Day's discussion on the invention and use of flash photography in *Lynching in the West*, 57–59; Susan Stewart, *On Longing: Narratives of the Miniature, the Gigantic, the Souvenir, the Collection* (Durham, NC: Duke University Press, 1993), 136.

65. Litwack, *Trouble in Mind*, 283–84; James Allen, Hilton Als, John Lewis, and Leon F.

Litwack, *Without Sanctuary: Lynching Photography in America* (Santa Fe, NM: Twin Palm Publishers, 2000), 174.

66. Goldsby, *A Spectacular Secret*, 283; J. Marshall Beier, "Grave Misgivings: Allegory, Catharsis, Composition," *Security Dialogue* 38, no. 2 (June 2007): 251; John E. Carter, "Making Pictures for a News-Hungry Nation," in *Eyewitness at Wounded Knee*, ed. Richard E. Jensen, R. Eli Paul, and John E. Carter (Lincoln: University of Nebraska Press, 1991), 50, 58.

67. Jeffrey Meikle, "Paper Atlantis: Postcards, Mass Art, and the American Scene," *Journal of Design History* 13, no. 4 (2000): 267–86; Steve Hendricks, *The Unquiet Grave: The FBI and the Struggle for the Soul of Indian Country* (New York: Thunder's Mouth Press, 2006), 61.

68. Harvey Young, "The Black Body as Souvenir in American Lynching," *Theatre Journal* 57, no. 4 (2005): 639–57. W. E. B. DuBois wrote that the public display of lynch victim Sam Hose's body parts in the window of an Atlanta grocery store in 1899 influenced his shift toward more directly engaged political activism; see DuBois, *Dusk of Dawn: An Essay Toward an Autobiography of a Race Concept* (New York: Harcourt Brace, 1940), 602–3.

69. "Troops Guard Duluth After Lynching of 3," *Minneapolis Journal*, June 16, 1920.

70. Litwack, *Trouble in Mind*, 294.

71. Saidiya V. Hartman, *Scenes of Subjection: Terror, Slavery, and Self-Making in Nineteenth-Century America* (Oxford: Oxford University Press, 1997), 1–2.

72. The exhibition Witness: Photographs of Lynchings from the Collection of James Allen opened at Ruth Horowitz Gallery in New York in 2000; it was subsequently reorganized as Without Sanctuary: Lynching Photography in America.

73. Patricia J. Williams, "Without Sanctuary," *Nation*, February 14, 2000, 9.

74. Shawn Michelle Smith, "The Evidence of Lynching Photographs," in Dora Apel and Shawn Michelle Smith, *Lynching Photographs* (Berkeley: University of California Press, 2007), 41.

75. Grace Hale, quoted in Catherine Carstairs, "Defining Whiteness: Race, Class, and Gender Perspectives," *International Labor and Working-Class History* 60 (Fall 2001): 204–5; Grace Hale, "Exhibition Review: *Without Sanctuary*," *Journal of American History* 89, no. 3 (December 2002): 993.

76. Susan A. Crane, "Choosing Not to Look: Representation, Repatriation, and Holocaust Atrocity Photography," *History and Theory* 47, no. 3 (2008): 309–30; see also Janina Struk, *Photographing the Holocaust: Interpretations of the Evidence* (London: I. B. Tauris & Company, 2004).

77. John Tagg, *The Burden of Representation: Essays on Photographies and Histories* (Amherst: University of Massachusetts Press, 1988), 188; Roland Barthes, *Camera Lucida: Reflections on Photography*, trans. Richard Howard (New York: Hill and Wang, 1981), 118–19.

78. On anti-lynching campaigns, see for example Gail Bederman, *Manliness and Civilization: A Cultural History of Gender and Race in the United States, 1880–1917* (Chicago: University of Chicago Press, 1995), 45–76; and Jacqueline Dowd Hall, *Revolt Against Chivalry: Jessie Daniel Ames and the Women's Campaign Against Lynching*, rev. ed. (New York: Columbia University Press, 1993).

79. "Murnian Declared Unfit for His Job, Grand Jury Finds That Public Safety Head is Incompetent for Place," *Duluth Herald*, June 23, 1920.

80. For an account of his trial, see Fedo, *The Lynchings in Duluth*, 158–62, 172, and the Duluth Lynchings Online Resource.

81. Census statistics noted in the Duluth Lynchings Online Resource.

82. Fedo, *The Lynchings in Duluth*, 172–73.

83. Sinclair Lewis, *Kingsblood Royal* (New York: Random House, 1947); Jennifer Delton, "Before the White Negro: Sin and Salvation in *Kingsblood Royal*," *American Literary History* 15, no. 2 (Summer 2003): 311–33.

84. Bob Dylan, "Desolation Row" *Highway 61 Revisited* (1965), Columbia, CL 2389, vinyl LP (© 1965; renewed 1993 Special Rider Music); Mark Allan Jackson, "Dark Memory: A Look at Lynching in America Through the Life, Times, and Songs of Woody Guthrie," *Popular Music and Society* 28, no. 5 (December 2005): 663–75. For the response of American artists to lynching, see Helen Langa, "Two Antilynching Art Exhibitions: Politicized Viewpoints, Racial Perspectives, Gendered Constraints," *American Art* 13.1 (1999): 10–29, and Marlene Park, "Lynching and Antilynching: Art and Politics in the 1930s," *Prospects* 18 (1993): 311–65.

85. Lydecker and Sommer, *Duluth: Sketches Of the Past*.

86. Heidi Bakk-Hansen, "Duluth's Lingering Shame," *Ripsaw News* (Duluth, MN), June 7, 2000.

87. "Clayton Jackson McGhie Memorial Discussion Guide," Clayton Jackson McGhie Memorial Web site, http://www.claytonjacksonmcghie.org/discussionguide.php (accessed August 14, 2006); Taylor quoted in "It's Not Just History," part 6 of "Postcard From a Lynching," http://news.minnesota.publicradio.org/projects/2001/06/lynching/page6.shtml.

88. Monica Davey, "It Did Happen Here: The Lynching That a City Forgot," *New York Times*, December 4, 2003; Grytdahl, quoted in "Duluth Still Deals with Racism" from "Postcard From a Lynching," http://news.minnesota.publicradio.org/projects/2001/06/lynching/sidebar.shtml.

89. Carla Stetson, interview with author, August 9, 2005. Unless otherwise noted, all subsequent quotes from Stetson stem from this interview.

90. The song itself was written by Lewis Allan (pseudonym, Abel Meeropol). Filmmaker Joel Katz made *Strange Fruit* in 2002.

91. "If you're south of the Canadian border . . . ," blog entry on "Uppity-Negro.com," March 10, 2004, http://www.uppity-negro.com/2003/12/if_youre_south_of_the_canadian.html (accessed August 14, 2006).

92. "Clayton Jackson McGhie Memorial Discussion Guide."

93. Memorial Board, Clayton Jackson McGhie Memorial Web site, at: http://www.claytonjacksonmcghie.org/whowewere.php (accessed May 3, 2007).

94. Shoshana Felman, "The Return of the Voice: Claude Lanzmann's *Shoah*," in *Testimony: Crises of Witnessing in Literature, Psychoanalysis, and History*, ed. Shoshana Felman and D. Laub (New York: Routledge, 1992), 204; Kelly Oliver, *Witnessing: Beyond Recognition* (Minneapolis: University of Minnesota Press, 2001), 20.

95. Cohen, "The American National Conversation about (Everything but) Shame," 1088.

96. Oliver, *Witnessing*, 7.

97. The three young men are Eddie Glenn, Delon Grant, and Dan Kachingwe; Carla Stetson, interview with author, February 10, 2008.

98. Dominick LaCapra, "Trauma, Absence, Loss," *Critical Inquiry* 25 (Summer 1999): 698.

99. *Reconciliation* was designed by sculptor Stephen Broadbent, who also created iden-

tical statues dedicated in England and the Republic of Benin as part of a sculptural program focused on the slave trade.

100. See also Derek H. Alderman and Rachel Campbell, "Symbolic Excavation and the Artifact Politics of Remembering Slavery in the American South," *Southeastern Geographer* 48, no. 3 (2008): 338–55. Savannah's sculpture bears some similarity to Meta Warrick Fuller's seven-foot sculpture *Emancipation* (1913), which was cast in bronze in 1999 and installed at the National Center of Afro-American Artists and the Museum of African American History, Boston.

101. Dan Chapman, "Savannah Struggles Over Inscription," *Atlanta Journal-Constitution*, February 23, 2001.

102. Kate Wiltrout, "A Dream Comes True," *Savannah Morning News*, July 28, 2002; letter to the editor, *Savannah Morning News*, August1, 2002, letter to the editor, *Savannah Morning News*, August 13, 2002, both noted in Derek H. Alderman, "Coastal Heritage as a Contested Landscape: The Politics of Remembering Slavery in Savannah, Georgia," in Proceedings of the 14th Biennial Coastal Zone Conference, New Orleans (July 17–21, 2005), 3.

103. Dell Upton, "Remembering the Civil Rights Movement," *Design Book Review* 40 (Fall 1999); 22–33; see also Owen J. Dwyer and Derek H. Alderman, *Civil Rights Memorials and the Geography of Memory* (Chicago: The Center for American Places at Columbia College, 2008); and Victoria J. Gallagher, "Displaying Race: Cultural Projection and Commemoration," in *Rhetorics of Display*, ed. Lawrence J. Prelli (Columbia: University of South Carolina Press, 2006), 177–96. Some northern cities also feature civil rights memorials, such as the Indiana University South Bend Civil Rights Heritage Center at the Engman Natatorium, a formerly segregated public swimming pool.

104. Jeremy W. Peters, "A Slavery Apology, but Debate Continues," *New York Times*, January 13, 2008; Darryl Fears, "House Issues an Apology for Slavery," *Washington Post*, July 30, 2008; Avis Thomas-Lester, "A Senate Apology for History on Lynching," *Washington Post*, June 14, 2005. In 2009 the Senate approved a resolution apologizing to Native Americans "for years of 'ill-conceived policies' and acts of violence" by United States citizens; see "A Symbolic Apology to Indians," *New York Times*, October 8, 2009.

105. Darryl Fears, "Seeking More Than Apologies for Slavery," *Washington Post*, June 20, 2005; Pam Belluck, "Panel Suggests Brown U. Atone for Ties to Slavery," *New York Times*, October 19, 2006.

106. Aaron Lazare, *On Apology* (New York: Oxford University Press, 2004), 41; Ali Mazrui, quoted in Elazar Barkan, *The Guilt of Nations: Restitution and Negotiating Historical Injustices* (Baltimore, MD: The John Hopkins University Press, 2000), 302. The Organization of African Unity was founded in 1992 to study the possibilities of restitution for slavery from Europe and the United States.

107. Yonni Chapman, guest blog post on Unsung Founders discussion board, Orange Politics.org, http://orangepolitics.org/2006/10/unsung-founders-discussion/ (accessed May 11, 2007); "Do Ho Suh, Maquette for *Public Figures*," http://www.publicartfund.org/pafweb/projects/03/metrotech/metrospective_suh_s03.html (accessed May 11, 2007).

108. James W. Loewen, *Lies Across America: What Our Historic Sites Get Wrong* (New York: New Press, 1999), 161; Kirk Savage, *Standing Soldiers, Kneeling Slaves: Race, War, and Monument in Nineteenth-Century America* (Princeton, NJ: Princeton University Press, 1997), 155–61.

109. W. Fitzhugh Brundage, "Meta Warrick's 1907 'Negro Tableaux' and (Re)Presenting

African American Historical Memory," *Journal of American History* 89, no. 4 (March 2003): 1368–1400; see also Renee Ater, *Remaking Race and History: The Sculpture of Meta Warrick Fuller, 1907–1921* (Berkeley: University of California Press, forthcoming).

110. Nathan Irvin Huggins, *Black Odyssey: The African American Ordeal in Slavery* (New York: Vintage, 1990), xi–xii.

111. Ira Berlin, "American Slavery in History and Memory and the Search for Social Justice," *Journal of American History* 90, no. 4 (March 2004): 1251.

112. A brief sampling of slavery-centered exhibitions organized in recent years includes Legacies: Contemporary Artists Reflect on Slavery (New-York Historical Society, 2006); Lest We Forget: The Triumph Over Slavery (The Schomburg Center for Research in Black Culture and the New York Public Library, 2004); Landscape of Slavery: The Plantation in American Art (Gibbes Museum of Art, Charleston, South Carolina, 2007); and Materialising Slavery: Art, Artefact, Memory and Identity (National Gallery of Jamaica, 2007). On the "slavery heritage" industry, see G. M. S. Dann and A. V. Seaton, eds., *Slavery, Contested Heritage and Thanatourism* (New York: Haworth Hospitality Press, 2001).

113. Ron Eyerman, *Cultural Trauma: Slavery and the Formation of African American Identity* (Cambridge: Cambridge University Press, 2001).

114. Julia M. Klein, "Slavery Divides Again," *New York Times*, March 12, 2008. Slavery museums are not unique to the United States; the International Slavery Museum in Liverpool, for example, opened in 2007.

115. Barkan, *The Guilt of Nations*, 307.

116. Michael Eric Dyson, "Essentialism and the Complexities of Racial Identity," in *Multiculturalism: A Critical Reader*, ed. David Theo Goldberg (New York: Blackwell, 1994), 221.

117. Pat Ward Williams, *Accused / Blowtorch / Padlock* (1986), collection of the Whitney Museum of American Art. The artist also produced other versions of this piece. For a discussion of black women artists and representations of racial violence see Phyllis Jackson, "Re-Living Memories: Picturing Death," *Ijele: Art EJournal of the African World* 5 (2002), http://www.africaresource.com/ijele/issue5/jackson.html (accessed November 4, 2007).

118. By 1998, more than eighty thousand individual claims had been paid, at a cost of more than $1.6 billion; see Barkan, *The Guilt of Nations*, 31. On objections to the inclusion of Masaoka's words, see the Japanese American Voice Web site at http://www.javoice.com/ (accessed November 7, 2007).

119. Buckley, quoted in Heather Hammatt, "Touchstones of Memory," *Landscape Architecture*, June 2002, 68; Clinton, quoted in James M. Goode, *Washington Sculpture: A Cultural History of Outdoor Sculpture in the Nation's Capital* (Baltimore, MD: The Johns Hopkins University Press, 2008), 16.

120. Barkan, *The Guilt of Nations*, xviii.

121. Kimberly Edds, "New Museum Revives Painful Memories for Internees," *Washington Post*, April 26, 2004; Edward Epstein, "Internment-site Preservation Okd," *San Francisco Chronicle*, December 6, 2006. During hearings on the camp preservation bill (HR-1492), National Park Service representatives expressed their opposition to its passage on the grounds that it would authorize funding to non-NPS managed projects. As of 2007, the NPS managed only two of the ten camps: Manzanar and Minidoka.

122. Toni Morrison, "A Bench by the Road," *World Journal of the Unitarian Universalist Association* 3, no. 1 (January / February 1989): 4; Felicia R. Lee, "Bench of Memory at Slavery's Gateway," *New York Times*, July 28, 2008. The society launched its bench project at

Princeton University in 2006 with a "Biography Bench" given to Morrison; other benches are planned for sites relevant to Morrison's novels and to African American history, such as the site in Mississippi where Emmett Till was murdered in 1955.

123. For histories, see Michele Bogart, "Public Space and Public Memory in New York's City Hall Park," *Journal of Urban History* 25, no. 2 (1999): 226–57; and Sarah R. Katz, "Redesigning Civic Memory: The African American Burial Ground in Lower Manhattan" (PhD diss., University of Pennsylvania, 2006); on slave population statistics, see Christopher Moore, "A World of Possibilities: Slavery and Freedom in Dutch New Amsterdam," and Jill Lepore, "The Tightening Vise: Slavery and Freedom in British New York," both in *Slavery in New York*, ed. Ira Berlin and Leslie M. Harris (New York: New Press, 2005), 38, 60.

124. William Diamond, quoted in Andrea E. Frohne, "The African Burial Ground in New York City: Manifesting and Representing Spirituality of Space" (PhD diss., Binghamton University, State University of New York, 2002), 48; on the *Tilted Arc* affair, see Harriet F. Senie, *The Tilted Arc Controversy: Dangerous Precedent?* (Minneapolis: University of Minnesota Press, 2001).

125. As noted in Katz, "Redesigning Civic Memory," 59–60.

126. Katz, "Redesigning Civic Memory," 87.

127. Frederick Douglass, "Free Blacks Must Learn Trades," in *Frederick Douglass: The Narrative and Selected Writings*, ed. Michael Meyer (New York: Modern Library, 1984), 350.

128. U.S. Department of the Interior, "Secretary Norton Announces President's Designation of African Burial Ground as a National Monument," news release, February 28, 2006, http://www.doi.gov/news/06_News_Releases/060228.htm (accessed March 23, 2008).

129. Barkan, *The Guilt of Nations*, xvi; see also Robert F. Drinan, *The Mobilization of Shame: A World View of Human Rights* (New Haven, CT: Yale University Press, 2002).

130. Marita Sturken, "Memorializing Absence," in *Understanding September 11*, ed. Craig Calhoun, Paul Price, and Ashley Timmer (New York: New Press, 2002), 382; Dominick LaCapra, *Writing History, Writing Trauma* (Baltimore, MD: The Johns Hopkins University Press, 2001), 53.

131. George Shulman, "Only Cans and Bottles Can be Redeemed: Suffering and Redemption in American Political Rhetoric," paper delivered at the annual meeting of the American Studies Association, Washington, D.C., November 5, 2005; Maeve Cooke, "The Ethics of Post-Holocaust Art: Reflections on Redemption and Representation," *German Life and Letters* 59, no. 2 (April 2006): 268–270.

132. LaCapra, *Writing History, Writing Trauma*, 40.

133. Tomkins, quoted in Sedgwick and Frank, *Shame and Its Sisters*, 156.

134. Memorial Board, Clayton Jackson McGhie Memorial Web site, http://www.claytonjacksonmcghie.org/wherewearegoing.php (accessed May 3, 2007).

135. Brooks, quoted in Errin Haines, "Re-Enactment of 1946 Lynchings Planned," AP wire services, July 17, 2005, http://wesclark.com/jw/lynching_reenactment.html (accessed January 23, 2006), and Shaila Dewan, "Group Lynching is Re-created in a 'Call for Justice,'" *New York Times*, July 26, 2005.

136. "A Lynching Memorial Unveiled in Duluth," *New York Times*, December 5, 2003; see also Read's memoir, *The Lyncher in Me: A Search for Redemption in the Face of History* (St. Paul, MN: Borealis Books, 2008), 129–31.

137. Barbara Haataja, quoted in Davey, "It Did Happen Here"; "American Renaissance" posting by "mikemason," July 16, 2005, and "betty," July 25, 2005, http://www.amren

.com/mtnews/archives/2005/07/georgia_lynchin.php (accessed April 4, 2006); Associated Press, "Georgia Lynchings Re-Enacted: 1946 Event Re-Created in Hopes of Jarring Memories, Consciences," MSNBC.com, July 25, 2005, http://www.msnbc.msn.com/id/8700457/ (accessed August 5, 2009).

138. Before the site was transferred to the National Park Service, for example, it was owned by the Los Angeles Department of Water and Power.

139. Robert Hayashi, "Transfigured Patterns: Contesting Memories at the Manzanar National Historic Site," *The Public Historian* 25, no. 4 (Fall 2003): 57, 69; Elena Tajima Creef, *Imaging Japanese America: The Visual Construction of Citizenship, Nation, and the Body* (New York: New York University Press, 2004), 139–40.

140. Associated Press, "Name of Park at Prison Camp Site is in Dispute," *New York Times*, June 25, 2006, http://www.nytimes.com/2006/06/25/us/25park.html?ex=1184212800&en=5a52c7b261093223&ei=5070 (accessed June 25, 2006); Maria Tumarkin, *Traumascapes: The Power and Fate of Places Transformed by Tragedy* (Carlton: Melbourne University Press, 2005), 12.

141. Sara Ahmed, *The Cultural Politics of Emotion* (New York: Routledge, 2004), 106, 15.

Chapter 6

1. Elvia Díaz, "Statue of Spaniard Loses Foot," *Albuquerque Journal*, January 8, 1998.

2. Erik Eckholm, "A Grim Tradition, and a Long Struggle to End it," *New York Times*, April 2, 2008; on the Visitors Center, see their Web site, http://www.rio-arriba.org/departments_and_divisions/onate_center.html (accessed May 20, 2008).

3. Díaz, "Statue of Spaniard Loses Foot."

4. Allan J. Ryan, *The Trickster Shift: Humour and Irony in Contemporary Native Art* (Vancouver: University of British Columbia Press, 1999).

5. Marc Simmons, quoted in Nancy Plevin and Ben Neary, "Vandals Maim Bronze Sculpture at Visitor's Center," *Santa Fe New Mexican*, January 8, 1998; Ray Rivera, "Hero or Villain: How Should We Remember Don Juan de Oñate?" *Santa Fe New Mexican*, January 11, 1998 Tom Chávez, quoted in Rivera, "Hero or Villain"; Irene Brandtner de Martinez, letter to the editor, *Santa Fe New Mexican*, February 5, 1998.

6. Cindy Bogert Bibo Lamm, letter to the editor, *Santa Fe New Mexican*, February 5, 1998; P.J. Lopez, letter to the editor, *Santa Fe New Mexican*, January 22, 1998; Andrew Lauriano, "Oñate Honor Opens Old Wound," *Albuquerque Journal*, January 11, 1998; Maurus Chino, "Haubu Hanu: Oppression Affects All People," *Counterpunch* (October 27–29, 2006), http://www.counterpunch.org/chino10272006.html (accessed August 12, 2008).

7. Richard McCord, "The Scars of History Take Time to Heal," *Santa Fe New Mexican*, January 11, 1998.

8. See, for example, Douglas Seefeldt, "Oñate's Foot: Histories, Landscapes, and Contested Memories in the Southwest," in *Across the Continent: Jefferson, Lewis and Clark, and the Making of America*, ed. Douglas Seefeldt, Jeffrey L. Hantman, and Peter S. Onuf (Charlottesville: University of Virginia Press, 2005), 169–209; Michael P. Carroll, *The Penitente Brotherhood: Patriarchy and Hispano-Catholicism in New Mexico* (Baltimore, MD: The Johns Hopkins University Press, 2002), 1–4; and Jake Kosek, *Understories: The Political Life of Forests in Northern New Mexico* (Durham, NC: Duke University Press, 2006), 50–61.

9. "Lincoln Statue is Unveiled, and Protesters Come Out," *New York Times*, April 6, 2003.

10. Paul Davenport, "Arizona 9/11 Memorial Called Insult to America," Associated

Press State & Local Wire, September 26, 2006; Randal C. Archibold, "Effort to Rework Arizona's 9/11 Memorial Fails," *New York Times*, April 17, 2008.

11. On King street naming, see Derek H. Alderman, "A Street Fit for a King: Naming Places and Commemoration in the American South," *Professional Geographer* 52, no. 4 (2000): 672–84.

12. Michael E. Ruane, "Unhappy with 'Confrontational' Image, U.S. Panel Wants King Statue Reworked," *Washington Post*, May 9, 2008; Michael Birnbaum, "Arts Panel Members Satisfied with Changes to King Statue," *Washington Post*, June 20, 2008.

13. Brent Staples, "Putting a Price Tag on the Legacy of Martin Luther King," *New York Times*, November 28, 2001; Ronald Smothers, "Issue Behind King Memorial: Who Owns History?" *New York Times*, January 15, 1995; Brett Zongker, "Kin Charges Group Building Memorial for Use of King's Words and Image," Boston.com, April 18, 2009, http://www.boston.com/news/nation/washington/articles/2009/04/18/kin_charges_group_building_memorial_for_use_of_kings_words_and_image/?rss_id=Boston+Globe+—+National+News (accessed May 1, 2009).

14. Jeffrey Gettleman, "Rocky Mount Journal: King Statue, A Unity Symbol, Severely Tests the Dream," *New York Times*, December 13, 2003; Brenda Goodman, "City Abandons Dream of Statue of Dr. King," *New York Times*, November 30, 2005; Rip Woodin, "Last Word on the Statue," *Rocky Mount (NC) Telegram* (24 May 2007). By contrast, a statue of King that Blome made for Milwaukee's YMCA in 1998 was well received.

15. Ben Evans, "Selection of Monument Sculptor Criticized," *South Bend (IN) Tribune*, August 26, 2007; Mitchell Landsberg, "MLK Monument Outsourced, Critics Say," *Los Angeles Times*, July 23, 2007; Patricia Cohen, "The King Memorial: Dreams at Odds," *New York Times*, September 24, 2007; Ariana Eunjung Cha, "A King Statue 'Made in China'?" *Washington Post*, August 15, 2007.

16. Cha, "A King Statue 'Made in China'?"; Caitrin McKiernan, letter to the editor, *Los Angeles Times*, May 22, 2008.

17. Howard Schuman, Barry Schwartz, and Hannah D'Arcy, "Elite Revisionists and Popular Beliefs: Christopher Columbus, Hero or Villain?" *Public Opinion Quarterly* 69, no. 1 (Spring 2005): 2–29; Carla Rahn Phillips and William D. Phillips, "Christopher Columbus in the United States Historiography: Biography as Projection," *History Teacher* 25, no. 2 (February 1992): 128. See also Frances FitzGerald, *America Revised: History Schoolbooks in the Twentieth Century* (Boston: Little Brown, 1979), and Tony Horwitz, *A Voyage Long and Strange: Rediscovering the New World* (New York: Henry Holt, 2008), 3.

18. John Sanko, "Indians Protest Columbus Day," *Rocky Mountain News*, October 10, 1989; "Columbus Statue Smashed in San Jose," *San Francisco Chronicle*, March 10, 2001. See also James Loewen's discussion of contemporary Columbus iconoclasm in *Lies Across America: What Our Historic Sites Get Wrong* (New York: Simon & Schuster, 2007), 46–48.

19. See Robin Nieto, "Columbus Statue Toppled in Venezuela on Day of Indigenous Resistance," Venezuelanalysis.com, October 13, 2004, http://www.venezuelanalysis.com/news/734 (accessed May 27, 2008).

20. Robert S. Nelson and Margaret Olin, eds., *Monuments and Memory, Made and Unmade* (Chicago: University of Chicago Press, 2003), 205.

21. Jane Kromm, *The Art of Frenzy: Public Madness in the Visual Culture of Europe, 1500–1850* (London: Continuum, 2002), 1–2, 9–10.

22. Seneca, *Moral and Political Essays*, ed. and trans. by J. M. Cooper and J. F. Procopé (New York: Cambridge University Press, 1995), 18–19; Martha Nussbaum, *Upheavals of Thought: The Intelligence of Emotions* (Cambridge: Cambridge University Press, 2001), 160;

William V. Harris, *Restraining Rage: The Ideology of Anger Control in Classical Antiquity* (Cambridge, MA: Harvard University Press, 2002).

23. Deborah Cox, Karin Bruckner, and Sally Stabb, *The Anger Advantage: The Surprising Benefits of Anger and How It Can Change a Woman's Life* (New York: Broadway Books, 2003); Mark Ames, *Going Postal: Rage, Murder and Rebellion: From Reagan's Workplaces to Clinton's Columbine and Beyond* (New York: Soft Skull Press, 2005), 74–77; Andrew Ferguson, "Road Rage," *Time*, January 12, 1998, 44.

24. See "The State of the News Media 2008: An Annual Report on American Journalism," http://www.stateofthenewsmedia.org/2008/narrative_cabletv_audience.php?cat=2&media=7 (accessed June 2, 2008); see also Peter Hart, "The 'Oh Really?' Factor: Bill O'Rielly Spins Fact and Statistics," *Fair: Fairness and Accuracy in Media*, May / June 2002, http://www.fair.org/index.php?page=1108 (accessed June 2, 2008); and Rory O'Connor and Aaron Cutler, *Shock Jocks: Hate Speech and Talk Radio* (New York: AlterNet Books, 2008).

25. Silvan Tomkins, "Anger," in *Shame and Its Sisters: A Silvan Tomkins Reader*, ed. Eve Kosofsky Sedgwick and Adam Frank (Durham, NC: Duke University Press, 1995), 207–12; Arjun Appadurai, *Fear of Small Numbers: An Essay on the Geography of Anger* (Durham, NC: Duke University Press, 2006), 100.

26. Michael Fumento, "Road Rage Versus Reality," *Atlantic Monthly*, August 1998, 12–17; Barry Glassner, *The Culture of Fear: Why Americans Are Afraid of the Wrong Things* (New York: Perseus, 1999), 27–28; Peter Wood, *A Bee in the Mouth: Anger in America Now* (New York: Encounter Books, 2006), 191.

27. Philip Fisher, *The Vehement Passions* (Princeton, NJ: Princeton University Press, 2002), 175; George W. Bush, "Address to a Joint Session of Congress and the American People," September 20, 2001, http://www.encyclopedia.com/doc/1G2-3401804866.html; George W. Bush, State of the Union address, January 20, 2004, http://millercenter.org/scripps/archive/speeches/detail/4542 (accessed May 20, 2008).

28. Amy Gutmann and Dennis Thompson, *Why Deliberative Democracy?* (Princeton, NJ: Princeton University Press, 2004).

29. Carol Tavris, *Anger: The Misunderstood Emotion* (New York: Simon & Schuster, 1982), 21; Arlie R. Hochschild, *The Managed Heart: Commercialization of Human Feeling* (Berkeley: University of California Press, 1983); Victoria L. Brescoll and Eric Luis Uhlmann, "Can an Angry Woman Get Ahead? Status Conferral, Gender, and Expression of Emotion in the Workplace," *Psychological Science* 19, no. 3 (March 2008): 268–75.

30. Custer was reinterred at West Point in 1877. The two-hour battle was preceded and followed by a separate charge under the command of Major Marcus Reno; for further details on the battle see James Welch, *Killing Custer: The Battle of the Little Bighorn and the Fate of the Plains Indians* (New York: Penguin, 1994). The memorial cost $1,000 and was made by the Mount Auburn Marble and Granite Works, Cambridge, Massachusetts; see Jerome A. Greene, *Stricken Ground: The Little Bighorn Since 1876* (Norman: University of Oklahoma Press, 2008), 31.

31. Edward Tabor Linenthal, *Sacred Ground: Americans and Their Battlefields*, 2nd ed. (Urbana: University of Illinois Press, 1993), 130–31, 139; see also Linenthal's essay "From Shrine to Historic Site: The Little Bighorn Battlefield National Monument," in *Legacy: New Perspectives on the Battle of Little Bighorn*, ed. Charles E. Rankin (Helena: Montana Historical Society Press, 1996), 306–19. For an overview of the park's history and management see Greene, *Stricken Ground*.

32. Michael A. Elliott, *Custerology: The Enduring Legacy of the Indian Wars and George Armstrong Custer* (Chicago: University of Chicago Press, 2007).

33. Joy S. Kasson, *Buffalo Bill's Wild West: Celebrity, Memory, and Popular History* (New York: Hill and Wang, 2000), 5, 246–48; Patricia M. Burnham, "Custer's Last Stand: High-Low on Old and New Frontiers," in *Seeing High and Low: Representing Social Conflict in American Visual Culture*, ed. Patricia Johnston (Berkeley: University of California Press, 2006), 124–41.

34. Patricia Nelson Limerick, *The Legacy of Conquest: The Unbroken Past of the American West* (New York: W. W. Norton, 1987).

35. Greene, *Stricken Ground*, 170; Linenthal, *Sacred Ground*, 138, 143–44; Robert Utley, *Custer and Me* (Norman: University of Oklahoma Press, 2004), 149; see also Russell Means, *Where White Men Fear to Tread* (New York: St. Martin's Press, 1995), 357–58.

36. Linenthal, *Sacred Ground*, 159–61; Linenthal, "From Shrine to Historic Site," 314; Means, quoted in James Hagengruber, "Built Out of Protest: Memorial to Warriors Had Passionate Beginning," *Billings (MT) Gazette*, June 25, 2003. The plaque was deaccessioned after the opening of the Indian Memorial; see Greene, *Stricken Field*, 236.

37. For details, see the Indian Memorial Design Competition guidelines, http://www.nps.gov/archive/libi/competition.htm (accessed June 6, 2008).

38. The call for design entries ran from July to October 1996; see Charles E. Rankin, "An Indian Memorial for the Little Bighorn," *Montana, The Magazine of Western History*, Summer 1997, 58–59.

39. *The Indian Memorial at Little Bighorn Battlefield National Monument* (Tucson, Arizona: Western National Parks Association, 2003); see also http://www.nps.gov/libi/winning-design-entry.htm (accessed June 6, 2008).

40. Colleen Cutschall, quoted in "Professor of Visual Art Designs Sculpture for U.S. Monument," Brandon University (Manitoba) press release, (November 18, 2002, as noted on her Web site, http://www.sisterwolf.com/index.html (accessed June 16, 2008).

41. *The Indian Memorial at Little Bighorn Battlefield National Monument*, n.p.

42. Richard Slotkin, "Signifying on the Little Bighorn," in Rankin, *Legacy*, 289.

43. Wolfgang Schivelbusch, *The Culture of Defeat: On National Trauma, Mourning, and Recovery* (2001; New York: Henry Holt and Company, 2003), 3, 29–32; on the Alamo, see Richard Flores, *Remembering the Alamo: Memory, Modernity, and the Master Symbol* (Austin: University of Texas Press, 2002).

44. Jeffrey Ostler, *The Plains Sioux and U.S. Colonialism From Lewis and Clark to Wounded Knee* (New York: Cambridge University Press, 2004), 351.

45. Judy Holland, "Capitol Statues Switched as Subjects' Fame Fades," *Minneapolis Star Tribune*, March 29, 2008.

46. Rebecca Solnit, "The Struggle of Dawning Intelligence: On Monuments and Native Americans," *Harvard Design Magazine*, Fall 1999, 54.

47. A Tennessee appeals court overturned the decision in 2005, forbidding Vanderbilt from eliminating "Confederate" from the building's façade, but the university omits the word in all of its maps and in-house references.

48. Derek Alderman, "A Bumpy Road," *Planning*, January 2008, 18.

49. "Despite Objection, Redskins Will Remain Redskins," *New York Times*, October 24, 1991.

50. Philip J. Deloria, *Indians in Unexpected Places* (Lawrence: University Press of Kansas, 2004), 2–9.

51. Erika Doss, "*Shoot-Out*: Poking Fun and Challenging Myths in Western American Art," in *Redrawing Boundaries: Perspectives on Western American Art*, ed. Laura Caruso and Peter Hassrick (Denver: Institute of Western American Art, 2007), 44–55. *Shoot Out* is currently located on a rooftop sculpture court at the Denver Art Museum. For other Denver area sculptures depicting Native Americans see Troy Lynn Yellow Wood, "Trauma and Memory: The Importance of Imagery to Native Peoples," *Sculpture Review* (Winter 2006): 32–35.

52. Gretchen Ruethling, "Honoring Warriors From Both the Past and the Present," *New York Times*, June 10, 2006; "Annual Journalism Scholarship Winners Announced," *News From Indian Country*, May 12, 2008, 23.

53. Scott Aust, "Students Present Statue Protests," *Rapid City Journal*, March 10, 2004; John Villani, "Glenna Goodacre," *Southwest Art* (September 1991): 85. Goodacre's sculpture was based on a smaller piece called *Banished*, designed in 1979.

54. "Prairie Edge Replaces Controversial Statue," *Rapid City Journal*, March 20, 2008.

55. Letter from Chief Standing Bear to Gutzon Borglum, December 4, 1931, as noted in Albert Boime, "Patriarchy Fixed in Stone: Gutzon Borglum's 'Mount Rushmore,'" *American Art* 5, no.1–2 (Winter / Spring 1991): 161; Chief Standing Bear's explanation of Native American heroes, widely quoted in Crazy Horse Memorial literature, is based on a now "lost" letter to Ziolkowski according to memorial representatives; see John Taliaferro, *Great White Fathers: The Story of the Obsessive Quest to Create Mount Rushmore* (New York: Public Affairs, 2002), 329.

56. Taliaferro, *Great White Fathers*, 330.

57. Robb DeWall, *Korczak, Storyteller in Stone*, 5th ed. (Crazy Horse, SD: Korczak's Heritage, Inc., 2000), 44; see also Kathryn Eischeid, "Native American as Nature's Nobleman: Identity and Representation at the Crazy Horse Memorial," (master's thesis, University of Colorado, Boulder, 2005). The Crazy Horse Memorial Foundation claims to have sponsored college scholarships totaling over $1 million for Native American students; see "Annual Journalism Scholarship Winners Announced," 23.

58. Carole Blair and Neil Michel, "The Rushmore Effect: Ethos and National Collective Identity," in *The Ethos of Rhetoric*, ed. Michael J. Hyde (Columbia: University of South Carolina Press, 2004): 156–96.

59. Gutzon Borglum, "Colossal Sculpture: Its Value to Civilization" (pamphlet), Mount Rushmore National Memorial (Mount Rushmore National Memorial Committee, 1931), 16; Gutzon Borglum, "Carving Mountains into Monuments," *New York Herald Tribune*, August 21, 1927, as cited in Blair and Michel, "The Rushmore Effect," 165nn58–59.

60. Vine Deloria, Jr., preface to *Custer Died For Your Sins: An Indian Manifesto* (1969; Norman: University of Oklahoma Press, 1988), xi, ix.

61. Charmaine White Face, quoted in Tony Perrottet, "Mount Rushmore," *Smithsonian* 37, no. 2 (May 2006): 80; Charlotte Black Elk, quoted in Avis Little Eagle, "Desecration of Mountain Angers Lakota: Completion of Memorial Not on the Near Horizon," *Indian Country Today* 16.2 (12–15 June 1996): B-3; Gerard Baker, quoted in Perrottet, "Mount Rushmore," 81.

62. Taliaferro, *Great White Fathers*, 350–57, 400; for other accounts of the 1970 AIM occupation of Mount Rushmore, see John Fire / Lame Deer and Richard Erdoes, *Lame Deer: Seeker of Visions* (New York: Simon & Schuster, 1972), 91; and Means, *Where White Men Fear to Tread*, 168–70.

63. Mark David Spence, *Dispossessing the Wilderness: Indian Removal and the Making of the National Parks* (New York: Oxford University Press, 1999), 4; Robert H. Keller and

Michael F. Turek, *American Indians and National Parks* (Tucson: University of Arizona Press, 1998), 48–51.

64. Larry J. Zimmerman, "Plains Indians and Resistance to 'Public' Heritage Commemoration of Their Pasts," in *Cultural Heritage and Human Rights*, ed. Helaine Silverman and D. Fairchild Ruggles (New York: Springer, 2007), 152; see also Michelene E. Pesantubbee, "Wounded Knee: Site of Resistance and Recovery," in *Religion, Violence, Memory, and Place*, ed. Owen Baruch Stier and J. Shawn Landres (Bloomington: Indiana University Press, 2006), 85–86; Mario Gonzalez and Elizabeth Cook-Lynn, *The Politics of Hallowed Ground: Wounded Knee and the Struggle for Indian Sovereignty* (Urbana: University of Illinois Press, 1999); and Mary Nolan, "The Politics of Memory in the Berlin Republic," *Radical History Review* 81 (Fall 2001): 128.

65. Keller and Turek, *American Indians and National Parks*, 233.

66. Renée L. Bergland, *The National Uncanny: Indian Ghosts and American Subjects* (Hanover, NH: University Press of New England, 2000), 4.

67. James B. Meadow, "'Honor to All the Fallen Warriors,'" *Rocky Mountain News*, June 26, 2003.

68. Enos Poor Bear, Sr., "Peace Through Unity," February 5, 1998, http://www.usd.edu/iais/bighorn/docarchive/theme.html (accessed June 24, 2008).

69. More recent headstones erected to Native Americans omit the word "homeland."

70. Wendy Brown, *States of Injury: Power and Freedom in Late Modernity* (Princeton, NJ: Princeton University Press, 1995), ix.

71. Brown, *States of Injury*, 98; Little Bighorn Battlefield National Monument park ranger Gerald Jasmer, interview with author, June 6, 2008. For a different view on nationalism at the site, see Michael A. Elliott, "Indian Patriots on Last Stand Hill," *American Quarterly* 58, no. 4 (December 2006): 987–1015.

72. Baker, quoted in "After 120 Years, a New Battle at the Little Bighorn," *New York Times*, June 23, 1996; Frederick Turner, "No Surrender," *Outside Magazine*, August 1997, 119–20.

73. Wells, quoted in "After 120 Years."

74. Turner, "No Surrender," 118.

75. Quoted in Gary S. Trujillo, "Custer Loses Again," *Progressive*, September 1991, 11.

76. James B. Meadow, "127 Years Later, the Other Side Speaks," *Rocky Mountain News*, June 24, 2003; Meadow, "Honor to All the Fallen Warriors."

77. Gwen Florio, "Little Bighorn: Thousands Gather to Honor Warriors," *Salt Lake Tribune*, June 26, 2003.

78. Hagengruber, "Built Out of Protest."

79. Becky Bohrer, "Hundreds help dedicate Indian Memorial on battle's anniversary," *Daily Camera* (Boulder, CO), June 24, 2003; Lorna Thackeray, "Thousands See Dedication of Indian Memorial at Little Bighorn," *Billings (MT) Gazette*, June 26, 2003); and James Hagengruber, "Activist Means Steals the Show at Dedication," *Billings (MT) Gazette*, June 26, 2003.

80. Patricia Nelson Limerick, "The Battlefield of History," *New York Times*, August 28, 1997; letters to the editor, *New York Times*, September 3, 1997.

81. James E. Young, *The Texture of Memory: Holocaust Memorials and Meaning* (New Haven, CT: Yale University Press, 1993), 27 (for his discussion of the Gerzes' monument—officially titled the Harburg Monument against Fascism, War, and Violence—and for Peace and Human Rights, see 28–37). For one critique of the monument see Noam Lupu, "Memory Vanished, Absent, and Confined: The Countermemorial Project in 1980s and

1990s Germany," *History & Theory* 15, no. 2 (2003): 130–64. Michel Foucault, *Language, Counter-Memory, Practice*, ed. Donald F. Bouchard (Ithaca, NY: Cornell University Press, 1977), 139–64.

82. See Nicolas Argenti, "Ephemeral Monuments: Memory and Royal Sempiternity in a Grassfields Kingdom," and Susanne Küchler, "The Place of Memory," both in *The Art of Forgetting*, ed. Adrian Forty and Susanne Küchler (New York: Berg, 1999), 21–52, 53–72.

83. Letter from Millie Santillanes, project director and coordinator of the Oñate Cuartocentenario Committee, to Jose L. Rodriguez, chairman, Albuquerque Arts Board, May 19, 1997, Oñate Cuarto Centenario Committee Files, Albuquerque Arts Board, Albuquerque, NM. For further details, see Phillip B. Gonzales, "'History Hits the Heart': Albuquerque's Great Cuartocentenario Controversy, 1997–2005," and Kathy Freise, "Contesting Oñate: Sculpting the Shape of Memory," both in *Expressing New Mexico: Nuevomexicano Creativity, Ritual, and Memory*, ed. Phillip B. Gonzales (Tucson: University of Arizona Press, 2007), 207–32, 233–52, 283–86. See also Kathy Freise, "The Creative Terrain of *Numbe Whageh*: Creating Memory, Leading to Center," *American Indian Culture and Research Journal* 31, no. 3 (2007): 81–98.

84. Katy June-Friesen, "Recasting New Mexico History," *Weekly Alibi* (Albuquerque, NM), October, 20–26, 2005, 35.

85. Houser, quoted in Barbara Ferry, "Oñate Statue's Journey Nears End," *Santa Fe New Mexican*, April 18, 2007. The statue is the second in an anticipated series of twelve aimed at illustrating El Paso's history, hence the name of the sponsoring organization. The first statue, of Franciscan friar Fray Garcia de San Francisco, was dedicated in downtown El Paso in 1996.

86. Public comments noted in Aurelio Sanchez, "Protests Interrupt Talk by Oñate Sculptor Houser," *Albuquerque Journal*, September 25, 2005; "Statue to be Renamed," *Albuquerque Journal*, November 6, 2003.

87. Simmons, quoted in "Oñate's Journey"; Maurus Chino, comment on "New Mexico In Focus, Episode 204," a panel discussion held on July 16, 2008, following the KNME-TV (El Paso) airing of *The Last Conquistador*; see the video of the panel at: http://www.knme.org/newmexicoinfocus/blogger/2008/07/episode-204-last-conquistador.html (accessed August 6, 2008). Ibarra and Valdez, quoted in Robert Nott, "One Culture's Washington, Another's Genghis Khan," *Santa Fe New Mexican*, July 24, 2008.

88. Sonia K. Katyal, "Semiotic Disobedience," *Washington University Law Review* 84, no. 2 (2006): 501.

89. Larry J. Reynolds, "Patriot and Criminals, Criminal and Patriots: Representations of the Case of Major Andre," *South Central Review* 9, no. 1 (Spring 1992): 77–79; John Seelye, *Memory's Nation: The Place of Plymouth Rock* (Chapel Hill: University of North Carolina Press, 1998); Katyal, "Semiotic Disobedience," 499. On distinctions between vandalism and iconoclasm, see Dario Gamboni, *The Destruction of Art: Iconoclasm and Vandalism Since the French Revolution* (New Haven, CT: Yale University Press, 1997), 17–20.

90. David Lowenthal, "Fabricating Heritage," *History & Memory* 10, no. 1 (Spring/Summer 1998): 7, 11.

91. Alfred Gell, *Art and Agency: An Anthropological Theory* (New York: Clarendon Press, 1998), 65; Michael Taussig, *Defacement: Public Secrecy and the Labor of the Negative* (Palo Alto, CA: Stanford University Press, 1999), 3.

92. Robert Bevan, *The Destruction of Memory: Architecture of War* (London: Reaktion Books, 2006), 8.

93. Annie E. Coombes, *History After Apartheid: Visual Culture and Public Memory in a Democratic South Africa* (Durham, NC: Duke University Press, 2003), 19, 37, 53; see also Albert Grundlingh, "A Cultural Conundrum? Old Monuments and New Regimes: The Voortrekker Monument as Symbol of Afrikaner Power in a Postapartheid South Africa," *Radical History Review* 81 (Fall 2001): 95–112.

94. Sanford Levinson, *Written in Stone: Public Monuments in Changing Societies* (Durham, NC: Duke Univ Press, 1998), 68–71; Benjamin Forest and Juliet Johnson, "Unraveling the Threads of History: Soviet-Era Monuments and Post-Soviet National Identity in Moscow," *Annals of the Association of American Geographers* 92, no. 3 (2002): 524–47; see also the 1994 documentary *Disgraced Monuments*, directed by Laura Mulvey and Mark Lewis, which focuses on the fate of Soviet-era memorials in post-Soviet times.

95. Ralph Rugoff, "Monuments for the USA," in *Monuments for the USA*, exhibition catalogue (San Francisco: California College of the Arts Wattis Institute for Contemporary Arts, 2005), 4–11; Sam Durant, *Proposal for White and Indian Dead Monument Transpositions, Washington, D.C.* as illustrated in *Monuments for the USA*, 54. Durant's *Proposal* was shown at Paula Cooper Gallery in New York in the fall of 2005, featuring thirty scaled-down replicas of the Indian War monuments as well as pencil drawings and a maquette of the reconfigured National Mall.

96. Lucy Lippard, *The Lure of the Local: Senses of Place in a Multicentered Society* (New York: New Press, 1997), 86; W. Jackson Rushing III, "'In Our Language': The Art of Hachivi Edgar Heap of Birds," *Third Text* 19, no. 4 (July 2005): 365–84 (Heap of Birds is quoted on p. 384).

97. Solnit, "The Struggle of Dawning Intelligence," 57.

98. George E. Marcus, *The Sentimental Citizen: Emotion in Democratic Politics* (University Park: Pennsylvania State University Press, 2002), 8; George W. Bush, quoted talking with filmmaker Lionel Chetwynd, in Elisabeth Bumiller, "White House Letter: Film Maker Leans Right, Oval Office Swings Open," *New York Times*, September 8, 2003; Audre Lorde, "The Uses of Anger: Women Responding to Racism," in *Sister Outsider: Essays and Speeches* (Trumansberg, NY: Crossing Press, 1984), 124, 127.

99. Judy Baca, interview with author, June 4, 2006. Unless otherwise noted, all subsequent quotes by Baca stem from this interview. See also Steven W. Hackel, "Sources of Rebellion: Indian Testimony and the Mission San Gabriel Uprising of 1785," *Ethnohistory* 50, no. 4 (Fall 2003): 643–69.

100. Gloria Anzaldúa, *Borderlands / La Frontera: The New Mestiza* (San Francisco, CA: Spinsters / Aunt Lute Book Company, 1987), 3.

101. David Pierson and Patricia Ward Biederman, "Protest Over Art Forces Police to Draw the Line," *Los Angeles Times*, May 15, 2005; see also Sarah Schrank, *Art and the City: Civic Imagination and Cultural Authority in Los Angeles* (Philadelphia: University of Pennsylvania Press, 2009), 1–2.

102. Turner, quoted in Adam McKibbin, "Save Our State vs. ANSWER: a conversation with Joe Turner of Save Our State and John Beacham of ANSWER LA," *The Red Alert*, August 2005, http://www.theredalert.com/features/saveourstate.php (accessed July 19, 2008). In 2009, Turner let the California corporate registration for SOS lapse and was no longer affiliated with the group (which reformed under different leadership).

103. Fred Alvarez, "A Street-Fighter Mentality on Illegal Immigration," *Los Angeles Times*, June 27, 2005; Zeke Barlow, "Activist Feels a Calling to Oppose Illegal Immigration," *Ventura County Star*, July 8, 2005.

104. "Report Links Hate Groups, Anti-Immigrant Activism," *Los Angeles Times*, March 10, 2008; Turner, quoted in Miriam Jordan, "An Immigrant Fight, Grassroots Groups Boost Their Clout," *Wall Street Journal*, September 28, 2006.

105. "The Battle for Los Angeles," Save Our State Web site, http://saveourstate.org (accessed May 25, 2005); Turner, quoted in McKibbin, "Save Our State vs. ANSWER."

106. On right-wing radio's anti-immigration rage see, for example, Susy Buchanan, "Nativism on Air," *Intelligence Report, Southern Poverty Law Center* (Winter 2005); http://www.splcenter.org/intel/intelreport/article.jsp?aid=590# (accessed October 22, 2009).

107. Pierson and Biederman, "Protest Over Art"; Turner, quoted in McKibbin, "Save Our State vs. ANSWER."

108. Judy Baca, Baldwin Park press release and Arts manifesto, June 12, 2005, http://www.sparcmurals.org/sparcone/index.php?option=com_cont (accessed October 7, 2005).

109. Mike Davis, *Magical Urbanism: Latinos Reinvent the US City* (New York: Verso, 2000), 147.

110. Joseph Lelyveld, "The Border Dividing Arizona," *New York Times Magazine*, October 15, 2006, 40.

111. Wendy Brown, "Porous Sovereignty, Walled Democracy," lecture at the Simpson Center for the Humanities, University of Washington (April 22, 2008), http://depts.washington.edu/uwch/katz/20072008/wendy_brown.html (mp3 file; accessed June 20, 2008).

112. William L. Hamilton, "A Fence With More Beauty, Fewer Barbs," *New York Times*, June 18, 2006; Davis, *Magical Urbanism*, 60–61.

113. Lisa Duggan, *The Twilight of Equality? Neoliberalism, Cultural Politics, and the Attack on Democracy* (Boston: Beacon Press, 2003), xii.

114. Suzanne Lacy, comment on SPARC Web site May 15, 2005, http://www.sparcmurals.org/sparcone/index.php?option=com_cont (accessed October 7, 2005).

Index

Page numbers in italics refer to figures.

15863713R00268

Made in the USA
San Bernardino, CA
08 October 2014